CONTESTED WORLDS

Contested Worlds

An Introduction to Human Geography

Edited by
MARTIN PHILLIPS
Senior Lecturer in Geography, University of Leicester

ASHGATE

Published by
Ashgate Publishing Limited
Gower House
Croft Road
Aldershot
Hants GU11 3HR
England

Ashgate Publishing Company
Suite 420
101 Cherry Street
Burlington, VT 05401–4405
USA

Ashgate website: http://www.ashgate.com

British Library Cataloguing in Publication Data
Contested worlds : an introduction to human geography
  1. Human geography
  I. Phillips, Martin, 1961-
  304.2

Library of Congress Cataloging-in-Publication Data
Contested worlds : an introduction to human geography / edited by Martin Phillips.
     p. cm.
  Includes bibliographical references and index
  ISBN 0-7546-4112-0
  1. Human geography.   I. Phillips, Martin, 1961-

GF41.C576 2005
304.2--dc22

2004056936

ISBN 0 7546 4112 0

Typeset by Saxon Graphics Ltd, Derby
Printed and bound in Great Britain by MPG Books Ltd., Bodmin

Contents

List of Boxes

List of Figures

List of Figures

List of Figures (in Boxes)

List of Tables

List of Tables

List of Tables (in Boxes)

List of Plates

List of Plates (in Boxes)

List of Contributors

Dr. Hazel Barrett — School of Natural and Environmental Sciences, Coventry University, Coventry CV1 5FB

Dr. Angela Browne — School of Natural and Environmental Sciences, Coventry University, Coventry CV1 5FB

Dr. Ed Brown — Department of Geography, Loughborough University, Loughborough LE11 3TU

Professor Mark Cleary — Department of Geographical Sciences, University of Plymouth

David Cook — Department of Media Arts, The Waikato Polytechnic, Private Bag 3036, Hamilton 2020, New Zealand

Professor Keith Hoggart — Department of Geography, Kings College, University of London, London WC2R 2LS

Dr. Phil Hubbard — Department of Geography, Loughborough University, Loughborough LE11 3TU

Dr. Martin Phillips — Department of Geography, University of Leicester, Leicester LE1 7RH

Dr. Peter Vujakovic — Department of Geography and Tourism, Canterbury Christchurch University College, Canterbury CT1 1QU

Dr. Craig Young — Department of Environmental and Geographical Sciences, Manchester Metropolitan University, Manchester, M1 5GD

Part One:
Introduction

Chapter 1

Contested Worlds: An Introduction

Martin Phillips

Worlds of Contest: An Introduction

This book will explore the contested worlds of contemporary human geography. As has become very evident over the course completing this book, the world is full of contests and contestations, many of which are violent and bloody. When this book was initially commissioned, the thought of two aeroplanes being flown into and demolishing one of the world's largest buildings and causing the death of some 2,700 people was to most people unimaginable. It was widely argued that the end of the 'Cold War' between East and West would herald the onset of a period of world peace. However, since that time there has been two 'Gulf Wars' (1990, 2003), the second of which was rhetorically linked to a wider 'War on terrorism' and which also involved an invasion of Afghanistan in 2002. There have also been a series of 'Balkan Wars' in the 1990s, plus a host of other 'civil' wars in places such as Eritrea, Haiti, Rwanda, Somalia and Uganda. Rather than being a period of peace, the late twentieth and early twenty-first century might be characterised as a period of widening warfare, terrorism, genocide and torture.

Contests do not necessarily take such violent forms, and many are much more benign. In sport, for example, contests connect with spectacles and rituals, although increasingly sport is connected to other forms of contest, which although in a sense non-violent in that there is no actual or implied use of physical force, could be seen as highly violent in having all manner of dramatic consequences on people's livelihoods and lifestyles. These other contests are those that revolve around competition between firms for market shares, lower costs and continued profits, and also between politicians for peoples' votes and support. There are also contestations between people with different sets of beliefs and attitudes. Although these may at times connect to the previously mentioned forms of contests, and also to ideological debates and conflict, at other times they may simply lead to indifference, inactivity and silence as people fail to recognise the needs, aspirations and indeed presence of people who are in some manner different from themselves. People may inhabit physical locations which are proximate spatially and temporally but they live in quite different circumstances and, for a series of different reasons, in effect inhabit quite different worlds.

The contested nature of the contemporary world, or indeed worlds, has often been filtered out from geographical accounts. Philo (1991) has suggested that much of geography over the last 50 years has been frightened of considering things which 'maybe have worryingly "political overtones"', preferring instead to seek out some 'uncontestable geography' (Whittlesey 1945). However, Philo suggests that this restriction, along with a distrust of studying intangible things, has come to be challenged and replaced by less restricted visions of geography. Many of these visions, particularly those linked to notions of radical or critical geography, might be seen to be infused as much by some form of 'imagination of power' (Said 1986) as by any particular 'geographical imagination'.

This neglect of contestation is problematic given that many contests can be seen to be, in one way or another, highly geographical. Acts of warfare, terrorism, genocide and torture, for example, are often connected to territorial conflicts, with people seeking to gain access to particular areas of space and/or expel other people from particular places. Violent conflicts may also relate to access to particular aspects of nature, and hence may be seen as geographical if one ascribes to the notion that geography is about people-nature relations (see Unwin 1992).

The more benign forms of social contest can also be seen as having clear geographical dimensions, not least in that they are often organised using spatial distinctions. Not only do many sports make use of spatial zones or positionings but sports are often organised according to spatial areas of various scales in that there are national, regional and local teams and competitions. Furthermore the spatial scale at which sport is being practised may be shifting, with growth in the number and spatial extent of international competitions: in rugby, for instance, recent years have seen the creation of world, hemispherical and continental competitions. Furthermore, as MacEwan (2001) notes, many national leagues, such as the English soccer Premiership, have become increasingly globalised through the employment of players from other countries. MacEwan adds that localised differences in sport do remain, and it is also evident that shifts towards more globalised forms is often the subject of varied contestations. In Britain, for example, 'local' supporters often complain about the presence of overseas players in 'their club' and about the impacts that competing in 'overseas' competitions has on performances in 'domestic' leagues and tournaments, while concerns have also been expressed about the impacts of these changes on the performances of 'national' teams. The practices of sport may well be becoming more globalised, but for many people national, regional and local identities and performances still matter greatly.

Economic and political contests are also played out through geography. Competing firms, for example, are often differentiated spatially, both through being sited in potentially quite different areas, and also through fragmenting their activities and placing them into different areas, a process, which Massey (1984) characterises as a *spatial division of labour*. Massey and a series of other geographers have explored the reasons for these divisions, and also highlighted how these divisions have often been reformulated as firms seek to gain some competitive advantage over their rivals.

As well as spatial divisions of labour, there are spatial divisions in markets and in the regulation of economies. A classic view of a market, which according to people such as Walker (1988) still underpins much contemporary economic thinking, is of a bounded place – a market-place – in which buyers and sellers become physically co-present in order to fix prices and enact exchange. Such markets may now be seen as quite anachronistic and instead we are seen to live in a world of global markets, whereby goods, services and money are bought and sold across fast distances and also at increasing speed. Authors such as Harvey (1989) have argued that the contemporary world is experiencing *time-space compression*, while others such as Lash and Urry (1994) have argued that people now live in a *world of flows*, many of which are increasingly globalised. However, once again, the movement towards what is often characterised as *globalisation* (see Daniels *et al.* 2001) is contested, and contested in a number of quite difference ways.

One aspect of contestation is concern over the impacts of globalisation: the late 1990s and early years of the 21st century have, for instance, seen a series of demonstrations against globalisation. Much is made in these protests about power and how globalisation may entail a reduction in people's abilities to influence what goes on the particular places where they live, work, think and play, and there are calls to create more localised forms of economic and social interaction. Less dramatically, a series of academics have sought to contest the idea that people are living in a world of global flows and interactions (e.g. Hirst and Thompson, 1996; Scott, 1997). Amongst the arguments that have been made is that not everywhere in the world is equally part of the world of the global economy. This economy is a capitalist one, which means, amongst other things, that things only flow to those that have the money to purchase commodities. As I have outlined elsewhere (Phillips and Mighall 2000), this feature means that some people are denied access to many of the commodities of the globalised economy, including that most basic of products, food. Furthermore, as people such as Corbridge (1993), Castells (1998), and Thrift and Leyshon (1997) have highlighted, there exists areas across the world where people are deemed not to have sufficient money to borrow money; as such these areas and the people living in them have become divorced from the global money economy. Geographers have arguably been slow to recognise and represent how these people cope – or do not cope – with such a positioning beyond the limits of capitalism.

Politics also makes use of space in that it is frequently constituted *territorially*. That is, it makes use of spatial striations such as zones or districts. This use may be just for administrative purposes or to may be used to create systems of representation and accountability, as in Britain where people elect a 'local representative' who then, supposedly, represents the interests of 'their constituency' in systems of national, regional and local government. There are divisions of responsibility and accountability being created within and between the systems of government, and these themselves have been the subject of contestation, and indeed have been repeatedly reworked, not always in any one clear direction. In recent years, for example, there has been moves to create more local and regional systems of government, to foster more interaction between units of government (so-called 'joined-up government'), to create new national forms of government, and to establish heightened levels of supra-national governance.

Amongst the reasons why changes in systems of representation and decision-making are often contested is that they transgress existing spatial associations that people have made with other people and with particular territorial complexes. In other words, people come to live in geographically constituted *imagined communities* (B. Anderson 1991), whereby they feel they have some common bond or interest with others in an area even though they may never have met them and indeed will never be able to meet with all but a minute proportion of them; and/or, feel a sense of *place attachment* in that they come to value various attributes located in a particular area. Imagined communities and place attachments can take a variety of forms, can be formed in a variety of ways, and are subject to contestation. Jess and Massey, for instance, have suggested that 'issues of place' have 'become both more salient and more fraught' with senses and identities of place being,

> frequently disputed – sometimes by groups living in 'the same' place, sometimes between 'insiders' [who may feel that they belong to or are part of a particular place or community] and 'outsiders' [who may feel excluded from being a member of a place or community], sometimes in ways which open to question all of these categories (Jess and Massey 1995: 134).

Not only are there all manner of geographical contests occurring in the contemporary world, but their outcomes affect the worlds in which people live. The potential of political and military contests to change the lives of people caught up in them appears quite obvious, although arguably they figure relatively little in geographical accounts, at least those concerned with the present. There has, however, been a growing recognition by geographers about the military and political conquest of space, place and nature associated with European imperialism and colonialism, and the often devastating impacts this often had on the human and non-human populations (see Godlewska and Smith 1994; Mannion 1997; Phillips and Mighall 2000).

Success and failure in the market place has figured rather more strongly in the pages of human geography texts, as indeed has sport. A series of studies (e.g. Bradley 1990; Kotler *et al*. 1993; Williams 1997), for example, have highlighted how success on the sporting field can bring huge benefits to some people and to some areas; conversely failures may have serious financial problems as well as personal disappointments. This points to the increasing *commodification* of sport and also in some cases to the processes of globalisation mentioned earlier. The combination of these two sets of processes can, indeed, be seen to be affecting all sorts of aspects of social life, bringing with it all manner of geographically related processes. Taking on board Massey *et al*.'s (1999: 2) claim that 'human geography's take on the world derives from its standing on the ground of the triad of space-place-nature', then by way of illustrations one might, first, point to how success and failures in globalised commodity production have contributed to processes of *social-spatial differentiation* which have both accentuated and reconfigured existing spatial divisions, such as those of city and countryside, First and Third Worlds, East and West, rich and poor regions. Second, fortunes in globalised commodity production have knock-on effects which contribute to the construction of new forms and senses of place, and the undermining of established constructions of place, as when a major company, or indeed a whole industry, dis-invests from a locality. Third, the globalised commodity production involves the exploitation of both material and symbolic natures, practices which some claim are unsustainable into the future.

Contested Geographies

The preceding section has sought to provide brief illustration of the contested nature of the contemporary worlds in which people live. More sustained discussion of some of these issues, and many more besides, is contained in the chapters that follow. However, before outlining some of the content of these chapters and the structure of the book as a whole, it is important to highlight one other aspect of contestation and its relationship to geography, namely that the notion of geography is itself contested. While for Massey *et al.* (1999), human geography's 'take on the world' stands in the ground staked out by peoples' relations with space, place and nature, one might add that this ground has been far from stable with various geographers at various times seeking to very much tilt geography towards particular elements of the triad, even to detach one or two of its elements from providing any support for notions of geography, or else adding other elements onto the construction of geography. Livingstone (1992) has indeed characterised geography as a 'contested enterprise' with different people taking geography to mean differ things and/or seeking to do geography in different ways. Massey *et al.* (1999: 17) may be seen to also acknowledge this when they write that 'the construction, maintenance and relative power of particular geographical imaginations is a terrain of contestation', although they also note that academic geographers are not the only group of people who make geographies and direct much of their discussion of the contested construction of geography to these other groups. However, it is important to recognise that when studying academic geographies one is also very much entering a terrain of contestation.

There are different ways of reacting to this contestation. As mentioned earlier, many geographers have effectively shied away from areas of conflict, seeking instead to find some uncontestable horizons for geography. Another widely adopted approach has been to seek closure of contestation by asserting the primacy of particular concepts of geography and geographical practice over others. A key issue here is on what grounds might one say one view of geography is better than another. For much of modern geography notions of science, truth and utility (or usefulness) have provided important, and highly related, criteria for casting judgement on particular geographies and geographers. Today, however, many geographers have come to recognise that these concepts are themselves highly contested: there are, for example, a range of different definitions of science and truth, while what is useful to one person may well be detrimental to others. A third approach is to accept contestation as a chronic (that is a constantly recurring) and potentially critical (as in vital) feature of doing geography. If we live in worlds which are highly differentiated and which are full of all manner of conflicts and contestations, then we should probably expect our geographies to exhibit similar characteristics.

In editing this book I have very much adopted this third perspective. Authors were approached who were known both to be studying a range of different geographies and for taking rather different perspectives or approaches to 'doing geography'. Furthermore, although some of the commonalities between the variously authored chapters has been pulled out, there was no attempt to make the contributors tow a common line, or indeed cover a fixed agenda. The authors were simply asked to make their own geographies, addressing issues which were of concern to them and which are widely present within the syllabi of undergraduate geography degrees. They were also asked to highlight concepts which were of particular significance to understanding these issues (these appear in italics in the text – a practice which has already been adopted within this chapter), where necessary providing some commentary and illustration of these concepts through box sections. Many of these 'key concepts' have indeed been the focus contestation, with a range of quite different interpretations being advanced about the meaning or implications of particular ideas.

Contested Worlds: An Introductory Summary

So what contested worlds, geographies and concepts does the book cover? The book is divided into three broad parts. The first part includes this short introduction and a much longer chapter which explores in more detail contestations over the subject of geography. In particular, Chapter 2 considers in some of the *philosophical debates* which have come to surround human geography in recent years and outlines some of the different ways of 'doing geography' that have been proposed. An understanding of philosophical concepts and debates is now of considerable importance within human geography generally and Chapter 2 has been written as a general introduction to these concepts and debates. It is, however, also hoped that the chapter will act as a useful introduction to some of the concepts and approaches adopted by the various authors of the other chapters in the book.

The second part of the book explores issues that are widely seen to be of international, indeed global, reach and significance. In Chapter 3, Ed Brown reflects on the theoretical turmoil and conflicts surrounding the study of the *development* of the *Third World*, terms themselves that have been highly contested. The chapter highlights how the philosophical debates and arguments addressed in the preceding chapter have been worked out within, and have indeed themselves in part been constituted out of, more specific debates relating to the development, or lack of development, of many countries of the world. The chapter also highlights how notions of development straddle, at times quite uneasily, academic and policy-making arenas.

Chapter 4 by Hazel Barrett and Angela Browne also addresses the idea of development, and likewise recognises both the variety of contested interpretations of its nature, causes and consequences of development, and also how policy debates within institutions like the United Nations and the World Bank variously parallel, draw-on, and contradict, academic debates within geography and associated disciplines. The focus of this chapter is, however, much more particular in that it focuses on the specific role of *population/environment relationships* within development. The chapter notes the considerable emphasis currently given to increasing population numbers, particularly within parts of the so-called 'Third World', but demonstrates that the issue of population and environment relationships cannot be simply reduced to a question of numbers. The chapter draws on a series of case studies located in sub-Saharan Africa to illustrate some of the alternative ways in which population and environment relationships have been considered, beginning with the ideas of Thomas Malthus first articulated at the end of the eighteenth century.

Whilst the issue of population-environment relations has long been an issue of debate, in Chapter 5 Peter Vujakovic considers an issue which has risen to prominence in the late twentieth century, namely the break up of a global *geopolitical order* which has been seen to have dominated relationships between states since the middle of that century. The chapter highlights geographical aspects of state power, some of which have been briefly touched on in this chapter. So, for example, the chapter discusses the significance of *territoriality* within the formation of states, and how territoriality has often been closely connected to military power and conflict. The chapter also highlights how that most geographical of texts, the map, was of significance within the performance of territoriality and state power; and how associations of people and place are of significance to state power through *nationalism*. The chapter also addresses inter-state relations and how these may be implicated in the formation of some new global geopolitical order. The chapter also follows up, and in a sense constitutes something of a contradiction to, the view expressed earlier relating to geographers' neglect of armed conflict. So, throughout the chapter attention is drawn to the use of military forces to secure and/or thwart particular geopolitical objectives.

While the second part of book looked at issues of general, global concern, in the third part attention switches to issues of more particular, one might say 'regional' concern. The term *region* is open to a range of interpretations and has long been the subject of considerable contestation amongst geographers. Within this complexity and contestation a common view is that regions point simultaneously to both 'the partitional (the world can be exhaustively divided into bounded spaces) and [the] aggregative (... spaces can be fitted together to form a larger totality)' (Johnston *et al.* 2000: 687). To these common notions of the regional, there has also been increasing recognition of three further aspects of regions. First, the regional is a 'process of becoming': there are processes of partition and aggregation which foster the formation of regions but they rarely if ever come to full-fruition in clearly recognised regions. Second, the processes of regionalisation often do not lie in the region, but rather regions are constituted from the 'outside in' and/or from the 'inside out'. A third new ingredient in the study of regional geographies has been a recognition that people partition and aggregate space – and associated geographical entities such as places and natures – into regions in their imaginings as well as through their actions. Furthermore these imaginings can have significant material consequences, leading people into actions to foster or contest processes of regionalisation in general, or particular constructions of regions.

The four chapters in the third part of the book provide clear illustrations of both the common concern with regions as partitions and aggregations and the three further ingredients listed above. So, for example, in Chapter 6 Keith Hoggart explores whether the European Union, an aggregation of nation-states and national economies, is partitioned by social inequalities. The chapter also discusses regionalisation from the 'outside in' as it considers the role of globalisation in partitioning Europe into a mosaic of smaller worlds exhibiting considerable levels of inequality between, and often within, them. The chapter also draws attention to the role of national cultures and institutions in responding to globalisation, and also in fostering sub-national regional inequalities. The chapter thereby provides illustrations of the significance of culture in procedures that simultaneously partition and aggregate political-economic space. It also directs attention to issues of who does the aggregation and division, and in whose interests are they acting. There is clearly a politics to regionalisations which needs to be recognised, and indeed possibly contested.

Chapter 7 by Mark Cleary also addresses the partitioning of regional space, although the focus of attention is now South-East Asia, and more particularly the countries in the regional ASEAN grouping. Once again attention is paid to the differentiations within the region, and to how these variously reflect 'outside in' processes relating to globalisation and the legacies of European colonialism, and also 'inside out' processes. The principal focus of attention with regard to the latter relates to processes of national 'development', and the chapter thereby connects to many of the issues discussed in Chapter 3. The countries of South-East Asia have often been described as a success story in development, moving from positions in the mid-twentieth century of colonial dependency and economic/political un- or under-development, to some developed-world status and riding high in various waves of the contemporary global economy. In Chapter 3 many critical questions were raised about the discourses of development, and likewise Chapter 8 raises questions about the costs and inclusiveness of the *development stories* commonly constructed about the so-called 'tiger-economies'. Such questions include ones relating to: i) the treatment of the material environment and whether this provides a basis for a sustainable future for this region, or indeed more globally; ii) the degree of inequality between people living in different parts of the region, and indeed between people living in proximate locations to each other; and iii) the treatment of people who have different ways of life and the rights particular peoples may have over particular spaces and associated entities of natures.

The final chapter of Part 3 addresses a region that is very much 'in a process becoming' in that it addresses Eastern and Central Europe, areas which through much of the twentieth century formed a central element of the USSR, or *Union of Soviet Socialist Republics*, and an associated 'Communist bloc'. In this chapter Craig Young discusses how the countries of this region have been impacted by the dissolution of Communist nation-states, identifying a series of economic, social, political and cultural transformations. He argues that the changes occurring in the region should not be seen as a simple transition from a communist, or *state-socialist* system, to a western, *capitalist economy*. Instead, he argues that there are a series of complex, geographically uneven and highly contested transformations occurring in this region, based in part on the legacy of spatial differentiation created in previous regimes and also through competing visions as to the desirable futures and strategies of development. It is concluded, for instance, that it is far from clear exactly where the developmental stories and strategies of 'democratisation', 'marketisation' and 'regional autonomy'/'decolonisation' will eventually lead these counties, although it is highly likely that their outcomes will be both spatially and socially variable. In other words, whilst some places and some people may well value and gain advantage from these changes, other places and people may resist and become disadvantaged by them.

The issue of spatial and social differentiation forms the focus of Part 4 of the book, which explores the theme of local worlds and the inter-relation of people and places. In particular, this part of the book explores notions of social and spatial centrality and marginality. In Chapter 9, Phil Hubbard explores the concept of *marginal places* (see Shields, 1991 for a fuller discussion of this idea) and highlights the significance of spatial representation in the formation of social stereotypes and associated practices of discrimination and exclusion. He argues that some places get stigmatised as being home to various marginal groups, or 'outsiders', and once these areas get this reputation, then people living in these areas, who may well be quite different from the stereotypical image, become subject to heightened marginalisation as people and resources from the social centre shun these places.

Whilst Chapter 9 seeks to highlight how place, and specifically place images, can materially affect people, in Chapter 10 I focus on how people affect, and indeed create and recreate places, seen as both material and symbolic products. In this chapter attention also turns from places of the margin to places of the centre, with attention focusing on who is involved in creating change in these places. The specific

changes discussed are those associated with *gentrification*, a term which is broadly used to refer to physical and social restructuring of an area. The chapter, however, highlights the contested nature of this term and how the gentrification has been variously defined and interpreted by people with different philosophical outlooks. The chapter argues that while gentrification has often been understood as a restructuring of places of the centre by the agency of people and institutions of the centre, it may also involve people of the margins, either as important but rather neglected agents of gentrification itself, or as people being socially and spatially marginalised by the processes of gentrification, which can materially and symbolically 'displace' people from certain areas of space.

Chapter 11 also focuses on peoples' relationships with symbolic and material places and spaces. Here the focus is on the spaces of the nation and rurality: of country and countryside. In this chapter, David Cook and I explore the way that the nation of New Zealand has often been seen as a marginal space, quite literally at the other side of the world from a centre of colonial power, Britain, and also how rural spaces have often been seen as marginal. Urban places are often seen as central places by dint of the range of activities which take place there, and as a consequence rural areas may be seen as being marginal, and indeed as becoming increasingly marginal, through the low density of activities which are seen to go on there. However, the chapter goes on to question these constructions of country and countryside, highlighting amongst other things how: i) areas of the countryside may be important places of production for many of the resources which sustain places of the centre; ii) centres and margins, even when considered with a spatial rather than social emphasis, are relational terms (being distant or far-away is always a measure from somewhere); iii) socio-spatial relationships of centre and periphery are multiple in character and rarely add up to create a stable position of centre or margin; and iv) being positioned at the margin does not necessarily entail constraint and domination, but may constitute worlds in which there are potentialities for creativity and empowerment.

Contesting Contested Worlds

It is on this last, seemingly positive note, that I will end this introduction to *Contested Worlds*. Hopefully you will feel inclined to read the various chapters in this book and consider the issues touched upon in this introduction, and indeed many other issues raised by these chapters which have been sidelined within the writing of this introduction. When reading these chapters you may wish to bring other issues to the fore, to contest the interpretations made of these chapter in this introduction, and indeed to contest some of the claims made in these chapters. Indeed I hope that this will indeed be the case. Human geography today is being made in all manner of quite different ways, some of which are very evident in this book and others of which are not. This book is very much written as an introduction to some of the various worlds of contemporary human geography and the contestations which lie within and betwixt them. There are now all manner of human geographies, which perhaps inevitably leads to geography being a highly contested enterprise. However rather than seek some uncontested horizon l would argue that contestation needs to be recognised as a key strand in the making of new, stimulating and empowering human geographies.

Chapter 2

Philosophical Arguments in Human Geography

Martin Phillips

Philosophy in Human Geography: An Introduction

The preceding chapter highlighted the contested character of human geography, both in the worlds beyond the 'academy' and within the texts, conversations and practices of academic geography. The bulk of chapters focus on attempts to understand the worlds of geography beyond the academy, although attention will frequently be made to the worlds, words and ideas of academic geographers. This chapter, however, will focus exclusively on the words and ideas of human geographers in that it will seek to outline some of the philosophical issues and debates conducted within recent and contemporary Anglo-American human geography. The chapter will seek to provide some insights as to why philosophy might matter, both to the conduct of human geography and more widely. To assist in doing this, the chapter makes use of a distinction between *epistemology* and *ontology* to differentiate and discuss a range of philosophies which have been of significance within human geography – or at least Anglo-American human geography – since the mid-twentieth century. Ontologies refer to 'theories of what exists' and epistemologies to 'theories of how we can know what exists'. Philosophies may be seen to reflect particular sets of ontologies and epistemologies, although the emphasis placed on and degree of interconnection between epistemology and ontology can vary considerably between philosophies, as should become evident through the course of the chapter.

From Empiricism to Positivism

Unwin (1992) suggests that a widely held image of geography, often derived from people's school education, is that it revolves around the collation and recitation of a series of 'facts' about places. Unwin adds that such public understandings are very poor reflections of contemporary geography in Higher Education, although one might argue that they do reflect the character of this geography in past times, and indeed at least some of its current manifestations. It is also a sense of geography which can be described as *empiricist*.

Empiricism is a term used to describe the view that knowledge is constructed exclusively through sensual experiences of the world, particularly though visual observation. The term is often associated with British philosophers of the sixteenth and seventeenth centuries, such as John Locke and David Hulme (see Dunn *et al.* 1992; Peet 1998), although it is now generally applied to any works which imply that validity in knowledge construction stems exclusively from sensed experience. As such it connects to the common place understanding that geographical research involves the collection and representations of observations, while learning geography becomes the memorisation and recitation of these facts.

Such a conception of geography figured strongly in academic geography in Britain and the USA from the 1930s. In Britain, for example, the geography of this time has been characterised as 'capes and bays' geography, concerned with surveying and describing, often in quite a systematic manner, the physical and human aspects of various landscape features. A classical study was Steers' (1946) *The Coastline of Britain* which literally went around the coast describing the physical and human features found there. Other studies moved away from the coast, but still sought to write geography as observational descriptions of phenomena found in an area. Stamp (1946), for example, used some 22,000 school children as field assistants to map the land-use in grid-squares across the British Isles, while more generally use was often made of a regional frame to bound descriptions of human and natural landscape forms.

There were a series of discussions about how to define regions (e.g. Kimble, 1951; Hall 1935; James 1952; Whittlesey 1954) which drew in a range of work from France, Germany and the USA, although often these debates were rather left behind within studies which simply took as read that regions existed. Livingstone (1992: 311), for example, suggests that the *regional geography* of this time often 'degenerated into a plodding, enumerative exercise lacking both intellectual vigour and moral zest', while Philo (1991: 4) claims that the mid-twentieth century saw a 'restricted vision of geography' being established which was 'frightened about permitting geography to consider phenomena which are immaterial (which are not tangible, not easily countable and mappable) and which may have worrying "political overtones"' (see also Phillips 1998b; Philo 1994a).

Many regional geographers saw themselves as being non-philosophical and indeed often assigned pleasure in doing geography to its non-philosophical character. However, even those who were constructing geography as a non-philosophical discipline were making philosophical claims and assumptions. They were, for example, effectively claiming that knowledge can be created entirely or primarily through the operation of the senses. Often this claim was made implicitly: people just constructed their geographies through collecting together a series of observations. In other cases the argument was advanced more explicitly. So, for example, Carl Sauer, a leading figure in US geography from the 1920s claimed that,

> geography is first of all knowledge gained by observation … one orders by reflection and reinspection the things one has been looking at, and that from what one has experienced by intimate sight comes comparison and synthesis (Sauer 1956: 296–7).

This empiricist view of knowledge, although widely held in the Western world (MacNaghten and Urry 1998), is problematic in, at least, two respects. First, what people sense appears to be, in part, preconditioned by peoples' thoughts: people see, hear, smell, taste and feel what they expect to see, hear, smell, taste or feel. As a result two people may sense the same situation quite differently if those two people have quite different expectations. Second, an empiricist perspective implies that knowledge cannot be created with regard to things that cannot be sensed. Yet many things about which people claim knowledge are not directly accessible to the senses. These things range from the microscopic to the macro-scale, and also include things such as ideas, emotions and experiences which are commonly supposed to influence how people act but which cannot be physically sensed, although you may sense some telltale signs which you interpret as being indicative of a particular thought, emotion or experience. Similarly, many of the forces widely seen as significant in the operating in the physical world are not directly observable: Newton may have observed the apple falling but he did not directly observe the force of gravity pulling on the apple.

Empiricist studies hence employed a particular epistemology, or theory of knowledge, and one which when articulated fully has been widely seen as problematic. Many of these studies also adopted what Sayer (1992) described as an *atomistic ontology*. That is, they see the world as being composed of a jumble of discrete objects which come together for reasons which are created internally to each object but which may have impacts which affect other objects. In many a regional geography the region is conceived in terms of a set of discrete objects, such as firms, households and people, each of which make their own decisions about such things as where to locate, and when and what to move. Such decisions may mean that some of these elements of the region come into collision: firms may all decide to locate in one area, or people all decide to move from the countryside to the city or vice-versa, and when this happens new conditions are created which in term may set the elements of the regions moving in new directions. As will be discussed later, such ontology can be criticised for failing to recognise the extent to which seemingly distinct entities may be quite fragmented and/or may operate in connections with other, perhaps quite different and/or distant entities.

Despite being highly problematic, empiricism dominated much of Anglo-American geography from the early twentieth century at least until the 1950s. At this time, however, another set of philosophical ideas came to exert an influence on much of geography, although at the time their influence was dimly recognised. These ideas were those of positivism or, rather more precisely 'logical positivism', which argued, simplifying greatly, for the mathematical formulation of theories which were acceptable as true knowledge only after they had been tested in relation to predicted empirical observations. However to understand what logical positivism meant in geography and why it emerged, it is useful to consider it in relation to the distinction already made between epistemology and ontology.

Logical Positivist Ontologies in Geography

The first text to make an explicit link between geography and logical positivism was David Harvey's (1969) *Explanation in Geography,* although several commentators on the history of geography (e.g. Gregory 1978; Unwin 1992) have argued that many of the connections were made much earlier in an article by Fred Schaefer (1953) entitled 'Exceptionalism in geography'. Schaefer was friends with Gustav Bergmann who in the 1920s had been part of a philosophical discussion group known as the Vienna Circle which had initially outlined notions of logical positivism, and who subsequently wrote extensively about it (Bergmann 1954, 1957). Such associations suggest that Schaefer was well versed in the ideas of logical positivism even though he did not actually use these terms in his article. It is certainly clear that many of the arguments Shaefer made were fully compatible with those made by explicit logical positivists such as Bergmann. Indeed, Bergmann edited the paper just prior to publication, following the sudden death of Schaefer due to a heart attack, and Luckerman (1989: 55) has suggested that this skewed the paper away from geographical debates and even more towards the concerns of Bergmann and 'the logical empiricist school of positivist philosophy in the USA'.

One of the initial starting points of Schaefer's paper was that geography was too static: it lacked change and progress. He complained, for example that geography was: 'too complacent. Some fundamental ideas have remained unchallenged for decades though there is ample reason to doubt their power' (Schaefer 1953: 226); and that, 'the progress of geography was slower than that of some other social sciences such as, for instance, economics' (p. 227). He suggested that this situation was the by-product of what he called *exceptionalism* – 'a whole group of ideas which are variations of a common theme: geography is quite different from all other sciences, methodologically unique, as it were' (p. 231). Schaefer argued that such ideas fostered the notion that geography was '*the* "integrating science", completely different from other disciplines ... [with] unique importance', but that the actual results of geographical research where 'somewhat lacking in those startling insights which one is led to expect from such exuberant characterizations of the field' (p. 227). The reason for this, Schaefer claimed, was that much of geography failed to progress beyond description to explanation, a movement which according to Schaefer 'means always to recognize ... [phenomena] as instances of laws'. According to Schaefer geography 'had to be conceived as the science concerned with the formulation of the laws governing the spatial distribution of certain features on the surface of the earth' (p. 227).

This strident claim as to what geographers ought to do serves to highlight one of the features of logical positivism, namely its adoption of a *law-based ontology*. Phenomena and events were seen to be, in large part, the outcome of universal processes, that is processes which operated in a manner which was uniform across, and therefore in a sense independent from, time and space.

Such a view of explanation stands in some contrast to the regional, empiricist focused geography discussed earlier, and much of Schaefer's article took the form of a critique of such geography, through criticism of what he saw as some of its principal advocates, namely Kant, Hettner and most particularly Hartshorne. Hartshorne (1939a; 1939b) had written a major text entitled *The Nature of Geography* which Schaefer read as a justification of an *idiographic* regional geography. The term idiographic had been used by the German philosopher Windelband at the close of the nineteenth century (Windelband 1980) and was picked up by Hettner (1905) and then Hartshorne. The term was used by Windelband to characterise approaches that focused on specific events and phenomena and sought to explain them in relation to a particular, probably unique, combination of circumstances and processes. This was contrasted with a *nomothetic* approach which sought to explain events and phenomena in relation to general processes.

Schaefer read Hartshorne as an advocate of the study of the unique, remarking for example that 'Geography according to Hartshorne is essentially idiographic' and that he took the view that, 'Whenever laws are discovered or applied one is no longer in the area of geography' (Schaefer 1953: 240). Hartshorne took great exception to Schaefer's characterisations of his, and indeed other peoples' work, claiming that 'almost every paragraph, almost the great majority of sentences in the critique, represent falsification, whether by commission or omission' (Hartshorne 1955: 243). A series of latter commentators (e.g. Entrikin 1981; 1989; Gregory 1978; 1982b; Guelke 1977; 1978; Luckerman 1989) have all argued that the differences between Schaefer and Hartshorne have often been overplayed, and that Hartshorne did not, as Schaefer implied, see geography an exclusively idiographic enterprise. Indeed he argued explicitly against such a view:

> A geography which was content with studying only the individual characteristics of its phenomena and their relationships and did not utilize every opportunity to develop generic concepts and universal principles would be failing in one of the main standards of science (Hartshorne 1939a: 383).

However, as Agnew (1989: 122) remarks, what set Hartshorne apart from Schaefer and the logical positivist philosophy was that he did not see the generation of universal principles as the end-point and purpose of analysis (Hartshorne 1939a: 387). Rather they were 'merely a scientific tool' (Hartshorne 1939a: 387) to be used, where necessary, in a scientific 'seeking to know' (Hartshorne 1959: 168). For Schaefer (1953: 248), however, science simply 'searches for laws'.

Despite the criticisms of Schaefer's arguments by Hartshorne, it was the former's notion of science as a search for laws which came to dominate much of geography from the 1950s and 1960s. Two broad types of laws came to be developed in geography. First, there were attempts to derive 'spatial laws'. Geography came to be seen by many as being a 'spatial science' concerned with establishing universal laws about space, or more precisely the spatial arrangement of things in space. This view was clearly expressed in Schaefer's article where it was claimed that:

> Spatial relations are the ones that matter in geography, and no others. Non-spatial relations found among phenomena in an area are the subject matter of other specialists such as the geologist, anthropologist or economist (Schaefer 1953: 228).

As Gregory (1982b: 190) notes, Schaefer's proposal for a geography focused on spatial relations was itself 'in an important sense ... exceptionalist' in that it sought to 'outlaw' various geographies as being non-geographical and/or non-scientific. As mentioned earlier, a number of studies have argued that in the mid-twentieth century a 'restrictive vision of geography' was established which shied away from getting geography entwined with the intangible and the political. This vision was often enacted in definitions of what geography was and in discussions of the relationship and boundaries between human geography and other disciplines. These points were very much in evidence during Schaefer's espousal of geography as spatial science where he both sought to establish clear boundaries between geography and other social sciences in terms of their objects of study, and also bemoaned geographers for falling to keep within these restrictions. So, for example, he claimed that geographers:

do not always clearly distinguish between, say, social relations on the one hand and spatial relations among social factors of the other. Actually one may safely say that most of what we find in any given area is of primary interest to the other social scientist. For instance, the connections between ideology and political behaviour, or the lawful connections between the psychological traits of a population and its economic institutions do not concern the geographer ... Like all others the geographer had better cultivate his [sic] speciality, the laws concerning spatial arrangement ... the geographer's specific task in the analysis of regions is limited to spatial relations only. Accordingly, even the most complete geographical analysis of any region gives only partial insight into it (Schaefer 1953: 231).

In other words, Schaefer argues geographers needed to restrict themselves to the study of spatial laws even though such study would lead, at best, only partial explanation of particular situations and places.

Schaefer's proposal for a geography focused on spatial laws was explicitly resisted by people such as Hartshorne and appears to have been largely ignored by many other contemporaneous geographers (see Johnston, 1997: 60; Livingstone, 1992: 316–322). Despite this, as Unwin (1992: 115) notes, '[p]aradoxically ... the ideas expressed in his 1953 paper ... came to dominate the practice of geography in the 1950s and 1960s'. In particular, geography did become for many a 'spatial science', engaged in formulation of some form of spatial laws. One of the earliest examples of work on spatial laws was the *social physics school* which sought to explain human behaviour using mathematical formulations of spatial laws. Stewart and Wartnz, two leading figures in this approach, argued that geography has become 'thwarted' (Stewart and Wartnz 1958: 167) from becoming a 'well organised science' because of an over-emphasis on uniqueness. Geography, they argued, should be 'macroscopic' rather than 'microscopic' in focus, focusing on 'space-occupying systems' (p. 168) and searching wherever possible to discern the general over the particular. Much of the work of people associated with the spatial science school sought to formulate laws relating to the influence of distance on social interaction, and there was considerable use of mathematics, both to 'quantify data' and to express theory. Frequent connections were also made to physics, with Stewart exclaiming:

> There is no longer any excuse for anyone to ignore the fact that human beings, on average and at least in certain circumstances, obey mathematical rules resembling in a general way some of the primitive 'laws' of physics (Stewart 1947: 485).

Stewart was an astronomical physicist by training and he, along with Warntz, made frequent connections between social and physical forms and processes. Stewart and Warntz (1958; 1959), for example, argued that people and/or social organisations interact with each other in a way which is analogous to the way inanimate physical objects relate to each other through the forces of gravity. In other words, just as the gravitation force between two objects was conceptualised as directly proportional to the product of their masses and inversely proportional to the distance between them – then so the level of communication, or population movement or some other form of human interaction between two places, was seen as being proportion to the population of these places and inversely proportional to the distance between them.

Similar ideas about the need to develop spatial laws emerged from a variety of other places, including the universities of Washington (in Seattle), Iowa, Wisconsin, Lund (in Sweden) and Cambridge and Bristol (see Johnston 1997; Unwin 1992). Despite significance differences in some of their arguments, these geographers were all broadly convinced that geography needed to become a 'spatial science' concerned 'to specify the fundamental *laws of spatial organisation* present in both natural land- scapes and human activities' (Cloke *et al*. 1991: 66).

While many geographers in the 1950s and 1960s worked within the restrictions placed on geography by Schaefer, many more geographers can be seen to have trans- gressed his strictures and turned instead to what according to his arguments would appear to be 'non-geographical laws'. This possibility was indeed recognised by Schaefer (1953: 248) who argued that 'most of the laws of physical geography … are not strictly geographical laws' but rather 'specializations of laws independently established in the physical sciences geographers'. Schaefer suggested that geogra- phers might 'take as we find them' laws from a variety of natural and social sciences, 'apply them systematically to the various conditions that prevail on the surface of the earth and analyse them with particular attention to the spatial variables they contain' (p. 248).

This prediction proved a good one, with geography becoming a 'magpie disci- pline' (Unwin 1992: 137) borrowing universal laws from a range of other disciplines. Schaefer highlighted the use by physical geographers of laws established in other physical sciences and indeed this has been very evident. Unwin (1992) highlights how geomorphology in the 1950s was heavily impacted by the incorporation of ideas from geology, physics and engineering, while human geographers drew most notably, albeit selectively (see Gregory and Urry 1985), on principles developed by econo- mists, sociologists and, somewhat latter, cognitive-psychologists. There was also some borrowing by human geographers of ideas from the physical and natural sciences. The incorporation of Newtonian physics through the development of gravity models has already been mentioned, while another important source of ideas, albeit rather indirectly, was biology. Urban geography in particular was heavily influ- enced by ecological concepts introduced, arguably rather unknowingly, through the incorporation into geography of work by the so-called *Chicago School* of sociologists (see Chapters 9 and 10). Many human geographers came to see spatial patterns of activity as representing an outcome not of some universal 'spatial laws', such as the impact of a 'friction of distance', but rather to see spatial patterns as manifestations of 'economic' or 'behavioural laws'. Geographers saw themselves as 'law users' rather than 'law creators' (Guelke 1977): taking laws 'discovered' by biology, physics, economics, sociology, or psychology and testing them against spatial patterns of behaviour. The late 1960s and 1970s saw human geographers searching out a whole variety of 'economic' theories with some spatial element to them, or else if there was none, 'spatialising them' by proposing a series of expected spatial outcomes and then testing this spatialised theory against spatial patterns. Examples include Taafe *et al*.'s (1963) spatialising of Rostow's (1960) stage theory of modernisation, and various Von Thünenian, Christallerian and Löschian spatialisations of land rent theory (see Haggett 1965).

While many human geographers participated in such activities, Cloke *et al*. record that during the late 1960s and through the 1970s:

even within the ranks of the spatial scientists a measure of unease quickly began to emerge about the ability of their cherished 'laws' and 'models' ... to account adequately for observed patterns of location and movement within society (Cloke *et al.* 1991: 66–7).

To put it bluntly, the theories being tested did not stand up to their spatialised testing. While the Taffe and Gould model, for instance, might appear to explain the transport system of West Africa, it did not appear to fit convincingly in any other places. Similarly, while the spatialised rent theories might account for pattern of agriculture in south Germany or the distribution of housing in a few western cities, neither appeared be particularly good when tested against the situation in underdeveloped countries or indeed in many parts of the so-called 'developed world'. Some geographers began to question assumptions which underlay the theories they were using and to recognise that many of the assumptions they were making to construct their theories were untenable. Elements of this critique will be discussed later, but before then it is important to consider the epistemological aspects of logical positivist philosophy and spatial science.

Logical Positivist Epistemology in Geography

Geography as spatial science was not simply about looking for universal processes or laws but it also involved new ways of constructing and evaluating knowledge. That is it involved transformations in the predominant epistemology of geography, which has earlier been identified as empiricist. Logical positivism, and indeed an earlier form of positivism associated with the work of Auguste Comte (see Box 2.1), shared with empiricism a concern with observation as a way of establishing the truth of something, although particular emphasis was placed on the replicability and precision of observations. Secure, truthful, certain knowledge was seen to be the product of 'testing' through repeated observations unambiguously expressed through precise, quantified terminology. Closely associated with replicability and precision were calls for the adoption of a so-called 'scientific methodology', with the emphasis within logical positivism being very much placed on singularity of approach. Physics, for example, was often held up as the exemplar of a logical positivist science and its methodologies were seen to be of universal applicability over the physical and social sciences, and indeed into the arts and humanities. Linked to this, and also to the emergence of computer technologies able to mathematically process ever greater amounts of information, the production of geographical information became increasingly focused on 'quantification' – that is expressing things in terms of numerical values and formulae – and Unwin (1992: 135) comments that the application of such methodologies often became 'an end in itself', a claim that is lent support by the subsequent admission of one well known quantifier that he 'overwhelmed' himself with data, acquiring virtually any which looked analysable, which was then often 'manipulated ... almost *ad* infinitum' (Johnston 1984: 41–44).

Box 2.1: Comtean positivism

Almost 100 years prior to the Vienna School's elaboration of the notion of logical positivism, the Frenchman Auguste Comte sketched out another positivist philosophy. Indeed Comte coined the term 'positivism' to characterise a system of thought, or 'new world religion' as he called it, which he proposed would, as Unwin (1992: 31) puts it, 'provide general rules for the benefit and improvement of society'. Comte was highly concerned about the social situation in France in the early nineteenth century and was keen to stress both what he saw as positive features and to criticise what he saw as disorderly, irrational change. As Livingstone (1992) notes, although Comte has often been associated with the Enlightenment movement which stressed social change through the application of rational thought (see later in the text), he himself characterised his work 'retrograde' or as we might put it now, conservative. Comte's positive social features included tradition, familial associations and social inequality, which he set up against individualism which he described as the 'disease of the Western World' (quoted in Livingstone 1992: 320). What Comte did share with advocates of Enlightenment was a 'progressivist' mentality and a faith in the powers of human reason and science.

Comte proposed that rules for the improvement of society would be created out of knowledge created through science which followed certain principle. He outlined five basic principles which he saw as necessary for the creation of positive knowledge and thereby social improvement and order. These 'positive principles' were each contrasted with other, for Comte, less beneficial ways of acting and thinking. The five dualism he set up are listed below, in both French and in an English translation:

– Le réel versus le chimerique (the real/actual versus the imaginary)
– La certitude versus l'indescision (the certain versus the undecided)
– Le precis versus le vague (the precise/exact versus the vague)
– L'utile versus l'oiseaux (the useful versus the vain)
– Le relative versus l'absolute (the relative versus the absolute)

Comte's notion of *le réel* was very much a continuation of empiricist philosophy. Comte argued that the 'actual' or the real was only that which could be sensed. Anything that could not be directly sensed was viewed by Comte as being 'imaginary' or 'le chimerique', or as he also often called it, 'metaphysical'. Indeed Comte proposed that there were three distinct types of knowledge or ways of thinking: i) the 'theological' where events in the world were seen to be governed supernatural entities; ii) the 'metaphysical' where events where seen to be governed by some abstract force – such as the human spirit or the force of nature; and iii) the 'scientific' or 'positive' where events were explained in terms of 'the regular connection between empirically observable phenomena'. Academic disciplines, and indeed whole societies, could according to Comte be characterised as being within particular ways of thinking and could 'progress' by moving from the theological to the metaphysical, and from the metaphysical to the scientific. Hence scientific knowledge was given privilege – indeed one could really only describe the results of science as 'knowledge' – and the other forms of thought were downgraded to superstitions or 'metaphysical speculation'.

Given that for Comte science was seen to progress through the formation knowledge based on observation, anything that could be empirically observed could be subject to scientific inquiry. Comte in particular was keen to extend the notion of science from the physical sciences into the social. Anything not amenable to observation came to lie beyond the remit of scientific study and, given Comte's privileging of science over other forms of knowledge, became effectively relegated to a position of unimportance. The unobservable hence was given the dual identity of 'unfathomable mystery' and 'ultimate irrelevance'. As Gregory (1978: 26) comments, while 'Comte did not believe that *all* questions could be answered in positivistic term … he did claim that "if they could not be so answered then they could not be answered at all – so that there was no point in asking them"'.

A *second principle* of Comte's philosophy was closely linked to the rejection of metaphysical speculation. This principle was that of 'certainty' or 'la certitude'. Positivism was about providing clear, so-called 'objective', answers to questions rather than leaving issues open for people to answer for themselves in a multitude of ways. Positivist, scientific knowledge was knowledge about which there was agreement amongst those qualified to make judgements about an issue. This agreement was made possible, so Comte argued, where there was 'commonality of experience': where several independent observers see the same thing and draw the same conclusions, then there is more likelihood that this interpretation may be taken as valid. To assist in creating such certainty then scientists need to outline very clearly the conditions that were present when they made an observation such that someone might be able to replicate these conditions and hence should observe similar results. This notion of replicability is central to notions of 'experimentation' in physical science but for Comte was also possible outside the laboratory so long as scientists followed a very clear methodology which could be reproduced by others: hence as well as direct certainty produced through a 'commonality of experience' there was also 'methodological certainty'.

The *third principle* connects closely to the idea of methodological certainty. Comte did not merely ask for transparent methodologies in science, he also suggested that there were particular methodologies, or ways of creating knowledge, which were better than others. In particular he argued that precision was needed in generating knowledge and that this was best obtained by constructing 'theories' which allowed 'induction' of law-like hypotheses. For Comte the purpose of science was not to the accumulation of observations per se but the connection of observations to theories which consisted of 'laws', or statements about things taken as 'universally true, independent of time and space' (Johnston et al.1994: 320).

While the first two principles were very much about 'epistemology', the third principle has clear connections to the principle of ontology. For Comte, societies, and indeed the physical environment, were very much 'orderly constructions' in that behind all their apparent diversity and chaos he foresaw universal attributes or processes. This ontology of universal processes was often assumed rather than explicitly justified and may well be seen to reflect Comte's social conservatism. However the lack of justification can also be associated with positivism's epistemological principles with allowed observation to be the only form of justification. Positivism as a philosophy had the rather ironic effect of 'beheading' or devaluing philosophy: there appeared to be little value in trying to explain why such laws existed because to do so would probably lead one into producing a series of statements which would be far from certain, precise and observable. Rather the value of the positivist position was seen to be signalled by the growth in the adoption of its principles: if people could produce law-like interpretations which were in accord with positivistic principles, then its assumptions might be seen as being proved correct. Hence Comte's *fourth principle*, that the value of positivistic knowledge was demonstrated by its use. More particularly Comte argued that positive knowledge would be revealed by its 'instrumental effects' – the impact it had to change things in line with its own predictions – and by its 'rationality', particularly the way previously disconnected events could be connected to laws and these various laws in turn could become integrated together. Science for positivists is the accumulation and integration of theoretical laws which have been shown to accord with regular observations.

The final principle of Comte's positivism was *Le relative* which meant that all knowledge is provisional rather than final. Somebody might come along and challenge previously accepted knowledge, either on the grounds of some new observations which did not concur with those previously made, or by offering a new law that appeared more rational (that is connected with a wider range of accepted ideas) or could be connected with a greater range of regular occurrences.

Although logical positivism placed considerable emphasis of the construction of knowledge through the senses, the epistemology it advanced did break away in one critical respect to that associated with empiricism and Comtean positivism, 'inasmuch as it accepted that some statements could be validated without recourse to experience' (Gregory, 1978: 33). More specifically, logical positivists of the Vienna School set up a distinction between two types of knowledge. First, there was the knowledge created in accordance with the principles of empiricism and Comtean positivism: that is knowledge justified by reference to repeated observation. This knowledge consisted of *synthetic statements* which were taken to be true only after having been connected to empirical observation, and empirical observation undertaken through the principles of 'the scientific method'. Knowledge could, however, it was argued take another form, one not recognised by empiricists or Comtean positivists. This second form of knowledge was made up of *analytical* or *a priori* statements which were taken as being true even though they had not been, and indeed crucially could not be, formally tested against empirical observations.

This is a significant epistemological shift in that it implies that at least some ideas might be taken as being true even though they have not been empirically justified. For some logical positivists such as Carnap (1935) the number and form of analytical statements was very limited, relating exclusively to the realms of logic and mathematical formulation. Elements of such a view can also be discerned within Harvey's (1969) book *Explanation in Geography*, which referred to logical positivism as a philosophy focused on 'the logic of sound explanation' and argued that, following its lead, 'we may rightly insists that an explanation should be logically sound, before we even consider its philosophical underpinnings' (p. 6). One might add that this argument can be criticised for failing to recognise how 'logic' might itself be seen as a philosophical concept, although it can be seem to fully congruent with a logical positivist epistemology in which logic constitutes an axiomatic form of knowledge.

Harvey (1969: 8) himself argued that the identification of logic as an apriori epistemological principle was a characteristic only of 'logical positivism of an extreme kind' and that 'the whole procedure of explaining' should be seen as 'highly dependent upon … speculative objectives'. His book still focused on 'sorting out … those aspects of analysis that are a matter of logic and those aspects which are contingent upon philosophical presupposition', with a clear focus on the former. However, geographers more generally began to incorporate a series of 'speculative objectives' into their analysis, most clearly through the formulation of '*deductive theories*'. These theories were by definition seen as 'apriori constructs', although not necessarily in the sense implied in the logical positivist notion of 'analytical statements'. For many geographers deductive theories were what Chisholm (1975: 147), perhaps rather misleadingly in the present context, refers to as *positive theories*, which he defines as theories which seek to 'account for some empirically observed regularity or set of associations'. Such theories can be constructed deductively or inductively, but in each case the theory is only accepted as knowledge once it has been connected to sense observations. In other words, theories are synthetic statements. However, Chisholm argues that deductive theories do not have to be simply used as 'positive theories', or theories of 'what is', but may also be *normative theories*, or theories of 'what should be'. Chisholm argues that many of the theories incorporated into geography in the 1950s and 1960s were of this latter type, although often not recognised as such. So, for example, he argued that the central-place theories of Christaller and Lösch were normative in character, seeking 'not to show the world actually is, but how it should be' (Chisholm 1975: 125); and further that any attempt to criticise these theories because of a failure to correspond with empirical observations was fundamentally mistaken. Rather these theories should be used to plan how to order the world – hence a planner might use them as a guide for how to act in order to '*impose* his [sic] views on the real world' (Chisholm 1975: 146 emphasis added) – or 'to provide a yardstick against which to judge the efficiency of the real world' (pp. 146–7).

Chisholm's normative theories were is a sense akin to the analytical statements of logical positivism in that they were seem as being immune from empirical refutation. As argued elsewhere (Phillips 1998b: 124), logical positivist studies although often conditioned by a focus on what could be empirically sensed did in some cases involve 'utilizing a social imagination which was, at least in theory, … distanced from social experiences and interests'. For instance, Von Thünen's classic work on agricultural land-use, *The Isolated State*, began by asking the reader to make a series of quite unrealistic assumptions, such as 'a very large town at the centre of a fertile plain which is crossed by no navigable rivers. Throughout the plain the soil is … of the same fertility' (Hall 1966: 124). In a sense a logical positivism allowed an opening up of thought beyond simply that which could be connected with sensed observation. However, in other ways this approach produced highly circumscribed theories. In particular the notion of what should happen was often centred on universalising particular elements of the present and little radical transformation of the present into the future was ever envisaged within these theories. Furthermore these theories often neglected how present circumstances were themselves transformations from earlier states: they were *ahistorical theories*. These theories also neglected the complexity of the present and how some elements of the present may well have interests and consequences which run counter to the aspects privileged by the theorist. The theories of Von Thünen, for example, have been criticised by people such as Barnbrock (1976) for being based on an idealisation of capitalism. Somewhat later, Philo (1992b: 201) also noted how the theories of spatial science ignored a whole range of social differences, thereby creating images of the world as being inhabited by 'little armies of faceless, classless, sexless beings', dutifully enacting certain capitalist principles such as minimizing costs and maximising personal profits or utility. In time many geographers have come to reject these omissions, and even at the time when geography was becoming more of a quantitative and logical positivist spatial science, some geographers were beginning to question assumptions which underlay these constructions of geography. It is to these lines of critique that attention will now switch, beginning with a critique advanced by self-styled *humanistic geographers*, and then moving to so-called *radical* and *structuralist* critiques.

Humanistic Geography

Whereas much of logical positivist geography sought to put space and science at the centre of human geography, humanistic geography can be said to put people at the centre. The term humanistic relates to a number of closely related concepts, such as 'humanness' or 'humanity' (what constitutes being human), the 'humanities' (fields of inquiry into the conditions of humans) and being 'humane' (caring for humans). These terms, and the general notions of humanism, emerged in the fourteenth and fifteenth century European Renaissance when people began to challenge existing modes of religious and secular thought on the basis of whether or not these ideas fitted in with people's interests and capabilities. Rather than simply accepting things as the will of a sovereign king or God, people began to question the validity of particular ideas on the grounds of human reason and freedom. Human thought and actions were seen to be able to make a difference, to change things, and hold the potential for making the world a better place for people to live in. Put simply, humanism valued people, seeing them as a central agency in creating the world and considering their interests to be paramount over everything else.

Humanistic geography can be seen as an attempt to connect geography to these human centred values: hence definitions of humanistic geography as 'an approach to human geography distinguished by the central and active role it gives to human awareness and human agency, human consciousness and human creativity' (Johnston *et al.* 1994: 263). Cloke *et al.* (1991: 58) similarly claim that 'the bottom line for humanistic geography lies in the objective of bringing human beings in all their complexity to the centre-stage of human geography'. They add that this emphasis was pursued 'in conscious opposition' to what they see as 'the curiously "peopleless" character of much that had previously passed off as human geography' (Cloke *et al.* 1991: 58). As one of the authors subsequently argued, many 'logical positivist' studies in so-called 'human geography' appeared:

> either deserted of people – think of all those geometric representations of settlements …
> that render them eerily still, silent and devoid of life – or are occupied by little armies of
> faceless, classless, sexless beings dutifully laying out Christaller's central place networks,
> doing exactly the right number of hours farmwork in each of von Thünen's concentric rings,
> and basically obeying the great economic laws of minimising effort and cost in negotiating
> physical space (Philo 1992b: 200).

Cloke *et al.* (1991: 58) add that when one looks more closely at the notion of bringing people into human geography it actually has two major components. First, there is a need to recognise that geographers are human and therefore their human characteristics, their humanity, will influence how they do geography. This feature applies as much to physical as to human geography: all geographical research is human geography in the sense that it is done by people. The second issue, of specific relevance to human geography is the need to recognise the full range of characteristics that the people studied have. These components can be seen to relate respectively to the epistemology and ontology of humanistic geography.

Arguments for a More Humanistic Ontology

Humanistic geography suggested a rather different ontology from those employed by spatial science. Spatial science basically argued that people behaved in, or should behave in, regular, predictable ways. As Cloke *et al.* (1991: 69) comment, spatial science viewed people in a manner akin to some inanimate objects: it '"objectified", "reified" or (in Olsson's more memorable term) "thingified" the people under study', portraying them as disembodied and dehumanised 'entities':

> whizzing about in space – travelling from place X to place Y; shopping at centre X rather
> than centre Y; selling produce at market X rather than in market Y – in a fashion little differ-
> ent from the 'behaviour' of stones on a slope, particles in a river or atoms in a gas (Cloke *et
> al.* 1991, p 69).

Even within the ranks of geographers involved in geography as spatial science there was some contestation about the desirability of such a conception of people, particularly by advocates of a *behavioural approach* to human geography (see Box 2.2). From the early 1970s the number and scale of objections to this portrayal of people began to increase, with a series of calls being made for the development a more recognisably 'human' human geography: a human geography which had an ontology centred around the realites of people and being human, as opposed to a geography in which people appeared virtually indistinguishable from inanimate stones or soil particles. So, for example, Entrikin (1976: 616) argued for a humanistic geography which rejected spatial science's 'overly objective, narrow, mechanistic and deterministic view of man [sic]' and was concerned with 'the aspects of man which are most distinctively "human": meaning, value, goals, and purposes'. Similarly, Ley and Samuels (1978: 2) called for a human geography which put 'man ... back together again with all the pieces in place, including a heart and even a soul, with feelings as well as thoughts, with some sense of secular and perhaps transcendental meaning'.

Box 2.2: Behavioural approaches to geography

In the 1960s some researchers began to question some of the behavioural assumptions which underpinned theorising within spatial scientific geography. In particular they began to question whether theories based on neo-classical economic laws relied on a notion of an 'economic rational man' which was, first, far from universal and, second, might indeed be completely untenable. A key early study which touched on both issues was by Wolpert (1964). With regard to the first issue, Wolpert argued that many Swedish farmers were 'satisfisers' rather than 'optimisers': that is they were not really concerned about maximising profits by keeping costs down and maximising revenues, but were happy just to do enough to have a reasonable standard of living.

Wolpert also highlighted how even if farmers were seeking optimal decisions they often did not arrive at them, in large part because of limitations in their knowledge. This finding points to a fundamental criticism which can be made about the ontology of human behaviour underlying many neo-classical theories advanced within logical positivist spatial science. Specifically, many of these theories employed some notion of 'economically rational behaviour' associated with a so-called 'economically-rational *man*' (note the gendering of the term). This was, as Blakemore (1981: 96) notes, a representation or theory of human of behaviour which assumes that people seek the maximisation of self-advantage or profit and posits that: 'Given perfect knowledge and a perfect ability to utilise such information in a rational fashion, economic man maximises returns and minimizes costs'. However, as geographers such as Wolpert demonstrated, such assumptions are highly unrealistic in that not only are people not always profit maximisers but, more fundamentally, people vary in their abilities to process information and their knowledge is always 'bounded' or restricted, not least by issues of geography. People can never be perfect decision-makers because they never have knowledge of what existed everywhere. Rather people had spatially delimited knowledges, or as it was variously termed by behavioural geographers, 'cognitive/mental maps' (Downs and Stea 1973; Gould and White 1974), 'perceptual fields' (Potter 1976; 1977; 1979) or 'behavioural environments' (Boal and Livingstone 1989; Kirk 1952;

1963). As demonstrated in Walmsley and Lewis (1993), a series of behavioural studies on topics such as location decision making by firms, residential decision making and migration, shopping behaviour, and use of recreation and leisure facilities, all showed human behaviour being conditioned by peoples' spatialised perceptions, and how this perception was itself conditioned by geographies of behaviour.

Such studies raised fundamental questions about the value of theories and models developed by spatial scientists, and for people such as Burton (1963), Brookfield (1969) and Mercer and Powell (1972) represented a move towards a non-positivist (and for the last two authors, at least, a humanistic) human geography. Other geographers, notably Golledge and various co-workers, claimed that behavioural geography remained wedded, in large part, to a positivist approach (see Couclelis and Golledge 1983; Golledge and Couclelis 1984; Golledge and Rushton 1984; Golledge and Stimson 1987). Behavioural geography can indeed be seen to sit astride positivist and humanistic philosophies. Epistemologically it appeared highly positivist in the stress often given to scientific methodology; a detached, so-called 'objective', attitude to research; hypothesis construction and testing; quantified measurements and mathematical formulations. Ontologically, the positioning is a bit more ambiguous in that, as in positivist spatial science, considerable emphasis was given to connecting theoretical ideas with observed regularities across space and there was a universalising view of people which centred on them being rational decision makers. However, in contrast to the neo-classical theoretical assumptions which underpinned much of spatial science, within behavioural geography rationality was always 'bounded' and could take many forms apart from profit maximisation. Behavioural geographers were hence quite happy to accept that people would act in what from the outside would appear to be highly unpredictable ways, this unpredictability stemming from the degree to which people's aims and perceptions corresponded to or differed from other people's and from the theoretical predictions of the researcher. Overall one can conclude that behavioural geographers rejected some elements of the theories and explanations of spatial science whilst, at the same time, enacting some of the same epistemological and ontological fundamentals.

Notions of a heart and a soul, of feelings and of meanings, would all have been viewed as imaginary rather than real by positivists such as Comte and any consideration of them viewed as unnecessary metaphysics. Likewise within geography as spatial science, such notions would have been largely excluded from consideration either on the grounds that they were incapable of precise and replicable observation, or that they were merely distortions from some underlying rational order. However, for humanistic geographers such notions were seen as central to conceptions of humanity in general and to understanding the behaviour of individual people.

Humanistic geographers were also sceptical about whether human behaviour was conditioned by universal laws, instead emphasising how people's behaviour was often highly 'irregular' and not really linked to 'rational calculation' as implied within positivist and behavioural approaches. By contrast, humanistic geographers argued that much of human activity was both highly irregular and might be seen as 'non-rational' if not 'irrational'. In other words, it might well be conditioned by things other than rational calculation of the costs and benefits of any particular action. People's behaviour, for example, might be conditioned by habit and routine; by emotions and experiences about which people are only dimly aware and only partly able to account for; and through the unconscious, which by definition is not open to conscious thought and decision making.

Such arguments led humanistic geographers away from many of the sources of inspiration used by spatial scientists, such as physics and neo-classical economies, and towards a variety of other literatures. Some geographers of a behavioural persuasion turned to cognitive psychology; others such as Meinig (1983), Pocock (1981) and Porteous (1985) turned to art, history and other subjects in the humanities; while yet others turned to philosophy, with a range of approaches being promoted, including *phenomenology, existentialism, idealism, pragmatism* and *symbolic interactionism*. Fuller details of these approaches are provided in Boxes 2.3 to 2.6, but simplifying greatly it is possible to see idealism as an attempt to discover conscious thoughts that influence human behaviour; phenomenology as being concerned with how people relate, consciously, sub-consciously and unconsciously, to objects in the world; existentialism as having a focus on the experiences people gain in the world; and pragmatism/social interactionism as concerned with ideas formed in the context of social activities.

Box 2.3: Phenomenology

An early port of call in the search for a philosophical grounding for humanistic geography was phenomenology. Philosophically, this term is generally traced back to the work of Edmund Husserl, a German philosopher writing in the late nineteenth and early twentieth centuries. Husserl was very critical about the application of natural science perspectives and methods onto the study of human culture and society, arguing that each academic discipline had its own particular 'domain of investigation' (Christensen 1982: 51) and probably associated particular methodologies, which should relate to *essences* (or *eidé*). These essences were essential, 'deep' meanings formed by how people relate to things in the world around them. For Husserl there were 'transcendental', that is universally present but not necessarily consciously recognised, relationships between people and objects. People both experience and become conscious of objects in the worlds around them and also possess intentions towards objects in terms of how to relate to them: are these things to be used as 'objects' without any thought of these entities having such things as consciousness, emotions and rights; are these things to be ignored for having no use; or are these entities 'subjects' to be treated in a manner which acknowledges various normative rights and human faculties.

As discussed in the text, Husserl's *transcendental phenomenology* shared with positivism a universalised ontology, although there are important differences between positivist 'universal laws' and Husserl's 'intentional essences' (see Cloke *et al.* 1991; Pickles 1985). Epistemologically, differences between phenomenology and positivism were even more clear-cut, with Husserl being very critical of the empiricist notion that knowledge is constructed through the senses. For Husserl much of what makes phenomena of significance is not accessible through direct experience in that people relate to things un- and subconsciously as well as consciously. Indeed, Husserl suggests that consciousness often blinds people to what is of most significance; a problem which he felt was characteristic of much of scientific thought in the early twentieth century (see Husserl 1965). Husserl was not anti-science but rather felt that scientific theories and methods often got in the way of grasping the essences of phenomena. He advocated that all existing ideas about phenomena should be forgotten, or 'bracketed out', so that the resulting essences could be recognised (a process known as *phenomenological reduction* or *epoché*). Once this was done, he argued, it would then be possible distinguish distinct sciences, each with their own field of investigation centred on one or more essences.

As discussed in the text, these ideas were employed by some humanistic geographers to argue for a refocusing of human geography on people's relationships to place, space and nature. It is also suggested that over time there was a general movement away from Husserl's transcendental phenomenology towards the *constitutive phenomenology* of people such as Merleau-Ponty and Schutz (e.g. Buttimer 1976; Ley 1977). As Gregory (1978: 126) notes, Schutz rejected Husserl's concern with uncovering the 'essences' of social phenomena and its associated discarding of people's preconceptions. For Schutz these preconceptions constituted a central ontological focus because it was through these that people made sense of and acted upon the world in which they lived. Shutz's phenomenology was concerned with intentionalities directed at myriad constituents of everyday life rather than seeking transcendental intentionalities from which to construct a framework for the conduct of science. Geographers drawing on the work of Schutz have often focused their studies on the *taken-for-granted* understandings developed in people's everyday environments or *lifeworlds* (see Ley 1977). This work has taken the varied everyday experiences of people much more seriously than was the case with much of the work inspired by Husserl's transcendental phenomenology, and has as a result come to address issues of concern to people inspired by existentialism: indeed the writings of Schutz and Merleau-Ponty has been described as *existential phenomenology* (Cloke *et al.* 1991: 72; Peet 1998: 39–45).

Box 2.4: Existentialism

Existential philosophies can be seen to focus on how people exist in and experience the world. In many philosophies experience is seen as either a problem to be over come, as in structuralism, or else is reduced to some narrow variant of experience, such as sensed observations in empiricism and positivisms, or cognition in behavioural and idealist philosophies. Existentialism, as Peet (1998: 36) puts it, 'recurrently deals with the emotional life, the feelings, the moods and the effects through which people are involved in the world'. It seeks to address the whole range of ways of experiencing and existing in the world, although particular existentialists have often focused on particular forms of experience and existence.

Initial references to existential philosophers by humanistic geographers often focused on one of two claims about human experience and existence. Humanistic geographers such as Relph (1970; 1976), Tuan (1971) and Pickles (1985), for example, drew on the work of the German philosopher Heidegger who addressed notions of space and place in his books *The Question of Being* (Heidegger 1958) and *Being and Time* (Heidegger 1962). Heidegger argued that Western philosophy had adopted overly abstract, dehumanised, notions of these concepts. By contrast, Heidegger argued for the development of an ontology which focused on how people related to space in their everyday lives, and which saw peoples' relationships with space as being embodied and experiential as opposed to external and geometrical. He suggested, for example, that people relate to things in their world through what he described as *deseverance* and *directionality* where the former constitutes a 'de-distancing' whereby people feel close to things that they are familiar with or feel they understand, while the latter relates to the extent to which people are orientated towards something (see Peet 1998: 41). Deseverance connects closely to notions of *place attachment* and *dwelling* which were the focus of Relph's interest in the work of Heidegger. Further details of Relph's work is provided in the text, which also relates claims that his existentialism creates an overly romantic view of place attachment as well as adopting an overly monolithic conception of what the human person or being (or *dasein* as a Heideggerian philosopher might call it) is.

In some contrast to the romanticism of Relph's appropriation of Heidegger, although not to the monolithic construct of the human subject, Samuels (1978; 1981) draws on the existentialism of Buber (1957) and Sartre (1958) to suggest that a universal aspect human existence was being alienated from the world around us: of being 'set apart from the world around them' so that, in turn, they can 'enter into relationships' with parts of that world (Walmsley and Lewis 1993: 17).

Notions of alienation are central to many strands of Marxism, and as Peet (1998: 113) notes, Sartre moved from an 'existential phenomenology to awards an existential Marxism'. The notion of 'setting apart' so as to 'enter into relations with' may indeed be seen to describe the subject-object relations which characterise human productive activity. Despite such clear connections, calls to make use of Sartre's *existential Marxism* by people such as Baker (1984) have not really been followed up within geography. Instead what has emerged most strongly from geography's encounter with existential philosophy is a broad *geographical existentialism* (Cloke *et al*. 1991) which, although making little or no reference to the likes of Heidegger, Buber or Sartre, is concerned with how people experience the worlds around them, such as Rowles' (1978a; 1978b) studies of elderly people's experiential involvements with places and places.

Box 2.5: Idealism

Idealism is a term which has been widely used to characterise philosophical arguments and positionings. It can be seen to have been broadly used to refer to people who either adopt: i) an ontology whereby people's ideas, or conscious thoughts, determine much, if not all, of what goes on in the world (or *metaphysical idealism* as it is often called (Johnston et al 2000: 367)); or ii) an epistemology whereby knowledge is limited to that which is perceived (or *epistemological idealism* (Johnston *et al.* 2000: 367)). The term idealism is often associated with the German philosopher Hegel, and the critique of him by Marx. Hegel argued that historically societies moved through a series of 'spiritual forms' or cultures, and that this movement was a progressive one in that each stage represented a resolution of some problematic features earlier cultures. History for Hegel was seen to centre around the perfection of human consciousness.

Marx, however, vehemently rejected Hegel's view of historical development characterising his own work as 'historical materialism' to distant himself from Hegel's idealism. He argued in the book *The German Ideology* (Marx and Engels 1970) that Hegel and other idealists had misunderstood historical development and that rather than culture driving human activity and historical change, consciousness was created by human activity, most notably through developments in productive activity. It was from such arguments that notions of the economy determining culture have been taken by many Marxists, although these claims have also been widely contested within Marxism (see Chapter 3). The relationship between culture and economic practices and relationships was a key feature of debates between humanistic and Marxist geographers in the late 1970s and early 1980s (see Chouinard and Fincher 1983; Duncan and Ley 1982), and also resurfaced in discussions of postmodernism and post-structuralism, philosophies which were identified by people such as Harvey (1992) as exhibiting a *discursive idealism* which needed to be replaced by more materialist forms of analysis (see later in text).

Human geographers have made little direct use of Hegel's idealism, although notions of paradigm shifts (Box 2.1) and other 'Whiggish' accounts of the development of geography might be seen to rely on some broadly Hegelian logic (see Doel 1993). More direct connections were made to idealism by Guelke (1974; 1981; 1982a; 1982b) who turned to the *historical idealism* advanced by the historian Collingwood (1956). Collingwood argued that 'all history is the history of human thought' in the sense that all actions were, he claimed, the result of reasoned thought. Hence anyone wanting to understand human actions in the past, or a product of such actions such as the formation of a textual document, image or landscape feature, needed to address the thoughts that lay behind the action. This was to be achieved either by seeking to reconstruct those thoughts directly or to put one's self in the position and mind set of those actors and to 'rethink their thoughts' in a process of empathetic understanding, or *verstehen* (Guelke 1974).

Guelke's turn to historical idealism was stimulated by unease with positivistic approaches in human geography in general and historical geography in particular (see Guelke 1975; 1977; 1978). However, despite his criticisms of positivist approaches, Guelke's idealism has itself been seen to constitute a continuation of positivism (Harrison and Livingstone 1979). Guelke, like behavioural geographers, retained an epistemological emphasis on detachment as a route to objectivity and on verification through methodological certainty (see Box 2.2), and also an ontological emphasis on rational cognitive decision making. Where Guelke's idealism did differ from behaviouralism was in its emphasis on explaining individual actions and not seeking to formulate universalised notions of human cognition and behavioural patterns.

Box 2.6: Pragmaticism and symbolic interactionism

Logical positivism in geography is widely associated with the work of the so-called 'Chicago School' of urban sociologists (see Box 9.1). However, in the 1980s people such as Jackson and Smith (Jackson and Smith 1984; Smith 1984) argued that this work had been very selectively interpreted by spatial science and that much of it was inspired by humanistic concerns, and particularly by 'pragmatic' and 'interactionist' philosophies of people such as Charles Peirce, John Dewey, William James and George Herbert Mead. There are important differences between these writers, and in particular between the pragmatism of the first two and the symbolic interactionism of the latter two (Smith 1984: 354). However, these writers all sought to recognise the everydayness of knowledge construction: in their everyday actions and interactions people are making interpretations about the world, evaluating the value of these interpretations, and often reformulating them in the light of subsequent experiences.

Pragmatism and symbolic interactionism very much build similar ontologies as the constitutive phenomenology of people such as Schutz (see Box 2.3), although they tend to emphasise interpersonal, subject-subject relationships (or *inter-subjective* relations) as opposed to the subject-object relationships which was often the principal focus of phenomenologists. Pragmatists also very much focused on epistemological issues and on applying arguments about the construction of everyday knowledges to their own knowledge. As Hoy and McCarthy (1994: 8) comment, for pragmatists all practices 'including epistemic practices like theorizing – have to viewed in their socio-cultural context if they are to be properly understood'. Scientific knowledge, as much as any other form of knowledge, was seen to be created inter-subjectively, to be highly fallible and likely to need constant revision, and to gain its validity through its application within social practices.

The arguments of people such as Jackson and Smith, and also Ley (1977) and Duncan (1978), were not really followed up by other human geographers. Recent years have, however, seen a revival of interest in pragmatism within the social sciences and philosophy, with people such as Habermas (1978; 1987b; 1988) suggesting they pointed to key issues of 'practical understanding' which distinguish the study of human world from the study of the non-human (see Unwin 1992, especially: 35–41). Another source of renewal has been the work of Rorty (1979; 1982), who has championed a return to pragmatism in a critique of representation and universalising theories which, as discussed later in the text, has very much been caught up in the formulation of postmodern and post-structural geographies

Although humanistic geographers often criticised the spatial scientist's search for universal laws, in many ways they reproduced this search in their own work. Humanistic geographers, particularly those influenced by existentialism and phenomenology, often described the purpose of their human geographies in terms of uncovering some universal relationships or attachments that people had to such geographical objects as 'place', 'landscape', 'nature' and 'space'. The precise ways in which these relationships were understood varied considerably between humanistic geographers. Tuan (1971; 1976) and Relph (1976; 1985), for example, draw on the phenomenology of Husserl (see Box 2.3) to imply that scientific approaches to geography were obscuring some basic 'true' or 'essential' meanings of geography. A clear illustration of this is provided by Tuan (1976: 268) who claimed that humanistic geography had 'as one of its tasks, the study of geographical knowledge' in all its forms, forms which should be seen to range 'from the "mental maps" of migrating birds to our own "mental maps"', from 'implicit knowing to explicit knowledge', including but not simply the 'highly conscious and specialist' geographical 'lore promoted within … the culture of academic departments'. Relph (1985: 16) made very similar claims, arguing that a 'sense of wonder about the earth and its places' was a key motivator of people's initial interest in geography and that this 'original' aspect of geography had become 'submerged', either being excluded as being of no significance or as being obscured within the analytical generalisations of spatial science.

Slightly earlier, Relph (1976: 14) had drawn on the notion of 'dwelling' as outlined by Heidegger (see Box 2.3) to develop similar arguments. In particular, he argued that a fully human, 'authentic' sense of place lay in a sense of belonging or 'insiderness' which came from 'a direct and genuine experience of the entire complex of the identity of places – not mediated or distorted through a series of quite arbitrary social conventions about how that experience should be' (Relph 1976: 14). For Samuels, by contrast, the human condition was one of alienation from place:

> the sine qua non of human existence is objectivity (i.e. detachment or estrangement), which is nothing other than the act of making things (the world) distant from one-self ... All men are conditioned by distance and are – by definition – alienated ... All men, insofar as they are human ... are ontologically alienated. The differences among men (culturally and historically), in this regard, are a function of their success in overcoming, reinforcing or revolting against their alienation (Samuels 1978: 26–9).

Where such humanistic geographies differed from the work of spatial scientists was that they sought to uncover the universal not in spatial arrangement, in ordered sets of dots, lines and hexagons on a map, but instead in some 'basic', 'essential' or 'authentic' way in which people related to their worlds. As Cloke *et al.* (1991: 81) record, much of humanistic geography was hence seeking, 'to tease out the "transcendental" (universal, timeless, placeless) essences supposedly embodied in how all people experience space, place and environment'.

Cloke *et al.* add, however, that 'what has also surfaced on occasions is a concern for the more "everyday geographies" of the places in which we live and labour' (p. 81). They point particularly to the work of Ley (1974; 1977; 1988) and his use of the Schutz's notion of 'lifeworld' (see Box 2.3 and 2.6), which was also the focus of work by geographers such as Buttimer (1976) and Seamon (1979) and was picked up in the social theories of Habermas (1984; 1987b) and Giddens (1984) which were themselves to exert a considerable influence on some geographers.

Overall, two broad ontological positions can be identified within humanistic geography. First there was a strand that corresponds to what Pickles (1985: 45) has described as *phenomenological geography*. This was an approach to humanistic geography which sought to demonstrate that people have some form of universal relationship to geographical objects such as place, space, landscape or nature. Second, there were other geographers who concentrated much more on describing the diversity of perceptions and emotions people had about these objects. This corresponds to what Pickles describes as *geographical phenomenology*, although Cloke *et al.* (1991: 83) suggest that the term *geographical existentialism* might be more appropriate.

In the 1970s advocates of both ontological positions used the term 'humanistic' to characterise their work. However, by the late 1980s and early 1990s some of the human geographers involved in the second strand of research began to describe their work more in relation to other philosophies, notably those of postmodernism (e.g Ley 1989b; 1993). As part of this movement towards a more postmodern perspective, and also in association with the emergence of *feminist geography* (see Box 2.11), there emerged some criticism of the universalising strand of humanistic geography. Rose, for example, argued that their was an 'authoritarian' or 'positional claim' claim embedded within the humanistic celebration of notions of place:

The implication of this celebration of place is that those of us who are not interested in place are less than alive, less than human, less than the sensitive geographers who are aware of such important things (Rose 1993a: 50).

Humanistic geographers such as Tuan and Relph universalised their own interest in places (and equally, one might add, in such geographical entities as space, nature and landscape) in that they implied it was an interest shared by everybody. They also implied that understanding place was a complex task requiring skills such as empathy, sensitivity, artistry and creativity. As Rose notes, the implications of such views are that anyone who is not interested in place is either less capable or less interesting than those who are.

Rose goes on to critique some of the assumptions made by humanistic geographers. She argues, for instance, that humanistic geography falsely assumes that men's experiences of place can be taken to represent some universal/essential human relationship to place. She argues that when humanistic geographers talked about belonging and dwelling they tend to draw upon a highly gendered conception of home, seeing it as a place of rest, of recreation and re-creation. Rose argues that while this may be men's experience of the home, it is often not the experience of women for whom the home is often a site of exploitation, repression and confinement.

Such criticisms may be seen to have caused movement away from humanistic philosophies, particularly by those adopting the second ontological position which does not adopt the same universalising position critiqued by Rose. However, caution is needed because the movement occurred somewhat in advance of Rose's critique. One reason for this is that the movement may have related rather more to epistemological concerns than to a sustained ontological critique.

Humanistic Epistemologies

As mentioned in the introduction to this section, humanistic geographers not only argued for a greater recognition of people as the subject of human geography research but also argued for a greater recognition of the role that people had in the creation of knowledge. Positivism, in both its Cometean and logical forms, was a 'normative' epistemology in that it was concerned with how people *should* construct knowledge rather than how they actually did do it, which it implied was often not as it should be. Positivist knowledge if correctly created was seen as 'objective' knowledge unaffected by the 'subjectivity' of the researcher and divorced from such things as personal values, emotions and experiences. Humanistic geographers argued, however, that in reality subjectivity entered into all stages of the research: from the choice of research topics, through into 'every stage of data categorisation, collection and analysis' (Mercer 1984: 165), and right through into selection of how to present findings. As Cloke *et al.* (1991: 59) comment, for humanistic geographers there is no knowledge which is not 'indelibly' marked by 'human attributes and products'. Notions of objectivity were hence seen by many humanistic geographers as spurious. Furthermore, humanistic geographers often also argued that notions of divorcing knowledge creation from human values was undesirable in that it discouraged researchers from considering how their research might actually help people. Humanistic geographers, on the other hand, argued that a concern for the well-being of people, or of human kind if one adopted the more universalising approach, should be a central reason for doing geography. The purpose of doing geography for them was not about producing knowledge for its own sake, but rather producing knowledge that would make the world a more humane place, a world in which people might feel at home.

Such an epistemological view posed serious challenges to geographers, particularly those schooled into empiricist and positivist ways of knowing. In response to this challenge, humanistic geographers turned in a variety of directions. Some, such as Berdoulay (1978), Buttimer (1978) and Jackson and Smith (1984), turned for inspiration to the ideas and practices of earlier, and now seemingly neglected geographers and associated researchers. Other humanistic geographers looked to the practices – both in terms of research methods and with reference to wider practices of writing, disseminating and legitimating their research – of other, seemingly, nonscientific disciplines. Hence, Harris (1971, 1978) extolled the virtues of historians, Hart (1982) and Meinig (1983) those of the artist, and Jackson and Smith (1984) those of the anthropologists. A third route away from the methodology of science was a turn to philosophy, and in particular to philosophers who had actively criticised positivistic philosophies and/or developed seemingly radically different ideas.

As previously mentioned, one early port of call for humanistic geographers was the phenomenology of Husserl (Box 2.3). One of the attractions of his work for humanistic geographers was that he had argued, most prominently in a series of lectures in Prague in 1935 (see Husserl 1965), that the techniques of the physical sciences could not be extended into the study culture and society. In particular he argued that European society was at a point of 'crisis' because of a 'sickness' which stemmed from application of natural science perspectives and methods onto the study of human culture and society. Husserl took a largely negative view of the empirical and positivist sciences and argued that there was a need for people to forget, or 'bracket out' their preconceptions, including those established through scientific methods, when studying phenomena. Husserl argued that all objects had an essential meaning or *essence*, that the purpose of science should be to recover that essence, and this recovery could be achieved by *phenomenological reduction* in which all existing ideas about an object are forgotten and the resulting 'pure relation' is thereby revealed (see Box 2.4). Tuan and Relph drew on such arguments to suggest that the deployment of phenomenology within geography would provided a way of 'bracketing out' scientific and academic presuppositions and thereby permitting geographers to see things as they really are, including the recognition of the centrality of the notion of a sense of place.

There are, however, a number of major criticisms which have been levelled at the notion of 'bracketing out' presuppositions (see Billinge 1977) and there was a perceptible, and arguably unsurprising, movement in the philosophical arguments of humanistic geography into those which can be said to lie more under the rubric of 'existentialism' than 'phenomenology', although the dividing line between the two is not always clear, particularly in the writings of geographers. One reason for this was that the turn towards experience as an object of study, which can be said to be a definitive feature of existentialism, was prefigured in much of the earlier philosophical writing, of which geographers in the early 1970s were arguably only dimly aware. For instance, Husserl's notion of 'bracketing out', of which Tuan and Relph made so much, had already been rejected by Alfred Schutz when he developed his 'constitutive' or 'existential phenomenology' (see Box 2.4). Rather than wishing to bracket out social preconceptions, Schutz made the constitution of these preconceptions his focus of attention. He did this through the concept of 'lifeworld', which has been defined as "the culturally defined spatiotemporal setting or horizon of everyday life" (Buttimer 1976: 277). Schutz argued that people live and act within a 'reality or 'world' which is constituted through their own preconceptions of reality, which in turn are created through current and past experiences (see Schutz and Luckman 1973).

Given this precedent, it is arguably unsurprising that after a short period of time humanistic geographers began to 'talk less in terms of transcending the everyday and more in terms of studying those everyday meanings etched into the *lifeworlds* of particular peoples, societies or cultures' (Cloke *et al*. 1991: 72–73). In other words, they moved from Pickles (1985: 45) 'phenomenological geography' towards a 'geographical phenomenology' or 'geographical existentialism'. One might add that they may well have moved less as a consequence of reflection on the relative ontologies of these approaches and rather more as a result of the epistemological dilemmas the former approach raised. Having said this, however, it is also important to recognise that philosophical debates always occur set within a social context which may itself play a profound role in determining their outcomes. A 'phenomenological geography', for example, would not only fall foul of criteria of technical utility favoured by positivist geographers and hence be likely to be seen 'as an irrelevant failure' (Unwin 1992: 146), but it might also, as Gregory (1978) notes, been seen as a failure against other, more socially practical criteria; including those espoused within the radical and structuralist philosophies to which attention will now move.

Radicalism and Structuralism in Geography

So far philosophies have been discussed with regard to both epistemologies and ontologies. However, philosophical positionings are often far from clear-cut as is well evidenced by the emergence of radicalism and structuralism in human geography (see also Box 2.2 on behavioural geography). Many accounts of the human geography in the 1970s combine radicalism and structuralism, positing them as a third philosophy, standing against both positivism and humanism (see Johnston 1983b; 1997). However, in the following account radicalism will be discussed solely in association with epistemology, before considering structuralism as both ontology and epistemology. It is felt that this structure gives a clearer sense of some of the strands of philosophical ideas and contestations which characterised this period and produced a complex of mosaic of inter-related but significantly different approaches which have defied attempts to formulate some 'all-embracing, single descriptive, adjective' (Johnston 1997:209). Significant shards in the mosaic to be surveyed in the following section include anarchic, critical, feminist, Marxist, political economic, radical and structuralist geographies.

Radical Geographies and the Politicisation of Epistemology

As outlined in the preceding section, a central element within humanistic geography was an epistemological critique of spatial science's notion of objectivity. One of the main messages of humanistic geography was that subjectivity lay at the centre of knowledge production and could not be simply ushered away by the employment of some particular set of methodological principles. However, another line of epistemological critique emerged in geography in the 1970s, and this line of critique was often directed as much at humanistic as to positivistic geographies. The line of critique sought to politicise knowledge: to show how knowledge production and use is intimately connected into the operation of social power and associated conflicts and struggles.

Positivistic science sought to isolate scientists from their social context: the best scientist was seen to be one who is unswayed by personal values or political direction. This has been described as a *scientistic* understanding of science, one which sees science as some activity above or divorced from society (Phillips 1994a). This is a very widespread viewpoint, indeed Said (1995: 10) has argued that, 'the determining impingement on most knowledge produced in the contemporary West ... is that it be non-political, that is, scholarly, academic, impartial, above partisan or small-minded doctrinal belief'. He adds, however, that,

> ... in practice the reality is much more problematic. No one has ever devised a method of detaching the scholar from the circumstances of life, from the fact of his [sic] involvement (conscious or unconscious) with a class, a set of beliefs, a social position, or from the mere activity of being a member of society (Said 1995: 10).

Humanistic geographers, whilst generally not adopting scientistic self-understandings, did tend to separate knowledge production off from social context, with knowledge often being viewed as a product of individual consciousness with little or no regard as to how this might connect to, or indeed differ from, the understandings of others. Furthermore, whilst some humanistic geographers argued that it had at its core a social interest in making the world more humane, this concern appears somewhat peripheral to many of its studies. Indeed some 'hints of ... elitism' have been identified within humanistic studies (Johnston *et al.* 1994: 85), while, as already discussed, Rose (1993a) sees embodiments of a masculinist authoritarianism. There was certainly no real attempt to document the social impacts of humanistic geography – to see whether these studies really did make life more humane – and hence one can suggest that humanistic geography remained as much, if not more, of an 'ivory tower' exercise than did spatial science.

However, whilst academics of both humanist and scientific persuasions might have seen themselves as producers of knowledge isolated from society, people outside academia often tend to judge subjects on what 'use' they are in the so-called 'real world', which generally means their worlds. Planners and policy makers, for example, often look to academics to suggest policy changes; business organisation often look to academics to provide marketable products; while governments look to academics to solve political problems and to provide a good return on their investments. During the late 1960s and early 1970s a number of geographers began to feel that such people were beginning to look at geography and ask questions about the amount and value of the knowledge they were receiving from geographers. Prince (1971: 52), for example, suggested that geographers were beginning to experience 'a deep sense of failure' which was at least in part due to people outside geography not taking geographers seriously. Prince argued that the knowledge that geographers were producing was 'not being put to good use' in that it was not being applied to solving problems. In particular Prince argued that geographers had learnt much about 'ways and means of reducing hunger, disease and poverty, but little had been achieved' (p. 152). He also suggested that, 'educated people had not been instrumental in stopping a barbarous war [Vietnam] and that, within their own universities, they had failed to bring about overdue reforms' (Prince 1971: 152). In other words, Prince was suggesting that the knowledge of academic geographers might be an irrelevancy: ignored by policy makers and completely ineffectual in influencing events such as an overseas war or even how one runs a university.

For many geographers thoughts about the value of geographical knowledge were expressed in essentially monetary terms: if policy makers were viewing the products of geographers as irrelevant then they would presumably stop funding geographical research and teaching (e.g see Abler 1993; Berry 1970; Chisholm 1971). Other geographers, however, expressed concern about the links between knowledge and society in less directly self-interested terms. In the early 1970s various geographers, perhaps most notably Richard Peet, argued that geography needed to be changed to make it *socially relevant*. Peet (1977: 33) claimed that geography needed to be changed from being an 'eclectic irrelevancy', in which academic geographers studied whatever comes into their head or attracts their interest, into a 'study of urgent social problems'. These calls for social relevance were often connected into notions of an *applied geography*, although discussions of the latter often drew very heavily on arguments relating to disciplinary self-interest and also in the 1970s had a very clear public policy focus (see Coppock 1974; Harvey 1974; White 1972).

While geographers such as Prince were basically blaming the rest of society for not taking geographical knowledge seriously, for Peet the blame for the low esteem of geographical knowledge lay much more with the geographers themselves. Geographers were, he argued, failing to apply their knowledge, their spatial theories, to clearly evident social problems:

> It must be obvious to anyone who has ever travelled in the United States that over wide areas ... and in large segments of central cities either the majority or a large minority live in poverty .... Why is it then that, faced by widespread poverty, we have done so little work on the geography of poverty (Peet 1971: 99).

To help rectify this omission and thereby help solve the problem, Peet undertook a spatial analysis of 'poor, hungry America'. This was basically an attempt to apply the techniques of spatial science to resolving social problems, and can be seen as a forerunner of a variant of applied geography characterised as *welfare geography* (see Smith 1977; 1979).

Gradually some geographers, including Peet himself (see Peet 1975), did begin to question whether one could really hope to solve social problems using the techniques of 'spatial science'. Increasingly the view developed that they were not, in large part because some of the processes which were creating social problems were being perpetuated by the knowledge being produced by 'spatial scientists'. Particularly significant in this regard was David Harvey's arguments on ghettos (Harvey 1972; 1973). Harvey, who a few years earlier written *Explanation in*

Geography (Harvey 1969) which was seen by many people at the time and since as the fullest exposition of geography as a logical positivist spatial science, was by early 1970s arguing, like Peet, for a geography orientated towards solving social problems. The purpose of studying ghettos should, he argued, be 'to eliminate ghettos' (Harvey 1973: 137; cf. Berry 1972;). This would be achieved, he argued, if geographers could identify the causes of ghettos and the policy makers could remove these causes.

Harvey argued that geographers had for some time known about the cause of ghettos, namely 'competitive bidding for the use of land' (Harvey 1973: 136). Ghettos are created, Harvey argued, because some people do not have enough money to bid for all but the most run down of areas. He also argued that that the role of competitive bidding in determining land-use had been long recognised in spatial science, it was after all the basis of Von Thünen's theory of land-use first elaborated in 1826 and as mentioned earlier, widely adopted within geography as spatial science. But if the cause has long been recognised then why do ghettos still exist? Harvey raises the problem which had troubled Hugh Prince a couple of years earlier. Harvey, however, goes on to specify an answer to this problem, suggesting that in part it stems from policy makers unwillingness or inability to enact the full implications of the theory, namely the removal of the competitive bidding system for land (or the land-market) (see also Harvey 1974). Another contributory factor, he argued, was geographers providing 'second best solutions' which did not fully follow the course of action suggested by their theories but were offered up as part of a concern to do something to alleviate aspects of a problem. However, for Harvey, by doing this geographers were simply colluding in the perpetuation of the problem they are studying. Knowledge becomes, in his words 'suffused with apologetics for the *status quo*' and the theories advanced becomes 'status quo theory', which he defines as:

> a theory which is grounded in the reality it seeks to portray and which accurately represents the phenomena with which it deals at a moment in time. But by having ascribed a universal truth status to the proposition it contains, it is capable of yielding prescriptive policies which can result only in the perpetuation of the *status quo* (Harvey 1973: 150).

Status quo theory is a theory that accurately describes the world *as it is*, but which does not ask the question 'Is the way the world is, the way the world *should be*?' It does not have what Behabib (1986) calls 'anticipatory-utopian' ambitions as well as 'explanatory-diagnostic' ones (see Johnston, 1994a: 88). It thus universalises the present, foreclosing the possibilities of future change, and often also ignoring the extent to which the present situation did not exist in the past. So, for example, not only does neo-classical economics, on which Von Thünen and spatial science drew heavily, fail to consider if social life should be organised by market relations, but it also often ignores the extent to which market society is a modern creation, a point which Harvey went on to discuss later in his book *Social Justice and the City* (Harvey 1973, chapter 6).

However, sticking with his discussion of theory and the study of the ghetto, Harvey contrasts 'status quo theory' with two other types of theory: 'counter-revolutionary' and 'revolutionary' theory. The former he defines as:

a theory which may or may not *appear* grounded in the reality it seeks to portray, but which obscures, be-clouds and generally obfuscates (either by design or accident) our ability to comprehend that reality. Such theory is usually .... logically coherent, easily manipulable, aesthetically appealing, or just new or fashionable; but it is in some way quite divorced from the reality it purports to represent. A counter-revolutionary theory automatically frustrates either the creation or the implementation of viable policies (Harvey 1973: 150).

Counter-revolutionary theory is a theory which, in important respects, fails to help people understand the world. Harvey argues, however, that the failures of such theory should not be taken to imply that they have no impact or consequence. Rather, he suggests they may have very series social implications, such as diverting people's attention away from significant issues and/or actively justifying actions which serve particular interests and do not address issues such as social inequalities and injustices.

The final type of theory identified by Harvey is 'revolutionary theory', which he suggests is,

theory which is firmly grounded in the reality it seeks to represent, the individual propositions of which are ascribed a contingent truth status (they are in the process of becoming
true or false) ... A revolutionary theory offers real choices for future moments in the social
process by identifying immanent choices in an existing situation. The implementation of
these choices serves to validate the theory and to provide the grounds for formulations of
new theory. A revolutionary theory consequently holds out the prospect of creating truth
rather than merely finding it (Harvey 1973: 151).

Revolutionary theory therefore seeks to explain both how the world is, and how it could be. Revolutionary theory addresses ways of living which are not necessarily part of an existing situation. Such a theory could be seen as 'radical' or 'revolution-ary' in the sense that it seeks fundamental changes from existing situations, and indeed in the 1970s there were a series of calls to develop more 'revolutionary' and 'radical' forms of geography. A range of different forms of radical/revolutionary theory were proposed including anarchism (see Brietbar 1975; 1981; Dunbar 1981); liberalism (Harvey 1973, part 1; Morril 1969/1970; Muir 1979) and Marxism (Harvey 1973, part 2 and 3; Peet 1977), with much debate centring of the logics of their interpretations and their respective degrees of radicalism in both theory and practice (Clark and Dear 1978; Duncan 1979; Mannion and Whitelegg 1979; Muir 1978; 1979; Overton 1976; Peet 1978; Walmsley and Sorenson 1980). Others, notably Gregory (1978) talked of 'committed explanation' as part of a 'critical geog-raphy' which is was both critical of itself and, crucially, was a 'critique of the status quo' (Newby and Buttel 1980: 2; see also Phillips 1994a). Today such critiques are not seen as so all encompassing as the terms revolutionary and radical seem to imply. Rather a series of particular critical geographies, connected to the interests of partic-ular people, have been developed, notably *feminist geography* (Box 2.11), *queer geography* and *post-colonial geography*.

For Gregory (1978: 76) a 'critical geography' also had to encompass 'structural explanations', and indeed as outlined earlier many commentators on philosophy and human geography have combined radical/critical geography with structuralism. It is important, however, to note that not all of those who had broadly ascribed to notions of radical or critical geography have embraced structuralism. So, for example, Marxism, one of the early sources of inspiration and argument for radical geographers and frequently equated with structuralism – Johnston (1983a: 178), for instance, claimed that 'marxism is a variant of the philosophy of structuralism' (cf. Johnston 1997: 214) – has in a series of works been given humanistic arguments and positionings. Examples of this include the existential Marxism of Sartre (see Box 2.4 and also Baker 1984; Peet 1998) and also the 'critical theory' of people such as Habermas (see Habermas (1978; 1984; 1987b; 1988) and for general commentary, Unwin (1992) and Phillips (1994a)). Furthermore, many of the 'particular critical geographies' mentioned above have been in varying ways highly critical of structuralism but have retained committed to bring about social change. I will return to many of these critical geographies and to critiques of structuralism later in this chapter, but before that it is worth pausing to consider some of the epistemological and ontological claims made during geography's engagement with structuralist philosophies.

Structuralist Epistemologies

In both empiricist and positivist epistemologies observation was seen as central to the establishment of knowledge. One of the most significant features of structuralism was that it down-graded the status of observation as a guarantor of truth. As Gregory (1978: 76) records, structuralist approaches were 'a form of enquiry which locates explanatory structures outside [of] the domain of immediate experience and problematizes the relationship between theory and observation'. Within the geography of the 1970s and 1980s when structuralist philosophies first started to be drawn upon by geographers, these ideas were often phrased in terms of looking not at 'surface appearances' but at 'deep structures', although this spatialisation of the ideas of structuralism is not necessarily helpful in getting to an understanding of structuralism and its consequences for geography. Peet (1998: 112), for example, claims that structuralism is 'the most misrepresented and under-appreciated period in social and geographical thought'.

This call to move from surface to deep structure may in part be seen as a way of devaluing explanations of positivists: just as spatial scientists had damned empiricists for 'not explaining just describing', so structuralists could disparage spatial scientists for 'simply describing the surface appearance of phenomena and not examining their deep causal structures'. However, geographical engagement with structuralism should be seen as more than simply rhetoric in that significantly different epistemological positions were advanced within structuralism vis-à-vis empiricism and positivism. So, for example, structuralists tended to reject the simplifications inherent in logical-positivist forms of explanation. As Peet put it, for structuralists 'explanation does not consists of moving from the complex to the simple, but in replacing a less intelligible complexity by one that is more so' (Peet 1998: 115). The structuralist anthropologist Lévi-Strauss was, for example, highly sceptical about whether empirical regularities lead to explanation. He argued that interacting variables might produce quite different outcomes, a situation he likened to a jig-saw cutting machine which has a cam shaft which is constrained to a limited range of movements but the order of which may vary and which can thereby produce an extremely large number of different puzzles (Lévi-Strauss 1960). Lévi-Strauss also envisaged that interacting variables might produce outcomes only some of which are realised. He therefore recommends the supplementation of empirical observations with consideration of logical models which explore all possible interactions between variables (see Gregory 1978; Lévi-Strauss 1973; Walmsley and Lewis 1993).

Lévi-Strauss was also highly sceptical about studies which relied on people's own accounts of situations and their causes. In part this was simply an additional consequence related to problems of explaining though observation: if researchers found it hard to develop plausible explanation of situations why should other people to be able to do this. However, Lévi-Strauss suggested a further reason for avoiding using the accounts of research subjects, claiming that these accounts, which he described as 'conscious models', may be positively misleading:

> conscious models ... which are usually known as 'norms', are by definition very poor ones, since they are not intended to explain the phenomena but to perpetuate them. Therefore structural analysis is confronted with a strange paradox well known to the linguist, that is: the more obvious structural organization is, the more difficult it becomes to reach it because of the inaccurate conscious models lying across the path which leads to it (Lévi-Strauss 1953: 527).

Lévi-Strauss argued for the development of 'unconscious' models or theories to explain reality. These were not so much theories of the role of the unconscious but rather models which made little or no use of the expressed views of research subjects.

A similar sceptical attitude is also evident within Marxist discussions of ideology. As outlined clearly in Thompson (1984; 1990), while the term ideology is often used to simply refer to a particular set of beliefs, within the work of Marx it was often used as a pejorative term to imply a set of beliefs which were in some sense false and which actively misled people. The conception of ideology was picked up by Marxists such as Althusser (1969; Althusser and Balibar, 1970) who not only proposed a structural social ontology whereby societies were seen to be composed of economic, political-juridicial and ideological structures (see Castells (1977)), but also made an epistemological distinction between 'science' and 'ideology'. As Gregory summarises it:

> Althusser suggests that *ideology* fastens on the manifest appearances of the social world and reproduces them as categories in an unexamined discourse ... Science [seeks] to construct and reconstruct sets of theoretical relations which transforms the structures of the social world (Gregory 1978: 109).

Science for Althusser does not involve simply reporting the ideas and accounts of research subjects, but rather an examination of these in the light of theoretical ideas. Furthermore, science also involves researchers working on their theoretical ideas, examining long held ideas and being prepared to, perhaps, give up established ways of thought that seemed previously 'so clearly correct, so forcefully guaranteed' (Mephan 1973: 116), in large part because they corresponded with our everyday, and in Althusser schemata 'ideological', experiences of the world. Science hence became 'examined discourse', counterpoised to unexamined ideologies which merely reproduced existing realities and ideas (see Gregory 1978; cf. Gregory 1994).

Structuralist Ontologies

The basic preposition of structuralism with reference to ontological issues is that empirical phenomena are created through the operation of 'structures'. This statement, however, raises the question, what constitutes a structure? The answer to this question is, as the following quote from Kroeber demonstrates, often far from easy to answer:

> 'Structure' ... tends to be applied indiscriminately because of the pleasurable connotations of its sound ... everything which is not wholly amorphous has a structure. So what structure adds to the meaning of our phrase appears to be nothing, except to provoke a degree of pleasant puzzlement (Kroeber 1948: 325).

Some of the commentaries on structuralism in geography arguably do little to dispel such puzzlement with a wholes series of terms being promoted, such as 'empirical', 'functional' and 'transformational structuralism' (Walmsley and Lewis 1993); 'structure as construct' and 'structure as process' (Johnston 1983b); 'superstructures', 'infrastructures' and 'deep structures' (Johnston 1997); 'observable structures', 'collectivist (social) structures' and 'neuro-structural (formalist) structures' (Gregory 1978).

Whilst such a plethora of terms can be a source of confusion to people encountering these terms for the first time they do point to an important aspect of the term structure, namely that it can be seen to refer to quite a range of different things. Table 2.1, for example, highlights some of the different terms and characteristics that have been equated to the concept of structure, plus lists some illustrative examples.

It should be noted that these conceptions of structure are not mutually exclusive and the works of the authors listed in Table 2.1 generally contain elements of some of the other conceptualisations. For example, Giddens retains the idea of structure as a non-observable, underlying feature whilst emphasising the notion of structure as resource. He also arguably makes some use of the notion of structure as constraint, although for some critics not enough use of this idea is made (Thompson 1984). In contrast, Marxist approaches of various persuasions, including the 'structural Marxism' associated with people such as Althusser (Althusser 1969; Althusser and Balibar, 1970) and Castells (1977), placed considerable stress on constraints, often via a critique of a *voluntarism* identified in other approaches. Humanistic, behavioural and logical positivist spatial science were all criticised for over-emphasising 'choice', albeit in slightly different forms. Spatial science and behavioural approaches, despite their differences, both emphasised rational decision-making or, to put it another way, the exercise of choice over options is given central place. Humanistic geography, whilst critiquing the focus on rationality, still emphasised the exercise of human choice of options, often expressing it in terms of human creativity or human agency.

The voluntarist critique can be over-done: as noted earlier, spatial science established a reified image of people uniformly deciding to act in some particular way; some humanistic geographers implied that there were essential reasons for people attitudes and behaviour; while behavioural geographers considered decisions as always being bounded, particularly by the limitations of people's perceptions.

Table 2.1: Notions of structure

Concept of structure	Characteristic	Examples
Pattern	Structure is viewed as discernible order within series of observation	Radcliffe-Brown (1952); Rumley (1979)
Infrastructure	Structure viewed as the support for the empirical, often using a skeletal analogy. I.e. structures are not observable but give the visible its form	Lévi-Strauss (1973), Harvey (1973)
Relations	Structure viewed as set of relations between elements	Saussure (1966), Sayer (1992)
Constraint	Structure viewed as an external feature, or rule, which restricts what people may do	Althusser and Balibar (1970), Castells (1977).
Resource and rule	Structure viewed as enabling as well as constraining features, bound up in the production and reproduction of everyday life and society	Structuration theory of Giddens (1979; 1981; 1984; 1985) and Gregory (1982a)

Having said this, the exercise of choice was a central feature of these approaches, albeit often tempered, and even contradicted, by other theoretical principles. Many Marxists and structuralists were adamant that human choice was of extremely limited significance being always bounded, not only by perceptions but also by broader social processes and relations of power.

This argument was strongly articulated within human geography with reference to studies of urban housing. As discussed earlier, spatial scientists had expended considerable effort in developing universalised theories and models of spatial differences in urban housing and much of the behavioural critique of this approach centred on an examination of decision making relating to the selection of a place of residence (see Knox 1987; Walmsley and Lewis 1993). In the 1970s, this focus itself became subject to criticism, with people such as Gray (1975; 1979), Pahl (1969; 1970) and Williams (1976) arguing that decisions about where to live were always undertaken within an already determined set of options, such as an established range of housing stock with a more or less already present residential population, and within a series of constraints, such as finance and the space-time locations of work and consumption. As outlined in Chapter 10, such arguments led: first, to the formulation of *urban managerialism* which focused on how agencies such as building societies, banks and local authorities acted as so-called 'urban managers' or 'gatekeepers' to control access to the resources of urban space; and second to the widespread adoption of concepts derived from *Marxist political-economy*.

As also discussed in Chapter 10, Marxist geographers were not only highly critical of the voluntarism of spatial science, behaviouralism and humanistic geography, but were also critical of two other aspects of their ontologies. First, as has already been discussed in connection with the politicisation of epistemology, notions of universal laws – and one might equally add, transcendental relations – give no room for the possibilities of future change, and also often ignore the extent to which the present situation did not exist in the past. They in effect 'naturalise' the present, or their analysis of the present, by giving it the appearance of being universal and unchangeable. This point has been well made by Cater and Jones (1989) who suggest that the 'human ecological theory' advanced by people such as Burgess (1924; 1925) and Park (1936) and adopted widely within geography as spatial science, was effectively an 'unanswerable justification of the status quo' in that it adopted the view that there was 'a natural desire' amongst people to acquire as much living space as possible and given this desire and the physical limitation of space, there was 'inevitably' a process of competition in which – and here there were strong parallels being forged to Darwinian style theories of evolution (but see also Livingstone 1992) – the powerful would win out at the expense of the weaker. As Cater and Jones note, the implication of Burgess' theory was effectively that:

> residential segregation, housing inequality, slums and homelessness are inevitable facets of the human condition, programmed into our very genes. All attempts to impose change whether by reform or revolution, are mere futile tilting at the unalterable laws of the universe. 'What exists exists because it must exist' (Cater and Jones 1989: 47).

Some forms of structuralism may be equally subject to charges of naturalism. Gregory (1978), for example, argues that Lévi-Strauss' structuralism constructs human history as the meshing, unmeshing and remeshing of a series of essentially invariant structures. There is change, but only between one structured combination and another, with history becoming little more that working through all these combinations, and at times repeating old combinations. Marxism – which here is taken to designate works which show 'an indeptedness to Marx and Engles and /or later interpretations of Marx's work' (Castree 1994) – although often equated with structuralism has had a strong, although by no means always commanding, historicist streak to it. As geographers like Harvey (1984) have emphasised, Marxism has been described as *historical materialism* and had as one of its central propositions that human societies are 'historical' rather than 'universal' creations.

A third area of Marxist critique of spatial science, behavioural geography and humanistic geography was on the emphasis given to individual human agency. In contrast to the 'atomistic ontologies' of spatial science, behavioural geography and humanistic geography, both Marxist and structuralist tended to favour more *relational* and *holistic ontologies*. Indeed it was commonalities in this area that led people such as Harvey (1973) to suggest that these approaches could be married together. Harvey, for example, argued that Marx might be seen to be a form of 'operational structuralist' akin to that advanced by the psychologist Piaget. Within a relational ontology things get meaning, function or causal powers (and these terms have varied between various forms of structuralism) in relation to other features, features which constitute the 'elements of a structure'. So, for example, the *linguistic structuralism* of Saussure (1966) argued that the meaning of a word derives from its relationships with other words and meanings; in the *functional structuralism* of Talcott Parsons (1951) social agents act in a manner which enables the continued performance of particular social functions; while in the 'realism' of Sayer (1992) landlords get causal powers by virtue of their relationships through the ownership of property vis-á-vis their tenants. Furthermore, within many forms of structuralism the focus is on relations at the expense of particular elements. Hence, Fortes (1949: 56) claims, 'when we describe structure ... we are, as it were, in the realm of grammar and syntax, not of the spoken word', while Piaget (1970: 9) argued that 'operational structuralism ... adopts from the start a relational perspective, according to which it is neither the elements nor a whole that comes about ... but the relations among elements that count'.

Piaget explicitly distanced his structuralism from both atomistic understandings and also from a holism in which some 'supra-individual' outcome, or social 'totality', acts both autonomously from its constituent elements and to determine the actions of these elements. However, Duncan and Ley (1982), amongst others, have claimed that structuralist explanations often adopt this viewpoint. They argue, for instance, that the writings of Marxists geographers such as Harvey (1973), Castells (1977) and Santos (1977) often posited capitalism, or the capitalist mode of production, as a totality which determined how people, agencies and institutions behave.

Duncan and Ley's (1982) critique of the holism of work that they identified as constitutive of an emergent 'structural Marxism' can be criticised for ignoring the extent to which both proponents of structuralism such as Piaget and also Marxist geographers such as Harvey explicitly rejected such a holism. Their identification and critique of structural Marxism, conjoined with others within and outside of geography (e.g. Giddens 1981; Gregory 1978; 1982a; Hindess and Hirst 1977; Ley 1982; Thompson 1978), did, however, very much set the agenda for much of the ontological discussions in human geography over the course of the following decade. Not only was Marxism, as already mentioned, frequently conjoined with structuralism, but both were almost as frequently charged with neglecting 'human agency', and in particular the differences that an individual person might make to their own circumstances. Furthermore, a series of attempts were made to bridge the gap between structural(/)Marxist explanations and the more human agency centred explanations of behavioural and humanistic geographies. Among the philosophies proposed as part of this 'search for a common ground' (Gould and Olsson 1982) were 'structuration theory', 'realism' and 'regulation theory', brief descriptions of which are provided in Boxes 2.7 to 2.9.

Box 2.7: Gidden's structuration theory

Structuration is a term which is very much associated with the work of one person, the sociologist Anthony Giddens. In a series of books in the late 1970s and first half of the 1980s (e.g. Giddens 1979; 1981; 1984; 1985) Giddens identified the relationship between *agency* and *structure* as being *the* central problem of social theory, and claimed that this relationship had become so problematic because the relationship had been viewed as a *dualism* rather than as a *duality*. The former term implies two categorically different phenomena, whilst the latter term implies two differentiated but related terms.

Structuration was an attempt to bring structure and agency together as a duality, whereby actions were seen to be conditioned by and at the same time reproduce social structures, and, conversely, where social structures were seen to be the condition and outcome of social action. To achieve this integration Giddens proposed that structures need to be conceptualised as *rules and resources* which both constrained and also enabled actions, while actions conceptualised as having a *recursiveness* whereby their consequences constituted the conditions of future action. Giddens further proposed that actions and their consequences could be stratified between those about which people had some consciousness or practical awareness (rationalised and reflectively monitored actions and systemically predictable outcomes) and those about which people had little awareness (unconscious conditions of action and unexpected consequences of actions).

Box 2.8: Realism

In its broadest sense, the term realism relates to notions that there is some reality which exists independently of people senses, perceptions and interpretations (Cloke *et al*. 1991: 132). Such a view is often contrasted to notions of 'idealism', when that term is taken to imply to imply that reality is constituted through what people think exists (see Box 2.5), and is also term which could quite reasonably be applied to describe a range of other philosophical positions including empiricism and positivism. However, within contemporary human geography and many associated social sciences, the term realism has come to refer to rather more specific philosophical arguments, many of which actively critique notions of positivism and empiricism. The precise constellation of arguments and choice of terminology to characterise them has been subject of some discussion, but broadly one can suggest that terms such as *transcendental realism* (Bhaskar 1978), *scientific realism* (Bhaskar 1986) and *critical realism* (Pratt 1995; Yeung 1997) have been used to differentiate more specific, and anti-positivist and anti-empiricist, philosophical positions from the more general sense of realism as defined above. A variety of terms have also been coined to describe the general sense of realism and to differentiate it from the more specific variants: hence one has *naive realism* (Gibson 1981) and *empirical realism* (Bhaskar 1978).

A key element of the more specific, non-positivist and non-empiricist forms of realism has been a rejection of the empiricist epistemology whereby knowledge of the real is seen to created solely by that which can be sensed (see Box

2.2). By contrast realists such as Bhaskar (1986) argued that some of the most significant aspects of reality cannot be sensed. Bhaskar suggested that there were three *domains of reality*: the *empirical*, which consists of people's sensed experiences; the *actual* which includes events which generate particular experiences; and the *real* which encompasses structures and mechanisms which generate events. These three domains connect but only partially and only in one direction, namely from the real to the actual, and from the actual to the experiential. As a result, so Bhaskar argues, experience cannot be used to access all the real, although the real can be used to interpret the experiential.

This notion of reality and the role of people's senses in creating knowledge of that reality clearly distinguishing this form of realism from empiricism and positivism. It does, however, raise the question of how is knowledge to be created if it is not through correspondence of thought and experience. In developing answers to such questions realists have often made reference to notions of '*abstraction*', or 'thought experiments' (Foord and Gregson 1986), and '*practical adequacy*' (Sayer 1992).

Abstraction involves the identification in thought of the significant constituents of a situation or process, and according to Sayer (1992: 88) 'should distinguish the incidental from essential characteristics ... [and] neither divide the indivisible nor lump together the divisible and the heterogenous'. Sayer goes on to distinguish between *rational abstractions*, which are seen to have the characters just listed, and *chaotic conceptions* which 'arbitrarily divides the indivisible and/or lumps together the unrelated and inessential' (Sayer 1992). The former problem, the division of the indivisible, is seen to stem in part from the widespread adoption of *atomistic ontologies* (see section on empiricism) and an associated failure to distinguish between *external/contingent relations* and *internal/necessary relations*. The first relationship refers to those established between things which are constituted independently from each other, although possibly affecting each other. The latter refers to relationships between things which actively constitutes the things involved in the relationship such that these things could not exist as they are outside of the relationship. So, for instance, a person cannot be a tenant without their also being a landlord, and if there is no landlord and no payment of rent then it is meaningless to talk of someone as being a tenant.

The problem of lumping together the unrelated and inessential relates to the above discussion of internal/external relations. It also very much relates to a second set of distinctions introduced by realists such as Sayer, namely a distinction between the *abstract* and the *concrete*. The former refers to very selective abstractions, namely those which 'isolate in thought a one sided or partial aspect of an object' (Sayer 1992: 87). The concrete on the other hand refers to 'a combination of diverse elements or forces' (p. 87). A concrete abstraction is hence constituted out of combining a series of abstract abstractions.

Realism in its more specific forms sets up a series of terminological distinctions and claims about how we should best theorise reality. However an outstanding issue is how does one judge the value of particular theorisations or 'thought experiments'. It is to address this issue that realists such as Sayer have introduced the notion of 'practical adequacy', which suggests that we accept theories as having some potential validity if they 'generate expectation about the world and about the results of our actions which are actually realized' (Sayer 1985: 69). This notion would seem to bear parallels with the focus on practice which is characteristic of pragmaticism (see Box 2.8), although Sayer does not really expand on his notion of practical adequacy as much as might have been expected given its centrality to his construction of a realist epistemology.

The discussion of realism has focused so far primarily on epistemological issues, an emphasis which reflects Cloke *et al.*'s (1991: 95) contention that epistemological issues have predominated in the formulation of realism. It should, however, already be clear that ontological issues were quite central to the formulation of the realist epistemology: witness the distinctions between the empirical, the actual and the real and between atomistic contingent relations and internal/necessary relationships. Frequent mention is made by realists to notions of *ontological depth* (e.g. Bhaskar 1979), which means that reality is composed of a range of different entities which cannot be explained simply by recourse to some other set of entities. Often this is described in terms of a *layers of reality*, each of which is seen to have its own *emergent powers*.

This notion of ontological depth had two particular resonances within geography. First, it may be seen to provide a framework for linking human and physical geography without reducing one down to the other (Richards 1990; 1994; Unwin 1992). Second, it provided a warrant for a new structuralist ontology whereby the layers of reality were widely seen to consist of events, mechanism and structures, with the last of these being widely construed as being simultaneously both the empirically most inaccessible and the causally most significant (see for example Sayer 1992).

Box 2.9: Regulation theory

Regulation theory is a variant of Marxist political economy which argues that capitalism is unable to secure the conditions of its own reproduction through time because of the contradictions built into its very construction. Classical Marxist political economy also took this view, suggesting that capitalism would dissolve under the strain of its own contradictions. However, there has been little evidence to suggest that capitalist social relations are declining in their influence; indeed more and more areas of the world and more and more aspects of social life are arguably coming under their sway. The failure of capitalism to collapse has long been used to signal the failure of Marxist theory, but in the 1970s a number of French theorists such as Aglietta (1979) and Lipietz (1985; 1987) claimed that the failure of capitalism to collapse did not mean that Marxist political-economy was wrong in its assessment of capitalism as being inherently contradictory and crisis ridden. Rather what Marxism had failed to account for in its theorisations was the way that these contradictions and crises were being managed or 'regulated'.

A variety of mechanisms of regulation have been proposed. Aglietta (1979), for example, argued that the Marxist concept of a *mode of production* needed to be supplemented with the notion of a *regime of accumulation* which relates to mechanisms ordering the circulation and consumption of commodities, the distribution of income and investment and the social organisation of production (see Dunford 1990). For capitalist accumulation of profits to continue without crises, the regime of accumulation has to be in balance with the mode of production; if not there can be crises such as over-production and a surplus of commodities; or surplus, un-invested, capital and surplus labour power, leading to unemployment (see Harvey 1982). Aglietta suggested that one long success-ful regime of accumulation was *Fordism* where a mode of mass production was combined with mass consumption sustained by standardised and relatively high wage levels, Keynsian economic policies to ensure high levels of employ-ment and collective consumption through a welfare state. However, in the 1970s and 1980s this regime of accumulation was seen to be in crisis and a new *post-fordist* regime of accumulation seen to be emerging, although there has been considerable debate as to whether this has actually been achieved and what its form(s) might take (see Peck and Tickell 1994; Tickell and Peck 1995).

The concept of regime of accumulation focused on the economic dilemmas of capitalist accumulation and their regulation. The contradictions and prob-lems of capitalism are not, however, exclusively economic in character, and some theorists have suggested that social, political and cultural life is as much the subject of regulation as are economic relations. In this context the notion of a *mode of social regulation*, or *MSR* as it is widely abbreviated to, has been proposed as a supplement to the notions of mode of production and regimes of accumulation (see Cloke and Goodwin 1992; Dunford 1990; Jessop 1990; Peck and Tickell 1992). The mode of social regulation is seen to refer to processes of 'societalization' (Jessop 1990: 179) whereby disparate sets of practices become bound together in such a way that the regime of accumulation comes to func-tion and any problems regulated. The mode of social regulation is seen to encompass institutions of formal governance, or 'real regulation' (Clark 1992), plus a range of less institutionalised, habitualised practices, such as consuming certain products, working in particular ways, engaging in certain forms of poli-tics (and refraining from others). Such practices may constitute many of the relations critical to particular regimes of accumulation and thereby to the repro-duction of capitalist production, although such consequences may be far from the mind of those engaged in these practices. There are clear connections which could be drawn here to structuration theory's notion of structures as the unin-tended consequence of action (see Box 2.9), although there has been a tendency within regulation theory to see modes of social regulations simply as a mecha-nism for regulating problems constituted within capitalist production and

regimes of accumulation, rather than actively constitutive of economic structures. This tendency arguably still persists despite explicit claims from some
advocates of regulation theory that the concept of mode of social regulation
should be 'afforded equal analytical value' (Peck and Tickell 1992: 349) to
economic centred concepts such as 'regimes of accumulation', 'accumulation
systems' and 'modes of production'.

These philosophies stimulated a whole series of writing and debates in human geography in the 1980s and 1990s. However, despite important differences between them
and previous philosophies, and indeed between themselves, they can be seen to have
revolved around a common ontological concern with finding some way of combining
structure with agency. They also all shared some, more or less explicit and more or
less substantive, connection to the work of Marx. Overall, Gregory's (1994: 102)
phrase 'middling Marxisms' might be an appropriate term with which to characterise
them. As other chapters in the book clearly demonstrate, the furrows of the
structure/agency debate are still routinely ploughed by human geographers, often
drawing on one or other of these approaches. However, in the 1990s a raft of new
concerns drifted into human geography, concerns which seemed to blow away much
of the ground for a common search centred around structure and agency. These new
concerns were associated with a variety of what might be described as 'post-philosophies'.

The Arrival of the 'Post-philosophies'

The search for some common or middle ground characteristic of much philosophical
musing in the 1980s came to be disrupted almost as soon as it had begun by the transportation into geography of a range of philosophies and theories which frequently
contained a 'post-' epithet: hence one had 'postmodernism', 'poststructuralism',
'postcolonialism', 'post-Marxism', 'post-feminism', 'post-developmentalism', to
mention but a few of the most prominent. These philosophies raised a series of new
claims and set off a series on new debates, not least over what these terms meant:

> The participants in the discussion seem to agree on one thing; that there is the greatest
> possible disagreement as to what postmodernism is … It resists comprehensive definition
> and appears, at the same time, to accept the content so arbitrarily that some commentators
> are deluded into regarding this arbitrariness itself as an essential characteristic of postmod-
> ernism (Voss and Schütze 1989: 119; see also Chapter 3).

There has also been discussion of the relationship between these various terms.
Rosenau (1992), for example, argues that the terms postmodernism and poststructuralism 'overlap considerably' and that '[f]ew efforts have been made to distinguish
between the two, probably because the difference appears of little consequence'. Peet
(1998), on the other hand, makes much of the difference between postmodernism and
poststructuralism, although personally I associate much of what he designates as

being postmodernism with poststructuralism, and vice versa. A third position can be
discerned within the work of Gregory (1994) who whilst arguing that he does 'not
think that postmodernism, poststructuralism and postcolonialism can be folded …
directly and indiscriminately into one another' (p. 182), nevertheless does chart some
'complex braiding of intellectual currents' (p. 134) between them. This third position
is broadly the approach adopted here, although emphasis is placed on delimiting
some lines of difference which may lie between postmodernism and post-structuralism, in at least some of their expositions.

Postmodernist Geographies

As the quote from Voss and Schütze indicates, there has been considerable contestation about what the term postmodernism might be, and indeed contestation about the
value of even attempting to define it. However, Cloke *et al.* (1991) have suggested
that the term postmodernism is often used in two particular ways. First, to designate
an 'object of study': that is people study some *postmodern object*. Within geography
a variety of 'postmodern objects' have been identified, including: postmodern buildings (Jameson, 1991; also Chapter 10) and postmodern cities (Dear, 2000; Soja,
1995, 1996, 2000; Watson and Gibson, 1995; also Chapter 9); postmodern cultures
(Harvey 1989; Jameson 1991); postmodern (or as it is often also described, 'post-
fordist') economies (Harvey 1989; McDowell 1991b); 'post modern societies' and,
more generally, of living in a condition of *postmodernity* (Harvey 1989).

Two features tie these postmodern objects together. First, they are seen in some
sense or another to be new objects which can be contrasted with something that went
before and which was designated as modern. The 'post-' epitaph in part therefore
encompassed notions of temporal change: it is, in part, 'a periodizing concept'
(Jameson (1985: 113); see also Phillips (1998b)). Second, these new objects have
been seen to be highly complex and fluid, in contrast to what went before which is
seen to have simple outlines and be largely static in form. In postmodern culture, for
example, identities are seen to be complex and fluid, features which have been
frequently illustrated with reference to pop-stars. Cloke *et al.* (1991) for example,
quote O'Hagan's (1990) claim that the pop-star 'Prince' was the first 'postmodern
pop icon' in that at times he appeared to resemble Jimi Hendrix, at other times James
Brown or Little Richard. Since then Prince has even sought to reinvent his own identity, moving from titling himself as 'Prince' to 'The Artist, formerly known as
Prince'. Another pop-star frequently associated with post-modernism is Madonna
(Fiske 1992; Kaplan 1988; 1992). Like Prince, Madonna is a pseudonym and
like Prince, Madonna has projected a whole series of identities for herself, many
of which bring together images generally separate or reversing their established relationships:

> Her video of 'Like a Virgin' alternates the white dress of Madonna the bride with the black
> slinky garb of Madonna the singer; the name of Madonna the virgin mother is borne by a
> sexually active female; the crucifixes adopted from nuns' habits are worn on a barely
> concealed bosom or in a sexually gyrating navel … In the video 'Material Girl', Madonna
> goes through a dance routine with tuxedo-clad young men in a parody of [Marilyn]

Monroe's number 'Diamonds are a girls best friend' from *Gentlemen Prefer Blondes*. During the number she collects jewellery from men … But despite a whore like gathering of riches from men … she toys with the men, showing that their jewellery has bought them no power over her (Fiske 1992: 309–310).

The mixing of identities can be seen as a feature of more everyday lives with, for example, people often dressing in different ways in different situations and indeed taking on board different identities in different situations. Urry (1995), for example, has suggested that contemporary leisure and recreation pursuits, and also contemporary political actions, may be constitutive of postmodern practices of identity formation whereby people elect to 'temporarily adopt new identities', such that:

> The quite librarian during the week may engage in war games at the weekend, while the staunch Conservative voter and believer in the rule of law might take to chaining themselves to trees about to be felled to make way for a road by pass (Phillips, 1998b: 45).

Furthermore, when participating in these activities people may well find themselves joined by all manner of other, quite different people. As a result there is blurring of commonly held links between personal and political identities and social positionings such as class or social status.

Complexity and fluidity are also evident within economies – with, for instance, the rise of 'flexible' and 'just-in time' production, and niche and fashion products – and in the physical landscape of cities, where, for instance, large rectangular buildings and street layouts have been replaced in many areas with multi-level buildings which incorporate a mix or pastiche of styles and where land-use is mixed and the street layout complex (see Chapters 9 and 10).

The second way in which the term postmodernism has been used identified by Cloke *et al.* (1991) is as attitude or approach. '*Postmodernism as attitude*' shares with '*postmodernism as object*' an emphasis on complexity and fluidity but applies it to the conduct of finding out about the world as well as to the character of that world. It also incorporates some elements of temporality, although the degree to which it signals a break from modern approaches has been the subject of some debate (see Berg 1993; Curry 1991; Harvey 1989; 1992). For some human geographers postmodernism reflects a new philosophy for doing geography, incorporating both distinctively different ontological and epistemological concerns.

Postmodern Ontologies

According to Holt-Jensen (1999: 134) postmodernism relates primarily to 'factual changes in our societies, and reactions to those changes'. Dear (2000: 317) also claims that '[p]ostmodernism is best understood as an ontological slant'. However, these statements are far from straightforward and indeed may be seen as rather problematic given that, as will be discussed in the next section, postmodernists have raised a series of epistemological challenges to what they see as modernist theories. Indeed, Dear himself has argued that two geographers closely associated with postmodernism, namely Ed Soja and David Harvey, may have failed to appreciate many of its epistemological challenges (see Box 9.3).

However, for the moment, the emphasis will remain on ontological issues. Connecting ideas of complexity and fluidity identified in various postmodern objects to the research process, postmodernism as attitude can be seen to have come to stress at least two lines of ontological arguments. First, it has been argued that people should be 'incredulous toward metanarratives' (Lyotard 1984: xxiv) or be 'inherently suspicious of … "grand theories"' (Cloke *et al.* 1991: 171). Meta-narratives can be seen as 'big stories' which serve to organise phenomena or events into some seemingly meaningful order or pattern. They may be seen as 'total histories' or 'grand historical visions', to use phrases from Philo's (1992a) discussion of the work of Foucault, which draw phenomena up round a central plot; 'a principle, a meaning, a spirit, a world-view, an overall shape' (Foucault 1972: 10). As well as being central elements within many historical ontologies, such narratives may, as will discussed in the next section, be important epistemologically. In his book *The Postmodern Condition* Lyotard (1984), for example, argues that while scientists often employ a scientistic self-understandings which see science as an autonomous activity best carried out in isolation from social, moral and political influences and contestations, in practice science can never validate itself simply by reference to its own procedures. Instead, Lyotard argues, science relies on 'metanarratives', such as the conduct of science is linked to the achievement of 'human emancipation' and/or the 'realisation of the human spirit' (Lyotard 1984: xxiii).

The term 'grand-theory' is more clearly ontological and does not have the temporal connotations arguably associated with the notion of narrative. The phrase has been traced back to Mills (1959; see Barnes and Gregory 1997) and can be said to involve claims to have understood how the world operates which centre around one or two concepts which are seen to provide the key to understanding because they correspond to some central phenomena or processes around which the world is seen to operate. This argument is clearly stated by Foucault in a series of texts which Philo (1992a: 140) argues can be interpreted as 'flagging (although in no sense exhausting the possibilities of) a "truly" postmodern geography'. So, for instance, Foucault (1972: 9) highlights how interpretations often proceed by seeking to demonstrate how a series or collection of events 'express one and the same central core'. By contrast, Philo (1992a) argues that Foucault seeks to establish a non-hierarchical ontology whereby 'certain things are [not] presented as somehow being more significant than the other things' (p. 145) and there is 'an expectation that probably there is no deeper essence, truth or whatever to be spoken about beyond the … "isness" of things in the world' (p. 147). Dear (2000) has argued that postmodernism 'holds out for a philosophical culture free from the search for ultimate foundations of everything', while Foucault (1982: 18) wrote: 'nothing is fundamental; that is what is interesting about society'. Similar notions of a non-hierarchical ontology also figure highly within the actor-network theory of Latour and others (see Box 2.10).

Box 2.10: Actor-network theory

Actor-network theory, or ANT as it is commonly known, is a philosophical approach which has emerged into geography in the mid 1990s out of work initially focused on the sociologies of science and technology, much of which were produced by people 'associated with, and in many cases located at, the Centre de Sociologie de l'Innovation of the Ecole Nationale Superieure des Mines de Paris' (Law 1992: 379). The theory focuses on agency but in a manner which is quite different from many previous approaches. In particular it seeks to explain how agency – or the power to do things – comes about, and suggests that agency is an effect produced by *networks* of heterogenously associated entities (or *actants* as they are often called) which encompass both the human and the inhuman. Law provides an illustration of this argument which draws quite directly of actor-networks initial origins in the sociology of science:

> 'Knowledge' … is the end product of a lot of hard work in which lots of heteroge-nous bits and pieces – test tubes, reagents, organisms, skilled hands, scanning electron microscopes, other scientists, articles, computer terminals, and all the rest – … are juxtaposed into a patterned network … and … concerted (or 'trans-lated') into a set of … scientific products (Law 1992: 381).

Law adds that actor-network theorists extended their arguments about the production of knowledge to suggest that 'agents, social institutions, machines and organization' could all be 'seen as a product or an effect of a network of heterogenous materials' (Law 1992: 381). Actor network theorists have sought a *flat ontology* which whilst recognising a multitudinous range of entities in the world rejected privileging any of these over others by being described as being causal (cf. Box 2.8): rather actor-network theorists 'insist on symmetry', assert-ing that '*everything* deserves explanation' and that everything should be 'approached in the same way' (Law 1994: 9–10).

One illustration of the implication of such arguments is provided by Murdoch who draws on actor-network theory to suggest that whilst previous approaches to understanding changing economic forms have often made use of 'explanatory concepts' like modes of production and social regulation, social structures and classes, these entities should be 'treated not as causes of events but as a set of effects arising from a whole complex network of relations' (Murdoch 1995a: 747; Murdoch 1995b; and Phillips 1998a, for a critique).

As Whatmore (1999) comments, there are two important implications of actor-network theory's concept of agency. First it 'decentres' agency, in that agency is seen to a product of a dispersed collection of actants rather than a property held within some clearly identified social location, such as the human person or some social organization or institutions. In this decentreing, actor-network theory can be seen to intersect with post-structuralist argu-ments (see text). On the other hand, the second aspect of actor-network theory identified by Whatmore, namely its break with 'the logocentric presumption that agency is an exclusively human attribute' (Whatmore 1999: 30) stands in some tension with a post-structuralist emphasis on '*social* construction' and on 'discourse'.

Philo (1992a: 149) argues that Foucault's non-hierarchical ontology does not mean 'that all there is in the world is chaos', but rather that there is '*some* order' (emphasis added) and that such order as there is 'lies resolutely in the things themselves and not in any theoretical order imposed from without' (Philo 1992a: 149). Likewise, within actor-network theory it has been argued that the focus should not be on order but on modes of ordering. For Philo the focus of a postmodern geography should be on 'the "local changing rules" that in particular times and places govern, and in a sense simply are, the observable relationships between the many things under study' (Philo 1992a: 150).

Such a claim might be interpreted as a call to revert to a philosophy of empiricism, but Philo is quick to add that observation should not, and indeed cannot, proceed without some influence from apriori expectations and imaginings. Elsewhere, Philo has argued for movement by geographers beyond observable materialities and toward recognition of a whole range of intangible and often barely discernible 'events, entities and structures' (Philo 1994a: 260; Philo 1991; see also Phillips 1998b). Philo argues for greater attention to be paid to the messiness and disorderly character of much of social life: to recognise, as Gregory (1989: 69) has put it, that much of social theory is 'totalising' in that it over-emphasises the coherence of social life, explicitly or implicitly assuming that 'social life somehow adds up to (or "makes sense in terms of") a coherent system with its own superordinate logic'. As Cloke *et al.* comment:

> Most of us have been educated in one way or another to suppose that the world has fundamental order to it .... Natural scientists ... believe that the natural world 'obeys' certain laws (those of Newtonian mechanics, those of Darwinian selection [for example]) ... social scientists have by an large taken on board a ... notion of order existing 'out there' in the 'real' world and have hence embarked on quest after quest for the 'true order' of the human world ... [T]his is the case whether we are thinking about approaches informed by 'Marxist science' or 'historical materialism' ..., by humanistic philosophies such as 'phenomenology' ... or by other 'grand theories' of the human world (Cloke *et al.* 1991: 186–7).

Many of the approaches to human geography previously discussed, often with an emphasis being placed on differences in their ontologies, can be seen to have posited some orderly focus to the social world and to have sought to develop some theorisation of the production of this order. By contrast, postmoderists seek to develop 'local ontologies' which are well attuned to specific situations: to the 'jumbling together' of 'substance-ridden things' in particular 'worldly spaces' (Philo 1992a: 157).

Such local ontologies connect closely to the practices of description, so quickly dismissed by both spatial science and structuralism. Both Gregory (1989) and Philo (1992a) connect postmodernism with the notion of 'thick description' outlined by the anthropologist Geertz (1973), whereby a single event may be situated in a series of 'layers of meaning' and hence can be researched and described in a series of different ways. Thick description is contrasted with thin description whereby only limited data is collected and used to characterise a situation, albeit often from a large number of cases. Such thin description can be seen to be a frequent creation of social surveys using standardised questions, while ethnographic methods of data generation long employed by anthropologists may be seen as productive of thicker descriptions. For Geertz (1973: 27) the aim of thick description was to 'draw large conclusions from small, but very textured facts' and to make 'broad assertions about the role of culture' (p. 144).

These aspirations might be seen as quite modernist, but later Geertz argued that ethnographers needed to respect 'local knowledges' and not simply evaluate other cultures according to the values inscribed in western cultures (Geertz 1983). All knowledge was seen to be affected by the local conditions of its production, and hence rather than talking of knowledge in the singular there was a need to recognise a plurality of knowledges, each with its own geographical and historical specificity.

Not only did Geertz's later works chime with the local ontology espoused by some postmodernists, but his notions of thick description and ethnography began to figure frequently in discussion of qualitative methods which were themselves becoming much more prominent within human geography in the 1980s. Indeed qualitative methods began to be widely seen as part and parcel of a postmodernist approach to geography, just as quantitative methods had become widely commonly equated with positivist philosophies.

A second ontological concern of postmodernism closely associated with its concern to avoid grand theory is a concern with *difference*, or as Cloke *et al.* (1991: 171) put it, 'an alertness to the many differences that distinguish one person or event or process or whatever from another, and an insistence on not obliterating these vital differences in the face of grand theoretical statements'. In part this means that rather than looking for similarities between events or process and developing explanations centred around these similarities, postmodernists favour focusing in on what way something is different from something else.

Cloke *et al.* (1991) comment that the 'alertness to difference has many consequences', with one of the most obvious, and arguably most reactionary, being to equate sensitivity to differences as simply a return to the 'idiographic' and to 'empirical studies' (e.g. Turnock 1999). While Gregory (1989) and Cloke *et al.* (1991) have indeed made connections back to notions like 'aerial differentiation' and the study of the unique places, they have also been adamant about the impossibility of theoryless observation. Furthermore, the study of difference does not simply equate with the study of the unique: as outlined in the review of Philo's arguments about Foucault's geography, the study of difference both recognises the possibilities of commonalities between situations (and hence may be seen as less than idiographic), whilst at the same time recognises the possibilities of order and disorder (the latter possibility was not recognised in the idiographic, hence the study of difference is more than the idiographic). Finally, it should be stressed that postmodernism emerged from outside of geography and hence has, not unexpectedly, sought to recognise differences other than the purely spatial or place specific. Indeed Cloke *et al.* suggest that amongst the most prominent differences identified by postmodernism are those between people:

> alertness to difference ... forces us to respect the myriad variations that exist between the many 'sorts' of human being studied by geographers – the variations between women and men, between social classes, between ethnic groups, between human groups defined on all manner of criteria (Cloke *et al.* 1991: 171).

Cloke *et al.* argue that much research of human geography has been rather insensitive to such differences, tending, as one of the authors later put it, to portray people as:

'Mr Averages': as being men in employment, earning enough to live, white and probably English, straight and somehow without sexuality, able in body and sound in mind, and devoid of any quirks of (say religious belief or political affiliation) (Philo 1992b: 200)

People have been, in Philo's view, too often reduced to *the same*: being portrayed as very similar to each other and, crucially, essentially mirroring the people who, in the main, study them. Hence, he argues, many of those people writing geography were 'white, middle-class, middle aged, able-bodied, sound-minded, heterosexual men' (Philo 1992b: 199).

Very similar claims have also made by feminist geographers with Rose (1993a), for instance, arguing that geography has been dominated by a *masculinist gaze* which claims to be universal but is in practice very partial because it views the world from the perspective of 'hegemonically masculine men', either assuming that other people view the world just as the powerful, heterosexual male does (and hence are 'the same'), or else that they are radically different and less significant (and are hence an *other*). Instances of these two practices have already been mentioned with regard to humanistic geography which, on the one hand, often constructed the home as a place of rest, recreation and re-creation, and on the other, set up aesthetic notions such as emotions, feelings and sensitivity as being beyond the limits of scientific reason. For the humanistic geographer, one could not 'explain' such entities as place, nature and landscape but only seek, at best, to partially understand their mysteries and attractions, a construct of otherness which Rose argues paralleled and drew upon those made about women within wider discourses of hegemonic masculinity in which women were viewed as being 'other' than men in being more emotional or more sensitive, and at the same time less rational and less understandable than men.

The privileging of sameness and the neglect of difference is not simply the outcome of personal biases, although these have no doubt played some part, but also connects to some long-established conceptual distinctions and restrictions routinely employed by human geographers. McDowell (1989: 138), for example, argued that the long neglect of gender by geographers was 'partly a question of scale' with geographers usually omitting 'the small-scale and the "private" from consideration' in favour of studying 'patterns and processes that take place outside, or in the "public" world of institutions, places, areas and regions'. Geographers, she argued, tended to 'not go inside the factory gates or the office doors with the workers' but to 'stop at the front door and ignore questions about the division of responsibility for work within the home or the structure of power relations within households'. She added that if geographers did go into 'interior worlds' of factories, offices and homes, then gender differences became much harder to ignore, and indeed might well be a central focus of attention (see McDowell 1995a; 1997a; 1997b). Many other long established divisions and restrictions have come to be questioned through human geography's engagement with postmodernism, and indeed with feminism (see Box 2.11), with a range of new geographies emerging beyond some previously established boundaries of the subject.

Box 2.11: Feminist geography

Feminist geography can be seen as a clear illustration of the 'politicisation of epistemology' and the emergence of a 'radical geography'. An explicit feminist geography emerged in the mid 1970s as a series of women sought to bring into their geographies some of the political concerns which had for sometime been articulated in a much wider feminist social movement. Feminist geography can be seen as a 'radical' or 'critical' discourse which seeks to change things not simply study them. In particular feminist geography seeks to critique 'women's oppression in society ... [and] the various ways that this is reproduced in geographical theory ... within geographical institutions' and within the various practices of geographers such as teaching, research and publication (Pratt 2000: 259).

As Rose (1993b: 535) comments, whilst feminist geography has often been ignored or marginalised in discussions of geography, it very much lies 'at the heart of debates about this thing called geography'. Feminist geographers have, for example, played major roles in, amongst other things: i) the critique of 'objectivism' and the highlighting of the situatedness of theory; ii) the promotion of heightened reflexivity in methodology; and iii) challenging the value of major theoretical dualisms, such as culture/nature, work/home and public/private. The range of impacts across ontological and epistemological issues, and across theory and practice, highlights how feminist geography might be seen as a major philosophical approach of equal, if not greater significance than, say, humanism, Marxism, structuralism or post-structuralism. However, after considerable thought and still a fair degree of unease, it has been decided not to add a section on feminism to the main body of text but to discuss it in this box section. The decision was taken because, despite its undoubted significance and distinctive elements, feminist geography and feminism more widely has exhibited a 'proliferation' of forms which pose all sorts of 'awkward' problems in terms of how they might fit into a disciplinary account such as presented in the text (see Rose 1993b). A particular problem which exercised the decision to right this box section was that whilst not wishing to reduce feminist geography to mainstream (for which also read 'malestream') philosophical positionings, it was still felt that much of the proliferation within feminist geography was reflective of, and in some cases clearly influenced, more widely constituted philosophical debates.

Following on from this, particular forms of feminist geography will be identified and discussed on the basis of relationship with some of the philosophies discussed in the main text. This will draw particularly on the discussions of types of feminist geography advanced by McDowell (1993) and Pratt (2000). The former distinguishes three forms of feminist geography based on epistemological differences, while the latter, drawing on the earlier work of Bowlby *et al.* (1989) makes rather more of differences in ontological conceptions, although also ending up with a three-fold differentiation. Drawing of these works it is possible to suggest at least four distinct forms of feminist geography which bear some association with the philosophical positions of empiricism, structuralism, Marxism, postmodernism and post-structuralism.

Feminist empiricism

An early focus of feminist geographers was on 'making women visible'. This was a broadly empiricist exercise which sought to highlight the 'gender blindness' of much of human geography which had tended to either assume that: i) women had the same concerns and interests as men, and hence that gender did not matter, or did not matter as much as other axes of social differentiation such as class or ethnicity; or ii) men were the principal agents in the major geographical processes constituted in the public sphere, with the influence of women being seen to the lie primarily within a private sphere, itself accorded little significance (see main text). Feminist geographers undertook a series of empirical studies highlighting differences between men and women in terms of their access to and use and experiences of space; the neglected role of women in public sphere processes such the restructuring of urban space (see Chapter 10); and how the women's activities within the 'private sphere' of household work determined the time-space co-ordinates of, and restrictions on, their everyday lives.

This feminist geography focused on issues of inequality, with gender being viewed largely in terms of different levels of constraint experienced by men and women, relating to the different 'social roles' they inhabited. Men were seen to, generally, inhabit rewarding social roles in the public sphere, such as being 'wage-earners' in the official, money economy. Women, on the other hand were seen to generally hold un- or poorly rewarded social roles in the private sphere or at the margins of the public sphere, such as undertaking unpaid 'reproductive labour' (i.e. domestic and caring work) and/or part-time, low paid work. These studies have been characterised as broadly liberalist in political outlook it that they focused on the distributional issues – were women getting a fair return for their work – and the reform of existing social institutions, such as labour markets and the welfare state. As such they had, as Pratt (2000) notes, clear similarities with variants of radical geography such as 'welfare geography' (see text).

Structuralist feminisms

At just the time when feminist geographers were using empirical studies to highlight and undermine the gender blindness of human geography, empiricist ideas were themselves coming under challenge, notably from radical and structuralist philosophies. Under the influence of these philosophies, and also from debates within feminism more widely, feminist geographers began to question the value of simply making women empirically visible. In particular it was suggested that empirical analysis might simply reproduce, and not put into question, women's oppression in that it seemed to view differential gender roles as pre-given, rather than look at how these roles were created. In other words, and to use phrasing oft used by structuralist geographers, empiricist feminism was seen to 'describe and not explain' gender differences. In the 1980s there emerged various calls to develop a more 'radical' feminist geography which, amongst other things, cast gender roles as a phenomena in need of explanation, and sought to explain them by considering them as the product of social relations and associated 'social structures'. Two particular versions of this structuralist feminist geography emerged: *socialist feminism* and *radical feminism*.

Socialist/Marxist feminism

As outlined in the text, a series of initial forays into a range of radical geographies in the 1970s gradually came to be replaced by a more sustained engagement with ideas drawn from Marxism. Drawing on this movement and broader debates within feminism, a number of feminist geographers began to argue that differential gender roles might be understood through a Marxist theoretical framework and that feminist concerns over women's oppression needed to integrated within a broader socialist critique of social exploitation and domination. McDowell (1986), for example, argued that women's oppression and exploitation stemmed from the demands of capitalism, particularly for as low a wage-labour rate as possible and for the reproduction of a labour force through time.

Radical feminism

Many feminists were unhappy with both liberal feminism and socialist feminism, and sought to theorise alternative explanation of difference gender roles. One widely canvassed suggestion was that differential gender roles were a product of 'patriarchy' which was conceptualised as collection of political, economic, ideological and psychological structures in which women's interests and concerns were subordinated to those of men (see Vogel 1983; Walby 1986; 1989; 1990). For feminists such as Stacey (1981) the structures of patriarchy predate those of capitalism and therefore logically cannot be derivative of them, although other feminists, notably Walby, sought to develop a 'dual-structure' theorization of gender roles which related them to both patriarchy and to capitalism (see also Foord and Gregson 1986).

Postmodern feminism

Despite their differences, empiricist, post-socialist and radical feminist geographies all retained many common philosophical and political elements. They all, as McDowell (1993: 306) comments, worked from a basic premise that men and women should be treated equally, but at present were generally not being so treated. They all also employed a dualistic gender ontology in which people were simply separated into male and female, men and women. A further commonality was that they all retained some belief in the power of objective rational thought to both disclose and potentially change social reality. In other words they all employed a variant of 'enlightenment thought' (see text).

In the 1980s and 1990s all of these taken for granted elements of feminist geography came under scrutiny. The notion of equal treatment, for example, began to be criticised for failuring to recognise and respect the differences that being a woman entailed. Seeking equality with men was seen to be equivalent to seeking to become like men, a project which rather ignored the negative aspects of male behaviour. Feminist geographers in particular began to highlight the undesirability of emulating many of the practices routinely employed by many male academic geographers, such as a willingness to talk for, and over, others. They also began to suggest that there might be positive benefits that being a women might bring to the construction of knowledge. Increasing the 'situatedness' of knowledge production was highlighted by feminists, it being suggested by some that women might have a distinctive position or standpoint from which construct knowledge. Notions of *standpoint theory* were advanced by Hartsock (1983), the character of which has been well summarised by Di Stenafano:

> the gender specific and differentiated perspective of women is advanced as a preferable grounding for inquiry – preferable because the experience and perspective of women as the excluded and exploited other is judged to be more inclusive and critically coherent than that of the masculine group (Di Stefano 1990: 44).

A variety of other variants of standpoint theories have been advanced, with some variants of post-colonial theory, for example, arguing that the view from 'the margin' or from 'the border' or from some 'nomadic' position might be more inclusive (see hooks 1990a; 1990b; 1988a; Spivak 1988b). Notions of objectivity were sometimes retained albeit substantially reconfigured, as in the work of Haraway (1988) who argued for an *embodied objectivity* which acknowledged that knowledge claims are always partial (in the sense of being both incomplete and being biased in favouring particular social groups and interests) but could be seen as truthful if those making them were made to be answerable and accountable for the consequences of their knowledge claims. For other feminists, standpoint theory pointed to the partiality of all theory, a view which has clear connections with notions of local knowledges as outlined by some postmodernists (see text). A series of debates within and beyond geography emerged in the late 1980s and early 1990s focusing on the relationship between postmodernism and feminism (see McDowell 1991a; 1992; Nicholson 1990; Pile and Rose 1992).

The rise of postcolonial and postmodern studies was also of significance to feminism in that they acted to fragment the dualistic gender ontology of men and women by suggesting that the experiences and interests of women might be quite different from each other, given that women might be positioned quite differently from each other in relation to lines of social differentiation such as age, class, sexuality, conialism, ethnicity and nationality. There has hence, emerged what might be described as a 'postmodern feminism' concerned to recognise the presence of both different sorts of women (and indeed different sorts of men) and also of problematic relationships between women as well as between men and women.

Postfeminism

The recognition of social differentiation and relations of exploitation and domination between women, as well as between men and women, poses considerable stresses on the politicised epistemologies of feminism and feminist geography, which had assumed that there was some common interest between women related to their unequal treatment vis-à- vis men. Much of the debate over postmodernism and feminism mentioned above centred around the seemingly divergent politics associated with each philosophy, a discussion which also figured in Marxist reactions to postmodernism (see text). Adding further complexity to these reflections has come the increasing engagement by geographers and feminists with post-structuralist ideas and an associated scepticism about the status of any categorisation, including those of male/female, man/woman. The notion of gender as a structural foundation of social life has come under question with the very distinction between two genders being seen by people such as Butler (1993) as as a social, indeed discursive, product. People become gendered and sexed through being socialised into and performing gendered/sexed identities; and people who do not act according to dominant scripts have often found themselves subject to a range of disciplinary procedures, such as social discrimination and expulsion, psycho-analytical therapies and medical operations. On the other hands, some people have sought to perform alternative identities, some of which actively transgress gender binaries, as in transvestism.

The transformation of gender from transhistoric/transpatial structural causal entity to a highly contingent and possibly very ambiguous outcome clearly raises new political questions for feminism. The term *postfeminist* has sometimes been used to characterise feminist work which adopts a performative, post-structural view of gender. This term itself, however, is subject to several politically quite different interpretations. For some, the term 'post-feminism' implies the end of feminism, either in the sense that feminism has been seen to have achieved its aims or, and in one sense more consistent with post-structuralist arguments, because there are seen to be no essential differences between men and women. For others, however, postfeminism is a continuation of feminism, albeit one which recognises no appeal to intrinsic gender differences and points to the possibilities of new performances of gender, such as, to name one prominent popular manifestation, *girl power* which seeks to create new, empowered visions of femininity. The extent to which in popular manifestations of girl power enact radically new gender identities and relationships have been the subject of much debate (see Heath 1997; McRobbie 1993).

Closely connected with the focus on social difference and the challenging of previous boundaries of geography has been the study of so-called *neglected others* (Philo 1992b). These are people who, in one way or another, 'stand outside the societal mainstream', who are 'other' than 'male, white, heterosexual, middle-class, middle aged, able-bodied and sound in mind' (Philo 1993: 430). As is well demonstrated in other chapters in this book (see especially Chapters 9, 10, and 11), the study of *others* formed a focus for much geographical work in human geography in the late 1980s and 1990. Indeed, Cloke *et al*. (1991: 191) have claimed that the 'blindness to the diversity of human groups' which characterised much of past human geographies 'is now being rectified'. Dear also claims that,

> in my mind ... the advent of postmodernism has had a liberating effect on previously silent voices, including those of feminists, disabled and disadvantaged people, gay and lesbians, and people of colour ... Such groups have benefited from the new legitimacies accorded to difference (Dear 2000).

There certainly has been an enlarging portfolio of people studied by human geographers: as well as studying various aspects of white, middle-class, middle-aged, male, straight society, geographers are now, as is demonstrated in other chapters in this book, producing studies of wide range of peoples, including: 'people of colour' (e.g Agyeman and Spooner 1997; Pratt et al 1998); the economically marginalised (see Chapters 9, 10 and 11); the elderly (see Chapter 11), the young (e.g. Holloway and Valentine 2000; James 1990; Matthews and Limb 1999); women (see Box 2.11); gays and lesbians (e.g. Bell and Valentine 1995a;1995b; Valentine 1993; 1997a); and many other 'others' besides. Furthermore, as is discussed in Chapter 10, it has also been shown that people lying outside or on the margins of conventional society can have major impacts on many of the things traditionally studied by geographers such as the gentrification of cities. However, as Cloke and Little (1997: 281) conclude in a collection of studies of otherness and marginalisation in rural spaces, not only does geography still remains 'desperately short of information on the lives and experiences of a whole range of neglected', but also there a danger that such studies that are done may constitute little more than a 'touristic' flitting into, and voyeuristic gazing on, the lives of others. Whilst the voices of others may be incorporated within the text of these studies, the power of authorship are generally firmly retained by the researcher and/or by agencies commissioning research and as a consequence these studies may produce little or nothing which is 'of relevance, use or interest to the subject(s) of that research' (p. 282). Indeed, there may well be major epistemological problems surrounding the notion of 'giving voice to others', problems very much recognised by postmodernists and post-structuralists.

Postmodern Epistemology

In relation to epistemology, postmodernism can be considered as involving a rejection of, or at the least a movement away from, modern views on knowledge. Since at least the Renaissance, and indeed probably well before then, the acquisition of knowledge is seen to be in one sense of another emancipatory. In the Rennaissance of the fifteenth and sixteenth centuries, for example, knowledge was seen bringing about freedom from dogmatic understandings and allowing a flowering of humanity, while during the 'scientific revolution' of the sixteenth century, knowledge, at least in its scientific variants, was seen to hold the prospect of 'liberation from both the drudgery and dangers associated with eking an existence out of the natural environment' (Cloke *et al.* 1991: 188). A connection between knowledge and emancipation was more explicitly and fully articulated in the 'Enlightenment' period of the seventeenth and eighteenth century, where the exercise of reason and the creation of rational knowledge was seen to create freedoms for personal expression and communal organisation, as well as breaking down constraints of economic necessity. The association of knowledge with emancipation continued into the twentieth century where it became synonymous with the notion of modernism, and this association can indeed be seen to infuse many of the philosophies which have processed through modern geography. Within positivism knowledge is seen to bring powers of prediction and control over the natural and social circumstances; for the humanistic geographer knowledge brings about improved understanding of oneself and others; for the structuralist knowledge allows one to look through appearances and reduce delusions about the world.

In contrast with these 'modernist philosophies', postmodernists have sought to turn away from, and in some cases completely reject, Enlightenment ideas and ambitions. In part this was because they recognised that the various projects of the enlightenment had a 'black side' (Habermas 1987a: 110) which, as Harvey (1989) notes, had either been effectively ignored or else seen as stemming from failures to apply enough enlightenment rationality (see Chapter 3 on the problems associated with notions of development). Such black sides have, however, been widely recognised by many people who might still be said to subscribe to the so-called *enlightenment* project. Leading theorists of the so-called 'Frankfurt school' of critical theorists have, for instance, written at length on the problems of enlightenment thought and practice (e.g. Adorno and Horkheimer 1979; Habermas 1984; 1987a; 1987b; 1989; Marcuse 1964) and yet have, in some sense or another, all retained retained a faith in the power of reason and social emancipation. By contrast, postmodernists such as Lyotard have argued that the enlightenment was not simply an 'incomplete', as yet 'unfinished project' (Habermas 1983; 1987a) with serious blemishes, but was a fatally flawed project which could never be completed.

A variety of different interpretations of why the enlightenment project could not be completed have been advanced, but one of the most influential in the context of postmodernism is arguably that of Lyotard (1984). As already mentioned, Lyotard argues that the pursuit of science is often connected, albeit in often roundabout routes, to 'metanarratives' such as 'human emancipation' and the 'realisation of the human spirit'. Lyotard was, however, sceptical about the value of these narratives and claimed that this scepticism, or 'incredulity', was widely shared. Connor provides a clear summary of Lyotard's arguments:

> Science is no longer held to be valuable and necessary because of the part it plays in the slow progress towards absolute freedom and absolute knowledge. With this loss of confidence in the metanarratives (and perhaps as a contribution towards such loss of confidence), comes the decline of general regulatory power in the paradigms of science itself. ... [S]cience develops into a cloud of specialisms each with its own incompatible mode of proceeding, or language game. None of these language games has recourse any longer to external principles of justice or authority; in this situation, the goal is 'no longer truth but performativity' ... – no longer what kind of research will lead to verifiable facts, but what kind of research will work best, where 'working best' means producing more research on the same lines, and increasing the opportunity for more (Connor 1989: 32).

Lyotard hence argues that people have lost faith in the meta-narrative that science leads, as Habermas (1971) put it, 'towards a rational society' and also that science has become so specialist and fragmented that there can be no meaningful communication and integration between scientists working in different areas or taking different approaches. Positivistic notions of gradual integration of sciences and accumulation of knowledges are, hence, both clearly rejected by Lyotard, as indeed is the notion that philosophy can act as some form of arbiter over the status of particular types of knowledge and their relationships. As Dear (2000: 36) puts it, postmodernism may be seen to signal the 'end philosophy' in that the ideas of philosophers become merely another set of debates, or 'language games'. Dear also suggests that postmodernism breaks down the significance of philosophy within academic disciplines as, '[a]ll paradigms, theoretical frameworks, and discourses are obliged to surrender their privileged status. They are, in principle at least, all equally important or unimportant' (Dear 2000: 36). Furthermore, as Bauman (1987) has highlighted, such a perspective on knowledge radically affects the status of academic knowledge: rather than being seen to produce forms of superior knowledge able to arbitrate between competing interpretations and solve problems, academic knowledge becomes simply one more story of no greater value than any other. More generally still, the arguments of people like Lyotard problematises the whole notion of truth, suggesting that what really matters is *performativity*, or the ability to have an effect.

This last argument of Lyotard connects closely to the arguments of several other people often associated with postmodernism. Foucault (1980), for example, argues that knowledge does not lead to emancipation from necessity and social control but is itself a form of power. Drawing in part on the writings of Nietzsche, a nineteenth century poet/philosopher who is often described as a fore-runner and/or father figure of postmodernism, Foucault argues that the desire or 'will' to create/have knowledge is also a desire/will to have power. Similarly it has been argued that the writings of the French philosopher/literary theorist Derrida reveal how the process of writing contains 'conscious and unconscious strategies of exclusion, and are rife with internal contradictions and suppressed paradox' (Dear 2000: 36). Furthermore, as discussed in Chapter 3, the work of a range of post-colonial theorists such as Said and Escobar have highlighted how a concern for others is translatable into a concern for power over others: notions such as truth, knowledge, representation and development are all, to adopt a phrase from Peet (1998: 235), 'emancipatory languages of domination'.

Three ideas have often been foregrounded in the postmodern critique of enlightenment notions of knowledge and truth. First, and closely connected to the critique of grand theory discussed previously, there have been calls to recognise the 'limits to theory' (Ley 1989a), and in particular its 'partial' character. Here arguments focus on the issue of representation, with, as Philo (1992a: 158) comments, there being 'deep scepticism about the ability of theoretical endeavor to represent' what is happening within 'the geography of things'. Amongst the reasons which might be advanced for this situation is the complexity and fluidity of the postmodern world which may make it increasingly difficult to, hitching a phrase oft banded about in the study of postmodern objects, to 'cognitively map' these geographies. However, more epistemologically fundamental are claims that theories, at best, have always both served to represent and obscure phenomena. There is a clear line of connection in the later arguments to the epistemology of post-structuralism, and elaboration of this aspect of representation will be left until then.

As well as stressing partiality, postmodern discussions of epistemology have also highlighted the *situatedness* of knowledge: how knowledge is always constructed from a position somewhere within society. This understanding is widely contrasted with 'objectivist' epistemologies such as positivism, which as noted previously, seek to enact a separation of the researcher from social involvement. As Duncan and Ley (1993) have noted, a particularly striking representation of the positionality of objectivism is provided in Joanne Sharpe's drawing *Topographical Survey* in which the researcher may be seen as a disembodied viewer able to survey a world from which they have somehow managed to detach themselves in order to obtain a privileged vantage point. One might even say that objectivism pictures the researcher as some 'remote sensor', able to survey the world via some orbiting satellite. However, such a location may be neither desirable nor, even more significantly, possible: even remote sensors, are always situated within society, reliant on myriad others to build, fund and operate the satellites and also requiring earth based observations to establish so-called 'ground truths' (Pickles, 1995). Haraway (1991: 308) has described the idea of being able to view everything from some privileged position as 'an illusion, a god trick'. Despite such arguments, objectivist positionings have been discerned not only within the writings of logical positivism but also in a variety of other 'modernist' and 'masculinist' accounts, such as David Harvey's analysis of postmodern cities (see Box 9.3).

A range of other, explicitly 'situated' positionings have, however, been advanced within an expanding *spatialisation of epistemology*: hence there have been calls to view things 'from below' (e.g. Haraway 1991); 'from the streets' (e.g. De Certeau 1984); from the 'margins' (e.g. hooks 1990a; 1990b), from the 'contact zones' and 'border' areas (e.g. Bhabha, 1994), from real-and-imagined 'thirdspaces' (e.g. Soja 1996), and through 'travelling' (e.g. Clifford 1992) and 'nomadism' (e.g. Deleuze and Guattari 1987). In addition there has also been a more general awareness that geographical researchers need to reflect upon and make reference to their own positionality, or to put it simply, tell people 'where you are coming from' (Cloke 1999: 47). In addition to drawing on some spatialised epistemology, referencing one's own positionality can, as Cloke notes, include situating the production of knowledge in personal experiences which might generate particular insights or perspectives on a situation. It is also often taken to imply situating the production of knowledge in relation to the capacities and incapacities which might be seen to stem from the position of the researcher in social relations of power, such as class, gender, ethnicity, nationality, colonialism, imperialism and so on (within a postmodern emphasis on difference the list might be seen as literally endless). The term positionality may also be seen to have a political edge to it as well. As mentioned in connection with radical geography, theories do not necessarily need to restrict themselves to the 'what is' but could also seek to explore the 'what could be'. Whilst Marxist and certain feminist and critical theorists sought some general, collective transcendence of the present, postmodernists have been sceptical about these ambitions and have instead focused on more personally situated, embodied transformations, often characterised as *identity politics*. Significant illustrations of this particularised political epistemologies include the various strands of *feminism* which aim to improve the situation of women (see Box 2.11), *post-colonialism* with its concern to transcend colonial relationships (see Chapter 3), and *queer theory* which seeks to challenge homophobia and hetero-normativity (see De Lauretis 1991; Geltmaker, 1992; Gibson-Graham 1998).

Criticisms of Postmodernism

The impacts of postmodernism on geography, and indeed most other disciplines in the social sciences and humanities, have been considerable. They have, also been highly contested. So, for example, while the preceding two sections have identified five philosophical arguments associated with postmodernism – distrust of meta-narratives and grand-theory; emphasis on difference; the problematisation of repre-sentation; recognition of situatedness of knowledge; and its particularisation of social critique – each of these has been the subject of criticism. Harvey, for example, has been highly critical of postmodernism particularisation of social critique, claiming, that 'postmodern thinking shuts off … other voices from access to more universal sources of power by ghettoizing them within an opaque otherness' (Harvey 1989: 117; also Harvey 1993). Harvey argues that postmodernists' emphasis on local knowledge and difference ignores both the extent to which there may be commonali-ties of interest between different peoples, and how localised differences may stem from extra-local social relationships, most particularly those of capitalism.

Harvey's emphasis on capitalist political-economy as the foundation of social difference has been subject to considerable criticism from feminists and postmod-ernists (see Box 9.3). In responding to these criticisms, Harvey (1992) raised another epistemological issue, claiming that while postmodernists were criticising his work as being 'wrong, misguided, or fundamentally misguided' (p. 322), they could only do so by 'deploying truth claims of their own'. Similarly, Sayer (1993a: 323) claimed that while postmodernists often argued that all knowledge was equally valid, they themselves often asserted 'what is the case and what is not the case'. These two geog-raphers were in effect giving specific instances of a broader argument advanced by Habermas (1987a), who claimed that postmodernists such as Lyotard and Foucault were guilty of 'performative contradictions' in that they often failed to enact their own arguments fully. In particular Habermas suggest that while postmodernists disparage meta-narratives and grand theories, they often employ them in their own writings (see Phillips 1994a; Fraser 1989).

A range of meta-narratives and grand-concepts have indeed been identified within postmodern thought. Curry (1991) and Berg (1993), for instance, have identified modernist notions of authorship and knowledge within purportedly postmodern texts, whilst more generally, Berg (1993: 491) has commented that while he is sympathetic to many aspects of postmodernism he still 'find it necessary to draw upon particular modernist narratives, such as "oppression", "justice" and "equity" in order to make normative judgements'. It is just such meta-narratives, or perhaps rather better, grand-concepts, that Fraser (1989) identifies in the work of Foucault, despite his explicit scepticism at the value of such notions (see also Driver 1992).

Postmodernism has not only been criticised for employing modernist meta-narra-tives and/or concepts, but also of creating some new ones of its own. Kellner (1988), for example, argues that Lyotard's account of postmodernism employs a 'master narrative' of the decline of the meta-narratives of modernity and sets up a grand, totalising concept, namely that local knowledges cannot communicate with each other. Honneth (1985) similarly suggests that Lyotard's rejection of meta-narratives is contradicted by the repeated emphasis on respecting difference and local knowledges.

The emphasis given to notions of difference, otherness and the incomensurabilities of language has also been criticised for neglecting other aspects of social life, such as commonality and collectivity. Harvey (1993: 61–62), for example, claims that one of the impacts of postmodernism has been 'to throw out the living baby of political and ethical solidarities and similarities across differences'. He argues that the commonalities do exist between 'differentiated social groups' (Harvey 1992: 310) and that it is important to recognise and identify these because they may well form the basis of politically significant alliances. Furthermore, he suggests that postmodernists tend to treat difference as 'an end in itself rather than a problem to be confronted', at least in the sense of having to work out which differences should be taken as 'positive ' and which might be seen as 'trivial, unimportant or downright objectionable' (p. 312). For Harvey postmodernism leads into relativism whereby all forms of difference deserve recognition, all forms of knowledge are accorded equally validity, and all manifestations of otherness are to be fostered. This view has been criticised for failing to recognise differences in difference: that is, how '[s]ome differences are playful, some are poles of world historical systems of domination' (Haraway 1990: 203). McDowell (1992: 70) argues that while postmodern academics may revel in the play of difference, for many other people '"otherness" and "exoticness" reflects structures of oppression and domination'. McDowell also comments that while feminists have long sought to reveal the multiplicity of, and difference between, viewpoints on the world and thereby deconstruct the Western intellectual tradition which priorities 'the male view of "the one" at the expense of the multitudinous "others"' (p. 60), this does not mean that multiplicity and difference is everything:

> Women are not looking for fragmentation but reconstruction and recentreing. Rather than the discovery of difference and the reiteration of the positionality of all social groups, divided by a range of social attributes … feminism demands the recognition that certain of these social differences reflect and reinforce broad structures of social domination that need over-turning (McDowell 1992: 60).

For McDowell, Haraway and Harvey, difference is both a social feature which is not universally to be celebrated and encouraged, and also is a feature which is, at least in part, constructed as a product of other aspects of social life, such as systems or structures of domination. For Harvey, central themes within postmodernism, one might even say its 'meta-narratives', are the revelation of how:

> the world is a complicated place, that it is always hard to grasp what is happening to us and to it, and that something can be gained from looking at the oddities and complexities rather than presuming simplicities (Harvey 1992: 311).

For Harvey, while these themes are useful, postmodern thinking should not be 'merely about complication without explanation' (p. 311) and there are important philosophical and political differences between seeking to 'give full play to differentiated identities once they have formed', and endeavouring to understand the

Contested Worlds

'social processes of construction of identities' and/or 'the social processes creating ...
a problem' such as homelessness (Harvey 1993: 64). As Fraser (1997) also
comments, dealing with problems such as homeless or unequal access to work may
involve actions which actively seek to undermine the relationships that constitute
some group's social identity: that is, if you could abolish homelessness then you
would undermine senses of identity amongst the homeless; if you equalised access to
employment for women you might undermine the basis for collective feminist identities (see Box 2.11).

For Harvey (1992: 316) some representations are 'more adequate than others' and
the formulation of 'proper and powerful' theoretical representations is a serious task
requiring careful thought and commitment. He does, however, acknowledge that not
only is there much to be learnt from postmodernism with respect its ontological
notions of difference, otherness and complexity, but also from its epistemological
concerns over situatedness and representation. Even here, however, Harvey has some
reservations. He argues, for instance, that many of the discussions of situatedness and
positionality are overly too simplistic, often failing to recognise the differences which
go up to may both situational contexts and the researcher. He claims that researchers,
just like the people they research, are not distinct and homogenous entities, but rather
are 'bundles of heterogeneous impulses, many of which derive from an internaliza-
tion of the "other"'. In making these arguments Harvey can be seen to be drawing on
arguments connected to notions of post-structuralism as much as, if not more than,
postmodernism; although in Harvey's writings these arguments are very much turned
against their originators.

Post-structuralism

Post-structuralism is a term closely associated with the term postmodernism and
indeed, as noted earlier, there are so many areas of commonality and over-lap
between the philosophies that they are often seen as synonymous. However, it is also
possible to discern some lines of difference. For example, while the term postmodernism had origins in art and architecture, post-structuralism had rather more philosophical roots: Pratt (1994), for example, places that the origins of post-structuralism
in the work of French philosophers such as Derrida, Lacan, Foucault and Kristeva.
Post-structuralism can also be said to be rather more structural in its emphasis than
postmodernism, which as argued earlier had a clear focus on human agency, particularly that of neglected groups. Post-structuralism by contrast, and as its name
suggests, seeks as Pratt (1994: 468) has put it, to 'draw on and extend some of the
important insights of structuralism'. Pratt goes on two identify two particular areas of
development, namely 'linguistics' and the concept of the 'human subject'.

When structuralist approaches to human geography were discussed earlier, mention
was made of the variety of structuralisms, including the linguistic structuralism of
Saussure. Within human geography, however, the emphasis was generally on structures
as social entities, as opposed to linguistic or indeed mental entities. Structuralism in
human geography became quickly associated with Marxism, with structures being
envisaged in terms of entities that connect people together in terms of social activities
such as work, the communication of meaning and the exercise of authority. Structures

hence became entities such as 'modes of production', 'state apparati' and 'ideological systems'. While reference was made by human geographers to the work of people like Piaget and Saussure whose conceptions of structuralism centred on mental or linguistic entities, there was no real sustained engagement with these ideas. However, in the late 1980s and particularly into the 1990s there was something of a return to the arguments of linguistic structuralists in particular, albeit engagement was now undertaken using the 'post-' epithet. Peet (1998), for example, has claimed that if one single feature might be used to characterise poststructuralist thought, 'it is the *linguistic turn* towards discourse, text, reading and interpretation' (emphasis added).

Within forms of social structuralism like Marxism the individual person, or *subject*, is seen to be conditioned by broader social forces. Linguistic structuralism basically takes the same ideas and relates them to the development of language: individual linguistic elements – such as words – are seen as having meaning by their position within the broader linguistic patterns of meaning. A word gets its meaning from its difference from and relation to other words and associated meanings. This may seem like a small point but it has profound consequences in that its goes again many everyday understandings of what a term means and implies there are no necessary connection between terms and objects. As such it has considerable epistemological and ontological significance.

Poststructuralist Ontologies

In the 1990s a number of geographers began to argue that poststructuralist ideas could usefully be applied to understanding a series of subjects of geographical interest, such as landscapes, places and spaces. An early strategy in such work was to conceptualise landscapes, places and spaces as 'texts', that is as conveyors of meanings. One example of this was Cosgrove and Daniels' (1988: 1) claim that landscapes were cultural images or symbols, 'structuring or symbolising surroundings' whether created through 'paint on canvas, in writing on paper, [or] in earth, stone, water and vegetation on the ground'. This notion of landscape as text both significantly differed from earlier approaches to landscape, such as Sauer's materially focused, largely empiricist, morphological analysis of cultural landscapes (see Jackson (1989) and Phillips (forthcoming-a)), and also paved the way for the adoption of post-structuralist ideas. In particular, Duncan (1990) and Barnes and Duncan (1992) drew on poststructuralist theories of language to suggest that the meanings of landscapes should not be seen to stem from the character of landscapes conceived as ensembles of material elements present within a particular area of space. Such a view can be seen to inform both empiricist accounts of landscapes, where meaning is constructed through observation of landscape elements by the researcher, and also humanistic conceptions whereby landscape meanings are constructed initially within the activities and experiences of people inhabiting an area and then are represented, and possibly reinterpreted, by the humanistic geographer in their research texts. By contrast, Barnes and Duncan (1992: 5) argue that landscape texts, be these of the researcher or of people inhabiting a landscape, should not be seen as 'referential duplications' of landscape elements, but rather should be viewed 'intertextually', that is produced out of, and in association with, other cultural texts.

Duncan (1990) develops these ideas through a study of the landscape texts associated with the Kandyian kingdom in nineteenth century Sri Lanka, identifying a series of 'textual communities' which draw together particular sets of texts to establish their interpretation of this landscape. This idea has, as is discussed in Chapter 10, been employed in the study of gentrification by Mills (1993), and notions of intertextuality have also been employed in discussions of place identities and imageries, and spatial distinctions such as urbanity and rurality.

Halfacree (1993: 26), for example, argues that many geographers and other academics have sought to distinguish rural space from other spaces (most notably those of the urban) essentially on the basis of 'properties which are seen to be inherent in the rural environment' and which, thereby, gave these spaces and the people inhabiting them some 'distinctive rural character'. He suggests that not only has the identification of such elements and characteristics proved problematic with many supposedly rural elements and social characteristics being found to be almost equally present in spaces designated as urban, but that there has been 'a failure to distinguish between the rural as a distinctive type of locality and the rural as a social representation', or the 'rural as space and the rural as representations of space' (Halfacree 1993: 34). Many previous studies had effectively sought to bring about some one-to-one correspondence between representations of space and the character of spaces: to create definitions of rurality which represented the distinctive characteristics of rural localities. However, Halfacree, and also Murdoch and Pratt (1993) and Pratt (1996), argue that there may be little or no connection between socially accepted notions of rurality (or the countryside) and the characteristics of locations designated as rural, in large part because social representations of space are constructed out a diverse range of constituents, many of which have little or no connections to a locality, or indeed to rural locations in general. Halfacree, for example, argues that many academic definitions of rurality draw upon non-academic, 'lay', understandings and that these in turn are made from an amalgam of other influences such as 'personal experiences and "traditional" handed-down beliefs propagated through literature, the media, the state, family, friends and institutions' (Halfacree 1993: 33).

Post-structuralist arguments had been in existence some considerable time before they were picked up by geographers. Barnes and Gregory (1997: 294) suggest that post-structuralist ideas were not initially developed 'with geography in mind', which in part may account for the laggedly take up of post-structuralism in geography. Slightly conversely, Doel (1999: 2) has suggested that there was an 'enormous, subterranean' presence of attempts to link post-structuralism and geographical concerns in 'fields as diverse as quantum physics, sociology, and philosophy'. Whichever interpretation is favoured, it was only in the 1990s that the presence of post-structuralist idea came to be felt in a sustained way within human geography. Not only did some geographers begin to appreciate their relevance of post-structuralist ideas to the study of traditional geographical subjects such as landscapes, place identities and spatial distinctions such as rurality and urbanity, but some also began to explore and adopt into geography some of the ontological subjects which had been constructed very clearly with post-structuralism in mind. In particular, discussions of post-structuralism had long tended to foreground notions such as *discourse*, *identity*, the *body* and, in a sense drawing all of the afore mentioned notions together, the *constitution of the human subject*.

The notion of discourse is very much linked to post-structuralist theories of language. A discourse can be seen as a particular way of 'talking about, writing or otherwise representing' the world and things in that world (Cloke *et al.* 1999: 335), and from a post-structuralist viewpoint at least, is seen as being the product of a range of signifying elements and practices. Discourse hence do not here refer simply to verbal communication and debate, but include and are created from written texts, visual and audio imagery, bodily actions and all manner of entities – including spaces, places, and non-human elements of nature – which are seen to have some cultural meaning associated with them. These texts, images actions and entities act together to generate meaning: they form the system or 'structure' of texts or signs from which meanings are created and through which each elements gets its meaning. Once more, it is the interplay of signs, rather than the inherent character of an element, that produces symbolic meaning.

Amongst the implications of this notion of discourse is that all aspects of geography have a discursive aspect to them (McDowell 1995b). Even economic geography which has, as Crang (1997) notes, often been cast as the 'other' of anything cultural, has come to be considered as a discursive construct (see for example Barnes 1992; 1996a). However, not only has the notion of discourse signalled that all aspects of geography are cultural, it is also widely seen to imply that culture has power, or as it has been variously called *material* or *performative effects*. This argument is clearly seen, for instance, in the policies and practices which have flowed from various 'discourses of development' as is discussed in Chapter 3.

Discourses are also widely seen in post-structuralist theories to be embedded within and regulated by relations of power, although there are some ambiguity about this issue, even within the work of one of the people most widely associated with this argument, namely Michael Foucault. Barnes and Gregory, for example, comment:

> Whereas in his earlier writings Foucault presents discourses as almost free-floating, abstract concepts, in his later writings he increasingly situates them on the ground within intricate social networks of power (Barnes and Gregory 1997: 140–141).

More specifically, Foucault conceptualisation of discourse shifted between works employing what he entitled an 'archaeological' perspective (e.g. Foucault 1970; 1972) and those adopting a so-called 'genealogical' one (e.g. Foucault 1977; 1980). Best and Kellner (1991: 40) comment that the former approach sought to identify 'the determining rules of formation of discursive rationality that operate *beneath* the level of intention or thematic content' (emphasis added). Employing an archaeological approach involved digging beneath and sifting through discourses to reveal the rules which structured people's representations of the world. It was hence very similar to structuralism in that it sought to look through what people were saying to reveal what might be structuring those words. However, Foucault distanced himself from structuralism and his archaeological approach might be better described as 'quasi structuralist' (Hoy 1986). One area of difference was that Foucault's archaeology did not involve digging deep for structures: for him the structures of discourse lay within discourse and not in any economic or political infrastructure or in the deep structures of the mind. Second, in clear contrast to the arguments of Levi-Strauss discussed earlier, the structures identified by Foucault were not seen as 'universal or immutable in character', but rather were seen as 'historically changing and specific' (Best and Kellner 1991: 40).

Foucault's genealogical approach continued, and indeed strengthened, the emphasis historical change. One of the criticisms levelled at Foucault's archaeological approach was that whilst it recognised the possibility of change it never addressed how change occurred: hence Barnes and Gregory's comments about 'free-floating discourses' (see also Dreyfus and Rabinow 1982: 27; Johnston 1997: 24). Foucault's use of the term genealogy signalled a search for the origins of discourse, both temporally and also ontologically: within his genealogy Foucault, amongst other things, both charted the 'historical lineage' from the present of problematic discursive constructs such as 'normal and abnormal, legitimate and illegitimate', and also tracked the 'family associations' which existed between discourse and power (Johnston *et al*. 2000: 292).

Within Foucault's genealogy, discourse and power were seen as inter-related, and indeed inseparable: while in his archaeology Foucault wrote of discursive rules constructing particular 'epistemes', or knowledge-discourses, which determined what might or might not be construed as true; in his genealogy he was argued that relations of power were 'linked in circular relations' to 'regimes of truth' (Foucault 1980: 131) in such a manner that people should think in terms of 'power/knowledge' as opposed to power *and* knowledge, which implies two distinct, if interacting, entities.

Foucault's genealogical approach and associated notion of power-knowledges have been widely taken up within geography with studies both exploring the constitution of power-knowledges within academic geography (e.g. Unwin 1992; Livingstone 1992; Driver 1992) and within the worlds of various others (e.g. Matless 1995; Tsouvalis *et al*. 2000). Much of this work has also made use of Actor-Network Theory (Box 2.10) which may be seen as an extension of some of Foucault's ideas. However, other people, including some often seen as adopting a post-structuralist perspective, have been quite critical of Foucault. Baudrillard, for example, has claimed that Foucault genealogical analysis was too structuralist:

> With Foucault power remains ... a *structural* notion ... with a perfect genealogy and an inexplicable presence, a notion that cannot be surpassed in spite of a sort of latent denunciation ... It is hard to see how if could be reversed ... there is simply nothing else on either side of it, or beyond it ... Power ... is the last term, the irreducible web, the last tale to be told; it is what structures the indeterminate equation of the world (Baudrillard and Lotringer 1987: 39–40).

For Baudrillard power was not the ground to which discourses needed to be earthed, but rather power was itself a discursive construct like any other. Power was, Baudrillard and Lotringer (1987: 40) argue, a 'simulacrum', a concept without a referent, inter-textually constructed out of an array of signifiers, all of which were also simulacra.

In Baudrillard's work one can see the clear employment of a 'post-structuralist' theory of language where the development of concepts and signs is seen to evolve though a logic which is independent of the character and movements of an external, non-discursive, referents. One of the fullest expositions of such a perspective in geography is provided by Doel, who argues, for instance, that:

There was a time when we foolishly thought that words (signifiers) presented, gave way to, or mapped onto, meanings (signified) and worlds (referents). Today, however, we should all be familiar with the genealogy of the free-floating and self-referential sign ... [T]he signifier moves *before* it ossifies into the terminus of signified or referent ... [T]he signifier is always in circulation, always on the move, always pointing towards something else, and something other, it is irreducibly nomadic: doomed to wander and fated to disseminate (Doel 1993: 386).

Doel argues that geographers should seek to follow these nomadic, rhizomatic, movements, developing a 'delirious cartography' (Doel 1996: 427) of the innumerable lines of flight of any signifier, by which he means anything – event, object, word, thought and so on – which 'chokes, binds or fascinates you' (Doel 1993: 239). Doel himself has developed a series of 'deconstructions' of all manner of entities, ranging from the writings of 'post-structuralist' social theorists such as Baudrillard, Derrida, Lyotard, Deleuze and Guattari (see Doel 1996; 1999), through into notions of space and geography (Clarke and Doel 1994a; Doel 1996), rural change (Doel 1994) and political geography (Clarke and Doel 1994b), and on into the conjunctive term 'and' (Doel 1996), the 'Holocaust' (Clarke *et al.* 1996) and a stack of tomatoes on a supermarket shelf (Doel and Clarke 1999). These are deconstructions not in the sense of destructive dismantling of a concept, account, image or discourse, but rather as an attempt to reveal the instabilities and extensions present in their very construction; to '(dis)locate and (up)root' (Doel 1996: 426). For Doel there is no depth to ontology: the world is composed of signifers which are not the product of some underlying causal, structural, social relations such as those of power á la Foucault's genealogy, but rather are part of a 'scrumpled geography' where everything is of equal potential significance and where there are labyrinthine lines of interconnection and disconnection.

At present, post-structuralist ideas have been incorporated into the study of discourse in two quite divergent ways. This can be clearly seen in studies of geography and colonialism, with many studies drawing on the ideas of Foucault and the closely associated ideas of Said (1995) to interpret various writings of European travellers and scientists as being the product of particular discourses and powers circulating within European society. In some contrast Barnett (1998) has sought to 'deconstruct' these writings by revealing how they contained ever so slight signifiers of the agency of colonised people. Barnett argues that colonial writing was often based on the knowledges of indigenous peoples, but this reliance was largely written out of accounts who instead tended to emphasis the superiority of European understandings. However, alighting on traces of reliance of colonialised subjects, Barnett seeks to read the texts of colonial geographers in a manner 'otherwise than was intended', to 'inflect these discourses in new ways', constructing European knowledges as both exclusionary rather than all encompassing, and reliant rather than powerful.

The differences marking off genealogical and deconstructive post-structuralisms can be seen to traverse the other ontological subjects foregrounded within the encounter with post-structuralism. Within the study of identity, for example, it is possible to identify studies which have argued that people's identities are discursively formed through the operation of powers constituted through social relations such as class, ethnicity, gender, race, sexuality and nationalism and/or through psychological relationships with others (for discussions of the last set of relationships see Pile 1996;

Rose 1993a; Sibley 1995). Within such accounts, identities are seen often seen as quite stable, fixed by relations of power: to create new social and /or psychic identities the power structures of society need to change. Other studies, on the other hand, have seen identities as highly fluid and unstable entities, formed out of complex articulations of signifiers. Anderson (2000), for example, has sought to develop a *postnational* approach which seeks to trace the 'cultural routes' though which national identities are constructed, routes which make take one far beyond the boundaries of any particular nation states. Some *post-colonial* studies have likewise emphasised the inter-connections and articulations of the identities of the coloniser and the colonised, noting how areas as distance as London and Perth may both appear equally at the 'edge of empire' (Jacobs, 1996). *Post-structural/postmodern/post-colonial feminists* (McDowell 1993; Pratt 1993), or as they might also be cautiously characterised *post-feminists* (see Box 2.11), have argued that genders are discursively constructed and performed rather than some inherent, structuring entity. Likewise some variants of *queer theory* have argued that sexual identity is a discursive construct, with people becoming sexed rather than simply born with a particular sexuality (see Butler 1993).

Poststructuralist Epistemologies

In addition to its impacts on what geographers have studied and how they have sought to understand phenomena, poststructuralism also has profound epistemological consequences. Post-structuralist theories of language imply that words and images do not necessarily correspond to a particular object or have distinct and stable meanings. This stands in clear contrast to the epistemologies that have underpinned much of geography. As discussed already with reference to postmodernism, the dominant view of theory development within geography has long been one of trying to get theories to 'correspond to', 're-present' or 'mirror' objects of study. In other words, there is an attempt to establish clear, stable and unambiguous relationships between a concept, its meaning and some object or event to which the concept is seen to refer. However, not only has achieving consensus on the lines of association proved immensely difficult but may also, given a post-structuralist theory of language, be fatally flawed; doomed always to failure because the meaning given to any term or concept always stems more from the meaning of other concepts than it does to any world beyond the concept. The term rural, for instance, implies notions of the urban and of the agricultural, both of which are themselves far from clear cut and rely on a series of other concepts.

Geographers for a long period had rather ignored such ideas, but during the 1990s an increasing number of geographers began to accept that the notion of representing objects and events in the world may be quite problematic and in some cases also to accept that there might be, as Baudrillard tellingly phrased it, 'no system of reference to tell us what happened to the geography of things' (Baudrillard and Lotringer 1987: 126). A series of authors (e.g Fischer and Marcus 1986; Cosgrove and Domosh, 1993) started to talk of a 'crisis in representation' and to, at the very least, question to what extent their concepts and theories related rather more to the cultural expectations held by themselves, their academic peers and the society in which they lived and worked, than it did to the character of some object or situations they were studying. There emerged an increasing concern to reflect on the origins of concepts rather than simply seek to elaborate new ones and to apply them to understanding particular situations. Hence, as well as studying the discourse of others, geographers have also sought to be *reflexive* about their own discourse, although as might be expected given the earlier discussion of discourse there have been quite divergent foci for reflection. One strategy, already discussed within the ambit of postmodernism, has been to seek to position geographical discourses in social relations of power such as class, gender, ethnicity, race and sexuality. Within works influenced by post-structuralism these positions are, however, often seen as ambiguous, uncertain and even tenuous. Rose (1997), for example, highlights how discussions of the position of the researcher vis-à-vis those being researched often suggest quite different positionings (such as needing to be in-side *and* detached from a situation) and how they require researchers be able to recognise their own positionality and yet a person's self may well not be transparently knowable, least of all by the self. Rose also ends by arguing that there 'is no clear landscape of social positions to be charted' (p. 317) but rather researchers negotiate and perform a range of positions when carrying out research, some of which may have effects which reconfigure the performances, positions and powers of others.

Rose very much seeks to connect discourse and action: knowledges are created through the performance of various research activities, ranging from conducting interviews and interacting with people 'in the field', through the writing of research accounts and into the dissemination of research as academic papers, seminar presentations and teaching. Other post-structuralist geographers have adopted a much more linguistic/textual focus to their study of geographical discourses, frequently either adopting a broadly 'archaeological' approach which seeks to situate particular concepts and associated knowledges within broader discursive networks or else seeking to 'deconstruct' them by revealing the inconsistencies that lurk within them. Barnes (1992), for example, can be seen to enact the former approach when he argues that neo-classical economic theories and the theories of Marxist political-economy were constructed using metaphors draw from physics and biology respectively; while later he examined the arguments used to justify the use of mathematics by quantitative geographers and sought to deconstruct them by revealing that 'submerged beneath the ostensible clarity and precision of mathematics are a series of metaphors, tropes, and rhetorical claims which subvert its central claims' (Barnes (1996b).

Despite the differences between Barnes' two studies, both focus very clearly on the realm of signs and signifiers rather than any worlds to which these might refer. Indeed Barnes very clearly resists making such a connection, claiming for instance that 'theoretical interpretations can reflect only other interpretations and not a bedrock reality' (Barnes 1992: 118), and that:

> there is no ultimate signified, and only a system of signifiers that is inescapable, there can only ever be the flux of meaning, and no constant presence … we can never have access to things in and of themselves (Barnes 1996b: 1025–6).

The implications of such arguments for people such as Strohmayer and Hannah (1992) is that theories and concepts cannot be made to refer or describe anything:

> Whenever we speak or write *about* a reality, the language we use *is not* the reality to which it is supposed to refer ... Descriptive language, no matter how precise and exhaustive, can never succeed in anchoring itself to a reality; it can only move 'sideways' through the realm of words (Strohmayer and Hannah 1992: 37).

They go on to argue that human thought and understanding is inexorably tied to the structures of language and that this 'mediation' by language 'render problematic such concepts as immediacy, truth, certainty, and independent reality' (p. 37). They add that they do not rule out the existence of such things as truth but merely that 'if there is truth, we are incapable of recognizing it *as such* with any certainty' (p. 39, original emphasis).

Strohmayer and Hannah's arguments have, however, been subject to criticism, albeit from two rather different directions. Sayer (1993a: 324–6) attacks their arguments from a realist perspective (see Box 2.8), arguing that whilst theories and explanations are 'unavoidably linguistic' and the notion of being able to say that one has definitely arrived at a true representation is 'untenable', it does not follow that there are no points of anchorage between language and other aspects of the world, nor that there is no value in the notions of truth (and indeed falsity). For Sayer there is not an endless 'horizontal' movement of flow of meaning but rather 'it is a precondition of communication and social life that a large proportion of signifiers and sense relations are relatively stable' (p. 326) both because without it language would become unintelligible and because particular interpretations appear more 'practically useful', and thereby might be seen as 'truer', than others.

Barnett (1993a; 1993b) criticises both Strohmayer and Hannah, and also Sayer. He argues that the latter presents a caricature of the arguments of post-structuralists and postmodernists and that he employs a very restrictive concept of language. By employing these techniques, Sayer develops an 'unsympathetic critique' of postmodernism and postructuralism, to which Barnett seeks to respond in kind (Barnett 1993b; see also Sayer 1993b). Stromhayer and Hannah identified very similar critiques in the work of Marxist writers such as Harvey (1989) and Jameson (1972) who they argue seek to 'domesticate' the two philosophies by failing to recognise the challenges they pose to established notions of theory and knowledge. Strohmayer and Hannah seek to 'let loose the beast' and recognise the full implications of the post-structuralist theories of language; yet Barnett (1993a) levies similar criticisms of them as he did of Sayer claiming that they caricature and homogenise work of a range of authors, plus misrepresents the arguments concerning language and representation of Derrida. In particular Barnett criticises Stromhayer and Hannah for failing to recognise that Derrida explicitly argued against an abandonment of notions of reference and representation and, connected to this, claimed that language and reality should not be conceptualised as 'ontologically distinct realms' (Barnett 1993a: 347). For Barnett:

> All language use rests on representation, and representation and reference are not something attached to language from the outside ... Derrida is not against representation, but is complicating our understanding of it (Barnett 1993a: 349).

In a sense, Barnett and Sayer come to quite similar conclusions, albeit through quite different routes. It is, however, also evident that there are major points of disagreement between Barnett and Sayer and that the issue of representation is certainly both complicated and contested. As Peet (1998: 215) notes, post-structuralist ideas concerning language and writing are often seen to imply that 'representation theories of truth are impossible'. However, the arguments of Barnett suggest that this argument may be far from clear cut.

Peet (1998: 215) also comments that even if representational theories of truth were possible, for post-structuralists they would inadequate in that 'even accurate description only begins to approach the nebulous realm of truth'. Despite Strohmayer and Hannah protests to the contrary, their theorisation of language does seem to render notions of truth rather redundant: they argue that it is not possible to possible to pin down truth 'with any certainty' (p. 39) but do not then go on explore whether there is any value in making truth or validity-claims, albeit ones which are seen as always uncertain, provisional and contestable. Thompson (1990: 320), drawing on the critical theory of Habermas (see for example Habermas 1984; 1987a; 1987b; and Phillips 1994a), has argued that social interpretations should be seen as 'inherently risky, conflict laden and open to dispute', while Habermas himself has argued that the key epistemological issues are not whether or not one puts forward truth claims – for him in the very 'act of uttering, language and the speaker are situated within, and hence make (albeit often implicitly) "validity" or "truth" claims' (Phillips 1994a: 111) – but how is it that some claims are accepted and others not, and what are the social consequences of accepting specific claims.

In making these claims, Habermas' work resonates somewhat with notions of 'practical adequacy' outlined by Sayer, not least because Habermas argues that 'language does not form or operate entirely within a linguistic realm, but that it is frequently used within practical contexts' (Phillips 1998c: 46–47). However, Habermas adopts a very broad definition of truth, seeing it as involving notions of 'rightness' and 'sincerity' as well as correspondence with the world of objects and events (see Phillips 1994a). These arguments raise an issue not explored by Strohmayer and Hannah, namely whether truth might both mean rather more than accurate representations of the real and come about in more ways than simply through correspondence of signs and referents. Indeed, Habermas distinguishes between 'world generative' and 'problem-solving' aspects of language (McCarthy 1987: 47), with the former referring to how in language people constitute and reformulate their understandings of the worlds they inhabit and the latter referring to the way these understandings act as a medium for dealing with problems in the world, problems which may have extra-, but not non-, discursive origins.

For Habermas both aspects of language are significant. Sayer on the other hand, may be seen to privilege the 'problem-solving capacity' of language, not least in his notion of 'practical adequacy'. Habermas (1987a), however, suggests that post-structuralists such as Foucault and Derrida focus on the world-generative, or 'performative' (Barnett 1993b: 366) aspects of language, to the expense of the problem-solving. Harvey (1992) can be seen to be making rather similar arguments when he argues that Deutsche (1991), and by implication Baudrillard, employ a 'discursive idealism' in which cultural representations, whilst not actually representing anything, are seen to be the primary forces constructing the social world. For Harvey not only does this view give too much autonomy and power to cultural productions but it also, conversely, fails to connect representations to social realities, such as poverty. He argues that 'some representations are more adequate than others' (p. 317) and that some things, such as the

presence and impacts of poverty, are 'real and accessible enough' whatever the epistemological issues surrounding notions of representation. Peet, like Harvey an early
advocate of radical/Marxist geography, has also been fiercely critical of much of the
work characterised here as poststructuralist (although Peet describes it as postmodern),
claiming that it is far too focused on representations:

> Representations of representations ... amounts to a new kind of fetish, that of representa-
> tionality. Its utter fascination with texts written about texts may produce a dense intertextu-
> ality which precludes contact with the world outside the fetishistic dream ... At its worst,
> postmodern geography is a kind of selfish, privileged self-gratification, displayed in essays
> which meander between personal idiosyncrasy and lazy bits of research ... Much postmod-
> ern geography consists of reading the poststructuralist literature, arguing interminably over
> its contents, and making what are actually simple, tentative steps towards the study of
> space, place and environment (Peet 1998: 226–77).

Peet's characterisation can be seen as rather misleading in that many post-structuralists
have been highly critical of the notion of representation, and have sought either to
dispense with it or at the least make people recognise that it is a much more complex
affair than is often realised. Furthermore, as Peet himself mentions, not all post-structuralists have been solely exercised by problems of representational accuracy and truth.
Much of the radicalness post-structuralism may well lie in its recognition of the world
generative aspects of language in ways other than through representation. Doel (1996:
433), for example, argues that the radicalness of post-structuralist thought lies in its
commitment to 'experimenting *fully* with what concepts can do'. Theory he argues, is
'just like a bag of tools, filled with so many prostheses for enhancing, extending and
intensifying though and action' (Doel, 1999: 37) and that what matters 'are the events
and effects' that theories give rise to, rather than 'their "truth" to "sense" content' (Doel,
1999: 4–6). Deleuze (1990: 321) likewise argues that a theory's power lies in its ability
to alter established meanings and to 'impose a new set of divisions on things and
actions'; while Baudrillard (1988: 57) argues that theory is a 'seducing sign', something
which 'one cannot avoid responding'. Doel (1999) also remarks on how Deleuze and
Baudrillard engage in 'theory-fictions', and one can also point to their use of parody,
irony and a humourous textuality which may be seen as aimed at continually provoke
readers to ask 'are you being serious'? Barnett (1993b: 366) notes that such textual
strategies are often met with 'cheerless and intolerant humour' as critics seek to point
out the absurdities in argument, but that in doing so one 'might wonder who the joke is
really on' (see also the debates over Smith's 'Rethinking sleep': Smith; 1996b, 1997;
Hamnett, 1997b; Pile 1997; Peet 1998). Recently Thrift (1996; 1999; 2000; 2004) has
argued for adoption of 'non-representational theory', and although his comments on this
notion at present remain programmatic rather than demonstrative, they do at least point
to the possibilities of looking at theory, and philosophy, in new ways.

Conclusion

In this chapter I have sought to present some insights into philosophical debates and
concepts as articulated in human geography during the course of the second half of
the twentieth century and into the onset of the twenty-first. It should be stressed that

the account presented is very much a personal interpretation and should hence not be seen as an objective account but rather a situated, positioned account. Readers may wish to disagree with the descriptions and emphases given in this account, and indeed there are numerous points in this account about which I am either uncertain and/or uneasy. Furthermore, despite its length, this account has clearly also been highly selective and reductionist. Philosophical debate even within a discipline which has long been highly resistant to things philosophical has burgeoned into a expansive, complex, varigated and highly contorted discourse. This chapter has attempted to chart some lines of similarity and difference, and there are various other cartographies of the philosophy in geography: Livingstone (1992), for example, charts a contested history of geography involving ten conversations; Unwin (1992) relies on a three-fold distinction between empirical-analytical, historical hermeneutic and critical science to make sense of the place held by geography; while Peet (1998) identifies eleven 'schools' of modern and postmodern human geographical thought. Doel wonders whether even this is sufficient to characterise the discipline:

> in Peet's two dimensional pictogram ... the majority of the figure is cast in grey tones, and the resulting grey areas stand in stark contrast to the historicised white streaks of post-enlightenment geography. One wonders what is lurking in the dark, uncharted and unattributed portions of geographical praxis (Doel 1999: 29).

He adds that in his view,

> It is futile to try to isolate discrete theoretical practices – each with its own system of ideas, conceptual approaches, phrase regime, frame of reference, proscribed territory, and logic of internal development – and to position each over and against the others (Doel 1999: 32).

The reason he gives is that, in his view, any philosophical practice would always 'be endlessly other', composed of multitudinous elements which not only do not add up to a complete unity but often connect one philosophy to another, in a series of contorted folds of influence and argument. Thinking in '-isms', he argues, 'invariably leads to the freezing of variation into monolithic and seamless constancy' (Doel, 1999: 32). Barnett makes similar comments, albeit specifically with regard to the reception and use of postmodern and post-structuralist writings:

> What needs to be resisted is the construction of particular philosophical and theoretical work into the toothless beast we have come to know as postmodernism – the effect of this construction is to invite cavalier engagements with work whose complexity and openness in posing its problematizations demands a reciprocal degree of modesty and respect in drawing out its consequences (Barnett 1993a: 346).

Such comments are useful warnings, as it is very easy when reading some accounts of philosophy in geography to be left with the impression that it largely involves picking one out of a number of pre-existing, clearly delimited philosophies. Hopefully I have avoided giving such an impression of philosophy in geography within this account, because I do feel such an account is highly misleading. It is misleading, for instance, because it ignores the evidence that even the acknowledged and apparently influential – the so-called 'master weavers' (Bodman 1991; 1992) or, depending of your own perspective, 'heroes' and 'villains' (Livingstone 1992: 5) of geography – have clearly struggled with philosophy, moving from one position to another: Harvey moved, for example, from positivism to Marxism; Duncan from humanism to post-structuralism; Gregory from structuralism, structuration and Habermasian critical theory to post-colonialism and post-modernism. If such people have struggled with philosophy and had significant changes of heart and mind, then it is perhaps not surprising that others find it hard to identify where they stand within the debates. Furthermore, movement from one philosophical positioning to another should perhaps be expected and indeed encouraged given that, as Doel (1999: 30) comments:

> Concepts, ideas, frames of reference, and theoretical practices are never created *ex-nihilo* or given as ready mades … They are fabricated and fashioned in particular contexts, from materials and practices that are … available to us (Doel 1999: 30).

Hopefully this chapter will have demonstrated some of the fabrications of philosophy in geography, given pointers to some of the contexts in which they have been produced and received, and also given you some materials to help fashion new, perhaps more becoming, philosophies in human geography.

Box 2.12: Chapter summary and suggestions for further reading

- Philosophical terms and debates have become a significant element of contemporary human geography, although geographers have often seemed reluctant to recognise their significance to the practices of doing geography

- It is suggested that it may be useful to think about philosophies in terms of epistemologies and ontologies: that is in terms of theories of knowledge and theories of what exists.

- A range of different philosophical positions have been discussed, including empiricism, Comtean and logical positivisms, humanism, radicalism/criticial theory, structuralism, post-modernism, post-structuralism.

- The need for care and thought in the description of different philsophies, and in understanding philosophical change, is highlighted.

I have previously reviewed some of the major texts on philosophy and geography (Phillips 1994), concluding that Livingstone's (1992) *The Geographical Tradition* and Cloke *et al.*'s (1991) *Approaching Human Geography* provide useful commentaries on a range of philosophies, while Unwin's (1992) *The Place of Geography* provides a more argumentative assessment. Since writing this review article there have been several new or revised publications which may also prove very useful. These include Peet's (1998) *Modern Geographical Thought*, which provides extensive reviews of philosophical discussion in both human geography and in wider social theoretical literature; Holt-Jensen's (1999) substantially revised and graphically enhanced *Geography: History and*

Concepts – a Students Guide; Barnes and Gregory's (1997) edited collection *Reading Human Geography*; and Hubbard *et al.*'s (2002) *Thinking Geographically* The new edition of Johnston *et al.*'s (2000) *The Dictionary of Human Geography* is a must read for anyone interested in philosophical debates in human geography, while Johnston's (1997) *Geography and Geographers* still provides a useful guide to some of the key people and debates in human geography. As well as these general texts, there have also been a series of more personal engagements with philosophy and human geography, including Gregory's (1994) *Geographical Imaginations*; Harvey's (1996) *Justice, Nature and the Geography of Difference*; Pile's (1996) *The Body and the City* and Doel's (1999) *Poststructuralist Geographies*.

Part Two:
Global Worlds

Chapter 3

Unravelling the Web of Theory: Changing Geographical Perspectives on Development

Ed Brown

Back in the 1960s and 1970s, lecturing on development theories was a rather well-defined domain of knowledge transfer. Authors on the subject used to be divided into 'the good' (neo-Marxists), 'the bad' (modernization theorists) and 'the ugly' (the computerized doomsday specialists) ... Now, well into the 1990s, things have changed. The good feel bad, the bad feel good, and the ugly underwent plastic surgery (Schuurman 1993: ix).

INTRODUCTION: THE DIVERSITY OF APPROACHES

The content and theoretical orientation of undergraduate geography courses tackling *'Third World' development* issues (See Box 3.1 on the concept of the Third World) have been transformed considerably over recent years. Students beginning such courses in the early twenty-first century will find themselves grappling with an area of study that has been the site of considerable theoretical turmoil and not a little conflict, much of it linked to philosophical debates discussed in the preceding chapter. So, whilst few will escape the now obligatory treatments of the *modernization* and *dependency* perspectives that dominated the field until the late 1970s, the majority of current students will also find themselves exposed to an at times bewildering variety of other schools of thought. These might include a wide range of different *Marxist* approaches, the *neo-liberal counter-revolution* in development policy formation and various schools of *ecopolitical* and *feminist* thought. Most recently, some will also have been introduced to *post-colonial* literatures and the complex philosophical terrain of *postmodern* approaches to social knowledge.

Box 3.1: The concept of the Third World

As long ago as 1986, Harris pronounced the death of the 'Third World' as a meaningful analytical concept. Approaching two decades later, the term appears to have suffered little from this and other attacks. Two important recent 'development' texts (Escobar 1995 and Kiely and Marfleet 1998), for example, both feature it in their titles. So where did the term originate and what has led to the range of different views on its current applicability?

Bell (1994) draws our attention to two specific usages of the idea of the 'Third World' and their different origins. The term's original meaning was political, emerging out of a conference in Bandung, Indonesia in 1955, where a group of African and Asian nations attempted to assert their unity, common interests and independence from both the capitalist and socialist worlds, presenting themselves as an identifiable alternative, non-aligned, 'third' world. This positive, self-referential, definition was, however, gradually to give way to the more familiar economic interpretation whereby the 'Third World' became defined through its lack of economic development and the pejorative stereotypes now popularly associated with the term (famine, drought, political instability, poverty and corruption) began to take root. In this sense, the 'Third World' gradually shifted from representing a dynamic political alternative to become a symbol of 'paternalism' and 'dependency' (Bell 1994: 174–175).

The term's association with such negative connotations, together with the end of the Cold War and the increasingly divergent experiences of the nations said to constitute the 'Third World', mean that attitudes such as Harris' are hardly surprising. For many, such concerns have been sufficient to lead to their complete abandonment of the term. For others, the 'Third World', for all its limitations, remains an important descriptive tool. Ray Kiely, for example, concludes his introduction to *Globalisation and the Third World* through an, at least partial, endorsement of Worsley's defence of the term back in 1984:

> Worsley has argued that, 'The Third World is not a myth. The various meanings with which the term "Third World" has been invested show family resemblances, even though they do not fully coincide. They have, that is, a common referent in the real world out there: the unequal, institutionalized distribution of wealth and illth on a world scale' (Worsley 1984: 339). Thus, while non-alignment makes less sense in a post-Cold War world, and there is no economic unity (and probably never was) among an extremely diverse set of nations, the reality of global inequality means that, for Worsley, the Third World continued to exist. While such a definition lacks analytical rigour … it at least has the merit of identifying such inequalities. The Third World therefore remains an important descriptive term, and it is in this sense that the contributors to this book continue to find it appropriate (Kiely 1998a: 16–17).

Overall, it is clear that quite what the 'Third World' represents has changed markedly over time and the term continues to signify different things to different people. Nevertheless, despite the obvious analytical and representational limitations, it remains a central concept within studies of development and is likely to remain so for the foreseeable future.

In a certain, perhaps over-simplistic, way this thematic and theoretical diversification is hardly surprising when one considers the dramatic ways in which the world has changed over recent years. The end of the Cold War and the continuing struggles over the direction of the *New World Order* now emerging from its ashes (see Chapter 5), together with the much discussed, if seldom specified, phenomena of *globalization*, have (just to mention two examples) fundamentally transformed the international political and economic environment within which developing societies find themselves. Furthermore, the increasingly divergent experiences of developing countries themselves have seriously problematised attempts to generalize about development and it is little wonder that theories that first emerged in the 1960s and 1970s do not appear to have the capacity to successfully interpret conditions in the new millennium.

Nonetheless, it would be over-simplistic to view recent transformations in the theorization of development as merely signifying the replacement of older inadequate theories by newer ones more able to interpret contemporary global change. The relationships between ideas and wider political and economic contexts are far more complex than any simple correlation between the waxing and waning of particular theories and changes in the wider world (see Forbes 1987). As an illustration, one only has to think of situations where adherents of a particular view of development have managed to gain the political power to implement policies derived from those views in the 'real world'. The rise and fall of particular theoretical perspectives on development is, therefore, linked not only to the changing nature of the global economy and polity, but also to the balance of ideological and political conflicts, the internal progression and reworkings of particular schools of thought and the changing nature of the academy itself (and its relationship to the wider world of politics and policy), issues which will be examined in more detail later.

The sheer range of approaches towards development issues can initially appear extremely intimidating. Much of the confusion often experienced in first encounters with the literatures of development arises, not only from the variety of perspectives involved, but also from the ways in which very different types of issues have traditionally been conflated under the broad banner of *Development Theory* (Martinussen 1997: 14). The 'catch all' term 'Development Theory' has been applied, not only to conceptual discussions of what 'development' is actually understood to mean, but also to more policy-related considerations of how particular ideas of development might be best implemented or of what features or conditions might inhibit the achievement of particular development objectives. It will be useful to bear these different dimensions in mind during the discussions that follow (see Box 3.2).

Box 3.2: Dimensions of development theory

Development studies is, by its very nature, a vast and divergent field of study. Coming to terms with the issues involved is not aided by debates which according to Martinussen (1997) obscure and confusingly mix various dimensions of issues, a similar language of development often being applied to quite distinct theoretical concerns. Martinussen identifies three distinct areas of development theorization, which he terms respectively – *'development concepts'* (or objectives), *'development theories'* and *'development strategies'*.

Martinussen's first term refers to fundamental ideas regarding what development is understood to mean (these are sometimes more formally formulated as specific development objectives). He argues that it is here that the influence of the individual values of each theorist can be most clearly seen, in that a development concept will always reflect notions of what *ought* to be understood by development (Martinussen 1997: 14). These concepts have frequently been hidden in development research as the meaning of development has often been assumed rather than articulated. Recent years have, however, seen direct considerations of such issues become more prominent as the purpose and impacts of 'development' have been increasingly contested.

Martinussen reserves the use of the 'catch-all' term 'development theory' for theories that seek to explain how the world is actually constituted (rather than how they feel that it ought to be structured). These theories address more specific questions such as: what conditions/structures are likely to influence progress towards particular development objectives or in what ways different social groups and geographical locations are likely to be affected by the processes of 'development'. For Martinussen, these theories, whilst not 'value-neutral,' are more amenable to empirical analyses of 'actual conditions and historical experiences' than the more 'value-laden' development concepts (later discussions in this chapter will question this distinction).

Finally, more policy-oriented questions as to 'the actions and interventions that can be appropriately used to promote strictly defined development objectives' (Martinussen 1997: 15) are denoted as *'development strategies'*.

The distinctions between these three different aspects of development theory are illustrated graphically in Figure B3.2.

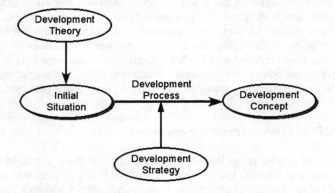

Figure B3.2 Development concepts, theories and strategies
Source: based on Martinussen, J 1997 *Society, state & market* (London: Zed Books). p. 15

The rest of this chapter explores these shifts in theoretical focus in more detail. Attention will focus initially upon a range of Marxist-influenced perspectives which came to dominate geographical discussion of development from the early 1970s, before then exploring critiques of that literature which emerged in the so-called 'impasse debate' of the mid-to-late eighties and beyond. Before this, however, some of the background to how geographers have approached the study of 'developing' regions since the Second World War will be traced.

THE EARLY EVOLUTION OF DEVELOPMENT GEOGRAPHY

During the immediate Post-War decades geographical studies of the non-Western world had largely consisted of detailed descriptive *regional geographies*, which, on the whole, were not placed within any clear theoretical framework (Forbes 1987: 57; see also Chapter 2). From the early 1960s, however, the theoretical vacuum in which development geographers appeared to work gradually began to be challenged. This reflected a growing attempt to develop the systematic side of geography (the analysis of process and causality rather than the simple description of regions) that was then occurring in many parts of the discipline (see Chapter 2). As a result, development geographers turned to the statistical techniques of the *Quantitative Revolution* (see Chapter 2) as part of a search for 'scientifically' testable spatial laws and patterns that might effectively chart the processes of 'modernization' across the globe.

These new, more systematic approaches derived their underlying models of causation from the dominant theories of social and economic modernization of the time (see discussions in the following section) and most research consisted of attempts to model and statistically analyse relationships between key factors suggested by those theories. This interest in modernization occurred, however, at a time when the central tenets of such theories were being subjected to far-reaching criticism in other fields. This, together with the increasing radicalism of geographers and a growing disillusionment with quantitative techniques, meant that geography's flirtation with modernization was short-lived.

Such factors set the scene for an engagement with more radical research agendas and the beginning of the 1970s witnessed the gradual establishment of a range of Marxist approaches that were to remain dominant in geographical treatments of development until the mid-to-late 1980s. These ideas first infiltrated into the discipline through an engagement with the neo-Marxist writings of Gunder Frank which had grown popular in wider academic debates about development during the 1960s. During ensuing years, drawing upon various critiques of Frank, geographers began to engage with a number of different Marxist perspectives. Many of the debates that have occurred since, both within the Marxist tradition and between Marxist theoreticians and others, mirror those that have occurred within the wider field of development studies and it is to those debates that we now turn. It is interesting to note, however, how development geographers have evolved from the theoretical vacuum in which they appeared to work before the 1960s, through a stage when they became consumers of theoretical developments in other fields (firstly through exposure to the empiricism and positivism of the quantifiers and secondly through the opening of the discipline to the influence of radical social theory) to a position where today geographers are making important and innovative contributions to the major debates (see Schuurman 1993; Crush 1995; Brass 1995).

The Rise of Marxist Development Theories

The idea of 'development' was reborn in the period following the Second World War as the colonial powers began to pursue a more developmental approach to the administration of their overseas territories in Africa and Asia and the colonies themselves began to demand and achieve independence. In addition, the successes of the Marshall Plan in the regeneration of post-war Europe had demonstrated what could be achieved through state-directed economic growth strategies involving large injections of capital, which, it was suggested, would prove equally successful in the pursuit of development in Latin America, Asia and Africa. Such ideas of rapid progress and modernization were, thus, placed at the centre of Post-War international concerns and, consequently, a new inter-disciplinary interest in 'development' studies, based around the emerging idea of the 'Third World,' began to take form.

The fundamental ideas about development that underpinned this new academic and political interest in the non-Western world were largely derived from two bodies of theory. The paradigm of the expanding capitalist nucleus emerged from the new *development economics* sub-discipline (based on the relations between discrete capitalist and traditional economic sectors; see Hunt 1989: 86–120) and *structural functionalist* approaches to social and political theory (loosely-based on the application of theories of biological evolution to the analysis of human societies; see Peet 1991: 21–42). Common to both was the visualization of development (or 'modernization') as a universal linear process, along which all countries progressed through a series of stages from a traditional (or undeveloped) society to a modern (or developed) society; a transition largely predicated upon the experiences of Western nations. Modernization theorists, thus, looked to the historical experiences of the evolution of capitalism in the West to provide indications of which norms and institutions were likely to facilitate or impede development in the emerging states of the Third World.

In sociology, authors such as Hoselitz (1960) utilized ideas drawn from Parsons' (1951) reworking of classical sociological theories of social relations in idealized traditional and modern societies to produce a series of indices of modernization. It was argued that once these indices (or norms) had been adequately theorized, then modernization (or development) could be characterised as the progressive expansion of 'modern' social attributes and the erosion of those deemed 'traditional'. The task for modernization theorists was, therefore, conceived as explaining how such social transformations occur, suggesting how they could be best facilitated and identifying those factors that impeded the process. In development economics, similar identifying developmental characteristics were also searched for, and much early research in the field was devoted to identifying internal barriers to economic growth which were seen as impeding developing countries from following the same stages of economic modernization which had occurred in the industrialized world (see Box 3.3).

Box 3.3: Aspects of modernization theory

The idea of a universal historical transition from a traditional (or undeveloped) society to a modern (or developed) society dominated the underlying conceptualization of development during the immediate post-war decades. Two ways of envisioning this transition were particularly influential: Bert Hoselitz's utilization of Talcott Parson's 'Pattern Variables' and Walt Rostow's 'Stages of Economic Growth'.

Pattern Variables

Sociological modernization theory owes much to Talcott Parsons' (1951) theories of evolutionary social change that were based around the ideas of adaptive specialization and changing value systems. In particular, he proposed a series of dichotomous 'pattern variables' that, he argued, illustrated the contrasting values and social roles of individuals in idealized 'modern' and 'traditional' societies. Bert Hoselitz (1960) was the most influential of a number of theorists who attempted to apply Parson's variables more specifically to the analysis of development and underdevelopment. Hoselitz suggested that many aspects of Third World societies could be characterized as representing the 'traditional' social roles identified by Parsons. As such, it logically followed that development could be defined as the gradual erosion of those traditional roles and values and their replacement by those of a modern Western society. As shown in Figure B3.3a, he argued that there were four main lines of contrast between the types of social relations prevalent in 'developed' and 'underdeveloped' societies.

For Hoselitz, therefore, underdeveloped countries are characterized by a low level of division of labour, poor social and geographical mobility and the overriding importance of kinship-ties and local customs. Developed countries, on the other hand, he claims enjoy a much more complex distribution of productive activity, more social mobility and greater opportunities for self advancement through personal achievement (Hoselitz 1960: 60).

Stages of Economic Growth

Economists also looked to Western history to provide them with models of economic development that could be applied in the Third World. The most influential of these was developed by Walt Rostow, an economic historian who was an adviser to the United States government during the Vietnam era. Based upon studies of the Industrial Revolution in Britain, he proposed the existence of specific stages to the achievement of a sustainable modern capitalist economy. All developing countries, he argued, could be located at one or other of these stages, which he identified as outlined in Table B3.3a.

Similarly to the Parsonian pattern variables, Rostow's model suggests common origins and goals to all societies. Here, however, the chief driving force of the evolutionary process is the economy and, in particular, the rate of

Underdeveloped Societies	Developed Societies

Particularistic Norms   **Universalistic Norms**
The roles played by individuals in Developed societies are seen as relatively universal in nature, being largely defined by objective criteria that
could be fulfilled by anyone (e.g. salesman-client relations). Most social
roles in Underdeveloped countries, on the other hand, are said to be
defined in terms of the particular circumstances of individuals which are
obviously not transferable (e.g. family relations etc.).

Quality (Ascription)   **Performance (Achievement)**
Social roles within Underdeveloped societies are seen as chiefly dependent upon the physical (non-achievable) attributes of individuals (class,
age, gender etc.); whilst individual performance and achievement are
assumed to have a much greater role in determining status within
Developed societies.

Functional Diffuseness   **Functional Specificity**
Social relations in Developed countries are said to be largely functionally
specific, in that their content is clearly definable and delimited, reflecting a
high level of division of labour. These types of roles are much less widespread in Underdeveloped countries where an individual's role within
society is said to be more diffuse (reflecting a wide range of different
dimensions – friendship, family roles etc.).

Self Orientation   **Collective Orientation**
Hoselitz argues that Underdeveloped societies are characterized by a high
level of personal self-interest (at least in terms of the attitudes of elites) in
contrast to a more collective orientation in Developed countries.
Interestingly, this reverses Parson's own interpretation of this variable, in
which he argued that it was Modern societies that exhibited more individualistic traits (Larrain 1989: 89).

Source: adapted from Peet 1991: 23 and Larrain 1989: 89–91

**Figure B3.3:   Contrasts between Underdeveloped and Developed societies
as identified by Hoselitz**

investment within it. Both models do, however, rather revealingly, focus on the
appearance of an entrepreneurial elite as the key to the development process;
Hoselitz seeing such a group as imperative in challenging the domination of
society by custom and tradition and Rostow viewing them as the source of
needed capital and economic dynamism. As Roxborough suggests,

Table B3.3: Rostow's stages of economic growth

Stage	Title	Key characteristics
1	Traditional Society	A 'natural' state of undevelopment where society is dominated by agriculture. Very limited levels of productivity, undeveloped political institutions and fatalistic value systems.
2	Pre-Conditions for Take-Off	Development of new ideas (often through the influence of external powers), political constitution as a nation state, development of trade and economic infrastructure, expansion of education and the emergence of entrepreneurship.
3	Take-Off	Growth becomes a permanent feature of society as the old blocks to steady growth are removed, the rate of investment growth exceeds the population growth rate and industrial and agricultural production are rapidly mechanized.
4	Drive to Maturity	A long period representing the technification and modernization of more and more areas of the economy, the level of investment rises to between 10 and 20 per cent of national income, increasing levels of industrial diversification, and a growing presence in the international economy.
5	High Consumption	Orientation of the economy towards the mass production of consumer goods and the creation of large economic surpluses (leading to competing demands for consumption, welfare, military spending etc.).

Source: derived from Spybey 1992: 22; Rist 1997: 94–104; Larrain 1989: 96–97

this emphasis on entrepreneurship and capital accumulation is the single most pervasive theme in the literature on economic growth. It always appears as *the* lesson to be learnt from Western experience and to be mechanically applied to the rest of the world so that they can repeat the transition (Roxborough 1979: 16).

Even this focus upon entrepreneurial ambition, however, does not address one of the major problems with these types of simplistic and ahistorical linear models of development, the fact that it is never made sufficiently clear quite how nations are supposed to advance from one evolutionary stage to the next or, indeed, why such a transition might be expected to take place (Berberoglu 1992: 10).

Such criticisms, moreover, highlight but one aspect of a much wider set of shortcomings which include:

- The theories' insufficient recognition of: (i) the different circumstances facing developing countries compared to those Western countries had faced in their industrial development during previous decades; (ii) the considerable impacts of colonial history; and (iii) the divergent characteristics and resource bases of individual countries (it is simply insufficient to amalgamate all non-Western countries under the notion of 'traditional society') (Roxborough 1979: 15 and Larrain 1989: 100).

- Failure to deal adequately with the relations between societies. Development is assumed, by and large, to be an endogenous process or, where external factors are given causal significance, they 'seem to produce similar internal effects in all … nations, directly and without any internal mediation' (Larrain 1989: 101–2).

- The Eurocentrism of assumptions that all societies will pass through the same historical stages and processes as Western countries; who, it should also be pointed out, often display considerable tendencies towards social roles that are supposedly characteristic of 'traditional' societies (Hettne 1995: 63).

For further discussions of these issues see Hunt (1989: 41–121); Hettne (1995: 21–75); Roxborough (1979: 13–41); Rist (1997: 93–108); Peet (1991: 21–42) and Larrain (1989: 87–102); or for the original authors themselves see Hoselitz (1960); Parsons (1951) and Rostow (1960).

These essentially Eurocentric and ahistorical ideas had never been without their critics but it was not until Gunder Frank synthesized the regional work of Latin American structuralist economists with the global neo-Marxist analyses of Paul Baran (e.g. Baran 1957) and postulated 'a model of underdevelopment', that one could begin to talk of the articulation of an alternative body of theory (often termed Neo-Marxist or, more widely, dependency). Dependency theorists attacked modernization perspectives for having virtually ignored the historical impact of colonialism and the inequitable nature of modern international economic relations, pointing out the very different economic circumstances facing developing countries compared to those that had existed in the development of industrial capitalism in the West (Frank 1966). They also challenged the assumption that Third World societies would progress through the same (or similar) stages that Western economies had in their transition towards modernity, arguing instead for a more historical and holistic approach such that 'the diffusion of capital, technology and culture from the capitalist centre to the periphery should not be conceived of as an ahistorical, "disembodied" process taking place in a vacuum' (Mouzelis 1988: 23–4).

Rather than blaming poverty, or lack of development, upon the traditional nature (or relative backwardness) of developing societies as modernization theorists had done, Frank argued that underdevelopment was an historical outcome of the functioning of the international capitalist system; suggesting that the possibilities for development (or the lack of them) were conditioned, if not determined, by the ways in which individual countries had been integrated into that system. The main feature of this system was, he claimed, the unequal relationship between the countries of *the core* and *the periphery*; with the wealth and affluence of the former seen as historically dependent upon the exploitation of the latter. In this analysis, therefore, poverty and underdevelopment in the periphery were not seen as resulting from the traditional nature of such societies (or internal barriers to development) but, rather, from their position within an international capitalist system which, since their first incorporation, has plundered their resources and appropriated their economic surplus; perpetuating, as Frank (1969) called it, 'the development of underdevelopment' through which such countries are condemned to economic stagnation (see Kay 1989; Larrain 1989).

These ideas gained credence at a time when the global post-war economic boom was beginning to run out of steam and the continued existence (or even extension) of poverty in the Third World, despite two decades of rapid economic growth, was beginning to be recognized. In this context, the popularization of Frank's ideas (and a growing engagement with a whole range of innovative theorizing about development emanating from the Latin American dependency school more widely – see Kay 1989) instigated a shift away from the search for internal obstacles to 'development' towards a more historically-informed consideration of the 'dependent' position of peripheral societies within the international capitalist system and the ways in which this had influenced the evolution of social relations and political institutions within such countries (see also Chapters 7 and 11).

The emergence of dependency theory certainly revolutionized thinking about development. It provided an effective counter to the Eurocentric assumptions of modernization theory and enabled a radical politicization of the whole debate about development. Nevertheless, despite these advances, some of the ideas central to dependency analyses were themselves soon facing heavy criticism (Schuurman 1993). At an empirical level, for example, the stagnationist argument of the dependency framework (that development efforts were doomed to failure given the position of developing countries in the international economy) was questioned by pointing to the economic advances that had been made in certain countries, as well as the lack of statistical evidence for surplus transfer (the chief mechanism said to underlie the transfer of resources from the periphery to the core).

The most stringent attacks on the perspective, however, were more conceptual in focus, often originating from more orthodox Marxists who claimed that dependency theorists had misunderstood and hence misused Marxist analysis. Such critics argued that dependency analysts assumed rather than explained the causes of underdevelopment (Weeks and Dore 1979); that they rarely had a very clear idea of exactly what they meant by the core 'exploiting' the periphery (Leys 1996: 15); and that their accounts of underdevelopment suffered from an unhelpful form of tautological reasoning – the reliance upon explanations already contained within the definitions of the terms employed (Larrain 1989: 188–89). Vandergeest and Buttel (1988: 684) illustrate this, pointing out how Frank defines underdevelopment as a lack of sustained industrial growth and yet, simultaneously, ascribes the causation of this underdevelopment to the same lack of sustained growth; a circular argument that leads nowhere. In a similar vein, Bernstein (1979) questioned the logical basis of Frank's depiction of the historical relationship between the core and the periphery, suggesting that Frank's definition of 'real' development (as opposed to the underdevelopment of the periphery) as 'self-sustaining and independent growth' was at odds with his argument that development in the core had *necessarily* been built upon the exploitation of the periphery, hardly a self-sustaining process (Bernstein 1979: 92).

One of the chief causes of these problems, the critics argued, was that Frank's analyses of underdevelopment rested upon an unhelpfully vague definition of capitalism as any economic system characterized by market relations and commodity production. Authors such as Laclau (1971) and Brenner (1977) argued that this robbed the concept of capitalism of its explanatory power and historical significance, since most societies had, at least to a certain degree, participated in market relations since Roman times (see also Weeks and Dore 1979: 65). Instead they insisted that, as had been argued by Marx (1973; 1976), that capitalism was better defined not in terms of the forms of commodity circulation it involved, but rather as a particular *mode of production* encompassing specific relations of production (namely the separation of direct producers from ownership of the means of production through the commodification of land and labour).

The emphases upon circulation within Frank's dependency theory also had the effect of limiting the specificity of analysis and inducing an over-reliance on broad and sweeping generalizations. If the problems of underdevelopment were seen to reside, ultimately, in the workings of the international economy and the extraction of surplus from the periphery, then dependency perspectives were bound to focus upon the functioning of that 'system' in search of a global explanation for underdevelopment. Such endeavours would always face the problems of over-generalization and over-simplification. This was unfortunate because the historically-sensitive nature of dependency approaches could logically have allowed for the identification of historically specific incidences of dependency in particular forms in different places. As Mouzelis argues:

> From the neo-Marxist point of view, the process of diffusion is understandable only if located within a matrix of domination/subordination relationships ... operating at both the national and the international level ... One would expect as a logical outcome ... a research strategy ... that ceases to treat the Third World in blanket fashion and draws attention to the enormous complexity and variation of the various countries of the so-called Third World. Instead of this, the neo-Marxist dependency tradition has proffered a plethora of theories which; in their attempts to account for the development or lack of development of the Third World as a whole, repeat some of the very mistakes that the neo-evolutionists committed in the early fifties (Mouzelis 1988: 26).

Dependency theories were also criticized for being overly economistic; with class relations, the nature and dynamics of the state and the evolution of political ideas in the periphery all seen as fundamentally determined by the changing needs of metropolitan capital accumulation. Frank, in his later works, went some way toward meeting these criticisms by claiming that his work was meant to complement class analysis rather than replace it. However, as Larrain (1989) argues, on the one hand Frank tries to re-emphasize the agency of distinct classes in the determination of historical processes but, on the other, he maintains that class practices are still fundamentally determined by the structural dependence of peripheral countries upon the core.

Finally, critics also questioned the political conclusions that seemed to emerge from the basic logic of dependency analyses – that the only possibility for development rested in withdrawing from the international economy and pursuing a more autarchic approach. Frank's advocation of this political strategy was based upon his analyses of the factors that had enabled the dramatic growth of the Japanese economy in the twentieth century and the economic progress which had been made in certain Latin American countries during the two wars and the Great Depression when their links to the global economy had been particularly limited. Frank's interpretation of those experiences, however, ignored the importance of locally-specific factors in determining those trends and was unable to explain how economic growth had been achieved by the South East Asian 'Tiger' economies under very different international conditions during the post war period (Corbridge 1986; see also Chapter 7). The somewhat more flexible *World Systems* approach of Wallerstein (1974) went some way toward modifying the Frankian approach to enable it to more successfully account for those successes, through the addition of what he termed the semi-periphery to Frank's dualistic core-periphery model.

Before briefly considering some of the directions in which the Marxist critique of dependency was to lead, it should be noted that the arguments advanced above have not gone uncontested. It has been suggested, for example, that much of the critique relies on a deliberately over-generalized account of dependency (often based around a loose reading of Frank's work) that fails to acknowledge the breadth of approaches to be found within the perspective (see Box 3.4).

Box 3.4: Varieties of dependency analysis

Since its heyday in the early 1970s, 'dependency theory' has been one of the most heavily critiqued theoretical perspectives on development. Many of the charges of over-generalization and circular reasoning have, however, been developed on the basis of a particularly deterministic and mechanical version of dependency writings, loosely based on the work of Gunder Frank. This reading of dependency has been used to construct an indefensible 'straw man' which can then be easily invalidated. More recently, however, there have been a number of attempts to re-evaluate the contribution of the *'dependentistas'* to the study of development.

First it has been claimed that dependency analyses did not seek to offer a coherent theoretical framework for the study of development, but simply aimed to rectify an analytical imbalance whereby the constraints imposed on 'developing' countries by their experiences under colonialism and their position in international divisions of labour were not acknowledged. Whilst the theoretical limitations of dependency analysis are relatively clear, the important advances in understanding generated at the time should not be forgotten. Second, the writings of dependency analysts are so diverse that it makes little sense to lump them all together. Recent contributors have, for instance, differentiated between: systematic models of 'the development of underdevelopment' proposed by Frank, and also apparent in the writings of Amin, Wallerstein and Emmanuel; and analyses of concrete situations where dependency is employed as a framework for assessing the *differential* impacts of colonialism, international economic relations and the spread of transnational capital upon the productive forms, social relations and political systems of the periphery (see Kay 1989, Lehmann 1990, Larrain 1989 and Palma 1989).

The central issues are explained well by Mouzelis (1988) who argues that there is nothing inherently wrong with examining changing *global* inter-relations, but problems arise when crude generalizations are made about 'necessary' outcomes:

> When one shifts the focus of analysis from the world system to the Third World, … theories which do not go beyond the periphery/ semi periphery dichotomy … soon run into difficulties … Thus dependency theory, in so far as it tries to create a *general* theory about the Third World without taking variations into account, cannot escape the fate of all contextless, universalistic theorizing in the social sciences (Mouzelis 1988: 28)..

At the same time, however, there is equal danger in empty rhetorical statements about the complexity and uniqueness of the individual circumstances of each nation, social formation or locality. Untheorized empirical investigations offer the same dead ends. What is needed is 'the hard, painstaking, macrohistorical, comparative work required for translating such statements into concrete analyses' (Mouzelis 1988: 28). Whether less deterministic strands of dependency theory could be of use in informing such research remains a point of controversy, with many commentators seemingly content to reject all forms of dependency analyses (see Booth 1985; Vandergeest and Buttel 1988; Corbridge 1990).

Whilst dependency theory has faded from fashion in radical circles in the West, in Latin America it, "has not been rejected but rather situated in its time as a necessary and fruitful critique of both modernization theory and the erstwhile strategies of the Communist Parties of Latin America" (Slater 1993: 429). In the years following its emergence, a wide and varied literature has appeared (see Kay 1989) which recognises its deficiencies but also stresses that it was,

> an intellectual/political movement… which argued, wrote and theorized back. This was the significance of dependencia and the fact that associated modes of reflection emerged in other parts of the South during the same years … In the encompassing context of North-South relations, the dependency writers constructed and deployed a geopolitical imagination which sought to prioritize

the objectives of autonomy and difference and to break the subordinating effects of metropolis-satellite relations. To the Western mind inculcated in the Cartesian tradition, 'dependency' seemed little more than a vague discontent, but in actual fact it was a key body of alternative critical thought (Slater 1993: 430).

The perceived inadequacies of the dependency framework stimulated an increasing engagement with a variety of other Marxist perspectives during the 1970s and early 1980s. Warren (1980) was perhaps the most extreme Marxist critic of dependency, arguing strongly for a return to what he saw as Marx's original emphasis on capitalism as an emancipatory, rather than a regressive, economic system; suggesting that whilst capitalism would eventually collapse under the weight of its own contradictions, there could be no socialist substitute for the capitalist stage of development. Warren saw Frank's depiction of capitalism imposing economic stagnation and 'underdevelopment' in the periphery as dangerously naive and, in contrast, argued that the spread of capitalist relations had, in fact, produced impressive levels of industrialization in many developing countries during the post-war years (Martinussen 1997). Warren suggested that where poverty and underdevelopment had persisted this was related to the perseverance of pre-capitalist social relations and a *lack* of capitalist development. Although Warren's work was welcomed by some for its attack on the more simplistic assumptions of dependency theory, it was quickly recognized to be as ahistorical as the accounts it so vigorously denounced. At the very least, the dependistas' critique of modernization had established that the problems of underdevelopment could not simply be expressed as the failure of capitalism to take root in developing countries which, in essence, was Warren's argument.

Conversely, other Marxist scholars argued that underdevelopment was related to the perseverance of pre-capitalist social relations but developed explanations of much greater theoretical complexity than those of Warren, drawing in large part from the *structural Marxism* of Althusser (e.g. Larrain 1989; see also Chapter 2). These theorists, whilst recognizing many of the problems identified by dependency analyses, saw these as reflecting, not some global process of exploitation, but rather specific 'articulations' of the capitalist mode of production with a diverse range of pre-capitalist ones. This *modes of production* school of thought suggested that, under certain conditions, the survival of pre-capitalist forms was actually functional to the needs of local capitalist accumulation, thereby warping the processes of development and in *some* cases promoting stagnation (Hettne 1995).

One of the main advances of this approach was that it shifted attention away from global theorizing towards national and local-scale studies of the articulation of modes of production and the historical processes which underlay underdevelopment (Ruccio and Simon 1986). This, at least to a certain degree, moved beyond the idea of a 'normal' development path present in most theories of dependency and in Warren's work, whilst also allowing analysis encompassing both global and national issues (Kiely 1995: 62). Debates arose, for example, concerning the different ways in which individual pre-capitalist modes of production co-existed with the capitalist, and how functional the former were to the latter although this arguably did result in an unhelpful proliferation of separately identifiable pre-capitalist modes, to the extent that every society seemed to have its own mode (see Foster-Carter 1978).

What set the modes of production school apart from the neo-Marxism of Frank *et al.* was the centring of analysis upon production and class relations rather than the sphere of circulation, and on the national level rather then the global (although the importance of international factors was recognized). This rejuvenated Marxism introduced a theoretical rigour to the study of development that was based upon a more detailed conceptualization of the structures of individual societies and the ways in which they are transformed. It also offered the possibility for much more informed and sensitive political analyses of the prospects for local opportunities and struggles (Corbridge 1986).

A further strand of Marxist theory, like that of Warren, recognized that industrialization had occurred in particular parts of the Third World (especially since the 1960s), but was much less dismissive of the claims of dependency theorists about the nature of that industrial development. Particularly associated with the work of Frobel and his associates (see Frobel *et al.* 1980), these theorists attempted to interpret dependent development through the nexus of international class analysis, rather than the sphere of circulation. In this way they suggested the existence of a *New International Division of Labour* (NIDL) which, they argued, could explain the development of the Asian *Newly Industrialised Countries* (NICs). Such ideas, through their underlying depiction of the changing needs and activities of international capital as the determining factors, lay open, however, to many of the criticisms levelled against dependency theories (see Jenkins 1987; Kiely 1995).

Whilst there were certainly different emphases and sharp divisions of opinion (as detailed in the preceding discussions), taken together Marxist and dependency perspectives certainly revolutionized the way in which studies of development were approached. They offered a range of concepts that allowed development issues to be much more effectively analyzed in their historical contexts. They also produced much more helpful theories of the dynamics of the international economy and how its structures affected the developmental trajectories of countries which found themselves in contrasting positions within it. Furthermore, other elements of the Marxian heritage offered important insights into questions of geopolitical power, of the nature and dynamics of the nation state and of what might be unique about capitalism as a mode of production and how it related to ideas of progress. All of this produced some important and innovative work that certainly succeeded in placing themes concerning poverty, exploitation and inequality at the centre of analyses of development.

Neo-Liberal Restructuring and the Crisis in Critical Development Theory

Part One: The Neo-Liberal Counter-Revolution

Whilst the critical engagement with dependency and other Marxist approaches certainly produced a range of more innovative approaches to development issues, it only had a limited impact upon official (or mainstream) thinking about development within the 'development community' (the international financial institutions, other international agencies and non-governmental organizations and the majority of national governments). Here, the imprint of modernization perspectives remained clearly visible, although there were some modifications during the course of the 1960s and 1970s as some of the radical critique considered earlier filtered through. As Leys explains,

> even the international 'development community' felt obliged to accommodate some of its (dependency) perspectives: for instance, the International Labour Office's 1972 call for 'Redistribution with Growth' and the World Bank's adoption in 1973 of the principle of meeting 'Basic Needs' were both influenced by the (unacknowledged) impact of dependency thinking (Leys 1996: 11–12).

All of this was, however, to change rapidly in the 1980s when something of a theoretical impasse began to be recognized both within mainstream development thinking and amongst its more radical critics (Schuurman 1993). To a certain degree, this reflected the economic depression that had hit the international economy at the end of the 1970s and its massive impact upon particular regions of the developing world, notably Latin America and Africa. Indeed, the economic and social effects of this were so intense that the 1980s are frequently referred to as the *Lost Development Decade* within these regions (see Box 3.5). Although the severity of these economic circumstances did, to a certain degree, validate some dependency and other, non-Warrenite, Marxist critiques of post-war development strategies, it also starkly revealed a worrying lack of concrete proposals for responding to the crisis. At the same time, it was becoming increasingly apparent that the existing schools of modernisation thought were largely unable to address the increasing diversity of Third World countries' experiences; whilst the highly fractious debates on aspects of Marxist theory that dominated the more radical literature seemed to bear little relevance to increasingly desperate struggles for economic survival.

Box 3.5: The Lost Development Decade: The crisis of the 1980s

Large parts of the Third World ran into deep economic problems during the international depression of the early 1980s. These problems were so severe, and represented such a reversal in 'developmental fortunes', that the 1980s have often been termed the 'Lost Development Decade'. This economic downturn reflected massive changes in the world economy, including: a collapse in Western demand, leading to declining prices for many developing countries' exports and negative shifts in their overall terms of trade; the oil price hikes of the 1970s; and changes in the economic policies of Western governments, particularly through the significant raising of interest rates. All of this led to increasing 'Balance of Payments' problems for many Third World countries, massive increases in debt repayments within a context of declining national revenues and the virtual disappearance of new sources of finance. The combination of these factors left the economies of many countries on the brink of collapse. In some senses, this economic crisis represented the final debunking of the idea of a recognizable Third World with common features and interests, in that, despite the global nature of the economic downturn, it was the regions of Latin America and Africa that were worst afflicted, whilst Asia remained

Contested Worlds

relatively unaffected. The huge financial impact of the crisis in Sub-Saharan Africa can be seen clearly from Table B3.5.

Table B3.5 Macro-economic indicators in sub-Saharan Africa

Economic indicator	Annual percentage changes	
	1965–1980	1980–1986
GDP	5.6	– 0.0
Agriculture	1.6	– 1.2
Industry	9.4	– 1.5
(Manufacturing)	(8.5)	(0.3)
Services	7.5	0.1
Government Consumption	8.1	– 1.0
Private Consumption	4.9	0.7
Gross Domestic Investment	8.8	– 9.3
Exports	6.6	– 2.1
Imports	19.5	– 7.7

Source: Ghai and Hewitt de Alcântara 1990: 17, Table 2.2

Latin America was also hit severely, with the overall standard of living in many countries returning to 1960s levels. Real per capita gross domestic produce (GDP) declined by 7 % across the region between 1980 and 1988, although that figure hides the fact that the decline was as much as 20 % in several countries. The Terms of Trade turned against the region by an estimated 22 % during the same period, whilst there were also massive falls in the levels of investment (and in the flow of other financial resources to the region), increasing unemployment levels and, perhaps most importantly, given the existing patterns of wealth and income distribution, a marked increase in inequality (Ghai and Hewitt de Alcântara 1990: 19–21). The overall impact of the crisis is effectively summarized in the two quotes which follow:

> By the end of the 1980s, the total debt of developing countries was over US$1,100 billion. As a result of this huge debt, the drive towards industrialization and economic restructuring for long-term development came to a halt in many countries. Instead, there ensued a desperate struggle to find resources to meet the short-term goal of debt repayment. As well as shaking the world financial system, the 'debt crisis' has also had serious repercussions for social and economic development in most of the Third World (Gibson and Tsakalotos 1992: 41).

> [F]or Sub-Saharan Africa, in particular, the 1980s became a disastrous decade and the subcontinent rapidly acquired the character of a marginalized Fourth World, increasingly recognized as requiring special action and special criteria. The other true part of this sad story is that the decade was 'lost' to development in the sense that attention shifted to debt settlement, stabilization, adjustment, structural change, liberalization etc. – often at the expense of everything that had

previously been understood as development, whether growth, employment, redistribution, basic needs or reduction of poverty (Singer 1989: 46).

Whilst these two quotes clearly illustrate the severity of the crisis effectively, they also point to a sea change in attitudes towards development which accompanied it. The ensuing international reaction reflected the dominance of neo-liberal interpretations of the causes of the crisis, whereby stress was placed upon domestic economic mismanagement and corruption which, it was claimed, left many developing economies unable to deal with unfavourable external tendencies. Whilst there is some truth in such charges they also served to draw attention away from the need for more systematic international action to address the disastrous external economic climate over which developing country governments certainly had little control.

Such factors enabled a very different set of ideas to come to dominate official development thinking in a process frequently referred to as the neo-liberal counter-revolution in development theory and policy (Toye 1987). This counter-revolution shared some of the criticisms that Marxist and dependency theorists had made of post-war development policies but proffered starkly contrasting explanations for development 'failures' and suggestions as to how they might be overcome. The neo-liberal position argued that the whole idea of bringing about development through directed state interventions within society was fundamentally misplaced and that development would only be achieved through the pursuit of free competition and the prioritization of market mechanisms: in effect a restatement of the universal applicability of neo-classical economics (Martinussen 1997). In some senses, these ideas were stark expressions of the more simplistic components of modernization theories, although the policy direction that led from these analyses was radically different (see Brohmann 1995).

The consolidation of such perspectives on the international stage was rapid. The late 1970s and early 1980s saw the election of Western governments committed to radical neo-liberal agendas and, under their influence, individuals holding such ideas came to dominate major international financial institutions and eventually the majority of national governments and other sectors of the development industry (see Escobar 1995). Within neo-liberal analyses, development issues became largely reduced to the imperative of 'getting economics right' which was translated into reducing state intervention to a bare minimum, liberalizing national and international markets and prioritizing the export sector (see also Chapter 12). More theoretical discussions of the workings of the international economy or the nature of individual societies became largely limited to the search for impediments that might serve to stop the spread of free market relations. As such, any Marxist-inspired discussions of exploitation or the structural causes of underdevelopment were viewed as irrelevant, although wide-ranging critiques of the social, political and environmental costs of neo-liberal policies did emerge (Rich 1994; Green 1995; Veltmeyer *et al.* 1997).

To a certain extent, these developments destabilised what had been a more or less general consensus on basic development concepts (to use Martinussen's terminology from Box 3.2). Up until the economic crisis of the late 1970s, the majority of development theorists, practitioners and planners had conceived of development in terms of a series of policies developed by nation states (or promulgated by international agencies) to meet a series of widely-defined development objectives. This meant that whilst Marxist and dependency positions on development never had a particularly direct influence on policy formation, and certainly did not have the impact claimed for them by critics such as Toye (1987: 115), some of the issues they pinpointed as underlying the failures of development efforts did at least filter into policy debates.

The consolidation of neo-liberalism as the dominant development discourse within the international institutions since the 1980s broke this consensus, promoting a much more limited econocentric idea of development and underplaying the potential role of directed social and economic transformation. What is, admittedly, still referred to as development is, in many senses, really simply the application of what are seen as 'correct' economic policies. The talk in Economics Ministries and the international financial organizations today, is not about the choice of a national development strategy but rather simply about 'appropriate' economic management. Any remaining commitments to longer-term development objectives have frequently been lost within rhetoric that calls for developing countries to adjust to the realities of international markets through liberalization, privatization and export promotion. As Leys puts it,

> it is hardly too much to say that by the end of the 1980s the only development policy that was officially approved was not to have one – to leave it to the market to allocate resources, not the state (Leys 1996: 24).

It is, however, important not to paint too monolithic a picture of neo-liberal ideas on development and the policies that have been formulated from them. It is clear, for example, that the nature of the policies 'recommended' by international financial institutions has altered over the years, as critiques of the impact of the *Structural Adjustment Programmes* (see Box 3. 6, and also Chapter 4) through which neo-liberal ideas were often implemented, have been responded to. This has led the World Bank to progressively re-introduce policies designed to alleviate the worst effects of poverty ('tack-on' social programmes), induce 'good governance' (through decentralization for example), or take environmental considerations into account. In essence, however, these could simply be viewed as 'add-ons' designed to ameliorate the social, political or environmental implications enduced through the pursuit of unfettered market liberalization. As expressed by Moore,

> theoretical and political jostling over such issues as sustainable development, state and/or market-led economic policies, and participation (or 'democratic governance') will take up much of the public stage. The World Bank, the IMF and their lesser kin will appear to take pragmatic and consensual approaches to their hearts … but will rest assured that their real neo-liberal agenda remains intact (Moore 1995: 16).

Box 3.6: Structural Adjustment Programmes

During the 1980s the impacts of the debt crisis saw a marked transformation in the operations of the international financial organizations in the Third World. Firstly, they became the most important provider of financial resources to the developing world and, secondly, the balance of their guiding principles shifted from professed developmental goals towards protecting the integrity of the global financial system and guaranteeing interest payments. These changes significantly enhanced the global power of these institutions who became a major influence in the promulgation of neo-liberal free market ideas across the globe. This was largely achieved through the application of 'conditions' (reflecting the adoption of neo-liberal policies) which borrowers had to comply with in order to gain access to funding.

In the case of the World Bank, these conditions took the form of *Structural Adjustment Programmes* (SAPs). These programmes (supposedly developed in tandem with borrower governments) were presented as a means of responding to the economic crisis and re-establishing growth and development in the developing world on a new footing. The policies reflected the Bank's adherence to neo-liberal analyses which stressed the role of internal mismanagement in the genesis of the crisis (e.g. see the Berg Report on the causes of economic crisis in Sub-Saharan Africa; World Bank 1981) and were designed to reorientate the economies of developing countries towards the international market place through liberalization, export promotion and the dismantling of the regulative and productive role of the state. More specifically, most SAPs have been made up of the major components identified in Table B3.6a, although it should be noted that the balance of elements has shifted somewhat over time.

Table B3.6: Major policy strategies and instruments of Structural Adjustment Programmes

Policy Strategies

Stabilization	The establishment of macro-economic equilibrium (in terms of the international balance of payments) and the righting of relative prices (in particular through the ending of inflationary pressures). Stabilization has often tended to occur as a separate shorter-term initial stage, before the longer-term adjustment process is embarked upon.
Privatization	An emphasis upon the selling of state interests in individual companies or the privatization of previously publicly-owned utilities. In some cases this has led to a markedly increased concentration of company ownership and/or greatly

	enhanced levels of foreign ownership (as well as several major instances of corruption).
Liberalization	Measures designed to open the economy to international trade. Restrictions on imports are normally lifted; the currency is often devalued to enhance the profitability of exporters and any protection of internal markets is removed.
Deregulation	The removal of restrictions on the economic activities of individuals and the drastic reduction of state intervention within the general running of the economy.
Fiscal Austerity	The reduction of government budget deficits through such measures as the laying off of public sector workers, cuts in the provision of public services and tax system reforms.

Policy Instruments

| Most programmes will include some of the following | – mass public sector redundancies
– currency devaluation
– abolition of price controls and reform of interest rates
– severe restrictions on credit provision
– withdrawal of subsidies
– stringent cuts in public spending
– privatization of public utilities
– reduction or abolition of import tariffs and quotas
– improved provision of export incentives and reduction in export taxes
– introduction or raising of fees for public services
– elimination of foreign investment controls
– deregulation of labour markets |

Sources: Veltmeyer, Petras and Vieux 1997; Pio 1992; Taylor 1997

From the perspective of the World Bank, the combination of these measures represent the best chance for economic recovery through their encouragement of economic efficiency, adjustment to changes in the international economy and the raising of productivity (more cynical observers might also add the guaranteeing of debt interest payments to that list). The obvious question is, 'has it worked?' Debate about the impacts of SAPs has been widespread and fierce. Most SAP supporters, and the World Bank itself, have focused upon the overall economic record of adjusting countries, claiming that they have outperformed non-adjusting countries. Others have, however, questioned the figures upon which such analyses are based, as well as whether it is the simple access to funding, rather than the policies implemented, that has produced any improvements noted (see Gibbon 1996).

Most criticism of SAPs has, however, not focused on their overall economic successes and failures but on the costs associated with their implementation (see Pio 1992). The packages include many policies (e.g. cuts in food subsidies, rises in the costs of public utilities and reductions in the coverage of social programmes) which worsen the precarious position of the poorest and most marginalized sectors, significantly intensifying the levels of income inequality. Questions have also been raised about their environmental impacts and the wider international geopolitical implications of SAPs for North-South relations and questions of national sovereignty (Ghai 1994). Finally, there has also been a wide-ranging debate about the relationship between economic liberalization of this type and democratic reform, political participation and the role of the state (Bienefeld 1995). Whatever one's view on the issues raised, the international financial institutions have certainly been forced into responding to some of the criticisms – although their basic policy stance has remained relatively unaltered (see Kiely 1998b).

Whilst neo-liberal ideas have not taken hold to any great extent in geographical studies of development (although see Auty 1995), it should be obvious from this brief account that they are important to understand since they now have a pervasive influence on how development problems are viewed in other academic disciplines (especially economics), provide illustrations of the importance of effective financial management, and have been instrumental in promulgating many recent global transformations via encouragement of privatization, liberalization, deregulation and integration. This last point is important because globalization is often seen as something just happening 'out there,' an objective natural process as it were. However, for processes of globalization to occur, favourable conditions have to be created via global and national agreement, legislation and so on. In this sense, neo-liberalism is the often obscured ideological core of globalization.

Part Two: The Impasse in Marxist Development Theory

The consolidation of neo-liberalism on the international stage has not gone uncontested: neither, practically, in terms of the development of alternative policy frameworks and specific critiques of the impacts of neo-liberal policies; nor conceptually, in terms of challenging the basis of neo-liberal thought. The crisis in development thought that accompanied, and indeed in some senses made possible, the rise of neo-liberalism has, however, problematised such efforts and the whole corpus of more 'critical' development theory continues to be characterized as facing something of a 'crisis' (Hettne 1995) or 'impasse' (Schuurman 1993). Politically, the rapid restructuring of the global economy and the hegemony of neo-liberal policy frameworks have served to dramatically limit the spaces open for the articulation of alternatives (although there have been some changes in neo-liberal policies in response to critiques); whilst, whatever their productive and moral limitations, the collapse of the 'actually existing' socialist nations of the Eastern Block also resulted in the removal of important sources of ideological and financial support for alternative development strategies.

Within conceptual studies there has also been an intense and wide-ranging critique of the previously dominant Marxist approaches to development considered in the previous section. This critique has, amongst other charges, accused Marxist development theory of: (i) lacking policy relevance; (ii) paying insufficient attention to feminist criticisms of the 'gender-blindness' of many Marxist positions (and, more generally, ignoring the insights offered by alternative, non-Marxist, critical analyses); (iii) working at an overly abstract and general level of analysis; (iv) exhibiting an over-arching economism; and (v) being unable to cope with the rapidly changing and increasingly global context of the 1990s (see Booth 1985, 1994; Edwards 1989, 1994; Marchand and Parpart 1995; Corbridge 1986, 1990; Schuurman 1993).

There is not the space here to go into all of the different dimensions of this critique, and the following discussion is therefore, by necessity, brief and partial. I make little direct mention of, for example, some important ways in which the development debate has been transformed over recent years through engagements with feminist theory (although many aspects of postmodern development theory discussed below does owe much to these literatures; see Parpart and Marchand 1995) nor the interaction between Marxist theory and environmental/sustainable development literatures (see Adams 1993; Eckersley 1992; O'Connor 1997; Pepper 1993, 1996; Redclift 1984, 1987; Phillips and Mighall, 2000). Instead, the chapter will look at the broad theoretical critiques of Marxist analyses of development and the work that has stemmed from it.

Perhaps the most influential expression of the doubts regarding Marxist approaches to development was Booth (1985), which spawned a heated debate (hereafter referred to as the *impasse debate*) on the applicability and coherence of Marxist approaches to development (see Sklair 1988; Mouzelis 1988; Vandergeest and Buttel 1988; Corbridge 1989, 1990; Schuurman 1993; Booth 1994). The central thrust of Booth's initial article was that Marxist development theories, both in their 'classical Marxist' and 'neo-Marxist' varieties, have a 'metatheoretical commitment to demonstrating that what happens in societies in the era of capitalism is not only explicable, but also in some stronger sense *necessary*' (Booth 1985: 773). This suggests that what happens in individual societies is comprehendable, and indeed in some senses predictable, from within Marxist theory, so long as a 'proper' understanding of the functioning of the laws of the capitalist mode of production is adopted. If this is done, so it is argued, then one can 'read off' significant aspects of individual economies and social formations from generalized laws of how capitalism works (Booth 1985: 773).

This intrinsic commitment to defining the mechanisms of social change in terms of the functioning of a range of abstract and universal laws of capitalism that operate, albeit differentially, across countries with widely divergent histories and cultures, was for Booth (1985: 774) the root inadequacy of Marxism as a conceptual framework. It inevitably leads, he argued, to an over-concentration upon the explanatory power of economic factors, which left Marxism unable to deal with cultural difference or political power without reducing them to epiphenomena of economic structures (see also Chapter 2 on critiques of Marxist structuralism). This has, it is claimed, left Marxism ill equipped to deal with the complexities of social change.

These types of arguments, together with the broader criticisms of the lack of policy relevance of Marxist analysis, led to attempts to articulate new directions for critical development research that might be less deterministic and less economistic. For

Booth this did not necessarily mean the abandonment of Marxist approaches to development per se. Rather, as he commented in his original article:

> Development ... does not need to be purged wholesale of questions and lower-order concepts derived from Marx, but specifically of abstract entities conceived as having 'necessary effects inscribed in their structure' or as being endowed with the capacity to shape socio-economic relations in accordance with their needs. Curiosity about the way the world is the way it is, and how it may be changed, must be freed not from Marxism but from Marxism's ulterior interest in proving that within given limits the world *has* to be the way it is (Booth 1985: 777).

Hence much of the work spawned by the impasse debate whilst attempting to break from Marxist tradition, has continued to work within political economy frameworks that owe much to Marxist concepts and methodologies. Such 'post-Marxist' work has taken several forms. The main tendency has been to shift attention away from general theories about the operation of capitalism or processes of development towards a focus on the diversity of experiences at national, regional and local levels. This has led to a proliferation of empirical, localized and, to a lesser degree, comparative research with a view to constructing 'middle range' theories sensitive to the immense diversity of situations in individual countries (Kiely 1995: 74; Vandergeest and Buttel 1988; Mouzelis 1988; see also discussion in Chapter 2 on 'middling Marxisms'). Whilst this is an advance on research that had tried to 'fit' individual experiences into pre-defined global explanations, as Booth himself acknowledges, it does not necessarily lead to the articulation of less deterministic theoretical positions:

> We face the danger that social researchers, disillusioned with the old theoretical certainties and perhaps also a little intoxicated by their renewed immersion in an ever-surprising empirical reality, will become very good at producing detailed case studies but rather bad at communicating the general implications of their work to a wider academic audience, not to speak of a wider public of development practitioners (Booth 1993, 59).

The issue here is the relationship between structures and agency which is, in essence, what the whole impasse debate has been about. The local-level of much recent work has implicitly or explicitly often emphasized human agency over structure, a position which is, for instance, reflected strongly in advocations of an 'actor-oriented' sociology of development (see Long and Van der Ploeg 1994; Long and Villarreal 1993; Long and Long 1992; and also Box 2.10 on 'Actor-network theory'). This approach, whilst recognizing 'the interplay and mutual determination of "internal" and "external" factors and relationships' is, nonetheless, most decidedly focused upon the micro or local level where the main emphasis is placed upon providing 'accounts of the life-worlds, strategies and rationalities of the different social actors involved' (Long and Villarreal 1993: 141). The approach arguably does little more than repeat the problems of structural determinacy in reverse. Booth, for example, argues that:

> Long and van der Ploeg ... vigorously refute the suggestion that their approach implies a neglect of the contexts of action. Nevertheless, today as in the past most local studies remain determinedly micro in both senses, the wider context being allowed to escape from view in a way that is disturbingly reminiscent of the bad old days of functionalist anthropology [and, I might add, of geography's regional descriptive phase] (Booth 1994: 18).

Such concerns have also been central to certain Marxist counter-critiques of the 'impasse' literature, which criticize the empiricism, abandonment of theory and prioritizing of agency over structure that they see characterizing much recent research. The reactions of Marxists to Booth's critique have, however, been more varied than this argument would suggest. Some responses have been relatively open and have made important contributions to the emerging debates. Others, however, have been more defensive. Tom Brass (1995) in his stinging review of Schuurman (1993) and Booth (1994) perhaps most exemplifies this reaction. Whilst Brass does make some important points about the sometimes unhelpful way in which Marxism has been portrayed in the 'impasse debate' (correctly pointing out that 'it is quite simply untrue that in a general sense Marxism adheres to a concept of an unproblematically unilinear determination of the political and ideological by the economic' (Brass 1995: 523)), he fails to illustrate how different Marxist traditions have dealt with those relationships. Many of his comments are either simply petty (as in his accussation that Stuart Corbridge's writing is 'largely content free' and 'fogeyish' (p. 519)) or unhelpfully vindictive (he terms the 'impasse debate' as 'self-styled, self-serving, eclectic, contradictory and largely irrelevant' (p. 517)).

Others, thankfully, have been more thoughtful in their responses. Some have attempted to defend the existing schools of Marxist analysis, as in Larrain's (1989) thoughtful reconsideration of dependency theory and Peet's (1991) (at least partial) defence of the structural Marxism of the modes of production school (Peet 1991). Others have pointed out, somewhat ironically, that the historical-comparative method that has evolved out of the issues raised in the impasse debate is precisely the type of approach that many Marxists have long been advocating for development research anyway.

This is not to suggest, however, that all Marxists have been dismissive of the issues raised through the impasse debate. Some certainly share a sense of unease about the ways in which Marxism has been applied to development debates, but suggest that, more widely, Marxist approaches have never been reducible to a set of 'laws' about societal development. They direct our attention towards other, often rather neglected, traditions of thought within Marxism that appear less econocentric and less deterministic, pointing out that many of the objections raised within the impasse debate actually been long recognised within these Marxist traditions. As Resnick and Wolf comment:

> Long before post-Marxism arrived and since, Marxists have intensely debated among themselves the merits and acceptability of classical Marxism and its alternatives within the Marxist tradition. Classical Marxism was *never* the only interpretation within the tradition (Resnick and Wolff 1992: 131).

The Marxist literature on development has, however, been heavily biased towards the more structural versions of Marxism in which little room has been left for the role of human beings in producing social change. Ironically, Althusser's structuralist Marxism, which has been so influential in Marxist development theory (and is essentially the caricature of Marxism portrayed by Booth) was, through the idea of the *relative autonomy* of the political sphere, an attempt to escape from the economism of previous formulations of Marxism. For Althusser, the economy is not meant to determine political forms, but only sets the limits as to what is possible in the 'last instance' and, as Althusser himself suggests, 'the lonely hour of the last instance', in fact, 'never comes (cited in Resnick and Wolff 1992: 132). As Kiely (1995) argues, problems remain because, despite attempts to de-economize Marxism, structural Marxists still tend to look for an over-arching theory of development within which social phenomena are interpreted (albeit in the last instance) as reflecting their func-tionality for capitalism rather than the struggles of agents within society.

Kiely, then, ends up agreeing with Booth's charges of 'necessitism' in the sense that structural schools of Marxist development theory persist in constructing overar-ching models of development and underdevelopment (or the functioning of capital-ism) that bear little relation to the actual experiences of agents in the real world. Nevertheless, he also criticizes those approaches that have reacted to this structural determinacy by stressing the absolute autonomy of agents from those structures. Instead of this false choice between general determinism or complete autonomy, he suggests that what is needed is:

> a theory that recognizes that there are 'laws' that operate in the global political economy, but that these do not operate in any mechanical way, and in particular their effects cannot be taken as explanations for the development of particular countries in the 'world system'. In other words ... the laws of motion of the global economy should be seen as tendencies, which can be altered by human action, both within and between countries (Kiely 1995: 103–104).

He bases this argument upon a reading of Marx in which capitalism is seen as an historical and social phenomenon produced through struggle rather than a natural universal phenomenon. For Kiely then,

> what is useful in Marx's work is a historical and materialist method, *grounded in empirical research*, that shows that phenomenal forms are historically and socially created. Marx's concern was therefore to build theory out of empirical research ... but didn't take facts as given ... such 'things' are neither universal nor natural (Kiely 1995: 80).

This somewhat different approach to Marxism, also apparent in the work of Mouzelis (1988; 1990) and perhaps most fully articulated in the work of Larrain (1986), has much in common with the comparative approach to research that has arisen out of the impasse debate and perhaps provides one way of providing a context within which the plethora of local and national research produced in recent years might, in time, begin to produce some more general theorization which does not rely on notions of some all encompassing necessary logic. This is an urgent task if the impact of the rapid changes within the international economy and polity of the last couple of decades are to be adequately understood and, more importantly, if the neo-liberal ideology that has promoted those changes is to be effectively challenged.

Part Three: The Encounter with Postmodernism

To some, the concerns raised through the 'impasse' debate do not go nearly far enough in their critique of development theory. Their reaction to the diversity (or 'difference') of the modern world is to call for a much wider negation of the possibil-ities for generalization, so that all that is left, and all that one can talk of (and even then with no particular authority), is the local and the specific. The recognition of diversity becomes an end in itself, rather than a means towards the rejuvenation of theoretical endeavours (Booth 1994: 14). Such perspectives relate to a much broader critique of modern social science encapsulated under the term *Postmodernism*.

As mentioned in Chapter 2, there is a broad array of perspectives that might loosely fall under the banner of postmodernism, and as a consequence, it is perhaps unwise to talk of *a* postmodern approach to anything. Palmer, for instance, suggests that postmodern and poststructuralist thought is,

> extremely difficult to pin down and define with clarity precisely because it celebrates discursiveness, difference and destabilizations: it develops, not as a unified theory, but as constantly moving sets of concentric circles, connected at points of congruence, but capable of claiming new and uncharted interpretative territory at any moment (Palmer 1997: 109–110).

Nevertheless, some commonalties of use can be suggested. Simon (1998), for example, makes a useful distinction between three particular ways in which the postmodern has been conceptualized: as *epoch*, as *expression* and as *problematic* (see also Dear 1988 on postmodernism as epoch, style and method; and also Chapter 2 on postmodernism as object and approach). Most people probably first encounter the idea of postmodernism in relation to the broad periodization of history (for which, in most cases, read Western history). In this usage, postmodernism refers to the onset of a new *epoch* of world history, or '*postmodernity*', which is seen to be markedly different to the modern period that preceded it in terms of economic, social, cultural and political organization and behaviour (see Chapter 2 on postmodernism as object).

As Simon (1998) outlines, the idea of a new postmodern historical epoch has been used, by some, as a context within which to explore the significance of the increasing diversity in the experiences of developing countries. The growing limitations imposed upon the ability of individual governments to develop coherent independent policy programmes, the destabilizing of the traditional nation state, the evolution of new forms of consumption and social expression and the increasing rapidity and depth in the integration of the global economy are all interpreted as reflecting this new postmodern era. Intimately linked to ideas of globalization, such discussions of postmodernity stress the inability of traditional social theory to comprehend these tendencies and complexities, because of, for example, its 'state-centric' and 'reductionist' character. However, it should be pointed out that such approaches might themselves have a tendency towards over-generalization, in that essentially Western analyses of postmodernity have been universalized to encompass all manner of social and cultural processes occurring in other regions of the globe.

The origins of the term postmodernity actually lie in the aesthetic fields of the arts and literature (particularly in architecture and the visual and performing arts) where the term was first used in the 1950s to signify a 'complex of anti-modernistic artistic strategies' that challenged the boundaries between 'art' and popular culture (Bertens 1995: 3). In this usage, the postmodern is conceptualized as a form of cultural *expression*, based around such features as the blurring of boundaries, 'playfulness' and pastiche. These features may even be interpreted as the cultural expression of the onset of the postmodern epoch suggested above (see Featherstone 1991).

For our purposes, however, it is the third aspect (or usage) of Simon's terminology which is the most interesting. Here, postmodernism is identified as an intellectual practice or *problematic*. As Bertens (1995: 6) explains, this usage of the term reflects the merging of the (essentially North American) aesthetic ideas of postmodernism with French post-structuralist philosophy. Postmodernism is, in this way, associated with a general questioning of the tenets of social theory through the abandonment of the idea that 'language can reflect reality'; that knowledge can be said to bear any true reflection of a reality that exists 'out there' beyond the form in which it is expressed. In other words, it is the conviction that, knowledge is always distorted by the environment in which it is formulated; 'that theories at best provide partial perspectives on their objects and that all cognitive representations of the world are historically and linguistically mediated' (Peet 1997: 73). To some of its advocates the chief challenge is, therefore, not to search for the forms of explanation that most closely approximate to reality (this is now seen as hopelessly impossible) but, rather to recognise that 'representations create rather than reflect reality'. This approach can be seen to bestow representations with an almost material status (Bertens 1995: 11).

By this point, some readers may well have thrown up their hands in horror and disbelief: how could ideas that evolved from the cultural milieu of post-industrial society and which emphasize language and forms of representation over the materiality of the 'real world,' possibly have anything of relevance to say to the study of development? I have to admit that this was my own reaction upon initially encountering attempts to introduce such themes into the development debate (see also Mohan 1997 and Simon 1988). I saw little to recommend what seemed to me to be essentially self-indulgent language games that had little to offer the struggle to articulate meaningful alternatives to the neo-liberal triumphalism of the times. Nevertheless, eventually, I have come round to the view that, despite the dense and, at times, virtually incomprehensible way in which it has often been articulated (although this a charge that could also be levelled at Marxist analyses), some elements of postmodern thought do offer important new perspectives on the traditional concerns of development theory or, at the very least, a healthy questioning of previously held certainties.

Following Best and Kellner (1991: 257), however, it seems useful to draw a distinction between more 'extreme' postmodern approaches, that allow for little if any interaction with traditional or 'modern' social theory, and more 'reconstructive' approaches that have attempted to use 'post-modern insights to reconstruct critical social theory and radical politics'. Within the more extreme forms of postmodern theory, admittedly rarely articulated within the development literature, any sense of causality has been abandoned altogether in favour of indeterminacy. In other words, their recognition of the partial and mediated nature of social knowledge leads such theorists to abandon any sense of causation in favour of an embrace of undecidability, difference and chance; in effect, abandoning social theory as an attempt to better understand society and casting all of the theorization thus far considered as being futile, authoritarian, repressive, warped and largely meaningless.

If we were to take this view – 'that "no" systematic knowledge of human action or trends of social development is possible' (Corbridge 1993: 456) – then it may well be, as Corbridge citing Giddens (1990: 47) suggests, that one finds oneself in the position whereby 'the only possibility would be to repudiate intellectual activity altogether – even "playful deconstruction" – in favour of, say, healthy exercise'. He goes on to argue that if we are to avoid this excess we must conclude that a recognition of the importance of language in mediating knowledge,

should not be taken to be equivalent to a break with reason itself ... It is perfectly sensible
to accept that our stories about the world are imperfect and do not represent some essential
truths, while insisting that some stories are better than others ... the critique of a privileged
vantage point need not imply a critique of the possibility of knowledge (Corbridge 1993:
456).

This does, of course, raise the question of how we decide that one 'story' is 'better'
than another; an issue that is still far from adequately explored even in the more politically committed postmodern work. However, it is an important issue if postmodern
approaches to development are not to render all social theory meaningless and self-
indulgent and if they are not to undermine the possibilities for change and political
action. In a world so riven by poverty and intensifying international inequalities, it
remains critically important to ensure that appreciation of the fluidity of the (post-)
modern world, and the contested nature of our categorizations and evaluations of it,
do not lead to a paralysis in meaningful critical analysis (Simon 1998: 241).

Thankfully, to my mind at least, most of the emerging postmodern approaches to
development lie nearer to the reconstructive side of Best and Kellner's distinction.
Indeed Peet (1998: 196) has suggested in relation to the influence of postmodernism
upon geography more generally that 'many ideas in what is supposedly poststructural
or even postmodern geography turn out as hybrids derived from blending these with
historical materialist notions', although not everyone sees this as beneficial (see Doel
1993; 1999). Most postmodern-influenced research on development issues, whilst
critical and suspicious of the claims of traditional social theory and insistent about the
importance of language in structuring understanding, does still seem to wish to talk in
terms of relations between forms of representation and a wider political world that
exists beyond them; even though this distinction would have no meaning to those
totally convinced by the more extreme postmodern and post-structuralist perspectives
(see also Chapter 2). However, as we shall see, the conceptual tools for exploring this
interface between representation and power remain, at present, sadly underdeveloped.

Deconstructing Development

in a quite fundamental way, the voices of postmodernism ... force us to ask ... what is
development, who says this is what it is, who is it for, who aims to direct it and for whom?
(Corbridge 1993: 454).

Thus far, our consideration of postmodern approaches has been conducted at an
extremely broad conceptual level. What remains to be shown is how such themes can
be brought to bear upon development issues. In essence, as one might imagine from
our preceding discussion, this has involves problematicizing the language used
within development research and exploring relationships between social knowledge
and political power. Some major foci in such research include: an interest in identity
construction; explorations of the limitations of the meta-narratives of Western social
theory in non-Western contexts; consideration of culture within discussions of the
politics of development; and reflections on the rights of 'experts' (even, or perhaps

especially, radical academics) to claim to speak for the interests of the poor and excluded. This final element has led to an intense process of academic reflexivity and self-doubt and a search for 'spaces' whereby such peoples might speak for themselves, rather than be represented through the words of others, however sympathetic.

There is not the space here for detailed consideration of all of the issues such work addresses, and indeed some of them have already been alluded to in Chapter 2. Instead, given the broad conceptual focus of this chapter, I wish to explore how engagement with postmodern social theory has been brought to bear, upon the concept of development itself. Central to such efforts has been examination of how particular ways of constructing the world (in this case via the all encompassing idea of development) originate and evolve over time and, perhaps more importantly, how they might be destabilized so that other previously marginalized ways of seeing might be articulated. Drawing on parlance of the postmodernists and post-structuralists, such a process is often referred to as the *deconstruction* of the dominant *discourses* of development (see Box 3.7). The earliest example of this type of approach can be seen in the writings of Edward Said who employed Foucauldian '*discourse analysis*' to reveal how the Western discourse of Orientalism cemented unequal relationships between Europe and Asia through its negative depictions of the latter (see Said, 1978). Said's influence was crucial in the emergence of a range of '*post-colonial*' literatures. These writings, based initially in literary theory, have sought to re-evaluate the legacy of colonialism through examining its cultural impact upon colonized societies. This has involved a re-reading (and destabilization) of colonial and post-colonial histories that highlights the role of representations in establishing relations of exploitation and marginalisation.

Box 3.7: The power of language – discourses and deconstruction

> Statements about the social, political or moral world are rarely ever true or false; and 'the facts' do not enable us to decide definitively about their truth or falsehood, partly because 'facts' can be construed in different ways. The very language we use to describe the so-called facts interferes in this process of finally deciding what is true and what is false (Hall 1992: 292).

This quote from Stuart Hall provides an excellent illustration of the centrality of language to the ways in which different sorts of knowledge are produced within society. The short piece from which it is taken (Hall 1992: 291–318) constitutes a particularly effective introduction to one of the most crucial elements within any consideration of such issues – the idea of *discourse*. In everyday usage, discourse, refers generally to spoken or written language; within social theory, however, it has been used more specifically to refer to how knowledge and social practices are constructed (Fairclough 1992: 3). Hall, therefore, drawing upon the work of Michel Foucault, defines a discourse as,

> a group of statements which provide a language for talking about – i.e. a way of representing – a particular kind of knowledge about a topic. When statements

about a topic are made within a particular discourse, the discourse makes it possible to construct the topic in a certain way. It also limits the other ways in which the topic can be constructed Hall 1992: 291).

What this suggests is that our knowledge of the world is structured and limited by these discourses. This social knowledge, in turn, influences our social practices, which illustrates the very real consequences and effects that discourses have upon society.

Knowledge is, then, fluid; representing a contestation for power and influence between a range of competing discourses. It is the outcome of this struggle that will determine how society views the 'truth' of any situation. As Hall goes on to point out, discourses are part of,

the way power circulates and is contested. The question of whether a discourse is true or false is less important than whether it is effective in practice. When it is effective – organizing and regulating relations of power – (say, between the West and the Rest) it is called a 'regime of truth' (Hall 1992: 295).

Recognizing that these 'regimes of truth' exist is one thing, attempting to escape from their confines quite another. One approach towards this end has been that of *Deconstruction* (Derrida 1976). This approach has involved 'deconstructing' the 'claims to truth' of dominant discourses through interpretations of their historical evolution that seek to reveal and destabilize how meaning has been constructed (particularly in terms of what has been seen as 'normal' or common sense and what has not) and, perhaps most importantly, how 'others' (those who are seen as different from us) have been represented. One central aspect of this has been to expose and, hopefully, reverse or displace, the importance within Western thought of binary opposites such as male/female and truth/falsity, 'whereby the nature and primacy of the first term depends upon the definition of its opposite (other) and whereby the first term is also superior to the second' (Parpart and Marchand 1995: 3). Such efforts it is argued, will reveal the incoherences of dominant forms of thinking and allow for the expression of other, previously marginalized, ways of seeing and knowing.

Said's influence has also been significant within recent, more general, examinations of the origins, dynamics and power of the idea of development itself. The very term, postmodernism, points to the direction of such work, suggesting the end (or transcendence) of modernity and, by inference, questioning the idea of human progress articulated through the enlightenment (see Chapter 2) and the very notion of 'development' itself. Since the early 1990s, a growing group of scholars have turned away from critiquing particular development strategies (or the inequalities of the context within which development is attempted) towards questioning the desirability of development itself and the impacts, in the 'Third World', of its consolidation as the dominant discourse ordering international relations and social transformation in the mid-to-late twentieth century. Probably the most important exponent of such analyses is the Colombian scholar Arturo Escobar, who succinctly outlines the rationale for such deconstructive efforts as follows:

> Development has been taken to be a true description of reality, a neutral language that can be utilized harmlessly and put to different ends according to the political and epistemological orientation of those waging it … from Modernization theory to Dependency or World Systems; from 'market-friendly development' to self-directed, sustainable or eco-development. The qualifiers of the term have multiplied without the term itself having been rendered radically problematic … No matter that the term's meaning has been hotly contested; what remained unchallenged was the very basic idea of development itself, development as a central organizing principle of social life, and the fact that Asia, Africa and Latin America can be defined as underdeveloped and that their communities are ineluctably in need of 'development' – in whatever guise or garb (Escobar 1997: 501–02).

What Escobar and others like him suggest is that the most important feature of 'Third World' societies is their entrapment within an all-pervading set of ideas, the *discourse of development*. This constitutes 'an interwoven set of languages and practices' (Crush 1995: xiii) that controls how meaning is bestowed and how the world has been imagined and hence acted upon (Escobar 1995: 5; Parpart and Marchand 1995: 3). To such theorists, it is in this realm of ideas and discursive frameworks that one must look for the 'power of development', reflecting a conviction that:

> the ability to control knowledge and meaning, not only through writing but also through disciplinary and professional institutions, and in social relations, is the key to understanding and exercising power relations in society (Parpart and Marchand 1995: 3).

Various studies have, then, begun to explore the 'archaeology' (see Chapter 2) of the idea of development; that is, the ways in which it has established itself as a form of 'common sense' truth about societies, and the manner in which it has disciplined and moulded the countries of the developing world to fit its own image of them. Such analytical efforts have, more often than not, been accompanied by strongly-worded denunciations of what has been done in the name of development and calls for its transcendence through the pursuit of new ways of thinking that might escape from the narrow confines of *developmentalism*.

These types of deconstructions of development (often termed *post-developmentalism*) are intensely critical of what they term the '*Development Industry*', or the plethora of institutions, academic disciplines and non-governmental organisations (NGOs) that make up the modern development community, interpreting the long history of development as a 'failed project', or perhaps more forcefully, as a major mechanism of imperial domination of the non-West. There are some remarkably ascerbic assertions made about development's failings; perhaps best illustrated through the often-quoted words of Esteva (1987: 135) that, 'you must be either very dumb or very rich if you fail to notice that development stinks'. Others are equally dismissive. Sachs (1992: 1–2), for example, talks of the project of development as a 'blunder of planetary proportions' and a 'crumbling lighthouse' whose light keeps receding into the dark'; whilst Escobar sums up the experience of development since the Second World War as a dream that,

progressively turned into a nightmare. For instead of the kingdom of abundance promised
by theorists and politicians ..., the discourse and strategy of development produced its
opposite; massive underdevelopment and impoverishment, untold exploitation and oppression (Escobar 1995: 4).

Some of this material can amount to little more than sloganeering – drawing on
'non-sequiturs,' 'unhelpful binary distinctions,' 'false deductions,' 'romanticism,'
'self-righteousness' and 'implausible politics' (see Corbridge 1998) – which can
attract one's attention away from the deeper, more analytical work on the politics of
knowledge (see Ferguson 1990; Escobar 1995; Crush 1995; Cooper and Packard
1997).

There is a brutal simplicity to the 'post-development' position, but it does beg
several questions. For one thing, it is open to question whether it is development as a
concept that is outmoded and untenable, or whether, as has long been argued by
Marxists and others, it has simply been misdirected. Furthermore, rather ironically,
whilst the essence of postmodern approaches revolve around the celebration of difference, diversity and complexity, post-development portrayals of the impacts of 'development' and the nature of development theory are incredibly monolithic and
over-generalizing (Peet 1997: 97). In relation to the former, Simon suggests that the
criticisms of post-war development outcomes may be somewhat overblown:

the very tangible achievements of many development programmes – albeit to different
extents and at different rates in rural and urban areas and in almost all countries of the
South – in terms of wider access to potable water and increasing literacy rates, average
nutritional levels, and life expectancy, for example, are often overlooked or ignored ...
The way in which often-diverse programmes, agendas and even principles espoused by
very different donor and recipient governments, nongovernmental organizations and
international financial organizations are dismissed by postdevelopmental critics using the
fashionable phrase, 'the development project' ... is unhelpful (Simon 1998: 221; see also
Corbridge 1998: 145)).

Furthermore, postmodern critiques of development, perhaps more than any of the
other approaches considered within this chapter, have tended to gloss over the differences between other alternative theories. There is, for example, a particular silence in
relation to the work of more radical development theorists: Escobar (1995), for
example, makes barely no mention of them. Where they are mentioned, then they are
viewed as merely representing reversals of orthodox ideas of modernization which do
not escape their basic conceptual frameworks. Peet suggests that this is an intrinsic
problem with discursive analyses of development:

the critical point here is not to make the easy claim that postmodern critics of development
theory overstate their position, but to argue that the analysis of discourse, with its linking of
oppositional theoretical traditions just because they oppose each other and therefore share a
vaguely defined 'same discursive space', is prone to this kind of overgeneralization ...
because it diverts attention from ... material contexts, conflating the different forms and
bases of power, merging conflicting positions on development into a single development
discourse (Peet 1997: 79).

Corbridge (1998) argues further that there is, in effect, not much new about post-
development accounts in that they assume, rather than explain, the mechanisms of

domination which they associate with the idea of development. The irony is that, in many cases, post-developmental deconstructions of the discourses of development are even more generalizing than the radical political economy perspectives that they are so scathing of. The vast complexities of development over space and time are, more often than not, reduced to the idea of an imposed Western mode of thinking and seeing that owes much (although this is never directly acknowledged) to the more simplistic formulations of dependency theory and cultural imperialism. There is also a tendency to romanticize the possibilities for the emergence of alternatives that might transcend development, most often associated with a championing of the liberating role of new social movements (see Escobar 1995). In essence, what this often boils down to is a glorification of 'tradition' (see Cowen and Shenton 1996: 456) and an, at least partial, misinterpretation of popular struggles for the fruits of modernity (even if those fruits are unachievable) as representing resistance to development (see Brown 1996).

This brief review of the influences of postmodern approaches within studies of development has been extremely cursory. The specific focus on post-development has been, I think, justified given the wide remit of the chapter, although it has perhaps diverted attention away from other, more subtle, attempts to stress the importance of representation (and particularly identity) within analyses of development (although see Chapters 7, 8, 11 and 12). What it has highlighted, however, is that, despite the limitations noted, postmodern approaches within development studies have been politically engaged and have certainly not suffered from the nihilism and detachment characteristic of some postmodern analyses in other areas of social theory: here, at least, there has not been a descent into navel-gazing language games. The emerging work on the discourses of development has forced a profound examination of the ways in which our knowledge of the world is constructed and articulated. As Foster suggests more generally, postmodern rejections of,

> grand historical narratives, of any central struggles that define history, indeed of any historical subject, coupled with its insistence on the constitution of our knowledge within diffused power relations, leads it to 'genealogical' investigations of power 'nearest to the body' – areas that social theory has been insufficiently attentive to in the past. Its concentration on discourse, as the sole constitutive element in social relations, has revealed much about the role of language in the ordering of power. Its researches have thus increased our critical understanding of many aspects of society previously neglected. In particular, it has had a deep influence on feminist analysis (although many would argue that the relationship has primarily been the other way around) racial formation theory, cultural theory, political conceptions of surveillance and control, etc. Its emphasis on what is most personal has struck a chord in a period in which the personal has become political (Foster 1997: 190).

Nevertheless, as our explorations of the post-development literature have revealed, postmodern approaches also leave serious questions about agency and power insufficiently addressed, through their tendency to abstract analyses of representation and discursive strategies from the economic and political forces which infuse them with power and authority (Peet 1997: 80). It seems that we have ended up exchanging a conception of power as ultimately based in material economic structures to one which sees it as primarily based around language and discursive domination; how such an approach can hope to encompass the very real dynamics of global economic inequalities and the intricacies of local production processes in a serious manner is open to severe doubt. As Jonathan Crush suggests in the introduction to *Power and Development*:

> though development is fundamentally textual it is also fundamentally irreducible to a set of textual images and representations. Even as they explore facets of the rhetoric and language of development, the essays in this volume implicitly reject the conceit that language is all there is (Crush 1995: 5).

Crush goes on to insist that such studies must make,

> conceptual space… for an exploration of the links between the discursive and the non-discursive; between the words, the practices and the institutional expressions of development; between the relations of power and domination that order the world and the words and images that represent those worlds (Crush 1995: 6).

As I have argued elsewhere (Brown 1996), quite how the links between the realm of ideas and political and economic contexts within which they are articulated are to be explored remains unclear at present. Even Escobar (1995) recognizes the importance of the material context of political power, yet he never adequately explores the linkages between dominant forms of representation and changing material contexts of the global economy. Others are also concerned by this. Slater (1996: 265), for example, in a sympathetic review of Escobar's book, questions the lack of engagement with the existing radical economic literatures, asking whether we are to 'assume … that radical economic analysis has no role in the needed reconstructions of thinking about North-South relations'. It seems that there is the potential for a fruitful interaction between the more responsive, historically sensitive and less deterministic versions of Marxism that have arisen out of the 'impasse' debate and the emerging explorations of the discursive aspects to the exertion of political power on the world stage. Quite how that research agenda is to be taken forward is, nonetheless, still very much open to debate (especially given the animosity so often displayed between Marxists and postmodernists). Two contrasting indications of some potential directions for such research lie, firstly, in the long yet currently marginalized traditions of Gramscian analyses of ideology and political praxis (see Moore and Schmitz 1995) and, secondly, in attempts to articulate some sort of 'postmodern materialism' or 'materialist postmodernism' that propose a continued engagement with Marxist interpretations of the economic sphere and yet refuse to give them causal priority (see Callari and Ruccio 1996, or for a critique, Albritton 1995). In the words of Resnick and Wolff,

> all that can ever be done – and all that any analyst ever has done – is to select some few influences and discuss their unique and different role in shaping the chosen event. Marxists, for example, have often chosen to stress economic influences and especially class influences … The problem arises … if and when any analysts … claim … that the influences they have chosen to study and the analyses they constructed based on them are not just *some* influences, but are indeed *the* crucial influences in some quantitative sense (Resnick and Wolff 1992: 132–3).

Summary and Conclusion

This has, by necessity, been a brief and partial journey through some of the major schools of thought that have influenced how geographers have approached development issues over the past forty years or so. I have already made excuses for some of the more obvious omissions so it is not worth repeating those here, save to say that my major intention was to focus on broad conceptual issues relating to how development has been understood and pursued. There also seems little point in offering a final synthesis of the diverse schools of thought that have been discussed. Instead, reflecting the current state of flux within the theorization of development, I wish to conclude the discussion via a series of broad themes and questions.

The second half of the twentieth century might quite conceivably be termed the 'age of development'. As we start a new millennium it appears, however, as if that age is now drawing to a close or, at the very least, what is understood by the idea of development is undergoing some dramatic changes. The international stage is dominated by the globalization of neo-liberal ideas concerned with the pursuit of free trade and the prioritization of market forces within more and more spheres of social activity. Traditional developmental agendas of poverty reduction, targeted industrialization and/or human and institutional capacity enhancement, whilst certainly still present, are, nonetheless, now framed within the confines of economic policies that do not emphasize or place strategic importance upon such concerns. Amidst such circumstances and the associated intensification of poverty and inequality in many parts of the world, there is an urgent need to refine our understanding of the ways in which the international economy is being transformed and the apparently chaotic cycles of political and cultural change occurring across the globe at a variety of different scales. The extent to which the approaches towards development reviewed within this chapter have enabled or hindered such academic endeavours obviously depends upon our own individual interpretation of those theories and the nature of the world around us.

The types of questions that have to be answered in arriving at our individual conclusions (or leanings) on these matters are many and varied; there are, perhaps, three of particular importance.

a) Does the idea of development retain any meaning in the early twenty-first century?

b) Is there anything unique (and knowable) about capitalism as an economic system and, if so, what do we know about how it operates and in what ways it is being transformed?

c) To what extent are we able to make generalizations about the impacts of global changes upon individual nations and communities and should we even be attempting to make such generalizations?

Box 3.8: Chapter summary and suggestions for further reading

This chapter has reviewed some of the threads of the complex web of theoretical ideas that surround notions of development and which can threaten to engulf the unwary student. In particular this chapter has highlighted:

- Variants of Marxist development theory that dominated geographical discussions of development from the early 1970s, including dependency and modes of production theories.

- How the rise of Marxist theory in development studies was challenged by the rise of neo-liberalism in international development institutions and also an academic critique which suggested that it did not sufficiently recognise diversity in the modern world.

- How the academic critique conducted initially from within a broadly modernist framework, but during the 1990s has become influenced by a postmodernist questioning of representational theory.

- Differences in postmodernism, particularly between 'extreme postmodernism' and 'reconstructive postmodernism'.

- How a reconstructive postmodernism has 'deconstructed' discourses of development, revealing how the very idea of development is used to establish and reproduce relations of domination and exploitation.

As should be evident from this chapter, there are a whole host of writings that employ some notion of development. The following may form useful starting points for further exploration of the issues surrounding the conceptualisation of development: Corbridge (1986) *Capitalist World Development*; Crush (1995) *Power of Development*; Forbes (1987) *The Geography of Underdevelopment*; Martinussen (1997) *Society, State and Market*; Peet (1991) *Global Capitalism*; Roxborough (1979) *Theories of Underdevelopment*; and Schuurman (1993) *Beyond The Impasse*.

Chapter 4

Global Crises? Issues in Population and the Environment

Hazel Barrett and Angela Browne

Introduction

Both population and the environment are commonly perceived to be in crisis. The so-called *Earth Summit* held in Rio de Janeiro in June 1992 (more formally entitled, the *United Nations Conference on Environment and Development*) and the *Cairo Population Conference* held in September 1994, reinforced these views, with alarmist media reports following. Debates concerning the relationship between population and the environment are however, not new and present day discourse on the subject can be traced back to Malthus' influential *Essay on the Principle of Population* published in 1798. Since then, the debate has broadened, with research demonstrating the highly intricate relationship connecting people with their environment. This chapter focuses on the complex theoretical debates concerning the linkages between these two emotive issues and uses examples from sub-Saharan Africa to illustrate them. We will begin by discussing, briefly, some general aspects of population distribution and growth, the notion of environment and contemporary sub-Saharan Africa.

Population

Discussions of population are often dominated by population size and fertility rates. These are clearly very important aspects of the human population. In 1999, the world's population exceeded six billion (UNFPA 1999; Barrett, 2000), with the last billion added in only 12 years. As Table 4.1 shows, more than half the world's six billion people live in East and South Asia, regions which include China and India. Yet these regions have moderate annual population growth rates of 1.2 per cent and 1.8 per cent respectively. The regions with the highest growth rates are sub-Saharan Africa, the Middle East and North Africa, with rates of over two per cent. The region with the lowest annual population growth rate is Eastern Europe and Central Asia, where an annual population growth rate of –0.2 per cent suggests there is no current population growth in these regions and that in the medium to long term population numbers will decline.

Table 4.1 shows, both population annual growth rates and total fertility rates are decreasing in all world regions. The world's total population is now increasing by 1.3 per cent per year, a reduction of 0.4 per cent in the average annual rate of population growth between 1980 and 1990. The rate is expected to continue to fall to 1 per cent

Contested Worlds

Table 4.1: Population characteristics of major world regions

	Population in millions	Population as % of world total	Average annual population growth rate %		Total fertility rate		Urban population as % of total population	
			1980–90	1995–00	1980	1995–0	1980	1995
Sub-Saharan Africa	596.7	9.8	3.0	2.4	6.7	5.2	23	31
East Asia and Pacific	1,858.0	30.8	1.6	1.2	3.1	2.2	21	31
South Asia	1,465.8	24.3	2.2	1.8	5.3	3.4	22	26
Eastern Europe and Central Asia	307.6	5.1	0.9	-0.2	2.5	1.4	58	65
Middle East and North Africa	354.0	5.9	3.1	2.1	6.1	3.7	48	56
Latin America	511.3	8.5	2.0	1.6	4.1	2.7	65	74
High Income Economies	935.0	15.6	0.7	0.3	1.9	1.6	75	75
World Total	6028.4	100.0	1.7	1.3	3.7	2.7	40	45

Sources: World Bank 1997: UNFPA 1999

by the year 2020. However a considerable *population momentum* is present because nearly half the world's population is below 15 years of age and it is expected that there will be enormous population growth when these young people become parents. At the beginning of this millennium it was estimated that an additional 78 million people per year were being added to the world's population. Of this increase, 95 per cent were living in developing countries (UNFPA 1999). United Nations medium term projections suggest that by the year 2050, the world's population will have reached 8.9 billion; assuming that total fertility rates and population growth rates continue to decline. Thus the demographic momentum is such that, even using the most optimistic assumptions, the world's population will increase by 3 billion people in the first fifty years of this century (UNFPA 1999). That will mean 50 per cent more people utilising the world's resources than at the end of the twentieth century.

Another major demographic trend is the rapid rate of urbanisation (Clark, 2000). In 1995 45 per cent of the world's population lived in urban settlements, a 5 per cent increase in five years. This trend is particularly noticeable in developing regions, where urban populations are growing at twice the rate of rural populations. By 2025 it is estimated that over 60 per cent of the world's population will live in urban areas, representing 4.6 billion people. Although cities contribute to economic development, accelerate the fertility transition and relieve pressure on rural areas, cities generate serious and increasing environmental problems (ActionAid 1992).

The Environment

Environment is a term which whilst often taken as being a central constituent of geography (see Chapters 2) is difficult to define. It is used in a variety of contexts and even when considered solely in association with population still acquires many meanings. It is, for example, often used interchangeably with the term 'nature' and taken to refer to resource endowments which provide for the sustenance of human life and economic activity. In other cases it is used to characterise spaces which surround particular populations. Sometimes these two meanings are conjoined, as when people refer to 'environmental changes' brought about by human activity. Peoples action in their local surroundings, for example, may bring about changes in vegetative cover, as with deforestation, which in turn may have further 'environmental impacts' such as altering the content and balance of nutrients in the soil and its capacity for regeneration. Furthermore all the possible meanings of population and environment take different shades of meaning and have different implications, depending on the spatial level at which they are considered.

Sub-Saharan Africa

The case studies used in this chapter are predominantly drawn from sub-Saharan Africa, a region which, although comprising approximately 10 per cent of the world's population, has the highest population growth rate and by far the highest total fertility rate of any of the major regions of the world (Table 4.1). The growth rate of its urban population, at 5 per cent per annum between 1980 and 1995, is the fastest regional value in the world today and represents an atypical model of urbanisation in historical terms, namely one that is *not* based on a synergy with industrialisation and development. Furthermore, Africa is widely reported to be a region of very difficult and harsh environments, with fragile soils, unpredictable and unreliable rainfall regimes, seasonal rivers and little opportunity for water control, except by massive engineering projects such as those on the Zambezi and the Volta rivers (Binns 1994). It is also the only region showing declining per capita food production (Dyson 1996).

The region has also been the scene of many recent global crises. During the 1980s and 1990s almost all of the world's famines occurred in Africa, and the widespread drought in southern Africa in the early 1990s was the worst ever recorded for that region. The problem of desertification, highlighted particularly in the 1970s in the Sahel region, is another sign of environmental stress. Although generally not densely populated, the region has pockets of very high population density where signs of environmental degradation are very evident. Even in areas of moderate or even low population density, environmental degradation is a serious problem.

For all these reasons Africa offers a good opportunity to review the contested theoretical perspectives associated with the population/environment debate. But it is also of interest because it is one of the poorest regions of the world, and according to Oxfam, the only region where the percentage of people below the poverty line is predicted to increase. The Oxfam study, published in 1993, reports that the numbers below the poverty line are predicted to rise from the 1990 level of 216 million (48 per cent of the then population) to 304 million (almost 50 per cent) in the year 2000 (Oxfam 1993). As this chapter will show, the relationship between population, poverty and the environment is now understood to be of very great importance in theoretical work linking population with environment.

Population-Environment Theoretical Perspectives

Population is the Problem

The view that population growth and the environment are linked has been articulated for more than two hundred years. Initially environmental factors, especially food production, were seen as a major constraint on the growth of human populations. More recently the relationship has been re-articulated, with population growth being posited as a major cause of resource depletion and environmental degradation. Proponents of this school of thought view population growth as a 'dependent factor', which needs to be controlled if environmental conditions and ultimately human well-being are to be improved. This view has, however, been criticised for its failure to distinguish between association and causation. Adherents regard the effect of population on the environment as universally negative and ignore the impact of other factors. Despite these criticisms the view that the relationship between population growth and the environment is detrimental to both parts of the equation is a popular one, with many alarmist books being published such as *The Population Bomb* by Paul Ehrlich in 1968 and *Only One Earth* by Barbara Ward and Rene Dubos in 1972.

Malthusian Pessimism The constraints to population growth and human welfare imposed by an environment with finite resources was first expressed by Malthus in the late eighteenth century (see Box 4. 1). He postulated that continued increases in population numbers could not be supported by the Earth's productive capacity to supply food and that in the absence of controlled human fertility, war, famine and disease would inevitably restore the balance between population numbers and the ability of the environment to provide for them. For Malthus food production levels were the limiting factor on population growth. His theoretical perspective viewed the social-environmental relationship as essentially static, with unchanging methods of food production and a limited supply of land. Thus the only solution to increasing population pressure on the environment is a demographic response.

Box 4.1: The population-food debate

In 1798 Thomas Malthus published his highly influential paper *Essay on the Principle of Population*, which investigated the relationship between population growth and food supplies. His fundamental thesis was that population is constrained by food supplies. He argued that population naturally increased in a geometric ratio, that is 2, 4, 8, 16, and so on, whereas food production increased only in an arithmetic ratio, namely 1, 2, 3, 4, etc. The inevitable outcome would be that population numbers would exceed food supplies (Figure B4.1a). The result would be famine, war, misery and increasing death rates (labelled 'positive checks' by Malthus) until the equilibrium between population and food supplies was restored. However Malthus argued that if population numbers could be controlled, then such a scenario could be avoided. He suggested that if 'preventative checks', such as moral restraint, sexual abstinence and late marriage were encouraged, then the balance between population growth and food supplies could be maintained (Figure B4.1a).

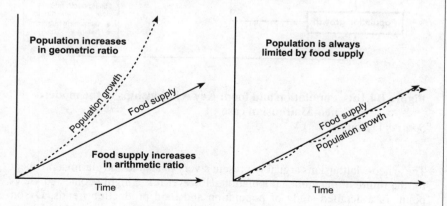

Figure B4.1a: Malthus' theory of population and food supply
Source: Barrett 1992: 22

The last two hundred years have provided little evidence to support Malthus' arguments. The world's population today is larger and better fed than it was when Malthus was writing. Although there have been localised and regional famines, the global catastrophe predicted by Malthus has not occurred. However there have continued to be commentators suggesting that societies are close to reaching some critical point with regards to population levels. Writers like Lester Brown (1991, 1994) and Paul Ehrlich (Ehrlich 1968; Ehrlich and Ehrlich 1990) all argue that global food production is increasingly coming up against various major constraints, the most serious being a shortage of land and water (Figure B4.1b). These, together with global warming and ozone depletion, are seen to be putting the world's population on course for a Malthusian disaster.

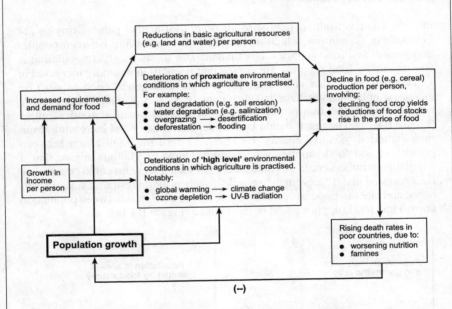

Figure B4.1b: Population and food: Key relationships in the modern neo-Malthusian case

Source: Dyson, 1996: 14

These neo-Malthusians arguably present a very plausible and alarmist prospect for the future of the human population. However it is a highly contested viewpoint. In a detailed study of population and food production trends, Dyson (1996) can find no evidence, at a global level to support the neo-Malthusian view. He states quite categorically, 'the 1980s and early 1990s have not been a particularly dismal period for global per capita food production' (p. 96). He concludes on this optimistic note, 'there is fair reason to expect that in the year 2020 world agriculture will be feeding the larger global population no worse – and probably a little better – than it manages to do today' (p. 208).

Within this approach the concept of '*carrying capacity*', which is explained in Box 4.2, has been used by advocates of the Malthusian perspective to suggest that there is a '*population threshold*' that a particular environment can support within a given level of technology whilst retaining its capacity for regeneration. Early examples of attempts to evaluate the carrying capacity of specific environments under traditional systems of agricultural production include Allan's work in Northern Rhodesia, first published in 1949 and Hunter's work in Ghana in 1966 (both re-published in Prothero 1974). Concerns about the ability of fast growing populations in developing countries to feed themselves gave the concept of carrying capacity a new lease of life during the 1980s (Higgins *et al.* 1982; Muscat 1985). However, the problems of assessing and measuring carrying capacity have meant that it has had limited analytical value, as Blaikie and Brookfield state:

> If carrying capacity changes with each turn in the course of socio-economic evolution, each new technological input or new crop introduction, and can also vary markedly according to the bounty or otherwise of rainfall in a given year, of what use is the concept? (Blaikie and Brookfield 1987: 29).

Box 4.2: The concept of carrying capacity in population geography

The essential debate concerning population growth and its relationship with resources and the environment has been greatly advanced by the development of ecological ideas, and particularly the concept of 'carrying capacity'. This concept has long been used by biologists and ecologists, but has only relatively recently been recognised by population geographers as a useful tool (see Barrett 1992). The carrying capacity of a 'natural system' can be expressed in terms of the maximum number of organisms that can be sustained by the food producing system without impairing the ability of that system to continue producing. If the numbers of organisms depending on a biological system become excessive, then the system will be slowly destroyed. For example, if an area of ocean is overfished, stocks will dwindle and the fishery will collapse; similarly, when forest cutting exceeds regrowth, forest cover will consequently decrease. The same concept has been applied to human populations.

Figure B4.2 demonstrates the possible consequences for a human population when carrying capacity is exceeded. As shown in Figure B4.2a, population overshoots the carrying capacity of the environment and its ability to support them and adjustment of the population takes place with the previously existing equilibrium being restored. In Figure 4.2b carrying capacity is exceeded but the human population continues to expand, consuming the biological resource itself. The result is that human consumption and numbers have to be reduced as the biological system collapses. In Figure B4.2c population expands but impending disaster is postponed by the application of technologies that raise the carrying capacity of the life support system.

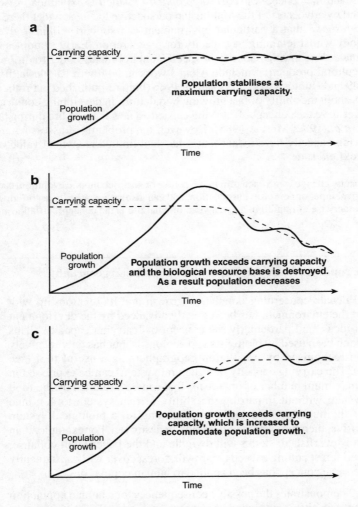

Figure B4.2a–c: The relationship between population growth and carrying capacity

Source: Barrett, 1992: 25

The concept of carrying capacity is particularly useful to population geographers when considering the concept of over population. It helps explain why some areas with low population densities, such as Africa with an average of only 18 persons per square kilometre, are believed to be overpopulated, while Western Europe, with a much higher population density of 155 persons per square kilometre, is not. Carrying capacities are not fixed through time. They are a function of technology and can therefore be raised or lowered. It is thus the level of economic development and technological application that determines a region's human carrying capacity. The concept thus illustrates that reducing population growth itself is often one part of a two-way solution. Investment in modern inputs, for example, can dramatically raise the population carrying capacity of croplands, although this very often is dependent on technological breakthroughs such as genetically engineered, high-yielding crop varieties.

Neo-Malthusian Alarmism Despite the enormous scientific and technical advances made since Malthus' time, the Malthusian view of impending catastrophe for the human population has not lost currency and still has its advocates. By the late twentieth century Malthusian concern had moved away from food production to embrace resource depletion. In the early 1970s a book entitled *The Limits to Growth* (Meadows *et al.* 1972) warned of the impending exhaustion of key natural resources unless population growth and levels of consumption were drastically reduced. Whilst this thesis was dismissed by many as alarmist, and its dire predictions have not become manifest, this seminal work highlighted the population-environment debate at a time when concern over the effects of human activity on the environment was growing.

The publication of *The Limits to Growth* heralded a shift within Malthusian perspectives. The preceeding Malthusian view was that the environment was the limiting factor to population growth was reversed. Instead the impact of population on the environment became central. In 1968 Paul Ehrlich articulated this relationship as a simple equation:

$$I = P \times A \times T$$

Where:

I   equals human impact on the environment
P   stands for population factors including size, growth rates and distribution
A   represents affluence and lifestyle measured by per capita consumption
T   stands for the technologies that supply A

Amongst these variables there is assumed to be a multiplier effect, with impacts compounding one another.

This formula suggests that environmental degradation is not solely correlated with the rate of population growth, but is a function of production technologies and consumption patterns (Commoner 1988). The formula is used to show how large populations in developing countries, despite widespread poverty and lack of access to technology, can impact heavily on the environment. On the other hand, the formula also demonstrates how relatively small wealthy populations in the industrialised countries can also have a detrimental impact on the environment. A report by the United Nations Fund for Population Activities (UNFPA) summarised this position by stating that two global groups are responsible for a disproportionate share of environmental degradation: the world's top billion richest and bottom billion poorest people.

The ascendance of this environment-centred paradigm was reflected in the publication of the United Nation's *World Commission on Environment and Development* report in 1987, entitled *Our Common Future*. This influential document considered environmental issues and concluded that environmental degradation and change resulted not just from the growth in population numbers. It suggested that patterns of consumption, resource use, production technologies, the global economic system and acute poverty also contributed to environmental degradation. The report called for *sustainable development* to help protect our environment for future generations.

The notion of sustainable development has been widely adopted within population-environmental discourse, although even within this environment-sentive debate, the nature of the relationship between population growth and environmental degradation has been the subject of much contestation. A number of international agencies including *UNPF, IUCNNR*, the *Worldwatch Institute* and the *World Bank* support the view that it is the increasing demands made on resources by high fertility levels and population growth which cause environmental damage and resource depletion. So, despite the recognition that there is a complex relationship between population and the environment, high population growth rates in developing countries are still largely blamed for environmental degradation (Jolly 1993: 13).

Population growth remained a favoured explanatory variable in accounts of environmental degradation for two reasons. First, the macro-economic, political and institutional factors, which for many non-Malthusians constitute the ultimate causes of environmental degradation, are widely perceived to be extremely resistant to change. Secondly, by contrast, population growth is perceived to be the easiest of factors to influence by policy intervention. Confronted with complex relationships, population continues to figure high in the environmental agendas of scholars and policy makers on the basis that 'while there is no systematic evidence to demonstrate that reducing population growth would actively lift the veil of poverty or regenerate environments, failure to do so will certainly worsen environments' (Shaw 1989: 207).

Population is a Positive Force

A counter-argument to the view that population is inevitably associated with environmental degradation has pointed to evidence that historically increasing population density has been associated with the evolution of more intensive and productive land-use systems. Thus, far from being detrimental, population growth can be seen as a major positive force for technological change. Unlike the neo-Malthusian view which perceives technology as ultimately environmentally destructive, this view suggests that technology can be used to improve environmental quality and conserve finite resources. However, a major criticism of this view is the assumption that intensification of production is necessarily beneficial. Agricultural intensification can lead to soil degradation or pollution from agro-chemicals, just as easily as it can result in improved land management. The key question to be answered is under what conditions does population pressure result in innovation rather than degradation?

Boserupian Optimism In contrast to the Malthusian and neo-Malthusian approaches to the population-environment debate, Boserup's seminal work *The Conditions of Agricultural Growth* claimed that 'population increase leads to the adoption of more intensive systems of agriculture in primitive communities and an increase of total agricultural output' (Boserup 1965: 118). According to Boserup, sustained population growth results in agricultural intensification characterised by the use of higher labour inputs and improved technology which make increased output possible through a more intensive use of land. Thus population growth in rural areas with low agricultural technology is viewed as a pre-condition for increasing agricultural output, enhancing land productivity and ultimately achieving economic growth and rural development. Within this approach population growth is the variable responsible for autonomous intensification in a closed rural system. Only migration can stop or delay the processes of intensification. Boserup's thesis is summarised in Box 4.3.

Box 4.3: Boserup's optimistic thesis

Boserup's (1965) *The Conditions of Agricultural Growth* challenges neo-Malthusian views that population increase leads to destruction of the land. Instead an alternative hypothesis is presented which recognises population as a positive stimulus to improving and intensifying the use of land. The hypothesis can be summarised as a five-phase sequential model, in which the agricultural system is adapted to an increase in population by progressive reductions in the fallow period, and increasing frequency and intensity of land use. The five-fold typology of land use, which Boserup (1965) describes as both a classification system and an evolutionary model, is as follows:

– *Phase 1*: Forest fallow cultivation, with long fallow periods
– *Phase 2*: Bush fallow cultivation, with medium fallow periods
– *Phase 3*: Short fallow cultivation, with short fallow periods
– *Phase 4*: Annual cropping, with no fallow period
– *Phase 5*: Multi-cropping, with two or more successive crops a year.

Within this model, increasing food needs of a growing population are met by increasing the length of time the land is in cultivation and shortening the time in fallow. By phase four, the fallow period has been eliminated, with the land being used every year by means of careful and intensive management, which preserves and enhances soil fertility. The most intensive system, multiple cropping, is found in the most densely populated regions of the world, especially the Far East. Boserup suggests that, under the pressure of increasing population, the shift in recent decades from more extensive to more intensive systems of land use has occurred in virtually every part of the developing world. In this way, 'regions which previously, under forest fallow, could support only a couple of families per square kilometre, today support hundreds of families by means of intensive cultivation' (Boserup 1965: 22).

Boserup's work has considerable relevance for Africa, which is predominantly within the extensive categories of land-use systems, is generally not densely populated, but has very high rates of population growth. Her optimistic view of the beneficial effect of population in stimulating agricultural intensification challenged the widely held view of the 1950s and 1960s that the soils and climate of the tropical zone limited the scope for intensification, thereby restricting the number of people that these areas could support. Boserup points out that where land is used intensively, for example in parts of Nigeria, the soils and climate are no different from where it is used extensively: the difference is that intensively used areas support dense populations whose farming methods have actually *increased* soil fertility.

The attractiveness of Boserup's theory is not in its empirical basis, which is relatively weak and largely based on the experience of pre-industrial Europe and Asia, but in the fact that it provides an alternative approach to Malthus. Although there have been some criticisms of Boserup's approach (see Lele and Stone 1989; Bilsborrow 1987; Bilsborrow and Ogendo 1992) the Boserupian view has recently become the centre of revisions and adaptations that reflect the re-emergence of the notion that population growth in present day developing countries may be a favourable condition for economic development in general and agricultural growth in particular. A detailed longitudinal study (1930–1990) undertaken in Machakos District in Kenya by Tiffen *et al.* (1994) found support for Boserup's theory. Their conclusion that 'human adaptability is sufficiently great to cope with population growth rates of 3 per cent per annum' (Tiffen *et al.* 1994: 261), in both high and low potential agricultural areas, ran counter to mainstream positions which favoured a neo-Malthusian perspective. This study effectively constituted a new 'paradigm' in the study of rural development in developing countries, and is summarised in Box 4.4. Other studies confirm these conclusions. One study of the evolution of technologies in tropical agriculture, for example, found that,

far from being immobile and technologically stagnant, 'traditional' societies have responded to changes in population densities and external markets with changes in farming systems and landuse patterns, as well as technological change, in systematic and predictable patterns (Pingali and Binswanger 1987: 50).

Box 4.4: The Machakos story

The Machakos study by Tiffen *et al.* (1994) covered the period 1930–1990, and documented the resource management practices of African smallholders in a predominantly semi-arid district in south-east Kenya. During the period studied, the population of Machakos District grew from 238,000 to 1,393,000 and the amount of land per person fell from 2.66 ha to 0.97 ha.

In 1930 the colonial department of agriculture wrote despairingly of the vast-scale of population-induced degradation, reflecting the official view that overstocking, inappropriate cultivation and deforestation, in an area already considered to be overpopulated, were to blame. But by 1990, not only had colonial predictions of land becoming a 'parched desert' not materialised, but land had actually been made considerably more productive by means of a range of investments made by the growing population. This growth in population was considered to be the trigger for intensification in the district: as landholdings shrank in size it became necessary to apply increasing amounts of labour and capital to the holdings to raise crop yields.

This was achieved in the following ways:

- terracing of the land to achieve soil and water conservation; this is now very widespread in the district, especially in more hilly areas
- adoption of an 'appropriate' multi-purpose ox-plough, useable by both men and women, to achieve faster tillage
- manuring the land instead of fallowing, the manure being derived from household stall-fed cattle and small-stock, thus achieving soil replenishment on annually cropped fields
- increasing use of drought-escaping (i.e. quick maturing) maize varieties, developed on a local agricultural research station, and utilised by farmers in conjunction with local and hybrid varieties to maximise their farms' potential.

These agronomic improvements were all permitted by a conducive economic and institutional environment, which gave farmers the opportunities and incentives to expand or diversify production. The authors of the study stress, in particular:

- market opportunities, eagerly seized by farmers, first for coffee and then for fruit and vegetables
- the acquisition of technical knowledge and experimental attitudes derived from formal schooling, travel, the missions and the market
- employment outside the district, bringing investment funds into farming
- investment of public funds (but not disproportionately to other semi-arid areas)
- security of title, with individual rights to land reinforced by statutory registration, which has now spread to most parts of the district.

In addition, the social environment has facilitated change, especially:

- flexible use of family labour, supplemented by hired labour or by collective work- groups (particularly for terracing)
- the crucial role of women both as farmers and as community leaders and participants.

The authors emphasise that the skills, enterprise and adaptability of the population brought about this farming revolution, which was driven by the increasing
scarcity of land and facilitated by a generally favourable external environment,
particularly since independence. The role of the state has been largely indirect,
in that it pursued an open market path to economic development, provided the
economic infrastructure, supported individual title to land and promoted channels for the communication of technology. The market, rather than enforcement
or external intervention, was seen as providing a stimulus to innovation. As the
authors say, 'What happened in Machakos did not contravene the laws of nature,
as the Malthusian paradigm would express them, but rather grew logically from
a conjunction of increasing population density, market growth and a generally
supportive economic environment' (Mortimore and Tiffen 1995: 86).

Tiffen *et al.* (1994) presented a new interpretation of the positive effects of the
dynamics of population growth in rural areas shown in Figure 4.1. It demonstrates a
situation in which population growth results not only in increased agricultural output,
but also in environmental regeneration as a result of 'the farmers' own investments of
labour and capital into land improvement and development, at times assisted by
external advice and capital' (Tiffen *et al.* 1994: 263). The study emphasises the
importance of government interventions and policy in assisting or impeding some of
the positive effects of population growth. The most important positive effects of
population growth identified in the study were: increased food needs; increased
labour supply; increased interaction of ideas leading to new technologies; and
economies of scale in the provision of social and physical infrastructure. The rate at
which these produce agricultural intensification depends on a number contextual
variables including government policy and access to credit.

Population as One of Many Factors

Both the Malthusian and Boserupian views have been criticised for being oversim-
plistic. They both ignore the complexity of causation and the role of economic, political and social factors. It is clear that population and environmental issues are affected
and influenced by socio-economic and political factors at local, national and international levels. It is these factors which create the conditions for environmental degradation, poverty and population growth. Proponents of this school of thought
recognise that the relationship between population and environment is a complex
one, in which the role of the political economy and social organisation
is central.
Political Economy. The general character of approaches associated with political
economy has already been discussed in Chapters 2 and 3. In this chapter we will
focus on a couple of specific studies of population-enviroment relations which highlight the significance of political-economic structures.
    Harrison (1992) suggested that the human population is part of an enormous
economic and political system, which is linked to the natural ecosystem by a whole
range of social factors. Using Ehrlich's formula as a basis, Harrison produced a

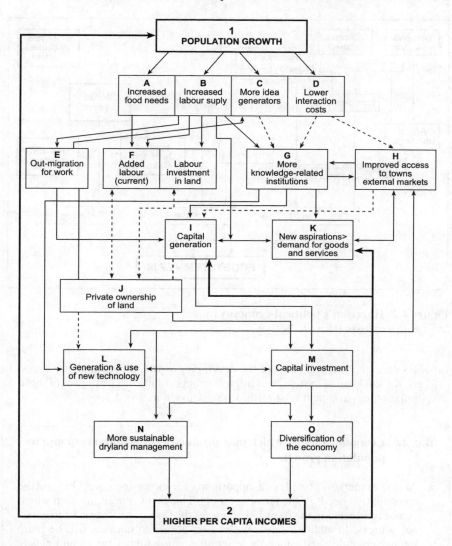

Figure 4.1: The positive effects of population growth
Source: derived from: Tiffen, 1994: 262

systems model which incorporated economic, political and social factors. Figure 4.2 shows that in this model the political economy of a society indirectly impacts on the environment through what he labels the 'proximate determinants of environmental degradation', namely consumption and technology. Clearly the economic and political environment is crucial in determining whether the positive effects of population growth envisaged by Tiffen *et al.* (1994) are realised. Among the many economic

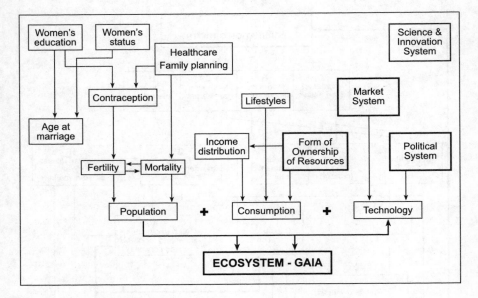

Figure 4.2: Harrison's political-economy model
Source: derived from: Harrison, 1992: 9

variables operating in rural areas of the developing world, three stand out: access to markets; the land tenure system; and migration opportunities. The impact of these on the population-environment relationship are discussed in Box 4.5.

Box 4.5: Economic factors which may produce a Boserupian response to population growth

a. Access to markets provides the opportunity for increasing output beyond the consumption needs of the farming family. This favours accumulation which can be reinvested in the farm and increases the flow of new ideas from external sources. In addition farms with better access to markets will be more intensively cultivated, since these families enjoy higher prices and elastic demands for their products. This in turn attracts migrants to the region looking economic opportunities. Thus population density is increased giving further impetus to intensification (Pingali and Binswanger 1987). Access to markets can, thus, have a beneficial impact on the population-environment situation by intensification and the adoption of good farming practices.

b. The land tenure system is of critical importance in determining human response to population growth, with changes in land ownership in turn being

---

affected by population pressure. Two characteristics of a land tenure system appear to be of the greatest importance: whether land is privately owned and the size of land holdings. Tiffen *et al.* (1994) found that in accordance with the terms of the agricultural intensification thesis, private rights to land in Machakos had strengthened since 1930 through changes in customary land tenure, and more recently government legislation. Where land was privately owned, the size of land holding and the intensity of landuse were usually inversely related, except where holdings had become so small as to be uneconomical (UN 1991). Where land was not privately owned, it was either open-access land (owned by the government) or common property (rights of access are regulated and enforced by the communities who own it). Open access and common property land systems are widely acknowledged as being disadvantageous in not providing incentives for investment in conservation and productivity raising technologies. In addition, as the land cannot be sold or mortgaged, farmers cannot get access to credit. However the assumption that communal land is prone to overuse, due to the lack of incentives for conservation that it offers, is disputed by Dasgupta and Maler (1990) who argue that local commons are far from open to all, with access subject to strict regulation and control by the community, which is very protective of the resource.

c. Labour migration can have positive and negative effects on the population-environment balance in rural areas. Boserup (1985) contends that in sub-Saharan Africa, migration from rural areas is not caused by over population or the marginality of the land in the sending regions, but rather by the lack of markets for agricultural surplus and poor transport infrastructure. As a result, in the sending areas, cultivation based on long fallow systems continue to be dominant and intensification is not attempted. Thus out migration from rural areas does not appear to have a negative impact on landuse and environmental degradation (UN 1991). The positive effects of migration that Tiffen *et al.* (1994) recorded in Machakos have also been observed in other African countries, including Zambia, where remittances from out-migrants have been positively associated with agricultural investment and equipment acquisition, with migrants returning with new cultivation practices and rural enterprises (Hansen 1992). It is suggested that migration can produce benefits to both exporting and importing areas, by altering population densities and by the introduction of new technologies, practices and investment.

Social factors are recognised by Harrison's model as important in the population-environment equation. These social factors focus particularly on gender issues, and include the education of women, the status of women and the work pattern of women. However he clearly attaches these factors to the 'population' part of the formula, seemingly not acknowledging that economic and political systems are also affected and altered by social factors. For Harrison population is one of three determinants affecting the environment. He suggests that population is part of a system of linkages with interacting effects on each other. However he admits that population is important and is often the dominant factor. Thus Harrison's model is very much within the neo-Malthusian mould.

The PPE Spiral Model. The complex inter-relationships between population, the political economy and the environment were recognised by UNICEF in 1994 and articulated in the *Poverty-Population-Environment (PPE) spiral*. This model, shown in Figure 4.3, treats PPE problems as a single issue, thus emphasising the reinforcing relationship between the variables. According to the model population growth tends to reinforce poverty, and poverty tends to reinforce population growth, forming a circuit. In turn, poverty forces growing numbers of people into environmentally vulnerable areas and the resulting environmental stress becomes yet another cause of their poverty. A synergistic spiral of increasing population growth, poverty and environmental degradation follows. It is not surprising then to find that the poorest 25 per cent of sub-Saharan Africa's population is concentrated in those areas which have been deforested, overgrazed and, as a result, are suffering serious soil erosion (WCED 1987, 25). An example of this synergistic relationship is demonstrated in Eastern Province, Zambia in Box 4.6.

Box 4.6: The PPE spiral in Eastern Zambia (based on author's fieldwork, 1995/96)

The Eastern Province of Zambia illustrates synergistic relationships of population, poverty and the environment in an area of low-to-medium population density but very rapid rate of population increase due to high fertility. The area's agriculture is dependent on rain-fed cultivation of maize, with groundnuts and cotton increasingly being grown for cash. Rainfall is always unpredictable, with a mean of 700–900 mm and a rainy season lasting from November through to March. The area was badly hit by drought in the early 1990s, with 1992/3 recording less than half of the seasonal rainfall norm. Population is increasing at the rate of 4 % per annum, much higher than the national rate of 2.3 %. This is explained by a very high total fertility rate, of 7.1 children per woman; the national rate is 5.6.

The farming system of the area relies almost entirely on manual labour, of men, women and children. Technological improvements have been minimal, with very little use of machinery, agricultural chemicals or modern crop varieties, except for cash crops. Labour supply is an absolute constraint on the amount of land that farmers can successfully cultivate using hand-tools: the more children a family has, the more land can be cultivated. Few farmers can afford to buy in labour, so families rely on children, from the age of 6/7, to help with farming tasks. The 'value' of children is consequently high and the resultant high fertility is being maintained throughout the reproductive age groups.

This area illustrates a region where the PPE spiral is evident. The area is one of bush fallow, with, at present, enough reserves of farmland to enable an

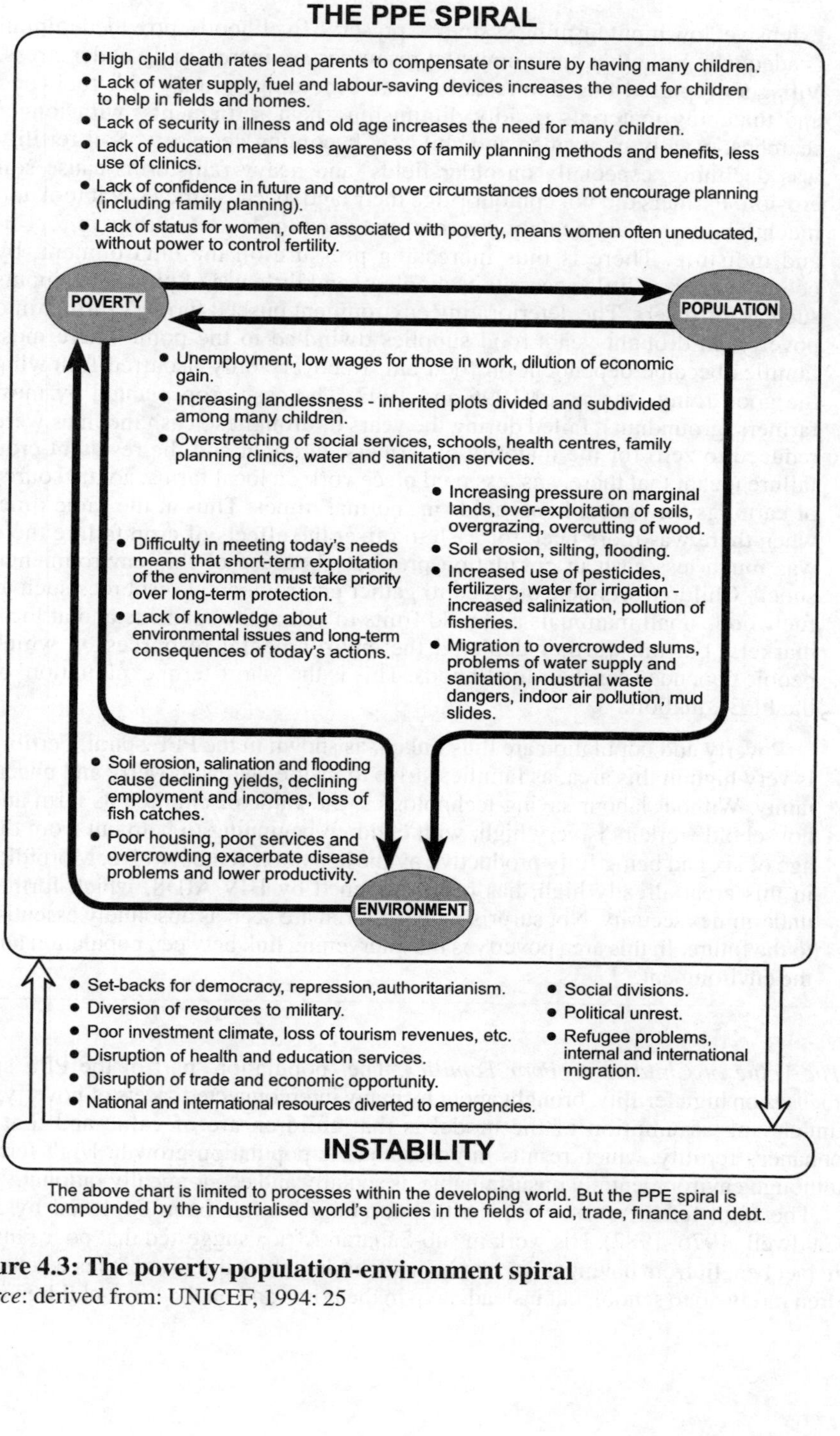

THE PPE SPIRAL

- High child death rates lead parents to compensate or insure by having many children.
- Lack of water supply, fuel and labour-saving devices increases the need for children to help in fields and homes.
- Lack of security in illness and old age increases the need for many children.
- Lack of education means less awareness of family planning methods and benefits, less use of clinics.
- Lack of confidence in future and control over circumstances does not encourage planning (including family planning).
- Lack of status for women, often associated with poverty, means women often uneducated, without power to control fertility.

POVERTY → **POPULATION**

- Unemployment, low wages for those in work, dilution of economic gain.
- Increasing landlessness - inherited plots divided and subdivided among many children.
- Overstretching of social services, schools, health centres, family planning clinics, water and sanitation services.

- Difficulty in meeting today's needs means that short-term exploitation of the environment must take priority over long-term protection.
- Lack of knowledge about environmental issues and long-term consequences of today's actions.

- Increasing pressure on marginal lands, over-exploitation of soils, overgrazing, overcutting of wood.
- Soil erosion, silting, flooding.
- Increased use of pesticides, fertilizers, water for irrigation - increased salinization, pollution of fisheries.
- Migration to overcrowded slums, problems of water supply and sanitation, industrial waste dangers, indoor air pollution, mud slides.

- Soil erosion, salination and flooding cause declining yields, declining employment and incomes, loss of fish catches.
- Poor housing, poor services and overcrowding exacerbate disease problems and lower productivity.

ENVIRONMENT

- Set-backs for democracy, repression, authoritarianism.
- Diversion of resources to military.
- Poor investment climate, loss of tourism revenues, etc.
- Disruption of health and education services.
- Disruption of trade and economic opportunity.
- National and international resources diverted to emergencies.
- Social divisions.
- Political unrest.
- Refugee problems, internal and international migration.

INSTABILITY

The above chart is limited to processes within the developing world. But the PPE spiral is compounded by the industrialised world's policies in the fields of aid, trade, finance and debt.

Figure 4.3: The poverty-population-environment spiral
Source: derived from: UNICEF, 1994: 25

extensive, low input farming system to preserve livelihoods, provided rainfall is adequate. But other environmental resources are increasingly under stress. Villagers reported that deforestation was becoming serious with fuelwood and thatching materials rapidly diminishing near settlements, with longer searches, usually by women and children, becoming necessary. Soil fertility was declining, especially on older fields, and heavy rainstorms cause soil erosion. Farmers did not contour ridge their land, because they say it took too much labour, but are acutely aware of the need to do so to preserve topsoil and moisture. There is thus increasing pressure on the environment, by people with very little access to technology and little use of purchased inputs such as fertilisers. The deteriorating environment pushed farmers further into poverty; in drought years food supplies dwindled to the point where most families became dependent on food aid. Recovery only occurred following the good rainy seasons of 1996 and 1997. The cash crop planted by most farmers, groundnuts, failed during the years of drought so cash incomes were reduced to zero for the majority of farmers. Drought and the resultant crop failure meant that there was less paid piecework on local farms, a vital source of earnings for poorer households in 'normal' times. Thus at the same time, when there was more need for cash to offset the effects of crop failure there was much less cash in circulation precisely because of this environmental shock. Children were encouraged to gather environmental resources such as fuelwood, small mammals and wild fruits to sell at the roadside and at local markets, but this further depleted the environmental resources on which people depended for their livelihoods. This is the 'short-term exploitation' of the PPE equation.

Poverty and population are thus linked, as shown in the PPE spiral. Fertility is very high in this area, as families strive to insure against poverty and uncertainty. Without labour saving technologies, the value of children as farm and household workers is very high, with children beginning to help out from the age of six and being fully productive by the age of eleven or twelve. Morbidity in this area, already high, has been worsened by HIV/AIDS, which further undermines security. Not surprisingly, children are seen as absolutely essential to the future. In this area poverty is the intervening link between population and the environment.

The Value of Children to Poor Families. The 'population' part of the PPE spiral focuses on high fertility, brought about by many interconnected facets of poverty. The underlying assumption of the model is that children are of value and that this enhances fertility, which results in unsustainable population growth. High fertility, although environmentally unsustainable, is socially and economically rational.

The high fertility associated with poor families has been explored by John Caldwell (1976, 1982). His work in sub-Saharan Africa suggested that poor families in fact benefit from having large numbers of children, because in societies where children rarely go to school, but instead, help in the home and on the farm, children make a valuable contribution to the household. Very often by the age of nine, children are producing more than they consume. As a result of his research Caldwell devised a theory entitled the *Intergenerational Wealthflows Theory*, to explain high fertility amongst poorer people in Africa. This theory is described in Box 4.7. What Caldwell suggests is that poor people make rational decisions in deciding to have large numbers of children.

Box 4.7: Caldwell's theory of intergenerational wealth flows

Caldwell's (1982) theory of intergenerational wealth flows combines elements of sociological and economic approaches to fertility, but views social change as the precursor and trigger of change in the economic relations within the family, and hence of fertility decline. This theory was constructed primarily on the basis of studies undertaken in developing countries, especially Nigeria, over a number of years. In summary, the theory states that high fertility is maintained by wealth flowing from children to parents within the family. Changes in the relative value and cost of children within the family operate to effect a reversal in the direction of wealth flow, which results in fertility decline.

In Caldwell's view it is the nature of the family that determines the costs and benefits derived from children, the direction of the net wealth flow, and the level of support for high fertility. Caldwell argues that while children undeniably incur costs in the village, which increase as the village economy becomes monetised, and also cause additional work to their mothers when they are young, their returns outstrip their costs. Children begin to perform tasks valued by the household from as early as five years of age, including housework, child minding, collecting and carrying water and fuelwood, helping out on the farm and possibly some income generating activities. Children also represent a guaranteed source of free labour in peak periods and an insurance against depletion of household numbers through high mortality. To the labour and financial help which children provide to their parents must be added the social benefits. Among the social benefits are increased ability of parents to enjoy more leisure to perform highly valued social functions, and the prestige and power that parents derive from a large family (Caldwell 1976: 233).

The notion that high fertility ensues from the rational choice of poor people has been contested on several counts. Cleland and Wilson (1987: 15–16) argue that the available contemporary evidence does not support Caldwell's assertion, while Cain (1982) draws on evidence from Asia to suggest that Caldwell 'has overstated the magnitude of the economic benefits provided by children and underestimated the variability in their economic value within the region that he considers' (Cain 1982: 159–60). Schultz (1983) and Cain (1982) also criticise Caldwell's disregard for the principle of economic marginality. In Cain's words, the great majority of the populations of the developing world are poor …As such, the marginal utility of their income will be higher, the costs of children's consumption will represent a higher proportion of the family budget, and their behaviour is more likely to reflect constraints rather than choice (Cain 1982: 163).

Cain believes that there must be another explanation, namely that children provide an insurance against risk for poor families.

Cain (1982) distinguishes between children as instrumental within two differenti-ated family strategies: of 'gain' and of 'loss prevention', or survival. He points out that 'while Caldwell does not ignore the role of children in providing insurance, particularly physical security, he has focused much more on the opportunities created by children' (Cain 1982: 163). In other words, he focuses on children as a mechanims of 'gain' rather than as 'loss prevention'. In Cain's view, the insurance risk value of children is the most important in terms of maintaining high fertility:

> Unlike child labour and old age security, it is possible to see how the insurance value of children could economically justify large numbers of children (within the limits of natural fertility, that is) in high-risk settings: the combination of uncertain child survival, diverse sources of risk, a premium on sons, and the probability of great loss in their absence could argue for such a reproductive strategy (Cain 1982: 177) .

Thus population growth is a response to poverty, an insurance risk strategy in times of stress, but one which is often linked to environmental degradation.

Feminist Perspectives. As outlined in Chapter 2, feminist perspectives have profoundly impacted on geography, bringing amongst other things a growing aware-ness of the significance of the roles that women play in a vast number of geographical processes. Population-environment processes can be included in this list in that over the last 25 years or so, there has been a growing recognition of women's roles in establishing particular population-environment relations. A basic premise for much of this work has been that women are not only mothers, they are also environmental managers (Dankelman and Davidson 1988; Sen and Grown 1987). Two competing theoretical perspectives have been put forward for the analysis of women and the environment. The first of these is the *women and environment approach* which grew out of the *women and development* debate of the 1980s. This approach emphasises the importance of women in their roles as environmental resource managers and their vulnerability to declines in resource availability. This viewpoint advocates the need to develop environmental programmes directed at assisting women, which are parallel to, but separate from, men's programmes. (See Box 4.8)

Box 4.8: Women and the environment: The Green Belt Movement in Kenya

The Green Belt Movement in Kenya is an indigenous grassroots organisation that builds upon the link between women and the environment (see Ofosu et al, 1992). It was founded in 1977 by Dr Wangari Maathai with assistance from the National Council of Women of Kenya. At the time of its founding, soil erosion and deforestation in Kenya had created an acute shortage of wood, the major source of energy (fuelwood and charcoal) for more than 90 % of the country's rural population, as well as low-income groups in urban areas.

The Green Belt Movement was organised to encourage the planting and management of trees, both to provide fuelwood and to protect the soil. The Movement now includes some 1,000 tree nurseries with more than 50,000 women participating at these sites. In the last ten years more than 7 million trees have been planted, with a survival rate of 70 to 80 percent. Project organisers make tree planting an inome generating activity, especially for women. Millions of tree seedlings have been issued to small-scale farmers, schools and churches. Women are beginning to harvest fuelwood from their own trees, and fruit trees are bearing produce, providing both nutrition and income to the family. The project also promotes organic farming in order to improve soil fertility and food production.

The Green Belt Movement, through women's efforts and initiative in planting and managing trees, thus contributes to environmental conservation and sustainable rural development. The Movement has been replicated in 12 other African countries.

The second approach is derived from a philosophy which assumes that women have a natural affinity to nature, as opposed to men's urge to control and manipulate the natural world through science and technology. This approach is known as *ecofeminism* and suggests that the burden of environmental conservation and regeneration falls squarely on the shoulders of women, with men absolving themselves from environmental responsibilities. Advocates of this view seek respect and support for women's efforts to conserve the environment (Jackson 1993; Joekes *et al.* 1994).

But both these viewpoints are narrow in their conceptualisation of social relations and arguably demonstrate a limited understanding of the complexities and interactions between the genders in the pursuit of livelihoods in a region such as sub-Saharan Africa. Jackson (1993) and Joekes *et al.* (1994), for example, have both published detailed critiques of these perspectives. The women and environment approach is criticised for assuming it is in women's interests to conserve local resources when often these resources are needed immediately in situations of extreme poverty. The work involved in conservation also ignores the demands on women's time from motherhood and domestic tasks, as well as income generation. The underlying assumption is that gender roles are fixed, unchanging and universal. However, this assumption is increasingly being challenged. In the 1990s there was increasing evidence that African men help their female relatives much more than researchers in the 1980s assumed (Cromwell and Winpenny 1993). The ecofeminist school is also widely criticised, for the belief in at least some of its strands, that affinity to nature is biologically determined. This is a contradictory expression of feminism in that it ignores the function of social relations in allocating roles and that women are often subordinate to men (Boserup 1990). It may be women's status, lack of opportunity outside the household and poverty which make them apparently 'closer to nature', not their biological make-up.

From these criticisms a third view has emerged. This has been labelled a *developmentalist* perspective by Joekes *et al.* (1993). This view acknowledged that in many situations women do have primary responsibility for the use of natural resources, such as collecting fuelwood, water and wild foods. However, it accepted that these roles are not so universally ascribed to women as the literature would suggest. Women's and men's relationship to the environment is part of general entitlements and capabilities ascribed to individuals by social relations such as gender and class. Thus the wider socio-economic, political and cultural context of gender relations must be considered. There are clearly intervening factors which include access to land and resources, mechanisms of resource allocation and access to health and educational services. There is increasing recognition that the situation is further complicated by the international context of aid, trade and debt. The socio-economic context of gender-environment relationships are shown in Figure 4.4. It is becoming evident that an approach which places gender roles and environmental management

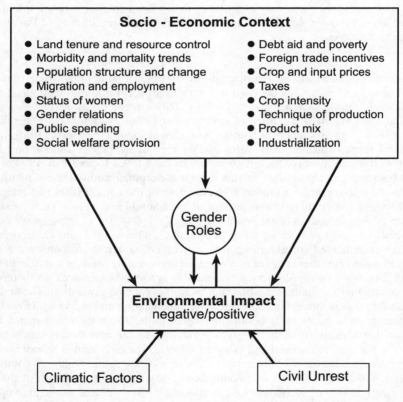

Figure 4.4: The socio-economic context of gender-environment relationships
Source: derived from Barrett and Browne, 1995: 36

in the international, national, regional as well as household context is essential, as they are all interlinked.

Conclusion

This chapter has investigated the complex links between what some commentators have argued are the two most pressing global issues of the twenty-first century, namely population and the environment. The chapter has examined a range of alternative theoretical perspectives and discussed a series of case studies that demonstrate how the theoretical work can be understood in practice. Some of the specific arguments and features of the Chapter are outlined in Box 4.9.

Box 4.9: Chapter summary and suggestions for further reading

This chapter has:

- Shown that despite decelerating rates of population growth in all major global regions, world population numbers are set to increase by about one third over the next 25 years due to inbuilt population momentum
- Presented and discussed opposing theoretical approaches to the population-environment debate, including the Malthusian, neo-Malthusian, Boserupian, political economy, synergistic and feminist views
- Examined the influence of socio-economic factors such as consumption, affluence, technology and poverty
- Illustrated theoretical viewpoints using case studies drawn from sub-Saharan Africa.

Useful texts you might wish to explore include: Binns (1995) *People and Environment in Africa*; Dyson (1996) *Population and Food*; Zaba and Clark (1994) *Environment and Population Change*; Marten (2001) *Human Ecology* and (dare we say it!) Barrett (1992) *Population Geography*.

The general argument of the chapter has been that theories which focus exclusively on either the influence of population on the environment or, conversely, on the influence of the environment on population are mistaken. There may hence be no room now for notions of cultural or environmental determinisms once popular in geography. Rather what is needed is a recognition that demographic and environmental processes are both affected by and in turn influence socio-economic factors, and it is in the context of this complexity that relationships between population and environment emerge.

Chapter 5

Nation States and Super-States: The Geopolitics of the New World Order

Peter Vujakovic

Introduction

One of the major geographical events of the late twentieth century was the disintegration of the Cold War *geopolitical order* which dominated the relations between states since the end of World War Two. The *bi-polar* world of the Cold War, dominated by the United States and the Soviet Union, provided stability which has yet to be fully replaced by a new geopolitical order. This chapter examines a variety of scenarios for the new international political architecture which might replace the former world order. The association of changes in geopolitical orders with the rise and fall of super-states will be examined, as will the fragmentation and (re)emergence of nation states in the contested space of the new Europe.

An outline of the geographical nature of the state and the significance of geopolitical world-orders as frameworks underlying global-scale politics and interstate relations provides an initial basis for discussion. The study of international relations and geopolitics has generally focused on the interaction between states as *mutually exclusive* territorial units. Concentration on the territorial state can, however, lead to a disregard for profound processes operating on world politics at other scales, from the local to the global (Agnew and Corbridge 1995). Later sections of the chapter will explore the changing relations between states and their potential roles in creating some future geopolitical order.

Geographical Aspects of the State

Power and Knowledge: The State and the Control of Territory

The term *state* is generally used to describe a bounded space, or *territory*, which is controlled by a single sovereign power with a monopoly of the means of violence needed to achieve control (Giddens 1985). The existence of a state also implies a formal government, with control over resources and population, which drafts and implements laws, and which defines the criteria for full membership of the state, or *citizenship*.

Taylor (1994) argues that the power of the state is founded on the geographical concept of *territoriality*. By controlling access to a defined space, the content (resources, population, infrastructure) of the territory can be regulated and fashioned by the sovereign power. The state can be regarded as a 'power container' which is able to appropriate a wide range of social functions through territorial control. The main functions of the state can be distilled as the waging of war, the management of the economy, the propagation of national identity and the provision of social services.

Mastery of territorial space is built on the control of knowledge. The advent of telecommunication networks in the eighteenth and nineteenth centuries was a critical factor in the consolidation of the territory of emergent European nation-states, with control of effective communication networks facilitating the regulation of people and resources within a territory, the dissemination of propaganda, and operations of war (see Box 5.1). The development of modern methods of survey and cartography has also been important. Although maps have historically been an important tool of government, from the mid-nineteenth century onwards they became crucial to the control and defence of territory. The Savoy Cadaster, initiated in 1728, became the model for state property surveys throughout Europe. Cadastral maps provide a detailed and rational basis for assessment of taxes and records of ownership (Kain 1993), but also assisted in the control and (re)allocation of land by the state. Cadastral maps, for instance, provided one of the main instruments with which the archetypal nation-state of France dismantled the feudal landscape after 1789. Furthermore, recent advances in survey technologies enhanced the ability of states to gather and control geographical information. The development of satellite remote sensing systems and Geographic Information Systems (GIS) are the consummate tools for territorial and military surveillance, providing a small number of technologically advanced states with ability to gather and control knowledge at the global scale. The capability of some states to gather *extra*-territorial information from space has been viewed as a form of neo-colonialism by Third World states.

Box 5.1: Technical networks and territorial control

The development of pre-electric semaphore telegraph in Revolutionary France was a significant factor in the creation of a unified territory and nation state. From its earliest use in 1793 (linking Paris to Lille) the telegraph system had, within fifty years, connected twenty-nine French cities, as well as important international outposts in Mainz and Turin (a network of about 5,000 kilometres) (Mattelart 1994).

Similarly, the evolution of railway systems in the 1880s was critical to the territorial integration and economic development of other major European powers, such as the newly unified Germany where former mini-states were integrated and regional particularities in custom and politics eroded (Henderson 1959). Railways also revolutionised war and the defence of national space. Much of the success of the Prussians in the Franco-Prussian War (1870) can be attributed to the superiority of their communications systems and their ability to rapidly direct troops and resources to key positions.

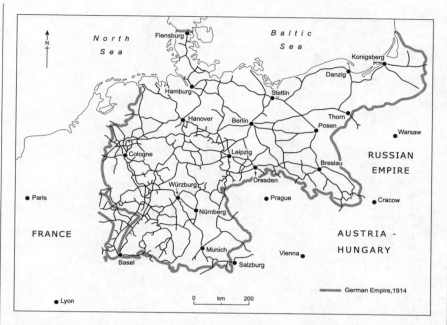

Figure B5.1a: Communications system in the German Empire, 1914

The formation of effective supra-national entities, such as the EU, also rely on efficient technical and transport networks. The geographically peripheral states of the EU are clearly at a disadvantage to those which cluster around the so-called 'Golden Triangle' of Amsterdam, Brussels and Cologne. Likewise, as the Pacific rim region begins to challenge the Atlantic as the core of the world economy, it is reliant on integrated communications systems such as those provided by submarine fibre optic links between Australia, west coast US and Canada, and Japan, Korea and south east Asia (Forbes 1999).

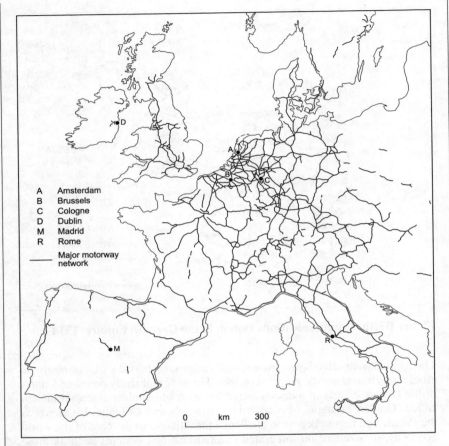

A   Amsterdam
B   Brussels
C   Cologne
D   Dublin
M   Madrid
R   Rome

⎯⎯⎯   Major motorway
      network

0   km   300

Figure B5.1b: Major motorways in the European Union in the 1990s

During the late twentieth century, however, control of information networks has arguably begun to slip away from national governments. The information 'super-highway' and systems of electronic financial transfer mean that national govern-ments are now much less able to control events within their own territory. New political movements, which transcend the territorial state, such as the 'green move-ment', have also called into question the ability of individual states to control inter-national affairs (Agnew and Corbridge 1995). Regional forms of political and economic integration, such as the European Union (EU), or the North American Free Trade Area (NAFTA), can be seen as attempts by governments to retain some form of control over a broader, but still defined territory. The relative success of such trans-state structures mean that it is "premature to proclaim the death of the nation-state" (Yeung, 2003; 105).

Territorial Integrity: The Spatial Dimension

The territorial extent of individual sovereign states varies enormously. The Russian Federation, with a total land area of over 17 million square kilometres, remains the world's largest single state despite the loss of territory following the disintegration of the Soviet Union (22.4 million square kilometres). At the other end of the scale are the *microstates* such as the Pacific island states of Tuvalu (24.6 km^2) and Nauru (21 km^2).

The implications of size for territorial integrity and control of strategic resources are by no means simple. Large territory does not, for instance, necessarily imply a wealth of resources. Compare the a number of the larger North African Arab states, with their relatively poor primary resource base, and some of the territorially much smaller, but oil rich Middle East states (Table 5.1). While heavily dependent on a single primary resource, these oil states are able to generate higher per capita GNP and spend much larger amounts on their armed forces, factors which influence internal stability and the defence of national territory.

One of the major predicaments facing states with large territories is the need to secure their borders. This is especially significant for states with poorly populated and potentially resource rich hinterlands. This problem is often addressed by state sponsored settlement policies and the construction of major transport arteries to secure contested frontier zones. Effective control of Imperial Russia's immense Eurasian territory, for example, involved massive investment in transport infrastructure. The Trans-Siberian and the Orenburg-Tashkent railways (completed c.1905) were critical to Russia's determination to expand its influence and retain control of its Asian assets (Hauner 1992; LeDonne 1997). The crucial importance of a strategic communications network was emphasised by the Russo-Japanese war of 1904–1905. Despite Russia's defeat, Mackinder (1919) was impressed by Russia's ability of to move a quarter of a million men over a distance of four thousand miles to fight the war in Manchuria. The defence of Russian territorial integrity remains dependent on the ability to move troops across extremely large distances, and persists as a source of anxiety for contemporary Russian geostrategists.

The problem of controlling an extensive hinterland has also been a major factor in the development of geopolitical thinking in South America. For example, post-war Brazilian attitudes towards Amazonia were initially dominated by the concept of 'living frontiers' (Hepple 1992). The military, in particular, regarded effective control of the hinterland as critical to the country's national development, as well as a means of thwarting the territorial ambitions of neighbouring states. The frontier mentality led to expansionist settlement policies for Amazonia, and the improvement of links with the transport system of the core region, for instance, the National Integration Plan (PIN) to construct the Transamazon Highway and other strategic routes (see Foresta 1992; Allen 1992; Phillips and Mighall 2000).

The configuration of the territory may also have an impact on the ability of the state to control population and resources. States which are compact in form should, theoretically, provide the least problems. Other forms, for example elongated territories like Chile or fragmented island group such as Indonesia, may have a number of disadvantages, including extensive border zones or weak central control of hinterlands.

Table 5.1: Armed forces and military expenditure in selected Arab states

	Area (km²)	Human Development Index (HDI) world ranking (1996)	GDP per capita ($US) (purchasing power parity) (1998)	Members of the armed forces per 1,000 of population (1997)	Military expenditure per capita ($US) 1997
Algeria	2,381,741	82	4,600	4.3	44.6
Egypt	1,002,000	109	2,850	7.6	55.3
Bahrain	707	43	13,100	18.4	462.6
Kuwait	17,818	53	22,700	9.0	1,592.8

Sources: Europa (1999) *The Middle East and North Africa 1999* (45th edition), London: Europa Publ.; Instituto del Tercer Mundo (1999) *The World Guide 1999/2000: A view form the South*, Oxford: New Internationalist Publ.; CIA (1999) *The World Fact Book 1999*, Washington: Central Intelligence Agency.

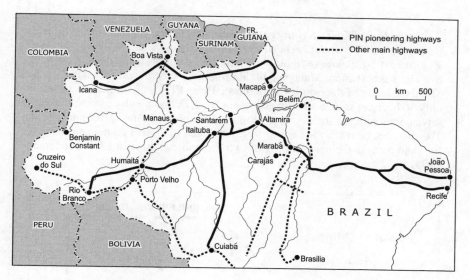

Figure 5.1: Brazilian highways

Location is also important. Coastal location, for example, provides access to ocean transport routes and to marine resources. However, the delimitation of maritime boundaries and territorial waters is often complex and the source of dispute between states (see Box 5.2). *Landlocked states* have special problems of their own. They are dependent on neighbouring states for access to ocean routes which are essential for trade and economic development. Prior to the recent changes in the world political map, there were twenty-four landlocked states world-wide (twelve of these in Africa), but the number has now risen to thirty-five (including seven ex-Soviet republics in Central Asia).

Box 5.2: Coastal states and control of the seas

Control of the seas adjacent to coastal states has become a significant geopolitical issue since the end of World War Two. The *Truman Proclamation* of 1945 set out US claims to the resources of the continental shelf adjacent to its coasts. The Proclamation precipitated a race by coastal states to claim control of marine resources, and led to a series of United Nation conferences, culminating in the 1982 *UN Convention on the Law of the Sea*. The convention introduced the notion of a 200 nautical mile (nm) (370km) '*Exclusive Economic Zone*' (EEZ) by which the coastal state secures exclusive rights to marine and mineral resources (Meredith *et al.*, 2000). About a third of the oceans lie within the EEZs.

Declaration of EEZs has triggered disputes between states, principally over fishing rights. There has also been a scramble to claim small outlying islands to legitimate more extensive rights. An interesting example is the dispute between five claimants (China, Malaysia, the Philippines, Taiwan and Vietnam) for the Spratly Islands of the South China Seas (Blake 1994), the largest of which is only 36 hectares in size and 2m above sea level. Economically useless in themselves, they provide the key to potential oil resources in the surrounding seas. The disputes between the various states have led to violent contestations with, for example, the Chinese sinking of two Vietnamese ships in 1988 (Anderson 1993).

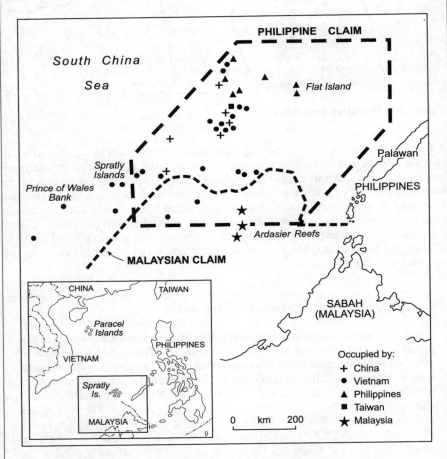

Figure B5.2: The Spratly Islands in the South China Sea

EEZs are crucial to the economy of island microstates in the Pacific and Indian Oceans. Tuvalu, for example, profits from a land to sea ratio of 1 to 30214. The establishment of EEZs have allowed them to control exploitation over relatively large areas of sea, to derive revenue from licensing foreign fleets, and to support local processing of fish products.

The Nation State

The concept of the *nation* is distinct from, although often connected to, that of the state. In contrast to the concept of the state as a spatialised 'power container', the notion of the nation can be seen to involve 'cultural association' between people and particular geographical locations or territories. The concept of a 'nation' involves people embracing what has been described as an 'imagined community' (Anderson 1991a), and according to Hobsbawm (1992) the 'nation idea' provides a surrogate for 'real' human communities which have been disrupted in the modern world.

Smith (1991) divides the concept of nation into two distinct types: a 'Western model', based on a legal-political community, common culture and a civic ideology; and a 'non-Western model' which sees the nation as a community of common descent, a 'super-family' or 'folk' (see also Ignatieff (1993) who makes a very similar distinction between civic/territorial nationalism and ethnic nationalism). Although both models hold the idea of a national territory or 'homeland' in common, the civic model allows transfer of allegiance between nations, while the 'folk' model does not.

Nationalism is a doctrine that often seeks to connect notions of nation to those of state organisation. The ultimate goal of nationalism is often the creation of a *nation-state* in which the territorial extent of a nation is seen to equivalent to the territorial limits of a single unitary state. A nationalist political agenda may arise within a given population for numerous reasons, and a variety of characteristic forms of nationalism can be identified (see Box 5.3).

Box 5.3: Nationalism and the state

The genesis of nationalism as a distinct political practice is identified with the late eighteenth century and the French Revolution. Nationalism is essentially a form of politics in opposition to other manifestations of the modern state, particularly the growth of powerful monarchical states in early modern Western Europe (Breuilly 1993). Breuilly (1993) identifies the following forms of nationalism:

- *Unification nationalism*: involves calls to bring together national territories and states. An example is the unification of the German mini-states during the nineteenth century when an appeal to a common 'national' culture and history providing justification for a Prussian led political programme of unification and opposition to the powerful Austro-Hungarian empire.

- *Separatist nationalism*: involves the break up of territorial states in order to bring them in line with the supposedly national boundaries. Often associated with the collapse of existing states or empires, such as the creation of nation states following the disintegration of the Austro-Hungarian and Ottoman empires. The rise of separatist nationalism within the Russian Federation (eg. in Chechnya) provides a contemporary example.
- *Anti-colonial nationalism*: 'liberation' movements seek to wrest control from a colonial power. Taylor (1993a) differentiates between liberation nationalism involving European settler groups (e.g. the United States) and indigenous groups (e.g. India, Vietnam).
- *Reform nationalism:* Originally a reaction to colonial pressures on existing state structures during the nineteenth century. Chinese nationalists, for instance, accepted the need for reorganization of the political structure of the state to counter external pressures (from Britain and other aggressive imperialist powers). A contemporary variant involves the state in an attempt to redefine its position within the changing world-economy. The present contest between western orientated and ultra-nationalist political groups in Russia may be regarded as a struggle to redefine Russia's place in the world.

Very few nation-states are composed entirely of a single, ethnically homogenous population, although China, Japan and Korea may be possible exceptions (Hobsbawn 1992). In fact, most nation-states have significant national minorities, while some states are essentially multi-national, composed of a variety of national groups and homelands. In many cases nationality may become territorially less than, and subordinate to the state, as was the case in the former Soviet Union, and remains so in the Russian Federation today. Forms of civic nationalism on the other hand, accept and even celebrate variety in its multi-national make-up, as exemplified by Switzerland and the USA. However, attempts to encourage or impose civic nationalism where little or no cultural cohesion exists, or where inter-ethnic tensions are extreme, can often be counterproductive. This is especially true where newly independent states have retained the borders imposed by former colonial powers. The conflict between Tutsi and Hutu groups in Rwanda and Burundi, and the long term conflict between the Muslim Arab north and the Christian/Animist south of Sudan, are cases in point. Historically successful examples of civic nationalism in the 'developed world' may even break-down, with consequential problems for people and the economy, when one or more groups feel that they are disadvantaged, such as is argued by some in relation to the French Canadian separatist movement (Kaplan 1994; Lo and Teixeira 1998).

In very few cases do inter-ethnic conflicts lead to the creation of new nation-states (Hobsbawm 1992). The fragmentation of Yugoslavia into several new unitary states is unusual (see Figure 5.2). The apparent success of Marshal Tito's Yugoslavia as an example of post-war civic nationalism concealed ethnic-nationalist tensions that had strong cultural-historical roots in earlier independent territorial states, such as Serbia and Croatia (Box 5.4).

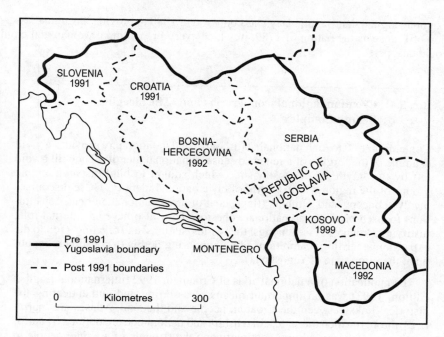

Figure 5.2: Break-up of Yugoslavia

While some commentators see evidence for the decline of nationalism and the nation-state, events in Europe during the early 1990s suggest that ethnic nationalism remains a potent force in world politics. The nation-state remains a robust dual institution in which two politically powerful territorial concepts, that of a *sovereign domain* (the state), and a *national homeland*, are fused together (Taylor 1993).

Nation-state and Identity: Myths and Icons

Devotion and duty of citizens to the nation-state are enhanced by identification of with specific national symbols or *icons*. These help to create a sense of belonging to a common culture. Obvious examples of national icons include the flag of state or the national anthem. Another important symbol is the identification of the nation with a real or fictitious person; in Britain, for example, the monarch, John Bull, or Britannia. Other icons include associations of national character with attributes of a specific animal; the British lion, the German eagle, the French cockerel or the Russian bear.

National symbols are often created as part of a wider national discourse established by the state or nationalist political movements. These form part of 'invented' histories and traditions with the aim of creating and maintain state cohesiveness (see Box 5.4). For example, public ceremonies can be created in order to bring people together in communal acts of national identification: Hobsbawm (1983, p.271), for

example, argued that Bastille Day was contrived in 1880 to provide 'an annual assertion of France as the nation of 1789, in which every French man, woman and child
could take part'.

**Box 5.4:   Croatian national iconography and 'The Sleeping
            Beauty Complex'**

Contemporary Croatian nationalist discourse and iconography provides a vivid
example of the forging of a renewed sense of national identity. They fill a void
left by the 'myth' of 'Yugoslavism', which sought to bind disparate ethnic
groups of the region within a form of civic national identity. These discourses
involve concepts and symbols (flags, coat of arms, national anthem, constitution) focused on ensuring national cohesion. They also have an external role,
justifying Croatia's place amongst the worlds 'nations' and creating a foil to the
expansionist territorial ambitions of neighbouring Serbia (a constituent republic of the rump state of Yugoslavia).

The publication of a national atlas of Croatia in 1992 (international English
edition, 1993) was an important means of asserting and authenticating the
historical links between the Croatian people and the land. Atlases are 'narratives' through which the state, citizenship, and nationhood are defined by cartographic evidence of cultural continuity and the struggle of a united people to
defend their territory. Maps have always played a crucial role in national determination in the Balkans (Wilkinson 1951), and the continued importance of
cartographic representation is clearly understood by the Croatians.

The version of Croatian history outlined in the atlas is an example of a narrative type known as the 'Sleeping Beauty complex'; a myth based on a 'golden
age of heroes' followed by period of decline, from which the nation-state
awakes to reclaim its proud past. The zenith of Croatia's cultural and military
history is identified with the kingdom that ruled over much of the present territory of Croatia and Bosnia-Hercegovina from the tenth to the twelfth centuries
(see Vujakovic 1995, Jordan 2004).

Nationalism relies on a potent cocktail of association between a people and a histori-
cal-cultural space. The map, as an expression of this spatial concept, can be critical in
this process, not simply in defining the territory of the nation-state, but as an icon
representing the bond between people and place. Anderson (1991a) recognises the
importance of 'map-as-logo', a potent emblem which is instantly recognisable and
can be endless reproduced on coins, postage stamps, and other artifacts which are
controlled and issued by the sovereign power.

Geopolitical World Orders

Geopolitics is the study of the geo-strategic and geo-economic relations *between* states (see Agnew, 1998; Tuathail, 1996; Sharp, 1999; Sidaway, 2001 for further discussions). The actions of individual states are not unconstrained, but take place within relatively stable political frameworks or *geopolitical world orders*, which provide commonly accepted conventions for interstate relations. The conventions by which individual states relate to one another are termed *geopolitical codes*.

Interstate relations during the past few hundred years have been influenced by the rise and fall of a limited number of major powers. These powers have been able to influence the codes of lesser states, creating a pervasive framework for the prevailing geopolitical world order. Sometimes this is realised through a balance of power between the powers, at others, a single state may achieve *hegemony* (military and economic pre-eminence) and determine the geopolitical order, such as *Pax Britannica*, the period of relative peace and free trade under British leadership in the mid-nineteenth century. However, such periods of relatively stability are often punctuated by phases of uncertainty. History suggests that hegemonic state will come to be challenged, as Britain was confronted by Germany at the beginning of the twentieth century, and the Soviet Union contested US hegemony after World War Two.

A variety of explanations have been offered for the ascendency and decline of major powers and hegemonic states. Paul Kennedy's (1988) classic survey of the situation from the end of the fifteenth century seeks to explain it in terms of the balance between wealth creation and military power. If a hegemonic state over-extends itself, by over rapid expansion of colonial territories, or involvement in expensive wars, the benefits may be outweighed by the costs, and the state may enter a period of relative decline, to be succeeded by a new hegemon. Other explanations seek to link the rise and fall to cyclical events in global politics and economics (e.g. Modelski's political 'long cycle model', or Wallerstein's world-system approach, in which cycles of hegemony are related to long waves in the world economy (for discussion of these approaches see Taylor and Flint 2000; Agnew and Corbridge 1995, as well as Chapter 3.

The Cold War Geopolitical Order

The German challenge to British hegemony in the twentieth century resulted in two global wars from which neither emerged as the dominant super-state or hegemon. The USA, instead, assumed this role as the only major power to emerge from the conflict with a robust, undamaged economy; in 1945 the USA accounted for over fifty percent of world manufacturing output. However, its position was immediately contested, ideologically and militarily, rather than economically, by the Soviet Union. This created a period of heightened world tension, in which the stand-off between the two superpowers was characterised as (the) *Cold War*, as opposed to a 'hot war' of armed conflict. The USA, as hegemon, framed a geopolitical discourse of 'containment' of the threat of 'Soviet expansionism' that dominated the geopolitical order during the period. The Cold War, nevertheless, provided relative stability within the global political system for nearly five decades. Where wars were fought, they were regional rather than global, often involving client states of the superpowers; for example, US attempts to contain expansion of Soviet sponsored communism in south-east Asia between 1969 and 1975.

While the Cold War can be interpreted as a period of confrontation, it also provided clear political benefits to both of the major protagonists in their attempts to maintain their dominant positions (Taylor and Flint, 2000). Internationally, it enabled them to orchestrate the geopolitical codes of their allies and to maintain strong bloc cohesion, it also diverted concern away from massive inequalities between the developed and less developed regions of the world.

The geopolitics of the Cold War were not universally accepted. A grouping of states, mainly from the so-called 'developing world', created the non-aligned movement as a potential 'third force' in world politics. The philosophy of the non-aligned movement was not one of neutrality, but the promotion of an active international policy and an 'independent political space' (Dodds, 2000) to protect its members from the interference of the major power.

The economic collapse of Soviet communism at the end of the 1980s contributed to the ending of the Cold War. The massive arms race between the super-powers had distorted their economies, but only the US was able to survive the impact of the debt created by military spending. For all practical purposes the Cold War ended with the US-Soviet summits in Reykjavik in 1986 and Washington in 1987 (Hobsbawm 1994).

Post-Cold War Geopolitics

The rapid and unexpected changes in world politics since 1989, especially the disintegration of the Soviet Union, require a radical rethinking of the future state of global politics. The collapse of the Cold War *bi-polar world-order*, based on the competition between the United States and the Soviet Union, has created a void which has not yet been demonstrably filled by a US dominated *New World Order*. The end of the Cold War cannot be seen simply as a victory for capitalism over Marxist-Leninism; the breakdown of the Soviet system was paralleled, if not pre-dated, by a period of relative US political and economic decline. It is for this reason that the Cold War is unlikely to be replaced by a stable world system completely dominated by the US, although its economy has recovered since the late 1990s.

The transition to a new, stable geopolitics is yet to happen. A range of scenarios exist, which can be summarised as follows.

Scenario 1: continuation of a geopolitical system characterised by competition for world hegemony between two or more super-states. This may, in the short term, take several forms:

a) **A unipolar world**, in which the USA maintains its hegemonic position largely unchallenged.
b) **A bipolar world**, in which there is a challenge to US hegemony from another super-state.
c) **A multi-polar system**, in which *several* super-states compete for pre-eminence, or create a balance of power. This itself may take a number of forms, for example, a division into global zones (e.g. 'Pacific Rim' versus a 'greater Europe').

Scenario 2: Increasing *globalisation* of the world system may lead to improved international cooperation and increasing interdependence or *One Worldism*, with a consequent decline in the territorial state as a key actor in international relations.

Scenario 3: Decent into chaos, in which *localism, regional conflict,* and *ethnic nationalism* undermine the ability of states to control people and territory. The security situation in Europe has already been complicated by the collapse of the Soviet Union, and with it the dismantling of the *Warsaw Treaty Organisation* (WTO) (although the extension of NATO membership has gone someway to fill this void), and the creation of numerous new independent states in European and Central Asian.

The following three sections will explore each of these possible futures in turn.

Pax Americana – A New Unipolar World Order?

A post-Cold War world in which the USA maintains its hegemonic position, despite some fluctuations in its economic fortune, is a possibility. However, totally stable world system dictated by US interests, a '*Pax Americana*', is unlikely to evolve as the events of 11 September 2001 and its aftermath indicate.

The US's *relative* economic decline during the later twentieth century must also be viewed in terms of the massive artificial lead it had at the end of World War II and its subsequent international role. The US accounted for roughly one half of world industrial output in 1945, the economies of the other major powers having been devastated by the war. Following the war, US military spending and overseas commitments diverted investment from national economic development, while its rivals (particularly Germany and Japan) were able to invest heavily in industry. However, upgrading of US manufacturing industry and development of new technologies since the late 1980s have provided the US with the capacity to maintain its position against economies like Japan, which are now suffering problems of their own.

The US has also shown itself willing to use its military strength to protect its interests and to act as a *global policeman*. The United Nations intervention following Iraq's 1990 invasion of Kuwait seemed to provided a clear message that the Cold War stand-off in international relations had been replaced by co-operative action under US leadership. The Gulf conflict afforded a perfect opportunity for the US to *script* a geopolitical discourse of an American led 'New World Order' (Sidaway 1998; and see Box 5.5).

Box 5.5: Scripting the New World Order

The 1991 Gulf War and the 1997 NATO intervention in Kosovo were both presented by the western media as a police action against a renegade state, which had demonstrated a serious threat to the New World Order. Such conflicts confirmed the pivotal role of Anglo-American domination of both military technologies *and* international news flows (Taylor. 1992). The US managed to engineer a widespread, although not universal, reading of its actions as those of an altruistic world power, providing leadership and the strength of will to enforce a New World Order, even at the possible expense of its own interests.

The myth of a New World Order was made acceptable to western publics by representation of the conflict in clinical terms, particularly the imagery of 'smart weapons' and 'surgical strikes' which pin-pointed military targets and avoided civilian deaths. The US had learned the lessons from the Vietnam War in which the media came to be regarded as the 'enemy within', undermining public resolve. In the Gulf, the media was totally reliant on the military for its information. Despite the appearance of pluralism, based on a wide range of editorial and journalistic styles, the world was essentially presented a single story.

To accept the myth of a New World Order uncritically would be to ignore competing discourses. The 1991 Gulf War, and the events of 11 September 2002 onwards, demonstrate the potential for global fractures along North-South lines, based on Islamic resistance to US cultural and economic imperialism. In 1991, Saddam Hussein received widespread support amongst Moslem populations (if not governments) which must be understood in terms of his willingness to stand up to 'the West' (Ahmed 1992), and despite his removal in 2003, it appears that radical Islamic groups are still prepared to oppose US intervention in Iraq, for example terrorist attacks on Iraqi polling stations during the first free elections in January 2005.

The message of the first Gulf War has nevertheless been diluted by subsequent events, particularly the US's inability to provide clear leadership in Somalia or the Balkans, or the failure of the 'subtle truncheon' of 'precision warfare' (Vujakovic, 2001) to limit the loss of innocent lives during the NATO intervention in Kosovo.

The cost of having to plan for an enormous range of military contingencies was, for a while, called into question. In the presidential debates of 2000, George W. Bush Jnr (Republican) argued that the US should use military force only under limited conditions, where vital national interests were under threat, while Al Gore (Republican) favoured intervention in a wider range peace-keeping type activities; Bush won the presidency (Houghton, 2002a). This view was, however, radically revised following the 11 September 2001 terrorist attacks on the New York World Trade Centre and the Pentagon. The US again showed itself willing to take up the mantle of global policeman in the so-called 'war against terrorism', which included ousting of the Taliban regime in Afghanistan (2002) and the removal from power of Saddam Hussein in Iraq (during the second Gulf War, 2003) – although it could be argued that was simply a reaction to attacks on US interests rather than a genuine return to a wider role in international politics. While the US has been superficially successful in the 'war against terrorism', it has been unable to impose real and stable peace on these regions, which remain unstable; more US soldiers have been killed in Iraq since the end of the 2003 war than during it.

If the US retains supremacy, it is likely to be because it diverges from the conventional form of a hegemonic state. Its real power has been institutionalised within a wide range of international organisations (e.g. the IMF, GATT, the World Bank) and via its material culture, represented by Ritzer (1993) as the *MacDonaldisation* of the world (see Crang 1998). Through these the US has pervaded the globe and enmeshed and constrained the activities of other states (Agnew and Corbridge 1995). However, some commentators have questioned the US's ability, rather than its willingness, to police a free trade order in which its economy looms large (Houghton, 2002b).

Emergence of New Super-state Challengers

Such interpretations of the New World Order raise questions such as: 'are there any prospects of individual states or groupings of states being able contest US hegemony?' and 'what factors might favour some states over others?'. Taylor (1993) notes that the history of hegemonic states has been one of ever-increasing size, culminating in the 'continental-scale' of the USA – could this be reproduced by a political *grouping* of states such as the European Union?

Parker (1983) identified a number of key geographical factors which he believed had contributed to the super-power status of the USA and the former Soviet Union:

a) Both held very considerable territories (USA 9 million square kilometres; USSR 22 million square kilometres)
b) Relatively large total populations, but low population densities
c) Core areas served by extensive hinterlands with major reserves of strategic resources
d) Relatively homogenous physical and climatological conditions centred on mid-latitude climatic belts
e) A single elite in a dominant position within a diverse ethnic/linguistic population; 'WASP' (White Anglo-Saxon Protestant) in the US, Muscovite Russian in the Soviet Union.

While these criteria may provide a baseline against which to judge potential super-states, there is a danger that this approach may lead to new forms of 'geographical determinism' (Smith 1992), in which other critical factors are ignored. The rise of Japan to potential super-power status in the late twentieth century, was premised not on territorial size and an extensive resource base, but on its economic power and *lack* of military commitments.

At least five leading contenders for hegemonic status can be identified, each of which will be briefly discussed in turn.

China – Global Megapower? China's massive territory and population, together with recent impressive economic growth rates, clearly place it in a position to play an important role in global affairs. The present political structure of China owes much to its relationship with other world powers during the last one hundred years.

The decline of the Manchu (Ch'ing) dynasty during the nineteenth century provided the conditions in which the rival imperialist powers of Europe, together with

Japan, competed for access to China's large but poorly developed hinterland. This rivalry, particularly between the regional powers of Russia and Japan, led to war and occupation of Chinese territory. Prior to World War Two, the strategically important region of Manchuria was occupied, first by Russia (1900–05), and then by Japan (1905–45). The Japanese 'puppet-state' of Manchukuo, formed in 1932, provided the spring-board for the Japanese invasion of further Chinese territory, including Peking (Beijing) during World War II. The victory of the Communists over the Chinese Nationalist forces following the war, ensured that a single state apparatus assumed control of the vast majority of China's population and territory for the first time since the beginning of the century.

The Cold War provided China with a period of relative stability, during which each of two super-powers – the US and the Soviet Union – saw it in their interests to maintain a unified China. Until the mid-1960s, the Soviets regarded China as an 'anti-American' force while the era of rapprochement with the USA, initiated by President Nixon in the 1970s, led to China being seen there as a 'counterweight' to the Soviet Union (Friedman and Lebard 1991). China took full advantage, particularly from the late 1970s under Deng Xiaopeng, to develop its economy and export trade. China achieved annual average growth in real GDP of 7.8 per cent during 1976–85, rising to over 13 per cent in 1993 (compared to USA, 3.1 per cent; Japan, 0.1 per cent) (IMF 1994), although growth had dropped to 7.1% by the end of the twentieth century (Turner, 2003). The fact that from the 1990s more than 5,000 enterprises have been allowed to trade directly with foreign companies, compared to the ten official trading corporations through which trade was channelled in 1979, is indicative of the opening up of China to the world economy (Edwards 1999). The tenth Chinese 'five year plan' (2001–5) and its 'Long Term target for 2010' continues to concentrate efforts on economic restructuring.

Some anxiety has been expressed about whether China's success as an economic power will be translated into the creation an aggressive military super-state in the Far East. This is unlikely for a number of reasons, foremost of which is the relatively low priority given to building military capability since the 1970s. In fact, spending on the armed forces fell from about 17.4 per cent of GNP in 1971, to 7.5 per cent in 1985, which Kennedy (1988) attributes to Deng's conviction that defence should be fourth in priority of China's 'four-modernizations', being placed behind agriculture, industry and science. Defence expenditure in 2000 had fallen still further to 5.3% of GDP (Turner, 2003). Table 5.2 provides a comparison of the defence expenditure of the major contenders for super-power status.

Another important factor is the increasingly close ties with which China is binding itself to its immediate neighbours, and more recently to Russia. Any confrontation within the region is likely to be economically disastrous for the Chinese. China has been more concerned to encourage regional cooperation, while stressing the likely threats to the region if its economy were to collapse; the 'nightmare' scenario of mass-migration (Cable and Ferdinand 1994). According to Cohen (1973) China, because of cultural concepts of the boundedness of place, is unlikely to seek *direct* control of areas that are not deemed to be 'Chinese'. It therefore appears that while China is likely to exert a profound global economic influence, it is unlikely in the short term to challenge the US for geopolitical hegemony.

Table 5.2: Potential Super-Powers? – Defence expenditure, 2000

Super Power	Total (million $US)	Per capita ($US)	% per capita
China	41,167	32	5.3
Japan	44,417	351	1.0
Russia	58,810	400	5.0
Germany	28,229	343	1.6

Source: Turner, B. (ed.) (2003) *The Statesman's Yearbook: The Politics, Cultures and Economies of the World*, Basingstoke: Palgrave

Japan – A Post-Hegemonic Power Throughout the late twentieth century Japan was seen as the natural successor, particularly in economic terms, to the US. Japan's demilitarised status, enshrined in Article 9 of its constitution, and its protection under a US strategic umbrella, enabled it to invest in modernising its industries, giving it a direct competitive advantage over the US with its problems of 'global overstretch'. Defence expenditure in 2000 represented only 1.0 of GDP (compare with other potential super-states; table 5.2).

Japan's potential as a global super-state would appear to hinge not on 'hard' power (military hardware), but on the 'soft' power of non-military influence, exercised, for example, through its prominent position within the IMF and the World Bank. Japan's economic power, acquisition of European and American companies and penetration of foreign markets during the second half of the last century has been phenomenal; by the early 1990s twenty-nine and thirty-four of the world's largest 100 banks and companies, respectively, were Japanese (Kennedy 1993).

Japan's economic status has, however, been put to the test, caught as it is between increasing costs at home and competition from the *Newly Industrialised Countries* (NICs) of south-east Asia (Freedman 1999; see also Chapter 8). The Japanese economy also suffered badly during the Asian economic crisis of the late 1990s, and is in need of major restructuring (especially of its banking sector) to transform it from a risk-reducing economy, to a risk-taking economy capable of competing with the other new industrialising economies of the region. The real GDP growth rate was –1.0% in 2001, but despite this, Japan still had the second highest GDP (after the US) in the world at the beginning of the twenty-first century (Turner, 2003). These economic factors are also exacerbated by an ageing population, high population density, and a poor territorial resource base. It is estimated that the children born at the turn of the century will incur a tax burden two and a half times present levels simply to maintain the state's welfare systems (Freedman 1999).

In geopolitical terms, Japan is more likely to seek a key position within a cooperative international system, rather than seek to replace the US as the global hegemon. This is a strategy that appears to be more likely to sustain the present world economic order from which Japan has generally benefited (Inoguchi 1987; cited in Takagi 1993). It has been suggested that, despite the financial and economic crisis in the industrialised states of Asia from the mid-1997, the long-term development of the region is unlikely to be hindered, and we may see the transition to a 'Pacific century', in which the Pacific will replace the Atlantic as the core of the world economy (Forbes 1999). What geopolitical implications might follow from such a shift at present remains uncertain.

Russia – At The Crossroads The disintegration of the Soviet empire produced a large number of new unitary states within Eastern Europe and central Asia. Of these successor states, only the Russian Federation can be regarded as a possible hegemonic contender and the only one that still fulfils the criteria outlined by Parker (1983). Other states, such as the Ukraine, may emerge as significant regional powers. Russia's potential to remain a significant rival to the US depends, however, on the degree to which the problems that contributed greatly to the collapse of the Soviet state continue to impede the new state.

The collapse of the Soviet state appears to stem in large part from the deterioration of its economy from the 1960s onwards, arguably induced by a lack of industrial modernization, together with high military spending (see also Chapter 9). It should also be noted that the Soviet Union's economy was in many senses 'underdeveloped', right from the initiation of Communist rule (see Phillips and Mighall, 2000). Attempts at political and economic 'liberalisation' in the late 1980s were insufficient to halt the collapse and it has been argued that Russian economic security is likely to be increasingly determined by its relationship with the West, and particularly with regard to the levels and direction of inward investment from the US and Europe. The loss of the territory, trade, and resources of the former Soviet republics (Russia's so called 'Near Abroad') is also likely to hamper Russia's economic progress. In response to changes in the region, Russia's internal security service set up a special department to promote Moscow's interests in the Near Abroad, and allegedly, to destabilise those which it deems hostile (Adams 1994).

A flagging economy also undermined Soviet attempts to thwart the centrifugal forces of ethnic nationalism by creating the illusion of a *Sovetskii narod,* a unified Soviet people. In 2000, it was estimated that 35% of Russia's population were living below the poverty line (up from 21% in 1997) (Turner, 2003). This problem may continue to persist within the Russian Federation where, unlike many of the other former republics, the population lacks a clear national identity. Although dominated by Russians (81.5%; 1989 census), much of the territory is the homeland of many other distinct ethnic groups (Smith 1985; Turner, 2003).

Russia appears now to be at a crossroads, it can either continue to liberalise and integrate within the world economy, or relapse into a 'fortress state' mentality, dependent on the territorial resources of a regional empire (see later discussions of *pan-regions*). This represents a traditional dichotomy in Russian thinking between *westernisers* and *slavophile Eurasianists* (Adomeit 1995). A renewal of pan-slavist ideals might ultimately take the form of forcible annexation of territory presently outside of the Federation (Yanov 1987). While this scenario is unlikely to occur within the near future, further deterioration of economic conditions in Russia could result in an ultra-nationalist government with pretensions to a pan-slavic 'Greater Russia' (See Box 5.6).

Box 5.6: Mapping a Greater Russia

In early 1994 the ultra-nationalist Russian politician Vladimir Zhironovsky provided a geopolitical vision of the future of Europe that had much in common with the spheres of influence agreed by the Soviet Union and Germany in 1939. His vision was of a Europe divided between a Greater Russian and a Greater Germany.

Figure B5.6: Zhironovsky's vision for Europe

Poland would again be repartitioned. Germany would acquire Austria, the Czech Republic and Slovenia, while Russia would retake the Ukraine,

Moldova, the Baltic republics, and possibly, Slovakia. He also supported the annexation of Macedonia, and parts of Greece and Turkey by a Greater Bulgaria (Mather 1994). The Zhironovsky Blok received only 6% of the vote in the 2000 national elections, but ultra-nationalist ideologies are likely to remain a potent force in Russian politics (see Chapter 8).

Whatever the long-term economic and geopolitical outlook for Russia, it is likely remain a significant regional power within Europe *and* Asia. Its continued ability to influence world events is also illustrated by its influence during the recent Balkan conflicts, reviving the boast of Catherine the Great's chancellor that, 'not a single cannon in Europe would dare fire a shot without our permission' (Yanov 1987:8). It is also interesting to note the development of closer relations between Russia and the US since 11 September 2001, as both states focus on the issue of terrorism, whether this emanates from Chechnya or Afghanistan.

Europe as Super-State – 'Pax Bruxellana' The history of the European Union (EU) can be seen as an explicit strategy to bind the states of western Europe, particularly Germany, into a community of economic cooperation based on a candid philosophy of peace, or a *Pax Bruxellana* (Galtung 1973). However, it may also be viewed as an attempt to rebuild a Eurocentric world based on a European super-state. This would redress the loss of European power in the post-war period, a period in which the centres of power became located outside of the region, in Washington and Moscow. Moreover, this super-state would form the core of a *uni*centric Europe, with its centre in the west (Figure 5.3)

In quantitative terms the EU fulfils few of Parker's (1983) criteria for super-power status. It is effectively a densely populated core area without a resource rich hinterland. However, strong links with former colonies, such as trading relation-ships with the ACP states (African, Caribbean and Pacific) via the Lomé Convention, provide a surrogate hinterland. A more radical development would be the creation of closer ties and the formation of a 'Eurafrican' or 'Europe-Maghreb' pan-region (see below).

The form that a European state may take will depend on the issue of national sover-eignty. One option would be a *supra*-national, 'United States of Europe', in which citizens owe allegiance to the super-state as the sovereign entity. This reflects a French sponsored vision of Europe, based on universalist principles of a civic nation-state (Weaver 1995). However, any such unitary state structure is likely to be hampered by the lack of a single dominant national/cultural group, and competition for leadership between several assertive nations.

A more likely outcome is an *infra*-national model, in which nations, or even regions, are the critical level of identity for their citizens. However, this second model is less likely to provide the characteristics of a traditional territorial state, especially in terms of foreign policy and defence. In fact, the emergence of regionalism (a 'Europe of the regions') may even begin to undermine the role of existing territorial states. For example, the *Four Motors* project, which involved the regions of Baden-Wuttemberg (Germany), Rhone-Alps (France), Catalonia (Spain) and Lombardy

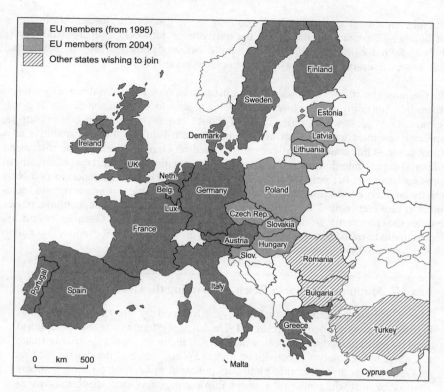

Figure 5.3: Make-up of the European Union

(Italy) exploited hi-tech communications systems to develop research, economic and cultural links with little reference to their respective state capitals (Ascherson 1992). This challenges the notion of Europe as a 'state-like' structure and it has even been suggested that the EU is a 'polymorphic' postmodern political entity, the existence of which highlights the inadequacies of the traditional model of the state (Bretherton and Vogler 1999). Its 'polymorphic' nature makes it difficult, however, to assess the eventual contribution that the EU will make as a global actor and potential super-power.

The issue of 'widening' versus 'deepening' of the EU will also affect the development of any state-like structures at the European level. The end of the Cold War has increased the need to widen the EU to include the former satellite states of the Soviet Union such as the Czech Republic and Poland. This may help to provide security and economic stability in Europe as a whole, but is likely to involve considerable economic costs (see Chapter 7) and may hinder any deepening of political integration (Stares 1992). The accession of ten central and eastern European countries (CEECs in 'Eurospeak') will add about 28 per cent to the EU population, but only increase its GNP by less than 4 per cent (McCormick 1999). Following Parker(1983), one might suggest this combination is particularly likely to retard the formation of a super-state structure capable of competing for hegemony in the foreseeable future. Although, as Buchan (1993) points out, the EU is 'the only one of the world's superpowers that is likely to *increase in importance* by the simple virtue of considerably, but legally and peaceably, increasing its territory' (p. 8; emphasis added).

The German Question The post-war settlement in Europe created a divided Germany, frozen into opposing super-power camps and unable to threaten the rest of Europe. Reunification did, however, refuel concern about Germany's ambitions within Europe, especially its intentions towards central and Eastern Europe, and its capability as a global actor. While much of this concern focused on Germany's economic role, as an industrial super-state dominating Europe, resurgent nationalism has created anxiety in both Germany and her neighbours (see Box 5.7). Much of the escalation in neo-Nazi activity and xenophobic extremism has arisen from the political immaturity and social unrest in East Germany. The reunified Germany remains an important economic power despite the problems of integrating the less efficient East German economy. Commitment to transfer resources from the prosperous west should eventually result in a stabilisation of both the social and economic situation in the east.

Box 5.7: Mapping the 'Forth Reich' – Scripting the German threat

The 'German question' is profoundly influenced by the manner in which Germany's past has been *re*presented. The images (stereotypes and metaphors) used by politicians, foreign policy makers and the news media invariably make reference to Germany's expansionist history. While much of the debate focuses on Germany as an 'economic giant', its potential to become a military super-state is an intrinsic aspect of a wider European geopolitical discourse which aims to tie Germany ever more closely to its European economic partners in the EU and its allies in NATO.

A potent element in news media discourse concerning Germany during the 1990s was the use of organic analogies of the state by the news media (Vujakovic 1993). These treat Germany, in historic terms, as an aggressive organism, in competition with other states for territory and resources. Paired or multiple maps have been used to contrast the reunified Germany with former manifestations that have threatened the balance of power in Europe (see Figure B5.7).

These images resonate with ideas from Germany's recent past. In the 1930s the theories of both the school of *Geopolitik* and the Nazi movement were informed by Darwinian concepts of the state espoused by the geographer Friedrich Ratzel. Ratzel regarded the competition for territorial control between states as comparable to the struggle for space found in nature. His concept of *Lebensraum* or 'living space' provided a purportedly 'scientific' legitimation for aspirations to create a pan-German state, with expanded territories in the east. Propaganda maps were used extensively to emphasise the vulnerability of Germany's position (due to territorial losses after WWI) and to argue for sufficient space for *all* German peoples, based on German cultural dominance throughout central Europe (Herb 1989).

Figure B5.7: Empires and the partitioning of Europe

Initial worries that a reunified and nationally resurgent Germany might make official claims on former territories east of the Oder-Neisse Line effectively evaporated after Chancellor Kohl agreed to settle the border by treaty with Poland in November 1990. Nevertheless, Kohl is thought to have resisted signing the treaty because of pressure from rightwing politicians and exiles who still wish to return to their former homes in Silesia and Pomerania.

A growing preoccupation with cultural identity and belonging amongst ethnic German's is unlikely to lead to pressure for a 'Greater Germany'. The growth of European 'regionalism', based on acceptance of local identities, provides an optimistic model for cultural integration within existing borders. For example the population of Bolzano in the Italian Tyrol is dominated by German speakers, and the Sudtiroler Volks Partie, which represents this group, is working for greater autonomy within the framework of the EU rather than for direct political links with Germany. This may become an acceptable way in which ethnic Germans and other minority groups can express their identity.

Germany may grow as both an economic and political power within central Europe, but it appears unlikely to become a military threat to the peace of Europe. Both the German state and its neighbours have evolved policies to ensure that it is deeply embedded within cooperative economic, political and pan-European defence structures; a 'European Germany, not a German-dominated Europe' (Kelleher 1992). However, post 11 September 2001, Germany has shown a willingness to become more directly involved in 'policing' a new international order, having deployed troops to Afghanistan – the first time that German armed forces have been used in this manner since World War II (Turner, 2003).

A Multi-polar World?

The idea of a world of several competing super-states is not new. Friedrich Naumann, in his book *Mitteleuropa* (1915; cited in Fitzgerald 1946: 117), envisaged a future in which five or six super-states of vast population and resources would compete for global supremacy. He argued for the creation of a Central-European super-state to be led by Germany.

Prior to the end of the Cold War, and the unforeseen demise of the Soviet Union, various attempts had been made to anticipate future forms of geopolitics based on a multi-polar system. Gittings (1982) for example, discussed the emergence of China as a potential *third* superpower. He drew an interesting comparison with George Orwell's book, *Nineteen-Eighty Four*, a vision of a geopolitics based on shifting alliances and antagonisms between three super-states of Oceania, Eurasia and Eastasia.

Taylor's (1993) review of Cold War futurology draws particular attention to the work of Galtung (1979), who envisaged a world dominated by several foci of power: the USA, the Soviet Union, Japan, China and western Europe. This group was also identified by Cohen (1982), who describes them as *first-order* states, capable of significant impacts beyond the geopolitical region which they dominate. Taylor extends this group further, to include latent super-states based on evolving intra-regional political or economic co-operation in areas such as Latin America, Africa, Southeast Asia, India and the Middle East.

The fragmentation of the bi-polar world followed from the doctrinal split between communist China and the Soviet Union in the 1960s, and increasing economic competition between the capitalist United States, Japan and Europe. The growth of intra-regional institutions in recent decades (e.g. the Arab League, the Latin American Free Trade Association) can also be seen as part of a tendency towards larger political units, capable of challenging the established powers. These groupings provide an opportunity for individual regional powers to create their own distinctive sphere of economic and political influence. A development along these lines was Turkey's success in establishing a Black Sea Economic Co-operation Zone during the 1990s (see Box 5.8).

Box 5.8: Black Sea Economic Co-operation Zone

Comprised of Turkey, Russia, Greece, Georgia, Albania, Ukraine, Romania, Bulgaria, Moldova, Armenia and Azerbaijan, the Black Sea Economic Co-operation Zone was set up in 1992. The new grouping provided Turkey with a regional influence reaching into both Europe and Central Asia. The move could be seen partly as a result of Turkey's frustration at failing to achieve full membership of the European Union and of the desire to carve out a sphere of influence, as befits a former Great Power. For the other members the alliance offered a range of promises, including regional stability, access to western markets and coordinated infrastructure development.

The organisation, now know as the Black Sea Economic Cooperation pact (BSEC), has a potential market of 400 million people and has the second highest oil and natural gas reserves of the world (*www.photius.com/bsec/about_bsec.html* (accessed 27.08.2003)).

Figure B5.8: Black Sea Economic Co-operation Zone

Galtung suggested a number of outcomes based on multiple power foci. One scenario envisages a less stable world of competitive super-states, each vying for economic advantage, with potentially disastrous consequences for poorer countries caught-up in these conflicts (Galtung 1973). He made the important point that a two superpower system is likely to be *less* unstable than a future multi-power system in which there are opportunities for a wider range of 'conflict configurations'; as an example, he postulated a clash between Japan and western Europe over the economic 'spoils' of the US empire in South America. With two superpowers a single prevailing conflict can be successfully 'institutionalised', as occurred during the Cold War. US and European anger over Japanese import restrictions in the 1980s and threatened trade wars between the USA and China or Europe in early 1990s could be regarded as symptomatic of a fragmenting global economic system.

Conflict could lead to another scenario postulated by Galtung, in which individual super-states attempt to dominate a specific region of the world in an effort to create the conditions needed for economic self-sufficiency and the defence of strategic resources. This scenario could lead to a modern version of *pan-regions* (see Box 5.9).

Box 5.9: Pan-regions

A classic attempt to create a pan-region originates from the Monroe Doctrine of 1823 by which the United States assumed the dominant role in the Americas and sought to exclude all European interference. The establishment of a pan-region is an attempt by a dominant state to achieve economic self-sufficiency (*autarky*) by exerting exclusive control over the resources within an extensive territorial unit. The German school of *Geopolitik* (1930s) advocated a division of the world into three major pan-regions, dominated by Germany, the United States and Japan.

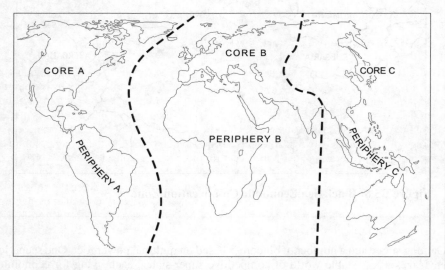

Figure B5.9: The pan-regions of the world

A world divided into pan-regions may not simply be a matter of academic speculation. O'Loughlin and van der Wusten (1993) note that real anxieties exist
concerning renewed developments of this type. They point to the reluctance on
the part of the EU to allow Germany to become the undisputed leader of the
community, and a similar unease among some states of South East Asia concerning Japanese economic dominance based on a latent 'yen bloc' encompassing
Seoul, Sydney and San Francisco (O'Loughlin and van der Wusten 1990).

Another possible outcome of the unfreezing of the Cold War bi-polar world, is a
global realignment on economic rather than ideological lines. Possible examples
might include the Pacific Rim which would include such super-states as China, Japan
and the US, counterpoised by a Greater Europe involving the EU and Russia
(Wallerstein 1983), although this currently seems unlikely.

Galtung's final scenario stresses the possibility of a rupture along north-south lines
into *world classes*. The Cold War geopolitical order, with its emphasis on east-west
relations, had deflected attention from north-south issues, although China had
professed leadership of the Third World during this period. The demise of state
communism as a competing global ideology has created a vacuum that some
commentators believe might be filled by the ascendancy of Islam, 'as the spearhead
of any future revolt of the periphery' (Taylor 1983a; p89). The events of 11 September
2001 indicate the strength of the opposition of some Islamic groups to US hegemony,
however, according to Mestrovic (1994) Islam is unlikely to completely replace the
East-West legacy of geopolitical order of the Cold War, in that divisions within the
Islamic world are of such an extent that they appear likely to undermine the formation
of a united front against the West in the foreseeable future.

A New World Disorder?

A variety of potentially destructive centrifugal forces can be seen acting against a
liberal global consensus. Chief amongst these is the resurgence of aggressive ethnic
nationalism that threatens to create a fragmented international state system built on
distrust and xenophobia. Equally disquieting is evidence that many regions of the
world are disintegrating into a state of chaotic 'localism'.

The collapse of the Soviet Union and Yugoslavia have led to the (re)creation of a
large number of nation-states based on ethno-territorial consciousness which had
been held in check by the Cold War geopolitics. The potential for further inter-ethnic
conflict throughout Europe and Central Asia has greatly increased since the end of the
Cold War. While the Soviet Union existed, it maintained a dual approach to managing
its 'nationalities problem': a long-term policy of complete assimilation through the
creation of a community of the 'Soviet people', was conjoined with a pragmatic
recognition of existing national identities. However, with this structure removed,
ethnic and irredentist conflicts have arisen both within the new Russian Federation
and in the newly independent republics. Examples include, the attempt by Chechnya,
in Central Asia, to secede from Russian control, or the declaration of a Trans-Dnestria
republic by ethnic Ukrainians and Russians living in the eastern part of the newly

independent republic of Moldova (formerly Soviet Moldavia), which is culturally Roumanian.

Similarly, in Yugoslavia, the post-war communist government created a relatively successful federal structure within a one party state, based on a system of six republics and two autonomous provinces which took account of ethnic diversity. However, this attempt to create a balance between ethnic consciousness and loyalty to the Yugoslav state backfired when multi-party elections were introduced in 1990. The new parties tended to develop along ethnic nationalist lines within the home republics, particularly in Croatia, Slovenia and Serbia culminating in the break-up of Yugoslavia (Breuilly 1993).

The collapse of the Cold War geopolitical order reactivated a geopolitical 'fault zone' in the Balkans, in which historic conflicts between nationalities threatened to draw in major powers, such as Russia and Germany, which have interests in the region. Germany's precipitous advocacy of international recognition of Croatia and Slovenia as independent states in 1991 has been seen by some commentators as part of a strategy to recreate *Mitteleuropa* (a distinctive central European cultural, political and economic zone) under German mentorship. Glenny (1991), for example, regarded the German position as part of a wider power struggle with the US and Japan for leadership of the New World Order. At the same time Germany extended its regional political and economic influence from Western Poland, through Bohemia and Moravia, to the western Balkans, further emphasising the historical splits between the western Catholic and eastern Orthodox Europe. This split is one of several suggested in 'The Clash of Civilizations', by Samuel Huntingdon (1993), in which the author argued that the new international (dis)order will be dominated not by the political-economic ideologies characteristic of the Cold War, but by a clash of world cultures, in part motivated by growing anti-Western sentiment. In Huntingdon's view, Sinic (Chinese) and Islamic culture loom large as alternative global influences, while Europe is split along the Western-Orthodox fault-line. His thesis is however contested as being simplistic, failing to recognise the complexity of interactions between cultures and the heterogeity within them (Agnew 1998; Dodds, 2000).

A crisis of geopolitics would be further deepened if the world enters a period of anarchic 'localism', characterised by chaos and violence associated with a weakening of the power of state. The state, particularly in parts of the Third World, has become powerless to intervene as local groups take forcible control of territory and resources. Growth in criminal control of large parts of the world's mega-cities is seen as symptomatic of this process. The activities of local war lords and criminal gangs are a growing problem throughout China, but especially in large cities like Guangzhou (formerly Canton) and Shanghai. Guangzhou, which lies within the province of Guangdong (economically the fastest growing region in the world), has been dubbed the 'Wild West of the Far East' (Harrison and Steinberger 1995). Tens of millions of people from other parts of China migrated to the province in search of work, driving its population up to 75 million. Many of these people have turned to forms of crime associated with the economic boom in the region; kidnapping of business people, drug smuggling and protection rackets. In recent years the death penalty has been extended, from treason and murder, to include crimes such as theft, drug-dealing, bribery and robbery with violence in recognition of these changes in Chinese society

– China executed over one thousand people in 1999 – more than any other state (Turner, 2003). Similarly, in Brazil the shanties of Rio de Janiero have been effectively transformed by drug barons into 'mini-states' in which by drug barons, the civic authorities are unable to exercise any governance.

According to the military analyst, van Creveld (1991), the future will be characterised by sub-state wars that will be small scale conflicts fought by criminals, or by religious, ethnic or economic groups. These will be protracted conflicts, with little distinction between combatants and non-combatants. Such conflicts already exist in areas of Europe like the former Yugoslavia, and also in parts of Africa such as Sierra Leone and Liberia where the nation state has almost totally collapsed. The clear distinction between 'war' and 'peace' will disappear with consequent problems for those who wish to police the 'New World Order'. Bellamy (1996), for example, argues that this will result in something close to the need to maintain a constant 'war footing', and that the role of the military with increasingly overlap with other professionals, such as aid workers – with consequent dangers for these other groups (for example the mass deaths resulting from a truck bomb placed in front of the United Nations building in Iraq in August 2003). As Seitz (2002) pointed out, six year after the end of the Cold War the world was still devoting US$1.4 million a minute to maintaining this 'war footing'.

Any widespread drift towards anarchy may result in changing attitudes to international intervention and the maintenance of a New World Order. Countries which have traditionally provided troops and resources for peace-keeping and humanitarian activities, such as Pakistan and Denmark, are likely to question their ability to maintain their commitments, while the US, Britain, and France, with relatively large military resources, may reserve these only for actions which they consider as vital to their own national security or political and economic interests, for example the 'war against terrorism' following the 11 September attacks on the US. Jean-Christophe Rufin, adviser to the French Defence Ministry, has suggested that the withdrawal of the UN presence from Somalia in 1994 constitutes something of a prelude to a general abandonment of the South by the North, with intervention only taking place if chaos is likely to spill over into the North. He believes that the rich states will be tempted to create a division of the globe reminiscent of the Roman world, in which those peoples beyond the limit of empire will be demonised as the 'new barbarians' (quoted on BBC in 1995). This view is certainly supported by western media representations of the crisis in the former Yugoslavia (Vujakovic 1993; Mestrovic 1994) and the ambivalent attitude of many politicians to the role of the UN and NATO in the former Yugoslavia. For some politicians, the containment of conflict in Europe's southern borders, rather than humanitarian concerns, became the pragmatic justification for committing and maintaining troops within the region.

Withdrawal by the North from a truly global order is presaged by the 'fortress Europe' mentality, a reaction to large-scale economic migration, especially from the former Soviet bloc countries. However, the 'ring-fencing' of Europe, or US isolationism, is unlikely to result in a division into hemispheres of order and chaos. There is evidence to suggest that contestation of the power of the state is also occurring in the North, as in the growth in the 1990s in the US of 'militias' groups opposed to what they saw as unwarranted Federal (state) control, or the gas attacks on Japanese metro trains by a fanatical religious sect (see Figure 5.4).

Globalisation: Challenging the Territorial State

At the other end of the geographical scale, processes leading to a global society are also likely to undermine the power of the territorial state. Globalisation, as understood by the sociologist Roland Robertson (cited in Dodds, 2000) is a process whereby social relations acquire borderless qualities as the world becomes increasingly integrated and interdependent. The concept of *one worldism* is also based on the notion that the globe has become the principle unit of economic activity, in which national economies (based on the territorial state) are 'reduced to complications of transnational activities' (Hobsbawm 1994: 15) and where national governance is focused on increasing international political integration and addressing the concerns stemming from a growing awareness of the global impact of environmental problems (Taylor 1989).

Globalisation does not, however, necessarily conflict with sub-state political movements, especially those associated with regionalism and decentralist green politics. Agnew and Corbridge (1995), point to the emergence of alternative political movements focused on human rights and ecological issues as a feature of globalisation threatening the primacy of the nation-state. Support for this is provided by the growth in number and membership of *non*-governmental organisations (NGOs) worldwide: between 1909 and 1988 the number of *inter*-governmental organisations

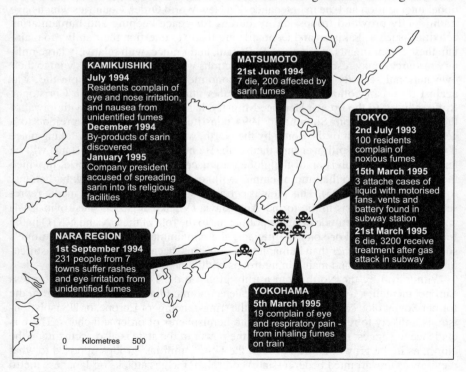

Figure 5.4: Japan gas attacks

grew from 37 to only 309, while international NGOs increased in number from 176 to 4,518 (Princen and Finger 1994; O'Riordan, 2000).

The global environmental movement is a notable instance of this new politics (Connelly and Smith 1999). Linked by email and international networking organisations, such as the *Environmental Liaison Centre International* (ELCI), NGOs have made important contributions to international policy and law. For example, the 1992 *United Nations Conference on Environment and Development* (UNCED) in Rio de Janeiro, included NGO representatives as part of some 150 official national delegations. The most successful example of the environmental movement's impact on geopolitical affairs is Antarctica, where environmentalists contributed to a dramatic policy shift, from proposals to allow mining operations to commence in Antarctica to a moratorium on any such activity (see Box 5.10).

Box 5.10: Antarctica: From real-estate to world park

Historically, a number of states have laid claim to sovereignty over parts of Antarctica (see Figure B5.10). However, under Article 4 of the *Antarctic Treaty* (ratified in 1961) these claims have remained in abeyance (Hansom and Gordon 1998; Phillips and Mighall, 2000). The treaty is in itself an unusual example of the ability of the international community to cooperate over an issue of territorial sovereignty, especially given the geopolitical issues concerned which include (Child 1988):

- Strategic control of sea-lanes, especially the key 'choke point' (Drake Passage) between Antarctica and South America.
- A potential focus of strategic military activities by the Cold War super-powers.
- Rival claims to strategic resources, both known (ocean fisheries) and anticipated (minerals).

The treaty was primarily inspired by fears that Antarctica would become a zone of military tension between the super-powers, and because of continued anxiety concerning the rival and overlapping claims of Argentina, Britain and Chile (Anderson 1993). The treaty banned all military activity and designated the region a nuclear free zone. The treaty states (twelve in 1961, growing to thirty-two in 1991) effectively manage Antarctica on behalf of the international community.

During the 1980s, members of the *Antarctic Treaty System* (ATS) began negotiating guidelines for mining activities on the continent (*Convention on the Regulation of Antarctic Mineral Resources Activities* (CRAMRA)). The issue was immediately taken up by environmental non-governmental organisations, who lobbied for Antarctica to be designated a World Park and for a ban on all mining. The high profile activities of both international and domestic environmental groups are believed to have had a decisive influence on the decision by two of the seven territorial claim states, Australia and France, to veto CRAMRA (Clark 1994; Hansom and Gordon 1998). Despite the shock that this

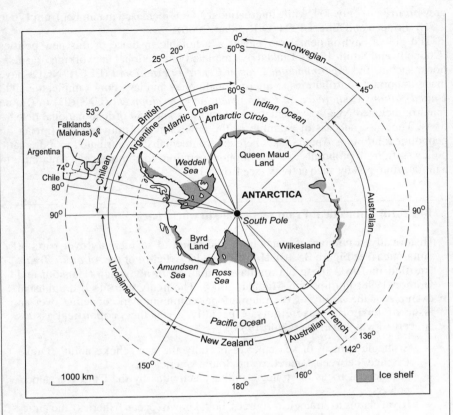

Figure B5.10: National claims on Antarctica

decision sent through the ATS, the World Park concept was taken up by Australia and France and led eventually to the 1991 *Madrid Protocol on Environmental Protection*, which imposes a fifty year ban on mining activity, although it does allow for mineral activity related to research (see Phillips and Mighall, 2000).

Ironically, one of the principal technologies by which these new political movements are becoming indisputably global has its roots in the defence of national territory, that is the Internet. The 'net', which provides a global communications network for a multitude of political groups, has its origins in the US's attempt to create a multi-centred computer communication system which would continue to function following a nuclear attack (Holderness 1994). The 'net' links millions of users world wide. Just as the railway and the telegraph allowed the state to master space during the nineteenth century, so personal global communications may presage the formation of a truly *global village* and the end of the territorial state. Unfortunately, the information revolution also provides opportunities for cyber-warfare that could result in widespread chaos with information, communication and financial systems crippled; aircraft and other transport systems disabled; and electricity supplies disrupted. In *cyber-war*, cities would not be levelled by firestorms, but the consequences could be just as serious (Bellamy 1996).

Summary and Conclusions

This chapter has focused on the nature of the state and its interactions with other states at the global scale. A number of key claims raised in the chapter are outlined in Box 5.11. The chapter began by discussing some general relationship between the state and geography, highlighting the territorial basis of state power and the connections and disjunctures between state territory and the spaces of national identity. The relationships between state power and identity are the subject of considerable contestation, a feature which will be explored in more depth in Chapter 8. The present chapter has focused more on the spatial scope of state power, looking at both the formation of territorial controls *within* and *between* nation-states.

The chapter addresses aspects of state-power through the notions of 'geopolitics' and 'geopolitial world orders'. In the later twentieth century there were suggestions that a US dominated 'New World Order' had arisen to replace the geopolitical order of the Cold War which had crumbled with the storming of the Berlin Wall and the slightly later dissolution of the Soviet Union. It has, however been argued that at present there is no clearly identifiable post-Cold War geopolitical world order despite US attempts to lead a New World Order. A range of alternative scenarios for the construction of a new world order are discussed, but overall post-Cold War geopolitics seems likely to remain in a state of flux, with complex political processes at the local and global scales as yet failing to mesh in a manner fully compliant with any of the proposed scenarios. Within this flux there is considerable scope for contestation, contestation which clearly has the potential to take the form of militarised conflict.

Box 5.11: Chapter summary and suggestions for further reading

The arguments advanced in this chapter have been:

- The power of the state is founded on the geographical concept of territoriality. By controlling access to a defined space, the content (resources, population, infrastructure) of the territory can be directed by the sovereign power.
- The mastery of national space is dependent on the control geographical knowledge and modes of communication.
- New technologies and the globalisation of economics has affected the ability of sovereign states to retain control of their territories

- The actions of individual nation states takes place within a sets of international relations that constitute 'geopolitical world orders'
- For much of the second-half of the twentieth there was a Cold War 'bipolar world-order', based on the competition between the United States and the Soviet Union.
- Since the close of the Cold War there has been a geopolitical void that has not yet been demonstrably been filled by an alternative and stable world order.
- Processes operating at the sub- and super-state scales appear to be undermining some of the traditional roles of the territorial state in geopolitics. These processes may presage a significant change in the operation of the form of geopolitical world orders which have dominated international relations in the modern world.

References which provide a useful general introduction to concepts of the state, territoriality and geopolitics include Storey's (2001) *Territory: The Claiming of Space*, Dodds' (2000) *Geopolitics in a Changing World* and Braden and Shelley's (2000) *Engaging Geopolitics* (Harlow: Longman, 2000); more advanced texts include Taylor and Flint's (2000) *Political Geography*, Agnew and Corbridge's (1995) *Mastering Space*, Agnew's (2002) *Making Political Geography* and Parker's (1998) *Geopolitics*. Other useful contributions to contemporary debates include Kliot and Waterman's (1991) *The Political Geography of Conflict and Peace*, Taylor's (1993) *Political Geography of the Twentieth Century: A Global Analysis* and Dodds and Atkinson's (2000) *Geopolitical Traditions*, while Breuilly's (1993) *Nationalism and the State* provides a comprehensive historical and theoretical overview of the subject of the nation-state. Useful journals include *Political Geography* and *International Affairs;* the latter is particularly interesting for the views expressed by diplomats and politicians as well as academics.

Part Three:
Regional Worlds

Chapter 6

Inequalities at the Core: A Discussion of Regionality in the EU and UK

Keith Hoggart

Interpreting the Complexities of Inequalities

This chapter will explore the inequalities which exist within the European Union, a region which is often seen as constituting one of the cores of the contemporary global economy and also, as discussed in Chapter 5, a potential candidate for geopolitical dominance. Central to the issue of what inequalities exist is the question of what is meant by inequality. We must be careful not to confuse inequality with distinction, for inequality does not mean 'difference' in the way that cultures differ or social groups crave to pronounce their 'uniqueness' (Bourdieu 1984). Inequality implies distinctiveness along a dimension where one position is graded as better, bigger, larger or somehow superior to another. But what are the key dimensions of inequalities?

Classical writings in sociology provide a clear message on this score. Here we find that three fundamental aspects of inequality are identified (Saunders 1993): *class*, *power* and *status* (see Box 6.1). Despite their centrality to conceptualisations of social hierarchies and the complex debates over their inter-relations (Scott, 1996), these three concepts still omit much that has interested geographers about inequality, as clearly evident in publications on the geography of *social well-being* that first appeared in the 1970s (see Box 6.2). Furthermore, dimensions of social difference that are central to studies of social well-being often cannot be translated directly onto a class, power or status hierarchy. Consider the quality of one's housing as an illustration. Although it is a simplification of reality, let us assume that wealth is a direct derivative of social class position. Even here, personal or household wealth is not linked directly to housing quality. One reason is state intervention. Despite some criticism of the quality of housing provided by local councils and housing associations (Dunleavy 1981; Page 1993), low-income tenants of their properties occupy accommodation that is far in excess of what they could afford in an open market place (Gauldie 1974; Nevitt 1978; Ryder 1984). This single example highlights an important message about inequality, which is that it has multiple, quasi-independent dimensions which overlap only in part.

Box 6.1: Class, power and status

Class conceptions are widely derived from Marxist ideas about a person's position with regard to processes of employment. There are varying degrees of complexity in schemes denoting class differences (see for example, Goldthorpe 1987; Wright, 1978, 1985, 1999). At their most simple level, classes are said to distinguish those who own 'means of production' (factories, land, capital, etc.), who are referred to as the *bourgeoisie*, and those who are employed by the bourgeoisie, the working class or *proletariat*. From this perspective, most of those who are commonly referred to as middle class are in fact employees, and so belong to the working classes, although people such as Wright (1978, 1985, 1999) have argued that the middle classes are 'contradictory class positions' involving features of the bourgeoisie and the proletariat.

To exercise *power* is to get others to act in a way that is your own best interests, even though they might not wish to act in this way. Power should not be confused with resources (money, obligation, employees, etc.), for resources need to be used to achieve desired goals, and there is unevenness in the ability to use resources effectively to achieve desired ends. Power also does not mean complete compliance. An attempt to change someone's behaviour might result in a compromise agreement, which still means that the end-product is closer to one's own preferences. Assessments of power are interpretations, given the need to assess magnitudes of influence on behaviour outcomes.

Status contrasts with class and power in that it refers to social prestige or respect. The way in which class, power and status do not overlap is readily seen for those who have a high level of prestige but who have insecure prospects as employees and exercise little power beyond their household. In farming areas a good example would be agricultural labourers who are recognised as very skilled workers by their colleagues, but who are paid low wages, have poor job security and are rarely able to persuade the broader community to respond to their wishes (Newby 1977). Note here that the status that agricultural workers can have in local communities is not reflected in their standing in national scales of occupational ranking. The basis and prestige of workers at a local level does not have to be reproduced beyond the locality. Similarly, those who exercise significant power locally might find their views carry little weight beyond the locality.

Box 6.2: Social well-being

According to Coates *et al.* (1977: 9) social well-being refers to a family of overlapping concepts that include level of living, quality of life, social satisfaction, social welfare and standards of living. Nine basic components of social well-being were identified by these researchers. These were nutrition, shelter, health, education, leisure, security, social stability, the physical environment and surplus income. Central to work of this kind were questions of distribution – who gets what, when and where (Smith 1977, 1979). These concerns have been carried into present-day geography in considerations of social justice (e.g. Blacksell *et al.* 1991; Smith 1994).

Further issues are apparent if one considers a second example, namely the uneven use of public space. Here it has been shown that women commonly feeling excluded from particular places, at least at specific times of the day, for fear of violent crime (Pain 1997). This brings out a combination of insights on inequality in living conditions, ranging from their uneven impact on people in the same location, their temporal specificity (differences between day and night), and also the way in which *non-events* are integral to inequalities (Box 6.3), in the sense that neither the specific person nor any individual might have been the object of a violent or even potentially violent incident in a location, yet fear of such incidents circumscribes activity spaces. But how significant are such non-events? This is a matter of *interpretation*. We might be able to get a handle on aspects of this by asking people who visit a location about their feelings toward it at different points in time. But it is more difficult to get a sense of the intensity of feelings amongst those who do not visit a particular place. After all, many of these people might be unaware of the place or find little that attracts them to it. But the centrality of interpretation in assessments of inequalities is not restricted to non-events, nor is it simply a function of value differences. It is also a fundamental component of all considerations of inequality. As Box 6.4 shows, this applies equally well when the issue under consideration is clearly visible.

Box 6.3: Non-events and social inequality – air pollution in Gary, Indiana

A good illustration of how a non-event can provide a significant clue to social inequity is provided in Crenson's (1971) comparative investigation of East Chicago and Gary, Indiana. Here he revealed how the City of Gary was substantially dependent for its tax revenue on a (heavily polluting) manufacturing plant owned by a large corporation (what was then US Steel). He argued that this dependence was linked to the failure of the City Council even to discuss the problem of air pollution, although this issue was regularly debated in the adjacent municipality of East Chicago (with no heavy economic dependence on a polluting industry). As with other researchers who point to associations between economic dependency and limited local government action (e.g. Phelan and Pozen 1973; Friedman 1977; Blowers 1983), the causes for inaction need to be teased out by researchers. These causes are not directly visible, but the absence of activity when this should be expected theoretically can provide a clue to causal processes (e.g. Buller and Hoggart 1986). However, on account of this invisibility, interpretations of causation are contentious, with positivist

investigators rejecting any suggestion that what cannot be seen can be used as
'evidence' of a causal relationship (see Polsby 1980, on Crenson and also
Chapter 2). Having noted this point, it should also be acknowledged that, in
research on power relations, researchers are commonly required to make
assumptions about causation, since much of the 'real meat' of causal processes
is out of sight (Hoggart 1991). Whether due to commercial or political sensitiv-
ities, the corporations and governments that have a significant effect on our
life-chances are not renowned for their openness in decision-making.

**Box 6.4: Inequalities as interpretations: The case of New Haven's
power structure**

Even if processes of power exertion are considered relatively visible, investigations of power relationships are self-evidently contentious. Following
Hunter's (1953) classic investigation, which indicated that Atlanta, Georgia,
was controlled by a non-elected local business elite, Dahl's (1961) book on
New Haven came as a god-send for those who cherish the image of the USA
as an 'ideal' democracy ('the land of the free and the home of the brave').
With numerous researchers, using (aspects of) Hunter's methodology,
concluding that city after city had an elitist power structure (i.e. a small, often
unelected, group decided key decisions on the city's future), Dahl provided
what seemed like a convincing challenge to Hunter. Not only did he conclude
that New Haven (Connecticut) had a pluralistic power structure (where
government decisions did not favour particular groups and the general citi-
zenry did have a substantial influence on City Hall), but he also cast doubt on
the applicability of Hunter's methodology; arguing that it was inclined to
favour elitist interpretations. Yet Dahl's conclusions have likewise been challenged as flawed. As Domhoff (1978) makes clear, the problem with Dahl's
approach is that he focused on the City of New Haven, when the structure of
US local government has resulted in the spatial segmentation of social
classes, so many issues in central cities are of little relevance to the suburban
wealthy (Johnston 1981; Cox and Jonas 1993). Domhoff shows that the
policy decisions Dahl investigated were of minor importance to the
metropolitan economic elite, who tended to live in the suburbs. As a
result, the image of a pluralist democracy that Dahl presented was an
illusion. The structure of government was such that issues debated in the
central city created few real challenges to wealthy suburban economic interests (Newton 1978).

As the example on Box 6.4 highlights, interpretations of inequality involve issues of
geographical scale. The remit for this chapter is to examine social differentiation
across locations. But while the central thrust of the material examined is concerned
with inter-local differences, it must be emphasised that *inter-local differences are*

not equivalent to intra-local ones (Urry 1981). There is an abundance of illustrative material on this score. In terms of electoral geography, for example, what is known as *Miller's Paradox* highlights how the local is not simply the national writ small (Box 6.5). Yet links between inter-local and intra-local inequities are not well conceptualised, a point which can be illustrated by research on income distributions. Until recently, the most notable geographical research on income differences focused on uneven average incomes across places. Occasionally, studies explicitly investigated income (e.g. Ray and Brewis 1976), but more commonly the issue arose in general treatments of regional economic performance (e.g. Clark *et al.* 1986). Sociologists and economists, by contrast, have long studied differences in intra-local income disparities (e.g. Betz 1972; McGranahan 1980; Bloomquist and Summers 1982). Yet, despite efforts to instill theoretical insight into links between intra-local and inter-local social processes, the conceptualisations presented in such investigations are rather tenuous, with empirical analyses carrying a notably descriptive tone (e.g. Hoggart 1987, 1989). For this reason, even admitting its narrow focus on *global cities*, the ideas of Sassen (1991) and others on the peculiar forces that combine to promote *social polarisation* need to be treated seriously. Contained within global city ideas is recognition of the importance of city competition for higher level financial and control functions. The acquisition of these functions is said to lead to a concentration of income and top occupational grades in global cities. It is argued that this has the spin-off effect of squeezing out middle-level occupational ranks, as well as encouraging growth in low-skilled work to service the production (journey to work, office cleaning, security, etc.) and consumption demands of the best paid (child-care, home cleaning, entertainment, shopping, recreation, etc.). Persuasive as Sassen's global city hypothesis might be in highlighting links between intra-local and inter-local income inequalities, it has not been subjected to sufficient rigorous evaluation.

Box 6.5: Miller's paradox

An intriguing inconsistency that has been identified for voting behaviour in the UK is the manner in which relationships between social class and ballot-box decisions have weakened over time at the level of individual voters, but have strengthened at the constituency level (Warde 1986). Put simply, while working class voters are now less likely to cast in favour of Labour and middle class voters have a lower propensity to support the Conservatives, the total Labour vote for a constituency is better predicted now than in the past by the share of constituency populations that are working class. The middle classes it seems are more inclined to vote Labour when higher proportions of the local population have manual occupations, just as the working class vote for the Conservatives is higher where the local representation of professional and managerial workers is high. In similar vein, a different set of associations and causal relationships link the socio-economic standing of areas to public service provision at inter-local and intra-local government levels (Burnett 1985; Hoggart 1991). The simple message is that both localised and translocal inequalities need to be considered when assessing socio-economic processes. Those living in administrative areas that in general are poorly served on a national scale might find themselves with high service standards for their administrative unit (e.g. Bradley *et al.* 1978), such that certain neighbourhoods within such administrations might be well served in national terms.

A primary reason for this, which restates Domhoff's criticism of Dahl (Box 6.3), is that the geographical scale at which global city relationships should be specified is open to question. If we are examining differences in local government service quality, it is relatively easy to conceptualise affected populations, for (usually) there are clear geographical boundaries for local authorities. Owing to the impact of commuting, decentralisation of (linked) office or manufacturing functions, and migration, the same cannot be said for global cities. Here administrative boundaries to demarcate arenas of global city impacts are not self-evident. Researchers inevitably end-up using arbitrarily drawn boundaries for the areas they investigate. This raises substantial problems for investigations. Thus, in Hamnett's (1996) thorough evaluation of London, he concludes that there is little support for Sassen's hypothesis that occupations in the capital are becoming increasingly polarised. But Hamnett only examines the London metropolitan area (the Greater London Authority area). Yet ever since the 1938 London Green Belt Act, urban growth in the capital has been encouraged to leapfrog the green belt, so settlements at seemingly ever greater distances from Charing Cross are tightly bound into a metropolitan-centred region. Some would argue that the green belt merely emphasised what had long existed, a message which is well articulated in Mackinder's observations:

In a manner all southeastern England is a single urban community; for steam and electricity are changing our geographical conceptions. A city in an economic sense is no longer an area covered continuously with streets and houses ... The metropolis in its largest meaning includes all the counties for whose inhabitants London is 'Town', whose men do habitual business there, whose women buy there, whose morning paper is printed there, whose standard of thought is determined there. East Anglia and the West of England possess a certain independence by virtue of their comparatively remote position, but, for various reasons, even they belong effectively to Metropolitan England (Mackinder 1907: 258).

Through New Town policies, London over-spill, and organisations like the Location of Offices Bureau, for some decades London's enterprises were officially encouraged to move from the capital, to other parts of the South East or even further afield. As a consequence, the effective area within which the income and occupational effects of London's global city standing are played out extends well beyond the administratively defined metropolitan area (Warnes 1991; Champion and Congdon 1992). Changes in socio-economic standing are perhaps more appropriately investigated by placing London in the context of the wider South East (see Hamnett 1986). Yet, once we incorporate areas beyond the green belt, the impact of London's global city standing becomes harder to establish, for relationships become extremely complex, as the impression made by being part of London's *urban field* intersects and interacts with more localised assertions of occupational and income diversity.

Further complexity arises from *cross-national differences*. This is something that Hamnett (1996) commendably draws attention to by emphasising that dissimilar welfare systems or regimes have distinctive impacts on the nature of inequalities between households and individuals. There is abundant evidence that nations develop distinctive welfare regimes as a result of cultural traditions, political compromises and controversial 'events' that spark or nurture specific forms of social provision (Ashford 1986). Understanding cross-national differences is critical to a fuller understanding of social inequality. This is not simply a matter of noting differences today but also of appreciating how nations respond differently to *globalisation* trends. To illustrate this we can examine the decentralisation of economic activities from cities. Reflecting the dynamism of economic systems, the geographical literature of the 1960s and 1970s was full of foreboding over the future of rural areas. Large cities, pundits claimed, were to be the power houses of national economies, with smaller places being hauled along in their wake – receiving spread benefits but not catching up (e.g. Berry 1970). How different from the 1980s and 1990s, when the same commentators highlighted the negative consequences of diseconomies in large cities and their unattractive social conditions (e.g. Berry 1980b). Today the arenas of rapid economic growth are different from the past, for the requirements of high-tech industries and the desires of manufacturers to introduce new working practices, steer investment away from traditional industrial heartlands (Hall *et al.* 1987; Mair 1992). At the same time, improvements in telecommunications, and sharper demand for office space in major metropolitan centres, has resulted in the decentralisation of lower-level office functions, as a cost saving measure (Marshall and Raybould 1993). This has led to complex organisational forms compared with the past (Li 1995; Lorentzon 1995). But what has decentralisation meant for changes in the spatial economy? The answer lies partly in the nature of the national political economy. A comparison of the UK with Germany can be used to illustrate this. In the case of the UK, the economy has been highly centralised, in terms of its *corporate control functions*, with London at the apex and other centres falling a long way behind. This is readily seen in the location of corporate headquarters for the largest firms in Europe (Figure 6.1). By contrast, in Germany, where the political structure is more decentralised and provincial governments (the *länder*) have considerable political authority (e.g. Jeffrey 1996), corporate head offices are more dispersed. In part this difference reflects divergences in political history, with Germany seeing the coming together of small states to create the present nation-state only in the nineteenth century (Borchardt 1991; see also Chapter 5), as opposed to the UK's evolution of into centralised, nationally-unified power structure over many centuries (Bulpitt 1983). Perhaps not surprising, then, pressures which encourage corporations to decentralise white collar workers from London produce few transfers beyond South East England (Marshall 1988: 84–88). Yet even for producer services, in Germany urban decentralisation is inducing growth in peripheral regions (Jaeger and Dürrenberger 1991).

Where does this place us with regard to understanding the patterning of socio-economic inequalities? First, in emphasising that inequalities are complex. The dimensions which are seen as most critical, their degree of overlap, the extent to which non-events are as important as events, and the different geographical scales over which processes need to be evaluated, all point to the centrality of interpretation and argument in evaluating social inequalities. Second, even within an accepted interpretative mould, patterns of inequity are subject to temporal shifts, some rapid and

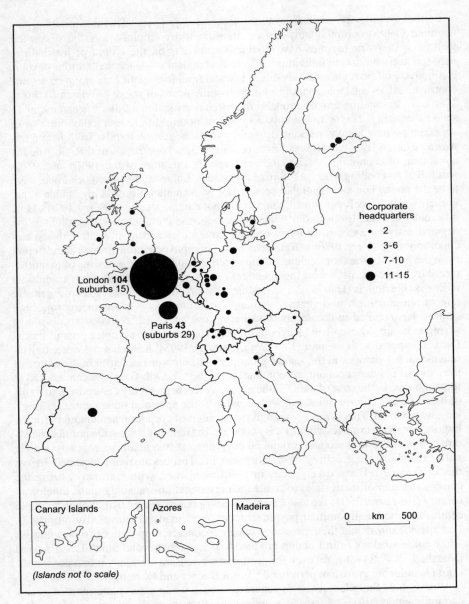

Corporate
headquarters
• 2
● 3-6
● 7-10
⬤ 11-15

London **104**
(suburbs 15)

Paris **43**
(suburbs 29)

Canary Islands   Azores   Madeira

0   km   500

(Islands not to scale)

Figure 6.1: **The location of the headquarters of the largest 500 manufacturing**
                firms in Europe, 1994

Note: Only centres with at least two headquarters are shown on this map.

Source: Time Books (1995)

others more gradual, which produce uneven impacts on people and places. Third, socio-economic change, and by implication inequalities across geographical zones and social groups, is conditioned by and itself helps condition national cultures (and regional and local cultures as well). Lastly, there is no direct correspondence between patterns of differentiation across locations and those that exist within them. This is a wider point than warning against the errors of the ecological fallacy (Robinson 1950); of assuming that a correlation between two social attributes that holds for area-units also pertains to individuals (cf. Warde 1986). Embodied within this point is recognition that many inequities that are visible at the intra-local level are disguised or not identifiable at the inter-local level (and possibly vice-versa). This is a significant caveat that must be set against this chapter, for its principal focus is on disparities between localities. In addressing this issue, the approach adopted has been to extract materials to illustrate the complexities and nuances of the geographical patterning of social inequality. In doing so efforts will be made to explore how globalisation, national cultures, sectoral changes and the organisation of corporate control, find expression in social inequities. This will be undertaken through an exploration of distinctions within the European Union and then, providing a finer tuning to examine temporal change and interactions between social processes, through a more detailed investigation of the geography of socio-economic standings within the UK.

Describing a European Economic Mosaic

Expressed in terms of gross domestic product (or GDP) per head, the wealth map of the European Union reveals a pattern of extremely low ratings in the South, with a band running from northern Italy through Austria and southern Germany as high spots. Outliers on this pattern include large cities like Hamburg, London, Paris and Stockholm, at the upper end, with the least wealthy group containing the Atlantic islands of Portugal (Azores, Madeira) and the overseas départements of France (Guadelope, Guyane, Martinique, Reunion). Highlighting the low standing of the South, if we examine the 19 sub-national regions on the European continent with the lowest GDP rates (this is the lowest 25 in the EU when the six overseas territories are excluded), we find seven in Greece, three in Portugal and three in Spain, with five in (the former East) Germany (Table 6.1). Despite the widely recognised economic problems of southern Italy (King 1987), only one region from this area appears in the bottom nineteen. The same single number, pertaining to the same region (Calabria), held for 1983, although for this year figures for the former East Germany are not considered accurate and have been excluded from the calculations (European Commission 1996: 134). Put simply, despite a lower income bias toward the South, there is no clean sweep of poverty stricken areas across the south of the continent, although the southern Italian GDP figures are below the EU mean average (European Commission 1996: 22). Likewise, we should not conceptualise northern European nations as universally wealthy, even in a relative sense. Even if the eastern *länder* of Germany are taken to be exceptional, much of Finland, Ireland, significant elements of northern and southwestern France, large tracts of the UK, and a scattering of regions in Belgium, the Netherlands and Sweden, all have per capita GDP figures that fall below the EU average. Moreover, unlike southern and Mediterranean Spain, the

Lisbon and Norte areas in Portugal, Ireland and the Rome region of Italy, most of these northern European zones had GDP growth rates some way below the EU average over the 1983–1993 period. For that decade, the real growth areas in the Union were in the Netherlands, central and coastal Spain and in those regions that bordered on Czechoslovakia and the east German *länder* (Figure 6.2). The important point here is the complex geography of income distribution. Thus, in terms of GDP per head, the wealthiest parts of the EU include some major cities (London, Paris, Rome, Stockholm), some intermediate cities (Antwerp, Hamburg, Stuttgart, Vienna), and some areas that are not known as major urban nodes (Scotland's Grampian region for one, albeit Aberdeen is in this area, with Luxembourg and Salzburg as further examples; Figure 6.3; Table 6.1).

Table 6.1: GDP per head in the richest and poorest regions of the EU, 1993

Rank		Richest 25 regions GDP EU = 100	Poorest 25 regions GDP EU = 100	
1	189	Hamburg (Germany)	37	Guadeloupe (France)
2	183	Brussels (Belgium)	42	Azores (Portugal)
3	164	Paris/Ile de France (France)	42	Alentejo (Portugal)
4	164	Darmstadt (Germany)	42	Madeira (Portugal)
5	162	Luxembourg	47	Reunion (France)
6	161	Vienna (Austria)	47	Ipeiros (Greece)
7	158	Oberbayern (Germany)	49	Centro (Portugal)
8	154	Bremen (Germany)	50	Voreio Aigaio (Greece)
9	144	Greater London (UK)	52	Mecklenburg-Vorpommern (Germany)
10	141	Stuttgart (Germany)	52	Martinique (France)
11	137	Antwerp (Belgium)	52	Thurginen (Germany)
12	134	Grampian (UK)	53	Sachsen (Germany)
13	132	Lombardy (Italy)	54	Sachsen-Anhalt (Germany)
14	131	Valle d'Aosta (Italy)	55	Dytiki Ellada (Greece)
15	127	Karlsruhe (Germany)	55	Extremadura (Spain)
16	127	Mittelfranken (Germany)	56	Iona Nisia (Greece)
17	127	Emilia-Romagna (Italy)	57	Guyane (France)
18	127	Ahvenanmaa (Finland)	57	Brandenburg (Germany)
19	125	Salzburg (Austria)	58	Kriti (Greece)
20	125	Trentino-Alto Adige (Italy)	58	Andalucía (Spain)
21	123	Dusseldorf (Germany)	59	Algarve (Portugal)
22	122	Liguria (Italy)	59	Thessalia (Greece)
23	121	Rome/Lazio (Italy)	60	Galicia (Spain)
24	119	Fruili-Venezia Guilia (Italy)	60	Antoliki Macedonia, Thraki (Greece)
25	119	Stockholm (Sweden)	61	Calabria (Italy)

Source: European Commission (1996: 134)

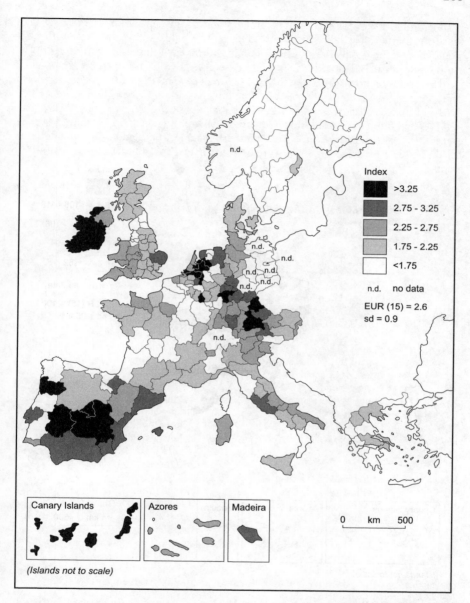

Figure 6.2: Average annual percentage growth in GDP by region, 1983–1993
Source: European Commission (1996: 23)

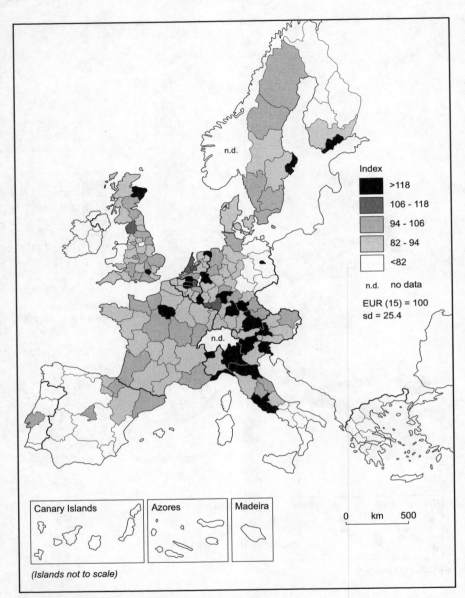

Figure 6.3: GDP per capita by region, 1993
Source: European Commission (1996: 23)

Yet a serious underlying problematic for the European Union is the perpetuation of large regional inequalities. Illustrative of this, the ratio for levels of GDP per head in the twenty-five wealthiest and the twenty-five poorest regions of the EU was some 2.5 in both 1983 and 1993. If anything the trend is perhaps toward more inequity, at least when expressed by the standard deviation for regional GDP scores (EU=100) which rose from 26.8 to 27.2 over this period, although the minor rise in these figures might be explained by the exclusion of the east German *länder* from the 1983 calculation. Certainly, despite EU structural policies, worrying tendencies favour the exacerbation of regional income disparities. In particular, the introduction of a Single European Market from '1992' reduced trade barriers, leading many commentators to expect market trends to heighten inequities in regional economic performance. Put simply, the intensification of regional integration is held to strengthen the market advantage of core regions (viz. the so-called 'vital axis' that runs from South East England to northern Italy), while penalising regions in the South and at the northern extremities (Dunford and Perrons 1994; Hadjimichalis 1994). The extension of the EU through the addition of new Member States likewise has brought new pressures for public expenditure and economic restructuring (Box 6.6). Yet stronger economic and political integration also raises fears over a loss of cultural identity, alongside concern over diminished national political autonomy and increased power for what is often portrayed as a 'remote' bureaucracy at the European-level. Arter captures the mood when describing reactions in Norway to proposals to join the EU:

> Cultural nationalism espoused the values of the living national community, of tradition and the Norwegian way of life as against the soulless supra-nationalism of Brussels and the remote bureaucracy in charge of the EEC (Arter 1993: 176–177).

Irrespective of whether such fears are exaggerated, the *Maastricht Treaty* and the *Single European Market* unleashed a potent combination of forces that have heightened tensions over European integration (Hadjimichalis and Sadler 1995), while extensions to the Union into Eastern Europe hold the prospect of increasing economic divergence (Budd 1997). Addressing such inequities will create significant political tensions, as the resources required to assist so-called 'lagging regions' will intensify demands for higher taxes at the European-level.

Box 6.6: Traumas of EU accession

Owing to differences in policies, there is inevitably a difficult transition to full EU membership. This applied even when EU expenditure was dominated by agricultural subsidies. To give an early illustration, Hill (1984) presents figures suggesting that the impact of the Common Agricultural Policy (CAP) on national economies ranged from a gain in Gross National Product of 8.8 per cent in Ireland to a loss of 0.6 per cent for the UK. These figures applied to the EU9. The additional of further countries to the Union has induced even greater threats of disruption. On the one hand, this is due to growing diversity in the socio-economic character of the EU. The accession of Portugal and Spain in

1986, for example, resulted in existing EU Member States insisting on increasing the normal period for full compliance with EU regulations for new members from five years to 10 years for certain agricultural products, largely for fear of the impact Iberian accession would have on their farm sectors (see Naylon 1981; Mykolenko *et al.* 1987). At the same time, a special regional development programme – the Integrated Mediterranean Programme – was introduced to provide extra funds to compensate southern France, Italy and Greece for the effects of Iberian accession on their economies. Adding to concern over the disruptive effects of EU expansion is the broadened remit of EU activities. Agriculture now accounts for a rapidly diminishing share of EU spending, with regulation and investment growing in the fields of environmental policy, manufacturing, regional policy and transport; all of which further complicate integration processes, as well as confronting new members with a broader set of policy compliance demands, that can clash with existing practices (e.g. Michalski and Wallace 1992).

Viewed nation-by-nation, economic disparities across the Union are indicated by the distribution *EU Structural Fund* payments (Table 6.2). Targeted at different kinds of economic problems, these payments have been extremely important for the poorer regions of the Union. The EU itself has estimated that its structural policies resulted in a 3 per cent equalisation of income in 1989–1993, with increased commitments to structural policies being expected to raise this figure to 5 per cent for 1994–1999 (European Commission 1996: 98). Examined in terms of the four poorest nations of the Union (Greece, Ireland, Portugal and Spain), the Commission has suggested that GDP growth was around half a per cent per year higher in Spain due to Structural Fund payments, and was close to 1 per cent higher in the other three nations. Indeed, it is estimated that the share of total capital formation accounted for by Structural Funds stands at 5 per cent in Spain, 13.5 per cent in Portugal, 16 per cent in Greece and 17.5 per cent in Ireland (European Commission 1996: 99). These are significant contributions to national economies, but achieving these rates has been expensive (Table 6.2). Moreover, the trend is toward growing demands on the Structural Fund budget. In part this is due to anticipated negative Single European Market impacts on peripheral areas (Dunford and Perrons 1994). Additional considerations arise from unexpectedly high rates of unemployment amongst some of the EU's new members. Finland and Sweden in particular have seen sharp rises in their unemployment rates since the late-1980s. In the Finnish case this arose from a collapse in export volumes to the Soviet Union, which resulted in unemployment growth from 3 per cent to 18 per cent, and beyond the immediate hinterlands of Helsinki and Turku the more common rate is greater than 25 per cent. Problems of macro-economic adjustment in the Swedish economy likewise saw a fall in the number of people in work of 13 per cent between 1990 and 1994, with the unemployment rate moving from 2 per cent to 10 per cent (European Commission 1996: 20). Further pressure for greater Structural Fund commitments has come from the reunification of Germany. Given the much touted postwar 'German economic miracle' (Borchardt 1991), it is perhaps surprising to see this nation receiving the third highest level of Structural Fund receipts (Table

6.2). Mostly this is the result of reunification. The costs to the public purse have been vast, with Germany being pushed toward significant changes in much valued public policies in order to reduce state spending; one clear example of which is the nation's changed position over higher payments for farm commodities (von Cramon-Taubadel 1993).

Table 6.2: Structural fund allocations, 1994–1999

Countries	Objectives						Total initiatives
	1	2	3	4	5a	5b	
Belgium	730	160	465	195	77	234	1860
Denmark	0	56	301	267	54	89	767
France	2190	1763	3203	1932	2238	1421	12748
Germany	13640	733	1942	1143	1227	1901	20586
Greece	13980	0	0	0 0	1083	15063	
Ireland	5620	0	0	0 0	304	5924	
Italy	14860	684	1715	814	901	1703	20678
Luxembourg	0	7	23	40 6	13	89	
The Netherlands	150	300	1079	165	150	232	2075
Portugal	13980	0	0	0	0	1410	15390
Spain	26300	1130	1843	446	664	2315	32698
United Kingdom	2360	2142	3377	450	817	1102	10248
Total	93810	6975	13984	5450	6134	11872	138190

Source: European Commission Directorate-General for Regional Policy and Cohesion (1996: 3)
Note: Objective 1: Regions whose development is lagging behind
Objective 2: Development of declining manufacturing areas
Objective 3: Combating long-term unemployment and labour market exclusion
Objective 4: Adaptation of workers to changes in production systems
Objective 5a: Development of fragile rural areas
Objective 5b: Adjustment of agricultural and fisheries structures

If the EU intends to bring about significant economic improvements in the nations of Eastern Europe that are negotiating to join the Union, we can expect that the cost to the public exchequer will be huge (Rueschemeyer 1993; Wild and Jones 1994); albeit Eastern Europe has already faced considerable economic upheaval without the benefit of large-scale EU resources (e.g. Inglot 1995; Buss and Yancer 1996). During such phases of policy restructuring, it is notable that social policies tend to decline, with poorer regions and people taking the brunt of cut-backs (van Kempen *et al.* 1992; Persson and Westholm 1993). With dates for entry into the EU set in advance, it will be difficult to ensure that the extension of the Union occurs at a time that is economically favourable. Potentially, this raises significant question marks against future regional policy commitments. If the likes of Sweden can experience such rapid downturns in economic performance (Table 6.3), the worry must be that taking-on a series of East European nations that are known to have unstable and relatively weak economies could place pressure on structural policies that will be difficult to resist and could result in a weakening of measures to aid poorer regions (Box 6.7). This is a serious concern, if the EU is correct in its assertions about the positive impact of Structural Funds on poorer regions (European Commission 1996; also Seitz and Licht 1995), and critics are accurate in asserting that the Single European Market will enhance the economic advantages of core regions (Hadjimichalis 1994).

Table 6.3: Gross Domestic Product per head, 1975–1994 (EU12=100)

	1975	1980	1985	1990	1994
Austria	103	107	107	105	112
Belgium	106	107	104	104	111
Denmark	108	106	114	105	112
Finland	98	97	102	103	89
France	113	114	111	110	105
Germany (West)	114	118	118	116	119
Greece	63	64	63	59	64
Ireland	62	64	65	71	83
Italy	96	104	103	103	102
Netherlands	110	106	104	101	102
Portugal	53	55	53	59	68
Spain	78	71	70	75	75
Sweden	121	112	114	108	96
United Kingdom	102	97	100	100	97

Source: European Commission Directorate-General for Economic and Financial Affairs (1996: 177)

Box 6.7: The shift to market economies and economic trauma in eastern Europe

After the fall of the Berlin Wall in 1990, the disruption created by rapid shifts towards market economy principles, plus the collapse of trade agreements that bound the former eastern European communist states together, was huge. Between 1990 and 1991, for instance, total national output is estimated to have fallen by 23 per cent in Bulgaria, 16 per cent in Czechoslovakia, 12 per cent in Romania and 8 per cent in the more market oriented Hungary (Bleaney 1994: 501). Even in the former East Germany, where the impact of the market economy was cushioned by substantial funding from the former West Germany, the impact was severe. As one illustration, Vogeler (1996: 439) reports losses of agricultural jobs between 1989 and 1994 of 45 per cent, 73 per cent and 84 per cent in the three case study areas he investigated, with accompanying farmland reductions of 29 per cent, 33 per cent and 37 per cent.

Elements in Regional Economic Disparities

But what of the underlying conditions that provoke the need for Structural Fund commitments? The first point to emphasise is that their combined effects are dynamic. This is an important message from the experiences of Finland, Germany and Sweden, amongst others, for their different regions have seen swift changes in economic standing (albeit it is likely that some of these are temporary in nature). In a European context, the southern region of Andalucía has long stood apart with its unemployment rate of around 35 per cent (Salmon 1992), with southern Italy continu- ing to languish in the economic league table, even as London and Paris retain their standing as high spots on their national income gradients. But the seeming stability that such extremes provide help disguise the shifting nature of regional economic fortunes. Evidence of rapid changes are readily available, whether we look at the impact of decentralised manufacturing growth in the Third Italy (Amin 1989), the expansion of regional tourist markets (Lewis and Williams 1989), land-based spin- offs from North Sea oil exploration (Button 1976), or the more complex interweaving of multiple economic trends that produce new geographies of employment and income growth (e.g. Naylon 1992). At a theoretical level, we can interpret such shifts as part and parcel of the ongoing acquisitive nature of capitalist production relation- ships, driven by a search for new opportunities to heighten profits (Markusen 1985; Massey 1995). At another level we can break down the components that enhance the prospects of one region being favoured over another in this reshuffling. In this regard, four elements in economic restructuring help illustrate the variety of pressures that lead to complex patterns of regional economic change.

Globalisation

For many people one of the primary changes that has affected society over recent decades has been the increased *globalisation* of the cultural, economic, political and social influences on people's lives (Waters 1995). In no sense is this meant to imply that extra-national impacts are anything new: the substantial effects that the opening-up of New World farming regions had on European agriculture provides a heady reminder of the long period over which 'global' events have made substantial local impressions (Tracy 1989; see also Chapter 11 for a discussion of European integration on the New World). However, as the decades have rolled on since the Second World War, pressures to reduce trade barriers and to integrate national economies have intensified. As dimen- sions of this we can see substantial growth in multinational corporate investment, with the result that inputs into production processes in the same company draw supplies from farther afield and from more varied national sources (Casson 1986). We can also note the imprint of improvements in telecommunications, so that it has become easier to communicate with (and control) operations at greater distances (e.g. Lorentzon 1995). Political hands have likewise contributed to the decline of national specificities, as with the formation of the European Economic Community, for which national leaders foresaw that tighter economic integration between European nations would be a mech- anism for reducing the chance of future armed conflict (see Chapter 5, and Milward 1992). Whatever the combination of forces that have increased interdependencies and linkages, the consequences have been marked.

At one level this is seen in the changing nature of market competition. Indicative of this, in a conceptualisation of market relations that was largely constrained by national regulation, O'Connor (1973) described a group of 'monopoly' sectors in which a few companies dominated the market. Unlike sectors such as tourism or many aspects of retailing, these monopoly sectors were characterised by the high cost of establishing new businesses within them, so that a few firms accounted for most production and/or sales. These were price-makers, rather than price-takers. Decisions by one company in such sectors could have a significant bearing on the cost consumers had to pay to purchase their commodities or services. Only a few decades ago, a clear example of a monopoly market sector was said to be motor vehicle production. But how different from today, when European and North American car manufacturers have lost their 'monopoly' position at home, under the force of increased competition from Japanese, Korean and increasingly other Asian producers (e.g. Rawlinson and Wells 1993). The significance of this is that some companies and even whole industries that for some decades appeared to exist in an extremely secure profit-making environment have seen themselves come under increasing competitive strain. For some companies, sharper competition has led to a relocation of production away from European nations towards sites with lower production costs, notably in the Third World (Fröbell *et al.* 1980). In many cases it has led to a restructuring of workplace operations, including partial or complete relocation to cheaper sites, whether this is for production or office staff (Marshall and Raybould 1993). At the same time, new multinational arrivals – the most obvious examples in a European context being the Japanese, and more recently the Koreans and Taiwanese (Jones and North 1991) – are adopting different locational criteria from those of earlier operators in the same industrial sectors. This has happened before, as with the siting of manufacturing plants by US corporations in interwar Britain (Green 1991). However, whereas the earlier wave was allied to new industries, much of the recent Asian multinational investment has involved well-established activities such as car production. Whatever the case, in combination globalisation forces are writing a new economic landscape; one that sees some regions and area-types grow while others experience relative decline.

National Cultural Traditions

Such globalisation effects do not occur in a random manner, but are conditioned by the national context in which economic change occurs. Clear empirical evidence for this comes from a number of studies which, in examining regional economic performance across Europe, have sought to identify circumstances associated with high and low rates of economic performance. This work demonstrates that, even given similarities in economic and social circumstances amongst regions in different nations, indices of economic performance reveal strong nation-specific effects that are additional to any effects that arise from similarities in regional economic structure (Cheshire 1993; Rodríguez-Pose 1994). In other words, whatever globalisation pressures, patterns of economic growth in Europe carry a notable national tone: regions within the same nation share many features in their economic performances irrespective of their dissimilar socio-economic circumstances.

What we can draw from this point is the power of national institutions to 'dictate' the circumstances in which economic growth occurs, although a word of caution is needed. The traumatic effects that currency speculations can have on economies has to be noted, with experiences like the removal of Sterling and the Lira from the European Monetary System in 1992 due to the actions of speculators revealing the limited power that governments have. Illustrative of this, McCutcheon (1995) shows how incentive packages offered by the Irish Government to draw-in foreign investment have varied in their attractiveness (or value to investors is perhaps a better description) because the actions of currency speculators meant that the 'real' cost of foreign investment in Ireland (as opposed to other nations) depended upon the value of the Irish Punt (as well as the exchange value for other currencies). What might have seemed like an extremely generous investment package at one point in time, was unattractive compared with other packages some months later, simply because the Punt gained in value relative to other currencies. Also to be recognised is the manner in which the 'ethos' or political culture of a nation is not determined simply by the state. This is not the place to go into this point in detail, but any serious student of European nations, or more particularly of the UK, should devote attention to understanding the peculiarities of national cultural traditions. Some very useful material has been published on the UK (Thompson 1965; Wiener 1981; Tylecote 1982; Ingham 1984; Taylor 1989; Rubinstein 1993). This draws out the peculiar impacts of close associations between a landed aristocracy seeped in agriculture and the finance sector, as opposed to ('ungentlemanly') manufacturing activity ('trade'), which, along with a focus on consumption rather than production, has resulted in an ethos amongst national economic elites that works against strong economic growth, favours short-term financial returns rather than long-term economic strength, attaches great importance to costly (status-bearing) overseas ventures, and downplays professionalism in favour of amateurism (Massey 1986; Sked 1987; Hallsworth 1996).

This does not mean that short-term policy changes are not important, nor that they cannot have significant long-term consequences (see Box 6.8). It does mean that even when we refer to rapid economic change – at the regional or national level at least – we are more commonly referring to shifts across decades rather than years. Shorter term economic adjustments, while perhaps carrying the seeds of long-term change, are more readily reversed, so that in the longer term their impression comes under the imprint of more deeply-seated forces. Thus, although the Thatcher and Major Governments of the 1980s and early 1990s made loud noises about the strength of the UK's economic performance (and how rapidly the economy was changing), this argument can only be sustained if judicious use is made of statistical evidence. As Table 6.3 shows, in the longer term the UK has not improved its economic standing in an EU context. If we carefully select a base year on which to make comparisons, high rates of growth can nevertheless be suggested for the years of Conservative rule. In 1979, for instance, GDP per head in the UK was 99.9 compared with the EU12 average of 100. Under the impress of Conservative Government policies, this fell to 97.2 in 1980, then to 96.1 in 1981 (European Commission Directorate-General for Economic and Financial Affairs 1996: 177). Despite these significant short-term drops, it is noticeable that little has changed in the longer term (Table 6.3). Politicians might seek to project an image of effectiveness, change, dynamism and radicalism, but there are deeply embedded cultural and social forces that limit possibilities for quick change in economic behaviour at the national level. Evaluations of the

Thatcher-Major years note that the economic circumstances of the UK have changed, in that we have significantly higher levels of (long-term) unemployment, much greater social inequities, and a diminished manufacturing base, but they also report no fundamental changes to national economic performance compared with other European nations (Brittan 1989; Vane 1992). We see evidence of this in one of the real powerhouses of economic growth; namely, research and development. Here the UK is saddled with a bias in its investment programme towards military applications, which are much less effective in promoting economic advancement than commercial innovations (Hicke and Lee 1994; Simmie 1995). One consequence of the resulting poor rate of innovation that is found amongst private sector companies in the UK is a reliance on innovations from overseas-based corporations (Eltis *et al*. 1992; Buxton *et al*. 1994). What we should not do is interpret this lack of innovation as a short-term issue. It is part of the culture of UK business that owes much to legacies from the past (Massey 1986).

These legacies are as much part of the governmental structure as the corporate structure of the nation. In the longer term this means that they have been embedded in the main lines of governmental policy. The efforts of recent decades to mitigate the impact of regional economic disequilibrium pale in comparison with these well-entrenched biases. Even if we could make rapid adjustments in the short-term, explicit spatial policies generally make a lighter impression on local and regional economies than seemingly aspatial policy initiatives. In the case of the EU, for example, Hadjimichalis (1994) points out that estimates place the benefits of the Single European Market at some 216 billion ecu a year, whereas the sum spent on Structural Funds are under 20 billion ecu. Such figures offer support for critical comments, such as those of Holland:

> One of the most striking features of the main range of Community policies to date is the manner in which they either outright contradict or do not significantly serve the main objective of reducing regional imbalance (Holland 1993: 186).

A key reason for this apparent contradiction is that seemingly aspatial policies have significant regional impacts. Examinations of Thatcher/Major taxation changes clearly reveal this, with vast shifts in national economic resources toward the South East from other regions (Johnston 1979; Hamnett 1997a), as well from the poor to rich (e.g. Dilnot and Stark 1986). Such increases have been associated with sharp (relative) rises in income inequality in the UK (Atkinson 1995), as well as having marked effects on national economic conditions (Box 6.8).

Box 6.8: 1980s short-termism and the long-term impacts on the UK economy

Hutton's (1996) *The State We're In* makes clear that one consequence of the devastation of the UK's manufacturing in the early 1980s is that new demand is likely to be satisfied by disproportionate increases in imports. The Thatcher Government of the early 1980s adopted a hands-off approach toward helping the manufacturing sector restructure (Gamble 1988), so that even those sectors that were viable in the long-term received scant help with short-term problems, so many companies folded. Alongside monetarist policies that forced the value of the pound upwards, and priced UK manufacturing out of world markets (Hannah 1989), the net effect of Government policies was to fuel decline in the manufacturing sector (e.g. Townsend 1983). Thus, manufacturing production fell by 14 per cent in 1980 and 1981, with profits in the sector falling by one-third. Compared with 1979, some two million fewer people were in work in 1983 (Hutton 1996: 70). Today, UK manufacturing industry no longer has the capacity to respond to substantial demand rises. The damage metered out to the economy in the early 1980s has heightened problems of economic regeneration. Hutton provides a succinct description of the quandary caused by the weakening of UK manufacturing industry:

> the economy and state now face a series of strategic dilemmas. There has to be economic growth to lower unemployment and improve the government's fiscal position but, if the current relationships hold, any significant economic growth would suck in imports so greedily that the balance of payments deficit would explode superimposed upon Britain's already heavy short-term borrowings. Because this is unsustainable, the finance markets would demand a policy change and interest rates would rise and the exchange rate would fall. Consumers would be squeezed savagely ... The difficulty is compounded because the City [finance sector] has reclaimed its ancient freedom to invest overseas which ... has meant a cumulative outflow of £87 billion between 1990 and 1993 ... if Britain's shrunken manufacturing base were able to support export growth of 5.5 per cent, this would prevent the current account deficit from becoming unsustainably large, but the most the wider economy can grow is by 1.5 to 2 per cent.... The terrible paradox is that modest growth is almost too much for Britain to bear. The economy is trapped by its own weaknesses (Hutton 1996: 79–80).

Sectoral Change

Accompanying nation-specific imprints on economic fortunes are uneven rates of change in different sectors of the economy. In part this is an issue of the balance between the private and the public sectors. In the UK this balance has shifted significantly toward the private sector over the last two decades. This has been achieved with few of the accompaniments that economists argue are essential for improving economic performance; commonly regional or national private sector monopolies have been created from previous public sector monopolies. In an international context, the *privatisation* of former state enterprises and activities in the UK has failed to foster competitive, innovative market relationships (Aharoni 1988). As in France, rather than carrying messages that promote gains in effectiveness, efficiency or service quality, the privatisation of UK enterprises has carried a heavy tone of ideology or too often of government revenue raising (Maclean 1995). The precise consequences of this are open to debate, but Dunford and Perrons (1994) quote some worrying conclusions from the work of Hansen and Jensen-Butler on Denmark. This holds that the multiplier effect that results from a rights-based, tax-funded welfare state system are significantly higher than a system of service provision based on private consumption, with a welfare state system having a major role in reducing regional and social inequalities. We can also trace negative impacts from privatisation on income inequalities (Atkinson 1995), for greater wealth amongst the already rich has a tendency to increase expenditure on services with limited local multiplier effects. A good illustration of this is tourism, where market segmentation is allied to differentiation of destination and vacation type by income, with those of higher income being more inclined to take (expensive) foreign holidays (Shaw and Williams 1994). Viewed in this light, nations like the UK, that have seen significant growth in income inequality, are building-up long-term problems for efforts to improve their relative economic standing.

Even without redistributions of income, shifts in economic bases are resulting in realignments in regional economic standing. This is readily apparent in decline in older manufacturing centres (Wood 1997), many of which are eligible for EU Structural Funds (Table 6.2). As Cheshire (1993) points out, larger urban-centred regions are more likely to be able to weather such storms, as they are inclined to have relatively diversified economic bases. However, this is not universally the case, with many city-regions in southern Europe becoming nodes of social disadvantage (Cheshire and Hay 1989). At the same time, the shift towards a more service-based economy and the growth of new high-tech industries is producing new economic surfaces of investment and employment. Most evidently this is seen in the transformation of (often coastal) rural landscapes into vibrant tourist centres (Pacione 1977; Lewis and Williams 1989; Tsartas 1992). Manufacturing industries that rely on new technologies, or that engaged in new fields of productive activity, also commonly favour new production sites (Hall *et al.* 1987; Amin 1989). In a sense, rises and falls in regional economic rankings are inevitable, for new economic spheres bring with them different requirements for 'ideal' locations, as well as their own aversions to practices and tones of existing economic incarnations. One example is the manner in which tourist destinations rise and fall in prestige, change their clientele and achieve uneven economic success over time (e.g. Nash 1979; Steinecke 1993; Marchena Gómez 1995). For zones like Mediterranean Spain this has contributed to a surge in economic advancement in recent decades (Morris 1992), with proximity to the coast bringing welfare gains at localised levels elsewhere in the Mediterranean (e.g. White 1985). However, it is important to note cross-national differences in economic change. In France and the UK, for instance, recent growth trends have tended to favour major urban fields, like the London and Paris regions, whereas in Germany it has been non-metropolitan regions in the south that have seen most growth (Dunford 1993).

Control Centres

As indicated earlier, one aspect of cross-national divergence is the dissimilar politico-economic histories of nations, with countries like Germany and Italy having experienced more recent accessions to statehood than France and the UK, so their territorial organisation has been centred around a multitude of *control centres* for much of their history. This should be expected to have a significant impact on the regional incidence of economic activity, for as Hymer (1975) suggests, the location of control centres is strongly related to the geography of economic well-being (Box 6.9).

Perhaps the Hymer model is somewhat exaggerated in the assertion that corporate head offices tend to be in regions with the strongest economies, as it describes a rather rigid, what might be interpreted a *Fordist*, mode of organisation (see Box 6.10). What the last few decades have clearly seen are more complex forms of corporate organisation (Lord 1992; Li 1995; Lorentzon 1995), with line outlets being embedded in local economies (Dicken *et al*. 1994), as well as the recent slimming of many headquarters operations (e.g. Marshall and Raybould 1993). Nevertheless, as Rodríguez-Pose (1994) suggests, we should not get carried away with images of a Fordist production system being replaced by a more flexible, more geographically varied and less regimented post-Fordist scheme. Many elements of Fordist control systems continue to make a significant contribution to the economic geography of European nations.

Box 6.9: Hymer's model of corporate organisation

Hymer (1975) conceptualises the organisational structure of corporations in terms of a series of levels of decision-making authority. At the top is the *(inter)national headquarters* level, which not only houses the senior decision-makers of the organisation but also produces demand for highly-paid specialist services, such as international lawyers, that could be in-house or in close proximity to the head office. At the same time, commonly owing to the costly nature of developing new products and the need to keep a tight check on evaluations of product cost, production feasibility, product success and market potential, workers in research and development and other high-paid corporate functions tend to be located close to headquarters. As such, regions which house a large number of headquarters units tend to have high average income levels, not simply on account of the salaries paid to corporate workers at this level, but also due to the income derived by specialist services that group around such offices. Below the (inter)national headquarters level there might be *regional or sectoral offices* level. These take charge of specific geograsphical markets or particular products/services and may have responsibility for decision functions that also exist at the corporate head office, although being a pale shadow of what exists at the higher echelons of the organisation. Mean average income, decision-making authority and the range of functions carried out at this (these) level(s) tends to be limited. Their incidence is still more noteworthy than *line units* (or *branch plants* Massey, 1984) – the factories or retail outlets – that form the lowest level of the corporate hierarchy. Here the authority vested in local decision-makers is slight (key product, production and marketing decisions primarily come from above), with salaries corresponding low. These units are important to the organisation but easily discarded if the need arises. Unlike office operations, which gain a peculiar strength from face-to-face contacts with state, financial and other corporate officials, the loss of a single line unit incurs comparatively small costs for the organisation as a whole (for one, other units can often take up any production losses). As a consequence, line units are more prone to closure than locally controlled enterprises (Clark 1976), as well as having less positive effects on their local economies (Shirlow 1995).

Box 6.10: Fordism and post-Fordism

Fordism refers to an array of social practices – particularly present but not confined to the workplace – captured in the phrase mass production and, in extreme form, encapsulated in Henry Ford's famous dictum that customers could have cars of any colour as long as they were black. In essence Fordism refers to the mass production of standardised goods, in which economies of scale in production were key elements in manufacturing processes. Fordism implies rather narrowly defined and rigid work tasks and organisational structures; a top-down mode of business decision-making. Outputs from Fordist procedures were limited in range (colour, design, style, add-ons, etc.). Post-Fordism is commonly seen to have emerged as an economic style in the 1970s. It is associated with more flexible production practices, as indicated in Japanese styles of production that result in goods being produced just-in-time (JIT) to meet demand, as opposed to the more characteristic just-in-case (JIC) scenario of Fordism (see Hill 1987 on Toyota, or more generally Mair 1992). Greater flexibility under post-Fordism is allied to dissimilar tempos of production, and the greater utilisation of out-sourcing for the supply of components in manufacturing processes. Fordism, by contrast, worked more to the principle of keeping production lines working at an even pace, so goods were more likely to be produced and stored for when demand picked up. Longer descriptions of these concepts can be found in Johnston *et al.* (1994).

When the distribution of corporate control functions across European space is examined, some succour is provided to the sentiment that corporate organisation is becoming less ordered. Comparing 1981 with 1994, for instance, there is a growing dispersion of head offices for the largest manufacturing firms across urban centres (see Table 6.4). Put simply more large companies are now found in smaller places. Backing this pattern, the headquarters distribution for the largest banks is less concentrated than that for manufacturing firms. However, whether we look at banks or manufacturing firms, London and Paris are the primary European centres of economic power (Sassen 1991). Yet it is instructive to note that there is no direct correspondence between centres of economic power and regions with the greatest wealth on the continent (Figure 6.3). This is seen in places appearing toward the top of the wealth league with few corporate control functions, such as the Grampian Region, Luxembourg or Salzburg, just as London's role as a continent-wide 'headquarters capital' is not matched by its wealth standing. This is not to say that Hymer (1975) was incorrect in ascribing wealth associations to corporate control functions. The notable decline in the standing of Stockholm might be noted in this regard, given the economic problems that beset the Swedish economy in the early 1990s (European Commission 1996). However, quite apart from organisational structures and accompanying business services being just one contributing factor in determining regional economic performance, we must recall that regional standings are heavily conditioned by nation-specific factors (Cheshire 1993; Rodríguez-Pose 1994) related to national economic performance and deep-seated peculiarities of politico-economic structures and cultural traditions. This should remind us of the importance of inter-relationships between national and cross-national processes. National factors feed into the determination of inter-state differentiation, just as trans-national change-carves deep cuts into the economic geography of nations.

Regional Divergence in the UK?

The significance of the messages contained in the last paragraph has been expanded upon in critiques of overly simplistic interpretations of globalisation (Hirst and Thompson 1996; Allen and Thompson 1997). Although pressures for global 'uniformity', or a sharing of trends, have increased (Waters 1995), there is interaction between transnational pressures and national/regional/local forces for change. One consequence is variety in responses to seemingly 'global' trends. Stated another way, globalisation impulses come with contexts attached (Allen and Thompson 1997). These contexts impose themselves in significant ways on the nature of social interactions and their outcomes. In this section such interaction effects are explored in the context of the geography of social inequalities within the UK. This examination reveals that nation-specific influences in economic restructuring processes have had the combined effect of intensifying regional disparities.

To understand regional disparities in economic fortunes in the UK it is necessarily to acknowledge the entrenched roots of a power-base centred on landed estates within the nation. These agricultural estates were large by European standards (Cannadine 1990: 19), while the early formation of a centralised state in England (compared, for instance, with the formation of nation-states in the later nineteenth century in Germany and Italy), meant that a closely-bound elite emerged that dominated cultural, economic and political affairs. Central to the function of this elite was London, which was the political capital and the centre of the social season – the coming together of the wealthy for part of each year. Important as it was as an economic centre, London owed its position of importance to its role as an entrepôt and as a producer of fine quality materials for the social elite. Despite its varied economic base, the city was not a significant player for manufacturing industries at the forefront of the Industrial Revolution (Green 1995). With the landed elite shunning the manufacturing sector, but finding an accommodation with financial institutions, the disposition within ruling circles was toward the nation's external relations; whether in the form of expansion into colonial acquisitions, increased trade or the maintenance of a strong currency. As Leys (1986) noted, the aristocratically-allied finance sector was happy to see a strong manufacturing base, if this strengthened trading enterprises. But if the economic desires of manufacturers deviated from those of finance, finance tended to be favoured by government policies.

The failure of the manufacturing bourgeoisie to become a ruling elite represents one of *the peculiarities of the English* for Thompson (1965). Yet Ingham (1984) makes clear that many of the supposed peculiarities of the English – as in the suppressing of national economic advantage to perpetuate the international role of Sterling – are eminently understandable as measures to favour the finance sector. Status distinctions between finance and manufacturing had the further consequence of weakening the impetus toward promoting rapid economic growth. This was seen in

Contested Worlds

Table 6.4: Location of corporate headquarters of the largest European companies

| | Manufacturing Firms | | Banks |
	1994	1981	1995
London	104	121	25
suburbs of London	16	9	
Paris	43	51	24
suburbs of Paris	29	22	
Stockholm	15	23	5
Madrid	11	9	8
Brussels	10	8	9
Helsinki	10	5	5
Frankfurt	8	11	15
Hamburg	7	14	3
Zurich	7	5	5
Cologne	6	6	4
Copenhagen	6	6	5
Essen	6	7	2
Munich	6	10	6
Amsterdam	5	6	6
Dusseldorf	5	5	6
Gothenburg	5	3	
Stuttgart	5	5	6
Balse	4	4	4
Edinburgh	4	2	2
Manchester	4	2	2
Berlin	3	3	3
Duisburg	3	3	1
Oslo	3	2	5
Turin	3	3	2
Amstelveen	2	2	
Birmingham	2	4	
Hanover	2	2	3
Milan	2	4	9
Rome	2	6	7
Rotterdam	2	7	
Utrecht	2	3	2
Vienna	2	4	11

Note: This list identifies the headquarters of the largest 500 manufacturing firms in terms of turnover, and the largest 500 banks in terms of assets. The data are from Times Books (1981, 1995) and *The Banker* (vol. 46, September 1995). Only places with at least two manufacturing headquarters in 1981 and 1994 are shown. 'London' refers to places with a London postal address, while its suburbs are in Greater London (hence places like Hayes, Middlesex, and Windsor are included). 'Paris' is département 75, with the 'suburban' départements 91–94.

bourgeois efforts to convert their accumulated economic capital into *cultural capital*, through the acquisition of stately homes, the 'purchase' of landed titles and the pursuit of a consumption-driven lifestyle (see Tylecote 1982; Howkins 1991); although manifestations of this were far from universal amongst leading manufacturers (Robbins 1990). Hence, despite the number of advocates of this 'cultural' explanation for the 'peculiarities' of the English, a word of caution is merited. Rubinstein (1990), for one, has argued that there is probably more strength in the view that any cultural peculiarities that existed arose from the uniqueness of the economy, rather than vice-versa. But irrespective of the precise bases of causation, an emphasis on consumption, status-laden symbols of class-distinction, and splits between finance-manufacturing, made deep impressions on geographical disparities in wealth within the UK.

The finance-manufacturing split, for one, has overt spatial reference points. Most obvious in the nineteenth century, we find this expressed in the stronger assertion of capitalist industrial mass production relations in the northern realms of the land, while places like East Anglia and the South West retained a strong agricultural bias, and the South East, or more particularly London, saw a disproportionate share of the state bureaucracy and the paraphernalia associated with the social season and the court. The divide was also expressed in terms of modes of production within agriculture, for in comparison with central and southern England, the rest of England saw much higher shares of land residing in the hands of the great land owners. In places like Middlesex and Cambridgeshire, for instance, the share of the land that under the control of yeoman farmers and small proprietors was significant by the later nineteenth century (Clemenson 1982). As we move into the twentieth century, this combination of a consumption-led environment, occupied as it was by a disproportionate share of the nation's middle ranking (state and company) officials, plus the absence of strongly supportive trade union sentiments, provided an attractive package for foreign (and particularly US) corporate investment. What added to the attractions of the South East in the inter-war years was the character of the new industries that these (often foreign) firms were establishing, primarily centred on selling household and consumption goods. The inter-war era thereby saw the emergence of new industrial zones in and around London, such as Western Avenue, the North Circular Road and the Great West Road which provided homes for US companies like Firestone, Gillette and Hoover, plus Dagenham, Luton and Slough. London had a number of attractions for such firms. For one, much like more recent inflows of Japanese corporations (Mair 1992), in settling away from the main loci of existing manufacturing production, incoming industries were better able to establish new work practices. In addition, with its port functions and nascent airline development, London was well equipped for (comparatively) rapid communication with other parts of the globe. Some sense of the role of London in these new industrial initiatives is gleaned from the fact that, between 1932 and 1938, 43 per cent of all new manufacturing plants in the UK were located in London (Green 1991: 25).

Further enhancing the South East economy was the concentration of national government work within the region. Quite apart from the administrative personnel the region housed – the numbers for which were disproportionately large compared to many countries, due to the colonial possessions of the UK and the role it then occupied in international relations – there was a substantial over-representation in the nation's defence industries (equalled 61 per cent of defence employment in 1931; Law 1981), along with an over-representation of governmental research institutes which (later) became an important base for the concentration of high technology industries in the region (Hall *et al*. 1987). All this provided a very distinctive landscape for London, with the growth of middle class suburbs in places like Bromley, Croydon and Hendon occurring with such vigour that the fear of urban sprawl led to the passing of the first green belt act in an effort to control further physical growth in the capital. This dynamism in the London-centred region stood in stark contrast with more northerly parts of the nation (Ward 1988). But the factors that made London and surrounding counties stand apart at this time were not simply a strong absolute performance. As far as regional economic imbalances were concerned, what was equally important was the devastating economic woes of many other regions (Massey 1986). Unlike the new industries of the South East, with their orientation towards local sales of consumer goods, the nation's 'heavy' manufacturing and mining industries had been conditioned by the UK playing a major role in world trade, over many decades. During the Great Depression in the 1930s, with nations reducing imports in the vane hope of preserving home jobs, these industries found their markets disappearing. Offering one illustration of the devastating impact this had, in the shipbuilding industry of North East England, some 60 per cent of the workforce was unemployed in the 1930s (Hudson 1989).

The emergence of such sharp regional economic disparities warns against too literal a reading of Dunford and Fielding's (1997: 265) statement that the crisis of Fordism that occurred in the 1970s meant that 'a significant divergence in the economic performance of British cities and regions was set in motion'. Critical divergences were well established long before the 1970s. Certainly there were government efforts to mitigate their effects, but the overall contribution of UK Government efforts to address regional imbalances is questionable, to say the least (Hudson 1989), and cannot be seen as making more than a marginal imprint at best (e.g. Edwards and Batley 1978). Indeed, in various ways government efforts worsened the situation of economically depressed areas. Set against a backcloth of continuing relative national economic decline (Sked 1987), UK Government encouragement of corporate mergers, so as to better equip companies to compete with giant foreign corporations, provides a ready example. No matter what impact this had on UK corporate performance, such mergers made clear inroads into the ability of peripheral regions to develop high-level corporate functions, and associated high income-generating support services. A key reason was the dominance of London as a corporate headquarters centre. As Goddard and Smith (1978) make clear, acquisition activity merely emphasised the central position of London as a centre of corporate power. Moreover, the process of acquisition commonly stripped peripheral areas of higher-level management functions. This is because, after merger or take-over, new companies commonly rationalise their operations by closing office, research and development and other higher-grade functions in peripheral zones, in order to concentrate activity close to corporate head offices (Leigh and North 1978), which are disproportionately in London and the South East. Enter the 1980s, with the Conservative Party holding to the ideological belief that higher rates of income inequality enhanced entrepreneurial incentives and so national economic performance, and we find governmental policies further increasing regional disparities (Johnston 1979; Hamnett 1997). To those who had, more was given.

Further intensifying regional disparity was growth in service industries. The 1970s, with its huge rises in oil prices, saw massive increases in OPEC oil revenues, which provided a significant boost to the UK financial services sector. A major reason was that petroleum was paid for in dollars, which generated a massive supply of (Euro)dollars. These were receipts in the US currency, held outside the USA. They could not readily find a home back in the USA due to the enormous deficits the US was running in its trade in physical goods and services (along with outflows of dollars in the form of US aid to other nations). Put simply, there was insufficient global demand for US products and services to soak up the vast quantities of dollars that had already seeped out of the US economy (Cox 1987). London had already become a central venue for the recycling, or economic utilisation, of these (Euro)dollars, helped in part by sharing a common language with the US, as well as by having an established reputation in international banking. Even before the oil price hikes, these (Euro)dollars had helped the UK banking sector fight-off competition that threatened to see London's world role decline. With the 1970s arrival of increased oil receipts, London's position received a further boost, as did the fortunes of the South East economy (e.g. Kettell and Magnus 1986). But this external prompt did not remove competitive threats to London's prominent position. In response to these challenges, the Conservative Government sought to enhance the competitive edge of London by deregulating financial markets in 1986 (the so-called 'Big Bang'). This induced a significant artificial boost to the London and South East economy. New office buildings designed for the requirements of a computer age sprung-up rapidly (Diamond 1991; Fainstein 1994). This major restructuring of London's office space could not have been achieved without strong national government support. This was willingly forthcoming, unlike the Government's response to manufacturing industries a few years earlier, with a critical element in this restructuring being the transformation of London's Docklands into an economic growth node (Brownill 1990). It is certainly the case that financial deregulation, alongside governmental insistence that this area of London was to be used to give employers opportunities to relocate and restructure their operations (e.g. the newspaper industry), meant that the capital city had an in-built demand for brownfield investment sites close to its centre (Hall 1991).

In this regard, as a venue of focused and substantial state aid, London's Docklands should have performed better than other Urban Development Corporations. Yet the contrast between Docklands and other urban aid zones raises the question of how appropriate such initiatives were for other regions (Stoker 1989; Moore 1990). On a broader front, there was a reluctance on the part of Conservative administrations to engage effectively in policies aimed either at mitigating regional disparities or assisting the poorest regions to overcome their structural economic problems (Turner 1994; McAleavey 1995). A combination of Government unwillingness to call on available European Union resources to help such areas, the diversion of European funds away from regional development into extravagances designed to make soon to be privatised companies more attractive to private investors, and considerable delays in funding allocations, led to severe criticism of the Conservative Government from Europe (see Plate 6.1), as well as efforts by local groups to by-pass the national government and appeal for assistance directly from Brussels (e.g. Turner 1994).

Delays put further grants for hard-hit regions at risk

Britain told to pass on EC funds for pits

Simon Beavis and
Martyn Halsall

THE Government has come under renewed fire for holding up European Community funds designated for areas hit by the run-down of the coal industry by failing to pay out an estimated £38 million it has already received.

The funds are the first tranche of £124 million of grants under the so-called Rechar programme, which was held up for almost two years until last February in a bruising dispute with the Commission.

But the Government's failure, six months after the settlement of the dispute, to begin using the money, has now brought warnings that further delays could jeopardise the UK's chances of drawing down the remaining £86 million designated to British coalfields.

News of the continuing delay comes at a time when ministers are wrangling over how to put together an aid package to help mining communities, having drawn up a list of 30 new pits to be closed in the run up to British Coal's privatisation.

The run-down of the industry was again underlined yesterday when BC announced it was to cut 580 jobs at the Daw Mill pit, the last remaining mine serving the rich reserves of the so-called Warwickshire Thick seam.

Last week the Guardian published a letter from Industry Minister Tim Sainsbury to Michael Portillo, the Treasury Chief Secretary, revealing a deep divide in government over new funding.

In his letter, Mr Sainsbury seeks Treasury support to back a fresh application for extra-Rechar funds, a suggestion the Commission has scotched, despite the delays.

Under the Rechar programme, which covers the period 1990 to 1993, a complicated system of accounting means that only portions of the total budget allocated to the UK are released at a time. Further money cannot be drawn down unless the original allocation has been spent.

The 11 Rechar programmes covering parts of Scotland, Wales and England, have begun receiving a flood of project proposals. But the process of approving projects and allocating funds has hardly begun.

Wayne David, Labour MEP for South Wales, warned that further money could now be lost to the UK if it failed to approve sufficient projects before the expiry of the programme at the end of 1993.

"It is quite scandalous what the Government is doing. It is hanging on to money earmarked for hard-pressed coalfields and playing politics with its own regions," he said.

Delays caused by the initial row have been exacerbated by the election. But the DTI plays down fears that the UK may run out of time.

It has been pointed out that the Government is free to spend money on projects up to two years after they are approved and could also apply to the Commission for an extension.

However the Commission has told the Government it is concerned about the delays. It has asked for assurances that lost time is made up.

One source involved in negotiations for Rechar funds, in which the DTI is the lead department, said last night: "There are some indications that it's not easy for local authorities to come forward with projects, given the way in which the Government has set the rules on this."

The amount of interest in Rechar schemes — "in which we are now at the beginning, even though we are half way through" — could build up into a more effective case for Rechar 2, said another source.

More than 400 local authorities in six EC countries this week launched a campaign for Rechar 2 amid fears that it should not be seen as the financial fuel for more UK pit closures.

Plate 6.1: Turning to Europe
'Britain told to pass on EC funds for pits', Simon Beavis and Martyn Halsall, *The Guardian*, 26 September 1992: 38.

This does not mean that government policies proved consistently bountiful for London and the South East. The artificial bubble created by the 'Big Bang' soon burst. The shake-up that resulted after the immediate euphoria of the 'Big Bang', added to the hang-over from Chancellor Lawson's boom-inducing policies, led to increased job insecurity, a shedding of white-collar jobs, and a collapse in house prices (Hutton 1996), with the South East taking the brunt of the cuts that resulted (e.g. Hamnett 1993). The mood created by this shift was well illustrated in the titles of newspaper articles (see Plate 6.2), although statements as to the demise of North-South divisions were replaced a few years later by declarations that the South was once more doing (relatively) alright (see Plate 6.3). As Martin (1995) makes clear, while there is no doubt that the South did lose more jobs in the early 1990s than more northern regions, these years constituted a temporary blip, rather than a fundamental realignment, of regional fortunes.

Critical for regional disparities is not what happens in the short-term but where longer term trends are leading. Viewed in this way we are still faced with a corporate economy that is heavily centred on London and nearby urban centres (Figure 6.1). Even when corporations bauk at the high costs of office space and employees' pay in London, their decentralisation efforts rarely take them outside the South East (Marshall and Raybould 1993). Higher paid and middle ranking white-collar work stays disproportionately in this region. This occurs in a context in which high technology industry is centred on southern locations (Hall *et al.* 1987). It occurs at a time when global economic trends are seeing a strengthening of service industries (and particularly of producer services); the very industries that give the South East its economic strength. It occurs against a backcloth in which government policies have not favoured the manufacturing sector, so this sector has seen its share of the UK economy fall, whether in terms of employment or production, with disproportionate shares of these losses falling outside the South East. It exists within a regional setting that has the potential for an enhanced centrality in a European context, given the greater ease of travel afforded by the Channel Tunnel. Quoting French ideas on these issues, Dunford and Fielding (1997) note that those countries that have poorer economic growth performances, such as the UK, the USA and potentially France, tend to have leading cities that are best described as a megalopolis. By contrast those with better economic performances are more inclined to have leading centres that are metropolitan (e.g. Milan and Munich), rather than megalopolitan. This is an interesting observation, although, as Dunford and Fielding note, it needs to be treated with some caution, given the positions of Seoul and Tokyo. At this point it is an observation – a comment on a pattern – no more.

As an explanation, the linking of settlement structure to economic growth rates carries too much of a ring of geographical determinism. It implies that the character of the central city is reflected in national economic performance, rather than vice-versa. Alternative explanations are easy to provide, assuming that we accept that London is a megalopolis in the first place, which seems highly stretched given green belt policies, and if megalopolis is taken to mean a city with an extensive urban field, then part of the explanation lies in transport networks, urban functions and size. But let us take the explanation as it stands. More satisfying than linking growth rates to urban features is acknowledging the positioning of nations within the changing international political economy. Offering a potential theoretical explanation, Pareto long

End of great divide as South-east is dragged into the jobless mire

Debate

Adam Tickell

••••••••••••••••••••

TWO YEARS of recession seem to have achieved something unthinkable for most of the past 30 years — the end of the British regional economic divide.

As the British economy boomed during the 1980s, a growing chorus of politicians, academics and journalists pointed to the fact that economic growth was a largely southern-based phenomenon. The Guardian ran 29 stories about the so-called "north-south divide" in the first six months of 1987 while Mrs Thatcher complained that northerners were "moaning minnies" who should "get on their bikes and find work".

The end of the north-south divide is most marked by changes in the geography of unemployment. The southern regions were the main beneficiaries of falling unemployment levels after 1986 — joblessness in the South-east was typically one-half or one-third of that in the north of England and on the "Celtic fringe". Since the middle of 1990, when unemployment levels began to rise again, there has been a marked evening out of unemployment rates, which are now marginally higher in the South-east than in Scotland.

Labour's industry spokesman, Derek Fatchett, argued in Manchester last November that "the new geography of Conservative economic failure means that, with the once affluent South-east now facing levels of unemployment previously only seen in the north, there is a need for a radical re-think of regional policy".

However, unemployment levels tell only part of the story. During the 1980s unemployment grew at the same time as the total number of people employed increased, because new people entered the labour market and part-time work grew.

The changing geography of employment is important. In the past two years, the total number of people employed in the UK has fallen by more than one million. The table shows that half of this decline occurred in just one region — the South-east, which has seen employment fall by 7.8 per cent.

Source: Employment Gazette

Financial service employment change 1990-92

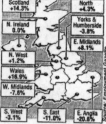

Scotland +14.3%	North +4.3%
N. Ireland 0.0%	Yorks & Humberside -3.8%
N. West +1.2%	E. Midlands +8.1%
Wales +16.9%	
W. Midlands -7.6%	
S. West -3.1%	S. East -11.0%	E. Anglia -20.6%

So the number of people working in the South-east region has fallen at twice the speed of the declines in the north of England, while Scotland saw a negligible increase in employment between June, 1990 and June, 1992.

Part of the explanation is simple. The south benefited from the economic growth of the eighties, which stemmed from the growth of financial services and consumer spending. Employment in financial services in the South-east, for example, grew from 10.8 per cent of regional employment in 1979 to 17.4 per cent in the peak year of 1990. More strikingly, in the same region more than three-quarters of people worked in services, compared to 60 per cent in the East Midlands. Because the recession started in the service sector, we would expect the region with the heaviest concentration of services to be hardest hit.

While the south of England is suffering from a continual erosion of the service sector, much of the north and west has experienced a growth in services during the past two years. The picture is slightly more complicated than the table suggests because public sector employment in the south has increased while private sector employment has collapsed. Financial service employment in East Anglia fell by 21 per cent, at the same time as it grew by 17 per cent in Wales (although Wales still has only 3½ per cent of financial service jobs).

With banks and insurance companies indicating future redundancies, it suggests the problems of the service sector in the south cannot be attributed solely to the recession and it is unlikely services can be as they

Selected regional economic indicators

| | Services employment change, 1990-92 | | Manufacturing employm't change, 1990-92 | |
	('000s)	(%)	('000s)	(%)
South East	-329	-5.9	-154	-13.8
East Anglia	-13	-2.4	-16	-9.7
South West	-4	-0.3	-51	-15.8
West Midlands	-21	-1.7	-104	-18.2
East Midlands	+20	+2.1	-39	-8.8
Yorks & Humber	-13	-1.1	-40	-8.7
North West	+10	+0.6	-74	-12.9
North	-3	-0.4	-18	-7.1
Wales	-10	-1.5	-21	-9.5
Scotland	+68	+4.8	-31	-8.4
N Ireland	+2	+0.5	-7	-7.1
United Kingdom	**-293**	**-1.9**	**-555**	**-12.1**

Source: Department of Employment Gazette, various issues.

were in the 1980s, the engine of the UK economy in general and the south in particular.

Before northerners start crowing, they should take a look at the decline of employment in manufacturing during the past two years. Unlike in the services sector, where economic decline has been concentrated in the south, falling employment levels in manufacturing have been dramatic — running at proportionately six times the decline in services — and fairly evenly distributed across the country.

There are more than half-a-million fewer people working in manufacturing than there were two years ago. Every region is suffering and particularly worrying is the fact that the three regions with most manufacturing industry — the South-east, the West Midlands and the North-west — have suffered the

largest percentage job losses. This means that the areas with most manufacturing industry are contracting at a faster rate than the norm.

In 1952, Ian McLeod espoused his version of one-nation Conservatism. It seems fitting that John Major, who has often expressed his admiration of McLeod, is presiding over the breakdown of the "two nations" economy of the 1980s. What is tragic and worrying is that the end of the north-south divide has been achieved by dragging the south into the mire, rather than by adhering to McLeod's insight that "the proof that we are one nation is that only in conditions of economic expansion can the needs of the problem areas be fully met".

Dr Adam Tickell is a lecturer in the School of Geography at the University of Leeds.

Indicators

TODAY — US: Purchasing managers index.

US: Construction spending.

TOMORROW — UK: Official reserves.

US: Fiscal 1994 budget released.

WEDNESDAY — US: Treasury 7 year note.

THURSDAY: No major releases today.

FRIDAY — US: Civilian unemployment rate.

US: Payroll employment.

US: Consumer credit.

Source: Chase.

Tourist rates — Bank sells

Australia	2.14	Hong Kong	11.35	Norway	10.23
Austria	16.75	India	43.43	Portugal	215.00
Belgium	48.75	Ireland	0.905	Saudi	5.66
Canada	1.865	Israel	4.014	Spain	167.50
Denmark	9.21	Italy	2.185	Sweden	10.54
France	8.08	Malta	0.535	Switzerland	2.145
Germany	2.385	Netherlands	2.69	Turkey	12,532
Greece	318.00	New Zealand	2.90	USA	1.4825

Supplied by NatWest Bank (excluding Indian rupee and Israeli shekel) as at close of business on Thursday.

Plate 6.2: The end of the North-South divide?
'End of great divide as South-east is dragged into the jobless mire', Adam Tickell, *The Guardian*, 15 August 1991: 11.

Home prices and unemployment show gap is no longer narrowing

North-South divide could be making a comeback

David Brindle, Social Services Correspondent

THE North-South divide may be reasserting itself after being eroded by the recession, government statisticians report today.

Movements in house prices and unemployment suggest that the four years of the gap narrowing have come to an end, according to Regional Trends, the annual digest of localised economic and social data.

House prices have risen each year since 1989 in the North, Northern Ireland and Scotland — in the latter by more than 30 per cent in five years. Prices in the South-east, South-west and East Anglia fell by about 20 per cent between 1989 and 1993.

However, price rises were recorded in the South-east and South-west last year.

Unemployment more than doubled in the South-east, South-west and East Anglia, but rose only marginally in Scotland and Northern Ireland.

Last year, however, unemployment fell in all regions, with the biggest falls in the South-west, East Anglia and South-east.

Alison Holding, associate editor of Regional Trends, said it was too soon to be certain of the economic indicators. But the

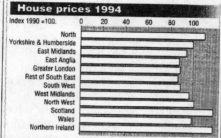

signs were that the "considerable narrowing of regional differences" had certainly slowed and might have stopped.

Ms Holding said the North-South divide had not always been clear-cut, with the West Midlands rivalling the South-east in terms of prosperity not long ago.

Regional Trends, published by the Central Statistical Office, this year marks its 30th anniversary. In its 1965 edition, the West Midlands was the region with the highest economic activity and lowest unemployment, average male earnings were on a par with those in the South-east and average household income was higher.

Other trends have changed little over 30 years. People in the North remain the biggest spenders on alcohol and tobacco and those in East Anglia still spend the least. In the North, more women (32 per cent) than men (28 per cent) are now regular smokers.

Scotland has the cheapest housing and the South-east the most costly — just as in the 1960s.

New inclusions in Regional Trends show fear of crime is highest in the North, and numbers of people who take part in voluntary activities highest in the South-west.

Regional Trends 30; HMSO; £34.95.

In brief

□ Workers in Scotland get the most paid holidays, while those in the East Midlands get the least, with one in six getting 15 days a year or less.

□ Northern Ireland has the cleanest beaches. Between 1990 and 1994, 75 per cent of its waters met European Union standards against an average of 56 per cent. The North-west had the worst record, at 12 per cent.

□ Children are getting healthier faster in Wales. Infant mortality there fell from 18.4 per 1,000 births in 1971 (UK average 17.9) to 5.5 in 1993 (UK 6.3).

□ Men in the South-east work the shortest hours (an average 40.9 a week) but earn the highest pay (an average £419.40 a week). Those in the West Midlands work the longest (42.2 hours) and those in Northern Ireland get paid the least (£319.20).

□ People in the North eat the most meat, those in Yorkshire and Humberside the most fish, those in the South-west the most vegetables and East Anglians the most fruit. Scots buy the most bread.

□ Fewer people are killed in road accidents in the South-east than anywhere else in Britain and the European Union (7 per 100,000 people).

Plate 6.3: The North-South divide re-established?
'North-South divide could be making a comeback', David Brindle, *The Guardian*, 22 June 1995: 12.

ago indicated that elites have a tendency to become complacent, to lose the edge
that drove them forward and led to them attaining a position of ascendancy (see
Pareto, 1968). Elites for Pareto do not simply rise and stay at the top of a power
hierarchy, but more commonly rise and fall. Placed in an international context, this
is precisely what has happened to the UK (Sked 1987; Rubinstein 1993), much as
the economic dominance of the USA has increasingly come to be challenged
(Block 1977; Cox 1987). Rather than seeing links to differences in urban structure,
which provides an internal definition of economic performance, a more satisfactory
theoretical account is to link the political economy of nations to their international
standing (and trends in both). Viewed as an aspect of traditions and processes in
(local, national and global) political-economies, we also find a more comforting
interpretation of why some nations do not have megalopolitan complexes. At least
in the case of Germany (Munich) and Italy (Milan), this can be seen in the late
formation of these polities as nations, with the result that a number of competing
'city-states' formerly existed. A similar position could be expected in federal states,
although this view can be questioned given the position of the USA (Gottman
1964). Without wishing to assert the 'correctness' of the interpretation, for no doubt
more 'exceptions' can be found, but merely as a means of stimulating discussion
and pointing to the way in which processes are nationally-grounded, it is as well to
note the weakness of land-use planning regulation in the USA (Gottdiener 1977;
Heiman 1988). In terms of its urban system, the federal nature of the USA is allied
to competing urban centres (Johnston 1982) rather than single city primacy, as in
France and the UK. But once seen at the local (and state) level, the flimsy fabric of
land-use regulation in the US does result in urban sprawl of a kind that leads to
megalopolitan spread. In its own right, this warns against any attempt to cast the
explanation for urban structure at one geographical scale. There is an integration
and interaction of forces at local, national and global scales, all of which bear on
social inequalities and economic growth.

Conclusion

This chapter has examined inequalities within the European Union. Some of the
specific arguments of the chapter are outlined in Box 6.11, but by way of a conclusion
let us take an argument from someone else. In what many see as a classic paper,
Kuznets (1955) puts forward the argument that the more economically advanced a
nation becomes the lower its rates of income inequality. Within a European context
we find some support for this notion, with inequality rates highest in the poorer
performing economies of the European Union (e.g. Ireland, Portugal, Spain, the UK;
Table 6.5), while countries whose longer term economies have shown greater
strength have relatively low rates of inequality (e.g. Germany, Netherlands, Sweden).

One point to take from this is that when we consider inequalities within a European
context it is not sufficient simply to compare issues like income rates or GDP per
head across nations or regions. A stark difference between, say, Germany and the UK,
is not simply that residents in the former have higher average incomes (Table 6.3) but
that the poorer members of society have incomes that are generally closer to that
average than is the case in the UK (Table 6.5). Moreover, with the UK seeing

Table 6.5: Income distribution within European countries and the USA

	Income level at decile points (median = 100)				
	Decile 10	Decile 25	Decile 75	Decile 90	Decile 90/ Decile 10
Belgium 1988	58.5	74.5	128.8	163.2	2.79
Finland 1987	58.9	76.5	125.5	152.7	2.59
France 1984	55.4	72.1	139.7	192.8	3.48
Germany 1984	56.9	75.0	132.7	170.8	3.00
Ireland 1987	49.5	66.7	150.9	209.2	4.23
Italy 1986	48.9	68.8	145.0	197.9	4.05
Luxembourg 1985	58.5	75.1	132.7	184.0	3.15
Netherlands 1987	61.5	75.7	135.0	175.0	`2.85
Norway 1986	55.3	76.0	128.7	162.2	2.93
Portugal 1980/1	47.4	69.2	143.5	203.2	4.29
Spain 1980/1	46.3	68.1	143.4	203.0	4.38
Sweden 1987	55.6	75.6	125.1	151.5	2.72
Switzerland 1982	53.9	73.6	134.3	185.1	3.43
Utd. Kingdom 1986	51.1	67.6	144.6	232.1	3.79
USA 1986	34.7	61.7	149.6	247.3	5.94

Source: Atkinson (1995: 47)

increased income inequities over the 1980s (Atkinson 1995), at a time of slow economic growth (Figure 6.2), the income trend for the poor in the UK sees them falling further behind their contemporaries in other European nations than is the case for wealthier segments of UK society. Indeed, as a result of growing income inequities, the better-paid strata of the UK population might be catching up with high-income residents in wealthier European nations.

Adding to the problems of the poor in the UK and many other European countries is the dismantling of many aspects of the welfare state (see Mohan 1989). The consequences of poor welfare state provision, as suggested by income distributions in the USA (Table 6.5), is an increasingly impoverished under-class, with heightened inequities placing serious question marks against the chances of relative improvement in the economies of countries like the UK (Hutton 1966: 169–192). The consequences of such inequities are not simply a matter of income, but stretch across the board, with significant impacts on the uneven incidence of ill-health (Townsend and Davidson 1982).

Such inequities also clearly have a geography, although this is more complex than simplistic dichotomies like North-South or urban-rural (Forrest and Gordon 1995). Moreover, these inequities are not only expressed in differential 'performances' across countries but in dissimilar benefit distributions within nations, by place, by social group and across dimensions of human well-being. By drawing attention to European-wide and UK-centred inequities between places, this chapter has sought to highlight how cross-national and national forces impose themselves in dissimilar ways on the geography of social inequality. This sets a context that needs to be borne in mind when examining disparities in people's lived experiences in single locations. Local expressions and nuances arising from such experiences are traced out in various other chapters within this book.

Box 6.11: Chapter summary and suggestions for further reading

The principal arguments of this chapter, and related sub-arguments, have been:

- Explanations for inequalities are complex, as there are multiple dimensions to inequity
    - inequities are difficult to interpret, being made apparent in events and non-events
    - ideology has a key role to play in interpretations of what causes inequities
- Local patterns of inequality are influenced by forces at national and transnational levels
    - these are made evident in national effects as patterns of regional economic change
    - they are evinced in different national responses to the same cross-national influences
- Patterns of socio-economic inequity in Europe are complex, even at a regional scale
    - notions like north-south, east-west, rural-urban, core-periphery do not capture this complexity easily
- Globalisation trends do not necessarily 'equalise':
    - global trends are contextualised in their impact
    - differences in (local and) national (political-economic) cultural traditions play an important role in determining impacts
- The organisation of economic institutions is important, as seen in:
    - corporate organisational hierarchies, and the way these are changing
    - governmental structures, as in differences between federal and unitary systems
- Economic change generates new inequities, as seen in shifts in sectoral balances
- Regional divergences emerge from national political-economic power structures
- Fundamental economic change at a national level is slow to emerge, because:
    - it requires adjustments in basic attitudes
    - it requires re-alignment in dominant power relationships

---

You should read the arguments put forward critically, seeking to confirm or reject then from other academic literature and from your own experiences. There are a range of studies you might turn to including: Clout (1986) *Regional Variations in the European Community*; Spooner (1995) *Regional Development in the UK*; Lewis and Townsend (1989) *The North-South Divide*; Cloke (1992) *Policy and Change in Thatcher's Britain*; and Hutton's (1996) *The State We're In*.

Chapter 7

Southeast Asian Development: Miracle or Mirage

Mark Cleary

Introduction

The economies of Southeast Asia have ranked amongst the most dynamic and rapidly-developing in the world. Over the last three decades the countries of this region have consistently out-performed the rest of the developing world providing an example of economic development to both academics and development practitioners alike. High export growth, the modernisation of farming methods and productivity and the widening of economic and social opportunity exemplify to many the so-called 'Asian miracle' (See Table 7.1). Explaining that growth takes us into the over-lapping fields of development economics and political theory. Thus the development of the four Asian 'tigers' (Singapore, Taiwan, South Korea, Hong Kong) may be viewed as resulting from the adoption of a range of *flexible production strategies* (see Box 7.1) using both foreign investment and domestic savings to drive economic growth and development. That economic growth has had important implications both for countries within the orbit of the new 'tigers', and for the nature of development theory itself. Some would also point to the increased economic cooperation between neighbouring nations in the region – especially the countries of ASEAN (the *Association of South East Asian Nations* – Brunei, Malaysia, Philippines, Indonesia, Singapore, Thailand, Myanmar, Laos, Cambodia, Vietnam) (see Box 7.2) as playing an important role in the emergence of the region as one of the most economically dynamic in the world.

Box 7.1: Flexible production strategies

The ability to switch production rapidly from one location to another is often a vital part of companies' strategies to maximise profitability. By so doing companies are able to keep costs as low as possible. In the late-1960s, international companies had evolved mechanisms which allowed them to move to production sites with lower costs. These lower costs might result from low wages, low social overheads and taxes or especially advantageous government policies. Governments of the first Asian 'tigers' were adept at attracting international companies by adopting policies which favourable inward investment. Companies in the footwear, textiles and plastics sector soon moved production

---

sites away from the developed world, with its higher costs, to Southeast Asia. In recent years, the search for lower production costs has led to a new migration of such industries to the low-wage areas of Southeast Asia such as Indonesia, the Philippines and Vietnam. The profitable research and development functions, together with new, capital-intensive industries such as biotechnology and software development have remained within the original 'tiger' economies.

See: Dicken, P (1993) *Global Shift: The Internationalization of Economic Activity*, London: Paul Chapman.

Table 7.1: Basic indicators

Country	GNP per capita	Growth rate 1980–93 (%)	Growth rate 1993/98 (%)	Life expectancy (yrs.)	Population per doctor	Access to water (%)
Singapore	15730	5.3	0.4	75	820	100
Indonesia	670	4.0	–13.2	60	7030	51
Philippines	770	–1.0	–0.5	65	8120	81
Malaysia	2790	3.2	–6.7	71	2590	78
Thailand	1840	6.0	–3.4	69	4360	77
S.Korea	6790	8.5	nd	71	1070	93
Hong Kong	15360	5.5	nd	78	1510	100

Source: Various sources, primarily the World Bank's *Annual Development Report* and the Institute for Southeast Asian Studies' *Regional Outlook*

Box 7.2: ASEAN

The *Association of Southeast Asian Nations*, or ASEAN, was established in 1967 as a forum for greater political and economic cooperation between Singapore, Malaysia, Indonesia, the Philippines and Thailand. Brunei Darussalam joined in 1984 and recent members include Vietnam, Cambodia, Laos and Myanmar (Burma). It has played an important role in maintaining good political relations in the region and as a forum for discussing and resolving issues of mutual interest. A recent initiative to establish an *ASEAN Free Trade Area*, effective by 2002, suggests an increased awareness of the role of trading blocs in the global economy. Fears about the development of exclusive trading blocs in the powerful European Union (the so-called 'Fortress Europe') is a matter of real concern in the region, and the *North American Free Trade Area* has been a prompt for much of the interest in developing an Asian trading zone.

The remarkable progress achieved in these countries through a range of development programmes has, perhaps inevitably, been episodic. The collapses in the currencies of a number of Asian countries in 1997–8 (South Korea, Thailand and Indonesia are the most striking examples) have sharply highlighted the fragility of growth and its high dependence on global markets and the confidence, or otherwise, of global financial market makers (see Yeung, 2002). High government expenditure coupled with massive lending to the corporate sector has damaged, at least in the short term, the economies of the region as the growth rates for 1998 in Table 7.1 show. The nature of development in the region highlights a number of issues relating to economic sustainability, resource exploitation and management, and cultural and social change. Growth strategies based on flexible structures of production and investment which can switch rapidly from one country to another in response to changing labour and market conditions, can bring both 'miraculous' growth and rapid economic collapse. Equally, the international companies in the clothing, electronics and computing industries which have established themselves in many parts of the region, attracted by low labour costs, especially amongst the female work force, low social overheads, generally stable government and a culture of hard work, can quickly shift elsewhere if economic or political circumstances change. Growth has been real and concrete in Southeast Asia and, as Rigg argues (1997), for all its problems, the development process has brought real advances to the peoples of the region. But that growth is fragile, as recent events have shown, and the development process needs to be examined critically if we are to understand its impact on the varied societies and cultures of the region.

This chapter seeks to do that in four ways. First an introductory section examines the characteristics of the region in terms of resources – both natural and human – and will review some of the ways in which geographers have looked at Southeast Asia. Having sketched the background to the region and its place in the development literature, the second section, 'Riding the tiger', examines the striking economic growth of the region, looking particularly at Singapore and Malaysia. Development has of course made huge demands on resources and the third section examines the management of resources and some of the conflicts that have arisen over their use. This is considered in relation to three issues – urban management, the rural environment, and the treatment of marginal groups in remote but economically and politically valuable areas. The final section examines the changing place – and perceptions – of the region in the global economic order. Is the region now firmly set as a trade bloc to rival the US or the EU? And how is that changing global order likely to affect the way we view Southeast Asia?

The Regional Context

The development of geographical writings on Southeast Asia has inevitably been coloured by its colonial past. British, French and Dutch writers on the region have produced a rich literature on the societies and cultures of the region and have articulated a range of models seeking to explain the economic structures, especially in the colonial period. However, as Fisher (1964) noted in his classic account of the region, it was not until the collapse of European military powers under the Japanese invasion of 1941, that the geo-strategic importance of the region was fully recognised. The sometimes violent process of decolonisation in the region – and, in particular, the wars of liberation in Indo-China in the 1960s and 1970s – further stimulated interest in the societies of the region by geographers as well as by anthropologists and sociologists (see, for example, the review by King 1994). By the early 1980s, the literature was dominated by a focus on the rapid economic growth in the region – phrases such as the 'Asian miracle' or the 'Tiger economies' rightly stressed the rapid pace of growth in this developing region, a pace which contrasted with the stagnant growth rates of some Latin American economies or the even poorer performance of Africa. Here, it seemed, was development that 'worked', a model for developing economies elsewhere. By the early 1990s, the stance was a little more critical, a little less laudatory. The 'cost' of development was brought sharply into focus by resource issues such as tropical deforestation and the impacts of climate change, or by a range of labour and human rights issues. Political instability in Indonesia where centre-periphery tensions (exemplified by the independence struggle in East Timor) and ethnic unrest (evident in Borneo and the Moluccas) have flared up in recent years has also underlined potential tensions in the region. A growing group of observers (excellently reviewed in Rigg 1997) are perhaps now questioning the 'Asian miracle': is there really enough space at the top table for all the aspirant economies or will some inevitably fall by the wayside?

The geographic focus of this chapter is restricted to the countries of ASEAN primarily for reasons of space. But there are also quite compelling intellectual reasons too. First, in Singapore, the countries of the region have a telling model of economic and social development which, consciously or otherwise, has been a catalyst for change. Secondly, the region has in Malaysia and Thailand two rapidly-developing economies whose growth rates, based in part on inward investment from Singapore companies, have been amongst the highest in the developing world. Thirdly, the exploitation of the natural resources of the region, in particular timber, have created serious and seemingly intractable environmental and cultural dilemmas. Fourthly, in Indonesia and the Philippines, the region has two countries with particularly pressing rural development problems.

The region straddles the equator (see Figure 7.1) and is dominated biogeographically by *Tropical Rainforest Formations* (TRF) (see Box 7.3). These diverse and ecologically rich forest types are varied in both extent and character and cover large areas, particularly in upland southeast Asia. These formations, together with the other characteristic landscapes of the region – low-lying mangrove forests, grasslands and river deltas – reflect a range of changing physical and human conditions. Extensive logging, for example, has dramatically reduced forest cover in parts of Thailand and the Philippines, as well as posing threats to forest sustainability in Malaysian and Indonesian Borneo. The basic climatic regime is one of high temperatures with relatively little daily or seasonal variation, heavy rainfall and high humidity, and a range of monsoon rainfall regimes. Close to the Equator the rainfall of around 2,500 mm per annum is distributed fairly evenly through the year. As one moves away from the Equator, a more marked dry season is apparent. This can range from one or two months on the Thailand-Malaysia border to around four months in the mountains of northern Thailand. Alongside these broad climatic features, local conditions such as tropical typhoons can be important, especially in the Philippines.

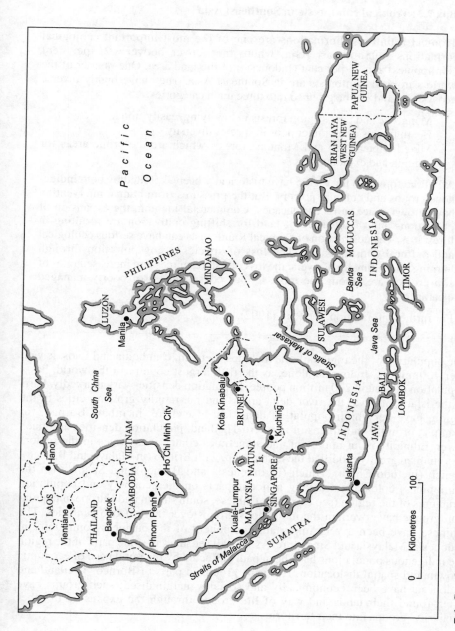

Figure 7.1: Southeast Asia

Box 7.3: Tropical rainforests in Southeast Asia

Tropical Rainforest Formations are one of the most important ecological formations in Southeast Asia, where they cover between 21 per cent (Philippines) and 75 per cent (Indonesia) of the land area. One-quarter of the world's tropical rainforests are in Southeast Asia. They have highly diverse ecosystems and can be grouped into three main categories:

–   Mangrove and peat swamp forests in low-lying, easily flooded areas
–   Heath forests often rather poor in species diversity
–   Mixed-Dipterocarp and Montane forests which are the prime areas for logging and exploitation

All of the forests in the region have historically been exploited by both indigenous groups and colonial powers. But the pressures from human intervention have grown apace in recent decades. Commercial logging, the expansion of plantations and the clearing of land for shifting cultivation are resulting in forest loss. The destruction of Tropical Rainforests can have serious ecological and cultural consequences. The loss of species, smog pollution through burning, the silting up of rivers, the loss of fish resources and increased rates of soil erosion are among the most serious consequences of poorly-managed clearance.

For further information, see Park (1992).

The population of the region, if one includes Vietnam, Cambodia and Laos, is well over 400 million. Indonesia alone, as the fifth largest country in the world, has a population of around 200 million people. Population densities vary markedly. Parts of the island of Java, the river delta areas, and the rapidly growing cities in the region, have very high population densities; elsewhere, in inland Borneo, for example, or in the mountains of northern Thailand, population densities are much lower. Ethnicity is an important and sometimes contentious issue in the region. Colonialism greatly modified the ethnic map, with British (in Malaya and Borneo), French (in Indo-China), Dutch (in Indonesia and Borneo) and Spanish (in the Philippines) colonialism having major impacts on the economy and population structures of the region (see Box 7.4). Chinese, south Indian and European population groups have overlain the indigenous groups over the last two centuries. The Chinese have been a very important component of the business community in Indonesia, Malaysia and Singapore. As we will see later, in some parts of the region the indigenous populations have been badly affected by the rapid pace of economic growth and spatial dislocation. Hill tribe groups in parts of Borneo, Thailand and Indonesia have been economically and socially marginalised; such groups have often found their lands and way of life eroded through the expansion of other 'majority' groups into their territories.

Box 7.4: Colonialism in Southeast Asia

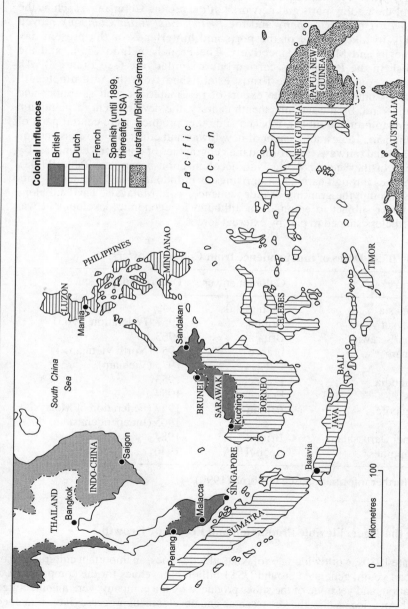

Figure B7.4: European colonies in the Southeast Pacific

Contested Worlds

European colonialism in Southeast Asia began in earnest in the eighteenth century when the trading companies of the Dutch and British sought to control the trading ports and networks of the region. Companies such as the *Dutch East India Company* and the *British East India Company* moved quickly to take control of the ports and hinterlands of the present-day Indonesia and Malaya respectively. The French in Indo-China and the Spanish in the Philippines carried out a similar role (see Figure B7.4). Colonial control was more firmly established from the mid-nineteenth century. Control of trade, the export of raw materials such as timber and minerals and, by the late nineteenth century, the development of plantation systems to produce rubber, tobacco and other products were central parts of colonialism. The establishment of new towns and cities and the construction of roads and railways transformed the geographies of colonised countries. By the end of the Second World War, decolonisation began (see Table B7.4a), sometimes through nationalist uprisings as in Indonesia and Vietnam, sometimes through the granting of independence, as in Malaysia. Thailand alone was never subject to colonialism although its economic development was nevertheless shaped in part by external forces.

Table B7.4: Dates of independence from Colonial powers

Country	Colonial power	Date of Independence
Indonesia	Netherlands	1949
Malaysia	Britain	1957 (Federation, 1963)
Sabah/Sarawak	Britain	1963
Vietnam	France	1954 (North Vietnam)
		1975 (Vietnam)
Cambodia	France	1953
Laos	France	1954
Singapore	Britain	1957 (Federation of Malaysia)
		1965 (Independent state)
Brunei Darussalam	Britain	1984
Philippines	Spain/USA	1946

For further information, see Osborne (1990)

Riding the Tiger: Flexible Production and Economic Growth

In the late 1980s, worldwide sales of Nike athletic shoes, an important cultural icon of American youth, generated around US$1 billion in revenues for the company, a US corporation, and yet none of the shoes produced by the company were manufactured in North America. Whilst the key research and development processes have remained in the USA, an elaborate system of sub-contracting, or 'partnership agreements', has diversified production in a range of different countries (Donaghu and Barff 1990). The manufacturing centres of countries in south and east Asia have come to hold a particular attractions to companies like Nike. The growing ability to sub-divide and specialise the production process, together with the presence of cheap, flexible labour and low overheads, have brought international companies across a wide range of industries – such as footwear, textiles, electronics and the semi-conductor industry – into Taiwan and South Korea (from the late 1970s), Singapore and Malaysia (from the early 1980s), Indonesia and the Philippines (from the early 1990s), and now, with economic reform, Vietnam.

These flexible production strategies have been pivotal in fostering economic growth in the region and have usually been referred to as *post-Fordist* patterns of economic growth (see Box 7.10). The period of sustained mass production and consumption in the West in the 25 years following World War Two, a period characterised by an accord between labour and capital and a degree of employment and welfare security, came to be referred to as *Fordist*. This gave way in the 1970s to recession in many countries in the west, to the dismantling of union and social welfare schemes, and to new, more flexible, production systems. From a diverse and at times contradictory body of economic and political theory, post-Fordism has become an organising and unifying concept for economists and development geographers alike. One of the major consequences of post-Fordist production methods has been the expansion of *trans-national corporations* (TNCs) into the developing world seeking cheap, flexible and non-unionised labour (Dicken 1992). East and Southeast Asia has been an important destination for many such companies. *Branch plants* (see Box 6.9) manufacturing a range of products from air-conditioners, through semi-conductors and computer products, to software and biotechnology, have been established in the region. From locations in the 'first generation' of *newly-industrialising countries* (NICs) such as Taiwan, Singapore and South Korea, production has shifted to a 'second generation' in Malaysia, Thailand and the Philippines. Massive foreign investment from the USA and Europe into that 'first-generation' was followed in the late-1980s, by Japanese and South Korean investment into the 'second-generation' of countries in the region.

The extent to which the economies of the region have been able to capitalise on the development of flexible production strategies has been one of the most striking features of the development process. The rapid growth of both the NIC's and their neighbours in the region provides, it has been suggested, a model for the economic development of other, poorer countries in the world. The 'Asian miracle' of rapid, sustained economic growth has been seen by some to provide lessons for the developed and developing world alike, in that a country such as Singapore, with only 3 million people, has become a significant industrial and commercial economy. What has been the secret of its success?

Since leaving the Federation of Malaysia in 1965, strong central economic planning, coupled with one of the highest levels of personal saving in the world, has facilitated the development of a range of export-oriented industrialisation programmes within Singapore. From an early focus on lower-value mass-produced goods, production has increasingly shifted to high-value products in the fields of micro-electronics, computing and biotechnology. Heavy investment in infrastructure and the establishment of a highly-educated and skilled workforce have ensured that continued technical development and innovation in the economy takes place. One of the most interesting features of the huge economic success of Singapore has been the heavy involvement of the state, a feature which contradicts many of the expectations of currently popular neo-liberal development theorists (see Chapter 3). From guidance of investment decisions to tight land use control, heavy investment in public housing and education and strong labour controls, the Singapore model of growth has involved heavy state intervention and planning in the economy (Savage *et al.* 1998). At a time when many governments in the west were seeking to disengage from the economy, Singapore's government remained committed to intervening in order to create the most appropriate investment conditions for sustained economic growth.

As lower-waged production in textiles, plastics or basic electronics has shifted to a new tier of 'second-generation' economies in the region, the 'first-generation' state of Singapore, with heavy state involvement through the creation of Science Parks, has diversified its own economic base and fulfilled a role as a source of capital and investment for the region as a whole. Given this apparent success, it is not unsurprising to find that *economic development strategies*, modelled to some degree on those of Singapore, are quite popular in neighbouring states like Malaysia and Thailand, despite failing out of favour among Western neo-liberal development specialists (see Chapter 3). Malaysia in particular, with its concerted drive towards the status of a major economic power by 2020 (the so-called *2020 Vision*), has actively sought to combine both domestic and foreign capital and investment in developing a strong, high value-added manufacturing base. The Proton car factory, in the dynamic growth zone around Kuala Lumpur, a joint-venture operation with the Mitsubishi Corporation in Japan, exemplifies such development efforts.

One of the most striking features of the development of manufacturing industry in countries like Malaysia, Singapore and Thailand has been a heavy dependence on young, predominantly female workers. As in the case of the 'first generation' NIC's, the successful growth of the electronics and, more particularly, the lucrative semi-conductor industries, has been based on a strategy of bringing young, unmarried female workers into industrial employment for the first time. For enterpreneurs, such a workforce is flexible, easily trained and reliable and often employed at low wage rates and working long hours. Many are rural migrants, making the jump from village to urban life. Within the factory environment, studies by sociologists and anthropologists have suggested that a range of mechanisms are used by employers to create a flexible and reliable work force (Ward 1990; Rasiah 1993). These include the use of quotas to increase competition between workers and the provision of tied accommodation and welfare facilities. Increasingly, it has been argued, the new Asian working class, the group on whose labour the tremendous growth of the 'tiger' economies has been built, is young, rural in origin and overwhelmingly female.

Resource Use, Management and Conflict

A Regional Picture

Southeast Asia has an abundance of natural resources ranging from tropical timbers and forest products through to minerals and hydrocarbons. Indeed, the presence of these resources was an important factor prompting European colonialism from the early eighteenth century onwards; their continued exploitation has been fundamental to post-colonial economic development of the region. Thus whilst the most dramatic growth has seemed to take place in the manufacturing sector (most notably electronics), that manufacturing growth developed, and has continued to thrive, in part on the back of intense exploitation of the region's natural resources. The export of these resources, most notably timber and hydrocarbons, has provided much of the government revenues needed for infrastructural development (roads, port facilities, airports), the expansion of utilities such as water and electricity, and the upgrading of education and training. It is hardly surprising, then, that conflicts over resource exploitation and management have intensified as the pace of economic growth has accelerated.

Perhaps the most fundamental pressure on resources and their management has been the sheer pace of demographic and economic growth in the region. Whilst overall population growth in the last two decades has been markedly lower than in south Asia, Africa or Latin America, average annual growth rates of between 1.5 per cent and 2.0 per cent (with the exception of Singapore which has very low population growth) have created considerable pressures in both rural and urban areas. Such demographic pressures, coupled with an expanding economy and services, have exerted considerable pressures on the management of natural resources.

In rural areas demand for that most basic resource, land, remains high with considerable landlessness and rural squatter populations in all the countries of the region except Singapore. In the Philippines an estimated 55 per cent of the rural population in the late 1980s was classed as landless whilst in Indonesia the figure reached 60 per cent (Cleary and Eaton 1996: 65). Even in countries traditionally regarded as having a surplus of land, such as Malaysia and Thailand, agricultural change, often resulting in the concentration of landownership in fewer hands, has tended to accentuate the problems of access to land. In urban areas, the continued influx of rural population, coupled with dramatic economic growth and industrial expansion, has also led to enormous pressures on land as cities like Bangkok and Kuala Lumpur seek to expand into the surrounding rural areas.

The continued drive to improve both infrastructure and utilities has also acted as a catalyst for significant conflicts over resource management. Road expansion, such as the pan-Borneo highway project and the development of the east and west coast motorway networks in Malaysia; the upgrading of major port facilities; and continued investment in water and electrical utilities have created major pressures. The provision of new hydro-electric power facilities, for example, have brought in their train both political and social conflicts. Malaysia provides good examples of this. There, the development of dam facilities such as the Pergau dam in Peninsular Malaysia or the Baku dam in Sarawak, have been highly controversial. In the latter case, the construction of the Baku dam in the Sarawak rainforests will lead to the displacement of up to 5,000 indigenous peoples as well as considerable damage to the rainforest environment. It is difficult to reconcile such conflicts with the clear need for greater and more secure electrical supplies, especially in Peninsular Malaysia where increases in demand for electricity can barely be met. Such pressures on resources in the booming economies of the region have been reflected in a number of endemic problems. Electrical blackouts, for example, remain a common feature in both Malaysia and Thailand, with many companies in the latter country being obliged to install their own generators in order to maintain production. Similar problems over water supply and waste disposal constitute what are usually regarded as 'blockages' in the economy, barriers to the maintenance of high economic growth. The solution to such problems brings in its train a range of resource management issues.

The continued drive to export primary commodities has created some of the most intractable issues in the region. Timber, one of the prime resources of the region, has been a vital source of export revenue for most countries. Malaysia and Indonesia together account for over 50 per cent of all the global trade in tropical hardwoods with major exports to Japan and Hong Kong in particular. Whilst the expansion of shifting cultivation has contributed to deforestation throughout the region, the increased demand for hardwoods on the world timber market has been the key catalyst. Logging rates in Malaysian Borneo, for example, more than quadrupled between 1965 and 1990. Logging revenues have been vital in stimulating regional and national growth. They also provide important revenues for state development projects in roads, health and education. Reconciling such benefits with the environmental and social damage caused by poorly-managed commercial logging projects remains a major problem (see Box 7.5).

Box 7.5: Timber and tribes

The relationships between logging companies, the government of Malaysia and the indigenous peoples of Malaysian Borneo (the states of Sabah and Sarawak) have been complex and controversial. Demand for tropical hardwoods in the chief markets of Japan and Hong Kong has meant that in Sarawak some 30 per cent of the total forest area was logged between 1963 and 1986, whilst in Sabah the area of commercial forests fell by nearly 70 per cent between 1972 and 1987. Much of the logging has taken place on land which, by the tradition of customary tenure, belongs historically to the indigenous *Dayak* groups of the rainforest. Lacking legal title to their land, they often have no knowledge that international logging companies are to log their lands and have little control over that process. The involvement of western environmental pressure groups, concerned at both the environmental and social consequences of uncontrolled logging, has often sharpened conflict with the national government arguing that logging is carried out only on state land. Whilst logging does bring vital revenues to the country and provides some employment and incomes for the local peoples, many *Dayaks* resent the lack of control that their communities have over the pace and management of the logging process.

The development of the Southeast Asian economies has therefore placed consider-able demands on the natural resources of the region. These demands have come in different forms, and will therefore potentially have had different impacts on different parts of the regions. To help explore these issues, and in particular address the management of resource and social conflicts relating to their use, three particular aspects of environment and development will now be considered: urban growth, the development of rural environments, and the treatment of marginalised groups in remote areas.

Managing Urban Growth

Some of the most difficult resource management problems have been those of the growing urban areas in Southeast Asia. From a relatively low base, urban populations have expanded dramatically and are predicted to rise through the next two decades. Much of the dramatic economic growth of the last two decades has been concentrated in urban areas and the dramatic growth of cities such as Bangkok and Chonburi in Thailand, Jakarta, Bandung and Yogyakarta in Indonesia, Kuala Lumpur and Johor Bahru in Malaysia, and Metropolitan Manila in the Philippines, has been built on the combined impact of industrial development and in-migration. The growth of the state of Singapore, whilst at a lower rate than other cities in the region, has nonetheless created difficult resource management issues.

Urban planning in the region is diverse, reflecting a varied colonial legacy coupled with different political and cultural systems (Shaw and Jones, 1997). The city of Bangkok, one of the largest and most overcrowded in the region, grew up as the capital of the kingdom of Thailand on the eastern bank of the Chao Phraya river from the late eighteenth century. Its growth, from a population of about 1.8 million in 1960 to a projected 11.5 million in the year 2000, has created enormous land pressures on what is an essentially cramped and marshy site (Rigg 1997). Inadequate housing, major pollution and waste disposal problems are all apparent, especially along the network of canals (*klongs*) that criss-cross the city.

Housing problems are reflected in the growth of so-called squatter settlements. Economic growth has been fuelled by massive in-migration into Bangkok creating enormous pressure on the housing stock. One estimate for the late 1980s suggests that close to 1 in 5 of the population of the city is housed in squatter settlements. These are established on both public and private land. Not all are illegal: many dwellers pay land rent for their tiny shacks and hovels, others are housed in much better conditions although, technically, they remain squatters on that land.

Public housing projects to rehouse that population have been slow and piecemeal. One of the central problems is a significant shortage of good building land. Indeed as Bangkok continues to expand the problem is exacerbated as more land is swallowed up by either industrial or retail development. Under-investment in service provision and roads has also contributed to the urban problems of the city. A lack of coordina-tion between planning departments and central government together with the lack of administrative authority available to the city's central planning body, the *Bangkok Metropolitan Administration*, also continues to hamper efforts at tackling the growing urban problems of Bangkok in a coordinated way.

Singapore provides a very different model of urban planning. The city became an independent state in 1965 with its decision to leave the Federation of Malaysia; from then it embarked on a programme of sustained investment in utilities, infrastructure and education in order to attract multinational capital. The maintenance of high annual growth rates, and the rapid emergence of the state to economic prominence as a new 'tiger' economy reflected the success of this strategy. Highly centralised land use planning, coupled with integration of transport, housing and industrial developments have been hallmarks of the city's strategy for managing resources on a small island with a population of some 3 million. The creation of huge public housing projects through the Housing Development Board, the building of major interlinked expressways and a Mass Rapid Transit System, and restrictions on the use of private vehicles through a punitive motor tax system have created a highly planned and regulated urban society (see Box 7.6).

Box 7.6: Urban planning in Singapore

With a population of around 3 million crowded onto a small island at the tip of the Peninsula Malaya, the state of Singapore faces potentially huge planning problems. Major expansion of public housing through the *Housing Development Board* (HDB), the development of an integrated transportation system, the growth of a high-tech manufacturing economy and the expansion of education have placed major strains on the land area. The *Urban Redevelopment Authority* (URA), set up in 1974, is the unitary body responsible for developing a centralised and co-ordinated planning system. Land reclamation in the coastal area, the careful zoning of business, industry and housing coupled with a Mass Rapid Transit system, cheap public transport and disincentives on private car ownership have been central to the planning system. The *Concept Plan* set up in 1991 provides a framework for the future development of the city. It includes the establishment of 4 major sub-regional centres, continued restrictions on private car use especially in the central area, and a programme of managing what remains of the city's historic heritage, particularly in the central area. A planned second causeway to link Singapore with Malaysia will act as a major corridor of growth in the north-west of the island.

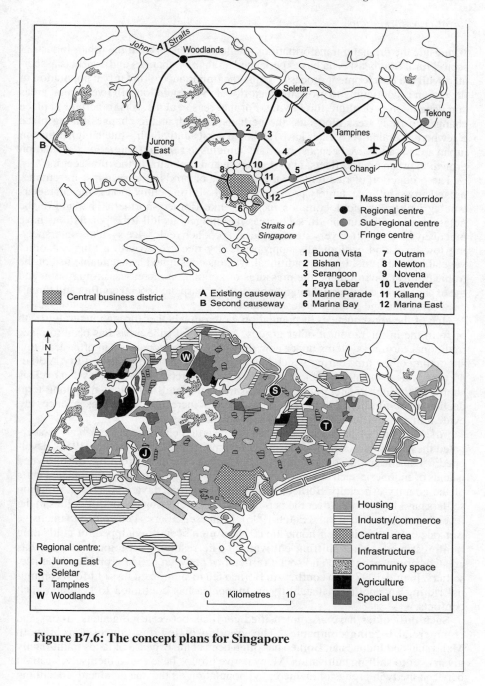

Figure B7.6: The concept plans for Singapore

Rural Transformations

Alongside the dramatic transformations that have taken place in the urban-industrial
sector, rural Southeast Asia has experienced a range of changes and conflicts associated with the development process. Whilst the importance of the urban population in
the region is continuing to grow, the majority of the population still live in rural areas
and depend on agriculture for a living. For that reason alone, it is important to place
changes in rural areas alongside the perhaps more dramatic changes taking place
elsewhere. Rural poverty rates have remained persistently high – much higher than in
urban areas – and have been an important stimulus to rural out-migration. Population
growth in urban areas reflects, in part, deep-seated problems in the rural sector.

The production of rice remains the mainstay of production systems. In remoter,
upland areas, hill rice, largely produced through shifting cultivation is the characteristic agricultural system, common in places like Borneo, northern Thailand or the
outer islands of Indonesia. In such areas the indigenous hill tribe populations have
practiced what are often very sustainable and productive dry rice systems, interspers-
ing low-level and ecologically appropriate dry-rice crops, with a range of other
vegetables and fruits. If such traditional systems constituted a sustainable use of the
tropical forest environment, the pressures of population increases, in-migration and
the expansion of commercial logging have often sharpened social conflict and threatened economic and ecological sustainability.

One of the consequences of population increase, whether through natural growth
or from the in-migration of other groups, in these hill tribe areas has been to place
traditional farming systems under new pressures. Such increases can often lead to a
shortening of the time during which land is left fallow to recover its fertility. A 30 or
40 year cycle is usually sufficient to allow the soil to recover fertility. As that cycle is
shortened through greater population pressure on the land, the potential for long-term
decline in the fertility of secondary forest areas is increased. Such consequences are
evident in parts of Borneo, northern Thailand and Sulawesi.

In some parts of the region government resettlement programmes have exacerbated these problems. The Indonesian government have, since the late-1950s developed a Transmigration programme to shift population away from the overcrowded
islands of Indonesia such as central Java and Bali to more remote, less populated parts
of the country especially Borneo, East Timor and Irian Jaya. Close to 2.5 million
settlers have been moved over the period 1954–1988 creating major difficulties in the
receiving regions (Cleary and Eaton 1996). Javanese settlers, accustomed to intensive
wet-rice cultivation in their home areas, have often been ill-equipped for cultivating
rainforest areas using shifting cultivation. The resultant ecological damage has
created serious economic and social difficulties between native groups and the new
settlers. In mid-1997 such conflicts in Borneo led to significant loss of life in communal rioting and political instability in Indonesia has continued to heighten such
conflicts.

Such difficulties have also intensified conflicts between indigenous groups and
commercial logging companies. The granting of logging concessions in both
Malaysian and Indonesian Borneo has often been at the expense of lands traditionally
given over to shifting cultivation. Many native groups have found themselves caught
between the twin prongs of an increased population on the one hand and a declining

land area on the other. Not surprisingly, social conflict and unrest have been endemic in inland Borneo over the last two decades. Western environmentalist groups have taken very strong interest in these issues with especially strong criticism being aimed at the Malaysian government for favouring logging interests over those of the indigenous peoples (King 1993). Pressures for forest clearance, both to increase timber exports and to allow the expansion of more profitable plantations, were also instrumental in leading to uncontrolled forest burns in late-1997, creating a major ecological disaster in the form of a choking smog in much of the region. This smog threatens to become an annual feature.

Wet-rice systems remain the characteristic form of agriculture in most of lowland southeast Asia. Based on highly intensive and complex systems of irrigation and terracing, the almost manicured landscapes of Bali or parts of Java reflect many thousands of years of cultivation. Highly productive, such agricultural systems can support some of the highest population densities in the world. Such systems, and the lives of the people who depend on them for a living, have been transformed by the *Green Revolution* (see Box 7.7). The adoption of new high yielding varieties (HYV) of rice from the late 1960s has produced dramatic increases in both production and productivity. By the late-1980s, HYVs were common throughout the region bringing dramatic increases in rice production. In the Philippines, where some 85 per cent of rice varieties in use were HYVs in 1993, six- or seven-fold increases in overall yields were reported. Some countries in the region, notably Thailand and Vietnam, are now major exporters of rice onto the world market, a dramatic shift from their position only a decade or so earlier.

Box 7.7: Green revolution

The term 'green revolution' is normally applied to a range of innovations which were developed in the 1960s to raise agricultural production and productivity in the developing world. At the forefront was the diffusion of new, hybrid rice and wheat varieties. In Southeast Asia, new rice varieties were rapidly adopted from the late-1960s in a drive to increase rice production in line with population growth. The results were sometimes spectacular with parts of the Philippines and Thailand recording spectacular improvements in output.

However, the Green Revolution also involved embracing a number of other mechanical and social innovations, some of whose benefits were far from clear-cut. The need for appropriate environmental conditions meant that only well-drained and irrigated land was suitable, necessitating the development of a range of irrigation machinery. Equally, changes in pricing policy also have been considered. Many countries in the region kept rice prices artificially low, often to assuage political protests from their rapidly expanding urban populations but in the process also discouraging farmers from increasing output. The best returns from the new innovation also necessitated expenditure on a range of fertilisers and chemicals, often bought from the West with scarce foreign currency.

Overall, most judgements of the impacts of Green Revolution in South East Asia are positive. It did dramatically improve output, it helped to ensure that the spectre of famine was lifted from the region, and, in some cases, allowed for a major expansion of rice exports. It did, however, have some damaging consequences. It may, for example, have led to the disappearance of many small farmers, consolidating the power of middle and large farming groups. The heavy use of fertilisers also led to problems of increased toxicity in the most intensively farmed regions. Changes in the nature of rice cultivation also led to the disappearance of many of the cultural and social rituals that were once embedded in rice-growing societies. The balance sheet, however, would in my opinion still seem to be positive overall, although other people might well contest this.

For further information, see Rigg (1991).

But the adoption of the *Green Revolution* technology has not brought universal benefits. The new HYV's achieve greatest effectiveness only when they are linked to specific irrigation requirements. The new technology has thus tended to widen regional disparities as well as make major demands in terms of capital investments. Given the large capital required for the irrigation, pesticides and fertilisers to facilitate the best yield increases, the benefits of the new technology have tended to accrue to the larger farmers. More and more smaller farmers, unable to afford the necessary credits to adopt the HYVs, have been squeezed off the land to swell the ranks of the urban poor. The disappearance of many of the traditional communal planting and harvesting methods associated with wet-rice systems such as the Javanese *bawan* harvesting system, have also acted to reduce labour demand in rural areas. Significant long-term impacts may also be apparent in the increasing levels of toxicity in irrigation systems due to high chemical inputs.

Marginalised Peoples and their Place in Regional Developments

Patterns of economic and social development in Southeast Asia have invariably been uneven. There are regions and peoples whose level of development, as measured by conventional criteria such as income, access to water and land, education, continues to fall behind that of others in the nation. In addition, such peoples are often marginalised by those groups making development decisions. They are, to use King and Parnwell's (1990: 2) phrase, 'the objects of development – they have things done to them – rather than being agents and active participants in programmes and projects'. Such peoples and places reflect perhaps the hidden face of the economic revolution in this region, and their development aspirations risk being sidelined in the pursuit of economic growth. Who, then, are these groups?

Perhaps the most important of these groups are the hill tribes of Southeast Asia. Most are located in the more marginal and isolated parts of the region, such as the 'golden triangle' of land between Burma, northern Thailand and Laos; on the island of Borneo; in interior Malaysia; or in the outer islands of Indonesia like Sulawesi and

East Timor. Many of these groups are the 'remnant' indigenous populations, often practising extensive shifting cultivation, living in physically demanding environments and often located in sensitive border areas. For such reasons, many of these groups have been subject to the imposition of power from outside, whether by colonial powers anxious to secure border regions or by newly-independent states seeking more land or resources. It is not hard to understand why. A high degree of mobility across border areas, farming systems that may appear archaic and damaging, and the adherence to languages and religions that may differ from those of the majority culture have led to policies which seek to undermine the viability and autonomy of such ethnic groups. Integrationist policies continue to be a feature of many governments in the region with attempts being made to draw border areas and remote interior lands into some secure relationship with a central state.

The case of interior Borneo illustrates this well. The term *Dayak* is generally applied to a whole range of indigenous groups living in the area, with the Iban, Kenyah, Kayan, Murut and Kedazan being perhaps the commonest groups (Cleary and Eaton 1995; Brookfield, Potter and Byron,1995). Such groups have historically practiced shifting cultivation in the rainforests of the island and their location, in an island divided between the states of Malaysia (Sabah and Sarawak), Brunei Darussalam, and Indonesia (the states of Kalimantan) have made them a target of political attention. A range of government policies have sought to reduce the power and autonomy enjoyed by these groups. The Transmigration programme of the Indonesian government, for example, has brought large numbers of Javanese migrants into Kalimantan leading to a reduction in the land available to indigenous groups for shifting cultivation. Education programmes have also sought to reduce local cultural autonomy and develop stronger national affiliations to the Java-based government of Indonesia. Missionary activity, whether Christian or Muslim, can also be viewed in a similar light.

Economic development, especially the impact of commercial logging, has also eroded the strength of indigenous groups. The expansion of timber concessions has dramatically reduced the area of land available for shifting cultivation leading to increased soil erosion and the out-migration of indigenous peoples to the timber-camps and towns of the coast. In the case of the nomadic Penan who depend on a hunter-gatherer economy, logging has virtually destroyed their traditional hunting grounds threatening the extinction of these peoples. Western environmental pressure-groups have often been vociferous in their condemnation of such impacts; whilst such attention has highlighted real concerns, much of its tone has simply alienated state and federal governments of the region. Economic development can hardly be halted, the revenues and benefits are real and concrete. What is perhaps required is the development of mechanisms to increase indigenous control of these resources. If timber concessions were controlled by Dayak groups, if their management and exploitation could be made more sustainable and accountable, then development without loss of cultural and social autonomy might be possible.

Similar development problems face indigenous groups elsewhere. In central Luzon in the Philippines, the indigenous Cordillera peoples have been affected by a range of development projects, the chief beneficiaries of which are located outside their region. The control of tribal lands has continued to be a critical factor. As elsewhere in Southeast Asia, many indigenous groups do not possess formal titles to the land they use. Oral tradition and epic histories rather than legal documents constitute the basis of their claims. The expansion of central government timber concessions in the mid-1970s onto traditionally tribal lands was a major catalyst for a range of central measures seeking to coerce the local population into accepting the 'benefits' of externally-imposed development projects. A range of resistances to such pressures, ranging from passive non-cooperation to armed insurrection, has continued to characterise the response to the indigenous groups to the efforts of the Marcos and Aquino governments to 'develop' the region (Otsuka *et al*. 1992).

What examples such as these illustrate is the contentious and politicised nature of economic development in Southeast Asia. The 'Asian miracle' is both contested and contentious in its effects. The remarkable pace of economic growth, of infrastructural development and of resource exploitation in the region has not been achieved without political, social and, at times, ethnic conflict. Such conflicts have sometimes led to the development of political programmes designed to address and redress perceived inequalities. One of the most important set of such policies has been the *New Economic Policy* (NEP 1971–90) and *National Development Policy* (1991–2001) of the Malaysian government. Formulated following a period of ethnic conflict between Chinese and Malay groups in Malaysia, the NEP sought to elaborate a development strategy to achieve certain economic and ethnic goals. It sought first to eradicate poverty through a strategy of sustained manufacturing investment. By increasing the size of the national cake, it was argued, the allocation of particular slices to particular groups would be an easier process. Secondly it sought to increase the share of wealth available to the majority Malay population . This was to be achieved partly through encouraging more Malays to move into the business sector, partly by seeking to restrain the continued growth in the economic power of the Chinese population. In its two decades of operation, the NEP has undoubtedly narrowed the gap between Malays and Chinese albeit within an economic environment of almost unparalleled growth (Idriss 1990). One of the challenges of the NDP will be to consolidate and extend that achievement in economic conditions which are likely to be rather less favourable in the future than they have in the past.

Conclusions: How Sustainable is Development?

The rapid emergence of the economies of Southeast Asia has reflected an important geo-strategic shift in the global economy towards the Asia-Pacific region. As southern China continues to achieve high growth rates the potential for growth in the region is enormous. But these high growth rates are not necessarily sustainable. Indeed, the degree to which growth in the region depends on global economic conditions has been sharply highlighted by the economic crisis in late-1997 brought about largely by high levels of both government and corporate debt incurred in the rapid drive for economic growth. But the growth of cooperation between the countries of the region provides potential for maintaining growth and development. Already the Southeast Asian nations have formed an increasingly powerful trading group under the auspices of ASEAN. Broader cooperation bodies, such as APEC (Asia-Pacific Economic Cooperation Forum) and EAEG (East Asian Economic Grouping), suggest that the emergence of the Asia-Pacific economies will have major effects on global trade, flows of investments and economic growth (Murphy 1995), and may also have future geopolitical significance as well (see Chapter 5).

This chapter has explored some of the factors identified with the economic transformation of South-East Asian economies, and some of the potentially problematic consequences of these changes. Box 7.8 summaries some of the principal lines of argument advanced in this chapter. Overall it can be suggested that the economic growth of this region has carried with it a range of social, cultural and spatial changes, some of which create conflict, others, a consensus based on shared benefits. The nature of that growth has perhaps affected the urban more than the rural environment. Rural poverty rates have remained obstinately high and it can be argued that the rural environment has received neither the investment nor the benefits that its size and importance perhaps warrants. Equally, in the more isolated rural regions, the cultural autonomy, not to say survival, of hill tribe groups is threatened by both economic and political change. The empowerment of such groups must remain one of the key tasks of development planners, agents and agencies into the next millennium. The benefits of economic growth are real and tangible. A secure and adequate food supply, clean water, access to education, access to utilities are the consequences of economic growth which are sought after and attained by less well-off groups. The devolving of economic power can undoubtedly improve further the conditions under which a large proportion of the population of this booming region live.

The issue of spatial and social equity remains, as it does in western economies (see Chapter 6), a difficult problem. Undoubtedly economic growth has created major inequalities. Regional growth rates have varied enormously: the booming economy of electronics, semi-conductors and manufacturing industry has created major regional differences. Equally, inequities in opportunities and wealth between different social groups has widened as the economies of the region have grown. As in the west, political strategies to improve the distribution of wealth remain fraught and problematic. To some extent, one distinguishing feature of economic growth in the region has been the attempt to reduce or subvert social and regional conflict through the inculcation of a particular national philosophy of growth and achievement. A higher degree of loyalty to group, community and national interests has been said to characterise the 'Asian way' of development, exemplified in Singapore, Malaysia or Indonesia. Such a philosophy, exponents such as Lee Kuan Yew (leader of Singapore from 1965–1990), or Mohamaed Mahathir (Prime Minister of Malaysia) argue, gives Asian societies their distinctiveness and social coherence. Arguments about the lack of democracy or accountability in such societies are treated with some disdain by such theorists. The resolution of conflict, they argue, is achieved by consensus and community pressures rather than through protest about the rights of the individual.

Such debates take one into the realms of political philosophy and the nature of democracy. Indeed they perhaps go to the heart of some of the issues of conflict and contestation which are central to the dramatic economic development in Southeast Asia since the early 1960s. That growth has been truly remarkable. In the space of a generation, the living conditions, educational achievements and employment prospects of millions of people in the region have been transformed. That transformation has, perhaps inevitably, had adverse consequences for some groups, for some regions, for some peoples. Indeed, whether such growth can continue to be maintained within the pressures of a changing global financial market, can also be questioned. But what the example of Southeast Asia perhaps shows is that the definition of 'development' and the identification of its programmes, policies, winners and losers remains a complex and difficult task.

Box 7.8: Chapter summary and suggestions for further reading

This chapter has undertaken the following:

- To consider the reasons behind the emergence of Southeast Asia as a dynamic, rapidly developing region and the extent to which such dynamism might be sustainable in the future

- To examine the nature of the development process in the region and whether it might provide a model for other regions of the world to follow

- To address the demands that the selected courses of development have placed on natural resources in the region, paying particular attention to problems surrounding the:
- Management of growth in the urban-industrial environment
- Development of rural Southeast Asia
- Treatment of indigenous peoples within projects of development

Useful references on South-East Asian development include: Cleary and Eaton (1995) *Borneo*; Dwyer (1989) *South East Asian Development*; Hodder (1992) *The West Pacific Rim*; Osborne (1990) *Southeast Asia*; and Rigg (1997) *Southeast Asia*. Useful regional journals which you might consult include *Pacific Review*, *Asia-Pacific Viewpoint*, *Singapore Journal of Tropical Geography* and the *Far Eastern Economic Review*.

Chapter 8

Post-Socialist East and Central Europe

Craig Young

Introduction

The post-1989 period has seen a vast portion of the world undergoing a contested process of change which is arguably quite unique in world history.[1] From that date, a huge region known as the Soviet Union and Eastern Europe which had integrated to form a '*Communist* bloc' has become a series of relatively independent states trying to negotiate a complex change from *state-socialist societies* (see Box 8.1 for discussion of terms). As a part of these changes these countries are, to varying degrees, being reinserted into the *capitalist world economy* from which they were relatively isolated, and are contributing new geographies to the complex economic, social, political and cultural mosaic of the contested world.

**Box 8.1: Communism, socialism and state-socialism
  (after Sakwa 1999 and Johnston *et al.* 1994)**

- *Communism*: a pure theoretical form outlined by the founders of the communist movements including Karl Marx, Frederick Engels and their successors. A body of ideas united by a common ideological tradition which takes as its basis the principle of communal ownership of all property. For Marx, full Communism was based on the common ownership of the means of production which could only come about in fully industrialised societies where goods were no longer scarce. With full Communism the state would wither away and differences between mental and physical labour, between nationality grouping, and between state and collective property would disappear.

- *communism*: the practice in those countries which proclaimed themselves on the road to Communism. This was the concept ultimately accepted by communist leaders themselves.

- *Socialism*: a term which refers to a body of writings, ideas and beliefs concerned with social justice and equality. In its most generally understood form it involves a social system based on the common ownership of the means of production and distribution. According to Marxist views the end-stage society of Communism is preceded by a transitional period of socialism, characterised by a dictatorship of the industrial proletariat.

- *State-socialism*: a term which indicates societies in which the dominant values are those of Marxism-Leninism. The dominant political institution is the Communist Party. There is state control of the means of production and central planning is a key element of the political organisation of the economy. Such societies tried to implement the ideals of eradicating or overcoming differences between town and country, state and collective forms of property, types of labour, and regional and national differences.

Thus state-socialist countries derived their support and legitimation from the claim that they were implementing Communist ideas, although they never actually achieved that ideal. In the 1970s, therefore, the concepts of '*actually existing socialism*' or '*really existing socialism*' were adopted to signify that the versions of communism adopted by communist leaders had diverged in practice from the ideal of Communism.

The complex transformation has immense geographical repercussions, ranging from transformations in geopolitical orders and processes of economic and political change at the level of the nation-state (as discussed in Chapter 5), through to local social, economic and environmental effects and responses, plus changes in the cultural landscape and identities. Whilst outlining the background to the key economic and political changes, the focus of this chapter will primarily be on the cultural geographies of this transformation. This is not to deny the fundamental changes in economic and political systems which the transformation involves, but to engage with the importance of the 'cultural' as an arena in which these changes are contested and possibly resolved, at geographical scales ranging from the global to the individual.

Culture is thus seen as a site of *ideology* (a set of meanings which serve to create and maintain relationships of domination and subordination through symbolic forms (Cloke, Crang and Goodwin 1999)) and of struggles between competing *ideological blocs*, as elite or dominant groups seek to impose their cultural values and meanings on other, subordinate groups. Culture is thus a place that reflects the ideological underpinnings of any given society, where the battle is fought between those who produce ideology and those who are supposed to consume it.

It is vital at the outset to understand the changes these countries are undergoing not as a straightforward *transition to capitalism*, whereby Communism is simply replaced by Western capitalism as the guiding principle of social life. Instead, they need to be conceptualised as a complex, geographically uneven transformation involving the emergence of different forms of economic, social and political organisation. This transformation is an arena of competing and highly contested sets of meanings about the future shape of these countries and societies.

Historical Background

What set the USSR and the countries of Eastern Europe apart from much of the rest of the so-called *Developed world* was that, from 1917 in Russia and 1945 in Eastern Europe, the form of their societies was defined according to the ideology of

Communism. Socialism – writings, ideas and beliefs concerned with social justice and equality – had long been an important but contested strand within European thought, particularly through the nineteenth century writings of Karl Marx and Frederick Engels. These ideas were refined into a Communist ideology in post-1917 Russia by the political leaders Lenin and Stalin.

In 1917 the tsarist regime which had ruled Russia since the fourteenth century collapsed rapidly. The resulting power vacuum was fought over by the Provisional Government and the *soviets*; councils composed of worker and soldier deputies, run by intellectuals from the socialist political parties. In the upheavals of the time, social and ethnic conflicts dominated, ultimately leaving the political field open to the *Bolshevik Party* led by Lenin. By political manipulation, then armed conflict, this party gained control over the territories within the former Russian Empire. While the Bolsheviks seized power in Russia explicitly with the aim of achieving world revolution, their main achievement was to create the first communist country in the world (Pipes 1994). This involved an ambitious programme of building socialism through radical economic, political and social change. Within this programme, culture was to play a significant role.

In Eastern Europe before 1945, Communism actually had a rather limited impact, with Fascism being more influential in the late 1930s. World War Two saw the region invaded by the Germans and then the Russian Red Army. Agreements between the Soviets and the Allied Forces led to the territory of 'Eastern Europe' being acknowledged as the responsibility of the Red Army. Even though in 1945 the Soviets had military control of Eastern Europe, Communist domination was not imposed overnight but gradually through Communist controlled social organisations, such as women's and youth associations and professional bodies. Soviet advisors were placed in government institutions, such as the army and the police, while trade agreements gave the *Union of Soviet Socialist Republics* (the USSR) direct control over important sectors of the economies of Eastern Europe. In the event there was little resistance to Communist takeover. The Red Army provided local Communists with material and psychological support, while transformations in the Soviet economy meant that the Communists were seen as successful practitioners of planned restructuring necessary to rebuild the war-torn economies. Furthermore, the Communists were the best organised political force in the area at the time, while their resistance record lent them credibility (see Crampton 1994).

Thus post-1917 Russia and post-1945 Eastern Europe could be distinguished from most of the rest of the developed world in that that their societies could be defined as 'state-socialist' (see Box 8.1). As will be discussed below, this had important implications for the nature of political organisation, the economy, society and culture. The communist states of Eastern Europe remained individual states but their political systems had much in common, principally the characteristic of one-party rule by a Communist Party in each country, heavily controlled by the Communist Party in Moscow. Internationally these states were impacted by the Cold War polarised geopolitical world order discussed in Chapter 5, with the countries of Eastern Europe being integrated into the Soviet sphere of influence by a network of bilateral treaties: the ideology of Communism was promoted internationally by the *Cominform* agency established in 1947; national economic plans were co-ordinated through *Comecon* (the Council for Mutual Economic Assistance) set-up in 1949; and multi-lateral military co-ordination achieved through the *Warsaw Treaty Organisation* (WTO) established 1955.

Although there was popular resistance to Communist rule this was suppressed, notably in Hungary in 1956 and Czechoslovakia in 1968. The 1970s and 1980s, however, saw growing disillusionment with state-socialism as the economic conditions within these centrally planned economies increasingly impacted negatively on the population, particularly through limitations on consumerism. Economic problems forced these communist states into borrowing capital from the West to prop up increasingly unstable economies. Politically, the Communist Parties became increasingly unpopular and to be seen by the majority of the population as an enemy. In Poland in particular, the Solidarity trade union movement became a symbol of dissatisfaction with the Communist regime from 1980. Over a long period, then, economic, political and social pressures were building against Communist rule. Economic decline helped to undermine the regimes' claim to legitimacy. Socialism had promised plenty for all, but had failed to deliver. Falling living standards contradicted the promoted ideology, and increasing exposure to Western media highlighted the difference in experience between East and West. As Smith (1999) noted, the entire state-projected image of state-socialism was undermined by the contrast between an ideology that viewed the decline of capitalism as inevitable and Communism as invincible, and the economic record of the communist states.

The appointment of Mikhail Gorbachev as general secretary of the Communist Party in 1985 created a political climate in which change became possible. In a series of speeches Gorbachev indicated that, in an effort to reform state-socialism to ensure its survival, individual states could have considerably more freedom to choose the direction of socialist development without fear of reprisal from the USSR. In the event, this opened the door for a series of popular revolutions in Eastern Europe in 1989 which swept away the Communist system (see Crampton 1994), while economic collapse in the USSR saw the end of the Communist regime there in 1991.

The result was that the previously relatively coherent regional formation (or 'super-state', Chapter 5), the Soviet Union and Eastern Europe, became a series of independent states in East and Central Europe (ECE) and Central Asia, plus Russia itself. These political processes ushered in a period of unique change which is having a considerable impact on today's contested world. These countries are undergoing significant political, economic, social and cultural shifts as they seek to manage the transformation from state-socialism. This period can be conceptualised as a process of post-socialist transformation. This term is further considered below, but first it is instructive to examine how the Communist regimes operated, and in particular how they used culture in their efforts to establish a new socialist society.

State-socialism

In the period from 1945 to 1991, the countries of the former Soviet Union (FSU) and Eastern Europe had adopted a common construction of society, state-socialism (see Box 8.1). The state-socialist societies were typified by one-party rule by a Communist Party. In addition to total political rule, the Communist Parties had control over the official economy. Thus in place of the capitalist model of private businesses operating in a market economy with some government regulation there was state control and ownership of the means of production. This involved attempts to eradicate private property and business as the basis of the economy, although the extent to which this was achieved varied considerably (see Frydman *et al.* 1993; Portes 1993).

Economic development in these communist states was a complex mix of economic decision making (such as considering the location of industrial development in a rational fashion) and Communist ideology. The latter point meant that economic decision making was influenced by attempts at achieving equity, such as trying to eradicate rural-urban differences by achieving a geographically even spread of industry, and also by propaganda aims. It was vital that state-socialism was seen to offer a viable economic alternative to capitalism, and thus spectacular economic success was necessary in the form of high-profile industrial developments. Rapid industrialisation was also important politically in the development of an industrial proletariat in societies which were largely dominated by a rural peasant society, who were often seen as reticent to adopt communist principles (Lenin 1956; Chayanov 1986; Verdery 1996).

This concern for industrialisation had two important implications for the nature of economic development. The first was an emphasis on the forced development of heavy industry, often in ways which made no rational economic sense: for example, every country sought to develop heavy industry such as steel making. Secondly, there was an emphasis on the collectivisation of agriculture, 'nationalising' land to create large-state owned farms, although again the extent to which this was achieved varied between countries (see Turnock 1997).

Central planning of the economy was achieved through the development and application of five-year plans by the Communist Parties. These plans gave detailed directions about how economic activity should be undertaken. They were implemented by the state apparatus, and at the local level by state-owned economic units (factories, farms and so on). Five-year plans were mainly concerned with specifying production targets which had to be met and the physical inputs which were required to achieve this. For example, the production target for, say, a shoe factory would be set at a certain level of shoes and the volume of inputs (leather, glue, thread etc.) required identified. The economic units measured were physical rather than in terms of market value: prices for many consumer goods were set by the state rather than by market forces. There were, hence, no measures of efficiency in market terms: profits and losses were not calculated, and there was no need to evaluate or stimulate market demand. The ideological aim of providing work for all also meant that there was considerable 'overemployment', in terms of optimum productivity, as the focus was on achieving the goal of zero unemployment.

This economic system produced a particular set of socio-economic relations in both production and consumption. In reality, the managers of economic units bargained hard over the terms of their five-year plans. They attempted to reduce production targets and to increase the amount of raw materials that they were provided with. Extra resources could either be hoarded to help with the following year's targets, or exchanged with other factories for other raw materials. Labour also had to be hoarded to meet the key production periods of the year, even if it was idle for much of the year. With the lack of properly developed consumer markets the key focus of competition between state firms was not for sales to customers, but for resources from the state. The result was the production of inefficient 'economies of shortage', of labour, materials and information (Verdery 1996).

Consumption was also organised very differently under state-socialism. Such consumer goods as were produced were not for 'sale' but were owned by the state which could redistribute them to ensure social provision and welfare. Redistributing goods to the population assisted in legitimating state-socialism through consumption. However, at the same time the redistribution of goods undermined state control over the means of production. The result was that heavy industry was preferred to consumer goods industries. The quality, availability and choice of consumer goods was very limited, again contributing to the 'economy of shortage'. The level and standard of consumption fell well behind that of the West, even for simple consumer goods such as food, and retailing and advertising were very poorly developed. The vast majority of people had to participate in informal or subsistence economies (e.g. producing their own food; engaging in petty theft from their workplaces;) and in informal barter and exchange systems.

This system did achieve some measure of success in terms of the ideology behind it. There was mass provision of employment, housing and social welfare. In some countries there was a degree of convergence in regional economic performance. However, the emphasis on heavy industry in the long run produced regional inequalities in economic development, and social inequalities were produced through the behaviour of the Communist Party. Loyalty to, and success in, the Communist Party was rewarded through an elaborate and hierarchical system of privileges. Special shops with a better range of goods, better education, jobs, holidays, housing and health care were available to Party officials, while the majority of the population often had to undergo austerity as the economy faltered. Corruption and preferment exacerbated these divisions and increasingly alienated the population from the Party. Pickvance (1997) gives an example of how these processes created inequality in access to housing in Hungary, as those in favour with the Communist Party were awarded better quality flats, and thus were more able to participate in the limited privatisation of housing in the 1980s to improve their standard of living and housing. Thus the operation of state-socialism, despite its ideology, created spatial and social inequalities which were to prove problematic in the continued existence of the system.

One-party rule and the state control of the economy by itself required the communist state to put a lot of effort into legitimating the control of the Communist Parties. As noted above, this was attempted through the redistribution of resources including preferential treatment for those in support of the Communist Parties. However, particularly in the later decades of state-socialism an increasingly poor economic performance, coupled with increasing exposure to the growing consumer culture of Western capitalism and increased alienation from the Communist Party, began to undermine the state's authority. Throughout the history of Communist rule, then, other processes were vital in attempts to secure legitimacy for the state (aside from the use of state power through the secret-police apparatus and the armed forces). Here the relationship between the authoritarian communist state and culture (a term which was understood in specific ways in that context) was significant. In order to build socialism the Communist parties, beginning in Russia from 1917, sought to create a new socialist society – the introduction and propagation of a new system of values and beliefs. By the end of the 1920s, Soviet society was structured in such a way that 'culture' was understood as the product of an ideology designed by a small group of Party elite for everybody else, in order to reinforce their power and strengthen the ideological underpinnings of Soviet society (Barker 1999). Culture was seen as an important mechanism for maintaining power and legitimating Communist rule. This was attempted through the state control of culture in three main ways. The first was the state control of the 'means of production' of culture, ranging from control of the institutions of the media through to control of the distribution of products such as typewriters. Secondly, to various degrees the communist states implemented strict censorship over cultural forms and their content. These were controlled through state organisations or committees which defined what was acceptable as culture and the values and meanings it should transmit. There was also control of people's everyday culture through the state secret-police apparatus. Thirdly, the authoritarian state actively produced culture as propaganda, whether this was literature, art, public monuments, architecture, design, film or photography.

Communism attempted a complete overthrow of previous society and its replacement with a new ideal state-socialist society. This involved attempts to maintain the support of the population for one-party Communist rule, through creating new notions of society in order to create allegiance to the new socialist order. In various ways, and at various scales, socialist regimes attempted to remake identities, to redefine senses of *self* and *other*, in a manner which accorded with the building of socialism. A key ideological goal was to homogenise society by reducing inequalities and assimilating social groups to create the 'socialist nation' in which the Communist Party could thus claim to represent everyone. These efforts focused on attempts to reshape identities, particularly in the creation of ideal identities for socialist men and women. This was attempted particularly through the Sovietisation of education and legal systems.

Despite often close historical ties with Western Europe, the countries of CEE were encouraged to see themselves as firmly part of a 'socialist bloc', with the West being regarded in terms of a hostile enemy or 'other'. Historical ties with Western Europe were abruptly severed in favour of a new orientation 'eastward' towards the Soviet Union (see also Chapter 5). Europe came to be conceived of as composed of two 'blocs', each with their own defence and trading organisations, and an allegiance to a different superpower. As has been mentioned in Chapter 5, the construction of new national histories was also central in this process. Pre-socialist historical trajectories were discredited, and new national histories were written to present the achievement of state-socialism as an historical inevitability. The rewriting of history also sought to emphasise, or invent, long-standing links with the USSR whilst at the same time denying historical links with Western Europe.

State-socialist Identity Projects

State-socialism was particularly concerned to mould people's sense of identity in three key areas in order to strengthen their allegiance to international socialism. The first of these was in the area of *gender identities* and people's relationship to their family. As Ashwin (2000) notes, the Soviet state promoted and institutionalised a distinctive gender order as a key organising principle of the Soviet system. The post-

1917 revolutionary Communist Party attempted to rework traditional patterns of gender relations in order to consolidate its rule. The disruption of the existing gender system, as an important basis of society, served both as a symbol of the triumph of the new regime and as a means of undermining the social foundations of the old order.

As Ashwin (2000) notes, gender thus became an important basis on which the duties of citizens to Communism were defined. Men and women had distinctive roles to play in the building of communism. Women were strongly identified as worker-mothers who had a duty to work, to produce future generations of workers, and oversee the running of the household. In return they theoretically received 'protection' from the state in their capacity as mothers and independence through their access to paid work. Men's identities were constructed as leaders, managers, soldiers and workers. They were to manage and build the communist system. Here, the state assumed responsibility for the fulfilment of the traditional masculine roles of father and provider, becoming in effect a universal patriarch to which both men and women were subject. Thus in the Soviet era the Communist authorities tried to construct gender relations in which the primary relation of individual men and women was supposed to be to the state rather than to each other, although they clearly did create differential relations between men and women.

A similar line of thinking underlay the attack on religion. Again the authorities felt it important to remove or undermine a strong source of identity which might challenge allegiance to the Communist cause and provide an alternative source of identity for individuals. From 1917 in the USSR, and in post-1945 Eastern Europe, anti-religious legislation was introduced, churches closed down and church property confiscated, religious education was banned and atheist propaganda promoted. Despite restrictive legislation, however, most countries retained some religious freedom, and only Albania in 1967 declared itself as an atheist country making religious practice a crime. Overall, however, efforts were focused on reducing religious affiliation, particularly through raising young people in the 'Communist spirit' at school.

Thirdly, *nationalism* was an important issue for the Communist authorities. The ideology of Marxism-Leninism posited that under conditions of developed socialism, with class antagonisms and international inequality eliminated and individuals socialised towards an international Communist community, national identity would give way to an international or a national Soviet identity (Kaiser 1997). Under a process of *sovietisation*, individuals, it was considered, might retain their sense of belonging to ethnocultural communities but this would be a non-political attachment which did not interfere with their allegiance to the Communist cause. Communist rule is thus sometimes stereotyped as the enforced removal of ethnocultural ties and national allegiances under an authoritarian state, since such nationalism was seen as alien to the project of creating an international fraternity of socialist states.

Within the USSR policies were developed which attempted to promote a sovietisation of the population, although Kaiser (1997) notes that these processes could be interpreted as a more nationalistic *russification* of the diverse peoples of the USSR. Linguistic russification, intermarriage with Russians, and assimilation to the Russian nation in effect made the sovietisation process one of *state nationalism*, with the end product more like a Russian nation-state built as the result of internal colonisation.

Forcible migration of people, and even deportation of entire nations during the 1940s, were conducted as part of demographic strategies to weaken indigenous nationalism and, in effect, strengthen russification. From this perspective, the USSR was viewed as a multinational empire seeking to become a Russian nation-state by assimilating non-Russians (Kaiser 1997). Events stereotypically taken to signify authoritarian communist rule destroying all forms of nationalism could thus be equally interpreted as evidence of a process of nation-making, with a Russian national identity becoming mass-based in the USSR and Russian nationalism becoming the dominant ideology within the state (Kaiser 1997).

However, the reality was even more complex. Soviet policy on nationalism varied considerably with change of leadership throughout the communist period (see Smith 1996). It was realised that within the huge diversity of the USSR, nationalist demands could prove damaging to the legitimation of Communist rule. The USSR thus developed a two-tier federal structure which recognised national and territorial differences. Official Soviet policy in the 1970s and early 1980s accepted the existence of a multi-ethnic society of culturally distinct yet integrated nationalities (Smith 1996). In this case, and in others, socialist regimes actually enshrined national differences through the adoption of federal structures, with different regions loosely corresponding to different nationalities (Verdery 1996). The federal structures of the Soviet Union, post-1968 Czechoslovakia, and Yugoslavia all served in effect to emphasise differences between particular groups, despite the official disapproval of nationalism. In addition to this, processes of russification actually strengthened nationalist feelings amongst indigenous groups subject to these policies in the USSR (Kaiser 1997). Other countries had a different experience of nationalism under communism. Romania is perhaps the best example, with nationalism being vigorously encouraged by leaders as a form of resistance to perceived Soviet imperialism, while in Poland the Communist authorities sought to homogenise the country's culture to encourage national cohesion.

Thus though the nationalism question was important for authoritarian communist states, in reality attempts at suppressing or modifying nationalism were only partially successful. Some federal state structures explicitly recognised national identity as an issue, and in others, attempts at promoting a central Soviet or Russian identity served effectively to strengthen nationalist feeling among minority groups (see Kaiser 1997). In any case, in many of the state-socialist countries of CEE ideas of nationhood were so deeply rooted in people's consciousness that even decades of Communist Party rule failed to remove them (see Verdery 1991; 1996). Indeed, Verdery (1996) suggests that in the shortage economy of state socialism, ethnic and national differences remained important in the maintenance of survival mechanisms which developed alongside the official economy, such as exchange and barter networks.

The Communist regimes needed to promote and legitimate their new vision of society, a process which involved the creation of a particular iconography of socialism. Two important examples of this are the attempts to transmit visions of the new social order through the visual propaganda of political posters, and the construction of urban landscapes which glorified the successes of state-socialism (see also Chapter 5 on maps as propaganda).

The Iconography of State-socialist Political Posters

The political poster became a key device for legitimating Communism (see Aulich and Sylvestrová 1999; Bonnell 1998). After the Bolshevik revolution of 1917 attempts to change the meaning of society faced the problem of a largely illiterate population and a war damaged mass communications industry. However, visual imagery was central to Russian culture, particularly due to the presentation of religion in the Russian Orthodox Church through the use of religious icons which were present in most people's homes and often embued with sacred qualities. The visual image as a means of transmitting meaning was thus familiar within Russian society and offered a simple and rapid means of communicating new meanings to society, giving political posters a significance which was not experienced in Western societies.

Simple visual forms offered a means for mass communication of the official narratives through which the state could make claims to legitimacy and control over public discourses. Socialist art became central to efforts aimed at developing new senses of the self and state, and from 1931 poster production in Russia was controlled by a single government department. The key to this was the production of new symbols and imagery. Thus in 1918 the hammer and sickle emblem representing working-class struggle was adopted as a symbol of Communism, and the Red Star was adopted as the symbol for the Red Army. The colour red was also significant as it represented revolution, and within Russian culture was also a very holy colour used in icons to denote figures worthy of veneration.

Early posters also played a role in attempts to construct acceptable versions of one-party rule by building the *cult of the leader*. Stalin in particular was portrayed in posters as 'leader' (leading the new socialist society to a glorious future), as 'father' (replacing traditional patriarchal family roles with the state), and as 'living god' (all powerful and substituting for religion). Political posters were also significant in attempts at creating the new socialist citizen. To support the forced industrialisation and the creation of an industrial proletariat the worker-icon became a central image in the new regime's propaganda. Portrayals of the idealised landscapes of collectivised agriculture were also common, reinventing the peasant woman as 'worker-mother', with 'equal rights' and liberated from the household to the world of work, thus also promoting the new gender order of state-socialism. In post-1945 Eastern Europe imagery stressed the notion of paradise being at hand (the radiant future of Communism is a reality); the contented, heroic industrial worker located in the landscape of heavy industry; and landscapes of technological progress (particularly vast, unfeasible landscapes of hydro-electric power generation), promoted as the Soviet example for the East European states to follow.

Plate 8.1 shows an example illustrating many of the design elements which were common to many posters as they sought to promote particular sets of meanings through the portrayal of landscapes and people. In the background the two key themes of centrally-planned development – heavy industrial production and mechanised, collectivised agriculture – are portrayed as highly technologically developed and successful, symbolically linked by the hammer and sickle. In the foreground a Communist Party official is handing a five-year plan to a worker. The caption reads 'Guarantee of five years of quality work!'. The image portrays the healthy, muscular worker as an active participant in the struggle for social and economic transformation along Soviet lines, guided by the Party. A broader set of meanings in the image are the idealised union of the city and the countryside, industry and agriculture, and the Party and the working class. Labour was an important moral category, portrayed as the means to forging a new Socialist society. Socialist agricultural labour was commonly represented as capable of freeing people from hunger and producing wealth in combination with industry. The image as a whole seeks to promote the perception of state-socialism as economically and socially successful.

Urban Spaces as State-socialist Icons

Another significant process was the use of the built urban environment in the promotion of successful images of state-socialism. Architectural and urban form have long been used as a means of expressing power and symbolising the establishment of a new political and social order. Landscape can aid in the projects and desires of powerful social interests and is important in structuring material social relations. In this sense landscape is a form of ideology in which meaning develops and circulates (see Mitchell 2000).

This was certainly the intention in the remodelling of the urban environment. Place names and street names were altered to celebrate the successes of state-socialism and promote key figures in Communism. The removal of street names celebrating significant pre-Communist figures was also a part of attempts to rewrite national histories in order to reorientate the population away from the nation as a source of identity.

This renaming was accompanied by the establishment of statues within the urban landscape. These statues glorified Communist leaders, heroes and martyrs, and also promoted the stereotypes found in propaganda posters such as the 'heroic worker'. Statues of Lenin and Stalin were particularly prevalent. Monuments were placed strategically within the urban environment in places where they would be involved in public life and also in the public ceremonies celebrating Communism. Thus they played a significant role in freezing particular values in the landscape as part of attempts to stabilise and legitimate state-socialism. Statues are also important as sites of collective memory, and like the renaming of places, the establishment of these statues was part of the process of creating discontinuity with the past (see Verdery 1999; Foote *et al.* 2000).

Considerably larger structures, in the form of massive industrial complexes and public buildings, were also created in the urban landscape. The *Huta Lenina* (*Lenin Steelworks*) in Krakow in Poland is a good example of the former. Established in the late-1940s, by the mid-1970s the plant employed 33,000 people and produced 6,700,000 tons of steel which contributed 45 per cent of Poland's output. Its other contributions were massive pollution and as a cultural symbol conveying a series of ideological meanings (see Dawson 1999). For example, it symbolised the intention of the Communist authorities to transform rural southern Poland into an area of heavy industry. It was also seen as a clear message of Soviet power to the people of Krakow who had not backed the communists in the late-1940s. Third, by attracting thousands to become steelworkers it attempted to impose an industrial proletariat on a city noted for its allegiance to the Catholic Church, academia and bourgeois values. Finally, it was intended to form a massive symbol of the success of Communist economic development.

Plate 8.1: An example of a political poster from the USSR (1976)
Poster text translates as 'Guarantee of five years of quality work!', and refers to the five-year plan in the centre of the poster being handed to the worker

Source: © and reproduced with the permission of Andrei Budnik.

Massive public buildings were another element of the urban landscape constructed to promote the ideals of state-socialism – the 'glittering icons' of Communism (Dawson 1999). An example is provided by the *Palac Kultury* (*Palace of Science and Culture*) located in Warsaw, Poland (see Plate 8.2). Begun in 1951 and completed in 1955, it was constructed as a 'gift' from the USSR, a symbol of Polish-Russian 'friendship', though during Stalin's reign (after whom the building was originally named) tens of thousands of Poles were deported to Soviet labour camps and religious activity was largely banned. At 234 metres high, the Palace towered over the cityscape and was visible from all over the city. Containing 3,288 rooms, four theatres, four cinemas, exhibition galleries, a Youth Palace and a 3,000 seat Congress Hall, it also played an important role in promoting Communist ideology, conveying a clear message to the Polish people. Its monumental size and socialist-realist architectural style were a challenge to the norms of Polish culture. It marked out a new urban landscape, and displaced the previously important landscape elements of Warsaw's Old Town, including the castles and churches. Again, it was a symbol of the new socialist society, and was materially involved in the appreciation of arts and science in the prescribed socialist way. The overall message of the building was that the USSR had become the dominant influence in Poland and development was to follow the Soviet path, a message reflected in a letter written by Boleslaw Beirut, First Secretary of the Polish Communist Party, to the Soviet Communist Party in 1955:

> This wonderful tall building built by Russian people-workers, technicians, engineers and architects ... will remain forever a monument of brotherly care among the nations ... a monument symbolising the greatness of the Russian nation and the entire family of the Soviet Union ... a monument of the great Stalin era, its overwhelming power and undefeated ideas ...' (cited in Mintor 2000).

The largest scale transformation of the urban landscape was the symbolic reconstruction of major cities. Moscow is the key example. The development of cities was guided by five-year plans, and Stalin's five-year plan of 1928 prescribed official design regulations to transform central Moscow into the nucleus of social and political life, expressing the glory of the Socialist state (see Bater 1980; Cavalcanti 1992, 1997; Ferkai 1992). Large squares were built and main routeways widened to accommodate public rallies, particularly those which contributed to the cult of Stalin. Immense boulevards were lined with uniform building frontages to provide long vistas. Nine-storey blocks of flats were built along the main streets. The architectural features and massive dimensions of the new buildings dominated the city skyline. These were built in what was known as a *socialist realist style*, an architectural form which combined the giganticism of skyscrapers with a range of other architectural styles, notably neo-Renaissance and neo-classicism (see Plate 8.2). This was imposed as a uniform style under Stalinism, where buildings were expected to symbolise the 'radiant future' which the Communist Party promised its citizens. The rebuilding of the city centre also involved considerable destruction of buildings which represented Moscow's past, particularly religious institutions. The overall effect was to recreate Moscow as the first city of the USSR, a symbol of empire and, in effect, a sacred place.

Plate 8.2: The Palace of Science and Culture, Warsaw, Poland

Source: author

Another example of the large-scale remodelling of the urban landscape under communism took place in Bucharest (see Cavalcanti 1992, 1997; Danta 1993). Under the reign of Nicolae Ceauçescu (1965–89) the Communist authorities attempted a complete remodelling of the settlement system to create a sameness across the country and to spread urbanism. In the 1980s Ceauçescu also undertook a complete transformation of central Bucharest, applying monumentalist approaches in architecture. Again, part of the aim was to destroy the visual past in the centre of Bucharest: some 40,000 people were evacuated by the armed forces to allow for an area five kilometres by one kilometre, constituting some 25 per cent of the city centre and containing a considerable amount of city's cultural and religious heritage, to be bulldozed. A major ceremonial route was created, the *Bulevardul Victoria Socialismului* (*Victory of Socialism Boulevard*), while at the centre of the project was the construction of the *Casa Republicii* (*House of the Republic*), some 270 metres long, 240 metres wide and 100 metres high, and possibly the largest structure in the world. The new urban landscape reflected Ceauçescu's desire for national unity, independence, and his intention to re-create Romanian society along Marxist-Leninist-Stalinist principles.

Tourism provided another arena within which this construction of an image of successful socialism was sought. Tourism was not a major priority for state-socialist governments and movements by international tourists were very tightly controlled and monitored. In the latter decades of state-socialism, tourism became more important for earning hard currency and also played an important ideological role in promoting the success of socialism, being deliberately constructed to project favourable images of state-socialism to the outside world and to visitors from other state-socialist countries, whilst limiting the contact between foreign visitors and the population. As Hall (1984, 1990) shows, the built environment was of major significance in these constructions of tourism.

It is necessary to conclude this section by highlighting the efforts expended by Communist Parties in changing the nature of society, although as Barker (1999) notes, a vision of society as divided into indoctrinated Communists and political dissidents opposed to Communist Party rule would be misleading. Soviet society was made up of 'sites of contestation' in which people's non-official life and daily life were partly comprised of various struggles with the dominant Party line. Between the Party line and dissent lay a vast arena where people lived their lives as a survival strategy and a means of getting by, which also incorporated everyday forms of resistance. Within this arena people still did much to define their own senses of identity, although the impact of the official view of society was significant. As Crampton (1994) notes, the Communist Party never managed to create the new mentality of 'Soviet man'. As discussed above nationalism was not eradicated and the family remained an important site of resistance within which former traditions, values and standards were preserved.

However, a key factor in the identity politics of post-socialism was the creation of new senses of identity. Identities are generally formed with reference to difference, to an 'other' who is not the same as 'us'. Verdery (1996) argues that the Communist Parties constructed their identities, and influenced those of their countries' populations, through identifying some form of 'enemy' intent on thwarting the work of building socialism (such as 'the Nazis' in World War Two, thereafter 'the West' and 'dissidents'). The effect in society was to create a binary sense of identity based on representations of 'us' and 'them'. This feeling was extended in the later years of state socialism when many people formed personal identities explicitly oppositional to communism. The populations of many socialist countries became increasingly alienated from the ruling Party during the 1970s and 1980s. Socialism was failing to bring prosperity for the majority, whilst the Party elite were regarded as enjoying greater privileges and luxury. The increasing use of surveillance by the socialist regimes along with the suppression of freedom further alienated the regime from people. Thus, far from enjoying the support of the people, the Party came to be regarded increasingly in terms of the 'other'. A highly distinctive social environment formed a distinctive sense of 'self', which was completed by the Party as 'enemy'. Such identities were relatively stable for as long as Communist Party rule – as a fixed point of reference – persisted, and have an important bearing on sources of post-socialist identity politics.

Post-socialist Transformation

Communist Party rule came to an abrupt end in Eastern Europe in 1989, and crumbled in the USSR to a final end in 1991. In fact, though the end of Communist rule in such a manner had not generally been expected, pressure for change had been rising within the state-socialist system since the 1970s and had even been predicted within Eastern Europe in some quarters. The very nature of state-socialist societies and economies, as described above, meant that they contained tensions and contradictions which ultimately produced their own downfall.

The reasons for the fall of state-socialism are complex. They included the effects of the poor economic performance of state-socialism in combination with a series of social and cultural changes (see Box 8.2 and Ramet 1995). Significantly communist regimes failed to solve the central problem of legitimation of one-party rule: despite attempts by Communist state, discontent among the population found various cultural outlets, including literature, poetry, religion and rock music, as well as provoking ethnic and class tensions (Ramet 1995). State-socialist systems were unable to create a reality of consensus, and recurrent demands for democracy indicated failure in the policies of socialist socialisation discussed above.

Box 8.2:   Key processes in the fall of Eastern European state-socialism (after Ramet 1995)

- Economic deterioration – the rapid economic growth of the 1950s and 1960s was replaced by the end of the 1970s with economic downturn. Increased borrowing from the Western capitalist nations in the 1970s lead to problems with servicing debt repayments which in 1987 took between 20–67 per cent of annual export earnings as interest rates rose rapidly. The result was that the population faced harder working conditions, lower real wages, shortages of consumer goods as these were marketed abroad, and energy shortages in order to help pay off national debts (Romania in particular suffered from harsh austerity measures). This lead to an increase in strikes in key industrial sectors and in alienation from the Communist regime.

- Mobilisation of new groups in the political system – in some cases state-socialism produced new social groups which provided influential in political change. Some policies actually heightened national and ethnic differences. The propaganda of the workers' democracy gave the working class a sense of political entitlement (for example, the Solidarity trade union movement in Poland). Social changes were produced by urbanisation, secularisation, education and sexual ethics, producing new movements among young people, women, and religious groups, for example.

- Defection of intellectuals – despite censorship academics, writers and other artists and intellectuals to varying degrees were able to voice dissent with the regime, in some cases forging alliances with the workers' movements, urging economic and political reform.

- Governmental inefficiency and corruption – inefficiency lead to a loss of state credibility among the population. Corruption became almost an alternative way of achieving things which the bulk of the population had to engage with. In the 1980s in several countries the authorities admitted corruption within government, but the attempts to deal with it (eg. trying and dismissing officials) heightened the regime's loss of credibility even further.

- Loss of credibility by the state-socialist regime – despite the Party's control of the media and the provision of misinformation surveys in the 1980s revealed a high level of disaffection with the regime among the general public and a very low level of credibility of the Communist Parties.

- Factions within the elite, loss of confidence by the elite – factionalisation among the political elite (eg. between reform minded and other Communists) weakened the Communist Parties' ability to rule. In the 1980s several Communist Parties admitted to past mistakes and harsh policies (including torture, execution and exile of citizens) which shook their credibility and self-confidence.

- Inept use of force – the 1980s saw many instances of use of force (state police and/or armed forces) to maintain the Communist regime

- Expectancy of change – throughout most of Eastern Europe the late 1980s saw increasing levels of belief that change could occur, and the continuation of strikes (as in Poland in 1988) demonstrated that people were still prepared to demand it.

A key aspect of this failure was the various attempts of Communist Parties to solve problems caused by poor economic performance without any major internal structural reform of the system. The picture varied from country to country, but in general the economic performance of state-socialist societies began to drop, particularly relative to the progress of Western capitalist economies from the 1970s. Individual countries began to fail to meet their production targets specified in the five-year plans: taking Czechoslovakia as an example, 31 percent of enterprises failed to meet their assigned production targets in 1987 (Ramet 1995). There were also qualitative deficiencies in production, with the poor quality of goods limiting sales on foreign and domestic markets, which in turn affected the standard of living within countries (Box 8.2) as export markets became increasingly important for earning hard currency.

To counter falling industrial output, in the 1970s state-socialist countries borrowed from Western industrialised nations to purchase new technologies to support exports to the West. The lack of competitiveness of resultant goods added to the problems of debt servicing, which took a large proportion of export earnings. The response was, to varying degrees, to introduce policies of reducing imports and introducing austerity programmes to save money to service debt. Romania was particularly badly hit, with power cuts implemented to reduce energy consumption and food products exported while domestic food consumption was drastically reduced. Throughout the region repeated shortages of consumer goods eroded confidence in the state-socialist system. Given the ideological and propaganda aims of Communism this represented a double crisis for the state, in both production and consumption, and such material hardships helped undermine the legitimacy of communist rule.

Managing these tensions by borrowing externally involved a fundamental shift – despite their ideological intentions state-socialist economies were opened to Western capital. Borrowing from Western economies offered a solution, but one which meshed state-socialist economies with the rapidly changing nature of global capitalism at a particular time in its evolution (see Verdery 1996). Borrowing and debt repayment increasingly brought state-socialism into contact with newly flexible capitalist systems (see Table 8.1). State-socialist economies increasingly had to try to cope with the nature of global capitalist systems at the very time that those global systems were undergoing fundamental change which made them more competitive and fluid.

This served to expose the limitations of the state-socialist economies, a situation which favoured reformist elements in the Communist Parties who were arguing for structural reforms in socialist development which at least partly depended upon the creation of a private sector. From 1985, President Gorbachev introduced policies of *perestroika* ('restructuring') and *glasnost* ('open-ness') in the USSR to bring about some structural change. An early strategy was to form *political capitalism*, a dual economy which was partly state controlled and partly open to capitalism. Over a long period of time, changes in attitude within the Communist Party and a series of wider social, cultural and political changes (see Box 8.2) combined to produce a profoundly destabilised political structure which ended so spectacularly in 1989–91.

What is more problematic is to define and understand what came next. In the early 1990s many observers predicted the establishment of Western forms of liberal capitalism on a *tabula rasa* left by the end of state-socialism. This view was particularly promoted in the world-views of the major international and monetary communities which heralded the victory of capitalism over Communism. The expected form of change was a straightforward 'transition to capitalism' along the lines of the developed Western world, through the importation of models of governance and economic development from the West supported by foreign direct investment into the region. Such policy positions were certainly adopted by governments of the newly independent states.

However, in reality post-socialism needs to be seen as a process, a highly *complex and contested transformation* to new and varied forms of capitalist development, integrating Western influences but spatially embedded in pre-existing socio-economic-political relations, that is within elements of state-socialist systems. Dingsdale (1999) identifies that this process of transformation is influenced by four key processes. Firstly, there is the need for these countries to integrate with ongoing processes of *globalisation* and *internationalisation*, including systems of foreign investment, western cultural forms and lifestyles, and international development policies. Secondly, processes of *Europeanisation* influence the relationship of these countries to Western Europe and the EU project of political and economic integration. Thirdly, there are the differing *policies of post-socialist governments* which have moved at different speeds in implementing key changes (see Box 8.3). Fourthly, these processes are interacting with *legacies of the Communist era*, such as outmoded and inefficient economic and administrative structures, unbalanced manufacturing profiles, a poorly developed tertiary sector, poor infrastructure, a repression of 'traditional' senses of identity, and highly centralised government.

No one simple model of change integrating the interrelationship of these different processes and their outcomes is possible. Though all these countries have a shared heritage of state-socialism, their experience of that system varied considerably. Their subsequent development trajectories similarly have varied considerably. Some, such as Poland, Lithuania and Hungary, have adopted *Western neo-liberal development* paths rapidly (see Chapter 3 for more on these) and are relatively advanced in *democratic state-building*, although they have periodically still re-elected socialist governments. In some cases, such as the Ukraine, Romania and parts of the former Soviet Union, the nature of change has lead analysts to compare it to a *transition from socialism to feudalism*, in the sense that as central control collapsed, power and authority became vested in local 'bosses' (officials and heads of state enterprises) who controlled personal demonetised economies with extensive barter systems (see Verdery 1996). Yet other countries, such as Uzbekistan and Kazakhstan, have experimented with market reform whilst preserving authoritarian forms of governance.

The picture is thus complex but some common characteristics of change can be identified (see Box 8.3). Most significantly, there is the end of Communist Party dominance over politics, the economy and society. This has lead to attempts at *democratisation* – the establishment of a multi-party democracy and civil society. Another important process has been attempts at the *marketisation* of economies, although there is considerable variation in the degree to which these have been successfully implemented. One overall outcome has been a fragmentation of political and economic space which is currently undergoing processes of *re-regionalisation* (see Dingsdale 1999). Table 8.2 demonstrates some of the complexity of this fragmentation, although the data need to be treated with caution and only used as a relative indicator of a country's development. The initial impact of the end of state-socialism was region wide economic recession (as indicated by the statistics for percentage change in gross domestic product (GDP) and industrial production 1990–91; see Smith 1997) which, combined with processes of marketisation, served to exacerbate economic inequalities in society. Since then, most countries have managed to recover positive economic growth and output by 2000, although as Table 8.2 demonstrates, there is considerable variation in economic development, with varying levels of inflation, unemployment, income and ability to attract foreign direct investment.

Box 8.3: The key characteristics of post-socialist transformation

Following Sakwa (1999) and Light and Phinnemore (1998) the key characteristics of post-socialist transformation can be summarised as:

- The end of Communist Party dominance over politics, economics and society.

- Attempts at democratisation – the establishment of a multi-party democracy and civil society. However, establishing a genuine multi-party system has proved difficult, as has the creation of a society with clearly understood rights for, and responsibilities of, citizens.

- A radical reorientation of foreign policy, particularly with regard to membership of Western organisations for economic (EU) and security (NATO) reasons. Also a pervasive belief that the only possible option for development is to enter the global economy.

- Attempts to introduce market economies to replace centrally planned economies. Key elements of market economies which have been unevenly introduced are:
    - The privatisation of stated owned property – the transfer of economic units (state owned factories and collectivised farms, land and buildings) from state ownership to private ownership.
    - The ending of the fixing of prices and exchange rates of currencies by the state to allow the market to determine prices (this is known as price liberalisation) and exchange rates (this is called establishing currency convertibility).
    - Attempts to attract private investment, particularly foreign investors, to inject capital and 'know-how' into post-socialist economies.

- Rapid changes in the class structure and the employment structure, accompanied by increasing social inequalities and social hardship.

- Rapid change in the area of identity politics, including the rise of nationalism and ethnic tension, and the complex working out of a multitude of cultural processes.

- A contested relationship with the Communist and pre-Communist past, particularly in the ways in which history is represented.

- The incomplete nature of the transformations with a key feature being the strong institutional, cultural and social legacy of the state socialist period in the post-socialist order. In elite politics, for example, many communist politicians continue to hold positions of power. There are many new institutions and practices as a part of post-socialism, but they are often hybrids of old and new practices, personnel and ways of operating. Continuity from the communist period is a key characteristic.

Table 8.1: The contrasting characteristics of state-socialist economies and flexible capitalism in the 1980s and 1990s

Characteristics of state-socialist economies	Characteristics of flexible capitalism
Large-scale heroic production, heavy industry	'Just-in-time' production, small batch production
Supply oriented	Demand oriented
Poor information flows, corruption, resistance to state	Information economy
Increased struggle of central government to retain control over resources	Increased role of finance capital in controlling economy rather than state, decentralisation of managerial control
Hoarding and freezing of resources, turnover time irrelevant	Rapid reduction in turnover time of capital through automation and electronics
Neglect of consumption	Increasingly sophisticated means of producing consumer need e.g. advertising
Lack of innovation	Accelerated pace of innovation
Focus on producing goods	Focus on producing events to aid consumption
'Closed' to inward investment	Globally mobile investment capital

Source: adapted from Verdery (1996)

While the post-socialist transformation involves complex processes of democratisation and marketisation, it also involves complex changes associated with the withdrawal of the social and cultural influences of Communist rule, a process which Smith (1999) has termed with respect to the post-Soviet states, *decolonisation* (see also Box 8.3). A key point for understanding the cultural geographies of post-socialist transformation is the demolition of the sources of identity which operated under

Table 8.2: Key characteristics of selected post-socialist countries in the former Eastern Europe and USSR

Region/country	Population in million 2000	Percentage change in GDP 1990–1991	Percentage change in industrial production 1990–1991	Percentage unemployment, 2000	Average monthly wage, in US$ 2000	Inflation rate 2000 (%)	Accumulated foreign direct investment stock, in US$ billions 1999/2000	GDP per capita in US$ 2000	Percentage change in industrial production 1999–2000
Baltic Europe									
Estonia	1.5	–13.6	–9.5	5.9	300	4.0	2.4	5,456^2	9.1
Latvia	2.4^1	–10.4	–2.1	7.8	267	2.4^1	3.9	4,136^2	3.2
Lithuania	3.7^1	–5.7	–26.4	12.6	275	2.5^1	2.1	4,425^2	–9.9^1
Central Europe									
Czech Republic	10.3	–11.5	–21.2	8.8	358	3.9	17.5	13,750	5.7
Hungary	10.0	–11.9	–16.6	8.7	315	9.8	20.2	12,230	18.2
Poland	38.6	–7.0	–8.0	15.0	463	10.1	28.0	9,440	4.3
Slovakia	5.4	–14.6	–19.4	17.9	279	12.1	3.6	12,260	9.1
Slovenia	2.0	–8.9	–12.4	11.9	869	8.9	2.7	16,790	6.2
Eastern Borderlands									
Ukraine	49.3	–8.7	–4.8	4.2	42	28.2	3.2	3,350^1	12.9
Balkan Europe									
Bulgaria	8.2	–11.7	–20.2	17.9	111	9.9	3.9	5,610	2.3
Croatia	4.5	–21.1	–28.5	27.5	602	6.2	3.6	7,600	1.7
Romania	22.4	–12.9	–22.8	10.5	133	45.7	5.4	6,240	8.7
Russia	146.9	–5.0	–8.0	10.2	81	20.2	18.6	7,620	9.0

Notes: 1 = figures for 1999, 2 = figures for 1998.
Source: Business Central Europe online (http://www.bcemag.com/statsdb). The geographical classification follows Dingsdale (1999).

state-socialism: Communist Party rule and the command economy. These relatively stable economic and political structures, which as discussed above were closely involved in processes of identity formation under state-socialism, were dismantled rapidly, even if in many countries there are significant continuities with the former system.

The sheer extent and significance of this aspect of post-socialist change should not be underestimated. As Verdery (1999) suggests, social life for many people in these countries has lost its moorings. Post-socialist change involves an entire re-ordering of people's lives and 'worlds of meaning', and the production and reproduction of new cultural identities at a range of scales. People's understanding of their lives has been suddenly turned upside down. Compelling sources of identity have disappeared, to be replaced with new ones which interact in complex ways with the legacy of the Communist era (Box 8.3). Cities, regions and states suddenly have had to cope with and compete in the new neo-liberal global context. Post-socialist countries have become highly contested within themselves and in terms of how they relate to the rest of the world.

Culture and the Contested Post-socialist World

The collapse of state-socialism and the Communist Party precipitated the removal of many of the certainties of social life and sources of identity. As Barker (1999) notes, however we chose to define 'culture' under state-socialism it was informed by its relationship to the centre, and with the collapse of the Soviet Union there is no longer a dominant culture to which all other cultures stand in some relation. There has thus been a shift from authoritarian Communist state rule, which aimed to homogenise society and create a new Socialist identity, to a new pluralism in the sources of values, attitudes and identities. The complex economic and social transformation of these countries has involved the introduction of a vast range of new influences on identity politics, place identity, nation-state building and consumption practices (see also Box 8.3). These engage in complex ways with pre-existing social relations, with different versions of the history of state-socialism and pre-state-socialism. The communist past has not been entirely eradicated and its memories and cultural values continue to play important roles in contemporary constructions of the differing and overlapping forms of identity. A key element of post-socialist transformation is the emergence of a new cultural landscape as people try to adjust to, shape and mediate new societal forms and relationships. This involves people renegotiating their relationships to their communist past and its legacy, and the incorporation of new 'Western' attitudes and expectations.

The change from state-socialism to a process of post-socialism has impacted significantly on identity at all levels. Identities are situated and contextual (see Crang 1998; Valentine 2001), and as the circumstances in which they are constructed and reproduced change, so too will identities be subject to redefinition, reformulation and contestation. It is unsurprising that senses of identity – whether defined at the level of the nation or the individual, the state or the region, or in terms of ethnicity and gender – are highly fluid and unstable in the post-socialist world. Senses of identity – of 'self' and 'other' – are being formed and shaped by new processes and are being constructed, reproduced and contested for entirely new ends. The post-socialist states have entered the world stage at a time when globalising processes such as the internationalisation of capital, the growth of regional trading blocs (particularly the EU), and the spatial diffusion of a world-wide mass media are restructuring the world. A key context is thus the complex and changing relationship between local and global. Access to the global economy is creating new demands and opportunities for regenerating local political and other identities (Smith 1999).

The politics of the past in the present also plays an important role in the shaping of the modern world (Nash and Graham 2000). How the past is remembered and represented in formal or official ways holds implications for present day understandings of social relationships, cultural identity and economic processes. As Graham (2000: 75) notes, 'powerful narratives of place, fixed with hegemonic representations of the past, remain fundamental to the modernistic ideas of [political] legitimacy and authority.' Nowhere is this more true, Graham (2000) suggests, than in the renegotiation of political control of space in contemporary Europe, a process which makes use of new or adapted representations of places and their histories. This process is central to the contested post-socialist transformation of East and Central Europe following the collapse of Communist hegemony in 1989. Here, political and economic transformation has been closely interwoven with a 'veritable orgy of historical revisionism' (Verdery 1999) aimed at creating new post-socialist identities, in part to legitimate and support new political and economic trajectories for these countries.

Key among these senses of identity are three which most concerned the communist state: church, family and nation. Religious revival has been strong in countries such as Hungary, the former Yugoslavia and the Ukraine, and the established religious organisations enjoy more freedom in those countries, such as Poland, where they managed to retain some place in society under communism. Alongside the return of traditional religion, there has also been a significant growth in new cults which have proved particularly appealing to members of society who are struggling to adjust to the changes ongoing in post-socialist societies (Ramet 1995).

In terms of gender, the collapse of the communist state has removed the institutional underpinning of the gender order forged in the Soviet era (Ashwin 2000). Women are no longer guaranteed work outside of the home, social benefits are being eroded, and motherhood is being redefined as a private institution and responsibility. Men are expected to reassume the traditional 'male' responsibilities which have now been abandoned by the state. The powers of the state to intervene in such matters are now restricted, and the material and institutional basis of old norms eroded. This has enshrined a new pluralism in which competing visions of the desirable form of gender relations can be expressed. On the one hand feminism, already active in some Communist countries before 1989, has become a significant force in debating the nature of gender roles. On the other, the way that the family under Communism acted as a means of preserving pre-Communist values has meant that expectations of a return to traditional gender roles and identities have emerged strongly.

With regard to the third key area, Kaiser (1997: 11) suggests that 'national identity and nationalism have become the cornerstones on which sociocultural, economic and political relations in the newly independent states...are being built.' Gorbachev's attempts at systemic transformation of the Soviet system and pursuit of *glasnost* policies from 1985 lead to increased demands for greater national self-determination within the former Soviet Union. The federal system had outlived its legitimacy and provided the basis on which the Union republics could challenge for greater autonomy, ultimately leading to the disintegration of the USSR along national territorial lines (Smith 1996). The resulting states, and those in ECE, now have to fashion a national identity out of their multi-ethnic communities, and independent nation building projects have become the predominant political action programmes in many post-socialist states.

Thus post-socialist national identities are being redefined for both internal and external consumption: that is, in relation to such questions as 'who are we?' and 'how do we want others to see us?'. One common theme in the building of national identity in almost all of the countries of ECE is that the former eastward orientation towards the former Soviet Union should be swiftly abandoned. These countries are now turning to the West and vigorously embracing the political and economic orthodoxy of Western Europe. Talk of a 'return to Europe' resonates through political discourse. The re-orientation towards the West is almost universal. Among those countries of ECE (Poland, Hungary, Czech Republic, and Slovenia) which have strong historical ties with the West, the desire to rejoin Europe is hardly surprising. However, a similar desire is also apparent among Eastern European countries (Romania, Bulgaria, the Baltic States and even Ukraine and Moldova) whose historical links with, and geographical proximity to, Western Europe are less strong. For many of these countries, membership of the political, economic and military structures of the 'West' – the EU and NATO – remains a key goal of foreign policy; only Belarus continues to look firmly eastward, seeking closer links with the Russian Federation. The reorientation to the West is a key force behind discourses of political identity which attempt a 'Europeanisation' of these countries, particularly through representations of their histories.

In many cases, the making of post-socialist national identities has been based on a noisy rejection of the socialist past and a search for new models. This is often accompanied by, yet another, process of historical revisionism which seeks to overturn the 'distortion' of history during the socialist period, by establishing a 'return' to an earlier historical trajectory which was 'interrupted' by the 'aberration' of four or more decades of state socialism. Often this involves the rediscovery and reassertion of a European heritage (Tunbridge and Ashworth 1996). In other cases it entails the harking back to a former 'golden age' of national greatness. As Graham (2000: 75) notes, 'rewritten narratives of the past create the alternative tropes of present belonging that must underpin the negotiation of acceptable political structures'.

Accompanying the process of redefining national identities for external consumption has been the emergence of, often violent, nationalism within post-communist states (see Chapter 5). In extreme cases, such as the former Yugoslavia and Chechyna, nationalism has been implicated in the collapse of states through war, or armed rebellion aimed at gaining independence. One of the most common explanations for such nationalism is the idea of the 'lid being taken off the boiling pot'. That is, that the old hatreds and enmities which were suppressed but not eliminated by Communist Party rule are now free to find expression since they are no longer suppressed by state socialism. However, Verdery (1996) argues that the situation is more complex. An understanding of post-socialist nationalism needs to take into account the nature of federal structures created by socialism which constitutionally enshrined national differences, while undermining other forms of organisational grouping. Once state-socialism collapsed, the nation or Union republic was one of the few organisational forms in existence for building post-socialist regimes, particularly in the context of a globalising world where a territorially bounded sense of identity may be of particular significance.

Verdery (1996) further argues that the particular circumstances of exit from state socialism experienced by individual states and nationalities have acted to exacerbate national tensions. In particular, once Communist Parties had ceased to exist, the 'other' against which senses of the 'self' had been defined similarly ceased to exist. What continued, however, was the mentality which tended to see questions of identity in terms of a simple 'us' and 'them' binary. In these circumstances senses of identity are reformulated with reference to new 'others', now often defined in ethnic or national terms. Such 'othering' of ethnic groups is further exacerbated by the very economic reforms which are seen as central to the post-socialist transformation, but which have heightened inequalities and aggravated social relations. So, for example, the establishment and operation of legal systems for privatising property has in some cases resulted in tension based on ethnic differences between the 'winners' and 'losers' in such processes.

With reference to Romania, for instance, Verdery (1996) suggests that different ethnic groups came to symbolise different aspects of post-socialist change – such as the disorder of the market economy or the loss of a feeling of wholeness – which have proved particularly disorientating. In Romania 'gypsies', Jews and ethnic Hungarians are singled out in this way. 'Gypsies' are visible in the petty commerce which has grown in association with market reforms. These market reforms in turn have caused unemployment, inflation and often required people to hold down two or more jobs. 'Gypsies', however, are seen as making a living through 'lazy' and illegal activities such as petty trading, which is seen (from state-socialist days) as inferior to production. To make a living from this, it is believed, they must be stealing goods which gives them an easy living and aggravates shortages. Market reforms have exacerbated inequalities and austerity for the majority of the population, but this is due to government pricing and taxation, the uneven effects of the market, IMF-imposed changes, privatisation and other aspects of transformation. However, it is easier to focus anger for these impacts on 'gypsies', who have become symbolic of these changes and their negative effects. Similarly, much anti-semitism arises from associating Jews with the Communist Party which wrecked people's lives, or with Western cosmopolitanism, which is now introducing new problems, and thus Jews have become symbolic of such problems. The Hungarian minority is similarly associated with the fragmentation accompanying the collapse of state-socialism, because of their demands for autonomy.

In some cases the processes of transformation have provoked ethnic and nationalist tensions which did not previously exist. Verdery (1996) recounts the case of land privatisation in one Romanian village. Ethnic Germans resident in Romania lost their land in 1945 when they were deported to Siberia for war-reparations labour. The land was given to poor villagers of Romanian ethnicity, who in turn were compelled by the communist state to give the land to a collective farm. In 1991 land rights of collective farms were given back to their previous owners, although ethnic Germans were given shares in the farm rather than actual land, which was given to Romanians. The

Germans successfully contested this in court, but a new German-Romanian ethnic antagonism had emerged between two groups who had previously peacefully co-existed. In addition, many post-socialist state-building processes tend to involve one section of the community, made up of members of the newly emergent titular national group, imposing political and cultural hegemony on the rest of the population, resulting in ethnic tension (Smith 1999). Thus rather than an essentialist return to inter-ethnic politics and violence, differing and overlapping forms of national identities are being newly constructed as a part of post-socialism.

In addition, the role of the former Communist Party leaders in exploiting nationalism for their own ends should not be overlooked. The phenomenon of 'communists turned nationalists' has manifested itself in many of the post-socialist states of ECE and the former Soviet Union. Many former Communist Party leaders were reluctant to relinquish their hold on power, and sought ways to legitimate their continuation in office. Since socialism was so discredited in the eyes of the population they could gain no legitimacy by adhering to the values of the former regime. Hence, for many rallying to the cause of the 'nation', and particularly its defence in the face of perceived threats, was an effective way of gathering popular support. Corneliu Vadim Tudor, leader of the Greater Romania Party, provides a good example. Previously a high-up member of the Ceauçescu regime, Tudor and his party have gained much support by exploiting the poor economic conditions in Romania. Their construction of Romanian nationalism has involved using the media to promote an image of an ethnically pure Romania (to the detriment of Hungarians, Jews and Roma) and an expansionist view of a 'Greater Romania' which will reincorporate parts of Moldova and the Ukraine.

The construction of nationalism highlights one of the central features of post-socialism, namely the significance of dealing with and representing the Communist past. At its most extreme Communist rule is associated with a repressive state which imprisoned, exiled, tortured and murdered its citizens. For millions it was a time of suppression of personal freedom and great personal hardship. At a range of scales, from the individual to the nation-state, people living under post-socialism are trying to forge new relationships with that past as a way of making sense of the new conditions that they find themselves in. Even young people, who may have only a vague memory of the latter days of state-socialism, are affected by the experience and collective memory of their elders (Barker 1999).

It is perhaps unsurprising that reactions have included a rejection of the communist period and attempted ensure of it as an historical aberration. In these revisions the pre-Communist past is joined directly to the 1990s in efforts to repossess a 'normal' past which can be woven into 'normal' presents and futures. More contested are efforts to commemorate and represent the period via museums, oral history projects and tourist products which seek either to preserve an accurate record of life under state-socialism, or to offer a particular version of it. Moreover, ECE and the former Soviet Union have even seen examples of a wish to return to the communist past. The re-election of former Communist politicians by citizens disillusioned with the progress of post-socialism is linked with growth in a sense of nostalgia for the period particularly among the older generation who have borne the brunt of the losses in jobs, state housing and social security. As well as a part of working through personal experiences of the Communist period, the representation of places for external audiences also involves other processes of dealing with the past. This process of dealing with and representing the past is thus central to many attempts at redefining identities under post-socialism, a point which can be illustrated by considering a number of other processes as well.

State-socialist Urban Landscapes within Post-socialist Societies

One arena in which the Communist past is contested is the legacy of the built environment of state-socialism. As discussed earlier, the built environment was one part of the cultural landscape which the Communist state used to transmit ideas and values about the new socialist order. Though the dismantling of the Berlin Wall is often used as a symbol of the fall of communism, many of these landscape features have survived and fix within the landscape a highly visible reminder of the Communist past. It is simply very difficult to remove massive industrial complexes and huge housing estates from the landscape, especially as they still constitute valuable resources in which people live and work. Again, Warsaw's *Palace of Science and Culture* provides a good example of how the built environment forms a focus for the contestation of the Communist past (see Plate 8.2).

The Palace of Culture has played an important role in changing place identities and people's relationship to their past in post-socialist Poland. The building remains the source of considerable feeling, with many Poles expressing open hatred of it. A saying has it that the best view in Warsaw is from the top of the Palace, because that is the only place that you cannot see the building itself from. In 1989 there was much support for plans to tear it down to eradicate the Stalinist past. It, however, still remains an important landscape feature in downtown Warsaw, partly because of the cost of removing it, and partly because its space is still a useful asset for tourism and commerce. Debate then centred on what to do with the building to try and disassociate it from its Communist past and even to demean its importance. One suggestion was to transform it architecturally, for example by cladding its exterior in glass. However, opposition was expressed at such literal attempts at covering up the Stalinist era. Other suggestions included remodelling the downtown area to incorporate taller buildings which would belittle it in the landscape. One Warsaw resident in favour of this option suggested that for him it would mean that 'My generation will achieve some triumph at last. The building that served as a symbol of Communist rule would be degraded' (Polish writer Jack Fedorowicz, cited in Stanislawski 2000). Another suggestion was to subvert the meaning of the building by putting a museum of Communism in it which accurately told the story of state-socialism and its demise. The use of the building to host international trade fairs and exhibitions has slowly brought the attribution of new meanings to the landscape associated with international capitalism: as Dawson (1999) notes, at one point a giant mobile phone was attached to the building to advertise a telecommunications company. This process has been reinforced by the growth of other buildings in downtown Warsaw, such as international banks, hotels and other multinational corporations, using Western architects and designers to create new ways of symbolising the way of life and the country.

As noted above, statues played a significant role in freezing particular values in the landscape as part of attempts to stabilise and legitimate state-socialism. The tearing down of these socialist statues has become almost a clichéd symbol of the fall of state-socialism (see also Verdery 1999). In fact, while many statues were removed from the landscape and destroyed, others have met different fates such as being preserved in museums or being retained in situ. While the former process is clearly a part of rewriting the past (yet again) to obscure Communism, the latter reveal another series of contested relationships with that past.

Two examples serve to illustrate this point. In Budapest, Hungary, many statues were torn down as the country gained independence in 1989. However, there was considerable debate over what the fate of those statues should be. While some wished them destroyed, others wanted them preserved as a memorial to the Communist past so that it was not forgotten. The debate highlighted the problems inherent in memorialising the Communist past. Whilst reluctant to attempt to completely erase that past, at the same time officials and the Hungarian public were anxious that such visible symbols of state-socialism did not hamper attempts at re-imaging Hungary as a modern, Western capitalist nation. In 1991 the city authorities decided that some statues should be retained and a park was designed to display them in 1993 (see Light 2000). Thus an open-air museum called *Statue Park* was created to hold these monuments (see Plate 8.3; it is also possible to 'visit' Statue Park virtually at http://www.szobopark.hu).

The park is designed to be a space for serious reflection on the nature of totalitarian regimes and their propaganda. Roughly half the park's visitors are foreign tourists and half Hungarians. Several relationships with the past are thus contested in this space. Many Hungarians are horrified that foreign visitors should wish to visit these reminders of the Communist past. However, some Hungarian visitors go to the park to remember the realities of that past, and some feel a sense of nostalgia for it. International tourists visit it because they have some kind of an interest in the legacy of Communism which is attractive to them in these destinations, a practice that Light (2000) terms *communist heritage tourism*. In one sense, Light (2000) suggests, this museum represents a positive, confident approach by Hungarian officialdom to its past. However, the park is spatially separated from the city centre where many of these statues originated, and accessing it involves either using public transport to the edge of the city, or paying to go on a tourist visit. This spatial separation serves to remove the visible legacy of the Communist era from those visitors who do not deliberately seek it out, and creates a self-contained, spatially separate 'memoryscape' for those who chose to remember (Light 2000).

A more extreme example is given by the so-called 'Stalin's World' park in Lithuania (the term was used in US news media). Lithuania suffered considerably under Soviet occupation, with around 300,000 Lithuanians deported to Siberian labour camps. After independence from the former Soviet Union in 1991, the Lithuanian Ministry of Culture appealed for a solution for the many hundreds of statues which were torn down. A local millionaire businessman incorporated them into a private museum similar to Statue Park. However, he also proposed building replica Siberian labour camps and a copy of the train station through which people were deported from Vilnius, complete with Red Army guards. Around 70 per cent of Lithuanians supported the idea of the park on tourism and local economic development grounds. However, as can be imagined, the park was also strongly contested. Local politicians and pressure groups opposed it on the grounds that it could glorify or trivialise the era of Soviet oppression. Members of Labora, a pressure group for

Plate 8.3:   A tourist examines one of the massive Communist era statues now on display in the Statue Park museum, Budapest, Hungary

Source: author

former political prisoners and partisans who fought the Red Army in the 1940s, actually expressed their opposition by going on hunger strike. The park's owner, however, argued that for the first time in nearly fifty years Lithuanians have a chance to look at their history from their own point of view, not the official Soviet one. The landscapes of post-socialism again reveal the contested nature of memory, heritage and history.

The use of the built environment and the memorialisation of Communism is also closely connected with the role of tourism in creating post-socialist identities (see Light 2000). International tourism presents a means by which a country can present itself to others. Through museums and heritage sites foreign tourists can be told a particular national story which acts to reinforce national identity. As the tourism market has developed it has thus become an important part of the process of representing the history of, and forging new identities for, the post-socialist countries. While the post-socialist nations wish to place the state-socialist era firmly behind them, the heritage of Communism is also an important source of revenue in that it holds an interest for tourists to these countries (see the discussion of Statue Park above). However, to celebrate or preserve such a legacy may compromise efforts to construct new post-communist national identities. Light (2000) discusses the example of the Berlin Wall in this context. The Berlin Wall became a symbol of the ideological division of post-1945 Europe and of the failure of the East German state to provide economic prosperity and generate popular support. The vast bulk of the Wall has now been demolished as a part of the process of reunifying Germany and declaring Berlin the new capital (see Cochrane and Jonas 1999). However, Berliners have called for the preservation of the Wall, and fragments of it (real and forged) circulate as tourist souvenirs. The route of the Wall is now marked for tourists in the roadway, and surviving elements have been preserved. Light (2000) suggests that the creation of these distinct 'heritage spaces', whilst preserving in part the meaning of the Wall, also act to consign it firmly to distant history.

Tourism raises the issue of how the post-socialist countries represent themselves and their pasts to international audiences. In addition to international tourist flows, important target groups for such processes are international investors and supranational political and military organisations which they are seeking to join (such as the EU and NATO). An important driving force in the creation of new place identities at the level of the national and local state is the need to re-image countries and localities as entities fit for integration with the modern world, specifically a world which is international, capitalist, Europeanised, and dominated by neo-liberal political and economic agendas. Thus *place promotion*, the 'advertising' of localities to target groups such as investors or tourists, has become an important economic process involving the re-imaging of countries and localities.

Place promotion is both an awareness raising exercise and an attempt to change people's attitudes towards a place in order to influence their behaviour. It has become increasingly important as localities attempt to manage the impact of globalisation and political change by competing to attract 'footloose' international investment, tourist flows, consumers and public-sector funding. In many places the restructuring of local economies and their exposure to the competitive global economy has led to de-industrialisation, the bankruptcy of large state-owned enterprises, and high unemployment. These problems have been intensified in certain localities by the fact that the centrally-planned economy often produced an over-reliance on key basic industries.

The demand for investment capital is high. However, central government funding is restricted and access to some Government funds is a competitive process. Private capital is scarce, and it is difficult for many cities to attract *foreign direct investment* (FDI). At the level of the state, the end of state-socialism exposed the newly independent countries to the highly competitive global economy, in which they have had to compete for international investment. Many cities also have a negative (often industrial) image, and the decentralisation of economic decision making powers to local self-government in many of these countries has allowed local authorities the chance to engage in place promotion. Thus in post-socialist East and Central Europe, inter-urban competition and the manipulation of place image have become increasingly important (see Young and Kaczmarek 1999; Purcell 1999). The record of post-socialist ECE and the former Soviet Union in attracting FDI has not been a good one in global terms, and as Table 8.2 illustrates there is considerable variation in the success of individual countries in attracting such investment (see accumulated FDI stock column).

A common element of place promotional efforts is the manipulation of local cultural and historical resources. In this process the past is incorporated in the present in ways which in turn shape our understanding of the past. As Philo and Kearns (1993: 26) point out, 'promotional initiatives can involve the creation of an impression of a truthful History with unavoidable lessons for the present ... in the course of meeting economic needs.' This manipulation and decontextualisation of history is central to many efforts to create new images for nations, states, regions and cities in post-socialist East and Central Europe.

As Johnson (2000) notes, representations of history play an important part in a larger network of circulated ideas about the nature of place and the past which impact on material practices in the present. Verdery (1999) suggests that these new versions of history allow post-socialist politicians to present themselves as heirs to a pre-communist past. They provide the material for symbolising a new order. Neo-liberal reform politicians and nationalists see the nation's fate as wrapped up in its economic vitality. Western politicians and investors see their best local allies as those who have put their Communist past behind them. As Purcell (1999: 10) notes in his study of how the Slovenian state represents itself in cyberspace, 'those deploying specific representations of space and representational spaces attempt to convince capitalists that the conditions for capital accumulation are present in the state.' For the Slovenian government this involves projecting an image of a modern, peaceful, non-Balkan, European, technologically advanced state. Their websites play down or even ignore the recent socialist past, including a simplified history which 'snips out' the Communist period from the timeline (Purcell 1999). Purcell (1999) details how these representations of Slovenia's history and development are tailored to signify a state which is open for business, investment and tourism, but also sufficiently harmonised with Europe to support EU and Nato membership.

The representation of the recent past is thus a 'politically mediated process circumscribed by wider debates in the post-communist period concerning the politics of memory and identity' (Light 2000). Official representations of post-socialist identity are often concerned with creating an identity for the state as democratic, pluralist, capitalist and largely oriented to the West. This identity is invoked to support further integration with Western Europe and to portray themselves as attractive locations for international investment. At the local level, this process has also become of major importance to the local economic development initiatives of post-socialist local states, entering into conditions of neo-liberal, inter-urban competition. The rewriting and re-presentation of history by the state for place promotion purposes is, hence, a key nexus for the creation of contested post-socialist place identities.

Another key area in post-socialism where the rapid but uneven penetration of foreign investment capital is combining with the legacy of communism is consumption. The landscapes of consumption have been transformed, with the growth of small street kiosks in most major cities and the arrival of multi-national retailers replacing the drab landscape of state-owned retailers and the hardships of constant shortages. Even those people who cannot afford to partake of the new consumer culture cannot escape its influence as advertising spreads via the media and in the built environment, with the layering of the symbolism of capitalism on the legacy of state-socialism often producing an unintended visual irony (see Plate 8.4). However, as Barker (1999: 18) notes, 'as we export everything from Disney to Barbie and Reeboks to the new Russia, we are exporting not only products but also the markers of an entire complex ideology.' The new post-socialist consumers are moving into an economic order that, like the system from which they have emerged, creates both ideologies and identities. The consumption of everything from food and clothing to soap operas is having a profound effect on senses of identity under post-socialism (as is the exclusion from consumption imposed by the inequalities of post-socialism). It is important to remember that although the current influx of Western culture into post-socialist societies is impressive in scope and quantity it is not the first. Whether officially accessible or not, Western culture has long been around, and this history also has an impact on what the post-socialist citizen makes of culture now.

Conclusion

With the fall of state-socialism the newly independent states of the former communist Eastern Europe and USSR are undergoing a long and contested process of post-socialist transformation (see Box 8.4 for a chapter summary and further reading). While these countries have a common, if highly differentiated, origin as state-socialist societies, it is by no means clear where attempts at democratisation, marketisation and decolonisation will lead them. Ten years after the final fall of the USSR many of these countries have made relatively little progress in the expected 'transition to capitalism'. Instead, a vast part of the world is still undergoing a highly contested process of attempting to develop new economic, political, and social forms of organisation to cope with the end of Communist dominance. They are doing so in the context of a time of change in the global economy and in how the local relates to the global, with an ongoing shift to more flexible capitalism and new regional alliances emerging, particularly with respect to the EU and to Russia. As these newly independent countries try to shape their development, their policies interact with these larger processes to create particular geographies of post-socialist change at the national, regional and individual levels. As this chapter has discussed, the analysis of the cultural geographies of post-socialist transformation adds much to our understanding of how nations

**Plate 8.4: The symbolism of international capital overlays the visible legacy of
the state-socialist built environment**
Here advertising by a multi-national corporation covers a block of state-socialist era
flats in Lodz, Poland

Source: author

and individuals are negotiating their way through their search for identity in the contested post-socialist world. It is a search that looks set to continue throughout much of the twenty-first century as the post-socialist societies contribute to the contested nature of the contemporary world.

Box 8.4: Chapter summary and suggestions for further reading

The chapter has:

- Given a brief historical account of the key changes affecting the region formerly known as the Soviet Union and Eastern Europe.
- Outlined the nature of society under state-socialism and in particular the way in which culture was produced, negotiated and contested within that system.
- Examined the transformation from state-socialism after the 'fall of Communism' in1989
- Discussed the contested cultural geographies of post-socialist transformation.

More detail on the historical background to the development and passing of state-socialism can be found in Pipe (1994) *Russia under the Bolshevik regime, 1919–1924* and Crampton (1994) *Eastern Europe in the Twentieth Century – And After*. Detailed accounts of the geography of state-socialism are provided in a series of books by David Turnock, with overviews of industrial geography provided in *Eastern Europe* (1978) and human geography in *The Human Geography of Eastern Europe* (1989), and also in Chapter 2 of his 1997 volume *The East European Economy in Context*. For an excellent insight into the operation of state-socialism and the process of post-socialist transformation at the micro-level, see Verdery (1996) *What Was Socialism and What Comes Next?* Social and political aspects of the transformation are well covered in Ramet (1995) *Social Currents in Eastern Europe*, while Pickvance and Smith's (1998) edited volume *Theorising Transition* provides a wide ranging collection of geographical studies of post-socialist transformation. Two key texts covering events in the former Soviet Union are Smith's (1999) *The Post-Soviet States* and Bradshaw's (1997) *Geography and Transition in the Post-Soviet Republics*, while the question of nationalism is extensively covered in Smith (1996) *The Nationalities Question in the Post-Soviet States*. A good account of the new cultural forms arising in post-Soviet Russia is given in Barker's (1999) *Consuming Russia*, whilst other overviews of recent changes include studies on *East Central Europe and the Former Soviet Union* by Turnock (2001) and Bradshaw and Stenning (2004).

Note

1 It is important to recognise that other countries are undergoing or have undergone a change from a situation where they have been run according to Communist principles, such as China, Cuba and a variety of countries in Africa, Latin America and Asia. Indeed, in 1987 it was estimated that 35% of the world's population lived under some form of Communism (Kornai 1992). The situation in the former-USSR and Eastern Europe is, however, unique in the sense of a whole relatively integrated region undergoing such change.

Part Four:
Local Worlds

Chapter 9

Places on the Margin: The Spatiality of Exclusion

Phil Hubbard

Introduction

All societies have places that are 'on the margins'. In simple terms, these are the places or locales where we find particular concentrations of 'outsiders', people excluded in various ways from participation in mainstream or 'normal' society. Of course, these spaces may not always be literally on the margins, in the sense in areas spatially distant from the command centres of the world economy, from spectacular new concentrations of leisure and entertainment or from areas regarded as aesthetically pleasing. In fact, they are often closely, and cruelly, juxtaposed with such areas. Yet such areas are a focus of simultaneous fascination and fear for most members of society, and indeed for many human geographers, as they represent specific spatial concentrations of those who fail to match mainstream ideas of how people should live and work. Typically, such areas might be characterised by large numbers of people excluded from the labour force, dependent on welfare and living in substandard housing. Simultaneously, this deprivation may be manifest in indicators of social pathology such as ill health, drug-dependence, vice and crime. Most people are probably aware of such places, even if they have never visited them, and generally seek to avoid them, regarding them as 'no-go' areas. It is the *stigma* surrounding these places that, I shall argue, leads to their relative isolation; once a place is labelled as degraded and deprived, its residents find it increasingly hard to be accepted by mainstream society.

What is therefore important from a geographical perspective is to understand how the character of these areas – social, economic, cultural, environmental – might contribute to the continuing marginalisation of specific individuals and groups, and, conversely, how the labelling or stereotyping of such areas comes to inform widely-held ideas of the status of such individuals and groups. In essence then, we are starting from the assumption that 'places on the margin' are places particularly associated with marginalised populations. But what do we actually mean by the term marginalisation? According to Winchester and White (1988), this is a difficult question to answer (see Box 9.1), but in general, it can be defined as referring to the ways in which some groups or individuals fail to match up to perceived norms or standards. One important aspect of their marginalisation is thus economic: people are no longer able to afford what might be perceived to be the normal necessities of life or enjoy an adequate standard of living. Such *material deprivation*, measured in terms of people's ability to purchase adequate shelter, clothing and food, is often pronounced among those who find themselves unemployed, yet it may also effect those who are employed in the lower strata of the labour market (see also Chapter 7). Based on an understanding of the dynamics of the capitalist mode of production where elite groups in the centres accumulate profit through the exploitation of workers in the peripheries (see Chapter 7 and 11), it might be argued that the marginalisation of the working classes is an inevitable result of the way dominant modes of production are organised. Moreover, that this economic marginalisation has traditionally been concentrated in specific places has been acknowledged since the inception of industrialised capitalism, as Engels' description of living conditions in the slums of nineteenth-century Manchester clearly demonstrates:

> After roaming the streets for a day or two, making headway with difficulty through the human turmoil, one realises that these citizens have been forced to sacrifice the best qualities of their human nature...the very turmoil of the streets has something repulsive against which human nature rebels...the brutal indifference, and the isolation of individuals increases the more people are crowded together in their squalid houses (Engels 1975: 64).

Box 9.1: Marginalisation

Winchester and White (1988: 38) suggest that marginalisation is a relative concept, in that the identification of a particular group as marginalised is not constant in time or constant between different societies and cultures. Nonetheless, they identify the following categories as indicative of the type of individuals and groups who find themselves on the margins of contemporary society: the unemployed (particularly long-term); the impoverished elderly; students; single-parent families (mainly female-headed); ethnic minorities; refugees; the disabled; illegal immigrants; 'down and outs' (homeless and street people); drug users; criminals; prostitutes (female and male); homosexuals. This list is, of course, an oversimplification, and it should be obvious that some individuals may belong to more than one category at a time. Moreover, it should be apparent that different processes – economic, social and legal – combine to determine the marginalisation of these groups in very different ways in different places.

Similar descriptions of the conditions of those who live and work in economically marginal locations have long been a mainstay of geographic research, with the 'Chicago School' of urban sociologists particularly noted for their 'thick' and detailed descriptions of life in the slum areas associated with economic hardship, immorality, crime and disease (see Chapter 2). Classic studies in the 1920s and 1930s by Park, Reckless, Burgess and Hoyt (see Box 9.2) thus focused attention on the way in which those living on the margins of poverty are typically found in marginal spaces, especially the *inner city*, suggesting that the relative economic power of different groups is manifest in their area of residence.

Box 9.2: The Chicago School

Generally regarded as the first sociology department to be established anywhere in the world, the University of Chicago Department of Anthropology and Sociology was founded in 1892 and became synonymous with urban sociology during the first half of the twentieth century. Although probably best known to geographers as the source of innumerable models of urban social structure (including Burgess' infamous and often-criticised concentric zones model), the work of the Chicago school was more diffuse and complex than is often acknowledged today. For example, although the writings of its most famous members, such as Thomas (1863–1947), Park (1864–1944), Burgess (1886–1966) and Wirth (1897–1952), drew in an often spurious manner on concepts derived from eugenics and social Darwinism, they were based on fastidious empirical research involving intensive qualitative fieldwork and observation. For example, Park (1925: 37) wrote of the need to observe and document the characteristic types of social organisation and individual behaviours evident 'in Bohemia, the half-world, the red-light district and other moral regions less pronounced in character', positing the marginal spaces of the city as 'laboratories' in which 'human nature and social processes may be conveniently and profitably studied'. Following Park's suggestion, members of the Chicago School were subsequently responsible for some remarkable *micro-sociological* descriptions of the customs and social practices of those found in marginal spaces, from Wirth's (1928) studies of the Afro-American inhabitants of the 'ghetto' to Reckless' (1926) descriptions of street prostitution. The Chicago School's advocacy of participant observation and *ethnographic* technique (literally, 'writing about a way of life') has remained extremely influential in urban sociology, particularly among those researchers who seek to shed light on the different social groups – or *subcultures* – existing on the margins of society (Thornton and Gelder 1997).

Yet in more recent times, geographers have switched their attention from economically-marginalised groups to examine the spatial distribution and marginalisation of a wider variety of social groups, including sexual minorities, the disabled, ethnic and racialised groups, single-parent families and so on. Here, economic hardship is not always as immediately apparent, yet these groups are similarly over-concentrated in so-called marginal areas. To understand their marginalisation, Winchester and White (1988: 38) argue that it is necessary to consider a second dimension of marginality; one that is social in nature. In this sense, it is apparent that many social groups and individuals are considered by controlling groups in society (often referred to as *hegemonic* groups) as challenging or undermining ideas of what is seen as a desirable or acceptable way of living and behaving. In contemporary Western society, the hegemonic group is normally white, adult, middle-class and heterosexual, and those who lie outside this social domain often find themselves labelled as 'deviant' or 'dangerous' because of the way they do not match up to these dominant constructions. For example, prostitutes are a socially marginalised group as they offer sexual services outside the socially-sanctioned institutions of domesticised monogamy and marriage, and thus are seen to disrupt the moral order of society. In this particular case, their marginalisation is reinforced through legal mechanisms which criminalise their lifestyles (Hubbard 1997). In other cases, however, although the lifestyle of the group is not criminalised (lone parenthood is not illegal, for example), it is still portrayed as being somehow undesirable and non-conforming, with its members often being subject to social stigma and prejudice.

Hence, there are a variety of different groups that, for a diversity of reasons, find themselves on the margins of society. Discrimination in the job market, in the housing market and in education frequently combines to further marginalise these groups, so they find themselves not only economically weak, but socially unacceptable. What it is important to realise, however, is that this process of *cumulative marginalisation* is a spatialised one, with specific marginal areas becoming associated with marginal groups over time. The placement of these marginal groups in such environmentally-degraded and poverty-stricken areas may then serve to enhance the powerlessness of this group. There is perhaps no better example of this than the systematic re-distribution of South Africa's coloured population under the Apartheid era, when the social and economic marginalisation of the native black population was underpinned by a racist ideology of enforced separation. While the hegemonic white population was able to enjoy 'Western-style' standards of living, the majority of the black population, who constituted 75 per cent of the country's total, were forced to live in the Homelands (or *Bantustans*) (see Figure 9.1). These amounted to only 13 per cent of the land area of South Africa, and were typically characterised by poor agriculture, lacked mineral resources and had little infrastructure. Hence, it was hardly surprising that the quality of life for the white minority and the coloured population differed so widely under the regime of the *Afrikaner Nationalist Party* which instigated the apartheid system, with whites having average monthly incomes six times higher than those of the black population in 1991 (Smith 1994).

The example of apartheid-era South Africa is clearly an extreme case of those not belonging to the hegemonic social group (in this case, any person not classified as white) being marginalised in a variety of ways, rendered effectively powerless in economic and political life. Yet it does serve to make the more general point that geographic marginalisation is not *just* a reflection of people's marginalisation but actually contributes to this process. Furthermore, although it might be imagined that processes of marginalisation are most apparent in the developing world, where shanty towns and *barrios* are home to millions, Western societies are also riddled by inequality and resulting marginalisation (for examples, see Chapter 7). Even in areas traditionally imagined as idyllic, such as the British countryside, there are many individuals who find themselves in relative disadvantage (Cloke and Little 1997). This is particularly the case in remote rural areas, where access to a range of employ-

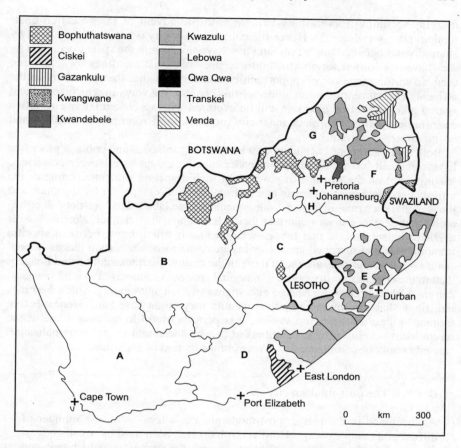

Figure 9.1: The 'black' bantustans (or homelands) established in the apartheid era by the 1951 Bantu Authorities Act

The ten areas account for 13 per cent of the land area of South Africa, but were the only spaces where the white minority allowed Black, Indian or Coloured groups to own land.

ment opportunities is often hampered by poor transport and a lack of service provision. Recent studies, for example, have suggested that the proportion of households whose income is less than 80 per cent of the mean household income for the area approaches 60 per cent in many English counties, with more remote study areas having more households in or close to poverty (Cloke *et al.* 1994).

Yet it is in the urban West that marginalisation is often most pronounced, with contrasts between spectacular sites of consumption and affluence (shopping malls, festival sites, gentrified housing developments and so on) and 'places on the margin' becoming increasingly evident with the advent of the so-called post-modern city (see Box 9.3). Hence the contemporary city is often characterised by sharp divides between the 'haves' and the 'have-nots', with the spaces occupied by the 'have-nots' often serving to reinforce their marginal identities by separating them from the range of job opportunities and services that the city offers to the affluent. Therefore, in the remainder of this chapter, the ways in which social and spatial marginalisation intersect will be explored with specific reference to urban case studies, particularly black inner city (or *ghetto*) environments in the USA and *no-go estates* in Britain.

Both examples represent situations where economic, social and political processes have combined in specific places to render specific groups as relatively powerless, leaving them on the margins of poverty. In such desperate situations, crime or the informal economy may represent one seeming form of 'escape' for local people, and the way that such marginal places subsequent become labelled as 'hotspots' of crimi-nality and deviance is an important theme throughout this chapter. Nonetheless, it needs to be recognised that the association that is often drawn between specific immoral acts and marginal areas (for instance, the idea that certain places 'breed' crime) is a spurious one, grounded more in the realms of representation and imagery than in the complex reality of life in marginal spaces. As Shields (1991: 5) suggests, marginal places 'carry the image and stigma of their marginality which becomes indistinguishable from any empirical identity they might have had'. Hence, before turning to these specific case studies, it is perhaps useful to examine some of the recent ideas developed by geographers as to why social and spatial marginalisation can only really be comprehended if we examine *images* of exclusion.

Box 9.3: The post-modern city

As discussed in Chapter 2, post-modernism is a term used in a number of diffuse and complex ways. However, it has often been used by urban geogra-phers to delimit a 'postmodern object', namely the type of city which emerged in the late twentieth century in response to a complex range of economic, social and political reorganisations. Soja gives a flavour of these changes, presenting Los Angeles as the quintessential post-modern city with many distinct urban forms:

> There is a dazzling array of sites in this compartmentalised corona of the inner city: the Vietnamese shops and Hong Kong housing of a redeveloping Chinatown; the Big Tokyo financed modernisation; the induced pseudo-SoHo of artist's lofts and galleries…the strangely anachronistic wholesale markets…the capital of urban homelessness in the Skid Row district; the enormous muralled barrio stretching eastwards toward East Los Angeles…the intentionally yuppify-ing South Park redevelopment zone hard by the slightly seedy Convention Center, the revenue-milked towers and fortresses of Bunker Hill (Soja 1989: 239–240).

What Soja is describing here is a new type of city permeated by all manner of divisions and fractures. This point is also made by Harvey (1989) who suggests that many cities, and indeed other areas, can be characterised as exhibiting a *condition of postmodernity* in which there is a plethora of cultural signs and images which come together to form a sort of messy social collage – or pastiche – of meanings within which there seems to be no overall order and within which individual people can find no stable bearings of meaning. Harvey suggests that this is largely an outcome of a new form of capitalism which he calls 'flexible capitalism'. He advanced four broad lines of argument to sustain this claim (see Cloke *et al.*, 1991: 182):

1) That there were close similarities in the way the postmodern city was being produced and the way capitalism works: 'I see no difference in principle between the vast range of speculative and ... unpredictable activities undertaken by entrepreneurs ... and the equally speculative development of cultural, political, legal and ideological values' (Harvey 1989: 344).

2) That much of the postmodern city is produced by and for people and institutions which are clearly capitalist in nature. Much of the postmodern city for example is designed by multi-national architectural firms, built by large-scale property-developers and construction companies, and inhabited by financial institutions and corporate headquarters

3) That the postmodern city is created out of, and acts to cover over, some of the problematic practices of capitalism. As Cloke *et al.* (1991: 182) note, Harvey argues that the practices of 'pastiche' employed in postmodern art and architecture can be seen as 'nothing more than an extreme manifestation of the relentless and structurally determined quest for new and unusual *commodities* to sell'. Harvey also argues that the postmodern city is designed to mystify people by making things appear more exciting, more individual, more open, more human scaled and yet still house corporate, multi-national firms which carry on their practices as before.

4) That both postmodernism and flexible capitalism are based on 'space-time compression' in which things which are distant in space can be accessed almost simultaneously. This is achieved culturally through the rise of the mass media and electronic communication and economically through the emergence of increasingly abstract forms of finance and the production of intangible, easily transportable, commodities.

Harvey's analysis is extremely ambitious suggesting as it does that seemingly disparate images and experiences can be connected to the dynamics of contemporary capitalism. It has, however, been strongly criticised, in large part for being insufficient postmodern in approach (for details of postmodernism as approach see Chapter 2). Dear (2000: 76), for example, claims that both Harvey and Soja offer 'profoundly modernist' accounts of the postmodern city. He suggests that this stems from:

1) The absence of any sustained engagement with 'the consequences of difference' (Dear, 2000: 766). Amongst the neglected difference identified by Dear are those of 'gender and feminism' which he claims are almost

complete absent within Harvey's (1989) *The Condition of of Postmodernity*. This point had indeed been made by several feminist geographers (e.g. Massey 1991; Deutsche 1991; Rose 1991) Amongst the arguments advanced are:

- That many of the images of modernism and postmodernism are quite clearly sexualised, and generally sexualised in a highly 'masculinist way'. Massey, for example, notes that while Harvey suggests that there has been a shift in art from modernist 'representations' to postmodern 'pastiches' and gives five illustrations to make his point: 'Every one of them is of a women, in every case a naked women' (Massey, 1991: 44). Hence rather than seeing the dominant forms of contemporary culture as being radically different from earlier forms, there is, Massey and Deutsche argue (and Harvey, 1992 concurs), a persistent patriarchal structure to it.
- That while the 'postmodern condition' of having no stable bearings and being unable to impose order one's surroundings may be novel to white, male, middle class academics like Harvey, it is a condition in which many people, including many women, have lived for some time. This point is particularly well demonstrated by Rose (1993a) who speaks of her personal feelings of space and how they are created through her gender. Watson and Gibson (1995) explore the experience of postmodern cities by different groups and how postmodern space may indeed be different in different areas of the world.
- Feminists such as Massey (1991) and Deutsche (1991) have suggested that culture has a 'social transformative' affect and that adopting a postmodern perspective of recognition of difference and the processes by which representations of the world are made, can lead to people adopting very different behaviours and a very different form of politics of change.

2) A lack of 'critical self-reflection about the author's own epistemological stances' (Dear, 2000: 76). In particular Dear comments on the 'almost complete absence of attention to language and rhetoric' (p. 77) and the uncritical adoption of Marxist metanarratives. Dear complains, for example, that while 'tacking an axe to postmodernism, Harvey leaves his own historical materialism almost totally unexamined' (p. 78). Harvey adopts a starkly modernist, even structuralist analysis of postmodernity, seeking to 'get behind' the fragmented features of postmodernity and to 'identify essential meanings' (Harvey, 1989: 74). As Cloke *et al*. (1991: 180) comment, Harvey employs an interpretation of the relationship between culture and the capitalist economy which appears quite close to a classical 'structuralist' one, whereby culture is seen to be determined by economic processes (see Chapter 2). Harvey also explicitly argues for the value of 'mega-theories' in general, and Marxism in particular: 'If there is a meta-theory with which to embrace all these gyrations of postmodern thinking and cultural production, then why should we not deploy it' (Harvey 1989: 337).

3) A 'misunderstanding/misrepresentation concerning the politics of post-modernity' (Dear 2000: 76). In particular, Dear charges Harvey with having double standards in his treatment of modernist politics based on rational thought and collective action vis-à-vis 'postmodern identity politics'. Whilst recognising authoritarian problems associated with the former, Harvey argues for a retention of the 'project of Enlightenment' (see Chapter 2), albeit in a new form. Discerning postmodernism to have other problems, notably such as relativism and individualism, Harvey responds by simply turning away from this philosophy.

Stereotyping and the Exclusionary Urge

While social marginalisation can be measured in material ways, such as through the physical exclusion of individuals and groups from the social institutions, rituals and practices enjoyed by hegemonic groups, it is important to note that this exclusion is also *symbolic*. Indeed, it could be argued that any differences between social groups are culturally-constructed – that is to say that they are creations produced (and repro-duced) through the realms of representation and imagery. Here, we may take the term representation to include all signifying practices and symbolic systems through which we come to understand the world and our place within it (Woodward 1997). Clearly, this can include a wide variety of contemporary media – films, TV and liter-ature being particularly important – which collectively order and structure the world into what is 'good' and 'bad', 'desirable' and 'undesirable', 'normal' and 'other'. In sum, it can be argued that the media is responsible for the construction and distribu-tion of *discourses*, frameworks of meaning (see Box 3.7), that often revolve around stereotypes of certain groups of people which provided a partial, simplified and distorted view of the lifestyles, habits and characteristics of often heterogeneous social groups. Although most people do not necessarily accept or internalise these stereotypes uncritically, it is inevitable that they find themselves drawing on these stereotypes in their social interactions, such is the difficulty in dealing with the complexity of everyday living.

What is especially significant about these stereotypes is that they are *ideological* in nature, in the sense they are generally created by (and in the interests of) hege-monic social groups, structuring the world mainly from the perspective of middle-aged, white, English-speaking, heterosexual, able-bodied, middle-class and educated men. Critical media studies have therefore demonstrated that these seem-ingly 'common sense' representations construct *hierarchies of difference*, with the media using specific metaphors and descriptions to suggest that marginalised groups are somehow less than normal (Cresswell 1996: 27). In his consideration of processes of social exclusion (see Box 9.4), Sibley (1995) argues that it is thus possible to identify a number of similarities in the way that marginalised groups have been depicted over the years, with terms relating pollution, dirt and disease frequently used to symbolise a distinction between order and disorder (see also Shurmer-Smith and Hannam 1995: 139–142). Hence, taking a number of different groups regarded as marginal – prostitutes, ethnic minorities, the homeless, travellers and so on – it is possible to see that key metaphors relating to bodily imperfection, disease and 'naturalness' are often invoked to suggest that some groups are beyond the realms of the acceptable.

Box 9.4: Social purification

In his consideration of 'geographies of exclusion', Sibley (1995) has offered one of the most thorough and theoretically-sophisticated explorations by a geographer as to how urges to marginalise particular social groups feed off images of difference. Drawing particularly on psychoanalytical ideas about the importance of maintaining self-identity (literally, maintaining the boundaries of the self), Sibley argues that the urge to exclude 'threatening others' from one's proximity is connected to deeply-engrained and often subconscious desires to maintain cleanliness and purity, many of which may be inculcated in early infancy. Following Douglas' (1966: 41) argument that dirt is 'matter out of place', he goes on to explore the ways in which this abject fear of the self being defiled or polluted is projected (or mapped) onto individuals and groups depicted by hegemonic society as deviant or dangerous. This engagement with psychoanalytical theory offers new ways for thinking about processes of marginalisation, implying that the way people seek to exclude other 'different' groups can only be understood with reference to the manner in which people identify with or against particular stereotypes on a psychic level. As yet, there has only been a limited geographic engagement with such ideas (Pile 1996), yet it is clear that such urges to purify are inherently spatial, with psychic spaces mapped onto social space as people attempt to purify their body, their surroundings and their locale through processes of boundary-erection – whether those boundaries are physical, symbolic or psychological.

An example of how stereotyped images often result in normal society rejecting a particular group is vividly illustrated in the media reporting of HIV/AIDS from the mid-1980s onwards. In the ensuing *moral panic* that followed diagnosis of the virus and its main vectors of transmission (i.e. as a blood-born and sexually transmitted disease), a sometimes hysterical media began to focus on the groups most readily identified as risk groups:

> The HIV virus has manifested itself in three constituencies in the West – blacks, intravenous drug user and gay men. The presence of AIDS in these groups is generally perceived not as accidental but as a symbolic extension of some imagined inner essence of being (Watney 1987: 8).

Hence HIV infection was portrayed as a condition affecting those whose 'inner essence' diverged from the expectations of normal society. Rather than being seen as a condition affecting normal hegemonic society, it was imaged as a threat to society that came from outside – that is, from those whose lifestyles disrupted notions of normalcy. In turn, ideas of sexual immorality, irresponsibility and willful hedonism on behalf of those groups most affected by the virus were used to create social barriers between healthy, normal society and these polluting influences. Consequently, this symbolic marking of HIV-infected groups as deviant became mirrored in their material marginalisation, as they began to suffer widespread discrimination, prejudice and neglect. As Wilton (1996) has shown, this has had clear spatial effects, with those infected with HIV characterised by *diminishing geographies* as their access to the normal spaces of the workplace, the home and the street have been subject to increasing constraint.

In his analysis of the constrained daily geographies of people with AIDS/HIV, Wilton stresses that the limits placed on an individual's daily world are the products not of AIDS/HIV in isolation but rather emerge from the surrounding social environment. He particularly highlights the social-spatial constraint displayed in neighbourhood resistance to such groups which may exclude them from community space – the so-called NIMBY (Not In My Back Yard) syndrome. Indeed, neighbourhood opposition to community facilities or welfare services is so widespread in Western society – particularly in suburban landscapes – that few stop to question why people might object to new development in their locality. Certainly, many NIMBY campaigns are fought with reference to the detrimental environmental effects (typically referred to by geographers as *negative externalities*) such as noise, water, air or visual pollution which might be caused by such developments. In turn, these might well have an economic impact on the locality, effecting house prices. Such economic impacts are, to an extent, quantifiable; what is less measurable is how community opposition might be related to processes of social stigmatisation and the desire to *purify* the suburb (see Box 9.4). Clearly people with AIDS/HIV represent a rapidly-expanding cohort with a highly stigmatised (and unique) social identity, and attempts to find favourable locations for facilities for this group typically meet with opposition from affluent suburban dwellers.

According to Dear and Wolch (1987) this spatial exclusion of people with AIDS/HIV is symptomatic of the more general community opposition displayed toward those seen as 'non-productive', albeit that people with AIDS/HIV stand as perhaps the most stigmatised groups in Western society (see Table 9.1). This community opposition to welfare-dependent populations – including the homeless, the elderly and the mentally ill – frequently results in the most visible concentration of facilitates being located in older service-dependent inner city areas where community opposition is muted. Over time, increasing numbers of the visible street homeless or 'down-and-outs' may find themselves isolated in such areas following the closure of more permanent facilities and residential homes (with an estimated 25 per cent of homeless in the UK are ex-mental patients). In turn, the presence of the homeless on the street creates anxiety on behalf of 'normal' populations:

> Evicted from the private spaces of the real estate market, homeless people occupy the public spaces, but their subsequent presence in the urban landscape is fiercely contested. Their visibility is erased by institutional efforts to move them elsewhere – to shelters, out of buildings and parks, to poor neighbourhoods, out of the city, to other marginal spaces (Smith 1996a: 89).

Table 9.1: Relative acceptability of human service facilities, United States

Facility type	Mean acceptability (1=low, 6=high)
School	4.75
Day care centre	4.69
Nursing home for elderly	4.65
Medical clinic for allergies	4.40
Hospital	4.32
Group home for mentally retarded	3.98
Alcohol rehabilitation	3.80
Homeless shelter	3.73
Drug treatment centre	3.61
Group home for mentally disabled	3.51
Group home for people with depression	3.47
Mental health outpatient facility	3.45
Independent apartment for mentally disabled	3.30
Group home for people living with AIDS	3.20

Notes: survey of 1326 respondents

Source: Takahashi, L.M. and Dear, M.J. (1997) 'The changing dynamics of community opposition to human service facilities', *Journal of the American Planning Association* 63: 83.

This 'ghettoization' of homeless ex-psychiatric patients, which formed the focus of Dear and Wolch's (1987) study of Toronto's changing provision of welfare services, serves to show that the spatial concentration of marginal groups is frequently a direct reflection of underlying exclusionary urges resulting from stigma of non-productivity. However, bearing in mind the range of responses uncovered in the study by Takashashi and Dear (1997: 81), it is worth noting that there is a *continuum of threat* which shapes community responses: the most consistently rejected and stigmatised groups are those stereotyped as deviant and dangerous, the least feared are seen as merely *different*.

Hence, although different groups and areas may well exhibit different reactions to people dependent on welfare services, spatial marginalisation can generally be read as a product of dominant *imaginary geographies* which cast minorities as 'imperfect' people, with either polluting bodies or devilish tendencies, who should 'therefore' be located 'elsewhere'. As Sibley (1995: 49) contends, this elsewhere might be 'nowhere', as when genocide or the moral transformation of a minority like prostitutes is advocated, or it might be some 'spatial periphery', like the other end of the world (as with British penal colonies in Australasia) or the edge of a city. In extreme cases, some nomadic groups who reject notions of domesticity and identification with a specific place find themselves regarded as constantly 'out of place' by hegemonic groups. In such ways, we can begin to see that social and economic marginalisation, underpinned by images of difference, results in very specific geographies. As the remainder of this chapter will explore, the subsequent 'placement' of marginal groups in marginal spaces can only really be explained with reference to widespread myths and stereotypes, images that often arouse deep-rooted anxiety on behalf of 'normal' groups and individuals.

Racialised Margins: The US Ghetto

Recent geographical research has suggested that many of the *geographies of exclusion* which permeate Western society are underpinned by racist processes of segregation, with images of marginal places often heavily racialised in nature (e.g. Smith 1989; Anderson 1991; Cohen 1996). Such research seeks to unpack those symbolic or imaginary geographies which portray ethnic spaces as marginal, demonstrating how such discourses sustain material differences between the predominantly white charter group and coloured ethnic minorities. Examples of the persistence of residential segregation among non-whites in particular can be demonstrated in many European cities, yet it is in the USA that racism has often served to place many black people in the poorest housing areas. Indeed, the association between areas of predominantly black residence and the poorest, often welfare-dependent 'ghettos' has become so pernicious that it serves to reinforce dominant white assumptions of the attitudes, behaviours and lifestyles of racial minorities, assumptions that may bear little resemblance to black people's urban experience. Events such as the Rodney King riots of 1992 – when the acquittal of a white police officer for the filmed beating of a black Los Angeles resident sparked the most intense public disorder seen for thirty years – have particularly consolidated the idea of the ghetto as a crime-ridden environment; although the areas of unrest were typically those of poorest income, high population densities and school dropout rates, it was the 'racial character' of these areas that was most highlighted in the subsequent reporting (Smith 1995: 160).

The idea of the ghetto as a dense concentration of danger and deviance has then become a particularly pernicious myth which has reinforced these assumptions of 'racial' inferiority. This association between the minority population and specifically criminalised places has been cemented over the years in a variety of media which uses the 'ghetto' as a coded term for the imagined deviance of black people. Even 'new wave' black films such as *Menace II Society*, *Harlem Nights*, *Jungle Fever* and *Straight Outta Brooklyn*, which seek to show something of the everyday struggle for survival on the streets in an authentic and sympathetic manner, ultimately serve to stereotype such places as landscapes of endemic violence and drug-dependence. As McCarthy *et al.* (1997) argue, the American middle-classes tend to know more about inner-city black people through long-distanced but familiar media images, than they do through personal everyday interactions. In this context, even John Singleton's 'realist' account of growing up in South Central Los Angeles, *Boyz 'n the Hood* can be seen as a corroboration of dominant white myths of an immoral inner city in which drugs, guns and teenage promiscuity are part of everyday life (Benton 1995). Such white fears and fantasies about the black inner city are acidly invoked in Wolfe's (1988) fictional account of the Wall Street trader, Sherman McCoy, who one night takes the wrong turning on his drive home only to be confronted with a side of New York that he remains cosseted from in his 'yuppie' housing development:

At the next corner, he turned – west, he figured – and followed that street a few blocks. There were more low buildings. They might have been garages, they might have been sheds. There were fences with spirals of razor wire on top. But the streets were deserted, which was okay, he told himself. Yet he could feel his heart beating with a nervous twang. Then he turned again. A narrow street with seven or eight storey apartment buildings; no sign of people, not a light in a window. The next block, the same. He turned again, and as he rounded the corner – astonishing. Utterly empty, a vast open terrain…here and there were traces of rubble and slag. The earth looked like concrete, except it rolled down this way, and up that…the hills and dales of the Bronx…reduced to asphalt, concrete and cinders (Wolfe 1988: 65).

This depiction of the Bronx as a wasteland inhabited by 'lots of dark faces' again reminds us of the ways in which fears of difference (in this example, based on skin colour) can provoke anxiety and feed the urge to exclude. From the perspective of the white narrator in Wolfe's book, the urban decay of the Bronx mirrors his perceived view of the city's black population as 'other': street people as opposed to his world of 'air people' (adopting Raban's 1990, description of those who can afford to distance themselves from marginal places).

For many African-Americans, ghetto life is similarly typified by anxiety, but an anxiety originating from fears of crime, isolation from a white mainstream and problems of poverty. In 1990 the average white household income was 1.72 times higher than that of black households, with one-third of black families remaining below the poverty line (Smith 1995). As the renowned feminist and cultural theorist bell hooks relates, this experience of living in the black ghetto is one that consistently reinforces feelings of subordination, marginality and inferiority:

To be in the margin is to be part of the whole but outside the main body. As black Americans living in a small Kentucky town, the railroad tracks were a daily reminder of our marginality. Across those tracks were paved streets, stores we could not enter and people we could not eat in, and people we could not look directly in the face. Across these tracks was a world we could work in as maids, as janitors, as prostitutes, as long as it was in a service capacity. We could enter that world, but we could not live there. We always had to return to the margin, to cross the tracks, to shacks and abandoned houses on the edge of town (hooks 1984: 9).

Indeed, until the 1960s it was not uncommon to find specific ordinances and zoning laws controlling the development of black neighbourhoods, with residents forbidden to enter the white city. Although such laws have long since been overturned, their legacy remains in racist practices of mortgage financiers, banks and estate agents, who may seek to maintain the blackness and whiteness of respective neighbourhoods in the interests of maintaining house prices. Similarly, the phenomena of 'white flight' has not been uncommon in many US suburbs; when the proportion of black residents in a neighbourhood reaches around 8 per cent, a rapid out-migration of white households begins (Short 1996: 223). It is thus unsurprising that the otherness of the African-American population is often embodied in stark segregation. Empirical evidence from Atlanta (Smith 1995), for example, suggests that 55 per cent of the city's census tracts are either 90 per cent black or white.

In the USA especially, this spatial concentration of urban poverty and its association with the black population, has been read as support for the idea of an *underclass* (see Box 9.5), a powerful metaphor which has been popularly adopted as a useful (if emotive) term to describe those who seemingly have little chance of being incorporated in the formal job market, left high and dry by processes of industrial decline and (especially in the US) welfare reform. According to one of the principal proponents of the underclass idea, the links between race and social problems are unequivocal:

> It is no secret that the social problems of the United States are, in great measure, associated with race...while rising levels of crime, drug addiction, out-of-wedlock births and, female-headed families and welfare dependency have been most dramatic amongst what has become a large and seemingly permanent black underclass inhabiting the cores of the city's major cities (Wilson 1987: 74)

Box 9.5: The underclass

There has been considerable debate whether the traditional class structures which existed in Western societies underpinned by industrial and manufacturing-based prosperity have fractured with the transition to a post-industrial economy. Although the term was originally coined by Myrdal (1962), it is the work of Wilson (1987) that bought widespread attention to emergence of an urban underclass – a fraction of society that is permanently excluded from the job market and caught in a 'cycle of deprivation' typically characterised by long-term joblessness, rampant street crime, high numbers of female-headed households, low skills and education and high welfare dependency. This work, and particularly Wilson's view that the underclass is inevitably racialised, has been controversially received amongst academics and policy-makers, particularly for its suggestion that the underclass is an 'undeserving' faction of the poor. In essence, this reiterates earlier (discredited) ideas that there is a group in society who do not wish to work, having been bought up in a culture discouraging participation in education, training or employment. This view, exemplified in Lewis' (1961) *culture of poverty* thesis, has gained much support from right-wing politicians who have used it as a justification for cutting welfare support to particular factions of society that they see as feckless or poorly motivated (especially ethnic minority groups and single mothers). Yet despite this, much of underclass literature does capture the importance of space in creating the underclass, with the relative isolation of the group from the opportunities and facilities on offer to mainstream society fundamental to their marginalisation.

Leaving aside for the moment whether female-headed households (or for that matter, out-of-wedlock births) should necessarily be considered as social *'problems'*, there is a strong racist undertow here which seeks to view problems of poverty and deprivation as the product of deviant, and invariably black, individuals and households. For example, the growth of a crack (cocaine) economy in many US cities has been depicted as a by-product of an African-American culture that encourages (and even celebrates) drug use.

Yet, in seeking to understand the growth of this new lower class faction (who we may or may not wish to refer to as an underclass given the connotations of inferiority that label confers), it is perhaps more useful to turn to the literature that has sought to understand their marginalisation against a backdrop of wider social and economic transitions. Lash and Urry (1994), in particular, have been at pains to emphasise how the growing number of socially and economically marginalised populations is intimately connected to the breakdown of industrialised capitalism and the subsequent shift to a de-industrialised, or post-industrial, society. Such dramatic changes, which began in the early 1970s against a backdrop of global competition and energy crises, have decimated the manufacturing industries which provided the backbone of Western economies, with the burden being particularly felt in the rustbelt regions which had previously prospered on the back of manufacturing success. In the USA, this hit much of the country's industrial heartland – cities like Baltimore, Philadelphia, Detroit, Cleveland and Pittsburgh – which were also areas typified by high proportions of African-Americans. On a more fine-grain scale, it was apparent that many of the jobs lost through manufacturing decline were similarly concentrated in inner city areas with higher proportions of black populations.

Thus the burdens of de-industrialisation were most acutely felt by African-Americans, and although it is important to acknowledge that there are twice as many poor whites in the USA than there are blacks, the white populations were less likely to live in areas of concentrated poverty (Kasarda 1990: 254). With the intensification of poverty and joblessness in black inner cities, it was perhaps unsurprising that social structures associated with industrialised capitalism began to break down:

> A socio-spatial analysis of today's underclass who inhabit a space characterised by a deficit of economic, social and cultural regulation. In such spaces, older organised capitalist structures – industrial labour market, church and family networks, social welfare institutions, trade unions – have dissolved or moved out…The resulting deficit of governance and regulation is the condition of social disorganisation of today's black ghetto (Lash and Urry 1994: 8).

This tendency for established community networks to breakdown in a period of significant economic stress was conversely exacerbated by an outmigration of an emerging mobile black middle class – those who had run the churches and community groups – as they began to prosper in a service-based economy (Smith 1995: 171). As Lash and Urry (1994) point out, this breakdown of community and social life is common in all sorts of spheres, but in more affluent areas, it has been replaced by a more individualistic information and communicative structure, with people able to maintain meaningful contact with the outside world through e-mail, internet and audio-visual technology. In the poverty-stricken spaces of the city, where this infrastructure does not exist, the result is the disintegration of community, anomie and loss of identity. It is in this sense we can talk of places on the margin as being 'unstructured': they are the 'wild places' in contrast with the tame spaces of, for example, the suburbs.

The way that these disparate economic, social and political forces combine to marginalise those living in US black inner cities is graphically shown in a recent analysis of the *urban desertification* of the Bronx, an area where two-thirds of the population are African-American or Hispanic (Wallace 1990). In this paper, the author presents a series of grim statistical comparisons which show strong correlations between rising homicide and murder rates, intensified substance and drug abuse, low birth weights and the incidence of AIDS and the location of African-American families. Such an overview brings home immediately the ways in which placement in a marginal space can effect one's life chances: AIDS is the most common cause of death for those aged between 25 and 44 in the Bronx; 45 per cent of residents are on public assistance; cirrhosis and homicide account for a third of all deaths. Yet Wallace (1990) avoids making any spurious connection between racial lifestyles and practices, on the one hand, and these devastating statistics on the other. Instead he seeks to explore the way the marginalisation of the Bronx is connected to broader institutional processes. In particular, he writes of the influence of the city council's redevelopment programme in prompting the wholesale 'desertification' or mass depopulation of the area, severely disrupting community social and health networks in the process (see Figure 9.2). Although such attempts at redevelopment may have been be borne of good intentions by the city council (i.e. the idea that poor quality housing should be destroyed), Wallace documents the massive disruption this caused for the remaining population, with that disruption measured in the rise of social unrest and criminality.

Hence, the marginalisation of black African-Americans is clearly and strongly related to their residential location in the city. Living in distinctive social spaces, which I describe as marginal places, ultimately serves to construct dominant assumptions of the cultural characteristics of the group, such as the misconception that black groups 'want' to live in such areas, or that the appearance of the area reflects their social values). It is perhaps useful here to refer to Shields' (1991) concept of a *socio-spatialisation* – the idea that places exist not only as physical realities, but more importantly as socially-constructed phenomena associated with particular values, events and groups. This process of place becoming imbued with meaning is, of course, problematic, and here we have glossed over the myriad of ways in which African-Americans seek to challenge dominant conceptions of their lives and spaces, appropriating their own space, yet the importance of space in shaping unequal relationships between dominant and marginal groups remains unquestionable: space is, after all, where social relations actually occur.

No-go Britain: Poverty on the Margins

The marginalisation of black populations in British inner cities has similarly been apparent since the first wave of post-War immigration. However, the processes of selective out-migration leaving a residual inner city ethnic population have generally not been as intense as in the USA. Measures of the ethnic segregation of the three million British who classify themselves as belonging to a non-white ethnic group (e.g. the *index of dissimilarity*) suggest that such populations are becoming more spatially dispersed over time. Hence, although a disproportionate number of Britain's Black-Caribbean, Pakistani, Indian or Bengali residents are located in electoral wards where proportions of ethnic minorities are high, the notion of the racialised ghetto is probably more relevant in the US. For example, recent studies of the 840,000 Indians resident in Britain show that they are becoming 'suburbanised' over time, becoming more strongly represented in owner-occupied housing, particularly in the outer suburbs of London (Moon and Atkinson 1997).

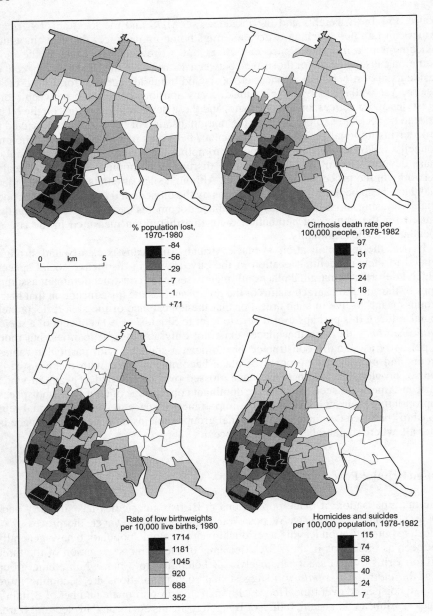

Figure 9.2: Bronx Health Authority Area
This shows a clear association between (a) percentage population lost 1970–1980; (b) cirrhosis death rate per 100,000 people 1978–1982; (c) rate of low birthweights per 100,000 live births 1980; and (d) homicides and suicides per 100,000 people 1978–1982 (from Wallace, 1990).

However, this does not mean that the marginalisation of such groups is not shaped by their very specific geographies, and the residential distributions of such groups have widely been interpreted as reflecting choice and constraint factors which are shaped by dominant constructions of race and colour. For example, Smith's (1989) studies of the half-million Black-Caribbeans living in Britain has strongly suggested that the over-enumeration of such groups in inner city areas typified by older age structures and high population densities is strongly related to their identification and stereotyping as criminalised 'others'. Her analysis of press reporting of crime in Birmingham showed a strong tendency for the local (white) press to focus salaciously on crimes (particularly 'street crimes') which occurred in the 'riot-prone' environment of Handsworth, while ignoring less 'newsworthy' but quantitatively more frequent crimes occurring in predominantly white areas (Smith 1989). In 1994, the controversial pronouncement by the Commissioner of the Metropolitan Police, Paul Condon, that the majority of London's muggers were black reawakened popular misconceptions that black youths are inevitably criminalised, and that black neighbourhoods are breeding grounds for vice and crime.

However, more recent events have perhaps served to deflect debates over the causes of crime away from spurious connections between 'race' and crime to the wider social and economic context in which crime occurs. Specifically, a seeming epidemic of urban unrest on a number of areas not typified by high concentrations of ethnic minorities, and particularly the phenomena of 'joy-riding' (taking vehicles without the driver's consent), has drawn attention to the particular combination of problems encountered on Britain's 'no-go estates' (see Figure 9.3). With sometimes sensationalist reporting focusing on neighbourhoods where GPs are afraid to visit, drugs are freely available and single parenthood is the norm, these areas (of mainly council-owned housing) have become Britain's equivalent of the US 'ghetto'. In particular, it is the association of these estates with crime and criminality that has succeeded in stigmatising these areas as the 'ghettos' of Britain:

> The sense of decline and neglect in many of these areas is palpable: the built environment in many of these areas has now taken on all the classic, ominous characteristics (boarded up windows, barbed wire surrounds) of the enclaves of high crime and violence associated with Los Angeles and its ghettos in the months leading upto the 1992 riots. Public space is often colonised by young men in baseball caps and cheap khaki (Taylor 1997: 6).

The label of 'no-go estate' has been increasingly coined by the popular and quality press alike to describe such areas where youth crimes are seen as endemic, although it is evident that the type of problems faced on different estates varies greatly across the country. Indeed, it is estimated that there as many as 2,000 council estates in Britain comprised of 500 or more housing units accounting for around two million people in total (Goodwin 1995), and that these vary from Modernist high-rise blocks to inter-war cottages with gardens (Power 1991).

It can therefore be argued that the general labelling of these areas as 'no-go estates' has served to stigmatise areas long-regarded as stable, everyday, or even mundane. An example of this is the Wood End estate, Coventry, which hit the headlines in May 1992 following unrest and rioting when police attempted to prevent groups of youths from using off-road motorbikes around the estate (see Plate 9.1). Unlike some 'no-go

LONDON:
Stonebridge, **Brent**
Parts of **Brixton**
Cato Road, **Clapham North**
Clapham Park, **Clapham**
Parts of **Hackney**
Redington House, **Islington**
Stockwell Park, **Lambeth**
Lancaster West, **Notting Hill**
Brunel, **Paddington**
Danebury Avenue, **Roehampton**
Aylesbury, **Southwark**
Gloucester Grove, **Southwark**
North Peckham, **Southwark**
Broadwater Farm, **Tottenham**

Wine Alley,
Govan,
Glasgow
Ferguslie Park,
Paisley

Scotswood,
Newcastle
Pennywell,
Sunderland
Raffles,
Carlisle
Ragworth,
Stockton-on-Tees

Manningham,   Chapeltown,   Orchard Park,
Bradford **Leeds**   Greatfield & Gypsyville,
                            Hull
Toxteth,   Moss Side,
Liverpool **Manchester**   Grange, **Grimsby**
Ordsall, **Salford**
Blacon, **Chester**   St Giles,
                      Lincoln

Handsworth,   Braunstone,
Birmingham   **Leicester**
                     Wood End,
                     Coventry

Ringland,   Blackbird Leys,
Newport   **Oxford**

Ely, **Cardiff**   **LONDON**
           Hartcliffe,
           Bristol

                                Moulsecoomb,
                                Brighton
North Prospect,
Plymouth

0   Kilometres   150

Figure 9.3: 'No-go Britain': Problem estates in Britain
Source: *Independent on Sunday*, 17th April, 1994

Plate 9.1: Wood End, Coventry: Police attempt to prevent the spread of public unrest
Source: Coventry Evening Telegraph, May 13 1992

estates' which are located in the inner city, Wood End is an example of an 'over-spill' housing estate developed on the northern edge of Coventry designed to accommodate a rapidly expanding post-war population. As with many other 1950s council estates, this was an essentially low-rise development of semi-detached and maisonette housing based on a neighbourhood centre, the Bell Green shopping centre, serving around 3,789 people (Census of Population 1991). The initial occupants of the estate were mainly the workers and families of those employed in Coventry's booming automobile industry, predominantly semi-skilled assembly workers for Chrysler and British Leyland in relatively well-paid and secure jobs. However, with the subsequent decline of the local motor industry and a 46 per cent decline in Coventry's manufacturing employment between 1974 and 1982 (Dunham and Healey 1994), male unemployment rose dramatically on the estate to 49 per cent in 1991, exposing the lack of social infrastructure and community facilities in the area. Problems of insufficient facilities were compounded by the isolation felt by many on the estate, which is located four miles from the city centre and has been poorly served by public transport. Furthermore, it was alleged that by the late 1970s, Coventry City Council were using the estate as a 'dumping ground' for problem families. Significantly, the 'riots' in 1992 occurred only two days after the Princess Royal, in her role as president of *Crime Concern*, had draw attention to the stigmatisation of schools and estates and made specific reference to Wood End, suggesting that by this time its reputation as a run-down and crime-ridden estate was firmly established. Subsequently, although attempts have been made to provide new health and school facilities, this reputation has, if anything, become more entrenched, with many who decided to buy their council house in the 1980s finding it impossible to sell their properties.

Box 9.6: Social polarisation

Social polarisation is most generally taken to refer to the widening of the gap between specific groups in terms of their economic, social and political circumstances and opportunities. Although the idea of an increasingly divided society is a particularly prevalent one amongst Western journalists and academics (see Chapter 7 and 11), the empirical evidence is inconclusive as to whether it is really meaningful to talk of polarisation, particularly with respect of occupational change. In this sense, it appears that the numbers of people employed in different strata of the labour market has not altered significantly over the fifteen to twenty years; the numbers employed in lower status employment relative to high status employment has not shifted markedly. However, what is in little doubt is that the amount of wealth accruing to each group has changed. For example, between 1979–1991, the average British income grew by 36 %, yet for the bottom tenth of the population it dropped by 14 % (The Observer 1997: 29). Similarly, the proportion of households living below 50 % of average income doubled from 8 to 16 % in the same period (Oppenheim 1996). Yet recent geographic analyses have stressed that these figures do not tell the whole story as the impacts of polarisation are unevenly felt:

The experience of polarisation and social divisions will be different in different places according to local economic, social, political and cultural factors...space and place play a role in the construction of inequalities between different groups (Woodward 1995: 77).

Hence it is important not to overgeneralise the effects of urban economic fragmentation as it impacts on different levels of the urban hierarchy. For example, Sassen's (1993) descriptions of polarised global cities such as New York and London, where the contrasts between the corporate city and the dying industrial city are extremely pronounced, may not be relevant in smaller towns and cities typified by lower immigration flows and lower order economic functions.

It is the residualisation and marginalisation of estates like Wood End that has been read by many as providing clear evidence of *social polarisation* (see Box 9.6), with their occupants subsequently described as Britain's underclass. Certainly, as in the USA, the burden of economic and welfare restructuring has fallen most heavily on those areas where the (relative) prosperity of residents had been most reliant on manufacturing-based employment. In 1981, around 5 per cent of Britain's electoral wards were characterised by extreme non-employment rates; with manufacturing decline, this had risen to 12 per cent in 1991, with male inactivity particularly pronounced in previously industrial areas (Green 1997). With manual labour skills no longer in demand, the numbers of long-term unemployed have risen dramatically, and combined with increasing numbers claiming incapacity and sickness benefits (as much as 15 percent in some areas), this leaves a combined non-employed population which has only a minimal chance of finding another a job without retraining and education. For example, in the local authority areas of Liverpool, Glasgow, Manchester, Knowsley (Merseyside), and the London boroughs of Tower Hamlets, Newham, Southall and Southwark, more than one in ten households had no earners by 1991. Moreover, it has been very evident that both economic inactivity and unemployment rates are exceptionally high on many estates, with evidence from twenty of Britain's most 'unpopular' housing estates (Power and Tunstall 1995) suggesting that unemployment rates were, on average, two and a half times higher than the surrounding local authority area, indicative of increasing social and spatial polarisation.

This spatial concentration of unemployment on these estates, especially among young men, has thus been postulated as the most important underlying cause of rioting and disturbances on these 'problem estates'. Figures for thirteen of those estates effected by serious disorder between 1991–1992 reveals that an average of nearly 80 per cent of their occupants were economically inactive or unemployed (see Table 9.2). In such circumstances, young people may lose aspiration or any hope of ever achieving stable employment, with isolation from the job market being perpetuated by the labelling of people from these estates as unemployable. A lack of economic infrastructure – including businesses, shops and banks – means there is little money circulating locally, and neither does the mythical black market, an informal economy based on petty theft, drug dealing and cash-in-hand trading, offer any sort of escape for the majority of residents in such areas. In fact, as Green (1997: 196–197) argues, the higher the level of economic inactivity in a locality, the less black market work may occur. Instead, many crimes occurring on such estates are not ostensibly economically-motivated, as Campbell's (1993) vivid account of life in the Blackbird Leys estate, Oxford, demonstrates:

> The lads had stopped making cars, but that did not stop them stealing them. The collapse in manufacturing work for men was succeeded in Oxford by the rise in car theft, a crime that was emblematic of the Eighties and Nineties ... Car crime on the estate was about much more than trade, however. It was about a relationship between young men, power, machinery, speed and transcendence ... It was the spectacle of the displays that vexed and humiliated the police, uniting thieves, drivers and audiences in alliance against the authorities (Campbell 1993: 32–33).

This notion of *resistance* against the authorities which had abandoned these areas, drawing attention to sites that had otherwise become rendered invisible in policy circles, stresses that car crimes are not motivated simply by greed or want, but a more complex dynamic which in part seeks to re-assert neighbourhood identities – particularly those of the residualised male.

Table 9.2:   Social characteristics of Great Britain, 13 'riot' estates and 20 'unpopular' estates from 1991 Census of Population

Social Characteristic	Great Britain average	20 'unpopular' estates	13 'riot' estates
Unemployment	10	34	31
Economic inactivity	36	44	45
Population under-16	19	31	31
Population under-24	33	46	48
Lone parents	4	18	15
Ethnic minority population	6	26	11
Pupils aged 15+ gaining 5+ GCSEs (grade A-E)	43	20	20

Source: Power, A. and Tunstall, R. (1997) *Dangerous Disorder: Riots and Violent Disturbances in Thirteen Areas of Britain, 1991–1992*, York: Joseph Rowntree Foundation.

The way the experience of living on estates is bound in to broader *power-space geometries* of globally-induced economic restructuring that has been examined by Massey (1996). She highlights one of the key contradictions for those living in these marginal places: while they might be tied into globalisation trends through satellite television, videos and even purchases of food, the majority of residents' lives are still intensely, and increasingly, parochial. Young men, who in previous years may have been ensconced in a world of work and leisure away from the estate, now found themselves spatially enclosed, 'trapped' in a space that they regarded as feminine (essentially, the space of the home). Without work, a regular source of income, or any real incentive to go and look for work, the traditional relationship between masculinity and spatiality broke down as these young men rarely left the estate for any particular reason. Moreover, with the feminisation of the workforce, and the increasing part-time employment of women in retailing and services, it was more likely that traditional gender roles were reversed. Yet, in the relatively secure space of a stolen car, Massey argues, masculine identities could be reasserted, played up and performed. Driving with speed – 'on the edge' – demonstrates the contempt of these men for authority, re-inscribing their mobility, albeit in a contradictory manner which may conflict with other estate dwellers, and certainly feeds into dominant stereotypes of these estates and their residents.

With a new Labour government elected in May 1997, variations of US-style work-fare schemes are being touted as one of the solutions to the problems of these no-go estates, with Tony Blair choosing the setting of the Aylesbury estate, Southwark, for his pronouncement that Labour was committed to getting people back into the labour market 'through empowerment, not punishment' (2 June 1997). Such tactics attempt to reduce welfare-dependency by compelling people to seek employment or lose benefit, targeting specific groups like Britain's half-million single mothers who, reportedly, make little effort to become incorporated in the labour market (perhaps unsurprisingly given the lack of good and affordable crèche facilities and after-school care). Such controversial tactics may well reduce the government's welfare expenditure; whether they reduce the over-concentration of unemployed and wageless households in the problem estates is questionable. Certainly, there will remain little incentive for people to work unless they have access to jobs that are relatively secure and which would generate an income which could support a household. Such problems are particularly pronounced in the estates because of rising levels of rent in the housing association and council housing sectors, where the only way some tenants can afford rents is to remain on housing benefit. Hence, one can see that living in such areas produces a number of disincentives for people to work hard to earn wages when they would perhaps be only marginally worse off if they remained economically inactive. Philo (1995: 12) there-fore concludes that housing association estates are Britain's new landscapes of poverty, and pessimistically argues that they are likely to remain so given the way they have become 'uncoupled' from the world of work.

Spacial Restructuring: Reclaiming the Margins?

As already noted, all societies have areas which can be described as marginal, whether they are places of poverty, sites of illicit activities or areas occupied by stig-matised populations (and perhaps all three). Often, the location of such marginal places has remained consistent over time, even if the individuals and groups it contains have changed (an example here might be the persistence of the inner city as a disordered and marginal place). This is clearly connected to the locus of power in society, with hegemonic society able to physically and symbolically claim the centres, whilst marginalising the powerless to peripheral areas:

> Centre/periphery distinctions tend frequently to be associated with endurance in time. Those who occupy centres establish themselves as having control over resources which allow them to maintain differentials between themselves and those in peripheral regions. The established may employ a variety of forms of social closure to sustain distance from others who are effectively treated as outsiders (Giddens 1991: 131)

In this chapter I have already described numerous examples of social closure by which hegemonic groups tend to isolate marginal groups in marginal places, including discrimination in the housing market, education and job markets. Other more blatant forms of spatial control – such as the British *Criminal Justice Act* (1994) – seek to criminalise actions central to the lifestyles of particular groups (in this case travellers and New Age communities), and restrict their access to specific areas of space (see Halfacree 1996). Recent studies particularly stress the role of the police as agents of social control, charged with maintaining the boundaries between 'problem areas' and respectable neighbourhoods (Herbert 1997).

Hence, we are left here with the impression that the social geography of the city is carved out by the rich and the powerful, who occupy specific spaces while relegating marginalised groups to areas typified by disinvestment and decay (Sibley 1990: 483). Although there is much support for this interpretation, it ignores the fact that the social spaces of the city are in 'high tension', with struggles for place conducted on an almost daily basis (evocatively termed *'turf wars'* by Wolch 1991). Hence, the labelling and identification of particular areas as marginal may shift over time, as marginal groups move (or are moved) elsewhere. For example, some marginal groups may well resist forms of social closure, perhaps ignoring the legitimacy of state policies or *transgressing* into forbidden spaces. Transgression (literally, the crossing of boundaries) principally occurs when marginalised groups appear 'out of place', challenging taken-for-granted (hegemonic) expectations about where they should locate (Cresswell 1996). When this occurs, hegemonic society may act hysterically (through the media, the judiciary and political institutions) creating a moral panic in society (such as that which surrounded the AIDS outbreak in the 1980s), triggering new forms of social and spatial control (such as the aforementioned Criminal Justice Act). However, other spatial transgressions, such as gay rights marches or 'black' carnivals in city centres, may challenge the assumptions of dominant (white, heterosexual) groups and subtly change the social order. In this sense, places on the margin can be seen as sites from which the relatively powerless can organise themselves into self-supporting cultures of resistance and co-operation. So-called *gay ghetto* areas in the USA (such as Castro in San Francisco, or West Hollywood in Los Angeles), for example, have been transformed from marginal spaces of persecution to relatively affluent centres of gay cultural life through political organisation, creativity and activism, creating new gay identities in the process (Forest 1995). In many racialised areas too, alternative economies may thrive (particularly in the cultural industries – food, music, fashion, arts and media), with ethnic entrepreneurs bringing different values and ideas to the attention of wider audiences, making them more mainstream in the process. This gradual *demarginalisation* process may, over time, bring such marginal places closer in character to those in the centre.

On the other hand, it is also worth noting that dominant society itself may attempt to claim back the margins, transforming landscapes of poverty and decay into prestigious ordered space through selective investment, redevelopment and *gentrification* (see Chapter 10). Such efforts are typically implemented under the rubric of urban policy in the West, with such investment in the physical and economic infrastructure being justified with reference to the living conditions of the worst-off in society. These policies are underpinned by an increasingly complex diversity of agencies and partnerships, blurring the distinction between public and private sectors. However, the net result of such improvement policy may be merely one of *displacement*, with marginalised populations unable to afford to live and work in improved, gentrified areas. The redevelopment of London Docklands, for example, provides ample evidence for this displacement thesis, with local residents, many of them former employees in the docks, rarely able to afford the 'yuppie' housing and forced to live elsewhere (contributing to the capital's growing homeless population. Similarly, Smith (1996) has graphically documented the way in which the 'improvement' of New York's Lower East Side resulted in the systematic eviction of the homeless from a number of shelters, parks and streets. He sees this as symptomatic of the continuing fear amongst the middle and upper classes of marginal populations, with the post-modern city characterised by increasingly vicious reactions against minorities, whether the unemployed, women, gays or immigrants. Hence, throughout Western cities we can find numerous examples where relatively powerless marginal popula-tions find themselves to be at odds with public policy and market forces, only to be shifted elsewhere. It seems in this respect that little has changed from Engels' day:

> The breeding places of disease, the infamous holes and cellars in which the capitalist mode of production confines our workers night after night, are not abolished, they are merely shifted elsewhere (Engels 1975: 73–74).

Although current dominant social, economic and political processes conspire to create specific places on the margin, it is still possible to envisage a situation whereby such places, and hence their populations, become demarginalised. This will clearly not come about through dominant groups attempting to reclaim the margins, but through more democratic urban policies which aim to improve such environments by providing affordable housing, new job opportunities and a full range of financial and social services.

Summary and Concluding Comments

In this chapter, an attempt has been made to consider those places described as being 'on the margins' of contemporary society, with the term marginality used here metaphorically to refer to those areas typified by high concentrations of marginalised populations. Although there is a rich tradition in geography of 'mapping' the location and conditions associated with such marginal places, this overview has focused on US inner cities and British housing estates in an attempt to illustrate the ways that contemporary social and spatial processes are related in intimate ways. Some of the principal arguments advanced in the chapter are listed in Box 9.7. Overall, the chapter suggests that any understanding of the production and reproduction of these marginal places necessitates the consideration of a broad range of social, political and economic dynamics as they are played out in a post-industrial and post-modern era, with cultural processes of representation regarded as central in this social-spatial dynamic.

Box 9.7: Chapter summary and suggestions for further reading

- Marginal places are generally 'poor places'; they lack developed economic, social or cultural infrastructure; and are typified by high rates of crime, health problems and poor environmental quality.

- These areas are particularly stigmatised as sites in which crime, deviance and immorality are prevalent, with hegemonic groups generally seeking to avoid these disordered spaces as a result. Hence marginal places are often distanced from elite areas of residence, with the physical, social and psychological boundaries between rich and poor society rigorously monitored.

- The spatial concentration and isolation of marginal groups in such settings tends to mutually reinforce their marginal status, with specific social, economic and cultural processes combining in particular ways to create a downward spiral of decline; once a place has obtained a reputation as a marginal location, it is unlikely to attract new investment of a type that will benefit its inhabitants.

- Given changing social, economic and political processes, marginal spaces may become de-marginalised, but this often has negative consequences for marginalised populations who are displaced to 'new' marginal spaces.

A good introduction to debates on the stereotyping of marginal groups is Woodward's (1997) *Identity and Difference*, while Sibley (1995) *Geographies of Exclusion* and Cresswell (1996) *In Place/Out of Place* provide geographical takes on the issue. McDowell's (1997c) *Undoing Place?* introduces some relevant 'new cultural geography', while Pacione's (1997) *Britain's Cities* and Galster and Hill's (1992) *The Metropolis in Black and White* addresses such issues as health, poverty, housing and crime in marginal places in UK and US cities respectively. Finally, Smith's. (1996) *The New Urban Frontier* teases out many of the links between post-modernism and the struggles for marginal spaces (see also Chapter 10 to follow).

Chapter 10

People in the Centre? The Contested Geographies of 'Gentrification'

Martin Phillips

Gentrification Studies in Human Geography: An Introduction

This chapter focuses on *gentrification* and *gentrifiers*. The former is often seen as a process of central importance in the construction of the contemporary geography of many areas, including central areas in many of the world's largest and most power laden cities. It has also been identified as being of significance in the changing geography of many rural areas (Phillips 1993), including, once more, some of the most power laden of such areas (see Chapter 7 of this book). Gentrification is therefore one aspect of the creation of 'places of the centre'. Gentrifiers are the people involved in this process and they may hence be seen to be 'people in the centre' in that they can be characterised as being in the centre of, and key agents within, the processes of making places of the centre. Gentrifiers may also be seen to be people in the centre in the sense that they are characterised as being part of a large and relatively powerful 'middle' class.

Notions of centrality and marginality may be seen as inter-relational, fluid and subject to contestation and this chapter seeks to highlight the contests over the delimitation and interpretation of what the processes of gentrification might be and who are the people involved. The chapter will highlight the notion of *agency*, of knowledgeable and capable people, but also draw attention to how agency is not necessarily constituted on the basis of individuals but is more often than not collective in character. In addition consideration will be given to issues of *power* and *inequality* and how the desires and preferences of one group of people are often created at the expense of others. The chapter will also highlight the notion of *difference* and how the seeming similar people engaged in similar actions may actually be significantly differentiated from one another. It will further be suggested that gentrification is not simply a process of the centre, nor gentrifiers necessarily people in the centre.

Within human geography gentrification has become both a major area of study and the subject of much debate. The term gentrification has been applied to a variety of situations, including both inner city and rural areas. It is a topic which has been the focus of attention for many advocates of alternative approaches to human geography. As part of these debates the meaning of the term gentrification, and the scope of gentrification studies, has shifted. In the following five sections attention will be paid to outlining some of the principal approaches which have been adopted to the study of gentrification, detailing how gentrification is understood within them, and considering how the approaches and interpretations impact on the issues of centrality and marginality.

The Origins of the Study of Gentrification

The term gentrification is often traced back to Glass (1964) who in a study of London wrote:

> One by one, many of the working-class quarters of London have been invaded by the middle classes ... Shabby modest mews and cottages ... have been taken over ... and become elegant, expensive residences. Larger Victorian houses, down graded in an earlier or recent period ... [to] lodging houses or ... multiple occupation – have been upgraded again ... Once this process of 'gentrification' starts in a district it goes on rapidly until all or most of the original working-class occupiers are displaced and the whole character of a district is changed (Glass 1964: 33).

Here one finds a clear sense that gentrification is about both the 'refurbishment' or doing up of an area, and about changes in its 'social composition'. This appears a very simple definition, but as will be shown, the term gentrification has spawned a whole host of conceptual arguments and debates, some of which has become quite heated (see for example Hamnett 1991; 1992; Ley 1986; 1987; Smith 1987a; 1992b). Furthermore, the term gentrification is one of the relatively few terms which has migrated from academic studies into popular discourses, appearing as the subject of cartoons and as the focus of a full-page advertisement in the *New York Times* (see Smith, 1996a). The scale of interest in the subject can also be gauged by the number of sites listed in an Internet search under the term 'gentrification': at the time of writing this chapter this was some 2,285 sites.

The term gentrification rose to prominence in the 1960s and 1970s, where it was often described as being equivalent, or closely connected, to terms such as 'redevelopment', 'upgrading', 'improvement' and 'urban renaissance'. This association is quite understandable given that gentrification was commonly associated with the refurbishment of housing stock. These terms came into prominence in the 1960s and 1970s when a series of *empirical studies* began to record that many inner city neighbourhoods appeared to be experiencing both physical renewal and social change. Classic examples included the London boroughs of Islington, Camden and Hackney which were the focus of attention of Glass (1964) and also areas in New York such as Soho, the Lower East Side and Harlem (see Smith 1996a).

The instances of gentrification in the 1960s were seen to be quite unusual and were therefore studied as idiosyncrasies. However, by the early 1970s gentrification was being recognised as occurring in a whole host of places. In 1976, for example, it was estimated that nearly half of the cities in the USA with a population greater than 50,000 were experiencing gentrification (Urban Land Institute (1976), quoted in Smith 1996a). By the early 1990s gentrification was being described as 'one of the "leading edges" of contemporary metropolitan restructuring' (Hamnett 1991: 174) and gentrification was identified in cities ranging from Birmingham to Baltimore and Budapest; from Philadelphia to Paris and Prague; from Sao Paulo to Sydney and San

Francisco; from Copenhagen and Malmo to Edinburgh, Glasgow and Dundee, and from New York to Tokyo. While gentrification is clearly associated with capital and primate cities, it has also impacted regional and local centres and has also been identified as occurring in rural areas (Phillips 1993).

The rise of gentrification as a topic of geographical research can, in part, be explained as a consequence of the rising visibility of gentrification. As gentrification spread from one or two localities to span areas across the global then it became difficult to ignore. However, much of the significance of gentrification for geographers stemmed from the way this phenomenon appeared to contravene the dominant 'theoretical ideas' of that time. In particular, the redevelopment of inner city areas seemed to run counter to the theories of urban change developed from the concepts of the 'Chicago School' and neo-classical economics. As discussed in Chapter 2, geography in the 1960s was dominated by notions of geography as 'spatial science' concerned to establish 'universal laws' about human behaviour and the use of space. A particularly significant example of this was the notion that cities were structured into spatial zones through which both housing and social groups were filtered, albeit in opposing directions. Hence, in the classic work of Park *et al.* (1925) the city was conceived in terms of concentric zones which, as you progressed out from the central business district of the city, became composed of higher quality housing and higher status individuals. Furthermore it was argued that over time, housing quality would decline and, as a consequence: i) higher status groups would move out to inhabit new housing areas; ii) lower class groups would move out to adjacent housing areas; and iii) there would emerge an *inner city* zone of dilapidation and either dereliction or, if there was a source of low status in-migrants, deprivation and delinquency (see Figure 10.1). These scenarios were seen to be more or less universal – what only varied was the extent to which these changes happened and whether there was, or was not, any low status in-migration to affect the fate of the inner city.

Empirical studies of gentrification highlighted that many inner city areas were experiencing neither dereliction nor expanding deprivation, but rather were becoming areas of repopulation. There was, as Smith (1979b) put it, 'a back to the city movement of people' which had not been foreseen by any of the theories of urban change which dominated geography in the 1960s and early 1970s. It was this contrast with theoretical explanations which led many geographers to study gentrification and in the process come to question some of the concepts circulating within geography and, in many cases, the positivist approach which was dominating geography at this time. This movement away from positivist explanation has, however, taken some time and has led to a series of quite distinct understandings of gentrification.

Positivist Explanations of Gentrification

Although gentrification posed serious problems to adherents of positivist explanation, it is important to recognise that some attempts have been made to apply this form of explanation. It is, I would suggest, possible to identify three broad ways in which positivists have approached the issue of gentrification. First, it has been suggested that gentrification is merely a small-scale localised phenomenon which simply represents a slight deviation from the general laws. This is the position

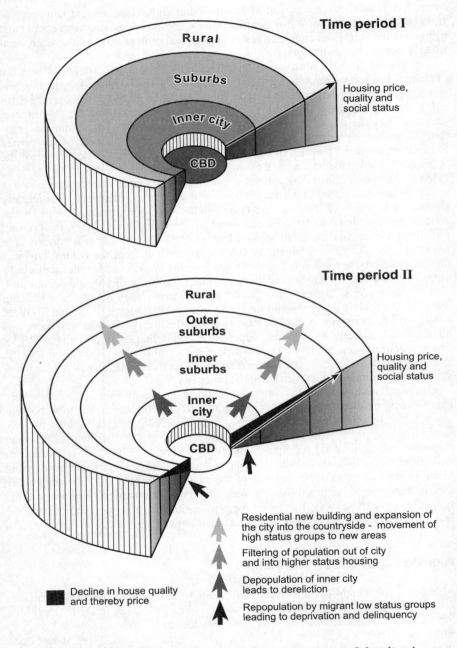

Figure 10.1: Urban filtering and the socio-spatial structure of the city: A positivist imagery

adopted by Brian Berry (1980a; 1985) who described gentrification as being merely 'small islands of renewal in seas of decay'. However, as the phenomenon of gentrification has spread it is increasingly hard to retain this view, although Bourne restated a similar view, claiming:

> the extent and impacts of gentrification have been exaggerated in the urban literature of the 1970s and 1980s, and that the process itself will be of decreasing importance as we move beyond the recession of the early 1990s (Bourne 1993: 183)

Bourne's arguments have, however, been criticised by Badcock (1993) who argues, amongst other things, that while gentrification may not be a universal feature of all cities, it is an important change within many and that it looks set to continue to be of significance beyond the early 1990s.

Another positivist response has been to accept that gentrification is quite a widespread phenomenon and to suggest that it has been created out of the emergence of new, quite widespread, factors which act to over-ride in particular places the universal laws of spatial behaviour. One of the most frequent cited over-riding variables has been government policy. Inner city areas are frequently perceived as being problem areas, and thereby areas in need of some form of government intervention or direction. In Britain, for example, the *City Challenge* programme represents one of a long line of policies designed to stimulate economic development in inner city areas and help finance the improvement of housing stock in these areas (see Imrie and Thomas 1993; Short and Bassett 1981).

There are some problems in this 'state centred' explanation of gentrification. First, a whole series of studies on regeneration policies has shown that generally they are, at best, extremely limited in their success (Diamond 1991; Hayton and Gray 1996; Oatley 1995). It is therefore difficult to square these interpretations with the suggestion that these policies could be responsible for what appears to be quite a dramatic change, indeed arguably a reversal, in the socio-spatial structure of many cities. Second, it is arguable that where these policies have been successful it is because they have fitted in with, rather than changed, the spatial dynamics of an area's economy: in other words policies have succeeded because there were other things besides the policy which were attracting people and investment into an area. Third, in many countries there has been, over the course of the 1980s and 1990s, a 'drawing back' or 'retrenchment' of the state, at just the time when gentrification appears to have been increasing in its frequency. It is hence once again hard to square these observations within a positivist style of interpretation.

It may be that government policies are not the correct intervening factor, and a number of other suggestions have been identified as intervening factors causing gentrification, including improved inner city transport and/or deteriorating suburban transport systems and private housing, and industrial developments. Once again, however, the issue is to what extent these factors are sufficiently widespread to be able to account for the global extent of contemporary gentrification. One may of course see these intervening factors in combination: to suggest gentrification is occurring in one area because of state policies, in another due to transport costs and so on. However, as Smith (1982: 141) notes, positivist studies, whilst arguing for the significance of universal laws, appear if this route is followed to end up explaining gentrification merely as 'a chance, extraordinary even … the accidental outcome of a unique mix of exogenous factors'. For Smith this is inadequate: he claims that the extent of contemporary gentrification is such that it should be seen 'not as an extraordinary event but as an increasingly ordinary event' (Smith 1982: 141).

In the above positivist explanatory strategies gentrification is seen to be the outcome of changes which are external or exogenous to the urban housing market. Another possibility is that gentrification is the outcome of changes which are internal to, or at least have an impact which becomes internal to, the urban housing market. At least two distinct examples of this form of explanation have been advanced. First, it has been suggested that during the second half of the twentieth century there has been a dramatic shift in the social structure of many countries with a rapid expansion in the size of the middle classes. This may be seen to have caused a spatial shift in the outcomes of the urban filtering process, although the way this process operates has not fundamentally changed (see Box 10.1).

Box 10.1:   Gentrification, urban filtering and the growth of the middle class

The dominant interpretation of the social structure of cities in the 1960s was that this was the outcome of a competitive filtering of social groups through housing which was seen to provide an equilibrium between house quality, house price and differences in social status. Those who had more income, the high 'class' groups, would be able to locate themselves in the better housing, while those in lower class positions would end up with poorer housing conditions. However, if there is an expansion in the middle class then you may get a situation where there is less outward filtering, and even perhaps a reversal in the direction of movement. This would occur where there is increased competition for suburban housing which is not met by an expansion in suburban housing, perhaps due to a lack of land or a concern to restrict suburban sprawl. With rising suburban housing costs, outward filtering would become less, which would mean that there would be a continued middle class presence in the inner city and in some circumstances a reverse filtering of the middle class from the suburbs into the inner city.

Another strand of positivist work on gentrification adopted a *behavioural perspective* and suggested that some modifications to the filtering model were necessary in order to be able to fully account for gentrification. In particular, questions were raised about the behavioural assumption built into the model of residential filtering that people 'naturally' prefer to live away from city centres. This assumption is explained in a variety of ways. In Burgess (1924, 1925) original model it appears as a sort of cultural norm: people are seen to want to live out of towns because it confers social status and because it is healthier and nearer to nature. In more neo-classical economic versions, such as Alonso's (1964) urban rent model, it relates to a rational decision made to balance the twin desires of proximity to the economic space of city centre and for living spaces.

Two key themes within behavioural geography are the complexity and bounded nature of decision making (see Chapter 2). Geographers adopting behavioural perspectives hence tended to emphasise the range of factors involved in decision making and how these were bounded by individual perceptions. In respect to gentrification studies, attention began to be paid to a range of motives which might lead people to move into inner city areas beyond the desire for economic centrality and living space. It has been suggested, for example, that gentrification may stem rather more from the leisure and recreational opportunities available in the city centre. Beauregard (1986) has suggested that gentrifiers represent 'up-scale consumers' who frequent trendy clubs, restaurants, bars, and shops, while Mills (1986) has argued that people may be attracted to inner city areas because of the availability of such recreational facilities as public markets, restaurants, jogging paths and marinas.

Recreation and leisure are often seen as consumptive, as opposed to productive, activities and evidence of their role in motivating people to live in inner city areas has led to a more general claim that 'consumption' provides the key to understanding gentrification, and there is frequent reference in the literature to *consumption-side* explanations of gentrification. One of the most frequently cited, and indeed probably one of the most fully elaborated, versions of this explanation has been developed by Ley (1980) in an article entitled 'Liberal ideology and the postindustrial city'. Although not explicitly on gentrification, this study centred on Vancouver has provoked considerable discussion and indeed heated debate (see Hamnett 1991; Smith 1992). Ley argued that from the late 1960s there had emerged in Vancouver a new, more consumption focused, urban form which stemmed from a concern amongst those responsible for planning the city's development to establish what was termed 'a liveable city', that is a city which was 'in harmony with human sensibility' (Ley 1980: 239), a city which 'people can live in and enjoy' (Ley 1980: 249). A particular housing development, the False Creek Development (see Box 10.2), was taken by Ley to represent the embodiment of a new *ideology of consumption*, although Ley suggested that this new ideology was not restricted to Vancouver but was 'felt to a greater or lesser extent in every major city in North America' (Ley 1980: 238). He also suggested that this ideology, or set of beliefs, was 'associated with shifts at the economic, political and socio-cultural levels of society' and in particular with the rise to power of a group of 'youthful, highly educated, middle and upper income ... professionals' who came to dominate local political and planning systems and then set about creating a city which conformed to their own tastes. In other words there was a dynamic interplay between the design and reconstruction of the built environment and the in-migration of a particular social group, an interplay which was centred around particular preferences about what and how to consume.

Box 10.2: The False Creek Development and the 'ideology of consumption'

The False Creek area of Vancouver has frequently been seen as an exemplary example of consumption based gentrification and has been the subject of a series of studies (e.g. Ley 1980; Mills 1986; 1993). False Creek is a small arm of the Burrard Inlet.

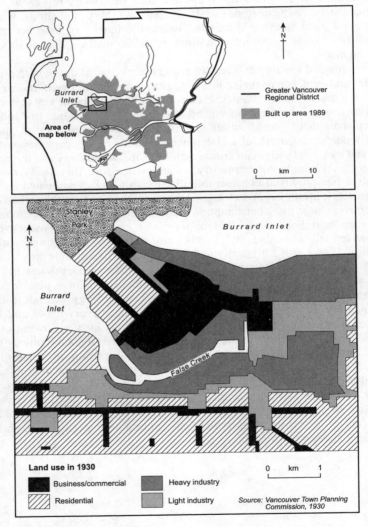

Figure B10.2: Vancouver – False Creek

The northern side of False Creek was cleared from forest in the late nineteenth century by the *Canadian Pacific Railway* and quickly developed to become part of the Central Business District or 'Down town' area of Vancouver. The southern side, on the other hand, became 'the industrial heart of the city' (Ley 1980: 253) with saw-milling, construction and engineering plants locating there, along with warehousing. The water of False Creek and the land on the southern bank became subject to serious environmental degradation and contaminated with toxic substances, sewage and a range of other pollutants (see Oke *et al.* 1992). However during the 1950s there was both a serious decline in the industries located along False Creek which in turn led to the area become an area of dereliction.

Plate B10.2a: **Disused factory and derelict landscape on the South Side of False Creek**

According to Ley (1980), in the 1960s and early 1970s there emerged amongst those responsible for planning the city's development a concern to establish what was termed 'a liveable city'. As part of this the False Creek area was redeveloped to provide 'a quality, liveable environment ' (Ley 1980: 253), a project which has been cited as an example of a *postmodern development* in that it avoids rigid land-use divisions and buildings are constructed using a mix of styles. It is also a landscape where consumption activities such as shopping, leisure and recreation play a large role. The development was, for example, constructed so that there was a continuous system of parks and marinas through which people could walk.

**Plate B10.b: The postmodern cityscape of the False Creek
                   Development**

Ley (1980) argued that such consumption landscape were being created in
cities across North America. However, Ley (1987) notes the contrast between
the development on the southern shores of False Creek and the subsequent
developments on the northern shores associated with 'Expo 86' which involved
'high-rise' and 'futuristic' buildings' and a rapid transport system, the
'Skytrain'.

More recently the areas within and surrounding the 'Downtown' area have
been redeveloped, again largely on the basis of large-scale and high rise corporate buildings. An area to the east of Vancouver's central business district
known as 'Downtown Eastside' has, in recent years, seen community initiated
attempts to regenerate one of the poorest areas of the city with high homelessness, crime and drugs problems, being displaced by corporate development,
much of it linked to an economic development strategy of making Vancouver
into a *global city*.

Plate B10.2c: Science World on the bank of False Creek
The dome was originally built as part of Expo '86 and is connected to
Downtown Vancouver by the Skytrain.

Plate B10.2d: The emerging high-rise cityscape of 'global city' Vancouver

The consequences of behavioural studies of gentrification can be seen to have been some movement away from the original tenets of positivist studies. In particular they can be seen to have led to rising recognition of the range of motivations which might lead people to live in an inner city location. Rather less overtly, however, they raised questions about the meaning of gentrification and the character of gentrifiers. The increased emphasis on consumption activities such as leisure and recreation, for instance, not only highlighted a range of other motivations in residential decision making apart from job and living space requirements, but also raised doubts as to whether the focus on residential refurbishment was sufficient. The arguments of people like Mills, Ley and Beauregard, for example, suggested that changes in housing may not be the only, nor indeed necessarily the most significant, change to the material landscape of the city which can be connected to gentrification (see also Zukin 1990).

A second consequence of more behavioural analysis which impacts the basic definition of gentrification is a suggestion that gentrification may not simply be linked to changes in the *class* composition of areas. Activities such as jogging, sailing and visiting clubs and bars, for example, may be seen to be activities which are particularly associated with younger people and a number of studies have argued that the characterisation of gentrifiers as middle class is insufficient: rather gentrifiers are *young* middle class people either in a single person household or in a childless household. Butler and Hamnett (1994), for example, argue that in gentrified areas of Hackney there are three times the national average of single-person households, although they argued that there was also quite a high proportion of households with young children. Beauregard (1986) has highlighted how the rise of gentrification corresponds temporally to widespread demographic changes stemming from behavioural changes such as an increased postponement, rejection and break-down of marriage and an increasing postponement or rejection of child-rearing. Such changes have led, so Beauregard (1986: 43) argues, to 'the creation of more single individual households and childless couples' whose 'consumption needs' are, he argues, best met in inner city locations. More generally, Beauregard, and also Rose (1984), have argued that there is a need to disaggregate the notion of gentrifiers beyond a simple designation of being middle class, and instead recognise that gentrifiers might differ quite substantially from one another, and therefore may be involved in gentrification for quite different reasons and in quite different ways.

A third strand of argument, however, has been to suggest that consumption is significant in understanding gentrification not so much as an alternative to class based explanations, but that it is itself caught up with changes in the nature of class relations in contemporary society. Much of the literature on gentrification posits a dichotomy between behaviourist, 'consumption-side' explanations of gentrification, and *structuralist*, *production-side*, explanations. As will be shown, such a clear distinction is hard to maintain but it still has been highly significant in geographical studies of gentrification.

Structuralist Interpretations of Gentrification

As discussed in Chapter 2, the 1970s witnessed the emergence of a range of structuralist approaches which broadly argued that people's actions are often determined by social forces – or *social structures* – many of which individual people may be unaware of. The precise nature of the social forces determining people's actions has been the subject of some contestation and a range of 'structuralist' interpretations have been advanced (see Chapter 2). In the context of gentrification studies, two particular strands of structuralist argument stand out: namely *managerialism* and *Marxist political economy*.

Managerialist Perspectives on Gentrification

Managerialist perspectives are often traced back to Pahl, an 'urban sociologist', who argued that social divisions of space should be seen as the outcome of a competition for 'scarce resources' created by a series of *urban managers* or *urban gatekeepers* who controlled, and severely limited, access to the resources of urban space (Pahl 1969; 1970). The emphasis on competition echoed many of the earlier positivist models of urban filtering but in contrast to these approaches Pahl did not suggest that this competition was a 'natural' feature of cities. He was also highly critical of the *voluntarist* nature of urban studies, complaining, for instance, they talked as if there were no constraints on what people do and talked solely in terms of 'diversity and choice'. By contrast Pahl argued that urban studies should 'be concerned with the social and spatial constraints on access to scarce urban resources and facilities' (Pahl 1969: 152).

As well as suggesting a more *critical* rationale for urban studies, Pahl proposed moving away from a focus on the individual and towards the study of urban institutions such as local government and planning authorities, financial institutions such as banks and building societies, architects, social workers and educationalists. Pahl argued that these institutions were responsible for creating the patterns of unequal access to urban space within which individuals operated and competed. He expressed this point as suggesting that the social and spatial division of the city and the decision making processes of individuals and households were 'dependent variables' created out of decision making by a few powerful organisations. The people in these institutions were seen as the 'managers and controllers of the urban system' and because their decisions affected everybody else in the city they were described as the 'independent variable' creating the social and spatial patterning of the city.

The origins of much of the early managerialist work actually lay in attempts to explain the reverse of gentrification, namely a continual downward spiral of degradation and deprivation in inner city areas. Work such as Rex and Moore's (1967) study of the Sparkbrook area of Birmingham suggested that the problems in this area stemmed largely from the impossibility of residents buying their own homes and thereby improving them. They suggested that this was due to the lending policies of building societies which refused to lend both to non-white 'ethnic groups' (a policy of social discrimination) and to lend to people buying in inner city areas (a policy of spatial discrimination). This later policy was often termed *red-lining* in that mortgage lenders often quite literally had maps in which red-lines were drawn around certain areas to indicate areas where the building society is not prepared to invest money in. Although redlining was sometimes quite explicit it also occurred less explicitly with mortgage managers having a mental, rather than paper, map of where they were not prepared to lend. A series of studies argued that such policies not only prevented inner city areas from improving but actively helped to create inner city decline and also suburban expansion (see Box 10.3)

Box 10.3: The consequences of 'redlining'

Knox (1987: 236) has noted that red-lining can be seen to initiate a decline in property values in the red-lined district and then onto 'neighbourhood deterioration, destruction and abandonment'. The argument is that with red-lining, there is a reduction in the number of people purchasing housing, and a gradual deterioration in housing stock. Once this becomes marked, local businesses start to go out of business, which leads to an out-migration of people from the area, with only the most disadvantaged groups remaining. This out-migration can lead both to a spread of the red-lined districts – some of the problem groups move away from the redlined district into other areas, which then become seen as risky investments – and also to a need for increased social services in the now deteriorating red-line district. Furthermore, the decline of mortgage lending in the initial and later red-lined zones frees up money for investing in purchase of homes in other, more 'profitable', areas of the city. Hence there is effectively a flow of credit from the redlined district to suburban areas. With this flow of finance, it becomes easier for people to purchase homes in the suburbs. In consequence, people tend to move away from city centres towards more suburban areas. This means that the migration of people towards the suburbs, which is described in spatial scientific and behavioural theories in terms of personal spatial preference can, in a managerial perspective, be seen as the consequence of the policies of financial institutions such as building societies.

If policies such as redlining may explain the flight to the suburbs, can they also explain the movement back into the inner city area? One factor might be the increasing criticism levelled at institutions which operated policies of social and spatial discrimination. Studies have shown that building society managers were increasingly unwilling to state that they operate redlining policy, although there has been some suggestion that they still do but just do not publicly acknowledge it. Another possibility is that the activities of other urban gatekeepers have overrode the redlining policies of financial institutions like building societies. As previously mentioned, there have been a series of policy attempts to regenerate the inner city. Some of these have included financial assistance to residents, such as the provision of improvement grants (see Hamnett 1973). However such grants are usually only given to households who own rather than rent their property: hence the provision of finance to enable the purchase of property still exerts a fundamental influence, delimiting whether or not a resident is able to get an improvement grant. In some areas, such as in New York, local authorities have sought to address this problem by selling off publicly owned property to encourage increased private property ownership. Another possibility is that building societies and other financial institutions now operate a *greenlining* policy (Smith 1996a: 23) in that inner city areas are now distinguished as areas where lending should be given. Smith (1996a: 23), for example, has suggested in New York's inner city area of the 'Lower East side',

> Areas that were once sharply redlined by banks and other financial institutions were sharply 'greenlined' in the 1980s. Loan officers were instructed to take down their old maps with red lines around working-class and minority neighbourhoods and replace them with new maps sporting green lines: make every possible loan with the greenlined neighborhood (Smith 1996a: 23).

Smith (1996a) suggests that there has emerged a 'frontier gentrification mentality' amongst housing developers whereby developers have 'a vivid block-by-block sense' of development opportunities and,

> move in from the outskirts, building 'a few strategically placed outputs of luxury' ... on the gold coats between safe neighbourhoods on one side where property values are high and the disinvested slums ... Successive beachheads and defensible borders are established on the frontier (Smith 1996a: 23).

Smith highlights the historical and spatial spread of gentrification within the Lower East Side area of New York (see Figure 10.2) and the way that the 'real estate industry' renamed the northern part of the Lower East Side as 'East Village' in order to 'capitalise on its geographical proximity to the respectability, security, culture and high rents of Greenwich Village' and offered low rents to artists and gallery owners to encourage a perception of the area as being a 'place of culture'. Once gentrification had begun, property prices escalated in this area forcing out some of these artist and galleries who then moved to the neighbouring areas of Soho and Williamsburgh in Brooklyn across the East River, thereby encouraging the process of gentrification in these areas as well. Indeed Smith suggests that it is possible to map an advancing frontier of gentrification spreading our from its initial outposts of Greenwich Village, Soho, and Chinatown and the financial district at the southern tip of the Lower East Side (see Figure 10.2).

Smith's arguments can be seen as a good example of how urban gatekeepers such as planners, estate agents and housing developers may play a key role in creating gentrification. Smith himself, however, adopts a Marxist political economy perspective which can be seen as a more structuralist account of gentrification than managerialism in that it suggests that the urban gatekeepers are not, as Pahl (1970) maintained, the independent, causal variable creating urban socio-spatial divisions, but were, as Saunders (1981) put it, merely 'intervening variables' which were themselves conditioned by larger, more powerful social forces.

Marxist Interpretations of Gentrification: The Work of Neil Smith

A key feature of structuralism is a rejection of the individualist focus of logical positivist and behavioural perspectives (see Chapter 2). This point formed one of the key starting points of Smith's Marxist inspired analyses of gentrification which have appeared in a whole host of writings (e.g. Smith 1979a; 1979b; 1982; 1987b; 1992; 1996a; Smith and Williams 1986). In one the first of these Smith argued that contrary

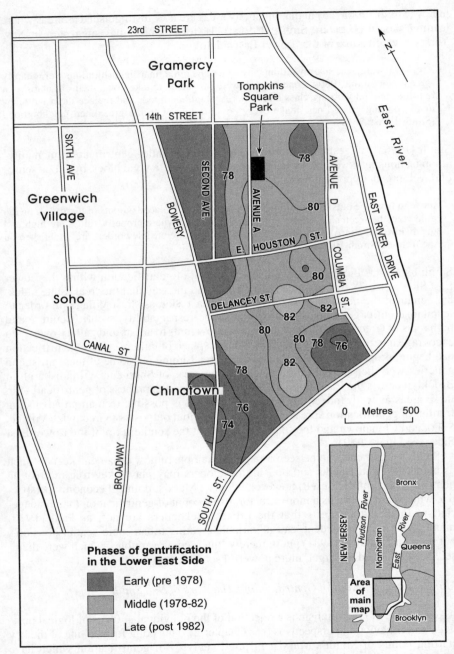

Figure 10.2: The spread of gentrification across the Lower East Side, New York
Source: based on Smith, N. (1996) *The new urban frontier* (London: Routledge).

to positivist and behavioural interpretations, gentrification should not be seen as a 'back to the city movement of people' – particularly a back to the city movement of the middle class – but instead should be seen as a 'back to the city movement of capital' (Smith 1979b). Smith suggested that the movement of people from suburban areas to the inner city was both over-stressed and insufficient to explain gentrification.

In support of his suggestion of an over-emphasis on back to the city movement of people, Smith argued that empirical research in Baltimore, Philadelphia and Washington suggested that only a minority of gentrifiers had moved to the inner city from the suburbs and most were people who had moved from elsewhere within the city limits (see Table 10.1). Even where gentrification was accompanied by a 'back to the city movement of people', for Smith the movement people should not be the sole focus of attention. He is, for instance, critical of the way that in many accounts gentrification is seen to be essentially a process of local social change created by middle class people choosing to move into an area, perhaps to take account of particular consumption opportunities available in this locality. By contrast Smith argues for an account of gentrification which is *collectivist*, which emphasises socially created *constraints* and which sees gentrification as a *productive activity*.

Table 10.1: The place of origin of 'gentrifiers' in three US cities

City and gentrified areas of city studied	City in origin (%)	Suburban in origin (%)
Philadelphia: Society Hill	72	14
Baltimore: Homestead Properties	65.2	27
Washington, DC: Mount Pleasant	67	18
Capitol Hill	72	15

Source: Smith, N. (1996) The new urban frontier: gentrification and the revanchist city (London: Routledge): 54.

For Smith, a key element of gentrification was that it was a process not only of social change but also a process of physical change: he argues, for instance, that gentrification if it is to have any specific meaning at all should be conceived as involving the investment of *productive capital* – that is money, resources and labour power – which change the physical structure of housing and other buildings in an area. He argued that the term gentrifier might be usefully replaced with the term *occupier developer* in order to 'highlight gentrifiers' roles as active agents in transforming as well as consuming the built environment' (Smith 1992: 122). Smith coined the term *sweat-equity* to refer to the way 'occupier developers' could improve the structure of their houses by 'investing' their own *labour power*. In other words, occupier developers bought houses and then did them up themselves.

Smith goes on to argue that although 'occupier developers' may be seen as the archetypal gentrifier – 'as the true gentrifiers' (Smith 1992: 122) – they are not the only agent of gentrification. He argues, for instance, that there are two other types of gentrifier developers: a) *professional developers* – that is firms or individuals who purchase properties, redevelop then and then sell them on to others for a profit; and b) *landlord developers* – that is firms or individuals who buy properties, redevelop them and then rent out these properties to others. Smith argues that all these agents of gentrification are significant, although he suggests that 'owner-developers' may be materially the least significant but are highly significant symbolically in that they are often seen to be individuals who through their own individual actions create buildings which accord with their own personal preferences and in the process rejuvenate run-down areas.

As well as arguing for the recognition of a variety of gentrifiers, Smith also argues against such *individualistic* interpretations of gentrification as given above. The purchase and renovation of a residential property generally involves the 'owner-developer' interacting with a range of 'profession agents of gentrification', including architects, bankers, builders, estate agents, mortgage lenders and planning officials (see Phillips 1993; Smith 1979b; Smith 1992). Smith therefore argues that gentrification, even when undertaken by 'owner-developers' should be seen as a form of *collective action* as opposed to an individual act. He argued that as well as the three types of developers, a whole host of other agents – including, for instance, financiers, builders, architects and planners – play a key role in determining the progress of gentrification: 'All the consumer preference in the world will amount to naught unless ... funding reappears: mortgage capital, in some form or another is a prerequisite' (Smith 1996a: 68).

This quote not only highlights Smith's notion of gentrification as a collective process, but also indicates a clear rejection of voluntarist and consumption based 'preference' theories. He suggests, for instance, that urban gentrification 'has been stimulated more by economic than cultural forces' and that one behavioural motive 'stands out above the others', namely 'the need to make a sound financial investment in purchasing a home' (Smith 1996a: 57). In this he can be seen to reject the drift towards emphasising consumption motivations begun by behavioural interpretations of gentrification. He can also be seen to express a structuralist distrust of statements of motivations for behaviour when he claims that: 'Whether or not gentrifiers articulate this preference [for profit], it is fundamental, for few would ever consider rehabilitation if a financial loss were expected' (Smith 1996a: 57). In other words gentrifiers are motivated by calculation of financial returns for gentrification although they frequently are not able to fully articulate this motivation.

Smith develops his broad arguments about gentrification in three particular ways: first he develops the concept of the *rent gap* to explain 'the history of investment and disinvestment at the neighbourhood' (Smith 1996a: 75); second, he suggests a theory of *uneven development* is necessary to set gentrification in its appropriate global context; and third, he outlines how gentrification can be seen to represent a mechanism of *class struggle*.

The rent gap concept stems from Smith's argument that gentrification is, in his view, essentially a process of property development, centred around a profit motive. Smith's concern in developing this concept is to be able to explain why particular areas experience the process of redevelopment known as gentrification. He basically suggests that this is the outcome of three key, but in some ways, contradictory features of property investments. The first feature is the extent to which private property rights create spatial monopolies. That is, once some one owns a piece of land they exercise control over how it is used. Smith suggests that from this control, landowners are able to derive rents. He then claims that this rent can be considered as having two forms – *actual rent* and *potential rent*. The former refers to the current value of a piece of land with any buildings, while the latter refers to the value of the land under a better land use. Second, he notes that that there is a considerable 'fixity' within capital investments in property which stems from the fact that the construction of buildings requires quite a considerable investment of resources and changes in the built form of an area requires both a further investment of resources and the destruction of previous investments. Thirdly, he notes that there are physical and social factors which lead to a slow decline in the value of investments in buildings. Given these three factors he suggests that it is possible to identify a cyclical process of investment, deinvestment and reinvestment which leads both to suburbanisation and to gentrification (see Box 10.4).

Box 10.4: The rent gap and the cyclical flows of capital flows

Smith suggests that gentrification should be understood as the outcome of the movement of capital – understood as resources and labour as well as money – and identifies a cyclical process of investment, deinvestment and reinvestment which leads both to suburbanisation and to gentrification.

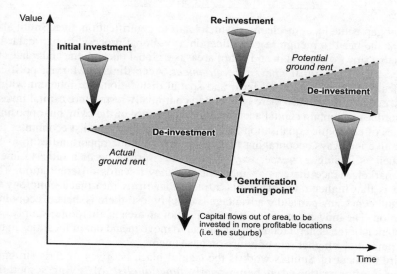

Figure B10.4: The rent-gap and cycles of investment and dis-investment

In the first phase of investment actual rents are close to potential rent in that it is assumed that the landowners will seek to maximise the level of rent they receive and will therefore opt for the development of the best possible landuse. However over time there is, Smith suggests, a general decline in actual rents and a steady rise in potential rents. The former stems from physical and social depreciation related to the physical degradation of existing building and stylistic/technological and economic change which means newer buildings are of higher value than older ones. These changes may also be significant in changing the potential rent of the area. However there is for a long period no change in land-use because of the 'fixity of capital investments' – people have invested money in these buildings and cannot afford the costs of redeveloping the area to a new use. However with falling actual rents there is decreasing investment in the area and indeed there is a flow of money and resources out of the area with those who have surplus cash investing in areas with higher potential rents. However the discrepancy between actual and potential rents may become so great that it does become profitable to redevelop an area. This point is termed by Smith the *gentrification turning point* and can, he argues, be identified empirically by mapping, for instance, a sudden decline in levels of tax arrears. At the gentrification turning point the existing capital value invested in the area is completely written off and new capital flows into the area to invest in the new built environment and bring actual rents back in line with potential rents. It is this flow of capital into an area which Smith argues constitutes gentrification. It is also a flow which is not an unexpected reversal of some seemingly universal process, but rather, so Smith argues, a totally expected reversal of flow.

If the rent gap is the local mechanism which leads to gentrification, then Smith also argues for the need to recognise gentrification as a global process. In particular he suggests that flows of capital in and out of areas is a global phenomena and relates to the processes of *capitalist uneven development*. According to Marxist political economics periods of boom and bust, and spatial dislocation, are inherent within capitalist economies because there is a need to continually restructure capital investment in order to maintain capital accumulation in the face of the twin, but opposing, tendencies of economic equalisation and differentiation. In capitalist economies the profit motive is always encouraging firms to look for unique opportunities to make profit, such as finding a cheaper way of producing something or a hitherto unexploited market. Hence there is an inherent tendency towards differentiation. The problem is that higher rates of profits attract other firms into that technology or market and hence any particular advantage is quickly lost: there is, hence, economic equalisation. The movement of capital in and out of an area is, therefore, simply one manifestation of the general tendency of capital to move in and out of localities in the endless pursuit of a higher rate of return on investment.

A third element of Smith's work is the central place he gives to class struggle. Marxism is often criticised as being overly *functionalist*: of saying something happens because something, generally 'capital', requires it to happen. This is often associated with a claim that Marxists give no role to human agents. While it is certainly the case that Marxists are generally highly critical of giving the individual as central a role as do, say, neo-classical economists or behaviourists, this does not mean that they give no role to human agents. Rather, as discussed earlier, it is that their key agents are often collectivities rather than individuals. Indeed one particular collectivity – or group of people – is given a high degree of agency, namely class.

Within Marxism there has been a long strand of argument which suggests that class struggle is a key subject of interest. This is often traced back to Marx and Engels comment that 'the history of all hitherto existing society is the history of class struggles' (Marx and Engels 1971: 35). Smith is keen to continue this emphasis in his study of gentrification and indeed he argues that there has been something of a *gentrification of gentrification theory* in which the class character of gentrification is ignored. In some ways Smith is as guilty of this as anyone else in that, as mentioned earlier, one of his initial starting points was that the focus within gentrification studies should be on the physical change in housing stock rather than on the social composition of people living in the area. However, subsequent to this, Smith (1995; 1996a) has sought to create a greater recognition of the class character of gentrification and to move away from thinking about it solely in middle class terms. Smith complains that in the 'gentrification of gentrification theory' middle class academic authors focus almost exclusively in their accounts on the agency of the middle class. It appears that gentrification is simply about middle class colonisation of an area. However, as noted in Chapter 9, gentrification is often accompanied by a process of *displacement* whereby people on the social margins of society are forced out of an area undergoing gentrification Although gentrification is often portrayed as the rehabilitation of derelict *and* unpopulated landscapes, run-down buildings are actually often home for many people. Such people are effectively 'written out' of many accounts of gentrification. Take, for instance, the city of Vancouver which appears in much of the literature as an epitome of a human-centred, 'consumption-side' gentrification. In some contrast to this image, and as mentioned in Box 10.2, the 'Downtown Eastside' area of the city is currently witnessing the displacement of a local initiated programme of community regeneration (run by DERA, the Downtown Eastside Residents Association) and, one should add, a displacement of the people of this area which the programme was designed to serve. Downtown Eastside was an area with a run-down physical and economic infrastructure and with a high concentration of low-income, elderly males and other *marginalised groups*, such as the mentally ill, teenagers who have left their parental home and a growing number of native Americans. While the DERA programme, which has been described as 'a remarkable model of community development' (Ley *et al.* 1992: 237), sought to regenerate the area through addressing the needs of these marginalised groups, from the mid 1980s these groups have increasingly been seen by the City authorities as the source of the area's problems. Local government policies have been altered to facilitate the demands of affluent gentrifiers while the marginalised population has been: a) left to live, and die, by their own devices; and b) become the subject of public condemnation, surveillance and regulation.

Smith (1996a) highlights similar processes in New York (see Box 10.5). Gentrification, often described in such pleasant and uplifting terms as 'urban improvement' or 'urban regeneration' and seen to be associated with the creation of a landscape of leisured consumption, as well as being described as being 'simply' an economic process, can be seen to have associated with it, in at least in some instances, a much grittier and violent side with, for instance, police charging 'anti-gentrification demos' and forcibly removing people from areas of gentrification.

Box 10.5:   Gentrification beyond gentrified theory: The working class and the gentrification of Tompkin Square

Smith (1996a) argues that studies of gentrification have tended to ignore or pacify the working class. They are ignored, in part, by considering gentrification as being a purely middle class affair and failing to consider the extent to which other social groups or classes may live in the areas undergoing gentrification and how they are displaced from these areas through gentrification. Smith highlights how Tompkins Park in the Lower East Side of New York (see Figure 10.2) came to be inhabited in the later 1980s by some 300 or so people, many of whom had been displaced from other parts of the Lower East Side as a result of the process of gentrification. This displacement occurred because many of the dilapidated buildings which had previously been let at low rents or used as squats were refurbished and sold to or rented by affluent gentrifiers, while other buildings were demolished to make way for new 'up-scale' developments. The displacement of people is often economic in that people on low incomes cannot afford the new gentrified housing and so have to move to other areas. This displacement is also often quite physical and violent with people being literally carried away from their 'homes'. Smith (1996a), for example, notes how the people living in Tompkins Park came to be evicted from the area by police, a process which led to over 120 complaints of police brutality.

As well as displacement of the working class within gentrification, Smith identifies a process of 'pacification' of the working class in that these groups are seen to quietly acquiesce to the physical and social restructuring of neighbourhoods. Smith, however, highlights how in New York and several other cities working class groups are actively resisting gentrification, for instance by organising demonstrations, squats, street art and vandalism. Such activity generally receives little academic attention and Smith notes how the agents of gentrification – both professional organisations and individual home owners – have acted in New York to efface this working class agency by having signs of protest and the protesters physically removed from areas.

Postmodernism and the Fragmentation of Gentrification

Smith's analysis of gentrification draws on a variety of strands of argument centred within Marxist political economy. In the 1980s human geography has been influenced by a wider variety of intellectual influences including those associated with some notion of *postmodernism* (see Chapter 2). The study of gentrification has not been immune from these changes, and indeed in many respects has been amongst the leading sites of contestation over the significance, or not, of ideas of postmodernism. At least two different arenas of interaction can be identified.

First, many of the areas described as having been 'gentrified' are said to incorporate the elements of 'postmodern architecture' and thereby become a 'postmodern landscape'. As outlined in Chapters 2 and 9, postmodernism can be seen to refer to an 'architectural style' which seeks to be different from the modernist conventions of high, rectangular, large-scale regularly laid out and uniform constructed buildings. By contrast, postmodern architects sought to introduce variations in building surface, shape and size, with much of this variation being derived from sticking together elements of different styles, to create a *pastiche*. Advocates of this form of architecture argued that it results in a more meaningful, more pleasurable and more human scale architecture. An oft quoted example of such architecture is the 'False Creek Development' in Vancouver (see Box 10.2).

A second element of postmodernism in human geography has been an emerging distrust of *grand theory*, where this is seen as claims to have understood how the world operates on the basis of one or two concepts which are seen to provide the key to understanding because they correspond to some central phenomena or process around which the world is seen to operate (see Chapter 2). Clear examples of grand theories are the theories of logical positivist spatial science, but it can also be seen to apply to other seemingly quite different approaches. Hence, Marxism, for example, can be seen to be a 'grand theory' through its use of concepts like modes of production and class struggle. By contrast, postmodernists suggest that there are multiple causes of phenomena and their importance will vary considerably from one situation to another. It can be said to favour 'humble' and 'eclectic' (a combination of diverse elements) theory and the formation of 'local knowledges', that is knowledge which is appropriate to a very limited number of instances.

So far, with the possible exception of empiricist studies, the perspectives on gentrification discussed so far have largely seen it in terms of being a manifestation of some singular and uniform process: that is, gentrification is seen as the outcome of some distinct gentrification process. Debate, and gentrification is a subject which has generated plenty of this, has been in terms of alternative suggestions as to what is this causal process. Logical positivists, for example, have seen it as the outcome of changing abilities to compete in the urban housing markets. Behaviourists have examined it as an outcome of changing in spatial preferences, while Marxists have viewed it as the outcome of changes in the value of particular parts of the city to a variety of capitalist property developers. However, a number of people such as Beauregard (1986), Clark (1991; 1992), Hamnett (1991) and Rose (1984) have come to question whether this is the only way the debate over theorising gentrification should be approached. The answer for some, although not all, of these authors is the adoption of a postmodern perspective on gentrification.

Hamnett (1991), for example, argued that the various theories of gentrification should be considered as 'partial' and 'complementary', rather than 'complete' and 'alternative' explanations of the same phenomenon. He argued that there is a need for the development of an 'integrated theory of gentrification' which takes the 'complementary' aspects of different theories and pulls them together. Both the 'complete but alternative' and the 'partial and complementary' views about gentrification theory can be seen to be what postmodernists would characterise as modernist 'grand theories': that is, they both are looking to develop an interpretation which establishes key concepts which are seen to be applicable across all cases of gentrification. Where they differ is only in the complexity of their conceptualisation: Hamnett's 'integrated theory' would appear to be, in theory, a much bigger theory than those of, say, Smith or Ley.

Rose (1984), however, can be seen to adopt a more postmodern perspective when she suggests that gentrification is a 'chaotic concept' which needs 'disaggregating' into a range of distinct processes and phenomena, each of which should be examined in their own right, and probably, she suggests, from different perspectives. Rather than seeing gentrification as a single process involving to some degree or another, lifestyles and changes in spatial preferences and/or the creation of housing developments and/or intra-urban residential movement, Rose argues that it might be better to disentangle each process and study it in its own terms. Hence, one might adopt a behaviourist approach for the examination of lifestyles and changes in spatial preferences, a Marxist approach for the study of the creation of housing developments and a neo-classical economic and/or behavioural perspective being used to explain intra-urban residential movement. Instead of having alternative explanations of '*the* gentrification process' or a range of more or less integrated theories building towards a new theory of '*the* gentrification process', one has a range of gentrification theories which refer to a range of 'gentrification process*es*', or perhaps more correctly to a range of situations which are often described as gentrification but should not be.

A third feature of postmodernism in human geography has been to emphasise, and indeed it is often said to 'celebrate', *differences*. That is, rather than seek to develop ideas which have universal, or at least large scale applicability, postmodernism argues for 'an alertness to the many differences that distinguish one person or event or process or whatever from another, and an insistence on not obliterating these vital differences in the face of grand theoretical statements' (Cloke *et al.* 1991: 171). In other words, rather than looking for similarities between events or process and developing explanations centred around these similarities, postmodernists favour a focusing in on what way something is different from something else and an explanation which then focuses on a) why those differences have been ignored, and/or b) an examination of the consequences of those differences.

Such ideas can be seen to have connections to the disaggregative approach to gentrification favoured by Rose. One of the reasons she argues for such an approach is that Rose, like Beauregard (1986), feels that there are actually a very wide range of gentrifiers. Rose and Beauregard argue that gentrification studies have too readily assumed that gentrifiers are all alike and that they are relatively affluent middle class people. Rose, like Smith (1996a), feels that too much of gentrification has focused on middle class affluence. For Smith, the important counter-point is the neglect and displacement of the working class by the middle class gentrifiers. For Rose (1984: 65), however, there are important differences within gentrifiers and as well as affluence there is also, she suggests, a substantial amount of evidence which points to 'the presence of considerable need' among gentrifiers. Hence rather than gentrification being a process for people securely in positions of power or in 'the centre', in many instances it is, she suggests, a process created by people who are, to some degree, socially marginalised. Rose coins the term *marginal gentrifiers* to refer to such people and she identifies three illustrative cases.

First, Rose highlights evidence of a high proportion of *first-time buyers* within gentrifiers and suggests that for this group gentrification is not so much an expression of spatial preference and affluence but rather one of the few ways into the housing market. In other words, young people looking to purchase a house may only be able to afford to purchase a run down house and hope to do it up in order to later trade up to a bigger and better, and probably more suburban, house. Second, Rose suggests that there are *reluctant gentrifiers*, who she characterises as people who previously rented accommodation but are forced to become property owners by their landlords, who may be in either the private or state sector. Such gentrifiers are effectively forced to become private property owners and once owning their own property then they have an interest in investment, although they would not have initially chosen this action. Third, Rose argues that much gentrification is undertaken by *constrained gentrifiers*. These people undertake gentrification activities, such as moving into a gentrified area and/or refurbishing a run-down house, not out of some lifestyle preference but rather because their residential options are constrained by major constraints, particularly with regard to employment opportunities or related to the performance of household tasks, or as it is often termed *reproductive labour*.

Rose suggests that these 'marginal gentrifiers' may be important agents of gentrification acting to transform the physical structure of an area and may alter the social structure of an area by displacing lower income groups from the localities into which they are moving. However to view them as powerful and exploitative agents is to ignore the extent to which they themselves have been excluded from many other housing markets and localities.

Recognition of difference not only leads to a recognition of hitherto rather neglected lines of economic differentiation and displacements, but, as discussed in Chapter 2, has also lead to a valuation of some neglected lines of social differentiation. Rose is a *feminist* and unsurprisingly perhaps this leads her to ask whether *gender differences* might also be significant in gentrification. So far, gentrification has been discussed in genderless terms: there has been reference to agents, to residents, to households and to social classes as if there is no gender differentiation amongst these entities. However, for Rose (1984; 1989) and also Bondi (1991; 1992, 1999) gender differences and relations may be crucial in understanding gentrification. Amongst the arguments they make in support of this is, first, how a rise in female participation in the paid labour market can be seen to stimulate gentrification. It can do this in two ways: first, by creating more affluent households through the expansion of *dual income households* and, second, because some women are now earning high individual incomes there are a growing number of high income single women households.

A second link between gender and gentrification is related to the performance of 'reproductive labour', or housework and childcare. Even with the rise of female participation in paid employment, women are generally also responsible for the majority of this sort of 'domestic' work. It has been suggested that the need to combine paid employment and reproductive work may contribute to gentrification because the inner city provides a location which enables householders to minimise the financial and temporal costs of both journeys-to-work and performing reproductive labour. As Markusen puts it:

Gentrification in large part corresponds to the two income (or more) professional household that requires both a relative central urban location to minimise journey-to-work costs of several wage earners and a location that enhances in household production (stores are nearer) and in the substitution of market produced commodities (laundries, restaurants, child-care) for household production (Markusen 1981: 32).

A third link between gender and gentrification relates to changes in the position of women within households and families, changes which may in part be associated with the rise of female participation in the labour force. There have, for instance, been a rising proportion of single women households and an increasing delay in child-rearing. It has been suggested that the inner city environment is particularly appealing to young single women and to people in childless couples.

Taken together these arguments all suggest that women are an important, and hitherto neglected agent of gentrification. Other work has highlighted other similarly neglected agents of gentrification. Zukin (1987; 1989), and also to a lesser extent, Smith (1996a), have highlighted how artists may be a key agent of gentrification in that they may move into areas because of low cost housing, and also perhaps a certain aesthetic preferences. Once in the area they act to raise the social tone of an area and hence encourage further gentrification. A rather different group are highlighted in the studies of Castells and Murphy (1982), Lauria and Knopp (1985) and Knopp (1990a; 1990b) who suggest that gentrification in some areas, such as in inner city San Francisco and New Orleans, is initiated by the movement of homosexuals into this area (see Box 10.6)

Box 10.6: Gay gentrification

Lauria and Knopp (1985: 152) have argued that 'the role of the "gay factor"… in urban redevelopment and gentrification', although often mentioned, has rarely been subject to detailed investigation as to 'the determination of exactly what this role is'. They suggest there may be at least two reasons for this: first 'a certain squeamishness regarding sexual issues' amongst academic researchers; and second, the complexity of the inter-relation. The first point connects to the arguments of postmodernist and others about the need for geographers to take people, and all there differences, seriously (see Chapters 2 and 12 for more on this). The second point has formed the focus of attention by Lauria and Knopp in a variety of studies. They argue that the inter-relation is not simply a contingent one – in some places there are people who are gentrifying who are homosexuals – but that there are a complex set of factors which in certain places come together to create what might be seen to be a process of gay gentrification. In Lauria and Knopp (1985) they argue, for instance, that during the 1970s social and economic opportunities for gay men expanded considerably in many inner city areas because: i) many of these areas became affordable, largely in the manner identified by Smith; ii) these areas afforded both greater anonymity and greater social interaction than did suburban and rural areas, and thereby both provided a space where homosexuals could escape homophobic oppression and a place where they could meet potential sexual partners; and iii) these areas were experiencing a growth in service-sector and clerical jobs which held a particular appeal to gay men in that because these jobs had traditionally been dominated by women,'heterosexual male culture' was 'less pervasive and oppressive' (Lauria and Knopp 1985: 160).

Lauria and Knopp also suggest, in a manner which parallels other studies of forms of gentrification (e.g. Beauregard 1990; Rose 1984; Smith 1996a; Zukin 1987, 1990), that there may be distinct phases or 'waves' of gentrification . This point is more fully elaborated in Knopp (1990b) who examines the gay gentrification of the Marigny district of New Orleans. He identifies three phases of gentrification. First, from the late 1960s through into the early 1980s there was a 'completely unorganised process' of gentrification whereby a few white, middle class professional, gay men decided individually to move into the area, in part because they felt alienated by the 'family-orientated suburbs' and because they feared to live in other 'black' inner city areas. From the early 1970s a second, more collectively focused phase of gentrification occurred centred around preserving the historical character of the area. According to Knopp this preservation movement had three important consequences: i) it created a strong sense of community identity; ii) the community came to have a higher political profile and influence within the New Orleans government and business communities; and iii) it fostered the social and political development of the gay community in the area in that many of the leaders of the preservation movement were openly gay and many gay men were encouraged, both directly and indirectly, to move into the area. The third phase of the gay gentrification of the area started in the mid 1970s. This phase involved more affluent gentrifiers and occurred when estate agents and housing developers came to recognise the economic power of gay gentrification and began specifically targeting gay men for advertising and marketing. Overall, Knopp (1990b) suggests that gentrification in Marigny was a complex combination of interests and events, and argues that although many of the key actors in the gentrification process were homosexual it is also important to recognise the role of other social differences, such as class, race and gender in constituting the gentrification of the area.

Post-structuralist Geographies of Gentrification

Closely connected to, and for some people indistinguishable from, postmodernism in human geography is *post-structuralism*. However, as discussed in Chapter 2, while the term postmodernism has much of its origins in art and architecture, post-structuralism is a rather more philosophical and linguistic in origin. Given these origins it is perhaps unsurprising that the clearest impacts of post-structuralism in the context of the study of gentrification have arguably been, first, a concern to reflect upon, rather than simply develop and use, concepts; and second, a movement towards analysing gentrification as, at least in part, a linguistic phenomenon.

A post-structuralist emphasis on the manner in which gentrification is 'conceptu-alised' can be seen in a number of recent studies. As highlighted in Chapter 2, within post-structuralism concepts are never seen as straight forward *representations of reality* but are rather seen as signs within complex systems of signs. Rather than seeking to 'discover' the concepts which 'correspond' or 'mirror' some object of study, within post-structuralism concepts need to be 'understood' in the context of their interaction with other concepts.

A clear illustration of such a perspective is, once more, provided by Smith (1996). As well as employing political economic concepts such as the rent gap, uneven development and class struggle, Smith also engages in analysis of various cultural meanings associated with the notion of gentrification. He notes, for example, how descriptions of gentrification, both academic and popular, frequently employ a language of *frontiermanship*. Newspapers describe gentrifiers using such terms as 'urban homesteaders' and 'urban pioneers' and the process of gentrification is likened to the 'Taming of the Wild West': the New York Times, for example, commented that 'The trailblazers have done their work: West 42nd Street has been *tamed*, *domesticated* and polished into the most exciting, freshest, most energetic new neighbourhood in all of New York' (New York Times (1983) quoted in Smith 1996a: 13 emphasis added).

Smith also notes that within advertising, television programmes and in films such as *Crocodile Dundee*, there has emerged a notion of the *urban cowboy* and he suggests that this image is also being produced within the new urban fabric of gentri-fied areas and indeed within the fabric worn by gentrifiers:

> Frontier is a style as much as a place, and the 1980s saw the faddishness of Tex-Mex restau-rants, the ubiquity of desert decor, and a rage for Cowboy chic ... The Western imprint on fashion is now much like a cattle brand – not too striking, but obvious to catch the eye. For city dudes, that means accents; a fringed jacket with black leggings; a shearling coat with a pinstripe suit; a pair of lizard boots with almost anything ... Americana West purveys diverse images of noble savages, desert scenes ... petroglyphs and pictographs, whips and spurs. Cacti and coyotes are everywhere (none real): a neon prickly pear is available for $350 (Smith 1996a: 15).

While the western frontier image is important in many areas, Smith also suggests that the frontier image is more widespread taking a range of different forms. He notes, for instance, allusions to the city as an 'urban jungle' and the rise of both 'jungle commodities' – leopard coats, antelope leather skirts, stuffed gorillas – and 'safari images' – the inclusion for instance of rhinoceros images on the back of 4 wheel drive vehicles (see Plate 10.1). 'Nature' too is incorporated into the urban fabric and commodities of gentrification with, for example, boutiques in the gentrified inner city offering consumer guides to natural history:

> The Nature Company ... is the apotheosis of this naturalised urban history, selling maps and globes, whaling anthologies and telescopes, books on dangerous reptiles and stories of exploration and conquest (Smith 1996a: 17).

Within Britain one can think of the widespread presence of companies with eco-friendly images, such as *The Body Shop*, within many areas of gentrification (see also

Plate 10.2). There is also interesting rural counterparts to these images, with an advertisement for 4-wheel drive vehicles (Plate 10.3) drawing together both American western frontier imagery – the lasso writing, the Colorado lettering, the invitation to say 'howdy' – together with a rose tinted image of English village life alongside the Thames (see also Phillips, 2002).

As Smith himself remarks, one common reaction to such imagery is to suggest that it has nothing really to do with gentrification: it is simply a meaningless coincidence. However, for Smith it does have significance in that he claims the frontier imagery acts as an *ideology* by bolstering the self-image of gentrifiers and naturalising the inequalities and exclusions which are created through gentrification. Zukin (1990: 42) similarly argues that the refurbishment of areas like Brooklyn or London's Brick Lane has involved the creation of a very selective image: what she terms a 'selective spatial history' whereby particular elements of the history of these areas, such as connections to mercantile wealth, are recreated in the physical refurbishment of buildings, while other elements of these areas' pasts are ignored, such as their long histories 'as boarding houses, Pakistani and Huguenot workshops and immigrant clubs'.

A similar perspective on gentrification is provided in the work of Mills (1993) who sees gentrification as a *text community*: that is as a set of 'texts', both official ones such as presented in property advertisements and more informal representations embodied in the attitudes and expressions of people living in or commenting on the area. Mills focuses in particular on the strategies by which gentrified areas – and once more her study area is False Creek, Vancouver – are presented and discussed by architects, estate agents and by people who have bought a property in this area (see also Mills 1986). She identifies a number of distinct ways in which the area is portrayed and interpreted: as 'a distinctive area for a living investment'; as 'city living at its best' and as a 'strategic location'. In the former case, the area is presented as where you want to be if you want to show, or even create, social status. Mills, for example, records how high-class lifestyles are promoted within the advertising and marketing of property: 'We don't just sell you a townhome, we offer an exciting new lifestyle' while the display homes have 'kitchens laid out with wineracks, microwave ovens, pasta makers and gourmet cookbooks; storage spaces is advertised for bicycles and windsurfers' (Mills 1986: 181). This is designed to appeal to those who have money, and also perhaps to appeal to those who want to give off the image of having money. Zukin (1995: 10) for example, has suggested that gentrification in effect 'creates urban oases where everyone *appears* to be middle class'. She notes how in public spaces such an appearance can quite quickly be assumed: even those with little money may be able to spend some time participating in middle case space by strolling around an area or at a cafe or bar in such an area. It is very difficult to assess the social class or wealth of someone simply from their appearance, particularly with the rise of fake Rolex and designer clothes. Apparent uniformity can conceal significant differences and Zukin is quick to point out that behind the public facade of affluence there is often considerable poverty: she notes how, for instance, in the backspaces of restaurant and bars, one finds not leisure and affluence but rather hard work, long hours, poor wages and racism.

A structuralist would attempt to look behind the image, to argue that it performs some function such as concealing inequalities. Mills adopts a rather more post-structuralist approach in that she focuses more on outlining the nature of the discourse and its relationships both with academic interpretations of gentrification and

Plate 10.1: 'On safari' in the gentrified city

Plate 10.2: Selling nature in the gentrified city

Plate 10.3: American West and idyllic rural England in the promotion of gentrification

with other interpretations of the developments in the area. Hence she notes that this interpretation corresponds well with the academic concept of conspicuous consumption and could be incorporated into Smith's notion of a rent gap analysis in that people are investing in houses in part as a way of establishing a new social status. However, she notes that not every text, either formal or informal, took this perspective.

Mill argues that a second set of texts appeared to present the area as 'city living at its best'. While in part these texts drew on notions of *positionality* or *social status* – it was 'best' because it was high class, luxury living – Mills suggests that there was a specifically geographical connotation to such texts in that they were constructing the False Creek and Fair View developments through a series of specifically spatialised assessments or *place images*. In particular, Mills argues that the area was seen to be best because it was close to, but not in, the city centre and, even more significantly, it was not suburban:

> I hope and pray that if I ever have to move … I'll still be able to live in the city. I do *not* want to live in the suburbs … even if one was forced into some awful situation like the family house … one can still do that in the city … I *like* cities, I like *busyness* – I want to be right here in the city. Being in a suburb is, like, forget it! It's not where I want to be (Interviewee quoted in Mills 1993: 159–160).

Another resident claimed,

> I've lived in Toronto, I'm a believer in, if you're going to live in the city, *live in the city*. I'm not a suburban person or a country person. I like living close to the urban areas (Interviewee quoted in Mills 1993: 159–160).

These quotations reveal expressions of clear spatial preferences, but preferences which may not be connectable to some rational assessment of the practical advantages and disadvantages of inner city versus suburban or rural locations. What they might be more connectable to, but which Mills herself does not really do, is a whole series of other cultural texts – both popular and academic – which have evaluated suburban spaces in mainly negative ways (Silverstone 1997; see also Ley 1996; Phillips 2004).

A third discourse identified by Mills does have a more practical, rationalistic, flavour. In these accounts, the Fair View/False Creek development is described in terms which are very similar to much of the academic discourse on gentrification in that attention is paid to the practical advantages that living in the location brings: advertisements stress the convenience and centrality of the city while residents interviewed talked of how the location and style of properties minimised, for example, journey to work times, reproductive labour costs and leisure costs:

> I like living in a town house because of the fact that you can just lock the door and go away, you don't have to worry about the garden and maintenance (Interviewee quoted in Mills 1993: 163).

> I think there's a real time advantage. I get from home to work in five minutes. I think that's a real advantage in my life particularly … because I go out in the evenings quite a bit (Interviewee quoted in Mills 1993: 163).

What is significant here is, first, how the discourse of people in this area reproduce the discourse of academics, and second, that even given this, Mills argues that such

discourses should not be seen as 'proving' the validity of a particular academic interpretation. Instead she argues for a need to recognise the existence of all the
discourses, not least because people themselves often draw, often in quick succes-
sion, on these seemingly quite distinct interpretations. She quotes, by way of illustration, a conversation between a wife and husband in which it is possible to identify the
three discourses at work:

Frances   I think it is going to ... become a place that people get quite committed
            to ... [Discourse 2]

Frederick I think it is going to be a very desirable place when ... people realise
            how convenient it is, how workable it is ... [Discourse 3]

Frances   I think [the fact that] these homes are here is going to encourage people
            to change there lifestyle ... people seeing its virtues not just as a place
            you can live cheaply on your way to somewhere [Discourse 1] but as a
            place with a lifestyle of its own. And the fact that it is here, people will
            adapt their lifestyles to here' [Discourse 3].

                                       (Mills 1993: 167, details of discourse added).

Summary and Conclusions

This chapter has focused on the people and processes of gentrification. The broad
arguments of the chapter are summarised in Box 10.7.

Box 10.7: Chapter summary and suggestions for further reading

- Gentrification is often taken to be about the doing up, or 'refurbishment' of
  the housing of an area, and an accompanying change in the social composition of the area.
- The precise character of gentrification has, however, been subject to
  repeated examination and contestation.
- Gentrification has clearly become a global phenomena and can be seen as
  a key feature in the construction and reconstruction of a range of contemporary 'spaces at the centre', such as global cities, regional centres and the
  rural residential spaces of the middle classes.
- The rise of gentrification caused problems for the prevailing 'spatial scientific' interpretations of the socio-spatial structure of cities.
- Although a variety of positivist explanations of gentrification might be
  advanced, gentrification has increasingly been understood through reference to arguments derived from Marxist political economy, feminism,
  postmodernism and post-structuralism.

The topic of gentrification has received considerable attention with a number of
books and a plethora of articles having been written of the topic. One of the best
introductions to the debates over gentrification is Smith and Williams' (1986)

Gentrification and the City while Smith's (1996a) *The New Urban Frontier* integrates a range of his earlier writings into an accessible, wide-ranging and challenging interpretation of gentrification. Other, more locality specific, interpretations are also be found in Zukin's (1989) *Loft Living*; Caulfield's (1994) *City Form and Everyday Life*; Ley's (1996) *The New Middle Class and the Remaking of the Central City* and Butler's (1997) *Gentrification and the Middle Classes*. To get a flavour of the at times highly antogonistic debates about gentrification see the articles by Ley and Smith in the *Annals of the Association of American Geographers* in 1986 and 1987, and the articles of Hamnett and Smith in *Transactions of the Institute of British Geographers* in 1991 and 1992. For a discussion of gentrification outside the city, see Phillips (1993, 2002, 2004).

More generally, it can be suggested that gentrification well illustrates the arguments of this book concerning constructed and contested nature of contemporary human geography both here with the world of academic texts and 'out there in the worlds of others' (Murdoch 1995b: 1214). The degree of struggle and contestation over the academic study gentrification can be off-putting. A well-known participant in the debate, for example, commented that he was left feeling disappointed and frustrated after reading one set of debates on gentrification (Clark 1992). He added that rather too often the gentrification debate is characterised by a certain level of 'conceptual blindness' amongst its protagonists as they fail to fully engage with and seek to understand the arguments of others, preferring instead to continue studying gentrification in accordance with their own 'idiosyncratic pre-conceived notions' (Clark 1992: 359). In addition he is also critical of what he describes as 'an infatuation with centre-pieces', or rather more pejoratively, as people playing 'king of the mountain' (Clark 1992: 360). That is, he is critical of people claiming to have discovered the true meaning or essential cause of gentrification. Recognising the constructed and contested nature of the concept of gentrification means that the researchers on gentrification may be well advised to adopt a fair degree of humility and caution: to have, as Law's (1994: 9) has put it, some 'modesty' in their accounts of situations by recognising that they will 'always be incomplete'. However, along with this humility there is also room for social commitment and critique: to be 'modest legislators' willing to speak about, albeit always 'defensibly to be sure', of things beyond our selves (Law 1994: 17). This point is very pertinent to the study of gentrification and Smith's arguments about the 'gentrification of gentrification theory'. While academic studies of gentrification may, almost by definition, be texts created by people 'in the centre' – that is written by people with some degree of power – and gentrifiers may often also be 'people of the centre', as this chapter has sought to demonstrate gentrification should not be see simply as a story of such people. In part this is because even within the people of the centre there are important differences in the powers that they have to construct their lives. It is also because the construction of places for the people of the centre is also about deconstructing other places and, all to frequently, the lives of other people.

Chapter 11

People in a Marginal Periphery

David Cook and Martin Phillips

Introduction: People in the Margins

Geographers have long sought to partition the world, and the people and multitude of other things that go up to make that world, into various zone or areas. As discussed in Chapter 2, a variety of strategies of partition have been utilised, ranging from abstract geometries of, say, central place theories; through the cognitive maps educed from people by behavioural geographers such as Gould and White (1974); into conscious and unconscious constructions of places within humanistic geographers; and onto the empowered and disempowered spaces of various critical geographies. It is in the latter geographies that notions of margin and marginality have often been spotlighted, although the precise hues of illumination have again varied considerably. As is well evidenced in many of the other chapters of this book, *political economist perspectives* of both a Marxist and more liberal hue have made much of spatial patterns of inequalities in social and economic resource provision and often partitioned the worlds into 'core' areas of wealth and affluence and 'peripheral' or 'marginal' areas of poverty and destitution. Furthermore, as shown in Chapter 3, in many analyses the wealth and affluence of the core was seen to be achieved by exploiting the periphery, which is seen as dependent on the core even though disadvantaged by it.

Although many people feel that there is much of value in such analyses, such political economic analysis have, at the very least, become somewhat displaced from a position of contested centrality within human geography (for more on this see Chapters 2 and 3). As noted in Chapter 9 the concept of economic marginalisation has become interpreted rather more inclusively. Hurd and Woodward, for example, argue that,

> we need to start thinking about the multiplicity of processes of 'marginalisation' that are at work ... which cross-cut in a variety of ways ... The term 'marginalisation' ... can be built into ideas of restructuring and exclusion; it also involves a host of other things – economic, political, social and cultural ... different people become marginalised in different ways (Hurd and Woodward 1991: 25).

Such widening in the concept of marginalisation can be seen as part of a broadening trend whereby a concern with economic and social welfare has, in recent years, become supplemented, and in the minds of some people (e.g. Sayer 1994), effectively replaced by a concern with culturally constructed lifestyles and identities. Notions of inequality and exploitation have become displaced by concepts of difference and recognition, arguably part of a broader shift in 'political imaginaries' from a *politics of distribution*, in which 'economically defined "classes" ... are struggling to defend their "interests", end "exploitation" and win "redistribution"', and towards an *identity politics* in which 'culturally defined groups ... are struggling to defend their "identities", end "cultural domination", and win "recognition"' (Fraser 1997: 2). Furthermore the dualism of core-periphery has become somewhat displaced by a new spatial lexicon which, according to Pratt (1992) commonly falls into three groups. First, there are terms such as 'nomadic', 'travelling', 'flaneur' and flow which in one way or another draw upon notions of mobility and detachment from place. Second, there are terms such as 'border', 'meeting place' and 'contact zone' which imply both difference and inter-relation. Third, there are notions of 'marginality and exile' which are often applied, like the other two sets of terms, as much to describe the position of the researcher than to refer to anything that the researcher might be studying. There has, as Keith and Pile (1993) observe, been a spatialisation of epistemology within, and beyond, human geography to go along side, and potentially disrupt, the long standing strategies of spatialising ontologies (see also Chapter 2).

The spatialising of ontologies and epistemologies has not been undertaken without contestation. Chapter 2, for example, highlighted how geographers have often criticised some of their number as having a 'spatial fetish'; of being obsessed to an unhelpful/unhealthy extent with things to do with space. This charge has been frequently levied at spatial science and its concern to represent the world as a composite of various geometric shapes, but it is a charge which has also been levied at more recent critical and postmodern/poststructuralist geographies. Unwin (2000), for example, has discussed the work of Henri Lefebvre which has been widely drawn upon by geographers with a range of different philosophical outlooks (e.g. Dear (2000); Gregory (1994); Harvey (1989); Pile (1996); Soja (1989; 1996; 2000)) and claims that it contains a fetishism of space which leaves 'the causes of the inequalities that influence human existence in space-time' rather over-looked:

> One of the most remarkable things about ... [Lefebvre's] discussion of ... geopolitical issues is that people never get a mention. It is not women, men and children to whom violence is meted out, it is not the voices of humans being slaughtered that cry out, it is not the pleading of the parent whose child is being violated that we hear, it is not the sounds of exploding warheads that reaches our ears – it is 'space' against which violence is directed (Unwin 2000: 23).

Although there may be much in this statement, it itself can be criticised for neglecting consideration of the way that space, and indeed other facets of geography such as notions of place, territory, landscape and nature, enter into the construction of violence directed against people, in both obvious and less obvious forms (see Chapter 1). It may also enter into resistances to such violence. Smith, for example, argues that space can,

> become a source of community for those oppressed by the social categories that society has worked with for so long – by ideas about, and practices around – 'race', class, gender, sexuality, age, nation, region and colonial status. Experiences of marginalisation and exclusion, and the spaces created by these processes, have been turned into a strategic resource. They have become a speaking position for voices which previously went unheard; a space in which old categories are resisted by new processes of identification (S. Smith 1999: 20).

Amongst these new processes of identification are those which have been described by Anderson (2000: 388) as 'relational thinking', involving 'ethics of engagement across groups' and indeed across conceptual boundaries. Anderson suggests that one of the 'many exciting developments in human geography today' has been the rise of studies 'which move beyond the binary fixes that inform such stock in-trade dualisms as center [sic] and margin, core periphery, urban and rural' (Anderson 2000: 388). This is not to imply that such distinctions are unimportant, but rather that we should not see them as immutable entities but rather as quite precarious, contorted, contested, changeable creations with a multiplicities of actual and potential conse-quences for people and other agencies of this world.

Rural People as Marginal

Rural areas have often been seen as being the spatial margins of modern society which is conversely seen to be centred on the urban. Bowler (2000: 129), for example, writes that 'the rural comprises those spaces left over once the urban has been accounted for'. Taking a general look at how the countryside is imagined, Short (1991) suggests that there has long been a view that the countryside and the people who live there are conservative, dull and slightly backward, conceptions which are often expressed through such notions as the 'country yokel' or 'hillbilly'. Country areas and their inhabitants are seen to have been by-passed by social developments such as industrial activity, modern communications, education and cultural innova-tion. Such notions of the countryside have been enacted not only within popular discourses but also in academic ones through such concepts as the *rural-urban continuum* and the *gemeinschaft/gesellschaft* distinction which informed many British 'community studies' undertaken between the 1930s and 1960s (see Box 11.1). Of particular significance in the present context is that these concepts effectively represented rural communities as spaces which 'lay outside the influence of moder-nity', although the 'forces of modernity were "closing in", threatening the future of traditional social systems' (Murdoch and Pratt 1993: 417). Although these concepts have both been subsequently critiqued, the view that rural areas are peripheral to modernisation can still be discerned within much contemporary geographical writing. Dear (2000: 7), for example, has claimed that, 'Cities – large and small, global and local, north and south – have become (for better or worse) the principal material expressions of contemporary human civilisation'. The city is hence seen as the place where things happen, where culture, even civilisation, is seen to reside. By implication the non-urban, which includes but may not be encompassed by the rural, is relegated to the unchanging and even the uncivilised.

Box 11.1: Key concepts within British community studies

In the 1930s, 40s and 50s a series of anthropologists, sociologists and geographers undertook studies examining the character and fortunes of 'communities'. Many of these studies focused on rural areas, and indeed, as Wright (1992) highlights, there was a clear concentration on remoter, more upland areas of Britain. This focus reflects two theoretical assumptions which underpinned, albeit often implicitly, these studies (Murdoch and Pratt 1993). First, it was felt that 'community' was more prevalent in areas which lay beyond, or at the margins, of modern urban/industrial societies. Second, the communities in these areas were seen to be under threat from an encroaching modern society in which notions of community were largely absent.

Although these ideas often remained barely articulated in many of these studies, they were, as Murdoch and Pratt (1993) note, at times formalised through use of a distinction between *gemeinschaft* and *gesellschaft* outlined by the German sociologist, Tönnies (1957). These two terms were seen taken to refer to two basic types of human relationships; the former relating to 'close human relationships developed through kinship … common habitat and … co-operation and co-ordinated action for social good', while the later was created through 'impersonal ties and relationships based on formal exchange and contract' in which 'no actions … manifest the will or spirit of … unity' (Harper 1989: 162–3). Using these ideas, rural areas were widely seen as places where gemeinschaft, or 'community' relations predominated, while modern, urban and industrialised places were characterised as being dominated by 'gesellschaft', or associative, relations. Furthermore, rural communities were seen to be in danger of being transformed into urbanised societies of gemeinschaft.

Notions of gemeinschaft and gesellschaft were often linked with another concept utilised by some community studies, most notably those contained in Frankenberg (1966), where a series of studies of both rural and urban places were placed within a conceptual framework of a 'rural-urban continuum'. This concept stemmed from a rejection of the notion that places could be defined as being either rural or urban. Such a view, propounded by people like Wirth (1938), argued that all urban places were essentially alike and all rural places were essentially alike, and that the differences between urban and rural places exceeded any differences between urban places and between rural places. However, writers such as Redfield (1947) argued that there was not a simple rural/urban divide but rather a series of subtle variations from a rural like place to an urban like place. In other words, there was a continuum stretching from completely – or as it was frequently described 'truly' – rural places to completely or 'truly' urban places.

The precise basis for the continuum was a matter of some considerable debate (see Phillips 1998b; 1998c), but in the 1960s a series of criticisms began to circulate about the notion of an urban-rural continuum and about the gemeinschaft/gesellschaft distinction. Criticisms were conducted at both empirical and theoretical levels. Pahl (1966), for instance, highlighted studies which suggested that relations of gemeinschaft and gesellschaft could often be seen in the same place, while Brody (1973) questioned the historical perspective advanced by many community studies, arguing that many of the customs and traditions cited as evidence of a long standing and at risk gemeinschaft, were in practice often scarcely a hundred years old. Wright (1992) has similarly argued that many British community studies paid insufficient attention to history and the 'detailed processes of historical change'. More theoretical criticisms include claims that Tönnies description of gemeinschaft and gesellschaft distinction reproduces a highly gendered division of public and private space (Phillips 1998b); that notions of community serve ideological functions such as displacing concern over class relations and conflicts (Bell and Newby 1971); and that relations of gemeinschaft and gesellschaft have social origins which are independent of the spatial characters of places (Pahl 1966). Pahl also argued that if the notion of a rural-urban continuum was to be used at all it should not be as a device for classifying settlements and their associated communities but rather should instead be interpreted in a more dynamic way as referring to the diffusion of processes of change. As illustration of such a perspective is provided by Lewis and Maund (1976).

Despite such criticisms, notions of gemeinschaft and gesellschaft, and the rural-urban continuum, continue to attract attention. Lewis (1979) and Harper (1987; 1989) have made connection to philosophies of humanism, while Day and Murdoch (Day 1998; Day and Murdoch 1993; Murdoch and Day 1998) and Liepins (2000) have made connections with postmodern and poststructuralist concerns.

There may be some good reasons for this view: rural areas have in many ways been marginalised within modernity. There are, however, problems with ascribing rural areas exclusively to the margins of contemporary society. Modern systems of telecommunications have, for instance, been brought about 'space-time compression' (Giddens 1990; Harvey 1989) and associated declines in the 'tyrannies of distance' which contributed to many rural areas becoming bereft of social developments and services. Rather earlier developments in transport technologies have also enabled people to travel longer distances more quickly and in many urbanised countries there has been an increasing trend towards people commuting from rural areas into cities for work, and also for retailing and leisure opportunities. In many countries there has been a decline in the number of people living in settlements defined as urban and a growth in people living in areas seen as rural, a situation which has been characterised as *counter-urbanisation* (See Box 11.2).

Box 11.2: Counterurbanisation and the growing significance of the rural

Counterurbanisation has been described as an 'ambiguous' (Cloke 1985; Dean *et al*. 1984) and even a 'chaotic' (Sayer 1985) concept. The term is often traced back to Berry (1976) who wrote that a 'turning point' had been reached in 'the American urban experience. Counterurbanisation has replaced urbanisation as the dominant force shaping the nation's settlement pattern'.

As Fielding(1982) notes, only two years latter the term counterurbanisation was seen to be a feature characterising all 'western' nations (see also Vining and Kontuly 1978). Yet despite the widespread adoption of the term there has still been widespread uncertainty about the value of the concept. Berry never really defines what counterurbanisation was, beyond suggesting that it is the opposite of urbanisation. However, as Robinson (1990) has noted, the term 'urbanisation' has been understood in at least three ways. First, it has been seen as a demographic phenomenon relating to an increase in the proportion of the population of an area living in so-called urban areas. Often these areas are themselves defined demographically, through such indices as total settlement populations or population densities. Urbanisation here may be seen to refer to growing concentration in the spatial distribution of people. Second, urbanisation has been viewed in more socio-economic terms, with urban areas being seen as spaces for the performance of particular functions, such as trade, industry or collective service provision. Growth in the performance of such functions is seen to equate to urbanisation as the growth in the significance of urban space within society. Third, urban areas have been seen as a behavioural environment, fostering distinctive forms of life: they are, for example, often seen as spaces where people engage in with large numbers of essentially apersonal interactions (or gesselschaft, see Box 11.1).

If counterurbanisation is the opposite of urbanisation then it would appear that there may be at least three distinct ideas of counterurbanisation – a demographic view, a socio-economic view and a behavioural view – or some composite of one or more of these views. Berry, for example, effectively sees counterurbanisation as a change in demographic, socio-economic and behavioural dimensions of life in that he argues it represents a complete reversal of the urban way of life. More often, however, counterurbanisation is seen to reflect a change in one element of urbanisation, namely the demographic trend towards concentration. Other elements of urbanisation, such as the behavioural, are seen very much to persist: indeed population deconcentration is frequently portrayed as a mechanism for the expansion in urban ways of life with rural communities often seen as be increasingly urbanised through the process of counterurbanisation.

The notion of counterurbanisation as a reversal of the demographic trends of urbanisation is common to most accounts of counterurbanisation, including that of Berry. He claimed that counterurbanisation can be defined as 'a process of population deconcentration', implying 'a movement from a state of more

concentration to a state of less concentration' (Berry 1980b: 16). The seemingly simplicity of definition is, however, quite misleading, not least because
deconcentration can occur in quite a number of ways. One can, for instance,
have deconcentration through growth of a great number of centres or else it
might stem from a decrease in the size and/or number of large
settlements. One can also have deconcentration through the growth of large
settlements, so long as these settlements grow spatially as well. To help clarify
the issue, a range of other terms and distinctions, such as decentralisation,
dispersal and suburbanisation have been advanced, although as Dean *et al.*
(1984) comment, many of the terms promoted as clarifying the debate were as
equally ambiguous as those which preceded them.

There have been several responses to this ambiguity, ranging from total
ignorance of any ambiguity, through to suggestions that the term counterurbanisation is essentially chaotic and should be abandoned completely. A useful
middle position is to suggest that the term is useful so long as one is specific
about what you mean by the term and which of the various definitions of counterurbanisation one is using.

One of the most widely used definitions of counterurbanisation in the British
context is that of Fielding (1982), who stated that counterurbanisation 'refers to
a process in which population change is inversely related to population size'.
Champion (1989) follows up this definition arguing that:

> In general, if population distribution is shifting in favour of larger urban places,
> then urbanisation is deemed the dominant process, but if smaller places are
> growing faster than larger ones, then counterurbanisation is occurring (Champion
> 1989: 84).

Using such a definition, Fielding (1990) has identified the following
chronology of change:

–   Until the 1950s urbanisation was the dominant trend in every country in
    western Europe with the largest settlements being the ones to which the
    largest number of people were migrating.

–   By the 1960s the 'core' countries of north-western Europe were exhibiting
    signs of counterurbanisation in that settlements low down the settlement
    hierarchy were experiencing growth.

–   The early- and mid-1970s saw the clear establishment of inverse relation-
    ships between population growth and settlement sizes with many urban
    areas declining in population numbers while many rural areas were
    increasing.

–   The early 1980s saw a diminishment of counterurbanisation with many
    large settlements growing at expense of smaller ones, at least in some parts
    of the core countries. There has also been a rise of inter-regional migration
    at expense of urban to rural movement.

Not everyone agrees with this chronology and it is explicitly of relevance only to Western Europe. One area of debate has been over whether the 1980s spelt the end of counterurbanisation or whether it has continued as a strong presence in the 1990s and beyond (see Champion 1994; Johnson and Beale 1995; Kontuly 1998). With reference to the spatial extent of the phenomena, counterurbanisation has been widely recognised as occurring in North America (e.g. Beale 1975; Frey 1989; Fugitt 1985), indeed it was in the context of the US that Berry used the term initially. Counterurbanisation has also been widely observed in Australia (Burnley 1988; Hugo 1994; Hugo and Bell 1998; Hugo and Smailes 1985; 1992; Sant and Simons 1993), and within New Zealand (Bedford 1983; Bedford *et al*. 1999; Kearns and Reinken 1994; Waldegrave and Stuart 1997).

The process of counterurbanisation suggests that rural areas may be becoming more not less central to contemporary society. This point is reinforced by suggestions of an *urban to rural shift* in manufacturing industry leading to a growing *industrialisation of the countryside* and, at least in the minds of commentators, contributing to the process of counterurbanisation (e.g. see Fothergill and Gudgin 1982; Champion and Watkins 1991). Furthermore, to shifts in manufacturing jobs can be added growing service sector employment, much of which is also attracted to rural locations (Thrift 1987). Amongst the reasons suggested for these shifts has been a perception that rural areas provide particularly beneficial environments in terms of people's well being. They are seen as natural areas set apart from the stresses and strains of modern, urbanised and industrialised society, even if they are almost equally as industrialised as the towns and show signs of urbanisation (See Box 11.2). Indeed, it has been suggested by people such as Williams (1985: 248) that notions of 'the country' have come to exert a cultural attraction almost in 'inverse proportion' to the extent to which these ideas are materialised in space.

It is also important to recognise that rural areas are sites at which many of the resources of urban living are produced such as water and food supplies, agricultural and mineral raw materials, and electrical power. Rural areas also act as important recreational sites for urban dwellers (Harrison 1991; Urry 1995), and indeed often act as the settings for the still and moving imagery of the mass media gazed upon by urban residents (Fish and Phillips 1999; Phillips et al, 2001). Furthermore, as Table 11.1 indicates, globally more people live in rural areas than in urban, and in many areas of the world a large majority of people are rural residents, albeit that in many countries the proportion is declining in the face of large rural-urban migration.

Not only may rural areas be quite central to contemporary societies but they themselves be seen as constituted through the various constituent processes of modernisation. Murdoch and Pratt (1993: 415), for example, argue that 'the rural ... is just as "modern" as the urban' and that indeed, as noted earlier, the very distinction of rural and urban may be seen as a creation of modern industrialised societies, with *urban industrialisation* being accompanied by a *de-industrialisation of the countryside* which left the economies of rural areas becoming dominated by agricultural activities to a much greater extent than they previously (see Phillips and Mighall, 2000)

Table 11.1: Indicators of rural marginality

Income level	Percentage of land under crops			Percentage of population living in non-urban settlements		
	1980	1996	% change, 1980–1996	1980	1997	% change, 1980–1996
Low	0.9	1.3	+ 0.4	78	72	–6
Lower middle	1.3	0.8	–0.5	69	58	–11
Upper middle	1.1	1.3	+ 0.2	38	26	–12
High	0.5	0.5	0.0	25	24	– 1
World average	0.9	1.0	0.1	61	54	– 7

Source: based on World Bank (1999)

Overall one can suggest that there are no unequivocal relationships between spatial and social positioning such that one can identify some forms of space as being in all cases central or marginal. Rather a particular spatial form, such as rurality or urbanity, can be variously positioned as central and marginal, and indeed may be being so positioned simultaneously. Furthermore these positionings may seen as rarely fully realised, in part because they are contested and in part because of the multiplicity of dimensions of marginalisation and centralisation. In addition, being placed at the margins with respects to one relationships may mean that one is well placed with respect of some other relationship: the margins may be a place of potentialities, of re-visioning, of 'radical openness' (hooks 1990b: 149; Soja 1996). The multiplicities, partialities and contestations surrounding the spacings of marginality are well illustrated by the case of Aotearoa/New Zealand.

Marginality and Centrality in Aotearoa/New Zealand

New Zealand, or Aotearoa as it was and is still called by its initial recorded human settlers, the Maori, has often been portrayed as a marginal/peripheral space. Harris (1993: 7) has characterised it as 'a small society, strategically isolated and economically vulnerable', while Bell makes a similar point, albeit striking a rather less serious tone:

> New Zealand was easy to find on any map: just look for a pair of small dots at the bottom of the world. Occasionally we'd come across a map of the world that left New Zealand off … Imagine: there were people out there in the rest of the world who didn't even know where we were (Bell 1996: 1).

Yet from the late eighteenth century the country had been incorporated into a 'world-system', the British empire. This incorporation was informal at first and then after the signing of the *Treaty of Waitangi* in 1840, as a formal colony. The country was very clearly impacted by British imperialism, although during the early nineteenth century its spatial marginality appears to have constituted something of a block into incorporation into British imperialism. By the 1830s the country had become one of the 'neo-European' spaces to which settlers were exported in the face of rapid population growth and a volatile, industrialising economy in Britain and other European countries (Crosby, 1986). In such spaces, agricultural production closely akin to that practiced in European countries soon emerged, initially to sustain the settlers and in the case of New Zealand, by the mid nineteenth century, to export to Britain.

As Figure 11.1 highlights, in the nineteenth and early twentieth centuries, exports from Aotearoa/New Zealand were dominated by a limited range of primary products, notably wool, meat and minerals. The country at this time has been referred to as 'Britain's farm', with people such as Perry (1994: 19) commenting that 'geographically it was part of the Pacific, but structurally it was part of Britain's rural hinterland'. There was some industrial manufacturing, but according to Armstrong (1978) such development was effectively stifled through a lack of capital as British financiers and local merchants, bankers and landed property owners saw potential for greater profits in the large scale expansion of agrarian production for exports. There was little processing of primary production prior to export (Schedvinn 1990). British industrialists and merchants, on the other hand, were able to sell manufactured products without having to compete against large-scale local producers, nor indeed much other overseas competition (Britton *et al.* 1992).

Even after Aotearoa/New Zealand had lost its formal colonial status in 1907, the country still retained political and economic ties to, and dependence upon, Britain. In the 1930s, however, the country's government tried to address its economic 'underdevelopment' by a policy of 'insulationism' (Cloke 1989; see also Larner 1998), whereby the importation of goods was restricted to help stimulate national production. Such strategies of 'import substitution' were once quite widely advocated by development experts but have been criticised for creating inefficient domestic production and foreign exchange shortages, with the latter in turn leading to a concern to generate greater export growth (see Mountjoy 1982). This was indeed the case in Aotearoa/New Zealand but the drive for export earnings was, as elsewhere, still very much conditioned by earlier colonial patterns of trade, with the country continuing as a producer of primary products for largely British markets. A reliance on the export of primary products has been seen by *dependency theorists* (see Chapter 3) as a condition which is likely to entail a country being located adversely with regard to unequal relations of exchange. The country's unequal trade position with regard to Britain was indeed highlighted when Aotearoa/New Zealand, and other Commonwealth countries, were, as Harris (1993: 8) puts it, 'discarded ... in favour of entry to the EC [European Community, now the European Union]', a move which was widely portrayed at the time as bringing additional economic benefits to Britain than could be obtained by though its trading connections with former colonies such as New Zealand. Although Aotearoa/New Zealand did manage to negotiate access agreements to British markets for its dairy produce in 1973, 1975 and 1992, the amount of foodstuffs exported to Britain declined dramatically from its 1970 levels.

The New Zealand Government's response to the effective closure of the country's principal export market was, first, to give further protection to its produc-

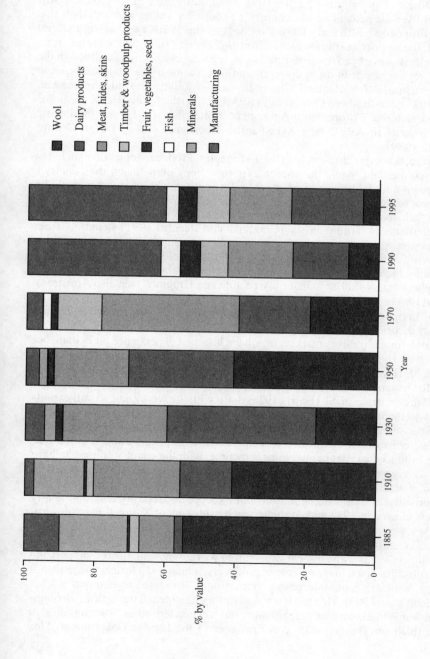

Figure 11.1: New Zealand's principal exports, 1885–1995
Source: derived from Robinson *et al.* (2000), Table 7.1

ers and, second, to seek to diversify its export markets, initially by searching out new markets for its existing export products rather than seek to export new products. As indicated in Figure 11.1, in 1995 wool, dairy and meat products still contributed over 40 percent of the country's exports by value, and although this figure has dropped significantly from the levels of the 1970s and before, over 60 percent of the export earnings came from the broad 'food and fibre sector'. Particular efforts have been made to forge new 'regional connections', although the concept of region has been quite diversely defined: variously as Australasia, as in CER (the Australia New Zealand Closer Economic Relations Trade Agreement, signed in 1983); the southern Pacific, as in SPARTECA (the South Pacific Regional Trade and Economic Co-operation Agreement, initiated in 1981); and the Pacific rim and Asia, as in APEC (the Asia-Pacific Economic Co-operation Group, launched in 1989).

There were, however, problem with these strategies. Producer-protectionism led to increasing public debt, while the chosen export strategy perpetuated the country's dependence on a limited range of products and meant that export incomes could be heavily impacted by falls in the international price of a relatively small range of products. Such falls materialised in the 1970s and 1980s with it being argued that there was an 'international farming crisis' (Goodman and Redclift 1991) stemming from over-production relative to purchasing power and consumption demands, and also from shifts in financial markets which led to higher rates of interest. Harris (1993: 8) argues that by the early 1980s 'in income terms New Zealand faced slippage into a semi-periphery status similar to that of Argentina and Uruguay' (see also Armstrong (1978) and Ehrensaft and Armstrong (1978) for a more production and class centred account of peripheral status; and also Chapter 3 on critiques of exchange-centred dependency theories).

The search for alternatives markets may have lessened dependence on Britain, but people such as Harris (1993) have been sceptical about whether there was actually much of a shift in the country's relative position within commodity markets. He claimed, for instance, that '[w]ith the exception of Australia, distance and "neighbourhood" are an irrelevance' (Harris 1971: 8–9), with the New Zealand still exporting largely to the northern hemisphere 'core' economies of Europe, North America, Japan and the so-called 'Asian Tigers' discussed in Chapter 7.

The crisis of income which Harris associated with a 'slippage' into a semi-peripheral status produced a crisis in government income, with the country coming to have 'a higher foreign debt per capita than all but a handful of developing countries' (Robinson et al. 2000: 251). In response there was a retrenchment of state activities through privatisation and deregulation, policies commenced by a Labour Party government elected in 1984 and continued on by subsequent National Party governments. A key aspect of the reforms was a reduction in government expenditure, which in 1984 had constituted over 40 per cent of the country's GDP (Le Heron and Pawson, 1996; Robinson 1993). Government expenditure was cut by reducing the support and financial subsidies given to New Zealand producers, which had a further consequence of making domestic economic policy increasingly orientated to external market success (Robinson 1993). This tendency was further heightened through an ideological shift towards market forms of regulation, often characterised as 'Rogernomics' in reference to Roger Douglas who was Treasurer of the Labour Government. This phrase had clear resonances to notions of 'Reaganism' and 'Thatcherism', so-called *far-right ideologies* with which Rogernomics had very close affinities, even if introduced by a Labour government.

The impact of such policies can be seen to have been a 're-internationalisation' of Aotearoa/New Zealand's economy after its period of insulationism, with Britton (1991) arguing that it led to flows of capital both into and out of the country. He also claimed that political and economic rhetoric of the time was that the country had to adopt a new internationalism, a point which is reinforced by Larner's (1998: 599) claim that from the early 1990s there were further shifts in the *spatial imaginary* of the country: rather than being represented as being some off-shoot or dependency of Britain, or a self-contained national economy engaged with trade with a range of other national economies, Aotearoa/New Zealand became increasingly portrayed 'as a node in the flows and networks of the Pacific Rim'. These flows not only involve capital but also labour with the Government seeking to deregulate the movement of people into and out of the country and to encourage the migration of people with professional and entrepreneurial skills and capital. Once again attention has come to be focused on the Pacific region, and also increasingly on Asia with some 162,000 Asian nationals migrating to Aotearoa/New Zealand between 1 April 1986 and 31 March 1998 (Bedford 1999).

Proponents of restructuring, internationalisation and globalisation claim that these changes will bring economic prosperity to the country, or at least more than could be achieved by other courses of action. It has also been argued that they bring cultural benefits, such as greater freedom of choice over lifestyle and living place. Many other people have, however, been highly critical of these changes. Britton, for example, argued that the move towards greater internationalisation may well make Aotearoa/New Zealand,

> both quite exposed to economic and political events beyond its control, and with less and less ability to control the economic means by which it achieves its national goals and creates the social life preferred by its citizens (Britton 1991: 20–21).

For Britton, despite the dramatic changes of the 1980s and 1990s, Aotearoa/New Zealand still remained 'a small country' with 'little negotiating clout in the market place' (p. 20), and as a result its communities and labour forces, if not its governmental and industrial leaders, were likely to experience further disadvantageous change. In other words, it still remained a peripheral, marginalised economy.

Having said this, many people now and in the past have taken a somewhat different view of the country, foregrounding positive aspects of its society, culture and, at times, its economy. Fairburn (1989), for example, has argued that once European colonisation had become firmly established there emerged amongst the colonists a view that the country provided the basis for an 'ideal society' where there was natural abundance, self-autonomy, order and an open society with no real status divisions. A series of positive descriptive labels and similes gained popular currency, such that New Zealand was a 'better' or 'brighter' Britain, an 'earthy paradise', a 'land of plenty', the 'land of Goshen' (the 'best part of the land', Genesis 47 v. 6), or a 'land of milk and honey' (Deuteronomy 6, v. 3). The notion of being 'Britain's farm', which could be construed as signalling dependence, could also be taken as a sign of productivity and of being able to surpass Britain in the production of a basic requirement for life.

Positive imagery of the country has continued subsequently, as recorded by the following commentary of growing up in the mid-twentieth century:

> Even as children we learned about this country's superiority over others. At Sunday school we gave shillings to very poor people overseas. Pictures on the collection envelopes of black people with leprosy and nothing to eat showed us that, by comparison, we were very rich indeed ... We were lucky: we lived in the world's only perfect country. England was second best. It rained there a lot, and people couldn't go out to the beach as often as we did. But we didn't have to send them money. We sent them butter instead (Bell 1996: 18).

Bell also records how other senses of national worth have been constructed through claims relating to economic welfare, such as the country having one of the world's highest 'standards of living'; to socio-political developments such as being the first to enact 'votes for women' and ban nuclear weapons; to sporting excellence, through the 'All Blacks' rugby team, the 'Silver Ferns' netball team and the 'Black Magic' America's Cup yachting syndicate. With the onset of a new internationalism, it has also been claimed that the country may provide a vision of future 'open society' where,

> economies and their associated labour markets were truly transnational, where people of quite divergent ethnic and cultural backgrounds felt 'comfortable' ... where local and national identities were accompanied by, and possibly even subsumed within, transnational identities (Summary of speech by David Caygill, Minister of Finance; in Le Heron and Pawson (1996: 350)).

This section has shown how Aotearoa/New Zealand has been variously positioned with respect to notions of centrality and marginality. It may share with its neighbour Australia what Anderson describes as an 'in-between' location, being placed,

> somehow 'down-under', it is thought to sit tenuously on both sides of the North/South divide, as a 'western' country under 'southern skies', making a push into Asia, while occupying a 'Third world environment' (Anderson 2000: 381).

It is also important to recognise that different people may occupy different position within, and be differently affected by, the socio-spatial practices and relations which may be seen to give Aotearoa/New Zealand its multiplicity of relations of centrality and marginality. Even those who have taken a very positive view of the situation of the country have, in some case, recognised that some people have been both marginal to, and marginalised by, such changes. Included amongst such people are many who might be said to be living in rural areas.

Marginalisation and Rural Aotearoa/New Zealand

The Centrality of Rurality within New Zealand

Rural areas have long seen as central to Aotearoa, both economically and culturally. Reference has already been made to the importance of the 'food and fibre' sector to the country's economy and the whole nation has often been ascribed a rural identity, as in references to it as 'Britain's farm'. As well as being sites of agrarian production, the rural areas of Aotearoa/New Zealand have also been locations for the production of many other economically valuable products, such as timber, gold, coal, hydro-electric and geothermal power. Furthermore, from close to the onset of colonialism, the country's countryside has been a tourist destination and by 1997 some 1.6 million people were visiting the country, at least 55 per cent who were 'on holiday', while a further 23 per cent were 'staying with friends and relatives' and quite likely to be also engaging in some tourist activity (Robinson *et al.* 2000: 263). To these overseas tourists, one can also domestic tourist and recreational visits, with New Zealanders in the early 1990s spending an average 18 nights away from their home each year (Cloke and Perkins 1998: 194). Although not all tourist visits are to rural locations, many rural areas have become popular rural destinations. Half of all overseas tourists, for example, visit one of its 13 national parks (Cloke and Perkins 1998: 195.)

Often drawing on their various economic uses have been a series of claims that rural areas are culturally central to Aotearoa/New Zealand and to the identities of its people. Bell (1996), for example, argues that a romantic image of rural life has been central to Pakeha national identity, right from the early stages of European colonisation. Similar arguments are advanced by Fairburn (1989) who claims that notions of New Zealand as an 'ideal society' often took an *Arcadian* form whereby people were seen to live in a natural environment which provided an abundance of the necessities of life and a simple and contented life.

Such Arcadian views are, they both argue, still prevalent today, not least in advertising branding slogans such as 'clean, green, beautiful' New Zealand (Bell 1996: 49). It is, however, easy to overplay the degree of continuity between colonial and contemporary representations of New Zealand and also to ignore the diversity of ways of understanding and valuing rurality. A key feature of the colonial Arcadia, for example, was on the productivity of the countryside, which as noted earlier, was often expressed in such colloquialisms, such as New Zealand was a 'land of plenty', the 'land of Goshen' and a 'land of milk and honey'. These phrases were often of Biblical derivation and the emphasis on productivity can be seen as a major constituent of what Short (1991) has described as the 'classical' Western, or Occidental, viewpoint on rural landscapes. This view valued landscapes which bear clear marks of human activity, and Fairburn (1989) highlights how 'harvest scenes' with regular and densely packed rows of wheat 'stooks' (stacks of about 12 bundles) were often commonplace is postcards and textual descriptions of New Zealand, while today tourists guides and the picture albums of tourists often contain images of pastoral order with animal stock grazing enclosed, homogenised grasslands (see Plate 11.1)

Within the classical perspective, areas which appeared to have little or no marks of human activity were seen as areas of nature and of a wilderness, or 'bush' as it was often described in Antipodean contexts, which was to be feared and if possible conquered or tamed by being transformed into more humanised landscapes. The humanising of landscape was frequently taken as a sign of social progress with, as Fairburn (1989) notes, the built environment of towns frequently being taken in the literature on colonial New Zealand as a sign of economic growth and the creation of civilisation. However, Fairburn also notes how towns were often portrayed quite negatively, in part because they represented some separation of people from nature, a separation which in Arcadian viewpoints is often seen to lead to social degeneration:

Plate 11.1: Touristic pastoral imagery

as Short (1991: 103, 30) comments, a recurrent theme within western thought has been that the cultivation of nature is 'an enobling experience', being 'wholesome, ... nourishing ... simple and less compromised by social convention'. Scenes of agrarian productivism and also scenes of active colonisation of the bush (see Plate 11.2) still retained connotations of being close to nature and a 'natural lifestyle', whilst at the same time were also capable of being interpreted as signalling progress in controlling nature. Such representations have been seen to be of considerable significance in informing senses of self-identity in colonial New Zealand (see Fairburn 1989; J Phillips 1996) and indeed in other settler societies like Australia, Canada and the USA (see Bunce 1994; Daniels 1993; R Phillips 1996; Short 1991; Turner 1963). They are also images which have contemporary resonance with Cloke, for example, arguing that:

> Whereas in Britain the bucolic rural idyll which influences in-migration ... centres of the 'thatched cottage surrounded by rose-garden in scenic setting' image, the psychic target of the New Zealand rural idyll more frequently involves ownership of land and carrying out some for[m] of agricultural enterprise, however small or part-time, on that land (Cloke 1986: 3).

Many of the images and descriptions of life in frontier societies were created by people who had quite a different relationship to agents of nature than did the people they were portraying. The development of photography emerged at about the same time as the onset of large scale European colonisation of Aotearoa/New Zealand and cameras were very quickly being used to represent this colonisation within what Bell (1996) describes as the 'view trade'. Knight (1981) identifies over 1,100 photographers as being active in New Zealand in the period before 1900, many of whom devoted a considerable part of their lives to travelling around and photographing various parts of New Zealand. Many of these photographers, and a slightly earlier set of landscape painters, created images variously described as 'romantic', 'picturesque' and 'sublime' (Bell 1996). These terms were promoted in European artistic and literary debates in the eighteenth and nineteenth centuries where subtle distinctions were often drawn between them. However, a common feature of all of them was a valuing of rural landscapes in ways other than as signifier of material productivity and human agency and control. So, for example, areas of wilderness were interpreted less as areas to fear, conquer and domesticate and more as places to value for their beauty, tranquillity, orderliness and even, for some, their 'deep spiritual significance' as 'a symbol of an earthly paradise' (Short 1991: 6; see also Phillips and Mighall 2000). Just as in Europe, 'romantic tourism' emerged with people visiting, and/or gazing at representations of, areas which appeared to be beyond, or at the margins, of human society. Attention was often focused on spectacular landscape forms, such as volcanoes, the Pink and White terraces at Tarawera (until they were destroyed by a volcanic eruption in 1886), and the lakes, inlets and mountains of the 'Southern Alps' and Fiordland. At other times the emphasis was on the flora and fauna of the country, and on what Bell (1996) has described as 'particular nature' or the plants, animals, insects, birds and climates found in particular places. She suggests that the unique flora and fauna, or the distinctive way more widespread forms of nature grow, are a distinctive feature of New Zealanders identity, epitomised in their self-identification as 'kiwis'.

Plate 11.2: Clearance of the Bush
Source: reproduced courtesy of Waikato Museum, Hamilton.

Spectacular landscapes and distinctive natures still figure highly in contemporary representations of Aotearoa/New Zealand, as indeed do more ecological and experimental/experiential notions of pure and exhilarating New Zealand (see Plate 11.3). Cloke and Perkins (1998) have highlighted how the country has recently become 'branded' by marketing consultants as a place of 'youthful experiment' and how this imagery has been reproduced in the growing adventure tourist industry. They argue that this expanding form of tourism is frequently marketed though images and texts which combine gazing on spectacular wild landscape with a focus on the adventurous conquering of a perilous nature (see also Bell and Lyall, 2002). In a sense there is a merging of a 'romantic gaze' with 'classical' notions of spaces of nature as a place to fear and conquer. However, the emphasis on natural productivity which was so strong in the classical viewpoint has been replaced with a concern accumulating experiences and developing senses of the self: by conquering wild nature you are seen to come to know yourself and to be able to do things which previously you had thought impossible.

As well as being a space of primary production and of spectacular, particular, ecological and adventurous natures, the rural areas of Aotearoa/New Zealand have also been valued as a place of idyllic and authentic community. Such evaluations of rural spaces are quite widespread and in the European context have frequently been connected with Tönnes' notions of *gemeinschaft* and *gesellschaft* (see Box 11.1). Although his arguments have been widely critiqued (see for overviews Harper 1987, 1989; Phillips 1998b, 1998c; Wright 1992), his notion of gemeinschaft or 'community' may be seen to resonate with many people's understandings of community, rural space and indeed, New Zealand. Perry (1994: 47), for example, has argued that notions of community have figured strongly within the country, even in its urban areas. He suggests that this in part derived the transference of ideas from Britain during the process of colonisation, a view which has also been taken by Arnold (1981) who claimed that British settlers brought with them notions of idyllic rural communities which had been fostered, even if not realised, in Britain. Fairburn (1989: 202) has noted that many Pakeha rural settlers were active readers of British newspapers and magazines, often displaying pictures from them on the walls of their homes and constructing from them mental imagery of 'community events, celebrations, recreations, and endless opportunities to chat, exchange opinions and ideas'.

Caution may be required, however, before connecting notions of community in rural New Zealand to British colonial influences. First, it is important to note the previous settlers of the country, the Maori and Moriori, were societies where relations of kinship, habitat and reciprocal actions all figured highly. They may hence be seen as societies where gemeinschaft relations might be seen to figure highly, although as discussed in Box 11.1 applying terms from European society is highly problematic. Second, people such as Jock Phillips (1996) have claimed that the experience of life on the frontiers of European colonialism created its own form of community, namely of comradeship, or as Phillips put it 'mateness', whereby people, or more specifically men, help each other out. Third, Fairburn (1989) has been highly sceptical about the significance of 'mateness', and indeed any notion of community, within colonial frontier society, suggesting, for example, that many men on the frontiers were itinerant loners, moving around places and jobs often in competition for isolated job opportunities and accommodation (see also Willmott 1985). Fairburn (1989: 172) suggests that land-owning rural settlers were 'buried in space', living in isolated

This image was accompanied by the following text in the original advertisement:

From the very top of Mt Alfred, your eye sweeps past distant peaks and down the Dart River Valley. You catch your breath. In air so clear and sharp, you get a high that is 100%

Plate 11.3: Clear, green, fresh New Zealand
Source: Photograph by Steve Bicknell, New Zealand

homesteads with virtually no transport and communication connections to any other people. However, he does acknowledge that from the 1880s onwards, a series of 'neighbourhood-creating associations' emerged, including local dairy factories at which farmers would 'take whole milk or cream ... and exchange gossip while waiting in the queue' and schooling, with primary schooling becoming 'nominally compulsory with the 1877 Education Act' (p. 171). During the late nineteenth century and early twentieth century there was a significant growth in small townships which were often the site for such institutions (see Chalmers and Joseph 1997; Fairburn 1989: 174), and a number of studies have identified various forms of communal and/or place attachment in such centres (e.g. Chalmers and Joseph 1998; Joseph and Chalmers 1995; 1998; Willmott 1985). Furthermore, representations of rural communities are quite prevalent in the media of New Zealand, with such communities frequently being presented as quite idyllic and/or in some sense 'authentically' New Zealand. A clear example of this was the promotion of the 1999/2000 America's Cup defence in Auckland whereby a series of images of rural people 'coming to the city' was used to convey a sense that the event was bringing out a sense of national community and was a sport of the 'real Kiwi man' (see also Perry 1994).

Overall, therefore it can be seen that rural spaces have been seen as quite central to Aotearoa/New Zealand, although there also appear to have been significant changes in how this centrality has been constructed, both economically and culturally. It should also be noted that this centrality has not always been uncontested: as Lees and Berg (1995) note, Aotearoa/New Zealand is currently one of the most urbanised societies in the world and there have been many people who have seen rural life as far from idyllic (Phillips forthcoming-b). Indeed from the 1980s onwards, the centrality of rural spaces to Aotearoa/New Zealand has been widely seen as being under threat, in part as a result of the repositioning and restructuring of the national economy discussed in the preceding section. Wilson, for example, comments:

> Given New Zealand's dependence on the agricultural industry and the severity of its political response to the international crisis, it would be expected that rural localities in New Zealand experienced dramatic economic restructuring (Wilson 1995: 418–9).

Kearns and Joseph take a similar view of the period since 1984, arguing that in the majority of rural communities,

> landscapes of opportunity have contracted ... employment is being lost and most residents must now have to travel further for basic services. In a minority of places, however, rural restructuring has led to enhanced political, economic or social opportunities (Kearns and Joseph 1997: 20).

They add that rural communities have been particularly hard hit by the restructuring because of 'their marginality within the national economy' (Kearns and Joseph 1997: 21), a 'position of subservience to macroeconomic trends' which is, they claim:

> an unfamiliar one for rural New Zealanders, as many recall clearly decades in which the economic and political dominance of rural productivity was unchallenged; New Zealand made its way in the world through the sale of abundant agricultural surpluses (Kearns and Joseph 1997: 21).

Restructuring and marginalisation of farmers

There have indeed been a series of attempts, by academics (e.g. Cloke 1989; 1994; 1996a; Le Heron 1991; 1993; Wilson 1994; 1995) and others (see Cloke 1996b), to document impacts of the post-1984 restructuring of the political-economy of New Zealand on agriculture and associated rural communities. As Cloke (1996a) emphasises, quite divergent views about the impacts of restructuring on agriculture have been advanced, in part related to differing standpoints from which these interpretation have been advanced. He suggests, however, that a number of farmer responses have been widely identified (see Box 11.3).

Box 11.3: Farmer responses to the restructuring of New Zealand's political-economy

Cloke (1996a: 315) summaries the findings of research on farmer responses to restructuring policies as follows:

–   A reduction in the levels of fertiliser use 'to below that required to maintain what was regarded as orthodox fertility of land'.

–   A reduction and in some cases complete cessation of all non-essential repairs and maintenance.

–   Ending plans to expand production into new areas of land, and a withdraw from production of areas only recently taken into production.

–   Reduction of expenditure on new equipment such as machinery. Total capital expenditure on farms apparently decreased by half between 1984/5 and 1988/9 (Britton *et al.* 1992).

–   Reduction of paid farm employment, either through an absolute reduction in the amount of labour applied to farm work or through a replacement of paid labour by household labour.

–   Reduction in the level of income drawn from farm businesses by farm families, again either though an absolute reduction or through relative decline. The latter stemmed from an increased use of non-farm sources of income; either through diversification into non-farm activities or the sale of family labour to non-farm employers (that is, an increase in off farm employment by members of the farm household).

A series of commentators, particularly in the mid-1980s, spoke of agriculture, and particularly family farming (Pomeroy 1996), being 'in crisis' and there being a 'rural downturn' (Coombes and Campbell 1996) or even 'rural collapse (Pomeroy 1996). Pomeroy (1996), however, concludes that such predictions were mistaken and that many rural areas have indeed been places of growing prosperity and population numbers. Such positive views are, as Cloke (1996b) notes, widely promulgated in governmental and agricultural institutions in the 1990s, although he adds that such views neglect both 'the short-term casualties of deregulation or the longer term effects' (p. 323, see also Liepins and Bradshaw (1999)). For example, while farm numbers may have stayed relatively stable during the course of restructuring, individual farmer households have left farming: Cloke (1994) suggests that across the country some 800 farm households may have been forced to relinquish ownership of their land. There also appears to have been some polarisation in land-holdings, with middle sized farms falling in number and, in some cases, having increased levels of debt brought about by attempts to expand during the period of crisis (Fairweather 1992; Wilson 1994). Even if these debts were not threatening the survival of agricultural business directly, they may have a significant longer term impact: Cloke (1996a: 323), for example, suggests that many farmers feel that they will not be able to pass on their farm holdings to their children, but rather hope to sell them to pay off their debts and to leave sufficient 'at least to pay for their children's education' and thereby 'passed something on to their next generation'. The experiences of their parents, together with an increasing range of non-agricultural jobs elsewhere, may also lead to a decreased desire amongst young people to take up farming (Fairweather 1995).

The Impacts of Restructuring Beyond Agriculture

Although New Zealand's rural areas are often conflated with agriculture, as Willis (1988: 222) comments, '"the rural population" includes a wider range of people than those simply involved in farming'. Pomeroy (1994: 595–598) notes that in 1986 less than half of those people in formal, remunerative work in rural areas were in primary industrial activity such as agriculture and she argues that there is a need to recognise that 'the issue of rural community prosperity goes beyond the farming sector'. Slightly later, Pomeroy (1996: 86) argued that the future survival of rural communities very much required the 'mobilisation of local resources ... beyond the farm gate', and noted that agriculturalists had indeed often turned to non-agricultural activities within their survival responses (see Box 11.3).

While Pomeroy seeks to emphasise the way non-agricultural activities may be used to sustain rural communities, a series of other studies have highlighted how agricultural restructuring and marginalisation may have knock-on effects which negatively impact aspects of rural economies. Cloke (1989: 45), for example, records that some rural shops, agricultural suppliers and contractors were 'severely affected' by a reduction of expenditure by farmers as part of their efforts to reduce their expenditure. Wilson (1995) developed a detailed analysis of *agricultural-rural economy linkages* and suggests that in Gore District, South Island, a large range of retail businesses experienced a fall in revenue during the agricultural crisis of 1986–1989, with some businesses closing or being taken over, while others relocated to nearby urban centres or laid-off people as businesses contracted. Wilson, however, also suggests that there were some longer-run positive changes, such as the adoption of new technologies, product range diversification and service quality improvements as struggling businesses sought to compete for a dwindling quantity of custom. However, it is important to recognise that increased competition brings about both losers as well as winners and both employers and employees will have had their lives considerably disrupted within these longer-term changes. Furthermore, as Cloke (1996a) notes, the disruption may be as much personal and psychological as it is economic.

It is also important to recognise that many non-agricultural rural activities were directly impacted by the political and economic restructuring of New Zealand. As Joseph and Chalmers (1998) have remarked, prior to the 1984 reforms the state had quite a substantial presence in rural areas and impact on the people living there. The state through central and local government was involved in the provision of banking and financial services, as well as welfare services like health care and education. Any retrenchment of state activities was clearly likely to have impacts beyond those discussed with reference to agriculture.

At times retrenchment took the form of effective withdrawal of the state from some aspects of public service provision. Studies have highlighted, for example, how the desire to reduce state expenditure on health care often translated into the closure of small rural hospitals, and community and residential care facilities (Joseph and Chalmers 1995; 1998; Joseph and Kearns 1996; Kearns and Joseph 1997). Such withdrawal of provision in a rural locality can produce problems of access to health care for those with limitations on their mobility, such as the elderly, the disabled, those on low income and those, such as child minders, with particular time constraints. Diminished accessibility to health care facilities may not only have health impacts with people failing to access care when they need it, but it has also been claimed that it might promote rural out-migration. Joseph and Chalmers (1998), for example, record how elderly residents made reference to people leaving rural communities to go to areas better served by health and care facilities, even though many of these residents hold a considerable attachment to living in their current rural places.

Retrenchment of the state in New Zealand, and indeed elsewhere, often did not take such immediate forms, not least because obvious removal of access to state services could, and indeed in many cases did, lead to political resistance (see Kearns and Joseph 1997). Often the retrenchment of the state was undertaken through privatisation and deregulation, which although often not so politically contested, could still have considerable impacts on rural people: Kearns and Joseph (1997: 22), for example, argue that 'private sector initiatives have shunned rural communities', largely because their 'dispersed populations' fail to provide sufficient business to produce profitability.

Another form of restructuring the state of significance to rural areas was, as Wilson (1995) notes, the transformation public sector institutions into 'state-owned corporations'. These organisation were kept in under nominal state control but were expected to be run as commercial corporation, often having 'no other public obligation than to earn a healthy dividend' for the government (Dunleavy 1999: 417). In many cases the formation of state-owned corporations was quickly followed by full privatisation. So, for example, the *Rural Bank*, which had previously acted as a form of agricultural protection through the provision of below market rate loans to farmers and administering government subsidies, was turned into a state-corporation in 1987, and then fully privatised in 1989 (Le Heron 1991). The state-owned *Bank of New Zealand* (or BNZ) was also privatised, and a loosening of banking regulations saw it become a subsidiary of an Australian bank. Another organisation impacted was the Post Office, which was subdivided into three parts: a banking element which was privatised to form *PostBank* (and later became part of the ANZ banking group); a telecommunications element (which was privatised as *Telecom*) and postal services. The last element, renamed as *NZ Post* remained in state ownership but was heavily marketised.

Although most of the former state run organisations cannot be seen as specifically rural organisations (the Rural Bank is the obvious exception), changes to their ownership and missions in many instances prompted a withdrawal of services from rural areas. These privatisation of BNZ, for example, was followed by a programme of branch closures affecting many rural areas (Britton *et al*. 1992; Joseph and Chalmers 1998), and there have also been closures of post-offices and banking outlets following the reorganisation of the Post Office. Furthermore, as Joseph and Chalmers note, service sector, and indeed agricultural, restructuring might also impact on community leadership and service provision:

> Multiple job holding has emerged as an important means of survival for the family farm ... and this has affected the capacity of farm families to take up their traditional roles as 'movers and shakers' in rural community organisations ... At the same time, restructuring in the private and public sectors has removed from rural communities professional people (in banks, pharmacies, local government offices, etc.) who provided leadership in rural communities ... [T]he increasing involvement of women in the rural workforce ... has meant that the involvement of women in voluntarism is now more likely to conform to the traditional male pattern – it will be more strategic than previously (Joseph and Chalmers 1998: 34; see also Box 11.3).

It is clear, however, that not all service closures stemmed exclusively from governmental restructuring of state activities. Kearns and Joseph (1997: 21), for example, comment that the decline in services often 'predates the recognition of restructuring as a transformative agent' and make reference to Cant and O'Neil's (1989) claim that there is a recursive reaction, or 'embrace', between service rationalisation and population decline. As Joseph and Chalmers (1998:29) explain, '[f]ewer people meant poorer services and poorer services meant it was less and less attractive for people to stay on in villages and small towns'.

One area which appears to have experienced such changes is the Waikato region, whose rural areas, as Chalmers and Joseph (1997) record, had become in the early twentieth century populated with a whole series of small settlements spaced out about 8 to 15 kilometres from each other and centred around a dairy factory, a hall, a general store and a garage. Figure 11.2 shows the distribution of factories for processing dairy products within the Waikato and Thames Valley in the early twentieth century, while Plate 11.4 shows Te Poi Memorial Hall, one of the large village halls which, as we write, still remains open. However, from the 1960s the communities who used such halls became subject to processes of marginalisation primarily through a combination of 'the consolidation of services away from villages and small towns' and 'changes in the organisation of commercial agriculture and food processing' (Joseph and Chalmers 1998: 29). The central dairy factory in Te Poi closed down in the early 1980s and the population of this settlement subsequently declined. In the 1990s residents of Te Poi, like residents in many other settlements across rural New Zealand attempted to revitalise their economies by localised 'place-marketing'. As Bell (1996) and Bell and Lyall (1995) document, much of this place marketing makes use of 'large roadside objects' which are constructed to both represent some localised association with experiences, occupations and objects which are nationally valued, and, at the same time, act as visual attractions in their own right and thereby help support or stimulate local tourist trade. Given the significance of rurality to national culture, it is not surprising that rural imagery figures prominently amongst these roadside objects: notable examples include a giant fibre glass sheep-shearer at Te Kuiti, a corrugated iron wool shop in Tirau made into the shape of a sheep and, in Te Poi, 'Big Cows' (see Plate 11.4).

Particularly critical for the fate of many rural settlements in the Waikato was the introduction of tanker lorries, which allowed the transportation of milk in bulk and thereby the centralisation of dairy processing into fewer larger units. The number of dairy factories in New Zealand fell from over 400 in 1955 to 259 in 1962 to 43 in 1990 (Rowlands 1971; Willis and Press 1997). The closure of dairy factories reduced employment in many small rural townships, although the total level of employment in dairy factories actually rose from 4,586 in 1961 to 6334 in 1990 (Willis and Press 1997). With no source of local employment, some people had little alternative but to move away from the small rural townships, and hence, as Joseph and Chalmers (1994) record, many of the most rural counties in the Waikato region experienced limited or negative growth between 1956 and 1976. In some cases the movement of people out meant that both public and private sector services found it hard to sustain sufficient business to remain open, and indeed in many cases they did close, often triggering further outmigration of people. The processes of change were often of a creeping nature: 'Gradually shops, schools and hospitals close; rural deliveries of mail, milk and newspapers become more infrequent, public transport is withdrawn. Essential services – sewerage, water and electricity – become more expensive (MacKay 1984 quoted in Chalmers and Joseph 1998: 158). By today, however, many of the small service centres suffered considerable out migration of both services and people, such that they appear as rather ghost like settlements, full of reminders of past events and personalities.

Joseph and Chalmers (1998) note, however, that many rural service centres retained services like schools, libraries, primary health care and some public transport until the restructuring of the 1980s. While it is clear that many rural communities were experiencing processes of marginalisation prior to the events of the mid 1980s, it also appears that the processes of restructuring acted as a further force which pushed some communities into a further spiral of decline.

It is, however, also important to note that the processes of political and economic restructuring did not necessarily lead to population decline. Waldegrave and Stuart (1997), for example, suggested that two restructuring policies acted to encourage urban-rural migration: namely a reduction of social benefit rates and an increase in public sector housing rents. Together these polices acted to decrease incomes and increase housing costs for people receiving benefits and renting public sector housing. One 'coping strategy' to deal with such a situation is to move to areas with lower housing costs, areas which, in New Zealand at least, often includes rural areas. Waldegrave and Stuart note an increased movement of people on benefits from large urban centres such as Wellington towards small towns in the Wairarapa region in the south of North Island. Kearns and Joseph (1997) advance similar arguments, noting also how restructuring serially impacted on low-income groups. So, for instance, restructuring resulted in increased unemployment levels, at just the time when social welfare benefits were being cut. Furthermore, people then responding to such

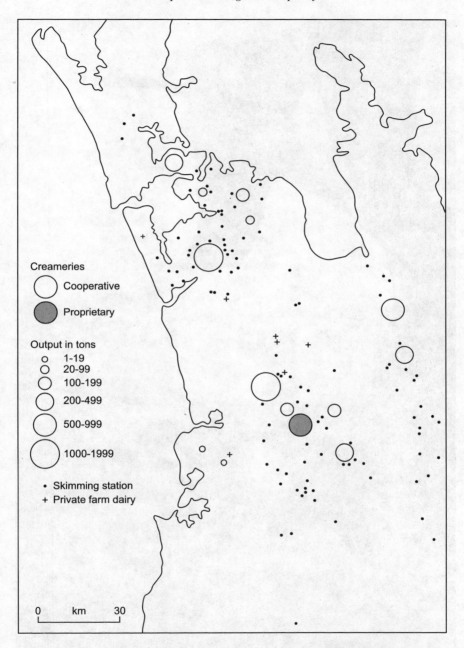

Figure 11.2: Dairy factories in the Waikato in the early twentieth century
Source: based on McKinnon, M. (1997) (ed) *New Zealand Historical Atlas: Ko Papatuanuku e Takoto Nei*, Auckland: David Bateman, plate 61.

Plate 11.4: Te Poi Memorial Hall and Big Cows

changes by migrating to rural areas with lower cost housing, might then find themselves with poor access to health and welfare services as these became rationalised and indeed commodified.

So overall, the countryside of Aotearoa/New Zealand appears to have been marginalised in a multiplicity of ways, many of which were closely associated with broadly focused strategies of political-economic restructuring. As discussed earlier, advocates of this restructuring claim that it holds the potential benefit of positioning the national economy more centrally within contemporary global flows of capital, commodities and people. Critics on the other hand, argue that it does little to change an essentially 'semi-peripheral economy' and that it has been conducted at considerable cost to people living in some places, including many rural areas. Rural areas may well be moving from a central position within a semi-peripheral economy to a marginal position in what may, perhaps, be characterised as a slightly less semi-peripheral economy. It is certainly evident that the population living in rural areas has declined significantly over the course of the twentieth century (see Figure 11.3). Having said this, rural spaces still appear to exert a considerable symbolic influence with Aotearoa/New Zealand and many still provide locations for economic activities of central national importance, notably agriculture, forestry, power and the new growth industry of tourism. Furthermore, as noted in Box 11.2 there have been some signs of 'counterurbanisation', and the movement of people to live in rural areas. However even within this centrality, and indeed within earlier positions of centrality,

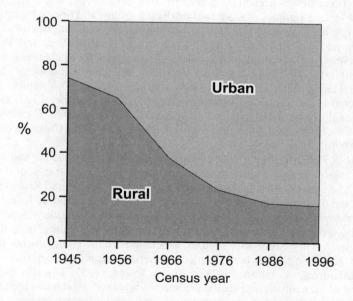

Figure 11.3: Rural/urban population in Aotearoa/New Zealand, 1945–1996
Source: Statistics New Zealand: Te Tari Tatau (1998) *People on the move … shifting around New Zealand* (Wellington: Statistics New Zealand – Te Tari Tatau)

some rural people have been marginalised, and it is such processes of marginalisation that our attention will now turn.

Marginalisation within Rural Space

So far we have been largely been discussing rural people as a singular category, as if all people in rural areas experienced similar conditions, be these of centrality, marginality or some complex multiple of various positionings of centrality and marginality. However, recent work in rural geography has come to recognise that people co-located in a particular locality might be quite differently positioned with respect to particular sets of social relationships, and that some people may be affected by some relationships whilst others are not. Philo (1992b), for example, argued that much of rural geography, and indeed rural studies more generally, had tended to neglect a range of social differences and associated groups and that:

> there remains a danger of portraying British rural people ... as all being 'Mr Averages', as being men in employment, earning enough to live, white and probably English, straight and somehow without sexuality, able in body and sound in mind, and devoid of any other quirks of (say) religious belief or political affiliation (Philo 1992b: 200).

Philo argued implicitly at first, and then more explicitly (Philo 1993; see also Murdoch and Pratt 1993; 1994) for a *postmodern recognition of difference* (see also Chapter 2). This call was heeded by many British researchers as there emerged in the late 1990s a series examples of studies of neglected groups and lines of social differentiation, including: women and gender differentiation (e.g, Hughes 1997; Little 1997; Little and Austin 1996); gays, lesbians and sexuality (Bell and Valentine 1995b; Valentine 1997a); people with disabilities and notions of able- and disabled bodies (Limb *et al.* 1995; Matless, 1995); children, the elderly and social constructions of age (Harper 1997; Jones 1997; 1999; Matthews *et al.* 2000; Valentine 1997b); people of colour and racialised identities (Agyeman and Spooner 1997; Kinsman 1995); national, regional and localised identities (Cloke *et al.* 1996; Cosgrove *et al.* 1996; Matless 1998); and lifestyle groups (Cloke *et al.* 1997; Cloke *et al.* 1998; Halfacree 1996; Sibley 1995).

As noted in Phillips (1998b; 1998c) some of the lines of difference had been the subject of research prior to Philo's postmodern intervention. A clear case of this in the New Zealand context is work of people such as Chalmers, Joseph and Kearns on rural health care and the lives of the aged in rural New Zealand. Chalmers and Joseph (1998: 157), for example, engage in a 'selective incorporation of postmodern concepts and interpretative repertoires' into rural studies, most notably a recognition of 'difference' and 'otherness'. They argue that such a 'wide-angled lens' complements previous work which sought to address both 'in-places experiences' and a recognition of socio-spatial restructuring. As outlined in Kearns and Joseph (1997: 18), this dual focus emerged out of 'humanistic and spatial analytical traditions', which was then invigorated with a 'political economic vantage point ...infused with a recognition of human agency' in the 1980s. One hence has a strand of research work which appears to sit well with postmodernist concerns, but which originally emerged out of a series other theoretical perspectives (see also Joseph and Chalmers 1995).

It is also relevant to note that whilst postmodernism has been welcomed by some New Zealand researchers, others have been rather more cautious. So, for example, while Lees and Berg (1995: 33–34) call for the development of a socio-cultural geography 'self-consciously adopting certain aspects of Anglo-American theory' such as postmodernism's 'rejection of totalisation', Kearns (1997: 4) argues that there is a risk that localised influences on theorisation will be neglected and that Aotearoan/New Zealand geographies will become 'branch plants of metropolitan theory'. Just as feminists have felt some sense of unease about the embrace of postmodernism squeezing out some of their own histories and politics (see Chapter 2), so many of the concerns of postmodernists had already been the subject of some long-standing reflection and debate within New Zealand. Indeed, feminist geography and the study of gender issues have been quite prominent within New Zealand geography well before the adoption into geography of notions of postmodernism (see Longhurst 1994; Stokes *et al.* 1987). Furthermore recognition of difference and the politics of knowledge construction highlighted within postmodernism (see Chapter 2), have been the subject of localised theorisation in relation to Maori and Pakeha geographies (see Box 11.4).

Box 11.4: Pakeha and Maori geographies

European colonists were often described by the pre-existing population of Aotearoa as Pakeha which variously translates as non-Maori, foreigners or white people. Since the onset of European imperialism and colonisation it has often been said that there are 'two New Zealands' (Pawson 1992), one Maori and one Pakeha, each with their own, often quite, quite divergent culture and ways of life. Furthermore, although the *Treaty of Waitangi* which made New Zealand a formal part of the British Empire involved Maori chiefs ceding sovereignty of the country to the British Crown, it also stated that Maori peoples had 'full exclusive and undisturbed possession of their Lands and Estates Forests Fisheries and other possessions which they may collectively or individually possess so long as it is their wish'. As Pawson (1992) notes, the preamble to the Treaty portrayed itself as a partnership. However, Maori peoples were in the years following the Treaty removed, often forcibly, from much of the land.

Geography was introduced as a higher education discipline in New Zealand only in the 1930s and according to Stokes for much of its initial thirty years made relatively little reference to the marginalisation of Maori in the installation of a European colonial economy and society.

Most Pakeha writers of regional history and historical geography have contented themselves with brief mention of the indigenous inhabitants, perhaps referred to the 'Maori' Wars, a particular local chief, where relevant, a garbled translation of a place name or two, and then proceeded to the much more interesting task of documenting the struggles of the hardy pioneer families in 'opening up' and 'breaking in' the land (Stokes 1987).

In the 1950s and 1960 rather more attention was paid by academic geographers in New Zealand – who as the above quote from Stokes indicates might be seen to be largely of Pakeha identity – to Maori people. In particular, Stokes argues, a series of geographers began to research *Maori problems*, which were largely conceived in terms of the extent to which Maori people might be seen to be integrated into or marginalised from a New Zealand society, conceived essentially in terms of the norms of Pakeha society. Hence there was a focus on the extent to which Maori were integrated into paid-labour markets, business enterprises, formal education systems and associated qualifications, and modern, urban societies. There was, with one or two exceptions highlighted by Stokes, very little attention paid to whether these norms were shared by Maori people. To use the language of contemporary postmodernism: Maori were reduced to the being 'the Same' of the Pakeha, or perhaps more often their 'Other of the Same' (for more on these terms see Chapter 2). What was produced, so Stokes argues, 'was a Pakeha geography of Maori'.

Stokes suggests that such geographies might be replaced by a 'Maori geography' which pays much more attention on the cultural viewpoints of Maori people. To do Maori research, she argues, 'you need knowledge and experience of participation in the Maori world', which, at a minimum requires that researcher 'serve a long apprenticeship of learning on the marae [or Maori community]' such that they become 'bicultural and preferably bilingual' (Stokes 1987: 121). It also involves, so Stokes argues, a movement away from the notions of detached researcher towards a more involved stance: 'The researcher must play many roles – to lead, advise, support, reinforce, be directed or whatever … The sternest critics will be Maori people who expect some benefit from the research to accrue to them' (p. 121).

These arguments clearly connect to notions of positionality and situatedness highlighted within debates surrounding postmodernism and other associated philosophies (see Chapter 2). Within New Zealand, however, they have emerged quite directly from localised political struggles. Whilst the 1950s and 1960s was a period where notions of 'social integration' and 'cultural assimilation' were to the forefront in many academic, administrative and political debates, in the 1970s such notions began to be openly contested by Maori representatives and activists who, like Stokes, argued for a clearer recognition of Maori difference from Pakeha society. Objections were frequently raised about Pakeha ability and right to speak about Maori issues and concerns. One high publicity example of this was the criticism levelled at the historical writer, biographer and journalist Michael King, who had worked for many years with Maori people and had sought to give some representation to their views and concerns within the press and television. After mounting criticisms about his representation of Maori history and people, King publicly announced that he felt it was no longer appropriate for him to work on Maori issues, and that Maori people should represent themselves (King 1985).

Stokes does not go as far as to suggest that a Maori geography should be constructed only by Maori, although notions of *standpoint theory* outlined in Chapter 2 might lead one to such a view. Gale (1996: 16) suggests that 'a Maori geography should be a creation of Maori themselves' but McClean *et al.* (1997) have claimed that there is a danger of reinforcing a 'Pakeha/Maori binary' and argue for greater recognition of hybrid identities: that is, a recognition of differences which are both 'Same and Other' rather than either 'Same' or 'Other'. They suggest that there is much for Pakeha academics to learn from Maori peoples and from a responsible and caring engagement with them.

Geographies of Difference in Rural Aotearoa/New Zealand

The significance of social differences relating to ethnicity and gender are cleary evident in a number of studies of rural Aotearoa/New Zealand. With reference to gender, it has been argued that the countryside has been highly masculinised, both culturally and socially. So, for example, Jock Phillips (1996) not only argued that key aspects of the country's culture and sense of national identity were centred around a rural, colonial frontier, but that this frontier, and associated senses of culture and national identity were heavily masculinised. The rural frontier was a Pakeha man's country: it was a place where a man could supposedly be 'a real man', as opposed to the city which was often seen as 'effeminate' because it was 'a place of voluptuousness and fashion, of luxury and ease, where men lived a soft life' (Phillips 1980: 251). The real man, and the frontier life, came to be seen as tough, rugged and physical where only the strongest, physically and mentally, would be able to survive and prosper. Women, children, and men who did not conform to the required masculine traits were marginalised within this construction of rurality: they were seen as people who were in one way or another out of place in the countryside, although women and children could be accommodated if they were placed in a domestic environment under manly protection (Berg 1994).

People such as Berg (1994), Law *et al.* (1999), Liepins (1996) and Longhurst and Wilson (1999) have all suggested that such images are still of major importance in contemporary Aotearoa/New Zealand, informing and being reproduced in popular and professional discourses. Liepins (1996), for example, has examined reporting on agricultural issues within newspapers and argued that women are either entirely absent from the papers or else appear in 'marginal positions' within them. Furthermore, women are, she argues, consistently 'constructed as wives, mothers and homemakers devoted to home, community service and ancillary work on the farm' (Liepins 1996: 5). In other words, women are portrayed doing work which is frequently seen as being in some way of lesser value than other forms of work: it is seen as being conducted 'at home' rather than at a 'real' workplace; it is seen as 're-productive', caring work rather than 'productive' work; it is seen as 'ancillary' rather than 'central'.

Views about the masculinity of rural life are often sustained by reference to the gender inbalances in population numbers. In the early periods of Pakeha colonisation there was a predominance of male migrants over female, but as Table 11.2 shows the gender imbalances in population numbers were most stark in areas classified as rural and in areas of gold mining activity. In urban areas, by contrast, differences in the proportion of male and females are quite minimal. During the course of the twentieth century the predominance of males decreased and from 1968 the number of females has slightly outnumbered males, reflecting the widespread tendency for women to outlive men. However, a male predominance is still evident in many rural areas: Chalmers and Joseph (1997), for example, suggest that the number of men exceeds those of women by 6 per cent in rural areas of the Waikato region.

Table 11.2: Distribution of adult population by gender and settlement type, 1874

Settlement type	Percentage of total population	
	Men	Women
Rural	37.4	17.9
Goldfields	12.8	3.9
Cities and towns	15.5	12.5
National figures	65.6	34.4

Source: derived from McKinnon *et al.* (1997)

However, while men may still outnumber women in rural areas, a series of studies have sought to highlight the central role that women play in many aspects of rural life. Begg (1988; 1994), for example, has sought to highlight the work and lives of women working on dairy farms. Begg also highlights how women may do important community work, an argument likewise made by Fairburn (1989: 253) who dates the formation of community in rural Aotearoa/New Zealand to, in large part, an 'influx of women' into voluntary associations from the 1920s. However, despite highlighting these contributions, Begg's studies also reveal continual devaluation of women's work, a point also made by Hatch (1992: 11) who claims that although women's contributions to the operation of a farm 'may be highly regarded' the work they do is often viewed as 'supportive, not primary'. Hence the symbolic marginalisation of women's work continues to persist, and can have significant material consequences.

Coombes and Cambell (1996), for example, note how gendered notions of work in the Catlins area of South Island led to different responses to agricultural crisis of the late 1980s. As noted in Box 11.3, two common albeit quite different responses were, first, to intensify the use of labour on the farm and second to seek alternative non-farm employment. Coombes and Campbell suggest that although the former strategy fitted in well with hegemonic notions of masculinity – working hard on the land was seen as a good, manly, pursuit – the latter strategy did not, and as a result 'in those cases where men did seek off-farm work, these jobs were almost exclusively situated in agriculture, even though such jobs were harder to find than positions in the local ski industry' (Coombes and Campbell 1996: 14). For women, notions of femininity connected less unequivocally with the two responses to the agricultural crisis. In part, participation in both on-farm and off-farm labour transgressed the norms of rural female activity and as a result highlighted existing contradictions between the norms and everyday experiences. On the other hand, these norms were being re-applied in valuations of female participation off-farm, although these valuations were in themselves quite contradictory. So, for example, participation by women in off-farm work was encouraged by some because these forms were not seen as masculine and, as already noted, many men were unwilling to apply for them. On the other hand, women working off-farm were seen to be neglecting their responsibilities for the 'home', where the home was seen to encompass not only the care and support of the family but also, in an ironic twist of earlier omissions, the farm. Coombes and Campbell (1996: 15) conclude that the agrarian crisis may have 'partly reconstructed' local discourses on female work, although discourses on masculine work remained apparently unchanged.

Turning to issues of ethnicity, although rural populations in Aotearoa/New Zealand have frequently been described in such ways that make no mention of ethnic differentiation there has arguably been rather more recognition of such differences than in countries such as Britain. In particular there has been some recognition that Maori peoples have formed a significant constituent of rural populations, albeit one declining sharply overall (see Figure 11.4). Studies of rural localities with high Maori populations often remarked on this, and general geographies of the country often made reference to changes in the urban and rural distributions of Maori and Pakeha. However, there has been a tendency in these *geographies of Maori* (see Box 11.4) to overlook that this population distribution was very much a product of the actions of European colonialism: as Pawson (1992: 24) comments, '[a]fter the wars of the 1860s, the iwi [or Maori tribes] ... held onto land remote from the main towns, much of it of marginal quality in European eyes'. The distribution of Maori post European imperialism became the base map from which subsequent variations were traced, in part because production of demographic data through a national Census commenced only after the formation of colonial government.

This neglect of the pre-colonial situation became foregrounded by the passing of the 1975 and 1985 *Treaty of Waitangi Acts* which set up a tribunal to consider claims for the return of land to Maori ownership. The original *Waitangi Treaty* of 1840 appeared to establish that all land was held by Maori who could sell it to the British Crown government, although there was considerable ambiguity in the translation of the Treaty between English and Maori versions (see Pawson 1992). However, even prior to its signing, and particularly from the 1860s onwards, there was occupation, purchase and forcible seizure of land by Pakeha settlers and private agencies such as *The New Zealand Company*. In 1862 the Crown effectively reneged on a key aspect of the 1840 Treaty by relinquishing its role as sole purchasers of Maori land, and there followed a series of private land purchases which not only massively reduced the amount of land under Maori 'possession' (see Box 11.5) but also left them with much of the most economically marginal land, as this was the land for which the Pakeha settlers were least willing to purchase.

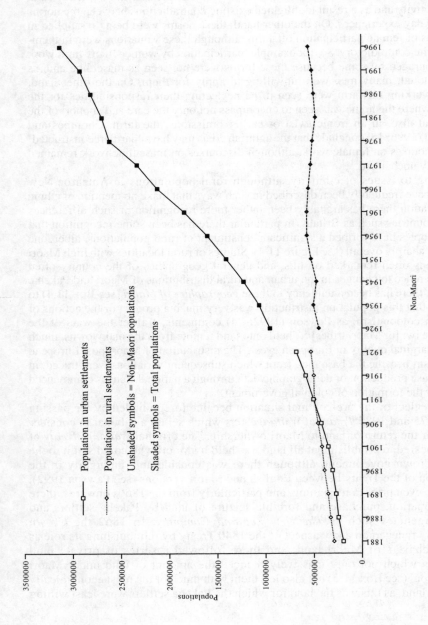

Figure 11.4: Changing urban and rural distributions
Source: Statistics New Zealand: Te Tari Tatau (1998) *People on the move ... shifting around New Zealand* (Wellington: Statistics New Zealand – Te Tari Tatau)

Box 11.5: Possession of land: Pakeha and Maori conceptions

Pakeha settlers in Aotearoa/New Zealand brought with them a conception of 'private property ownership'. Particular resources, goods and areas of space could be owned by a person or institution, who could then trade the rights of use and ownership to other people or institutions. Maori people, however, had rather different conceptions of possession. Stokes (1997) identifies 4 different ways in which rights of possession over land and resources were established with pre- and early-contact Maori societies:

- *Take whenua kite hou*: possession established through first contact or 'discovery'.
- *Take tupuna*: possession established through continuity of occupation
- *Take raupatu*: possession via conquest. Had to be followed by some form of occupation of the area, and also often accompanied by the formation of an alliance with the conquered people by marriage between members of leaders' families.
- *Take tuku*: gift or exchange of possession, given at special circumstances such as at a marriage or settlement of dispute.

These four forms of possession inter-connected and overlapped with each other to form a complex system of rights to use land and resources. These forms of possession were held not by individuals but by a range of inter-connective collective kinship groups, notably whanau (families), iwi (tribes) and hapu (sub-tribes). They were further formed inter-generationally, with rights of possession often being traced to the landings of particular canoes or 'waka' sailing from islands in Eastern Polynesia and subsequently from one part of Aotearoa to another (Royal 1997).

These notions of possession went largely unrecognised by Pakeha settlers, and indeed they were effectively undermined in the drawing up of legislation such as the 1862 *Native Lands Act,* which, as McKinnon (1997) records, was 'designed with Pakeha, not Maori, aspirations in mind'. The Act provided for Maori to have titles to land, but it was decided that no more than ten people could be named on any title deed. This completely denied the collectivity so central to Maori notions of possession.

For much of the next century, this reneging on an important aspect of *Treaty of Waitangi* was ignored by Pakeha New Zealand in what might be seen as a collective 'loss of memory' (Orange 1990). It had long been a source of resentment amongst Maori peoples and in the 1970s there was growing public recognition of the issues, recognition which led to the *Treaty of Waitangi Acts*. These Acts in turn have led to further attention being paid to the geographies of Maori at the onset of colonisation, not least because these geographies can form the basis of an appeal to the Waitangi Tribunal for the return of land and/or payment of compensation for land and resources appropriated in ways not consistent with the 1840 treaty. A number of

geographers have been involved in reconstructing the geographies of Maori possession and of the transfers of these to Pakeha ownership (see McClean *et al*. 1997;
Stokes 1992; 1996).

Much of the land being returned to Maori possession is rural land, with national
parks often being amongst the most favoured transfers (see Robinson *et al*. 2000).
Such transfers, together with financial payments and a sense of rising cultural recognition and status for Maori (or *mana Maori*), have been seen as stimulating a process
to 'return migration' to rural areas amongst the Maori population. As epitomised by
the book and film *Once Were Warriors* (Duff 1994; Tamihori 1997), the movement to
rural areas has widely been interpreted as a return to ancestral homelands, *marae*
settlements and a traditional, authentic Maori way of life. It has been objected,
however, that such an interpretation effectively legitimates a 'continued marginalisation' of Maori people as '*belonging somewhere else*' than within the places of mainstream New Zealand society (Matahaere-Atariki 1999: 114, original emphasis). On
the other hand, Lees and Berg have used the film to highlight the urbanity of much of
Aotearoa/New Zealand *and* of contemporary Maori. Despite the contemporary
emphasis given to Maori urban to rural 'return' migration, the majority of the Maori
population still live in urban settlements (see Figure 11.4). Furthermore, as studies by
people such as Davey and Kearns (1994) and Waldegrave and Stuart (1997) have
highlighted, return migration may be stimulated rather less by a renewed attachment
to Maori homelands and rather more by declining employment opportunities and
poor housing opportunities for Maori within cities. In addition, ways of earning a
living within rural areas may be quite removed from that implied by the 'traditional
idyll', not least because of the restructuring of agricultural production and service
provisions as discussed previously.

In the 1950s, 1960s and early 1970s when rural to urban migration was at its height
(see Figure 11.4), there was a tendency to focus attention on whether or not there was
a growing similarity between Maori and Pakeha populations. A growing Maori urban
population was sometimes taken as an indication of a growing *assimilation* of the
Maori into ways of life of the Pakeha majority (e.g Rowland 1972), but there was also
concern over the extent to which Maori remained marginalised in urban employment
and housing markets and within the delivery of health and education services. There
were also expressions of concern about differences in rural areas, most notably over
the use of land with Maori people being castigated for failing to adopt Pakeha forms
of agrarian production and settlement forms (see Frazer 1958). It was suggested that
these 'failures' produced high poverty levels amongst rural Maori, which in turn was
the cause rural outmigration. However, as discussed in Box 11.4, the notion of assimilation which underlay many of these studies came to be heavily criticised for its privileging of Pakeha ways of life over Maori and from the 1980s onwards there has been
a greater recognition of the need to pay attention to the values and opinions of Maori
people. So, for example while Frazer makes reference to 'an air of untidyness' and
links this to low levels of agricultural productivity, Stokes links rather similar observations a sense of 'comfortableness':

> There were no concrete paths … The lawn had not been mowed for a while. A dinghy lay
> upside down with nets draped over it … We greeted each other and started talking. A kettle
> was boiled and tea made. My son settled down and joined the other kids in demolishing the

remains of a packet of biscuits... I knew they could not afford chocolate biscuits but we were visitors who had been away for along time ... Maori places are comfortable places. We had been welcomed, eaten together, the kids played and my friend and I gossiped away the rest of the afternoon (Stokes 1987: 120).

Stokes argues, making reference to humanistic geographers, that this 'sense of place' is one amongst a range of others which might be studied by geographers (see also Chapter 2). Although there have been some attempts to develop such a geography of Maori (e.g. Murton 1979), it is a geography which still very much remains one of potential rather than having been realised. It is also one, which as outlined in Box 11.4, is positioned within highly complex and contested social situations.

Postmodern, feminist and Maori geographies have highlighted the presence of different people and senses of place which may exist in the countryside of Aotearoa/New Zealand. We ourselves have sought to present images of some of the different people who lived in one rural community, Rotowaro, and to 'give voice' to some of their views on and concerns about this place (see Cook and Phillips, forthcoming). This study is interesting in the present context as it reflects on three of the issues discussed in this chapter, namely those relating to cultural constructions of rurality; political-economic restructuring and marginalisation; and social difference and senses of place. The arguments advanced in this study will briefly be summarised.

People in the Marginal Periphery of Rotowaro

As discussed earlier, there has been a tendency to equate the rural with the agricultural and in the process, to neglect people involved other activities, including both people engaged in other productive activities, such as forestry, mining, and various service industries, and also those people not engaged in economically productive activities, such as children and their carers, the unemployed and the retired (for work on the last group, see Chalmers and Joseph 1998; Joseph and Chalmers 1995; 1998). Rotowaro, whilst fitting many cultural constructions of rurality – such as being a small settlement, or 'township', surrounded by open countryside and having, for at least some of its residents, a sense of being a 'solid community' of 'very loyal, very co-operative people' (Lyall Yarrow, quoted in Cook and Phillips, forthcoming) – was a mining and service settlement, with the former very much predominant. Indeed, whilst the Waikato region in which Rotowaro is located, is widely seen as an agricultural region, coal has been commercially mined in the region from as early as the 1860s and the northern part of the region has supported a number of extensive coalfields and associated settlements ever since (see Figure 11.5)

The settlement of Rotowaro was established in the early decades of the twentieth century, although by the late 1980s virtually every trace of it had been destroyed (see Plates 11.5–11.6), with the area being portrayed as 'lush pasture' on which cattle graze and 'a small clear stream nestles', with 'freshwater crayfish' and 'native fish' swimming along its course (Coal Corp, 1994). The short history of the settlement, and the representation of the area as having been returned to its 'natural state', might be seen as illustrations of Bell's (1996: 122) more general claim that settlements in

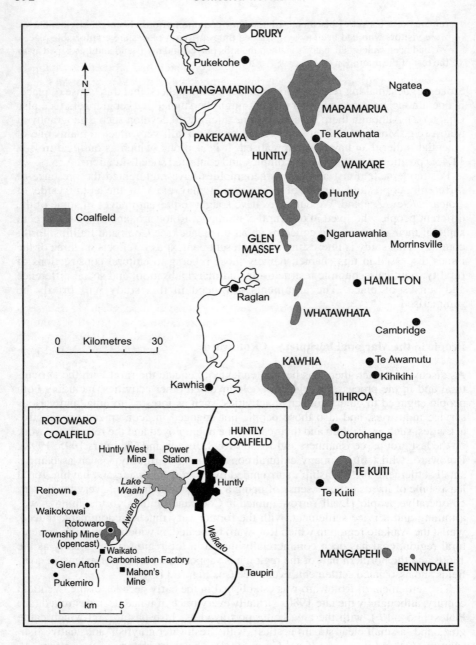

Figure 11.5: The coalfields of the Waikato

Aotearoa/New Zealand have often been highly ephemeral, thriving for a while and then declining as their economic bases becomes marginalised. Rotowaro may, however, be seen as a particular case of marginalisation, there being complete destruction of the settlement by the very industry which had secured its establishment, with the settlement being materially demolished to make space for an expansion in open-cast coal mining and then also symbolically erased by advertisements which promoted a return to pastoral rurality but make no mention of the previous existence – albeit relatively fleetingly – of a township which at its height numbered over 640 people.

In our study, we seek to give image and voice to the people of this settlement, and to represent some of the processes of marginalisation which not only accompanied the demise of the settlement but which also structured its relatively short history. We note, for instance, how the the lives and livelihoods of the settlement's residents had long been dominated by coal mining, with underground mine shafts extending under the settlement and causing subsidence such that people would 'walk … like a crab because of the tilting floor' and the village bowling green, itself established by the mining company, 'subsided down in one corner by six to eight inches' (Marj Thomas, quoted in Cook and Phillips, forthcoming). The residents of the community, dependent on income from the coal mining, came to accept 'living in a village which was subsiding', and indeed many also accepted hearing through letters deposited at the Post Office that the state-owned coal corporation intended to demolish the townshop on the grounds that 'An economic appraisal of the area is clearly in favour of winning the coal rather than preserving the township' (State Coal Mines, 1979). For other people, the decision represented abandonment by an organisation which had long failed to recognise the value of the people of Rotowaro and now thought that its 'citizens should expect to be pushed around, without explantation' (Yarrow, 1979). However, despite the formation of a 'Rotowaro Action Committee', State Coal Mines stuck by its decision, buying out property owners in the township and providing people who rented accommodation with alternative accommodation in the nearby urban centre of Huntly.

People's reponse to State Coal Mines' announcement and subsequent actions were varied, in part due social differences in their situations. The establishment of mining in the area had on several occasions been bound up with the marginalisation of Maori people, and at the onset of mining at Rotowaro, most of the miners were Pakeha. However, by the early 1980s some 58 percent of the population of Rotowaro was Maori, who formed the majority of the younger population of the township and often lived in rented accommodation provided by the coal corporation. By contrast, the older population was mainly Pakeha, many of whom had retired from working in the mines and had purchased their own homes in the village. Property owners had the advantage of receiving payment for their properties, and although many were very reluctant to move from the settlement initially, many were able to purchase property in the neighbouring urban settlement of Huntly. Many of the younger Maori residents, on the other hand, relocated to other rural areas in part because, as discussed earlier, these are areas with lower rental costs. This was particularly significant in that the closure of Rotowaro township coincided with the privatisation and restructuring of the State Coal Mines into the *Coal Corporation of NZ Ltd* and associated reduction in the workforce of the area by almost 500. As a result some families were being

Plate 11.5: Main Road, Rotowaro, 1987 (top) and 1989 (bottom)

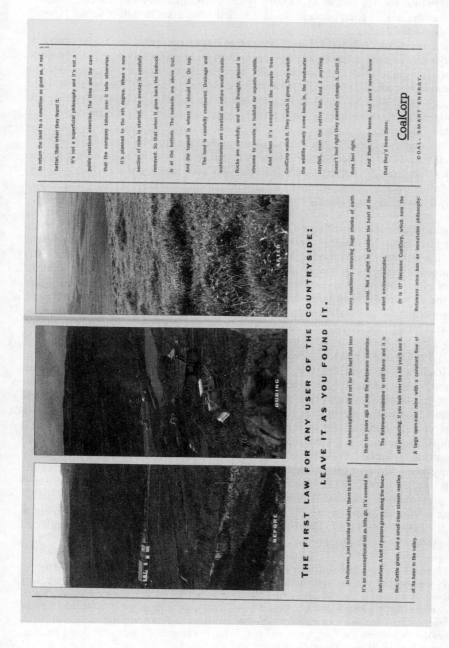

Plate 11.6: Return to nature/erasure of history

forced to look for new homes at the same time as loosing their employment. This was on top of the more general cuts in welfare benefits and rises in public sector housing costs discussed earlier.

Some residents of Rotowaro may be seen to have experienced serial marginalisation, but this was not a universal experience, even amongst the young Maori families. Twenty-four Maori families, for instance, became property owners by purchasing a house in Rotowaro and physically relocating them (see Plate 11.7). The purchase of the houses was enabled by loans from the *Department of Maori Affairs,* with people moving either to other nearby rural mining communities or to rural blocks of land owned by their hapu. For such families, the demolition of Rotowaro proved something of 'a blessing', restructuring their residentially and occupationally marginalised worlds in such a way that provided quite unexpected, and possibly quite empowering, opportunities: 'my uncle … always wanted to own his own home, but they [State Mines] wouldn't allow it … [now] we are looking at redundancies and yet we are going to own our own homes' (Nancy Buckley, quoted in Cook and Phillips, forthcoming)

The movement of Maoiri families to rural areas may not have been exclusively related to the economics of rental and home ownership. There is some evidence that many also wanted to maintain both a rural lifestyle and an ancestral connection to the land, the Rotowaro area having been first occupied in the late sixteenth and early seventeenth centuries by Maori, and becoming the focus of use by three *hapu* of the Tainui tribe. The so-called Land Wars, or *Raupatu*, of the 1860s had seen British colonial forces forcibly seize large tracts of land from Maori in the Waikato, although Maori people did gradually return to occupy some of the more marginal areas of the region. Through the *Treaty of Waitangi Acts* further land has been returned to Maori, although it has been argued that this has again been largely marginal land (Centre for Maori Studies and Research, 1986).

Attachment to rural lifestyle and a sense of connection to the area was not, however, restricted simply to Maori residents of Rotowaro. One Pakeha couple, for example, stated that they 'find no pleasure' in leaving the township and that if possible they would prefer to be relocated to 'a country area' where the 'pace of life is, as yet, by comparison leisurely' (Yarrow and Yarrow, quoted in Cook and Phillips, forthcoming). Indeed, for many of the residents, Rotowaro continued to exercise a presence long after the physical destruction of the community. In the Huntly West Mine in the neighbouring Huntly coalfield, for example, one of the shifts became known as the 'Rotowaro Shift' because it was composed of men who had previously worked at Rotowaro. Furthermore, the Rotowaro branch of the Country Women Institute, which was founded in 1939, continued to meet, again at Huntly (see Plate 11.8). Identifications with Rotowaro were also reproduced through less formal interactions:

> Whenever we have function, be it a funeral or a wedding anniversary, and Rotowaro people get together, all you can hear is the babble and the laughing, and always, always talking about 'Rotowaro in the old days'. And it is a joy to be there with Rotowaro people. We all have an affinity with one another, be it the coal mines, the school, we all have shared experiences. And even my own children who haven't lived in Rotowaro for years, still if you mention Rotowaro, they just smile and say 'Yeah, it was great living there' (Marj Thomas, interviewed in 1999 by David Cook)

Plate 11.7: Relocation of Rotowaro house to Maori ancestral lands, 1987

Plate 11.8: Meeting of the Rotowaro Branch of the Country Women's Institute, Huntly, 1999

Conclusion

The focus of this chapter has been on the people who inhabit, and at least in part create, worlds which have in some sense or another been labelled as, to use the phraseology of Shields (1991), 'places on the margin'. In particular the chapter has focused on people inhabiting rural space and the national space of Aotearoa/New Zealand. It is argued that while both spaces have been widely identified as being margin, caution needs to be exercised before employing this descriptor. So, for example, some rural areas appear to be far from marginalised, being quite centrally and advantageously implicated in many of processes of change in the contemporary (post-)modern world. There is hence a need to recognise that there are 'differentiated countrysides' (Murdoch and Marsden 1994).

In addition the chapter has illustrated how the social positionings of any particular rural space can change: hence many rural areas in Britain, for example, have changed from being central to an industrial economy, to being de-industrialised during a period of more general industrialisation, and now have been re-industrialised within a so-called post-industrial economy. Likewise Aotearoa/New Zealand, while long described as being, quite literally, at the furthest margins of British imperial and then trans-Atlantic centred global economies, has now been seen, by some people at least, to be now quite advantageously placed with respect to new 'core economies' of the Pacific rim.

Two further points of caution become apparent when one recognises the long running existence of a series of highly positive evaluations of Aotearoa/New Zealand. First, marginality and centrality can be constructed across a range of different practices, not simply in relation to economic performances. Success in sport, in lifestyle, in political innovation, as well as natural beauty and bounty, for example, have all been invoked as constituents of Aotearoa/New Zealand's centrality. Second, a marginal location may bring benefits, such as being immunised from problematic features of modern capitalist, industrialised and urbanised economies. Hence, one of the arguments advanced in this chapter is that notions of marginality, and indeed centrality, involve complex, multiple, changeable and differentially constructed and evaluated relations between social and spatial position (see Box 11.6).

Box 11.6: Chapter summary and suggestions for further reading

- Marginality and centrality are far from simple concepts and need to be used with some degree of caution, or 'reflexivity'

- Rural areas have been described as marginal spaces, but this is an over-generalisation as many rural areas are quite centrally and advantageously implicated in contemporary processes

- Certain countries, such as Aoterroa/New Zealand have been widely described as being on the periphery or semi-periphery, but economic core areas be may shifting to give it greater centrality and economic criteria may not be the only measure of social development

- Particular space forms may be quite central to a country's identity and social position, and in Aotearoa/New Zealand rural space has long been quite central

- Positions of centrality and marginality can change, and rural areas in Aoterroa/New Zealand may be becoming more marginalised.

- Within any one locality people may be quite differently positioned with respect to a complex array of social relations of power, and hence within a marginalised place some people may be far from marginalised and others may be subject to multiple forms of marginalisation.

- Margins may be places of opportunities as well as hardship, exploitation and exclusion.

For theoretical and substantive studies of marginalisation and the countryside, a useful starting point is Cloke and Little's (1997) *Contested Countryside Cultures: Otherness, Marginalisation and Rurality*. This book however has a strong British bias, and as yet there is no equivalent collection on rural Aotearoa/New Zealand, although the *New Zealand Geographer* does contain some relevant studies. Marginalisation as understood from a political-economic perspective figures highly in Le Heron and Pawson's (1996) *Changing Places: New Zealand in the Nineties* and in the earlier edition of this book by Britton, Le Heron and Pawson (1992), entitled *Changing Places in New Zealand: A Geography of Restructuring*. Other useful books on the human geographies of New Zealand/Aotearoa include Le Heron, Murphy, Forer and Goldstone's (1999) *Exploration in Human Geography: Encountering Place* and Robinson, Loughran and Tranter's (2000) *Australia and New Zealand: Economy, Society and Environment*.

Much of the positive imagery of Aotearoa/New Zealand centres on the rurality of the national space: although having a highly urbanised population, much of the land area of the country could be classified as rural and is widely seen as aesthetically beautiful, economically bountiful and socially bucolic. According to some observers, however, recent years have seen the centrality of rurality in Aotearoa/New Zealand coming under threat, in large part because of political-economic restructurings which have seen both a rolling back of the nation state and an opening up of economic practices to forces of globalisation. Hence, it is argued that rural Aotearoa/New Zealand might be described, cautiously and no doubt simplistically, as moving from a central position with a semi-peripheral economy to a marginal position in a possibly slightly less marginalised economy.

The chapter also argued that there is a clear need to recognise that people co-located in a particular locality – be that a locality of centrality or marginality – may not be identically positioned with respect of social relations of power. People in the same place may live within quite different 'power geometries' (Massey 1991), some of which are constituted through the people living in the bounds of this place and many of which are constituted in relationships which take far more extensive forms.

In the present chapter, attention is paid via a review of existing studies of rural Aotearoa/New Zealand to the social relations of gender, age, class and ethnicity. A case study of our own then addresses an extreme instance of marginalisation whereby a complete settlement has been removed from the landscape and people compelled, in some cases with considerable reluctance, to move elsewhere. The demolition of the settlement of Rotowaro, the relocation of its former residents and the evident disloca- tion of their lives was undertaken to enable the demands of a core industry, albeit one experiencing marginalisation, to be met. We noted, however, how even from the establishment of the settlement, processes of marginalisation were at work, with attendant exclusions and inequalities, as well as communal ties, services and senses of identity and belonging, becoming part of the everyday lives of people in the settle- ment. This everyday life was clearly irrevocably destroyed by the removal of the settlement, although we have shown that the turmoil associated with it were not exclusively negative experiences and that the settlement and its people still live on in the thoughts, words and activities of many of its former residents. Indeed, for some of its residents, particularly young Maori residents, the marginalisation of Rotowaro appears to have acted to establish a route out of the marginalisation they had faced in their everyday lives in the settlement.

Part Five:
Some Concluding Remarks

Chapter 12

Still Just Introducing the Contested Worlds of Human Geography

Martin Phillips

Given the emphasis on contested worlds and contested geographies it is, I feel, inappropriate to end this book with an attempt to reconcile the approaches, argument and content of its constituent chapters. Instead I wish to end by highlighting how this book, despite its length, is, I feel, very much just an introduction to contemporary human geography, its contests and some of the contested worlds it addresses. As Cloke *et al.* (1999) comment in the postscript to their *Introducing human geography*, 'all introductions to Human Geography are partial'.

Part of the partiality stems from the expanse, complexity and dynamism of human geography. Within only ten substantive chapters, there are clearly always going to be further places, spaces and worlds which could have been discussed. There is also much more that could have been said about each of the worlds which has been explored, and indeed each of the chapters has concluded with a list of further reading suggestions. Additionally, as has become very apparent during the writing of this book, contemporary worlds change very rapidly indeed. Many of these chapters have been substantially revised several times to catch up with the speed of events occurring in the worlds they were seeking to portray (particular thanks go out to the authors for doing these revisions). Having said this, by the time this book comes to be published, no doubt many of the things said will prove to have become outdated, with new transformations undermining many previously accepted certainties. There is need to continue exploring the worlds discussed in this book in the light of subsequent, texts, information and experiences.

Partiality not only comes through changes in the worlds geographers seek to study, but also by changes in how geographers see those worlds. As has been emphasised in this book, geography is a very contested discipline with a whole series of different approaches and ways of doing geography emerging at a seemingly ever-increasing rate (Mohan 1994). This book has sought to make accessible many of these changes and to highlight their significance in substantive studies of human geography. However, not only have new philosophies affected how traditional topics of geographical research have been understood and examined, but have brought forth new topics for investigation by geographers. Attention has, for example, been drawn within this book to the emergence of new research areas such as 'imaginative geographies', 'difference' and 'otherness'. There are further areas of geographical research which, if starting to write the book again, would now certainly warrant inclusion, such as: geographies of the body (see Longhurst 2000; Nast and Pile 1998, Pile 1996,

Pile and Thrift 1995; Teather 1999); and geographies of the mass media and cyberspace (see Clarke 1997; Crang *et al*. 2000; Dodge and Kitchin 2000; Phillips forthcoming – a). There is hence a need to supplement the contested worlds explored in this book with other perspectives and other worlds. These may not erase the worlds and perspectives discussed here, not least because not everything that is new is necessarily a development – i.e. an improvement – on from what is old (see Chapter 3), but neither should what has been accepted in the past necessarily set the course for the future of geography.

Partiality no doubt also comes from positionality of the book, its authors and its editor. As discussed in Chapter 2 it is hard to be fully cogniscent of positionality and how it is impacting on the texts you are writing. Some elements of positionality have been evident during the writing of this text. First, like several other introductory texts in human geography (e.g. Allen and Massey 1995; Cloke *et al.*, 1999; Massey *et al.*, 1999; Daniels *et al.*, 2001; Holloway and Hubbard 2001), the book is Anglocentric in its authorship and, hopefully to a lesser extent, its content. A key question which you should perhaps ask about this text, and others like it, is whether the inclusion of people from these worlds as authors rather than research subjects would have produced human geographies which would contest those which appear here. You might also reflect on how you would respond to those contests: whose accounts would you favour and why? There is clearly scope for further contested geographies to be written, by all manner of people.

References

Abler, R. (1993) 'Desiderata for geography', in R. Johnston (ed.) *The challenge for geography*, Oxford: Blackwell.

ActionAid (1992) *Lifestyle overload? ActionAid Development Report No. 5*.

Adams, J. (1994) *The new spies*, London: Hutchinson.

Adams, W. (1993) 'Sustainable development & the greening of development theory', in F. Schuurman (ed.) *Beyond the impasse* London: Zed Books.

Adomeit, H. (1995) 'Russia as a 'great power' in world affairs', *International Affairs*, 71: 35–68.

Adorno, T. & Horkheimer, M. (1979) *Dialectic of enlightenment*, London: Verso.

Aglietta, M. (1979) *A theory of capitalist regulation*, London: Verso.

Agnew, J. (1989) 'Sameness & difference', in J. Entrikin & S. Brunn (eds) *Reflections on Richard Hartshorne's The Nature of Geography*, Washington DC: Association of American Geographers.

Agnew, J. (1998) *Geopolitics*, London: Routledge.

Agnew, J. (2002) *Making political geography*, London, Arnold.

Agnew, J. & Corbridge, S. (1995) *Mastering space*, London: Routledge.

Agyeman, J. & Spooner, R. (1997) 'Ethnicity & the rural environment', in P. Cloke & J. Little (eds) *Contested countryside cultures*, London: Routledge.

Aharoni, Y. (1988) 'The United Kingdom: transforming attitudes', in R. Vernon (ed.) *The promise of privatization*, New York: Council on Foreign Relations.

Ahmed, A. (1992) *Postmodernism & Islam*, London: Routledge.

Albritton, R. (1995) 'The de(con)struction of Marx's Capital', in M. Zavarzadeh, T. Ebert & D. Morton (eds) *Post-ality*, Washington: Maisonneuve Press.

Allen, E. (1992) 'Jungle politics', *Geographical Magazine*, April: 28–32.

Allen, J. & Thompson, G. (1997) 'Think global, then think again – economic globalization in context', *Area* 29: 213–227.

Allen, J. & Massey, D. (eds) (1995) *Geographical worlds*, Oxford: Oxford Univerity Press.

Alonso, W. (1964) *Location & land-use* Cambridge, Massachusetts: Harvard University Press.

Althusser, L. (1969) *For Marx*, Harmondsworth: Penguin.

Althusser, L. & Balibar, E. (1970) *Reading capital*, London: Verso.

Amin, A. (1989) 'Flexible specialization & small firms in Italy', *Antipode* 21: 13–34.

Anderson, B. (1991) *Imagined communities*, London: Verso.

Anderson, E. (1993) *An atlas of world political flashpoints*, London: Pinter.

Anderson, K. (1991) *Vancouver's Chinatown* Montreal: McGill-Queens University Press.

Anderson, K. (2000) 'Thinking 'postnationally'', *Annals, Association of American Geographers* 90: 381–391.

Armstrong, W. (1978) 'New Zealand: Imperialism, class & uneven development', *Australian & New Zealand Journal of Sociology* 14: 297–303.

Arnold, R. (1981) *The farthest promised land*, Wellington.

Arter, D. (1993) *The politics of european integration in the twentieth century*, Aldershot: Dartmouth.

Ascherson, N. (1992) 'The New Europe', *Independent on Sunday* 9 February: 31–34.

Ashford, D. (1986) *The emergence of the welfare states*, Oxford: Blackwell.

Ashwin, S. (2000) *Gender, state & society in Soviet & post-Soviet Russia*, London: Routledge.

Atkinson, A. (1995) *Incomes & the welfare state*, Cambridge: Cambridge University Press.

Aulich, J. & Sylvestrová, M. (1999) *Political posters in Central & Eastern Europe 1945–95*, Manchester: Manchester University Press.

Auty, R. (1995) *Patterns of development*, London: Edward Arnold.

Badcock, B. (1993) 'Notwithstanding the exaggerated claims, residential revitalization really is changing the form of western cities', *Urban Studies*, 30: 191–195.

Bagnold, R. (1941) *The physics of blown sand & desert dunes*, London: Methuen.

Baker, A. (1984) 'Reflections on the relations of historical geography & the Annales school of history', in A. Baker & D. Gregory (eds) *Explorations in historical geography*, Cambridge: Cambridge University Press.

Baran, P. (1957) *The political economy of growth*, New York: Monthly Review.

Barker, A. M. (1999) 'The culture factory', in A. M. Barker (ed.) *Consuming Russia*, Durham, North Carolina: Duke University Press.

Barnbrock, J. (1976) 'Prolegomenon to a methodological debate on location theory', *Antipode*, 6: 59–66.

Barnes, T. (1992) 'Reading the texts of theoretical economic geography', in T. Barnes (ed.) *Writing worlds*, London: Routledge.

Barnes, T. (1996a) *Logics of dislocation*, London: Guilford Press.

Barnes, T. (1996b) 'Probable writing', *Environment & Planning A* 26: 1021–1040.

Barnes, T. & Duncan, J. (1992) 'Introduction', in T. Barnes & J. Duncan (eds) *Writing worlds,* London: Routledge.

Barnes, T. & Gregory, D. (eds) (1997) *Reading human geography*, London: Arnold.

Barnett, C. (1993a) 'Peddling postmodernism', *Antipode* 25: 345–358.

Barnett, C. (1993b) 'Stuck in the post', *Antipode* 25: 365–368.

Barnett, C. (1998) 'Impure & worldy geography', *Transactions, Institute of British Geographers* 23: 239–251.

Barnett, C. (1999) 'Deconstructing context: exposing Derrida', *Transactions, Institute of British Geographers* 24, 3: 276–293.

Barrett, H. & Browne, A. (1995) 'Gender, environment & development in sub-Saharan Africa', in T. Binns (ed.) *People & environment in Africa*, Chichester: Wiley.

Barrett, H. (1992) *Population geography*, Harlow: Oliver & Boyd.

Barrett, H. (2000) 'Six billion & counting', *Geography* 85: 107–120.

Bater, J.H. (1980) *The Soviet city*, London: Edward Arnold.

Baudrillard, J. & Lotringer, S. (1987) *Forget Foucault & forget Baudrillard*, New York: Semiotext(e).

Bauman, Z. (1987) *Legislators & interpreters*, Cambridge: Polity.

BBC/British Broadcasting Corporation (1995) 'Pulp Futures', Panorama BBC1, documentary broadcast 20 March 1995.

Beale, C. (1975) *The revival of population growth in non-metropolitan America. ERS-605*, Economic Research Service, US Department of Agriculture.

Beauregard, R. (1986) 'The chaos & complexity of gentrification' in N. Smith & P. Williams (eds) *Gentrification of the city*, London: Allen & Unwin.

Beauregard, R. (1990) 'Trajectories of neighbourhood change', *Environment & Planning D* 22: 855–874.

Bedford, R. (1983) 'Repopulation of the countryside', in R. Bedford & A. Sturman, (eds) *Canturbury at the cross roads*, Christchurch: New Zealand Geographical Society.

Bedford, R. (1999) 'Immigration in coherent societies', paper presented at the 'Third national metropolis conference: immigration with an international perspective', Vancouver.

Bedford, R., Goodwin, J., Ho, E. & Lidgard, J. (1999) 'Internal migration in New Zealand's settlement hierarchy, 1991–96', *New Zealand Journal of Geography*: 26–33.

Beeley, B. (1995) 'Global options: Islamic alternatives', in J. Anderson, C. Brook & A. Cochrane (eds) *Global world?* Oxford: Oxford University Press.

Begg, M. (1988) *Farm women in Piako County. Studies in rural change no. 15*, Christchurch: Department of Geography, University of Canterbury.

Begg, M. (1994) 'Rural women: a case study of dairy farm women', in D. Hawke (ed.). *Proceedings, New Zealand Geographical Society & the Australian Institute of Geographers Conference*, Christchurch: New Zealand Geographical Society.

Behabha, H. (1994) *The location of culture*, London: Routledge.

Bell, C. (1996) *Inventing New Zealand*, Auckland: Penguin Books (NZ).

Bell, C. & Lyall, J. (1995) *Putting our town on the map*, Auckland: Harper Collins.

Bell, C. & Newby, H. (1971) *Community studies*, London: Allen & Unwin.

Bell, D. & Valentine, G. (1995a) *Mapping desire*, London: Routledge.

Bell, D. & Valentine, G. (1995b) 'Queer country', *Journal of Rural Studies* 11: 113–22.

Bell, M. (1994) 'Images, myths & alternative Geographies of the Third World', in D. Gregory, R. Martin & G. Smith (eds) *Human geography*, Basingstoke: Macmillan.

Bellamy, C. (1996) *Knights in white armour*, London: Hutchinson.

Benhabib, S. (1986) *Critique, norm & utopia*, New York: Columbia University Press.

Benton, L. (1995) 'Will the real/reel Los Angeles please stand up', *Urban Geography* 16: 144–164.

Berberoglu, B. (1992) *The political economy of development*, New York: State University of New York Press.

Berdoulay, V. (1978) 'The Vidal-Durkheim debate', in D. Ley & M. Samuels (eds) *Humanistic geography*, London: Croom Helm.

Berg, L. D. (1993) 'Between modernism & postmodernism', *Progress in Human Geography*, 17: 490–507.

Berg, L. D. (1994) 'Masculinity, place & a binary discourse of theory & empirical investigation in the human geography of Aotearoa/New Zealand', *Gender, Place & Culture*, 1: 245–260.

Berg, L. D. & Kearns, R. A. (1996) 'Naming as norming', *Environment & Planning D* 14: 99–122.

Bergmann, G. (1954) *The metaphysics of logical positivism*, London: Longmans, Green & Co.

Bergmann, G. (1957) *The philosophy of science*, Madison: University of Wisconsin Press.

Bernstein, H. (1979) 'Sociology of underdevelopment vs. sociology of development?', in D. Lehmann (ed.) *Development Theory*, London: Frank Cass.

Berry, B. (1970) 'Commuting patterns', *Growth & Change* 1: 3–10.

Berry, B. (1970) 'The geography of the United States in the year 2000', *Transactions, Institute of British Geographers* 51: 21–53.

Berry, B. (1972) 'Revolutionary & counter-revolutionary theory in geography', *Antipode* 4: 31–33.

Berry, B. (1976) 'The counterurbanization process', in B. Berry (ed.) *Urbanization & counterurbanization*, Beverley Hills, California: Sage.

Berry, B. (1980a) 'Inner city futures', *Transactions, Institute of British Geographers* 5: 1–28.

Berry, B. (1980b) 'Urbanization & counterurbanization in the United States', *Annals, American academy of political & social science*, 451: 13–20.

Berry, B. (1985) 'Islands of renewal in seas of decay' in P. Patersen (ed.) *The new urban reality*, Washington DC: Brooking Institution.

Bertens, H. (1995) *The idea of the postmodern*, London: Routledge.

Best, S. & Kellner, D. (1991) *Postmodern theory*, Basingstoke: Macmillan.

Betz, D. (1972) 'The city as a system generating income equality', *Social Forces* 51: 192–198.

Bhabha, H. (1994) *The location of culture*, London: Routledge.

Bhaskar, R. (1978) *A realist theory of science*, Brighton: Harvester.

Bhaskar, R. (1979) *The possibility of naturalism*, Brighton: Harvester.

Bhaskar, R. (1986) *Scientific realism & human emancipation*, London: Verso.

Bienefeld, M. (1995) 'Structural adjustment & the prospects for democracy in Southern Africa', in D. Moore & G. Schhmitz (eds) *Debating development discourse*, Basingstoke: Macmillan.

Billinge, M. (1977) 'In search of negativism', *Journal of historical geography* 3: 55–67.

Billinge, M., Gregory, D. & Martin, R. (1984) 'Reconstructions', in M. Billinge, D. Gregory & R. Martin (eds) *Recollections of a revolution*, London: Macmillan.

Bilsborrow, R. (1987) 'Population pressures & agricultural development in developing countries', *World Development* 15: 183–203.

Bilsborrow, R. & Ogendo, O. (1992) 'Population-driven changes in land use in developing countries', *Ambio* 21: 37–45.

Binns, T (1994) *Tropical Africa*. London: Routledge.

Binns, T. (ed.) (1995) *People & environment in Africa*, Chichester, Wiley.

Blacksell, M., Economides, K. & Watkins, C. (1991) *Justice outside the city*, Harlow: Longman.

Blaikie, P. & Brookfield, H. (1987) *Land degradation & society*, London: Routledge.

Blake, G. (1994) 'The Spratly Islands', in T. Unwin (1994) (ed.) *Atlas of world development*, Chichester: Wiley.

Blakemore, M. (1981) 'Economic man', in R. Johnston, D. Gregory, P. Haggett, D. Smith, D. Stoddart (eds) *The dictionary of human geography*, Oxford: Blackwell, 1st edn.

Bleaney, M. (1994) 'Economic liberalisation in Eastern Europe', *World Economy* 17: 497–507.

Block, F. (1977) *The origins of international economic disorder*, Berkeley: University of California Press.

Bloomquist, L. & Summers, G. (1982) 'Organization of production & community income distributions', *American Sociological Review* 47: 325–338.

Blowers, A. (1983) 'Master of fate or victim of circumstance – the exercise of corporate power in environmental decision-making', *Policy & Politics* 11: 393–415.

Boal, F. & Livingstone, D. (eds) (1989) *The behavioural environment*, London: Routledge.

Bodman, A. (1991) 'Weavers of influence', *Transactions, Institute of British Geographers* 16: 21–27.

Bodman, A. (1992) 'Holes in the fabric', *Transactions, Institute of British Geographers* 17: 108–109.

Bondi, L. (1991) 'Gender divisions & gentrification', *Transactions, Institute of British Geographers* 16: 190–198.

Bondi, L. (1992) 'Gender symbols & urban landscapes', *Progress in Human Geography* 16: 157–170.

Bondi, L. (1999) 'On the journeys of the gentrifiers', in P. Boyle & K. Halfacree (eds) *Migration & gender in the developed world*, London: Routledge.

Bonnell, V. (1998) *Iconography of power*, Berkeley, California: University of California Press.

Booth, D. (1985) 'Marxism & development sociology', *World Development* 13: 761–787.

Booth, D. (1993) 'Development research', in F. Schuurman (ed.) *Beyond the impasse*, London: Zed Books.

Booth, D. (ed.) (1994) *Rethinking social development*, Harlow: Longman.

Borchardt, K. (1991) *Perspectives on modern German economic history & policy*, Cambridge: Cambridge University Press.

Boserup, E. (1965) *The conditions of agricultural growth*, London: Allen & Unwin.

Boserup, E. (1985) 'Economic & demographic interrelationships in sub-Saharan Africa', *Population & Development Review* 11, 3: 383–98.

Boserup, E. (1990) 'Population, the status of women & rural development', in G. McNicoll & M. Cain (eds) *Rural development & population*, Oxford: Oxford University Press.

Bourdieu, P. (1984) *Distinction*, London: Routledge & Kegan Paul.

Bourdieu, P. (1988) *Homo academicus*, Cambridge: Cambridge University Press.

Bourne, L. (1993) 'The myth & reality of gentrification', *Urban studies* 30: 183–189.

Bowlby, S., Lewis, J., McDowell, L. & Foord, J. (1989) 'The geography of gender', in R. Peet & N. Thrift (eds) *New models in geography, volume 2*, London: Unwin Hyman.

Bowler, I. (2000) 'Rural alternatives', in P. Daniels, M. Bradshaw, D. Shaw & J. Sidaway (eds) *Human geography*, Harlow: Prentice Hall.

Braden, K. & Shelley, F. (2000) *Engaging Geopolitics*, Harlow: Longman.

Bradley, D. (1990) 'Regeneration through sport', *The Planner* 76: 23.

Bradley, J. E., Kirby, A. M. & Taylor, P. J. (1978) 'Distance decay & dental decay', *Regional Studies* 12: 529–540.

Brass, T. (1995) 'Old conservatism in new clothes', *Journal of Peasant Studies* 22: 516–540.

Brenner, R. (1976) 'Agrarian class structure & economic development in pre-industrial Europe', *Past & Present* 70: 30–75.

Brenner, R. (1977) 'The origins of capitalist development', *New Left Review* 104: 25–92.

Brenner, R. (1982) 'The agrarian roots of European capitalism', *Past & Present* 97: 16–113.

Bretherton, C. & Vogler, J. (1999) *The European Union as global actor,* London: Routledge.

Breuilly, J. (1993) *Nationalism & the state*, Manchester: Manchester University Press, 2nd edn.

Brietbar, M. (1975) 'Impressions of an anarchist landscape', *Antipode* 7: 44–49; 154–164.

Brietbar, M. (1981) 'Peter Kropokin, the anarchist in geographer', in D. Stoddart (ed.) *Geography, ideology & social concern*, Oxford: Basil Blackwell.

Brittan, S. (1989) 'The Thatcher government's economic policy', in D. Kavanagh & A. Seldon (eds) *The Thatcher effect*, Oxford: Clarendon.

Britton, S. (1991) 'Recent trends in the internationalisation of the New Zealand economy', *Australian Geographical Studies*, 29, 1: 3–25.

Britton, S., Le Heron, R. & Pawson, E. (eds) (1992) *Changing places*, Christchurch: New Zealand Geographical Society.

Brody. (1973) *Inishkillane*, London: Allen Lane.

Brohmann, J. (1995) 'Universalism, eurocentrism, & ideological bias in development studies', *Third World Quarterly* 16: 121–140.

Brookfield, H. C. (1969) 'On the environment as perceived', *Progress in Geography* 1: 51–80.

Brookfield, H., Potter, L., Byron, Y. (1995) *In place of the forest,* New York: United Nations Press.

Brown, E. (1996) 'Deconstructing development', *Journal of Historical Geography* 22, 3: 333–339.

Brown, L. (1991) 'Global resource scarcity is a serious problem', in M. Polesetsky (ed.) *Global resources* San Diego: Greenhaven Press.

Brown, L. (1994) 'Facing food insecurity', in Brown, L. *et al.* (eds) *State of the world*, London: Earthscan.

Brownill, S. (1990) *Developing London's docklands,* London: Paul Chapman.

Buber, M. (1957) 'Distance & relation', *Pyschiatry* 20: 97–104.

Buchan, D. (1993) *Europe*, Aldershot: Dartmouth Publishing.

Budd, L. (1997) 'Regional integration & convergence & the problems of fiscal & monetary systems', *Regional Studies* 31: 559–570.

Bull, H. (1977) *The anarchical society*, London: Macmillan.

Buller, H. & Hoggart, K. (1986) 'Non decision-making & community power', *Progress in Planning* 25: 133–203.

Bulpitt, J. (1983) *Territory & power in the United Kingdom*, Manchester: Manchester University Press.

Bunce, M. (1994) *The countryside ideal*, London: Routledge.

Burgess, E. (1924) 'The growth of the city', *American Sociological Society* 18: 85–97.

Burgess, E. (1925) 'The growth of the city', in R. Park & E. Burgess & R. McKenzie (eds) *The city*, Chicago: University of Chicago Press.

Burnett, A. (1985) 'Urban political processes & resource allocation', in M. Pacione (ed.) *Progress in Political Geography*, London: Croom Helm, 177–215.

Burnley, I. (1988) 'Population turnaround & peopling the countryside?', *Australian Geographer* 19: 268–283.

Burton, I. (1963) 'The quantitative revolutiuon & theoretical geography', *Canadian Geographer* 7: 151–162.

Buss, T. & Yancer, L. (1996) 'Privatizing the Russian economy', *Environment & Planning C* 14: 211–225.

Butler, J. (1993) *Bodies that matter*, London: Routledge.

Butler, T. (1997) *Gentrification & the middle classes*. Aldershot, Ashgate.

Butler, T. & Hamnett, C. (1994) 'Gentrification, class, & gender', *Environment & Planning D* 12: 477–493.

Buttimer, A. (1976) 'Grasping the dynamism of the lifeworld', *Annals, Association of American Geographers* 66: 277–92.

Buttimer, A. (1978) 'Charisma & context', in D. Ley & M. Samuels (eds) *Humanistic geography*, London: Croom Helm.

Button, J. (ed.) (1976) *The Shetland way of oil*, Sandwick: Thuleprint.

Buxton, T., Chapman, P. & Temple, P. (eds) (1994) *Britain's economic performance*, London: Routledge.

Cable, V. & Ferdinand, P. (1994) 'China as an economic giant', *International Affairs* 70: 243–261.

Cain, M. (1982) 'Perspectives on family & fertility in developing countries', *Population Studies* 36: 159–176.

Caldwell, J. (1976) 'Fertility & household economy in Nigeria', *Journal of Comparative Family Studies* 7: 193–254.

Caldwell, J. (1982) *Theory of fertility decline*, New York: Academic Press.

Callari, A. & Ruccio, D. (eds) (1996) *Postmodern materialism & the future of Marxist theory*, Hanover: Wesleyan University Press/University Press of New England.

Campbell, B. (1993) *Goliath* London: Methuen.

Cannadine, D. (1990) *The decline & fall of the British aristocracy*, New Haven: Yale University Press.

Cant, G. & O'Neil, A. (eds) (1989) *Towards a land-use policy for rural New Zealand*, Wellington: Department of Lands & Survey.

Carnap, R. (1935) *Philosophy & logical syntax*, London: K. Paul, Tench, Trubner.

Casson, M. (1986) *Multinationals & world trade*, London: Allen & Unwin.

Castells, M. (1977) *The urban question*, London: Edward Arnold.

Castells, M. (1998) *End of millennium, volume III*, Oxford: Blackwells.

Castells, M. & Murphy, K. (1982) 'Cultural identity & urban structure' in I. Fainstein & S. Fainstein (eds) *Urban policy under capitalism*, Beverly Hills: Sage.

Castree, N. (1994) 'Teaching history, philosophy & theory', *Journal of Geography in Higher Education* 18: 33–42.

Castree, N. & Braun, B. (2001) (eds) *Social nature* Oxford: Blackwell.

Cater, J. & Jones, T. (1989) *Social geography*, London: Edward Arnold.

Caulfield, J. (1994) *City form & everyday life*, Toronto: University of Toronto Press.

Cavalcanti, M. (1992) 'Totalitarian states & their influence on city-form', *Journal of Architectural & Planning Research* 9: 275–86.

Cavalcanti, M. (1997) 'Urban reconstruction & autocratic regimes', *Planning Perspectives* 12: 71–109.

Centre for Maori Studies & Research (1986) *Rotowaro opencast coalmine technical report on Maori cultural & spiritual values*, Hamilton: Centre for Maori Studies & Research, University of Waikato.

Chalmers, A. & Joseph, A. (1997) 'Population dynamics & settlement systems', *New Zealand Geographer* 53: 14–21.

Chalmers, A. & Joseph, A. (1998) 'Rural change & the elderly in rural places', *Journal of Rural Studies*, 14: 155–165.

Champion, A. (1989) *Counterurbanization*, London: Edward Arnold.

Champion, A. (1994) 'Population change & migration in Britain since 1981', *Environment & Planning A* 26: 1501–1520.

Champion, A. & Congdon, P. (1992) 'Migration trends for the South', in J. Stillwell, P. Rees & P. Boden (eds) *Migration processes & patterns, volume 2*, London: Belhaven.

Champion, T. & Watkins, C. (1991) 'Introduction', in T. Champion & C. Watkins (eds) *People in the countryside*, London: Paul Chapman.

Chaney, D. (1994) *The cultural turn*, London: Routledge.

Chayanov, A. (1986) *The theory of the peasant economy* Madison: University of Wisconsin Press.

Cheshire, P. (1993) *European integration & regional responses, Single European Market Initiative working paper 1*, London: National Institute of Economic & Social Research.

Cheshire, P. & Hay, D. (1989) *Urban problems in Western Europe*, London: Unwin Hyman.

Child, J. (1988) *Antarctica & South American geopolitics*, New York: Praeger.

Chisholm, M. (1971) 'Geography & the question of relevance', *Area* 3: 65–68.

Chisholm, M. (1975) *Human geography*, Harmondsworth: Penguin Books.

Chouinard, V. & Fincher, R. (1983) 'A critique of "Structural Marxism & Human Geography"', *Annals, Association of American Geographers* 73: 137–46.

Christaller, W. (1966) *Central places in Southern Germany*, Englewood Cliffs, New Jersey: Prentice Hall.

Christensen, K. (1982) 'Geography as a human science', in P. Gould & G. Olsson (eds) *A search for common ground*, London: Pion.

Clark, D. (2000) 'World urban development', *Geography* 85, 1: 15–23.

Clark, E. (1991) 'On gaps in gentrification theory', *Housing Studies* 7: 16–26.

Clark, E. (1992) 'On blindness, centrepieces & complementarity in gentrification theory', *Transactions, Institute of British Geographers* 17: 358–362.

Clark, G. (1992) "Real' regulation', *Environment & Planning D* 24: 615–27.

Clarke, D. (1997) *The cinematic city* London: Routledge.

Clark, G. & Dear, M. (1978) 'The future of radical geography', *Professional Geographer* XXX: 356–359.

Clark, G., Gertler, M. & Whiteman, J. (1986) *Regional dynamics*, Boston: Allen & Unwin.

Clark, M. (1994) 'The Antarctic Environmental Protocol', in T. Princen & M. Finger (eds) *Environmental NGOs in world politics*, London: Routledge.

Clark, U. (1976) 'The cyclical sensitivity of employment in branch & parent plants', *Regional Studies* 10: 293–298.

Clarke, D. & Doel, M. (1994a) 'The perfection of geography as an aesthetic disappearance', *Ecumene* 1: 317–23.

Clarke, D. & Doel, M. (1994b) 'Transpolitical geography', *Geoforum* 25: 505–524.

Clarke, D., Doel, M. & McDonough, F. X. (1996) 'Holocaust topologies', *Political Geography* 15: 457–489.

Cleary, M. & Eaton, P. (1995) *Borneo*, Singapore: Oxford University Press.

Cleary, M. & Eaton, P. (1996) *Tradition & reform*, Kuala Lumpur: Oxford University Press.

Cleland, J. & Wilson, C. (1987) 'Demand theories of fertility transition', *Population Studies* 41: 5–30.

Clemenson, H. (1982) *English Country Houses & Landed Estates*, London: Croom Helm.

Clifford, J. (1992) 'Travelling cultures', in L. Grossberg, C. Nelson & P. Triechler (eds) *Cultural studies*, London: Routledge.

Cloke, P. (1985) 'Counter-urbanization – a rural perspective', *Geography* 70: 13–23.

Cloke, P. (1986) 'Observations on policies for rural communities in New Zealand', *New Zealand Geographer* 42: 2–10.

Cloke, P. (1989) 'State deregulation & New Zealand's agricultural sector', *Sociologia Ruralis* 29: 34–48.

Cloke, P. (ed.) (1992) *Policy & change in Thatcher's Britain*, Oxford: Pergamon.

Cloke, P. (1994) 'Agricultural deregulation', in P. Lowe, Marsden, T. & S. Whatmore (eds) *Regulating agriculture*, London: Fulton.

Cloke, P. (1996a) 'Looking through European eyes?', *Sociologia Ruralis* 36: 307–330.

Cloke, P. (1996b) 'Rural lifestyles', *Economic Geography*, 7: 433–449.

Cloke, P. (1999) 'Self-other', in P. Cloke, P. Crang & M. Goodwin (eds) *Introducing human geographies*, London: Arnold.

Cloke, P. & Goodwin, M. (1992) 'Conceptualizing countryside change', *Transactions, Institute of British Geographers* 17: 321–336.

Cloke, P. & Little, J. (eds) (1997) *Contested countryside cultures*, London: Routledge.

Cloke, P. & Perkins, H. C. (1998) 'Representations of adventure tourism in New Zealand', *Environment & Planning D* 16: 185–218.

Cloke, P., Crang, P. & Goodwin, M. (eds) (1999) *Introducing human geographies*, London: Arnold.

Cloke, P., Milbourne, P. & Thomas, C. (1996) 'The English National Forest', *Transactions, Institute of British Geographers* 21: 552–571.

Cloke, P., Milbourne, P. & Thomas, C. (1997) 'Living lives in different ways?', *Transactions, Institute of British Geographers* 22: 210–230.

Cloke, P., Milbourne, P. & Thomas, C. (1994) *Lifestyles in Rural England*, London: Rural Development Commission.

Cloke, P., Phillips, M. & Thrift, N. (1998) 'Class, colonisation & lifestyle strategies in Gower', in M. Boyle & K. Halfacree (eds) *Migration to rural areas*, London: Wiley.

Cloke, P., Philo, C. & Sadler, D. (1991) *Approaching human geography*, London: Paul Chapman.

Clout, H. D. (1986) *Regional variations in the European Community*, Cambridge: Cambridge University Press.

Coal Corp (1994) Advertisement, *North & South Magazine*, 102, September.

Coates, B., Johnston, R. & Knox, P. (1977) *Geography & inequality*, Oxford: Oxford University Press.

Cochrane, A. (1995) 'Global worlds & worlds of difference', in J. Anderson, C. Brook & A. Cochrane (eds) *Global world?*, Oxford: Oxford University Press.

Cochrane, A. & Jonas, A. (1999) 'Re-imagining Berlin', *European Urban & Regional Studies* 6: 145–64.

Cohen, P. (1996) 'Out of the melting pot & into the fire next time', in S. Westwood & J. Williams (eds) *Imagining cities*, London: Routledge.

Cohen, S. (1973) *Geography & politics in a world divided*, New York: Oxford Univeristy Press, 2nd edn.

Cohen, S. (1982) 'A new map of global geopolitical equilibrium', *Political Geography Quarterly* 2: 223–241.

Cohen, S. (1991) 'The emerging world map of peace', in N. Kliot & S. Waterman (eds) *The political geography of conflict & peace*, London: Belhaven.

Collingwood, R. (1956) *The idea of history*, Oxford: Oxford Univerity Press.

Commoner, B. (1988) 'Rapid population growth & environmental stress', paper presented to the United Nations Expert Group on Consequences of Rapid Population Growth, 24–26 August. New York, United Nations, mimeo.

Connelly, J. & Smith, G. (1999) *Politics & the environment*, London: Routledge.

Connor, S. (1989) *Postmodernist culture*, Oxford: Blackwell.

Cook, D. (1985) *Rotowaro*, Waikato: Waikato Museum of Art & History.

Cook, D. & Phillips, M. (forthcoming) 'Spiralling, travelling & haunting ruralities: images and voices of Rotowaro, New Zealand', in P. Cloke & M. Phillips *Representing rural culture*, London: Arnold

Coombes, B. & Campbell, H. (1996) 'Pluriactivity in (and beyond?) a regulationist crisis', *New Zealand Geographer* 52: 11–17.

Cooper, F. & Packard, R. (eds) (1997) *International development & the social sciences,* Berkeley: University of California Press.

Coppock, J. T. (1974) 'Geography & public policy', *Transactions, Institute of British Geographers* 63: 1–16.

Corbridge, S. (1986) *Capitalist world development*, Basingstoke: Macmillan.

Corbridge, S. (1989) 'Marxism, post-Marxism & the geography of development', in R. Peet & N. Thrift (eds) *New models in geography, volume 1*, London: Unwin Hyman.

Corbridge, S. (1990) 'Post-Marxism & development studies', *World Development* 18: 623–639.

Corbridge, S. (1993) *Debt & development*, Oxford: Blackwell.

Corbridge, S. (1993) 'Marxisms, modernities & moralities', *Environment & Planning D* 11: 449–472.

Corbridge, S. (1998) 'Beneath the pavement only soil', *Journal of Development Studies* 34: 138–148.

Cosgrove, D. & Domosh, M. (1992) 'Author & authority", in T. Barnes & J. Duncan (eds) *Writing worlds*, London: Routledge.

Cosgrove, D. & Daniels, S. (1988) 'Introduction', in D. Cosgrove & S. Daniels (eds) *Iconography & landscape*, Cambridge: Cambridge University Press.

Cosgrove, D., Roscoe, B. & Rycroft, S. (1996) 'Landscape & identity at Ladybower Reservoir & Ruttland Water', *Transactions, Institute of British Geographers* 23: 534–551.

Couclelis, H. (1991) 'Requirements for planning relevant GIS', *Papers in Regional Science,* 70: 9–19.

Couclelis, H. & Golledge, R. (1983) 'Analytic research, positivism & behavioural geography', *Annals, Association of American Geographers* 73: 331–339.

Cowen, M. & Shenton, R. (1996) *Doctrines of development*, London: Routledge.

Cox, K. & Jonas, A (1993) 'Urban development, collective consumption & metropolitan fragmentation', *Political Geography* 12: 8–37.

Cox, R. (1987) *Production, power & world order*, New York: Columbia University Press.

Crampton, R. (1994) *Eastern Europe in the twentieth century – & after*, London: Routledge. 2nd edn.

Crang, M. (1998) *Cultural geography*, London: Routledge.

Crang, M., Crang, P. & May, J. (eds) (1999) *Virtual geographies*, London: Routledge.

Crang, P. (1997) 'Cultural turns & (re)constitution of economic geography', in R. Lee & J. Wills (eds) *Geographies of economies*, London: Arnold.

Crenson, M. (1971) *The un-politics of air pollution*, Baltimore: Johns Hopkins University Press.

Cresswell, T. (1996) *In place/out of place*, Minneapolis: University of Minnesota Press.

Cromwell, E. & Winpenny, J. (1993) 'Does economic reform harm the environment?', *Journal of International Development* 5: 623–649.

Crosby, A. (1986) *Ecological imperialism,* Cambridge: Cambridge University Press.

Crush, J. (1991) 'The discourse of progressive human geography', *Progress in Human Geography* 15: 395–414.

Crush, J. (ed.) (1995) *Power of development*, London: Routledge.

Curry, M. (1991) 'Postmodernism, language & the strains of modernism', *Annals, Association of American Geographers* 81: 210–228.

Dahl, R. (1961) *Who governs?*, New Haven, Connecticut: Yale University Press.

Daniels, P., Bradshaw, M., Shaw, D. & Sidaway, J. (eds) (2001) *Human geography*, Harlow: Prentice Hall.

Daniels, S. (1993) *Fields of vision*, Cambridge: Polity.

Dankelman, I. & Davidson, J. (1988) *Women & environment in the Third World*, London: Earthscan.

Danta, D. (1993) 'Ceausescu's Bucharest', *Geography Review* 83: 170–82.

Danziger, J. (1996) *Understanding the political world*, White Plains: Longman.

Dasgupta, P. & Maler, K. G. (1990) *The environment & emerging development issues. Development Economics Research Programme, DEP No. 28* London: London School of Economics, STICERD Centre.

Davey, J. & Kearns, R. (1994) 'Special needs versus the "level playing field"', *Journal of Rural Studies* 10: 73–82.

Davis, M. (1991) *City of quartz,* London: Vintage.

Dawson, A. H. (1999) 'From glittering icon to …', *The Geographical Journal* 165: 154–60.

Day, G. (1998) 'A community of communities?', *The Economic & Social Review*, 29: 233–257.

Day, G. & Murdoch, J. (1993) 'Locality & community', *Sociological Review* 41: 82–111.

De Certeau, M. (1984) *The practice of everyday life*, Berkeley: University of California Press.

De Lauretis, T. (1991) 'Queer theory', *Differences* 3: 1–10.

Dean, K., Brown, B., Oery, R. & Shaw, D. (1984) 'The conceptualisation of counter-urbanisation', *Area* 16: 9–14.

Dear, M. (2000) *The postmodern urban condition*, Oxford: Blackwell.

Dear, M. & Wolch, J. (1987) *Landscapes of despair*, Princeton, NJ: Princeton University Press.

Deleuze, G. (1990) *Expressionism in philosophy*, New York: Zone.

Deleuze, G. & Guattari, F. (1987) *A thousand plateaus*, Mineapolis: University of Minnesota Press.

Derrida, J. (1976) *Of Grammatology*, Baltimore, Maryland: Johns Hopkins University Press.

Deutsche, R. (1991) 'Boys town', *Environment & Planning D* 9: 5–30.

Di Stefano, C. (1990) 'Dilemmas of difference', in L. Nicholson (ed.) *Feminism/postmodernism*, London: Routledge.

Diamond, D. (1991) 'Managing urban change' in R. Bennett & R. Estall (eds) *Global change & challenge*, London: Routledge.

Diamond, D. (1991) 'The City, the "Big Bang" & office development', in K. Hoggart & D. Green (eds) *London* London: Edward Arnold.

Dicken, P. (1992) *Global Shift*, London: Paul Chapman.

Dicken, P., Forsgren, M. & Malmberg, A. (1994) 'The local embeddedness of transnational corporations', in A. Amin & N. J. Thrift (eds) *Globalisation, institutions & regional development*, Oxford: Oxford University Press.

Dilnot, A. & Stark, G. K. (1986) 'The distributional consequences of Mrs Thatcher', *Fiscal Studies* 7: 48–53.

Dingsdale, A. (1999) 'Redefining "Eastern Europe"', *Geography* 84: 204–22.

Dodds, K. (1997) 'Classics in human geography revisited, commentary 1', *Progress in Human Geography* 21: 555–557.

Dodds, K. (2000) *Geopolitics in a changing world*, Harlow: Prentice-Hall.

Dodds, K. & Atkinson, D. (eds) (2000) *Geopolitical traditions*, London: Routledge.

Dodge, M. & Kitchen, R. (2000) *Mapping cyberspace*, London: Routledge.

Doel, M. (1993) 'Proverbs for paranoids', *Transactions of the Institute of British Geographers* 18: 377–94.

Doel, M. (1994) 'Something resists', in P. Cloke, M. Doel, D. Matless, M. Phillips & N. Thrift *Writing the rural*, London: Paul Chapman.

Doel, M. (1996) 'A hundred thousand lines of flight', *Environment & Planning D* 14: 421–439.

Doel, M. (1999) *Poststructuralist geographies*, Edinburgh: Edinburgh University Press.

Doel, M. & Clarke, D. (1999) 'Dark panoptican', *Environment & Planning D* 17: 427–450.

Domhoff, G. (1978) *Who Really Rules?*, New Brunswick, New Jersey: Transaction Press.

Donaghu, M. & Barff, R. (1990) 'Nike just did it ', *Regional Studies* 24: 537–552.

Douglas, M. (1966) *Purity & danger*, London: Routledge & Kegan Paul.

Downs, R. & Stea, D. (eds) (1973) *Image & environment*, Chicago: Aldine.

Dreyfus, H. & Rabinow, P. (1982) *Michael Foucault*, Chicago: University of Chicago.

Driver, F. (1992) 'Geography's empire', *Environment & Planning D* 10: 23–40.

Duff, A. (1994) *Once were warriors*, Auckland: Tamden Press.

Dunbar, G. S. (1981) 'Elisée Reclus, an anarchist in geography', in D. Stoddart (ed.) *Geography, ideology & social concern*, Oxford: Basil Blackwell.

Duncan, J. (1978) 'The social construction of unreality', in D. Ley & M. Samuels (eds) *Humanistic geography*, London: Croom Helm.

Duncan, J. (1990) *The city as text*, Cambridge: Cambridge University Press.

Duncan, J. & Ley, D. (1982) 'Structural Marxism & human geography', *Annals, Association of American Geographers* 72: 30–59.

Duncan, J. & Ley, D. (1993) 'Introduction', in J. Duncan & D. Ley (eds) *Place/culture/ representation,* London: Routledge.

Duncan, S. (1979) 'Radical geography & Marxism', *Area* 11: 124–126.

Duncan, S. (1989) 'What is locality', in R. Peet & N. Thrift (eds) *New models in geography, volume 2,* London: Unwin Hyman.

Dunford, M. (1990) 'Theories of regulation', *Environment & Planning D*, 8: 297–321.

Dunford, M. (1993) 'Regional disparities in the European Community: evidence from the REGIO databank', *Regional Studie*s 27: 727–743.

Dunford, M. & Fielding, A. J. (1997) 'Greater London, the South-East Region & the wider Britain', in H. Blotevogel & A. Fielding (eds) *People, jobs & mobility in the new Europe*, Chichester: Wiley.

Dunford, M. & Perrons, D. (1994) 'Regional identity, regimes of accumulation & economic development in contemporary Europe', *Transactions of the Institute of British Geographers* 19: 163–182.

Dunham, P. & Healey, M. (1994) 'Changing competitive advantage in a local economy', *Urban Studies* 31: 1279–1301.

Dunleavy, P. J. (1981) *The politics of mass housing in Britain 1945–75*, Oxford: Clarendon.

Dunleavy, T. (1999) *New Zealand television drama*, Unpublished PhD thesis, University of Auckland, Auckland.

Dunn, J., Urmson, J. & Ayer, A. (1992) *The British empiricists*, Oxford: Oxford Univerity Press.

Dyson, T. (1996) *Population & food*, London: Routledge.

Dwyer, D. (ed.) (1989) *South East Asian development*, London: Longman.

Economist, The (1990) 'With all her faults she is my country still: the state of the nation-state', *The Economist* 22 December: 73–78.

Edwards, C. (1999) 'Current economic trends in Asia & the Pacific', in Europa (ed.) *The Far East & Australasia 1999*, London: Europa Publications, 30th edn.

Edwards, J. & Batley, R. (1978) *The politics of positive discrimination*, London: Tavistock.

Edwards, M. (1989) 'The irrelevance of development studies', *Third World Quarterly* 11: 116–36.

Edwards, M. (1994) 'Rethinking social development', in D. Booth (ed.) *Rethinking social development*, Harlow; Longman.

Ehrensaft, P. & Armstrong, W. (1978) 'Dominion capitalism', *Australian & New Zealand Journal of Sociology* 14: 352–363.

Ehrlich, P. (1968) *The population bomb*, New York: Ballantine.

Ehrlich, P. & Erhlich, A. (1990) *The population explosion,* London: Arrow.

Eltis, W., Fraser, D. & Ricketts, M. (1992) 'The lessons for Britain from the superior economic performance of Germany & Japan', *National Westminster Bank Quarterly Review*, February: 2–22.

Engels, F. (1975) *The condition of the working class in England in 1844*, Moscow: Progress (first published, 1844).

Entrikin, J. (1976) 'Contemporary humanism in geography', *Annals, Association of American Geographers* 66: 615–632.

Entrikin, J. N. (1981) 'Philosophical issues in the scientific study of regions', in D. Herbert & R. Johnston (eds) *Geography & the urban environmnent*, Chichester: John Wiley.

Entrikin, J. (1989) 'Introduction', in J. Entrikin & S. Brunn (eds) *Reflections on Richard Hartshorne's* The Nature of Geography, Washington DC: Association of American Geographers.

Escobar, A. (1995) *Encountering development,* Princeton: Princeton University Press.

Escobar, A. (1997) 'Anthropology & development', *International Social Science Journal* 154: 497–515.

Esteva, G. (1987) 'Regenerating people's space', *Alternatives* 10: 125–152.

European Commission (1996) *First report on economic & social cohesion*, Luxembourg: Office for Official Publications of the European Communities.

European Commission Directorate-General for Economic & Financial Affairs (1996) *European economy: economic evaluation of the internal market 1996*, Luxembourg: Office for Official Publications of the European Communities.

European Commission Directorate-General for Regional Policy & Cohesion (1996) *Structural funds 1994* Brussels: Inforegio Information Sheet 15.

Fainstein, S. S. (1994) *The city builders*, Oxford: Blackwell.

Fairburn, M. (1989) *The ideal society & its enemies*, Auckland: Auckland University Press.

Fairclough, N. (1992) *Discourse & social change*, Cambridge: Polity Press.

Fairweather, J. (1992) *Agrarian restructuring in New Zealand*, Agribusiness & economics research unit, Lincoln University.

Fairweather, J. (1995) 'Changes in the age of farmers in New Zealand, 1971–1991', *New Zealand Geographer*, 51: 24–27.

Featherstone, M. (1991) *Consumer culture & postmodernism*, London: Sage.

Fellmann, J., Getis, A. & Getis, J. (1997) *Human geography*, Boston: WCB/McGraw-Hill, 5th edn.

Ferguson, J. (1990) *The anti-politics machine* Cambridge: Cambridge University Press.

Ferkai, A. (1992) 'Stalinist architecture', in P. György & T. Hedvig (eds) *Art & society in the age of Stalin*, Budapest: Corvina Books.

Fielding, A. (1982) 'Counterurbanisation in western Europe', *Progress in Planning* 17: 1–52.

Fielding, A. (1990) 'Counterurbanisation', in D. Pinder (ed.) *Western Europe*, London: Belhaven.

Finger, M. (1994) 'Environmental NGOs in the UNCED process', in T. Princen & M. Finger (eds) *Environmental NGOs in world politics*, London: Routledge.

Fischer, M. & Marcus, G. (1986) *Anthropology as cultural critique*, Chicago: University of Chicago Press.

Fish, R. & Phillips, M. (1999) 'Explorations in media country', in A. Ferjoux (ed.) *Environment et nature dans le campagnes*, Nantes: CNRS.

Fisher, C. A. (1964) *South-East Asia*, London: Methuen.

Fiske, J. (1992) 'British cultural studies & television', in R. C. Allen (ed.) *Channels of discourse, reasembled*, London: Routledge.

Fitzgerald, W. (1946) *The new Europe,* London: Methuen, 2nd edn.

Floyd, K. (1988) 'It's a waste', *Waikato Times* 5 November, Section 2, p. 1.

Foord, J. & Gregson, N. (1986) 'Patriarchy', *Antipode* 18: 186–211.

Foote, K., Tóth, A. & Árvay, A. (2000) 'Hungary after 1989', *Geographical Review* 90: 301–34.

Forbes, D. (1987) *The geography of underdevelopment,* London: Routledge.

Forbes, D. (1999) 'Towards the Pacific century', in Europa (ed.) *The Far East & Australasia 1999*, London: Europa Publications, 30th edn.

Forest, B. (1995) 'West Hollywood as symbol', *Environment & Planning D* 13: 133–157.

Foresta, R. (1992) 'Amazonia & the politics of geopolitics', *Geographical Review* 82: 128–142.

Forrest, R. & Gordon, D. (1995) *People & places*, Bristol: University of Bristol School for Advanced Urban Studies.

Fortes, M. (1949) *Social structure*, Oxford: Clarendon Press.

Foster, J. (1997) 'In defense of history', in E. Meiksins Wood & J. Foster (eds) *In defense of history*, New York: Monthly Review.

Foster-Carter, A. (1978) 'The modes of production controversy', *New Left Review* 107: 47–77.

Fothergill, S. & Gudgin, G. (1982) *Unequal growth*, London: Heinemann.

Foucault, M. (1970) *The order of things*, London: Tavistock Publications.

Foucault, M. (1972) *The archaeology of knowledg*e, Andover: Tavistock Publications.

Foucault, M. (1977) *Discipline & punish*, London: Allen Lane.

Foucault, M. (1980) *Power/knowledge*, New York: Vintage Books.

Foucault, M. (1982) 'Interview with Michael Foucault on space, knowledge & power', *Skyline* March: 17–20.

Frank, A. (1966) 'The development of underdevelopment', *Monthly Review* 18: 17–33.

Frank, A. (1969) *Latin America*, New York: Monthly Review.

Frankenberg, R. (1966) *Communities in Britain*, Harmondsworth: Penguin.

Fraser, N. (1989) *Unruly practices*, Cambridge: Polity.

Fraser, N. (1997) *Justice interruptus*, London: Routledge.

Frazer, G. & Lancelle, G. (1994) *Zhirinovsky*, Harmondsworth: Penguin.

Frazer, R. M. (1958) 'Maori land & Maori population in the Far North', *New Zealand Geographer* 14: 19–31.

Freedman, C. (1999) 'Japan: economy', in Europa (ed.) *The Far East & Australasia 1999*, London: Europa Publications, 30th edn.

Frey, W. (1989) 'United States', in A. Champion (ed.) *Counterurbanisation*, London: Edward Arnold.

Friedman, G. & Lebard, M. (1991) *The coming war with Japan,* New York: St. Martin's Press.

Friedman, J. (1977) 'Community action on water pollution', *Human Ecology* 5: 329–353.

Friedmann, H. (1993) 'The political economy of food', *New Left Review* 197: 29–57.

Fröbell, F., Heinrichs, J. & Kreye, O. (1980) *The new international division of labour*, Cambridge: Cambridge University Press.

Frydman, R., Rapaczynski, A. & Earle, J. (1993) *The Privatisation Process in Central Europe*, Prague: CEU Press.

Fugitt, G. (1985) 'The non-metropolitan turnaround', *Annual Review of Sociology* 11: 259–280.

Furuseth, O. (1998) 'Service provision & social deprivation', in B. Ilbery (ed.) *The geography of rural change*, Harlow: Longman.

Gale, L. (1996) 'Defining a "Maori geography"', *New Zealand Journal of Geography* April: 14–20.

Galster, G. & Hill, E. (eds) (1992) *The metropolis in black & white*, New Brunswick: Rutgers University Press.

Galtung, J. (1973) *The European Community*, London: George Allen & Unwin.

Galtung, J. (1979) *The True Worlds,* New York: Free Press.

Gamble, A. (1994) *The free economy & the strong state*, Basingstoke: Macmillan, 2nd edn.

Gauldie, E. (1974) *Cruel habitations*, London: Allen & Unwin.

Geertz, C. (1973) *The interpretation of cultures*, New York: Basic Books.

Geertz, C. (1983) *Local knowledge*, New York: Basic Books.

Gelder, K. & Thornton, S. (1997) *The subcultures reader*, London: Routledge.

Geltmaker, T. (1992) 'The queer nation acts up', *Environment & Planning D* 10, 6: 609–650.

Ghai, D. (1994) 'Structural adjustment, global integration & social democracy', in R. Prendergast & F. Stewart (eds) *Market forces & world development*, Basingstoke: Macmillan.

Ghai, D. & Hewitt de Alcántara, C. (1990) 'The crisis of the 1980s in Africa, Latin America & the Caribbean', in D. Ghai (ed.) *The IMF & the South*, London: Zed Books.

Gibbon, P. (1996) 'Structural adjustment & structural change in sub-Saharan Africa', *Development & Change* 27: 751–784.

Gibson, E. M. W. (1981) 'Realism', in M. Harvey & B. Holly (eds) *Themes in geographical thought*, London: Croom Helm.

Gibson, H. & Tsakalotos, E. (1992) 'The international debt crisis', in T. Hewitt, H. Johnson & D. Wield (eds) *Industrialization & development*, Oxford: Oxford University Press/Open University.

Gibson-Graham, J.-K. (1998) 'Queer(y)ing globalization', in H. J. Nast (ed.) *Places through the body*, London: Routledge.

Giddens, A. (1979) *Central problems in social theory*, London: Macmillan.

Giddens, A. (1981) *A contemporary critique of historical capitalism*, London: Macmillan.

Giddens, A. (1984) *The constitution of society*, Cambidge: Polity.

Giddens, A. (1985) *The nation-state & violence*, Cambridge: Polity.

Giddens, A. (1990) *The consequences of modernity*, Cambridge: Polity Press.

Giddens, A. (1991) *The constitution of society*, Cambridge: Polity, 2nd edn.

Gittings, J. (1982) 'China: half a superpower', in N. Chomsky, J. Steele & J. Gittings (eds) *Superpowers in collision*, Harmondsworth: Penguin.

Glass, R. (1964) *London*, London: MacGibbon & Kee.

Gleick, P. (1994) 'Water, war & peace in the Middle East', in L. Owen & T. Unwin (eds) *Environmental management*, Oxford: Blackwell.

Glenny, M. (1991) 'Germany fans the flames of war', *New Statesman & Society* 20–27 December: 14–15.

Goddard, J. & Smith, I. (1978) 'Change in corporate control in the British urban system 1972–1977', *Environment & Planning A* 10: 1073–1084.

Godlewska, A. & Smith, N. (eds) (1994) *Geography & empire*, Oxford: Blackwell.

Goldthorpe, J. H. (1987) *Social mobility & class structure in modern Britain*, Oxford: Clarendon, 2nd edn.

Golledge, R. & Couclelis, H. (1984) 'Positivist philosophy & research in human spatial behhaviour', in T. F. Saarinen, D. Seamon & J. L. Sell (eds) *Environmental perception & behavior. Department of Geography Research Paper No. 209*, Chicago: University of Chicago.

Golledge, R. & Rushton, G. (1984) 'A review of analytic behavioural geography', in D. T. Herbert & R. Johnston (eds) *Geography & the urban environment, volume 6*, Chichester: John Wiley.

Golledge, R. & Stimson, R. (1987) *Analytical behavioural geography*, London: Croom Helm.

Goodman, D. & Redclift, M. (1991) *Refashioning nature*, London: Routledge.

Goodman, D. & Watts, M. (eds) (1997) *Globalizing food*, London: Routledge.

Goodwin, M. (1995) 'Poverty in the city' in C. Philo (ed.) *Off the map*, London: Child Poverty Action Group.

Gottdiener, M. (1977) *Planned sprawl*, Beverley Hills, California: Sage.

Gottlieb, R. (1992) *Marxism 1844–1990*, London: Routledge.

Gottman, J. (1964) *Megalopolis*, Cambridge, Massachusetts: MIT Press.

Gould, P. (1979) 'Geography 1957–1977', *Annals, Association of American Geographers* 69: 139–151.

Gould, P. & Olsson, G. (eds) (1982) *A search for common ground*, London: Pion.

Gould, P. & White, R. (1974) *Mental maps*, Harmondsworth: Penguin.

Graham, B. (2000) 'The past in place', in B. Graham & C. Nash (eds) *Modern historical geographies,* Essex: Prentice Hall.

Gray, F. (1975) 'Non-explanation in urban geography', *Area* 7: 228–235.

Gray, F. (1979) 'The origins & use of theory in urban geography', *Geoforum* 10: 117–127.

Green, A. (1997) 'Income & wealth', in M. Pacione (ed.) *Britain's cities*, London: Routledge.

Green, D. (1991) 'The metropolitan economy', in K. Hoggart & D. Green (eds) *London,* London: Edward Arnold.

Green, D. (1995) *Silent revolution*, London: Latin America Bureau.

Green, D (1995) *From artisans to paupers*, Aldershot: Scolar Press.

Gregory, D. (1978) *Ideology, science & human geography*, London: Hutchinson.

Gregory, D. (1982a) *Regional transformations & industrial revolution*, London: Macmillan.

Gregory, D. (1982b) 'Solid geometry', in P. Gould & G. Olsson (eds) *A search for common ground*, London: Pion.

Gregory, D. (1989) 'Areal differentiation & post-modern human geography', in D. Gregory & R. Walford (eds) *Horizons in human geography*, London: Macmillan.

Gregory, D. (1994) *Geographical imaginations,* Oxford: Blackwell.

Gregory, D. & Urry, J. (1985) 'Introduction', in D. Gregory & J. Urry (eds) *Social relations & spatial structures*, London: Macmillan.

Guelke, L. (1974) 'An idealist alternative in human geography', *Annals, Association of American Geographers* 64: 193–202.

Guelke, L. (1975) 'On re-thinking historical geography', *Area* 7: 135–138.

Guelke, L. (1977) 'The role of laws in human geography', *Progress in Human Geography* 1: 376–386.

Guelke, L. (1978) 'Geography & logical positivism', in D. Herbert & R. Johnston (eds) *Geography & the urban environment*, London: John Wiley.

Guelke, L. (1981) 'Idealism', in M. Harvey & B. Holly (eds) *Themes in geographical thought*, London: Croom Helm.

Guelke, L. (1982a) 'Historical geography & Collingwood's theory of historical knowing', in A. Baker & M. Billinge (eds) *Period & place*, Cambridge: Cambridge University Press.

Guelke, L. (1982b) *Historical understanding in geography,* Cambridge: Cambridge University Press.

Guelke, L. (1989) 'Intellectual coherence & the foundations of geography', *Professional Geographer* 4: 123–30.

Habermas, J. (1971) *Towards a rational society*, London: Heinemann.

Habermas, J. (1978) *Knowledge & human interests*, London: Heinemann.

Habermas, J. (1983) 'Modernity', in J. Foster (ed.) *The anti-aesthetic*, Port Townsend, Washington.

Habermas, J. (1984) *The theory of communicative action, volume 1,* London: Heinemann.

Habermas, J. (1987a) *The philosophical discourse of modernity*, Cambridge: Polity.

Habermas, J. (1987b) *The theory of communicative action, volume 2,* Cambridge: Polity.

Habermas, J. (1988) *On the logic of the social sciences*, Cambridge: Polity.

Habermas, J. (1989) *The new conservatism*, Cambridge: Polity.

Hadjimichalis, C. (1994) 'The fringes of Europe & EU integration', *European Urban & Regional Studies* 1: 19–30.

Hadjimichalis, C. & Sadler, D. (1995) 'Integration, marginality & the new Europe', in C. Hadjimichalis & D. Sadler (eds) *Europe at the margins*, Chichester: Wiley.

Haggett, P. (1965) *Locational analysis in human geography*, London: Edward Arnold.

Haggett, P. & Chorley, R. (1967) 'Models, paradigms & the new geography', in R. Chorley & P. Haggett (eds) *Models in geography*, London: Methuen.

Halfacree, K. (1993) 'Locality & social representation', *Journal of Rural Studies* 9: 1–15.

Halfacree, K. (1996) 'Out of place in the country', *Antipode* 28: 42–72.

Hall, D. (1984) 'Foreign tourism under socialism', *Annals of Tourism Research* 11: 539–55.

Hall, D. (1990) 'Stalinism & tourism', *Annals of Tourism Research* 17: 36–54.

Hall, P. (ed.) (1966) *Von Thünen's Isolated State*, London: Pergamon.

Hall, P. (1991) 'The British enterprise zones', in R. E. Green (ed.) *Enterprise zones*, Newbury Park, California: Sage.

Hall, P., Breheny, M., McQuaid, R. & Hart, D. (1987) *Western sunrise,* London: Allen & Unwin.

Hall, R. (1935) 'The geographic region', *Annals, Association of American Geographers* 25: 122–130.

Hall, S. (1992) 'The West & the rest', in S. Hall & B. Gieben (eds) *Formations of modernity*, Cambridge: Polity Press/The Open Univeristy/Blackwell.

Hallsworth, A. (1996) 'Short termism & economic restructuring in Britain', *Economic Geography* 72: 23–37.

Hamnett, C. (1973) 'Improvement grants as an indicator of gentrification in Inner London', *Area* 5: 252–261.

Hamnett, C. (1986) 'The changing socio-economic structure of London & the South East 1961–1981', *Regional Studies* 20: 391–405.

Hamnett, C. (1991) 'The blind men & the elephant', *Transactions, Institute of British Geographers* 16: 173–189.

Hamnett, C. (1992) 'Gentrifiers or lemmings?', *Transactions, Institute of British Geographers* 17: 116–119.

Hamnett, C. (1993) 'The spatial impact of the British home ownership market slump, 1989–91', *Area* 25: 217–227.

Hamnett, C. (1996) 'Social polarisation, economic restructuring & welfare state regimes', *Urban Studies* 33: 1407–1430.

Hamnett, C. (1997a) 'A stroke of the Chancellor's pen', *Environment & Planning A* 29: 129–147.

Hamnett, C. (1997b) 'The sleep of reason'. *Environment & Planning D* 15: 127–8.

Hannah, L. (1989) 'Mrs Thatcher, capital-basher?', in D. Kavanagh & A. Seldon (eds) *The Thatcher effect*, Oxford: Clarendon.

Hansen, S. (1992) 'Population & the environment', *African Development Review* 4: 118–64.

Hanson, J. & Gordon, J. (1998) *Antarctic environments & resource,* Harlow: Longman.

Haraway, D. (1988) 'Situated knowledges', *Feminist Studies* 14: 575–599.

Haraway, D. (1990) 'A manifesto for cyborgs', in L. Nicholson (ed.) *Feminism/ postmodernism*, London: Routledge.

Haraway, D. (1991) *Simians, cyborgs & women*, London: Free Association Books.

Harper, S. (1987) 'A humanistic approach to the study of rural populations', *Journal of Rural Studies* 3: 309–19.

Harper, S. (1989) 'The British rural community', *Journal of Rural Studies* 5: 161–84.

Harper, S. (1997) 'Contesting later life', in P. Cloke & J. Little (eds) *Contested countryside culture*, London: Routledge.

Harris, C. (1971) 'Theory & synthesis in historical geography', *Canadian Geographer*, 15: 157–172.

Harris, C. (1978) 'The historical mind & the practice of geography', in D. Ley & M. Samuels (eds) *Humanistic geography*, London: Croom Helm.

Harris, N. (1986) *The end of the Third World*, London: Pelican.

Harris, W. (1993) 'New Zealand in the post Cold-War period', *New Zealand Geographer*, 49: 7–12.

Harrison, C. (1991) *Countryside recreation in a changing society,* London: TMS Partnership.

Harrison, D. & Steinberger, M. (1995) 'Bandits infest China's road to capitalism', *The Observer*, 6 August: 17.

Harrison, P. (1992) 'Getting beyond the question', in ActionAid (ed.) *Lifestyle overload? ActionAid Development Report No. 5*.

Harrison, R. & Livingstone, D. (1979) 'There & back again- towards a critique of idealist human geography', *Area,* 11: 75–9.

Hart, A. (1982) 'The highest form of the geographer's art', *Annals, Association of American Geographers* 72: 1–26.

Hartshorne, R. (1939a) *The nature of geography*, Lancaster, USA: Association of American Geographers.

Hartshorne, R. (1939b) 'The nature of geography', *Annals, Association of American Geographers* 29, 171–658.

Hartshorne, R. (1955) '"Exceptionalism in geography" re-examined', *Annals, Association of American Geographers* 45: 205–44.

Hartshorne, R. (1959) *Perspective on the nature of geography*, Chicago: Rand McNally.

Hartsock, N. (1983) *Money, sex & power,* Boston: North Eastern University Press.

Harvey, D. (1969) *Explanation in geography*, London: Edward Arnold.

Harvey, D. (1972) 'Revolutionary & counter-revolutionary theory in geography & the problem of getto formation', *Antipode* 4: 1–13.

Harvey, D. (1973) *Social justice & the city*, London: Edward Arnold.

Harvey, D. (1974) 'What kind of geography for what kind of public policy?', *Transactions, Institute of British Geographers* 63: 18–24.

Harvey, D. (1982) *The limits to capital*, Oxford: Basil Blackwell.

Harvey, D. (1984) 'On the history & present condition of geography', *Professional Geographer* 36: 1–11.

Harvey, D. (1989) *The condition of postmodernity*, Oxford: Blackwell.

Harvey, D. (1992) 'Postmodern morality plays', *Antipode* 24: 300–26.

Harvey, D. (1993) 'Class relations, social justice & the politics of difference', in M. Keith & S. Pile (eds) *Place & the politics of identity*, London: Routledge.

Harvey, M. & Holly, B. (1981) 'Paradigm, philosophy & geographic thought', in M. Harvey & B. Holly (eds) *Themes in geographic thought*, London: Croom Helm.

Hatch, E. (1992) *Respectable lives*: Berkeley & Los Angeles: University of California Press.

Hauner, M. (1992) *What is Asia to us?*, London: Routledge.

Hayton, K. & Gray, J. (1996) 'The costs of local job creation – lessons from City Challenge' *Town & Country Planning* 65: 21–23.

Heath, C. (1997) 'Spice Girls: too hot to handle', *Rolling Stone* 764/765: 197.

Heidegger, M. (1958) *The question of being,* New York: Twayne.

Heidegger, M. (1962) *Being & time,* New York: Harper & Row.

Heiman, M. K. (1988) *The quiet revolution,* New York: Praeger.

Henderson, W. O. (1959) 'Economic Development, 1815–71, in E. J. Passant (ed.) *A short history of Germany 1815–1945*, Cambridge: Cambridge University Press.

Hepple, L. W. (1992) 'Metaphor, geopolitical discourse & the military in South America', in T. J. Barnes & J. S. Duncan, J. S. (eds) *Writing worlds* London: Routledge.

Herb, G. (1989) 'Persuasive cartography in geopolitik & national socialism', *Political Geography Quaterly* 8: 289–303.

Herb, G. (1997) *Under the map of Germany*, Routledge: London.

Herbert, D. & Johnston, R. (1978) 'Geography & the urban environment', in D. Herbert & R. Johnston (eds) *Geography & the urban environment, volume 1*, London: John Wiley.

Herbert, S. (1997) *Policing Space*, Minneapolis: University of Minnesota Press.

Herod, A. (1991) 'The production of scale in United States labour relations', *Area* 23: 82–88.

Hettne, B. (1995) *Development theory & the Three Worlds*, Harlow: Longman.

Hettner, A. (1905) 'Das system der Wissenschaften', *Preussiche Jahrbücher* 122: 251–77.

Hicke, D. A. & Lee, S.-G. (1994) 'Regional economic impacts of federal R&D by funding source & performer type', *Regional Studies* 28: 619–632.

Higgins, G, Kassam, A., Naiken, L., Fischer, G. & Shah, M. (1982) *Potential population supporting capacities of land in the developing world*, Rome: FAO, UNFPA, IIASA.

Hill, B. (1984) *The Common Agricultural Policy*, London: Methuen.

Hill, R. (1987) 'Global factory & company town: in J. Henderson & M. Castells (eds) *Global restructuring & territorial development*, London: Sage.

Hindess, B. & Hirst, P. (1977) *Modes of production & social formation*, London: Macmillan.

Hirst, P. & Thompson, G. (1996) *Globalization in question*, Oxford: Blackwell.

Hobsbawm, E. J. (1983) 'Mass-producing traditions', in E. Hobsbawm & T. Ranger (eds) *The invention of tradition*, Cambridge: Cambridge University Press.

Hobsbawm, E. J. (1992) *Nations & nationalism since 1780,* Cambridge: Cambridge University Press, 2nd edn.

Hobsbawm, E. J. (1994) *Age of extremes*, London: Michael Joseph.

Hodder, R. (1992) *The West Pacific Rim* London: Bellhaven.

Hoggart, K. (1987) 'Income distributions, labour market sectors & the Goldschmidt hypothesis: the nonmetropolitan USA in 1970 & 1980', *Journal of Rural Studies* 3: 231–245.

Hoggart, K. (1989) 'Variation in intra-city income inequality in the Mid-Atlantic States', *Journal of Urban Affairs* 11: 379–396.

Hoggart, K. (1990) 'Let's do away with rural', *Journal of Rural Studies* 6: 245–57.

Hoggart, K. (1991) *People, Power & Place*, London: Routledge.

Holderness, M. (1994) 'Welcome to the global village', *Geographical Magazine* 66: 16–19.

Holland, S. (1993) *The European imperative*, Nottingham: Spokesman.

Holloway, L. & Hubbard, P. (2001) *People & place*, Harlow: Prentice Hall.

Holloway, S. & Valentine, G. (eds) (2000) *Children's geographies*, London: Routledge.

Holt-Jensen, A. (1999) *Geography*, London: Sage, 3rd edn.

Honneth, A. (1985) 'An aversion to the universal', *Theory, culture & society* 2: 147–57.

hooks, b. (1984) *Feminist theory*, Boston: South End Press.

hooks, b. (1990a) 'Marginality as a site of resistance', in R. Ferguson, M. Gever, M. Trinh & C. West (eds) *Out there*, Cambridge, Massachusetts: MIT Press.

hooks, b. (1990b) *Yearning* New York: Between the Lines.

Horsley, W. & Buckley, R. (1990) *Nippon – new superpower*, London: BBC Books.

Horton, R. E. (1932) 'Drainage basin characteristics', *Transactions, American Geophysical Union*, 13: 350–361.

Horton, R. E. (1933) 'The role of infiltration in the hydrological cycle', *Transactions, American Geophysical Union* 14: 446–460.

Horton, R. E. (1945) 'Erosional development of streams & their drainage basins', *Bulletin of the Geological Society of America* 56: 275–370.

Hoselitz, B. (1960) *Sociological aspects of economic growth*, New York: Free Press.

Houghton, D. (2002a) 'Manifest destiny & Realpolitik', in D. McKay, D. Houghton & A. Wroe (eds) (2002) *Controversies in American politics & society*, Oxford: Blackwell.

Houghton, D. (2002b) 'America as a global economic player', in D. McKay, D. Houghton & A. Wroe (eds) (2002) *Controversies in American politics & society*, Oxford: Blackwell.

Howkins, A. (1991) *Reshaping rural England*, London: Harper Collins Academic.

Hoy, D. (1986) 'Introduction', in D. Hoy (ed.) *Foucault*, Oxford: Blackwell.

Hoy, D. & McCarthy, T. (1994) *Critical theory*, Oxford: Blackwell.

Hubbard, P. (1997) 'Red-light districts & toleration zones' *Area* 27: 129–140.

Hubbard, P., Kitchin, R., Bartley, B. & Fuller, D. (2002) *Thinking geographically*, London: Continuum.

Hudson, R. (1989) *Wrecking a region*, London: Pion.

Hughes, A. (1997) 'Rurality & "cultures of womanhood"', in P. Cloke & J. Little (eds) *Contested countryside cultures*, London: Routledge.

Hugill, B. (1997) 'Britain's exclusion zone', *The Observer* 13 April: 29.

Hugo, G. (1994) 'The turnaround in Australia', *Australian Geographer* 25: 1–17.

Hugo, G. & Bell, M. (1998) 'The hypothesis of welfare-led migration to rural areas', in P. Boyle & K. Halfacree (eds) *Migration into rural* areas, London: Wiley.

Hugo, G. & Smailes, P. (1985) 'Urban-rural migration in Australia', *Journal of Rural Studies* 1: 11–30.

Hugo, G. & Smailes, P. (1992) 'Population dynamics in rural Australia', *Journal of Rural Studies* 8: 29–52.

Hunt, D. (1989) *Economic theories of development,* London: Harvester/Wheatsheaf.

Hunter, F. (1953) *Community power structure*, Chapel Hill: University of North Carolina Press.

Hurd, K. & Woodward, R. (1991) 'Some ideas of qualitative data & its use in understanding 'deprivation' in rural areas', *Rural lifestyles project research report*, Lampeter.

Husserl, E. (1965) *Phenomenology & the crisis of philosophy*, New York: Harper & Row.

Hutton, W. (1996) *The state we're in*, revised edn, London: Vintage.

Hymer, S. (1975) 'The multinational corporation & the law of uneven development', in H. Radice (ed.) *International firms & modern imperialism*, Harmondsworth: Penguin, 37–62.

Idriss, A, (1990) *Malaysia's new economic policy,* Petaling Jaya: Pelanduk Publications.

Ignatieff, M. (1993) *Blood & belonging*, London: BBC Books/Chatto & Windus.

IMF (1994) *World economic outlook*, Washington D.C.: International Monetary Fund.

Imrie, R. & Thomas, H. (1993) *British urban policy & the urban development corporations*, London: Paul Chapman.

Ingham, G. (1984) *Capitalism Divided?* Basingstoke: Macmillan.

Inglot, T. (1995) 'The politics of social policy reform in post-communist Poland', *Communist & Post-Communist Studies* 28: 361–373.

Jackson, C. (1993) 'Environmentalisms & gender interests in the Third World', *Development & Change* 24: 649–677.

Jackson, P. (1989) *Maps of meaning*, London: Unwin Hyman.

Jackson, P. & Smith, S. (1984) *Exploring social geography*, London: Allen & Unwin.

Jacobs, J. M. (1996) *Edge of empire*, London: Routledge.

Jaeger, C. & Dürrenberger, G. (1991) Services & counterurbanization', in P. W. Daniels (ed.) *Services & metropolitan development*, London: Routledge.

James, P. E. (1952) 'Towards a fuller understandinng of the regional concept', *Annals, Association of American Geographers* 42: 195–222.

James, S. (1990) 'Is there a 'place' for children in geography', *Area* 22: 378–383.

Jameson, F. (1972) *The prison-house of language*, Princeton, New Jersey: Princeton University Press.

Jameson, F. (1985) 'Postmodernism & consumer society', in H. Foster (ed.) *Postmodern culture*, London: Pluto Press.

Jameson, F. (1991) *Postmodernism, or the cultural logic of late capitalism*, London: Verso.

Jeffrey, C. (1996) 'Towards a 'third level' in Europe?', *Political Studies* 44: 253–266.

Jenkins, R. (1987) *Transnational corporations & uneven development:* London: Methuen.

Jess, P. & Massey, D. (1995) 'The contestation of place', in D. Massey & P. Jess (eds) *A place in the world?,* Oxford: Oxford University Press.

Jessop, B. (1990) 'Regulation theories in retrospect & prospect', *Economy & Society*, 19: 153–216.

Joekes, S. *et al.* (1994) 'Gender, environment & population', *Development & Change* 25: 137–165.

Johnson, K. & Beale, C. (1995) 'The rural rebound revisited', *American dempographics*, July: 46–54.

Johnson, N. (2000) 'Historical geographies of the present', in B. Graham & C. Nash (eds) *Modern historical geographies*, Harlow: Prentice Hall.

Johnston, R. (1978) 'Paradigms & revolutions or evolutions', *Progress in Human Geography* 2: 189–206.

Johnston, R. (1979a) *Geography & geographers*, London: Edward Arnold.

Johnston, R. (1979b) 'The spatial impact of fiscal changes in Britain', *Environment & Planning A* 11: 1439–1444.

Johnston, R. (1981) 'The political element in suburbia', *Geography* 66: 286–296.

Johnston, R. (1982) *The American urban system*, London: Longman.

Johnston, R. (1983a) *Geography & geographers*, London: Edward Arnold.

Johnston, R. (1983b) *Philosophy & human geography*, London: Edward Arnold.

Johnston, R. (1984a) 'A foundling floundering in world three', in M. Billinge, D. Gregory & R. Martin (eds) *Recollections of a revolution*, London: Macmillan.

Johnston, R. (1984b) 'The world is our oyster', *Transactions, Institute of British Geographers* 9: 443–59.

Johnston, R. (1997) *Geography & geographers*, London: Edward Arnold.

Johnston, R. J., Gregory, D. J. & Smith, D. M. (eds) (1994) *The dictionary of human geography*, Oxford: Blackwell, 3rd edn.

Johnson, R. J., Gregory, D., Pratt, G. & Watts, M. (eds) (2000) *The dictionary of human geography*, Oxford: Blackwell, 4th edn.

Jolly, C. (1993) 'Population change, land use & the environment', *Reproductive Health Matters* 1: 13–25.

Jones, O. (1997) 'Little figures, big shadows', in P. Cloke & J. Little (eds) *Contested countryside*, London: Routledge.

Jones, O. (1999) 'Tomboy tales', *Gender, Place & Culture* 6: 117–136.

Jones, P. & North, J. (1991) 'Japanese motor industry transplants', *Economic Geography* 67: 105–123.

Joseph, A. & Chalmers, A. (1994) 'Servicing seniors in rural areas', in D. Hawke (ed.) *Proceedings, New Zealand Geographical Society & the Australian Institute of Geographers Conference*, Christchurch: New Zealand Geographical Society.

Joseph, A. & Chalmers, A. (1995) 'Growing old in place', *Health & Place* 1: 79–90.

Joseph, A. & Chalmers, A. (1998) 'Coping with rural change', *New Zealand Geographer* 54: 28–36.

Joseph, A. & Kearns, R. (1996) 'Deinstitutionalization meets restructuring', *Health & Place* 2: 179–189.

Junas, D. (1995) 'Rise of the citizen militias', *Covert Action Quarterly* 52: 20–25.

Kain, R. (1993) The Savoy Cadaster, 1728–38', in P. Barber & C. Board (eds) *Tales from the map room*, London: BBC Books.

Kaiser, R. J. (1997) 'Nationalism & Identity', in M. J. Bradshaw (ed.) *Geography & transition in the post-Soviet republics*, Chichester: Wiley.

Kaplan, A. (1988) *Postmodernism & its discontents*, New York: Verso.

Kaplan, A. (1992) 'Feminist criticism & television', in R. C. Allen (ed.) *Channels of discourse, reasembled*, London: Routledge.

Kaplan, D. (1994) 'Two nations in search of a state', *Annals of the Association of American Geographers* 84: 585–606.

Kasarda, J. (1990) 'Structural factors affecting the location & timing of urban under-class growth', *Urban Geography* 11: 234–264.

Kay, C. (1989) *Latin American theories of development & underdevelopment*, London: Routledge.

Kearns, R. (1997) 'Constructing (bi)cultural geographies', *New Zealand Geographer* 53: 3–8.

Kearns, R. & Joseph, A. (1997) 'Restructuring health & rural communities in New Zealand', *Progress in Human Geography* 21: 18–32.

Kearns, R. & Reinken, J. (1994) 'Out for the count?', *New Zealand Population Review* 20: 19–30.

Keith, M. & Pile, S. (eds) (1993) *Place & the politics of identity*, London: Routledge.

Kellener, C. M. (1992) 'The new Germany', in P. B. Stares (ed.) *The new Germany & the new Europe*, Washington: Brookings Institute.

Kellner, D. (1988) 'Postmodernism as social theory', *Theory, Culture & Society* 5: 239–70.

Kennedy, P. (1988) *The rise & fall of the great powers*, New York: Random House.

Kennedy, P. (1993) *Preparing for the twenty-first century*, London: Harper-Collins.

Kettell, B. & Magnus, G. (1986) *The international debt game,* London: Graham & Trotman.

Kiely, R. (1995) *Sociology & development*. London: UCL Press.

Kiely, R. (1998a) 'Introduction' in R. Kiely & P. Marfleet (eds) *Globalisation & the Third World,* London: Routledge.

Kiely, R. (1998b) 'Neo-liberalism revised?', *Capital & Class* 64: 63–88.

Kiely, R. & Marfleet, P. (eds) (1998) *Globalisation & the Third World*, London: Routledge.

Kimble, G. (1951) 'The inadequacy of the regional concept', in L. Stamp & S. Wooldridge (eds) *London essays in geography*, London: Longmans Green.

King, M. (1985) *Being Pakeha*, Auckland: Hodder & Stoughton.

King, R (1987) *Italy*, London: Paul Chapman.

King, T. (1993) 'Politik pembangunan', *Global Ecology & Biogeography Letters* 3: 235–44.

King, T. (1994) 'The Sociology of South-East Asia', *Bijdragen Tot de Taal-, Land- en Volkenkunde* 3: 171–206.

King, T. & Parnwell, M. (eds) (1990) *Margins & minorities*, Hull; Hull University Press.

Kinsman, P. (1995) 'Landscape, race & national identity', *Area* 27: 300–10.

Kirk, W. (1952) 'Historical geography & the concept of the behavioural environ-ment', *Indian Geographical Journal* 25: 152–160.

Kirk, W. (1963) 'Problems of geography', *Geography* 48: 357–371.

Kliot, N. & Waterman, S. (eds) *The political geography of conflict & peace*, London: Belhaven.

Knight, H. (1981) *New Zealand photographers: a selection,* Dunedin: Allied Press Ltd.

Knopp, L. (1990a) 'Exploiting the rent gap' *Urban Geography* 11: 48–64.

Knopp, L. (1990b) 'Some theoretical implications of gay involvement in an urban land market', *Political Geography Quarterly* 9: 337–352.

Knox, P. (1987) *Urban social geography,* Harlow: Longman.

Knox, P. & Agnew, J. (1989) *The geography of the world economy*, London: Edward Arnold.

Kontuly, T. (1998) 'Contrasting the counterurbanisation experience in European nations', in P. Boyle & K. Halfacree (eds) *Migration into rural areas*, London: Wiley.

Kornai, J. (1992) *The Socialist system – the political economy of Communism*, Princeton: Princeton University Press.

Kotler, P., Haider, D. H. & Rein, I. (1993) *Marketing places*, New York: Free Press.

Kroeber, A. L. (1948) *Anthropology*, New York: Harcourt, Brace & Co.

Krushelnycky, A. & Kink, R. (1993) 'Zhirinovsky's sabre-rattling revives dreams of empire', *The European* 188: 17–23.

Kuhn, T. (1962) *The structure of scientific revolutions*, Chicago: University of Chicago Press.

Kuhn, T. (1970a) 'Logic of discovery or pyschology of research?', in I. Lakatos & A. Musgrave (eds) *Criticism & the growth of knowledge*, Cambridge: Cambridge University Press.

Kuhn, T. (1970b) *The structure of scientific revolutions*, Chicago: University of Chicago Press.

Kuznets, S. (1955) 'Economic growth & income inequality', *American Economic Review* 45: 1–28.

Laclau, E. (1971) 'Feudalism & capitalism in Latin America', *New Left Review* 67: 19–38.

Lakatos, I. (1970) 'Falsification & the methodology of scientific research programmes', in I. Lakatos & A. Musgrave (eds) *Criticism & the growth of knowledge*, Cambridge: Cambridge University Press.

Larner, W. (1998) 'Hitching a ride on the tiger's back', *Environment & Planning D*, 16: 599–614.

Larrain, J. (1986) *A reconstruction of historical materialism*, London: Allen & Unwin.

Larrain, J. (1989) *Theories of development*, Cambridge: Polity Press.

Lash, S. & Urry, J. (1994) *Economies of signs & space*, London: Sage.

Latouche, S. (1993) 'In the wake of the affluent society', in D. Lehmann (1990) *Democracy & development in Latin America,* Cambridge: Polity Press.

Latour, B. (1987) *Science in action*, Cambridge, Massachusetts: Harvard University Press.

Latour, B. (1993) *We have never been modern,* London: Harvester Wheatsheaf.

Lauria, M. & Knopp, L. (1985) 'Towards an analysis of the role of gay communities in the urban remaissance', *Urban Geography* 6: 152–169.

Law, C. (1981) *The defence sector in British regional development, Department of Geography Discussion paper 17*, Salford: University of Salford.

Law, J. (1992) 'Notes on the theory of the actor-network', *Systems Practice* 5: 379–393.

Law, J. (1994) *Organizing modernity*, Oxford: Blackwell.

Law, R., Campbell, H. & Schick, R. (1999) 'Introduction', in R. Law, H. Campbell & J. Dolan (eds) *Masculinities in Aotearoa/New Zealand*, Palmerston North: Dunmore Press.

Le Heron, R. (1991) 'New Zealand agriculture & changes in the agriculture-finance relation during the 1980's', *Environment & Planning A* 23: 1653–1670.

Le Heron, R. (1993) *Globalized agriculture* Oxford: Pergamon.

Le Heron, R. & Pawson, E. (eds) (1996) *Changing place*, Auckland: Longmann Paul.

Le Heron, R., Murphy, L., Forer, P. & Goldstone, M. (1999) *Explorations in human geography: encountering place*, Oxford: Oxford University Press.

LeDonne, J. (1997) *The Russian empire & the world 1700–1917*, Oxford: Oxford University Press.

Lees, L. & Berg, L. (1995) 'Ponga, glass & concrete', *New Zealand Geographer* 51: 32–41.

Lefebvre, H. (1991) *The production of space*, Oxford: Blackwell.

Leigh, R. & North, D. J. (1978) 'Acquisitions in British industries', in F. E. I. Hamilton (ed.) *Contemporary industrialisation*, London: Longman.

Lele, U. & Stone, S. J. (1989) *Population pressure, the environment & agricultural intensification: variations on the Boserup hypothesis, MADIA discussion paper No. 4*, Washington DC: The World Bank.

Lenin, V. (1956) *The development of capitalism in Russia* (Moscow: Foreign Languages Publishing House).

Lévi-Strauss, C. (1953) 'Social structure', in A. Kroeber (ed.) *Anthropology today*, Chicago: University of Chicago Press.

Lévi-Strauss, C. (1960) 'On manipulated sociological models', *Bijdragen tot de taal-land- en volkenkunde* 116: 45–54.

Lévi-Strauss, C. (1973) *Totemism*, Harmondsworth: Penguin.

Lewis, G. (1979) *Rural communities*, Newton Abbot: David & Charles.

Lewis, G. & Maund, D. (1976) 'The urbanisation of the countryside', *Geografiska Annaler* 58b: 17–27.

Lewis, J. & Williams, A. (1989) 'No longer Europe's best-kept secret, *Geography* 74: 170–172.

Lewis, O. (1961) *The children of Sanchez*, New York: Random House.

Ley, D. (1974) *The black inner city as frontier outpost*, Washington: Association of American Geographers.

Ley, D. (1977) 'Social geography & the taken-for-granted world', *Transactions, Institute of British Geographers* 2: 498–512.

Ley, D. (1980) 'Liberal ideology & the post-industrial city', *Annals, Association of American Geographers* 70: 238–258.

Ley, D. (1982) 'Rediscovering man's place', *Transactions, Institute of British Geographers* 7: 248–253.

Ley, D. (1986) 'Alternative explanations for inner city gentrification', *Annals, Association of American Geographers* 76: 521–535.

Ley, D. (1987) 'Reply: the rent gap revisited', *Annals, Association of American Geographers* 77: 465–468.

Ley, D. (1988) 'Interpretative social research in the inner city', in J. Eyles (ed.) *Research in human geography*, Oxford: Blackwell.

Ley, D. (1989a) 'Fragmentation, coherence, & limits to theory in human geography', in A. Kobayashi & S. MacKenzie (eds) *Remaking human geography,* London: Unwin Hyman.

Ley, D. (1989b) 'Modernism, postmodernism & the struggle for place', in J. Agnew & J. Duncan (eds) *The power of place,* Boston: Unwin Hyman.

Ley, D. (1993) 'Can there be a postmodernism of resistance in the urban landscape', in P. Knox (ed.) *The restless urban landscape*, Englewood Cliffs, New Jersey: Prentice Hall.

Ley, D. (1996) *The new middle class & the remaking of the central city*, Oxford: Oxford University Press.

Ley, D. & Duncan, J. (1993) 'Epilogue', in J. Duncan & D. Ley (eds) *Place/culture/representation*, London: Routledge.

Ley, D. & Samuels, M. (1978) 'Introduction', in D. Ley & M. Samuels (eds) *Humanistic geography*, London: Croom Helm.

Ley, D., Hiebert, D. & Pratt, G. (1992) 'Time to grow up?' in G. Wynn & T. Oke (eds) *Vancouver & its region,* Vancouver: UBC Press.

Leys, C. (1986) 'The formation of British capital', *New Left Review* 160: 114–120.

Leys, C. (1996) *The rise & fall of development theory*, London: James Currey.

Li, F. (1995) 'Corporate networks & the spatial & functional reorganizations of large firms', *Environment & Planning A* 27: 1627–1645.

Liepins, R. (1996) 'Reading agricultural power', *New Zealand Geographer* 52: 3–10.

Liepins, R. (2000) 'New energies for an old idea', *Journal of Rural Studies* 16: 23–35.

Liepins, R. & Bradshaw, M. (1999) 'Neo-liberal agricultural discourse in New Zealand: economy, culture & politics linked', *Sociologia Ruralis* 39: 563–581.

Light, D. (2000) 'Gazing on communism', *Tourism Geographies* 2: 157–76.

Light, D. & Phinnemore, D. (1998) 'Teaching 'transition' in Central & Eastern Europe through fieldwork', *Journal of Geography in Higher Education* 22: 185–99.

Limb, M., Matthews, H. & Vujakovic, P. (1995) 'Disabling countryside', in M. Talbot & A. Tomlinson (eds) *Policy & politics in sport, physical education & leisure*, London: Leisure Studies Association.

Lipietz, A. (1985) *The enchanted world*, London: Verso.

Lipietz, A. (1987) *Mirages & miracles*, London: New Left Books.

Little, J. (1997) 'Employment marginality & self-identity', in P. Cloke & J. Little (eds) *Contested countryside cultures*, London: Routledge.

Little, J. & Austin, P. (1996) 'Women & the rural idyll', *Journal of Rural Studies* 12: 101–11.

Livingstone, D. (1992) *The geographical tradition*, Oxford: Blackwell.

Lo, L. & Teixeira, C. (1998) 'If Quebec goes ... the "exodus" impact?', *Professional Geographer* 50: 481–498.

Long, N. & Van der Ploeg, J. (1994) 'Heterogeneity, actor & structure', in D. Booth (ed.) *Rethinking social development*, Harlow: Longman.

Long, N. & Long, A. (eds) (1992) *Battlefields of knowledge*, London: Routledge.

Long, N. & Villarreal, M. (1993) 'Exploring development interfaces', in F. Schuurman (ed.) *Beyond the impasse,* London: Zed Books.

Longhurst, R. (1994) 'Reflections on & a vision for feminist geography', *New Zealand Geographer* 50: 14–19.

Longhurst, R. (2000) *Bodies*, London: Routledge.

Longhurst, R. & Wilson, C. (1999) 'Heartland Wainuiomata', in R. Law, H. Campbell & J. Dolan (eds) *Masculinities in Aotearoa/New Zealand*, Palmerston North: Dunmore Press.

Lord, J. D. (1992) 'Geographic deregulation of the US banking industry & spatial transfers of corporate control', *Urban Geography* 13: 25–48.

Lorentzon, S. (1995) 'The use of ITC in TNCs', *Regional Studies* 29: 673–685.

Luckerman, F. (1989) 'The Nature of Geography', in J. Entrikin & S. Brunn (eds) *Reflections on Richard Hartshorne's* The Nature of Geography, Washington DC: Association of American Geographers.

Lyotard, J.-F. (1984) *The postmodern condition*, Manchester: Manchester University Press.

MacEwan, C. (2001) 'Geography, culture & global change', in P. Daniels, M. Bradshaw, D. Shaw & J. Sidaway (eds) *Human geography*, Harlow: Prentice Hall.

MacKay, P. (1984) *Rural health & related social issues in New Zealand*. Northland Community College.

Mackinder, H. (1919) *Democratic ideals & reality*, London: Constable.

Mackinder, H. (1907) *Britain & the British seas*, Oxford: Clarendon.

Maclean, M. (1995) 'Privatisation in France 1993–94', *West European Politics* 18: 273–290.

MacNaghten, P. & Urry, J. (1998) *Contested natures*, London: Sage.

Mair, A. (1986) 'Thomas Kuhn & understanding geography', *Progress in Human Geography* 10: 345–370.

Mair, A. (1992) 'Just in time manufacturing & the spatial structure of the automobile industry', *Tijdschrift voor Economische en Sociale Geografie* 83: 82–92.

Malthus, T. R. (1888) *An Essay on the Principle of Population*. London, Reeves & Turner, 9th edn (Originally published 1798).

Mann, M. (1984) 'The autonomous power of the state', *European Journal of Sociology* 25: 185–213.

Mann, M. (1986) *The sources of power, volume 1*, Cambridge: Cambridge University Press.

Mann, S. (1990) *Agrarian capitalism,* Durham: University of North Carolina Press.

Mannion, T. & Whitelegg, J. (1979) 'Radical geography & Marxism', *Area* 11: 122–124.

Marchand, M. & Parpart, J. (eds) (1995) *Feminism/postmodernism/development,* London: Routledge.

Marchena Gómez, M. J. (1995) 'New tourism trends & the future of Mediterranean Europe', *Tijdschrift voor Economische en Sociale Geografie* 86: 21–31.

Marcuse, H. (1964) *One dimensional man*, London: Routledge & Kegan Paul.

Markusen, A. (1981) 'City spatial structure, women's household work, & national urban policy', in C. Stimpson, E. Dixler, M. Nelson & K. Yatrakis (eds) *Women & the American city*, Chicago: Chicago University Press.

Markusen, A. R. (1985) *Profit cycles, oligopoly & regional development*, Cambridge, Massachusetts: MIT Press.

Marshall, J. N. (1988) *Services & uneven development*, Oxford: Oxford University Press.

Marshall, J. N. & Raybould, S. (1993) 'New corporate structure & the evolving geography of white collar work', *Tijdschrift voor Economische en Sociale Geografie* 84: 362–377.

Martin, D. (1996) *Geographical information systems*, London: Routledge.

Martin, R. L. (1995) 'Income & poverty inequalities across regional Britain', in C. Philo (ed.) *Off the map*, London: Child Poverty Action Group.

Martinussen, J. (1997) *Society, state & market:* London: Zed Books.

Marx, K. (1970) *Capital, volume 3* London: Lawrence & Wishart.

Marx, K. (1973) *Grundrisse*, Harmondsworth: Penguin.

Marx, K. (1976) *Capital, volume 1*, Harmondsworth: Penguin.

Marx, K. & Engels, F. (1970) *The German ideology*, London: Lawrence & Wishart.

Marx, K. & Engels, F. (1971) *Manifesto of the Communist Party*, Moscow: Moscow Publishers.

Massey, D. (1984) *Spatial divisions of labour*, London: Macmillan.

Massey, D. (1986) 'The legacy lingers on', in R. Martin & B. Rowthorn (eds) *The geography of de-industrialisation*, Basingstoke: Macmillan.

Massey, D. (1991) 'A global sense of place', *Marxism Today* June: 24–29.

Massey, D. (1995) *Spatial divisions of labour,* Basingstoke: Macmillan, 2nd edn.

Massey, D. (1996) 'Space/Power, Identity/Difference'', in A. Merrifield & E. Swyngedouw (eds) *The urbanisation of injustice*, Oxford: Blackwell.

Massey, D., Allen, J. & Sarre, P. (1999) *Human geography today*, Cambridge: Polity.

Masterman, M. (1970) 'The nature of a paradigm', in I. Lakatos & A. Musgrave (eds) *Criticism & the growth of knowledge*, Cambidge: Cambridge University Press.

Matahaere-Atariki, D. (1999) 'A context for writing masculinites', in R. Law, H. Campbell, & J. Dolan (eds) *Masculinities in Aotearoa/New Zealand*, Palmerston North: Dunmore Press.

Marten, G. (2001) *Human ecology*, London: Earthscan.

Mather, I. (1994) 'Zhirinovsky redraws the map of Europe', *The European* 195, 4–10.

Matless, D. (1995) '"The art of right living"', in S. Pile & N. Thrift (eds) *Mapping the subject*, London: Routledge.

Matless, D. (1998) *Landscape & Englishness*, London: Reaktion.

Mattelart, A. (1994) *Mapping world communication*, Minneapolis: University of Minnesota Press.

Matthews, H. & Limb, M. (1999)'Defining an agenda for the geography of children', *Progress in Human Geography* 23: 76–90.

McAleavey, P. (1995) 'European Regional Development Fund expenditure in the UK', *European Urban & Regional Studies* 2: 249–253.

McCarthy, C., Rodriguez, A., Buendia, E., Meacham, S., David, S., Godina, H., Supriya, K. & Wilson-Brown, C. (1997) 'Danger in the safety zone', *Cultural Studies* 11: 274–295.

McCarthy, T. (1987) 'Introduction', in J. Habermas (ed.) *The philosophical discourse of modernity*, Cambridge: Cambridge University Press.

McCarthy, T. (1991) *Ideals & illusions*, London: MIT.

McClean, R., Berg, L. & Roche, M. (1997) 'Responsible geographies', *New Zealand Geographer* 53: 9–15.

McCormick, J. (1999) *Understanding the European Union*, Basingstoke: Macmillan.

McCormick, T. (1989) *America's half-century*, Oxford: Oxford University Press.
McCutcheon, M. (1995) 'The tax incentives applying to US corporate investment in Ireland', *Economic & Social Review* 26: 149–171.
McDowell, L. (1986) 'Beyond patriarchy', *Antipode* 18: 311–321.
McDowell, L. (1989) 'Women, gender, & the organisation of space', in D. Gregory & R. Walford (eds) *Horizons in human geography*, London: Macmillan.
McDowell, L. (1991a) 'The baby & the bathwater', *Geoforum* 22: 123–133.
McDowell, L. (1991b) 'Life without father & Ford', *Transactions, Institute of British Geographers* 16: 400–419.
McDowell, L. (1992) 'Multiple voices', *Antipode* 24: 56–72.
McDowell, L. (1993) 'Space, place & gender relations', *Progress in human geography* 17: 157–179; 305–318.
McDowell, L. (1995a) 'Body work', in D. Bell & G. Valentine (eds) *Mapping desire*, London: Routledge.
McDowell, L. (1995b) 'Understanding diversity', in R. Johnson, P. Taylor & M. Watts (eds) *Geographies of global change* Oxford: Blackwell.
McDowell, L. (1997a) *Capital culture*, Oxford: Blackwell.
McDowell, L. (1997b) 'A tale of two cities', in R. Lee & J. Wills (eds) *Geographies of economies*, London: Arnold.
McDowell's (1997c) *Undoing place?*, London: Arnold.
McGranahan, D. A. (1980) 'The spatial structure of income distribution in rural regions', *American Sociological Review* 45: 313–324.
McKinnon, M. (1997) 'Native policy', in M. McKinnon (ed.) *New Zealand historical atlas: Ko Papatuanuku e Takoto Nei*, Auckland: David Bateman
McKinnon, M., Biggs, M. & Simpson, A. (1997) 'The colony in 1874', in M. McKinnon (ed.) *New Zealand historical atlas: Ko Papatuanuku e Takoto Nei*, Auckland: David Bateman.
McMan, D. (2001) *Whatiwhatihoe*, Wellington: Huia Publishers.
McRobbie, A. (1993) 'Shut up & dance', *Cultural Studies*, 7: 406–426.
Meadows, D., Meadows, D., Randers, J. & Behrens, W. (1972) *The limits to growth*, New York: Universe Books.
Meinig, D. (1983) 'Geography as art', *Transactions, Institute of British Geographers* 8: 314–328.
Mephan, J. (1973) 'The structuralist sciences & philosophy', in D. Robey (ed.) *Structuralism*, Oxford: Oxford University Press.
Mercer, D. (1984) 'Unmasking technocratic geography', in M. Billinge, D. Gregory & R. Martin (eds) *Recollections of a revolution*, London: Macmillan.
Mercer, D. & Powell, J. M. (1972) *Phenomenology & related non-positivistic approaches in the social sciences*, Department of Geography, Monash University.
Meredith, M., Wade, I., McDonagh, E. & Heywood, K. (2000) 'Managing the Oceans', on T. O'Riordan (ed.) *Environmental science for environmental management,* Harlow: Prentice-Hall, 2nd edn.
Mestrovic, S. (1994) *The Balkanization of the West,* London: Routledge.
Michalski, A. & Wallace, H. (1992) *The European Community* London: Royal Institute of International Affairs.
Mills, C. (1986) 'Life on the upslope', *Environment & Planning D* 6: 169–189.

Mills, C. (1993) 'Myths & meanings of gentrification', in J. Duncan & D. Ley (eds) *Place/culture/representation*, London: Routledge.

Mills, C. W. (1959) *The sociological imagination*, New York: Oxford University Press.

Milward, A. (1992) *The European rescue of the nation-state*, London: Routledge.

Mintor, K. (2000) The Palace of Science & Culture. Warsaw Voice OnLine, http://www.warsawvoice.com.pl/v611Buzz18.html

Mitchell, D. (2000) *Cultural Geography*, Oxford: Blackwell.

Mohan, G. (1994) 'Destruction of the con', *Area* 2: 387–90.

Mohan, G. (1997) 'Developing differences', *Review of African Political Economy* 24: 311–328.

Mohan, J. (ed.) (1989) *The political geography of contemporary Britain*, Basingstoke: Macmillan.

Moon, G. & Atkinson, R. (1997) 'Ethnicity', in M. Pacione (ed.) *Britain's cities*, London: Routledge.

Moore, C. (1990) 'Displacement, partnership & privatization', in D. King & J. Pierre (eds) *Challenges to local government*, London: Sage.

Moore, D. (1995) 'Development discourse as hegemony: towards an ideological history – 1945–1995', in D. Moore & G. Schhmitz (eds) *Debating development discourse*, Basingstoke: Macmillan.

Moore, D. & Schhmitz, G. (eds) (1995) *Debating development discourse*, Basingstoke: Macmillan.

Morril, R. (1969/1970) 'Geography & the transformation of society', *Antipode* 1 (1): 6–9 & (2): 4–10.

Morril, R. (1984) 'Recollections of the 'quantitative revolution's early years', in M. Billinge, D. Gregory & R. Martin (eds) *Recollections of a revolution*, London: Macmillan.

Mortimore, M. & Tiffen, M. (1995) 'Population & environment in time perspective', in T. Binns (ed.) *People & environment in Africa*, Chichester: John Wiley.

Mountjoy, A. (1982) *Industrialization & developing countries*, London: Hutchinson.

Mouzelis, N. (1988) 'Sociology of development', *Sociology* 22: 23–44.

Muir, R. (1978) 'Radical geography or a new orthodoxy', *Area* 10: 322–327.

Muir, R. (1979) 'Radical geography & Marxism', *Area* 11: 126–127.

Murdoch, J. (1995a) 'Actor-networks & the evolution of economic forms', *Environment & Planning A* 27: 731–57.

Murdoch, J. (1995b) 'Middle class territory?', *Environment & Planning A* 27: 1213–1230.

Murdoch, J. & Day, G. (1998) 'Middle class mobility, rural communities & the politics of exclusion', in P. Boyle & K. Halfacree (eds) *Migration into rural areas*, London: Wiley.

Murdoch, J. & Marsden, T. (1994) *Reconstituting rurality,* London: UCL Press.

Murdoch, J. & Pratt, A. (1993) 'Rural studies', *Journal of Rural Studies* 9: 411–27.

Murdoch, J. & Pratt, A. (1994) 'Rural studies of power & the power of rural studies', *Journal of Rural Studies* 10: 83–87.

Murphy, A. (1995) 'Economic regionalization & Pacific Asia', *Geographical Review* 85: 127–140.

Murton, B. (1979) 'Waituhi: ', *New Zealand Geographer* 35: 24–33.

Muscat, R. (1985) 'Carrying capacity & population growth', in D. Mahar (ed.) *Rapid Population Growth & Human Carrying Capacity Staff Working Paper 690*, Washington DC: The World Bank.

Mykolenko, L., de Raymond, Th. & Henry, P. (1987) *The regional impact of the Common Agricultural Policy in Spain & Portugal*, Luxembourg: Office for Official Publications of the European Communities.

Myrdal, G. (1962) *Challenges to affluence*, New York: Pantheon.

Nagel, E. (1962) *The structure of science*, New York: Harcourt, Brace & World.

Nash, C. & Graham, B. (2000) 'The making of modern historical geographies', in B. Graham & C. Nash (eds) *Modern historical geographies*, Essex: Prentice Hall.

Nash, D. (1979) 'The rise & fall of an aristocratic tourist culture Nice, 1763–1936', *Annals of Tourism Research* 6: 61–75.

Nast, H. & Pile, S. (eds) (1998) *Places through the body*, London: Routledge.

Naylon, J. (1981) 'Spain, Portugal & the EEC', *Bank of London & South America Review* 15: 122–130.

Naylon, J. (1992) 'Ascent & decline in the Spanish regional system', *Geography* 77: 46–62.

Nevitt, A (1978) 'Issues in housing', in R. Davies & P. Hall (eds) *Issues in urban society*, Harmondsworth: Penguin.

Newby, H. & Buttel, F. (1980) 'Towards a critical rural sociology', in F. Buttel & H. Newby (eds) *The rural sociology of advanced societies*, London: Croom Helm.

Newby, H. (1977) *The deferential worker*, London: Allen Lane.

Newton, K. (1978) 'Conflict avoidance & conflict suppression', in K. Cox (ed.) *Urbanization & conflict in market societies*, London: Methuen.

Nicholson, L. (ed.) (1990) *Feminism/postmodernism*, London: Routledge.

Ó Tuathal, G. & Dalby, S. (eds) (1998) *Rethinking geopolitics*, London: Routledge.

Ó Tuathal, G. (1999) *Critical geopolitics*, Minneapolis: Minnesota University Press.

Oatley, N. (1995) 'Competitive urban policy & the regeneration game', *Town & Country Planning* 66: 1–14.

O'Connor, J. (1973) *The fiscal crisis of the state*, New York: St. Martin's.

O'Connor, J. (1997) *Natural causes*, London: Guilford.

Ofosu, A. & Philleo, W. (eds) (1992) *Proceedings of the Global Assembly of Women & the Environment: partners in life, volume II*, Washington DC: United Nations Environment Programme & WorldWIDE Network.

O'Hagan, S. (1990) 'Pop's high priest of sex', *Sunday Correspondent*.

Oke, T., North, M. & Slaymaker, O. (1992) 'Primordial to prim order' in G. Wynn & T. Oke (eds) *Vancouver & its region*, Vancouver: UBC Press: 149–170.

O'Loughlin, J. & van der Wusten, H. (1990) 'Political Geography of panregions', *Geographical Review* 80: 1–20.

O'Loughlin, J. & van der Wusten, H. (1993) 'Political geography of war & peace', in P. Taylor (ed.) *Political geography of the twentieth century*, London: Belhaven Press.

Oppenheim, C. (1996) *Poverty*, London: Child Poverty Action Group.

Orange, C. (1990) *An illustrated history of the Treaty of Waitangi*, Wellington: Allen & Unwin.

O'Riordan, T. (2000) 'The sustainability debate', in T. O'Riordan (ed.) *Environmental science for environmental management*, Harlow: Prentice-Hall, 2nd edn.

Orwell, G. (1949) *Nineteen-eighty four*, London: Secker & Warburg.

Osborne, M. (1990) *Southeast Asia*, Sydney: Allen & Unwin.

Otsuka, K., Cordova, V. & David, C. (1992) 'Green revolution, land reform & household income distribution in the Philippines', *Economic Development & Cultural Change* 40: 719–741.

Overton, M. (1976) 'Towards a discussion of the natrure of radical geography', *Antipode* 8: 86–87.

Oxfam (1993) *Africa make or break*, Oxford: Oxfam.

Pacione, M (1977) 'Tourism', *Geography* 62: 43–47.

Pacione, M. (ed.) (1997) *Britain's cities*, London: Routledge.

Page, D. (1993) *Building for communities*, York: Joseph Rowntree Foundation.

Pahl, R. (1966) 'The rural-urban continuum', *Sociologica Ruralis* 6: 299–327.

Pahl, R. (1969) 'Urban social theory & research', *Environment & Planning A* 1: 143–153.

Pahl, R. (1970) *Whose city? & other essays on urban society*, Harlow: Longmans.

Pain, R. (1997) 'Social geographies of women's fear of crime', *Transactions of the Institute of British Geographers* 22: 231–244.

Palma, J. (1989) 'Dependency', in J. Eatwell, M. Milgate & P. Newman (eds) *The new economic development*, Basingstoke: Macmillan.

Palmer, B. (1997) 'Critical theory, historical materialism, & the ostensible end of Marxism', in K. Jenkins (ed.) *The postmodern history reader*, London: Routledge.

Pareto, V. (1968) *The rise & fall of elites*, Totowa, New Jersey: Bedminster Press (first published, 1901).

Park, C. (1992) *Tropical Rainforests*, London: Routledge.

Park, R. (1925) 'The city', in R. Park, E. Burgess & R. McKenzie (eds) *The city*, London: University of Chicago Press.

Park, R. (1936) 'Human ecology', *American Journal of Sociology*, 20: 577–612.

Park, R., Burgess, E. & McKenzie, R. (1925) (eds) *The city*, Chicago: University of Chicago Press).

Parker, G. (1983) *A political geography of community Europe*, London: Butterworths.

Parker, G. (1998) *Geopolitics,* London: Butterworths.

Parpart, J. & M. Marchand (1995) 'Exploding the canon', in M. Marchand & J. Parpart (eds) *Feminism/postmodernism/development*, London: Routledge.

Parsons, T. (1951) *The social system,* London: Routledge & Kegan Paul.

Pawson, E. (1992) 'Two New Zealands', in K. Anderson & F. Gale (eds) *Inventing places*, Harlow: Longman.

Peck, J. & Tickell, A. (1992) 'Local modes of social regulation?', *Geoforum* 23: 347–363.

Peck, J. & Tickell, A. (1994) 'Searching for a new institutional fix', in A. Amin (ed.) *Post-fordism*, Oxford: Oxford Univerity Press.

Peet, R. (1971) 'Poor, hungry America', *Professional Geographer* 23: 99–104.

Peet, R. (1975) 'Inequality & poverty', *Annals, Association of American Geographers* 65: 564–571.

Peet, R. (1977) 'The development of radical geography in the United States', *Progress in Human Geography* 1: 240–263.

Peet, R. (1978) 'The dialectics of radical geography', *Professional Geographer* 30: 360–364.

Peet, R. (1991) *Global capitalism*, London: Routledge.

Peet, R. (1997) 'Social theory, postmodernism & the critique of development', in G. Benko & U. Strohmayer (eds) *Space & social theory*, Oxford: Blackwell.

Peet, R. (1998) *Modern geographical thought*, Oxford: Blackwell.

Peet, R. & Thrift, N. (1989) (eds) *New models in geography: 2 Volumes*, London: Hyman.

Pepper, D. (1984) *The roots of modern environmentalism*, London: Routledge.

Pepper, D. (1993) *Eco-socialism*, London: Routledge.

Pepper, D. (1996) *Modern environmentalism*, London: Routledge.

Perry, N. (1994) *The dominion of signs,* Auckland University Press.

Persson, L.O. & Westholm, E. (1993) 'Turmoil in welfare system reshapes rural Sweden', *Journal of Rural Studies* 9: 397–404.

Phelan, J. & Pozen, R. (1973) *The company state*, New York: Grossman.

Phillips, J. (1980) 'Mummy's boys', in P. Bunkle & B. Hughes (eds) *Women in New Zealand society*, Auckland: George Allen & Unwin.

Phillips, J. (1996) *A man's country?*, Auckland: Auckland University Press.

Phillips, M. (1993) 'Rural gentrification & the processes of class colonisation', *Journal of Rural Studies* 9: 123–40.

Phillips, M. (1994a) 'Habermas, rural studies & critical social theory', in P. Cloke, M. Doel, D. Matless, M. Phillips & N. Thrift, *Writing the rural*, London: Paul Chapman.

Phillips, M. (1994b) 'Teaching & learning philosophy in geography from text-books', *Journal of Geography in Higher Education* 18: 114–122.

Phillips, M. (1998a) 'Investigations of the British rural middle classes: part 1, from legislation to interpretation', *Journal of Rural Studies* 14: 411–425.

Phillips, M. (1998b) 'The restructuring of social imaginations in rural geography', *Journal of Rural Studies* 18: 121–164.

Phillips, M. (1998c) 'Rural change', in B. Ilbery (ed.) *The geography of rural change*, Harlow: Longman.

Phillips, M. (2002) 'The production, symbolisation & socialization of gentrification', *Transactions, Institute of British Geographers* 27: 282–308.

Phillips, M. (2004) "Other geographies of gentrification', *Progress in Human Geography* 28: 5–30.

Phillips, M. (forthcoming-a) *Cultural geographies,* London: Sage.

Phillips, M. (forthcoming-b) 'Visions of (post-)rurality on Aotearoa/New Zealand', submitted to *New Zealand Geographer*.

Phillips, M. & Healey, M. (1996) 'Teaching the history & philosophy of geography in British undergarduate course', *Journal of Geography in Higher Education* 20: 223–242.

Phillips, M. & Mighall, T. (2000) *Society & exploitation through nature*, Harlow: Prentice Hall.

Phillips, M., Fish, R. & Agg, J. (2001) 'Putting together ruralities', *Journal of Rural Studies* 17: 1–27.

Phillips, R. (1996) *Mapping men & empire*, London: Routledge.

Philo, C. (1991) 'Introduction, acknowledgements & brief thoughts on older words & older worlds', in C. Philo (ed.) *New words, new worlds*, Lampeter: Social & Cultural geography Study Group.

Philo, C. (1992a) 'Foucault's geography', *Environment & Planning D* 2: 137–161.

Philo, C. (1992b) 'Neglected rural geographies', *Journal of Rural Studies* 8: 193–207.

Philo, C. (1993) 'Postmodern rural geography?', *Journal of rural studies* 9: 429–36.

Philo, C. (1994a) 'History, geography & the 'still greater mystery' of historical geography', in D. Gregory, R. Martin & G. Smith (eds) *Human geography*, London: Macmillan.

Philo, C. (1994b) 'Political geography & everything', *Geoforum* 25: 525–532.

Philo, C. (1995) 'Where is poverty?', in C. Philo (ed.) *Off the map*, London: Child Poverty Action Group.

Philo, C. & Kearns, G. (1993) 'Culture, history, capital', in G. Kearns & C. Philo (eds) *Selling places*, Oxford: Pergamon.

Piaget, J. (1970) *Structuralism*, New York: Basic Books.

Pickles, J. (1985) *Phenomenology, science & geography*, Cambridge: Cambridge University Press.

Pickles, J. (eds) (1995) *Ground truth*, New York: Guilford Press.

Pickvance, C. (1997) 'Inequality & conflict in the post-socialist city', in O. Källtorp, I. Elander, O. Ericsson & M. Franzen (eds) *Cities in transformation – transformation in cities*, Aldershot: Ashgate.

Pile, S. (1993) 'Human agency & human geography revisited', *Transactions, Institute of British Geographers* 18: 122–39.

Pile, S. (1996) *The body & the city*, London: Routledge.

Pile, S. (1997) 'Space & the politics of sleep', *Environment & Planning D* 15: 128–134.

Pile, S. & Rose, G. (1992) 'All or nothing?', *Environment & Planning D* 10: 123–36.

Pile, S. & Thrift, N. (1995) *Mapping the subject*, London: Routledge.

Pingali, P.L. & Binswanger, H.P. (1987) 'Population density & agricultural intensification', in D. Johnson & R. Lee (eds) *Population growth & economic development*, Madison, Wisconsin: The University of Wisconsin Press.

Pio, A. (1992) 'The social dimension of economic adjustment programmes', in P. Moseley (ed.) *Development finance & policy reform*, Basingstoke: Macmillan.

Pipes, R. (1994) *Russia under the Bolshevik regime, 1919–1924*, London: The Harvill Press.

Pocock, D. (ed.) (1981) *Humanistic geography & literature*, London: Croom Helm.

Polanyi, K. (1968) *Primitive, archaic & modern economies*, Boston: Beacon Press.

Polsby, N. (1980) *Community power & political theory*, New Haven, Connecticut: Yale University Press, 2nd edn.

Pomeroy, A. (1994) 'Rural New Zealand – structures & issues', in D. Hawke (ed.) *Proceedings, New Zealand Geographical Society & the Australian Institute of Geographers Conference*, Christchurch: New Zealand Geographical Society.

Pomeroy, A. (1996) 'Relocating policies for sustainable agriculture under the umbrella of rural development in Australia, USA & New Zealand', *New Zealand Geographer* 52: 84–87.

Popper, K. (1959) *The logic of scientific discovery*, London: Hutchinson.

Popper, K. (1970) 'Normal science & its dangers', in I. Lakatos & A. Musgrave (eds) *Criticism & the growth of knowledge*, Cambridge: Cambridge University Press.

Porteous, J. (1985) 'Literature & humanist geography', *Area* 17: 117–22.

Portes, R. (ed.) (1993) *Economic transition in Eastern Europe*, London: CEPR.

Potter, R. (1976) 'Directional bias within the usage & perceptual fields of urban consumers', *Psychological reports* 38: 988–990.

Potter, R. (1977) 'Spatial patterns of consumer behaviour & perception in relation to the social class variable', *Area* 9: 153–156.

Potter, R. (1979) 'Perception of urban retailing facilities', *Geografiska Annaler* 61B: 19–37.

Power, A. (1991) *Housing – a guide to quality & creativity*, London: Longman.

Power, A. & Tunstall, R. (1995) *Progress & polarisation on twenty council estates*, York: Joseph Rowntree Foundation.

Power, A. & Tunstall, R. (1997) *Dangerous disorder*, York: Joseph Rowntree Foundation.

Pratt, A. (1995) 'Putting critical realism to work', *Progress in Human Geography* 19: 61–74.

Pratt, A. (1996) 'Rurality: loose talk or social struggle', *Journal of Rural Studies* 12: 69–78.

Pratt, G. (1992) 'Spatial metaphors & speaking positions', *Environment & Planning D* 10: 241–244.

Pratt, G. (1993) 'Reflections on poststructuralism & feminist empirics, theory & practice', *Antipode* 25: 51–63.

Pratt, G. (1994) 'Poststructuralism', in R. Johnson, D. Gregory & D. Smith (eds) *The dictionary of human geography*, Oxford: Blackwell.

Pratt, G. (2000) 'Feminist geographies', in R. Johnson, D. Gregory, G. Pratt & M. Watts (eds) *The dictionary of human geography*, Oxford: Blackwell.

Pratt, G. & The Philippine Women Centre, Vancouver, Canada (1998) 'Inscribing domestic work on Filipina bodies', in H. Nast & S. Pile (eds) *Places through the body*, London: Routledge.

Prescott, J. (1987) *Political frontiers & boundaries*, London: Unwin Hyman.

Prince, H. (1971) 'Questions of social relevance', *Area* 3: 150–153.

Princen, T. & Finger, M. (eds) (1994) *Environmental NGOs in world politics*, London: Routledge.

Prothero, R. (ed.) (1974) *People & land in Africa south of the Sahara*, Oxford: Oxford University Press.

Purcell, D. (1999) *The Slovenian state on the Internet*, Ljubljana, Slovenia: Open Society Institute-Slovenia.

Raban, J. (1990) *Hunting mister heartache*, London: Collins Harvill.

Radcliffe-Brown, A (1952) *Structure & function in primitive society*, London: Cohen & West.

Ramet, S.R. (1995) *Social currents in Eastern Europe*, Durham, North Carolina: Duke University Press, 2nd edn.

Rasiah (1993) 'Competition & governance', *Journal of Contemporary Asia* 23: 3–23.

Rawlinson, W. & Wells, P. (1993) 'Japanese globalisation & the European automobile industry', *Tijdschrift voor Economische en Sociale Geografie* 84: 349–361.

Reckless, W. (1926) 'The distribution of commercial vice in the city', *Publications of the American Sociological Society* 20: 164–176.

Redclift, M. (1984) *Development & the environmental crisis*, London: Methuen.

Redclift, M. (1987) *Sustainable development* London: Methuen.

Redfield, R. (1947) 'The folk society', *American Journal of Sociology* 52: 293–308.

Relph, E. (1970) 'An inquiry into the relations between phenomenology & geography', *Canadian Geographer* 14: 193–201.

Relph, E. (1976) *Place & placelessness*, London: Pion.
Relph, E. (1985) 'Geographical experiences & being-in-the-world', in D. Seamon & R. Mugerauer (eds) *Dwelling, place & environment*, Dordecht: Martinus Nijhoff.
Resnick, S. & Wolff, R. (1992) 'Reply to Richard Peet', *Antipode* 24: 131–140.
Rex, J. & Moore, R. (1967) *Race, community & conflict*, Oxford: Oxford University Press.
Rich, B. (1994) *Mortgaging the Earth,* London: Earthscan.
Richards, K. (1990) 'Editorial', *Earth Surface Processes & Landforms* 15: 195–197.
Richards, K. (1994) "'Real' geomorphology revisited', *Earth Surface Processes & Landforms* 19: 277–281.
Rigg, J. (1991) *Southeast Asia*, London: Unwin Hyman.
Rigg, J. (1997) *Southeast Asia*, London: Routledge.
Rist, G. (1997) *The history of development*, London: Zed Books.
Robbins, K. (1990) 'British culture versus British industry', in B. Collins & K. Robbins (eds) *British culture & economic decline*, New York: St Martin's Press, 1–23.
Robinson, G. (1990) *Conflict & change in the countryside*, London: Belhaven.
Robinson, G. (1993) 'Trading strategies for New Zealand', *New Zealand Geographer* 49: 13–22.
Robinson, G., Loughran, R. & Tranter, P. J. (2000) *Australia & New Zealand*, London: Arnold.
Robinson, W. (1950) 'Ecological correlations & the behavior of individuals', *American Sociological Review* 15: 351–357.
Roche, M. & Pomeroy, A. (1996) 'Introduction', *New Zealand Geographer* 52: 1–2.
Rodríguez-Pose, A. (1994) 'Socio-economic restructuring & regional change', *Economic Geography* 70: 325–343.
Rorty, R. (1979) *Philosophy & the mirror of nature*, Princeton: Princeton University Press.
Rorty, R. (1982) *The consequences of pragmaticism*, Minneapolis: University of Minnesota Press.
Rose, D. (1984) 'Rethinking gentrification', *Environment & Planning D* 1: 47–74.
Rose, D. (1989) 'A feminist perspective on employment restructuring & gentrification' in J. Wolch & M. Dear (eds) *The power of geography*, London: Unwin Hyman.
Rose, D.B. (1999) 'Indigenous ecologies & an ethic of connection', in N. Low (ed.) *Global ethics & environment* London: Routledge.
Rose, G. (1991) 'Review: The Condition of Postmodernity, *Journal of Historical Geography* 17: 118–121.
Rose, G. (1993a) *Feminism & geography*, Cambridge: Polity.
Rose, G. (1993b) 'Progress in geography & gender', *Progress in Human Geography* 17: 531–537.
Rose, G. (1997) 'Situating knowledges', *Progress in Human Geography* 21: 305–320.
Rosenau, P. (1992) *Postmodernism & the social sciences,* Princeton, New Jersey: Princeton University Press.
Rostow, W. (1960) *The stages of economic growth*, Cambridge: Cambridge University Press.

Rowland, D. (1972) 'Processes of Maori urbanisation', *New Zealand Geographer* 28: 1–22.

Rowlands, C. (1971) 'Changes in the structure & organization of the New Zealand dairy industry since 1950', in R. Johnston & J. Soons (eds) *Proceedings of the Sixth New Zealand Geography Conference*, Christchurch: New Zealand Geographical Society.

Rowles, G. (1978a) *Prisoners of space?*, Boulder: Westview.

Rowles, G. (1978b) 'Reflections on experiential fieldwork', in D. Ley & M. Samuels (eds) *Humanistic geography*, London: Croom Helm.

Roxborough, I. (1979) *Theories of underdevelopment*, Basingstoke: Macmillan.

Royal, T. (1997) 'Nga tapuwae-nuku: journeys & migrations', in M. McKinnon (ed.) *New Zealand historical atlas: Ko Papatuanuku e Takoto Nei*, Auckland: David Bateman.

Rubinstein, W. (1990) 'Cultural explanation for Britain's economic decline', in B. Collins & K. Robbins (eds) *British culture & economic decline*, New York: St Martin's Press, 59–90.

Rubinstein, W. (1993) *Capitalism, culture & decline in Britain 1750–1990*, London: Routledge.

Ruccio, D. & Simon, L. (1986) 'Methodological aspects of a Marxian approach to development', *World Development* 14: 211–222.

Rueschemeyer, M. (1993) 'East Germany's new towns in transition', *Urban Studies* 30: 495–506.

Rumley, D. (1979) 'The study of structural effects in human geography', *Tijdshrift voor Economische en Sociale Geografie* 70: 350–360.

Ryan, D. (1995) 'Asserting US power', in P. Davies (ed.) *An American quarter century*, Manchester: Manchester University Press.

Ryder, R. (1984) 'Council house building in County Durham 1900–39', in M. Daunton (ed.) *Councillors & tenants*, Leicester: Leicester University Press.

Sachs, W. (1992) *The development dictionary*, London: Zed Books.

Said, E. (1986) 'Foucault & the imagination of power', in D. Hoy (ed.) *Foucault*, Oxford: Blackwell.

Said, E. (1995) *Orientalism*, Harmondsworth: Penguin.

Sakwa, R. (1999) *Postcommunism*, Buckingham: Open University Press.

Sallnow, J. (1989) 'Non-alignment in a polar world', *Geographical Magazine* 61: 22–25.

Salmon, K. (1992) *Andalucía*, Sevilla: Junta de Andalucía Consejería de Economia y Hacienda.

Samuels, M. (1978) 'Existentialism & human geography', in D. Ley & M. Samuels (eds) *Humanistic geography*, London: Croom Helm.

Samuels, M. (1981) 'An existential geography', in M. Harvey & B. Holly (eds) *Themes in geographic thought,* London: Croom Helm.

Sant, M. & Simons, P. (1993) 'The conceptual basis of counterurbanization', *Australian Geographical Studies* 31: 113–126.

Santos, M. (1977) 'Society & space', *Antipode* 9: 3–13.

Sartre, J.-P. (1958) *Being & nothingness*, New York: Philosophical Library.

Sassen, S. (1991) *The global city*, Princeton, New Jersey: Princeton University Press.

Sassen, S. (1993) 'Rebuilding the global city ', *Social Justice* 20: 32–50.

Sassen, S. (1994) *Cites in a world economy*, London: Pine Forge Press.

Sauer, C. (1956) 'The education of a geographer', *Annals, Association of American Geographers* 46: 287–299.

Saunders, P. (1981) *Social theory & the urban question*, London: Hutchinson.

Saunders, P. (1993) *Social class & stratification*, London: Routledge.

Saussure, F. de (1966) *Course in general linguistics*, New York: McGraw-Hill.

Savage, M., Barlow, J., Duncan, S. & Saunders, P. (1987) 'Locality research', *Quarterly Journal of Social Affairs* 4: 27–51.

Savage, V. R., Kong, L. & Neville, W. (1998) *The Naga Awakens*, Singapore: Times Academic.

Sayer, A. (1985) 'Realism & geography', in R. Johnson (ed.) *The future of geography*, London: Methuen.

Sayer, A. (1992) *Method in social science*, London: Routledge.

Sayer, A. (1993a) 'Postmodernist thought in geography', *Antipode* 25: 320–344.

Sayer, A. (1993b) 'A reply to Clive Barnett', *Antipode* 25: 369.

Sayer, A. (1994) 'Cultural studies & the economy, stupid', *Environment & Planning D*, 12: 635–637.

Schaefer, F. K. (1953) 'Exceptionalism in geography', *Annals, Association of American Geographers* 43: 226–249.

Schedvinn, C. B. (1990) 'Staples & regimes of Pax Britanica', *Economic History Review*, 43: 533–559.

Schultz,T. (1983) 'Book review of J. C. Caldwell's theory of fertility decline', *Population & Development Review* 9: 161–168.

Schutz, A. & Luckman, T. (1973) *The structures of the lifeworld*, Evanston: Northwestern University Press.

Schuurman, F. (ed.) (1993) *Beyond the impasse*, London: Zed Books.

Scott, A. (1997) (ed.) *The limits of globalization*, London: Routledge.

Scott, J. (1996) *Stratification & power*, Cambridge: Polity.

Seamon, D. (1979) *A geography of the lifeworld*, London: Croom Helm.

Seitz, H. & Licht, G. (1995) 'The impact of public infrastructure capital on regional manufacturing production cost', *Regional Studies* 29: 231–240.

Seitz, J. (2002) *Global issues*, Oxford: Blackwell, 2nd edn.

Sen, G. & Grown, C. (1987) *Development, crises & alternative visions*, London: Earthscan.

Sharp, J. P. (1999) 'Critical geopolitics', in P. Cloke, P. Crang & M. Goodwin (eds) *Introducing human geographies*, London: Arnold.

Shaw, B. & Jones, R. (1997) *Contested urban heritage*, Aldershot: Ashgate.

Shaw, G. & Williams, A. (1994) *Critical issues in tourism*, Oxford: Blackwell.

Shaw, R. (1989) 'Rapid population growth & environmental degradation', *Environmental Conservation* 16: 199–208.

Sheppard, E. (1993) 'Automated geography', *Professional Geographer* 45: 457–460.

Shields, R. (1991) *Places on the margins*, London: Routledge.

Shirlow, P. (1995) 'Transnational corporations in the Republic of Ireland & the illusion of economic well-being', *Regional Studies* 29: 687–691.

Short, J. (1991) *Imagined country*, London: Routledge.

Short, J. (1996) *The urban order*, Oxford: Blackwells.

Short, J. & Bassett, K. (1981) 'Housing policy & the inner city in the 1970's', *Transactions, Institute of British Geographers* 6: 293–312.

Shurmer-Smith, P. & Hannam, K. (1995) *Worlds of power, realms of desire*, London: Edward Arnold.

Sibley, D. (1990) 'Urban change & the exclusion of minority groups in British cities', *Geoforum* 21: 483–488.

Sibley, D. (1995) *Geographies of exclusion*, London: Routledge.

Sidaway, J. (1998) 'What is in a gulf?', in G. Ó Tuathal & S. Dalby (eds) *Rethinking geopolitics*, London : Routledge.

Sidaway, J. D. (2001) 'Geopolitics traditions', in P. Daniels, M. Bradshaw, D. Shaw & J. Sidaway (eds) *Human geography*, Harlow, Prentice Hall.

Silverstone, R. (1997) *Visions of suburbia*, London: Routledge.

Simmie, J. (1995) 'R&D & the "peace dividend"', *International Journal of Urban & Regional Research* 19: 194–207.

Simon, D. (1998) 'Rethinking (post)modernism, postcolonialism & posttraditional-ism', *Environment & Planning D* 16: 219–245.

Singer, H. (1989) 'The 1980s: a lost decade – development in reverse?' in H. Singer & S. Sharma (eds) (1989) *Growth & external debt management*, Basingstoke: Macmillan.

Sked, A. (1987) *Britain's decline*, Oxford: Blackwell.

Sklair, L. (1988) 'Transcending the impasse', *World Development* 16: 697–709.

Skocpol, T. (1979) *States & social revolutions*, New York: Cambridge University Press.

Slater, D. (1993) 'The geopolitical imagination & the enframing of development theory', *Transactions of the Institute of British Geographers* 18: 419–437.

Slater, D. (1996) 'Review of A. Escobar, "Encountering Development"', *Third World Planning Review* 18: 264–66.

Smith, A. (1997) 'Breaking the old & constructing the new?', in R. Lee & J. Wills (eds) *Geographies of economies*, London: Arnold.

Smith, A. D. (1991) *National identity*, Harmsworth: Penguin.

Smith, D. (1977) *Human geography*, London: Edward Arnold.

Smith, D. (1979) *Where the grass in greener*, Harmondsworth: Penguin.

Smith, D. (1994) *Geography & social justice*, Oxford: Blackwell.

Smith, G. (1985) 'Ethnic nationalism in the Soviet Union', *Environment & Planning C* 3: 49–73.

Smith, G. (1996) 'The Soviet state & nationalities policy' in G. Smith (ed.) *The nationalities question in the post-Soviet states*, Harlow: Longman, 2nd edn.

Smith, G. (1999) *The post-Soviet states*, London, Arnold.

Smith, N. (1979a) 'Gentrification & capital', *Antipode* 11: 139–155.

Smith, N. (1979b) 'Towards a theory of gentrification', *Journal of the Amercian Planners Association* 35: 538–548.

Smith, N. (1982) 'Gentrification & uneven development', *Economic Geography* 58: 139–155.

Smith, N. (1987a) 'Gentrification & the rent gap', *Annals, Association of American Geographers* 77: 462–478.

Smith, N. (1987b) 'Of yuppies & housing', *Environment & Planning D* 5: 151–172.

Smith, N. (1992a) 'History & philosophy of geography', *Progress in Human Geography* 16: 257–271.

Smith, N. (1992b) 'Blind man's bluff or, Hamnett's philosophical individualism in search of gentrification', *Transactions, Institute of British Geographers* 17: 110–115.

Smith, N. (1995) 'Gentrifying theory', *Scottish Geographical Magazine* 111: 124–126.

Smith, N. (1996a) *The new urban frontier*, London: Routledge.

Smith, N. (1996b) 'Rethinking sleep', *Environment & Planning D* 14: 505–506.

Smith, N. (1997) 'Beyond sleep', *Environment & Planning D* 15: 134–135.

Smith, N. & Williams, P. (1986) *Gentrification of the city*, London: Allen & Unwin.

Smith, S. (1984) 'Practicing humanistic geography', *Annals, Association of American Geographers* 74: 353–374.

Smith, S. (1989) *The politics of race & residence*, Cambridge: Polity.

Smith, S. (1999) 'Society-space', in P. Cloke, P. Crang & M. Goodwin (eds) *Introducing human geographies*, London: Arnold.

Soja, E. (1989) *Post-modern geographies*, London: Verso.

Soja, E. (1995) 'Postmodern urbanization', in S. Watson & K. Gibson (eds) *Postmodern cities & spaces*, Oxford: Blackwell.

Soja, E. (1996) *Thirdspace*, Oxford: Blackwell.

Soja, E. (2000) *Postmetropolis*, Oxford: Blackwell.

Spivak, G. (1988) 'Can the subaltern speak', in C. Nelson & L. Grossberg (eds) *Marxism & the interpretation of culture*, Urbana, Illinois: University of Illinois Press.

Spooner, D. (ed.) (1995) *Regional development in the UK*, Sheffield: The Geographical Association.

Spybey, T. (1992) *Social change, development & dependency*, Cambridge: Polity Press.

Stacey, M. (1981) 'The division of labour revisited or overcoming the two Adams', in Abrams P. (ed.) *Practice & progress* London: Allen & Unwin.

Stamp, L. (1946) *The land of Britain*, London: Longman.

Stanislawski, W. (2000) Coping with Stalinism. Transitions Online, www.tol.cz/jan00/poland.html

Stares, P. (ed.) (1992) *The new Germany & the new Europe*, Washington: Brookings Institute.

State Coal Mines (1979) Letter addressed to 'The Rotowaro Householders', dated 30 May.

Statistics New Zealand: Te Tari Tatau (1997) *Census 1996*, Wellington: Statistics New Zealand Te Tari Tatau.

Statistics New Zealand: Te Tari Tatau (1998a) *People on the move … shifting around New Zealand*, Wellington: Statistics New Zealand – Te Tari Tatau.

Statistics, New Zealand: Te Tari Tatau (1998b) *Tangata whenau … aspects of Maori society*, Wellington: Statistics New Zealand – Te Tari Tatau.

Steel, R. (1982) 'Regional geography in practice', *Geography* 67: 2–8.

Steers, J. (1946) *The coastline of England & Wales*, Cambridge: Cambridge University Press.

Steinecke, A. (1993) 'The historical development of tourism in Europe', in W. Pompl & P. Lavery (eds) *Tourism in Europe*, Wallingford: CAB International.

Stewart, J. (1947) 'Empirical mathematical rules concerning the distribution & equilibrium of population', *Geographical Review* 37: 461–485.

Stewart, J. & Wartnz, W. (1958) 'Macrogeography & social science', *Geographical Review* 48: 167–184.

Stewart, J. & Wartnz, W. (1959) 'Physics of population distribution', *Journal of Regional Science* 1: 99–123.

Stoddart, D. (1981) 'The paradigm concept & the history of geography', in D. Stoddart (ed.) *Geography, ideology & social concern*, Oxford: Basil Blackwell.

Stoker, G. (1989) 'Inner cities, economic development & social services', in J. Stewart & G. Stoker (eds) *The future of local government*, Basingstoke: Macmillan.

Stokes, E. (1978) *Coal Mining Settlement of the Huntly Region, Huntly Social & Economic Impact Monitoring Projec*t, Hamilton, University of Waikato.

Stokes, E. (1987) 'Maori geography or geography of Maori', *New Zealand Geographer* 43: 118–123.

Stokes, E. (1992) 'The Treaty of Waitangi & the Waitangi Tribunal', *Applied Geography* 12: pp. 176–191.

Stokes, E. (1996) 'Maori identities', in R. Le Heron & E. Pawson (eds) *Changing places*, Auckland: Longman Paul.

Stokes, E. (1997) 'Te whenua tautohetohe: land in contention, the Waikato region in the nineteenth century', in E. Stokes & M. Begg (eds) *Te hononga ke ti whenua: Belonging to the land*, Hamilton: Waikato Branch, New Zealand Geographical Society.

Stokes, E., Dooley, L., Johnson, L., Dixon, J. & Parsons, S. (1987) 'Feminist perspectives in geography', *New Zealand Geographer* 43: 139–149.

Storey, D. (2001) *Territory: the claiming of space*, Harlow: Prentice Hall.

Strahler, A. (1950) 'Davis' concept of slope development viewed in the light of recent quantitative investigations', *Annals, Association of American Geographers* 40: 209–213.

Strohmayer, U. & Hannah, M. (1992) 'Domesticating postmodernism', *Antipode* 24: 29–55.

Swenarton, M. (1981) *Homes fit for heroes*, London: Heinemann.

Taafe, E, Morril, R. & Gould, P. (1963) 'Transport expansion in underdeveloped counties', *Geographical Review* 53: 503–529.

Takagi, A. (1993) 'From hegemony to co-operation', in P. Taylor, (ed.) *Political geography of the twentieth century*, London: Belhaven Press.

Takahashi, L. & Dear, M. J. (1997) 'The changing dynamics of community opposition to human service facilities', *Journal of the American Planning Association* 63: 79–93.

Tamihori, L. (1997) *Once were warriors*, motion picture.

Taylor, I. (1997) 'Running on empty', *The Guardian* Wednesday May 14: 2–6.

Taylor, P. (1989) 'Britain's century of decline', in J. Anderson & A. Cochrane (eds) *A state of crisis*, London: Hodder & Stoughton.

Taylor, P. (1993) *Political geography* Harlow: Longman, 3rd edn.

Taylor, P. (1994) 'The state as container', *Progress in Human Geography* 18: 151–162.

Taylor, P. (1997) 'Classics in human geography revisited, author's response', *Progress in Human Geography* 21: 560–562.

Taylor, P. & Flint, C. (2000) *Political geography* Harlow: Longman, 4th edn.

Taylor, P. (1992) *War & the media*, Manchester: Manchester University Press.

Teather, E. (ed.) (1999) *Embodied geographies*, London: Routledge.

Terry, J. (1990) 'The Naming of Rotowaro', *Auckland-Waikato Historical Journal* 57.

Thompson, E. (1978) *The poverty of theory & other essays*, London: Merlin.

Thompson, E. (1965) 'The peculiarities of the English', in R. Miliband & J. Saville (eds) *The Socialist Register*, London: Merlin Press.

Thompson, J. (1984) *Studies in the theory of ideology*, Cambridge: Polity.

Thompson, J. (1990) *Ideology & modern culture*, Cambridge: Cambridge University Press.

Thornton, S. & Gelder, M. (1997) *Subcultures*, London: Routledge.

Thrift, N. (1987) 'Manufacturing rural geography', *Journal of Rural Studies* 3: 77–81.

Thrift, N. (1996) *Spatial formations*, London: Sage.

Thrift, N. (1999) 'The still point', in S. Pile & M. Keith (eds) *Geographies of resistance*, London: Routledge.

Thrift, N. (2000) 'Afterwords', *Environment & Planning D* 18: 213–255.

Thrift, N. (2004) 'Summoning life', in P. Cloke, P. Crang & M. Goodwin (eds) *Envisioning human geographies*, London: Arnold.

Thrift, N. & Leyshon, A. (1997) 'Financial desertification', in J. Rossiter (ed.) *Financial exclusion*? London: New Policy Institute.

Tickell, A. & Peck, J. (1995) 'Social regulation after Fordism', *Economy & Society*, 24, 357–386.

Tiffen, M., Mortimore, M. & Gichuki, F. (1994) *More people, less erosion*, Chichester: John Wiley.

Times Books (1981) *The Times 1000, 1981–1982*, London.

Times Books (1994) *The Times 1000, 1995*, London.

Tönnies, F. (1957) *Community & association*, London: Routledge & Kegan Paul.

Townsend, A. (1983) *The impact of recession*, London: Croom Helm.

Townsend, P. & Davidson, N. (1982) *The Black report*, Harmondsworth: Penguin.

Toye, J. (1987) *Dilemmas of development*, Oxford: Blackwell.

Tracy, M. (1989) *Government & agriculture in Western Europe 1880–1988*, Hemel Hempstead: Harvester Wheatsheaf, 3rd edn.

Tsartas, P. (1992) 'Socio-economic impact of tourism on two Greek isles', *Annals of Tourism Research* 19: 516–533.

Tsemenyi, B. (1988) 'The exercise of coastal state jurisdiction over EEZ fisheries resources', *Ambio* 17: 255–258.

Tsouvalis. J., Seymour, S. & Watkins, C. (2000) 'Exploring knowledge-cultures', *Environment & Planning A*: 909–923.

Tuan, Y.-F. (1971) 'Geography, phenomenology & the study of human nature', *Canadian Geographer* 15: 181–92.

Tuan, Y.-F. (1976) 'Humanistic geography', *Annals, Association of American Geographers* 66: 266–76.

Tunbridge, J. & Ashworth, G. (1996) *Dissonant heritage*, Chichester: Wiley.

Turner, B. (ed.) (2003) *The statesman's yearbook*, Basingstoke: Palgrave.

Turner, F. (1963) *The significance of the frontier in American history*, New York: Ungar Publishing.

Turner, R. (1994) 'Regenerating the coalfields', *Local Government Studies* 20: 622–636.

Turnock, D. (1997) *The East European economy in context*, London: Routledge.

Turnock, D. (1999) *A concise philosophy of geography*, Leicester: Department of Geography, University of Leicester.

Tylecote, A. (1982) 'German ascent & British decline 1870–1980', in E. Friedman (ed.) *Ascent & decline in the world-system*, Beverly Hills, California: Sage.

UNFPA (1999) *The state of world population, 1999*, New York: UNFPA.

UNICEF (1994) *The state of the world's children*, Oxford: Oxford University Press.

United Nations Secretariat (1991) 'Relationships between population & environment in rural areas of developing countries', *Population Bulletin of the United Nations* 31/32: 52–69.

Unwin, T. (1992) *The place of geography*, Harlow: Longman.

Unwin, T. (2000) 'A waste of space?', *Transactions, Institute of British Geographers* 25: 11–29.

Urban Land Institute. (1976) *New opportunities for residential development in cities. Report No. 25*, Washington, DC: Urban Land Institute.

Urry, J. (1981) 'Localities, regions & social class', *International Journal of Urban & Regional Research* 5: 455–473.

Urry, J. (1995) 'A middle-class countryside?', in T. Butler & M. Savage (eds) *Social change & the middle classes*, London: Routledge.

US Arms Control & Disarmament Agency (1990) *World military expenditures & arms transfers 1990*, Washington: US Arms Control & Disarmament Agency, 21st edn.

Valentine, G. (1993) 'Negotiating & managing sexual identities', *Transactions, Institute of British Geographers* 18: 237–48.

Valentine, G. (1997a) 'Making space', in P. Cloke & J. Little (eds) *Contested countryside cultures*, London: Routledge.

Valentine, G. (1997b) 'A safe place to grow up?', *Journal of Rural Studies* 13: 137–148.

Valentine, G. (2001) *Social geographies*, Harlow: Prentice Hall.

van Creveld, M. (1991) *On future war*, Oxford: Blackwell.

van Kempen, R., Teule, R. & van Weesep, J. (1992) 'Urban policy, housing policy & the demise of the Dutch welfare state', *Tijdschrift voor Economische en Sociale Geografie* 83: 317–329.

Vandergeest, P. & Buttel, F. (1988) 'Marx, Weber & development sociology', *World Development* 16: 677–697.

Vane, H. (1992) 'The Thatcher years: macroeconomic policy & performance of the UK economy, 1979–1988', *National Westminster Bank Quarterly Review* May: 26–43.

Veltmeyer, H., Petras, J. & Vieux, S. (1997) *Neoliberalism & class conflict in Latin America*, Basingstoke: Macmillan.

Verdery, K. (1991) *National ideology under Socialism*, Berkeley: University of California Press.

Verdery, K. (1996) *What was Socialism & what comes next?*, Princeton: Princeton University Press.

Verdery, K. (1999) *The political life of dead bodies*, New York: Columbia University Press.

Vining, D. & Kontuly, T. (1978) 'Population dispersal from metropolitan regions', *International Regional Science Review* 3: 751–758.

Vogel, L. (1983) *Marxism & the oppression of women*, London: Pluto Press.

Vogeler, I. (1996) 'State hegemony in transforming the rural landscapes of eastern Germany: 1945–1994', *Annals of the Association of American Geographers* 86: 432–458.

von Cramon-Taubadel, S. (1993) 'The reform of the CAP from a German perspective', *Journal of Agricultural Economics* 44: 394–409.

Voss, D. & Schütze, J. (1989) 'Postmodernism in context', *New German Critique* 47: 119–142.

Vujakovic, P. (1993) 'Maps, myths & the media', in P. Mesenburg (ed.) *Proceedings of the 16th International Cartographic Conference*, Bielefeld: German Society of Cartographers.

Vujakovic, P. (1994) 'Propagating the message', in T. Unwin (ed.) *Atlas of world development*, Chichester: Wiley.

Vujakovic, P. (1995) 'The sleeping-beauty complex', in T. Hill & W. Hughes (eds) *Contemporary writing & national identity*, Bath: Sulis Press.

Vujakovic, P. (2002) 'Mapping the War Zone', *Journalism Studies* 3: 187–202.

Walby, S. (1986) *Patriarchy at work*, Cambridge: Polity.

Walby, S. (1989) 'Theorising patriarchy', *Sociology* 23: 213–234.

Walby, S. (1990) *Theorizing patriarchy*, Oxford: Blackwell.

Waldegrave, C. & Stuart, S. (1997) 'Out of the rat race', *New Zealand Geographer* 53: 22–29.

Walker, R. (1988) 'The geographical organization of production-systems', *Environment & Planning D* 6: 377–408.

Wallace, R. (1990) 'Urban desertification, public health & public order', *Social Science & Medicine* 31: 801–813.

Wallerstein, I. (1974) *The Modern World System*, New York: Academic Press.

Wallerstein, I. (1983) *Historical capitalism*, London: Verso.

Walmsley, D. & Lewis, G. (1993) *People & environment* Harlow: Longman.

Walmsley, D. & Sorenson, A. (1980) 'What Marx for the radicals?', *Area* 12: 137–141.

Ward, B. & Dubos, R. (1972) *Only one Earth*, London: Deutsch.

Ward, S. V. (1988) *The geography of interwar Britain*, London: Routledge.

Warde, A. (1986) 'Space, class & voting in Britain', in K. Hoggart & E. Kofman (eds) *Politics, geography & social stratification*, London: Croom Helm.

Warnes, A. (1991) 'London's population trends', in K. Hoggart & D. Green (eds) *London*, London: Edward Arnold.

Warren, B. (1980) *Imperialism*, London: Verso.

Waters, M. (1995) *Globalization*, London: Routledge.

Watney, S. (1987) *Policing desire*, London: Methuen.

Watson, S. & Gibson, K. (1995) *Postmodern cities & spaces*, Oxford: Blackwell.

Weaver, O. (1995) 'Europe since 1945', in K. Wilson & J. van der Dussen (eds) *The history of the idea of Europe*, London: Routledge.

Weeks, J. & Dore, E. (1979) 'International exchange & the causes of backwardness', *Latin American Perspectives* 6: 62–87.

Whatmore, S. (1999) 'Hybrid geographies', in D. Massey, J. Allen & P. Sarre (eds) *Human geography today*, Cambridge: Polity.

White, G. F. (1972) 'Geography & public policy', *Professional Geographer* 24: 101–104.

White, P. E. (1985) 'Modelling rural population change in the Cilento region of southern Italy', *Environment & Planning A* 17: 1401–1413.

Whittlesey, D. (1954) 'The regional concept & the regional method', in P. James & C. Jones (eds) *American geography*, New York: Syracuse University Press.

Whittlesey, D. (1945) 'The horizon geography', *Annals, Association of American Geographers* 45: 105–108.

Wiener, M. (1981) *English culture & the decline of the industrial spirit 1850–1980*, Cambridge: Cambridge University Press.

Wild, T. & Jones, P. (1994) 'Spatial impacts of German unification', *Geographical Journal* 160: 1–16.

Williams, C. (1997) *Consumer services & economic development*, London: Routledge.

Williams, P. (1976) 'The role of institutions in the inner London housing market', *Transactions, Institute of British Geographers* 1: 72–82.

Williams, R. (1985) *The country & the city*, London: Hogarth Press.

Willis, R. (1988) 'New Zealand', in P. Cloke (ed.) *Policies & plans for rural people*, London: Unwin Hyman.

Willis, R. & Press, C. (1997) 'Growth & crisis in rural New Zealand, 1961–1991', in M. McKinnon (ed.) *New Zealand historical atlas: Ko Papatuanuku e Takoto Nei*, Auckland: David Bateman.

Willmott, W. E. (1985) 'Community at Tinui', *New Zealand Geographer* 41: 15–20.

Wilson, O. (1994) 'They changed the rules', *New Zealand Geographer* 50: 3–13.

Wilson, O. (1995) 'Rural restructuring & agriculture-rural economy linkages', *Journal of Rural Studies* 11: 417–431.

Wilson, W. (1987) *The truly disadvantaged*, Chicago: University of Chicago Press.

Wilton, R. (1996) 'Diminished worlds?', *Health & Place* 2: 69–83.

Winchester, H. & White, P. (1988) 'The location of marginalised groups in the inner city' *Environment & Planning D* 6: 37–54.

Windelband, W. (1980) 'History & natural science (Rectoral address, Strasbourg 1894)', *History & Theory*, 19: 169–185.

Wirth, L. (1928) *The ghetto*, Chicago: Chicago University Press.

Wirth, L. (1938) 'Urbanism as a way of life', *American Journal of Sociology* 44: 1–24.

Wolch, J. (1991) 'Urban homelessness', *Urban Geography* 12: 99–104.

Wolfe, T. (1988) *Bonfire of the vanities*, New York: Bantam.

Wolpert, J. (1964) 'The decision process in spatial context', *Annals, Association of American Geographers* 54: 537–58.

Women & Geography Study Group (1984) *Geography & gender*, London: Hutchinson.

Wood, G. (1997) 'Social & economic restructuring in old industrial areas', in H. Blotevogel & A. Fielding (eds) *People, jobs & mobility in the New Europe,* Chichester: Wiley.

Woodward, K. (ed.) (1997) *Identity & difference*, London: Sage.

Woodward, R. (1995) 'Approaches towards the study of social polarisation', *Progress in Human Geography* 19: 75–89.

World Bank (1981) *Accelerated development in sub-Saharan Africa,* Washington: World Bank.

World Bank (1997) *The world development report 1997*, Oxford: Oxford University Press.

World Bank. (1999) *Entering the 21st century*, New York: Oxford Univerity Press.

World Commission on Environment & Development (WCED) (1987) *Our common future*, Oxford: Oxford University Press.

Worsley, P. (1984) *The three worlds*, London: Weidenfeld & Nicholson.

Wright, E. (1978) *Class, crisis & the state*, London: New Left Books.

Wright, E. (1985) *Classes*, London: Verso.

Wright, E. (1997) *Class counts*, Cambridge: Cambridge University Press.

Wright, S. (1992) 'Image & analysis', in B. Short (ed.) *The English rural community*, Cambridge: Cambridge University Press.

Yanov, A. (1987) *The Russia challenge & the year 2000,* Oxford: Blackwell.

Yarrow, L. (1979) Letter on behalf of Rotowaro Action Committee to State Coal Mines, 26 June.

Yeung, H. (1997) 'Critical realism & realist research in human geography', *Progress in Human Geography* 21: 51–74.

Yeung H. (2002) 'The limits of globalization theory', *Economic Geography* 23: 3–23.

Yeung, H. (2003) 'Globalization', in A. Rogers & H. Vile (eds) *The student companion to geography*, Oxford: Blackwell.

Young, C. & Kaczmarek, S. (1999) 'Changing the perception of the post-Socialist city, *Geographical Journal* 165: 183–91.

Zaba, B. & Clark, J. (eds) (1994) *Environment & population change*, Liege, Ordina Editions.

Zukin, S. (1987) 'Gentrification', *American Review of Sociology* 13: 129–147.

Zukin, S. (1989) *Loft living*, New Brunswick: Rutgers University Press.

Zukin, S. (1990) 'Socio-spatial prototypes of a new organization of consumption', *Sociology* 24: 37–56.

Zukin, S. (1995) *The cultures of cities*, Cambridge, Massachusetts: Blackwell Publishers.

Index